Finance and Development

The research underlying this book forms part of a general research programme on finance and development funded by the Department for International Development (DFID). We thank DFID for their financial support. The interpretations and conclusions expressed in this book are entirely our own and should not be attributed in any manner to DFID.

Finance and Development

Surveys of Theory, Evidence and Policy

Edited by

Christopher J. Green

Professor of Economics and Finance, Loughborough University, UK

Colin H. Kirkpatrick

Hallsworth Professor of Development Economics, Institute for Development Policy and Management and Co-Director of the Regulation Research Programme, Centre on Regulation and Competition, University of Manchester, UK

Victor Murinde

Professor of Development Finance, University of Birmingham, UK

Edward Elgar
Cheltenham, UK • Northampton, MA, USA

Published by
Edward Elgar Publishing Limited
Glensanda House
Montpellier Parade
Cheltenham
Glos GL50 1UA
UK

Edward Elgar Publishing, Inc.
136 West Street
Suite 202
Northampton
Massachusetts 01060
USA

A catalogue record for this book
is available from the British Library

ISBN 1 84376 030 4 (cased)

Typeset by Manton Typesetters, Louth, Lincolnshire, UK.
Printed and bound in Great Britain by MPG Books Ltd, Bodmin, Cornwall.

Contents

PART II   HOUSEHOLDS, FIRMS AND FINANCIAL INSTITUTIONS

Contributors

Thankom Arun is a lecturer in Development Finance at the Institute for Development Policy and Management, University of Manchester. He started his career working in State Planning Organisation of Kerala in India, later working for the University of Ulster as lecturer in economics. His research interests are in the areas of development finance, particularly in micro/rural finance, regulation and corporate governance.

Martin Brownbridge is a consultant on fiscal and financial sector policies, currently working with Sigma One Corporation in Ghana. His previous positions include macroeconomic advisor to the Ministry of Finance, Planning and Economic Development in Uganda. He is the author, with Charles Harvey, of *Banking in Africa* (1998).

Paul Cook is Professor of Economics and Development Policy and Director of DFID-funded Research Centre on Regulation and Competition (RCRC) at the Institute for Development Policy and Management, University of Manchester. He has published numerous papers and books on issues relating to privatization, economic regulation and competition, and has acted as a consultant for a variety of international development agencies.

Edmund Valpy Knox FitzGerald is Reader in International Economics and Finance, University of Oxford; Director, Finance and Trade Policy Research Centre, Queen Elizabeth House, Oxford; and Professorial Fellow of St Antony's College, Oxford since 1992. He is also Visiting Professor of Economics at the Institute of Social Studies, The Hague; and Faculty of Economics and Business, Complutense University, Madrid since 1995. Educated at Oxford and Cambridge, his research interests include international capital flows to emerging markets; macroeconomic policy in open economies; economics of conflict and reconstruction; Latin America economic history. He has done advisory work for the OECD, UNCTAD and UK government (FCO, DfID) and is Head of International Economics, Oxford Analytica Ltd, Oxford.

Christopher J. Green is Professor of Economics and Finance in the Department of Economics at Loughborough University. Educated at Oxford and

Yale universities, he has been on the staff of the International Monetary Fund in the African Department and was an assistant adviser in the Economics Division of the Bank of England. His previous university appointments were at Manchester University and then at the University of Wales College of Cardiff where he was the Sir Julian Hodge Professor of Banking and Finance for ten years, before moving to his present appointment. He has also held visiting appointments at Yale University. His main areas of interest are in portfolio analysis, asset price formation, and financial markets in the industrial and developing countries, and he has published more than 60 refereed journal articles and books in these areas. He has been the coordinator of numerous research programmes, in particular several ESRC grants (including the Money Study Group), a number of grants for research on long-term stock market development in the United Kingdom (including two from the Leverhulme Trust) and two major EU-funded Phare/ACE research programmes on financial reform in central Europe. He was also a partner in a major DFID-funded research programme on finance for development and poverty-reducing growth (directed by Professor Colin Kirkpatrick) and a convenor of the ESRC research seminar programme on 'Finance for Development and Poverty Reduction' (directed by Professor Victor Murinde).

David Hulme is Professor of Development Studies at the Institute for Development Policy and Management, University of Manchester. He directs the Chronic Poverty Research Centre (www.chronicpoverty.org) and has particular interests in poverty reduction in Bangladesh.

Susan Johnson has a background in economics and agricultural economics and has a Doctorate in Development Studies from the University of Bath where she is a lecturer. She started her career working in an agricultural development project in Kenya for the UK's Department for International Development, later working for the international NGO ActionAid. Since 1997, when she moved to the University of Bath, she has specialized in impact assessment, gender and research into local financial markets and microfinance. She is currently a researcher in the ESRC funded research group on Wellbeing in Developing Countries, and a lead researcher in the *Imp-Act* programme – a global three-year action-research programme that aims to improve the quality of microfinance services and their impact on poverty.

Colin H. Kirkpatrick is Hallsworth Professor of Development Economics, Institute for Development Policy and Management (IDPM), University of Manchester. He is co-director of the Regulation Research Programme at the Centre on Regulation and Competition (CRC) and Director of the Impact

Assessment Research Centre (IARC), both at IDPM. His research interests are in the areas of utilities regulation in developing countries, international trade and sustainability impact assessment.

David T. Llewellyn is the Professor of Money and Banking at Loughborough University and Chairman of the Loughborough University Banking Centre. He has formerly held positions at Unilever (Rotterdam), HM Treasury (London), University of Nottingham, and the International Monetary Fund (Washington). He has been a Public Interest Director of the Personal Investment Authority (London) and has served as a consultant to banks and regulatory agencies in several countries. His main research interests are in the analysis of financial systems, the theory and practice of bank behaviour, the causes of banking crises and the theory and practice of financial regulation. He has researched and written extensively in the area of the theory and practice of financial regulation. Recent books include *The New Economics of Banking, and Financial Regulation: Why, How and Where Now?* (with Charles Goodhart and others). In 2003/4 he was a consultant to PricewaterhouseCoopers on an EU Commission project focused on the economic impact of the proposed Basle 2 Accord. He has served as a consultant to regulatory agencies in many countries. He is President of SUERF, the European Money and Finance Forum.

Samuel Munzele Maimbo is a financial sector specialist at the World Bank. Before joining the World Bank he was a Bank of Zambia Senior Bank Inspector (1995–7) and prior to that position, an audit assistant at PriceWaterhouse. He was also a Rhodes Scholar at the Institute for Development Policy and Management, the University of Manchester (2001) from where he obtained a PhD in Public Administration. He also holds an MBA (Finance) degree from the University of Nottingham (1998) and a Bachelor of Accountancy Degree from the Copperbelt University (1994). He is also a fellow of the Association of Certified Chartered Accountants and the Zambia Institute of Certified Accountants.

Imran Matin is the Director of Research and Evaluation Division of BRAC (previously, Bangladesh Rural Advancement Committee). He was formerly with the Consultative Group to Assist the Poor (CGAP) at the World Bank. He completed his PhD in economics from the University of Sussex. His research interest includes livelihoods, enterprise development, microfinance, social exclusion and extreme poverty.

George Mavrotas is a resident Research Fellow and Project Director at the World Institute for Development Economics Research of the United Nations

University (UNU-WIDER) based in Helsinki, Finland, currently co-directing two WIDER research projects on 'Development Aid: A Fresh Look' and 'Financial Sector Development for Growth & Poverty Reduction'. He taught for many years at the Universities of Oxford and Manchester before joining WIDER in January 2003. His main area of expertise is development finance broadly defined to include external finance (aid effectiveness, aid and poverty, capital flight, international capital flows) but also domestic resource mobilization (savings mobilization, financial sector development and finance and growth). His other research interests include quantitative development economics, primary commodity markets and the economics of education and training. He has served as an advisor to DfID, UNICEF, the World Bank, the Inter-American Development Bank and the EU, among others, and has extensive experience in working with governments in developing countries. He has published widely in leading academic journals including *Weltwirtschaftliches Archiv*, *Oxford Economic Papers*, *The Manchester School* and the *British Journal of Industrial Relations*, among others, and is co-author of *Commodity Supply Management by Producing Countries* (1997).

Victor Murinde is Professor of Development Finance as well as Head of the Finance Subject Group in the Birmingham Business School at the University of Birmingham. He completed his PhD in economics at Cardiff Business School, University of Wales Cardiff, in 1990. Thereafter he held positions as lecturer in Banking at Cardiff Business School, Senior Lecturer in Finance and later Reader in Development Finance at the University of Birmingham. During the academic year 2001–2, he held the distinguished Hallsworth Senior Research Fellowship at the Institute for Development Policy and Management, University of Manchester, on sabbatical from the University of Birmingham. He was awarded the *Doctoris Honoris Causa* of Tallinn Technical University on 17 September 2003. He has also worked as a consultant to the World Bank, the United Nations, UNCTAD, as well as a number of banks, private companies and governments in developing and transition economies. Professor Murinde has published over 40 articles in many leading journals and authored, co-authored and edited about a dozen books. He is the joint convenor (together with Professors Christopher J. Green and Colin Kirkpatrick) of ESRC Research Seminars on 'Finance for Development and Poverty Reduction'. His research interests cover corporate finance issues in emerging financial markets, development and international banking, and the flow of funds approach to macroeconomic policy modelling.

Rose W. Ngugi is a lecturer in the Department of Economics at the University of Nairobi as well as a policy analyst and Head of Private Sector Development Division at Kenya Institute of Public Policy Research and

Analysis (KIPPRA) in Nairobi. She completed her PhD in Finance at Birmingham Business School, University of Birmingham in 2002. She is active in various research forums including the African Economic Research Consortium where she is a senior researcher and has been a visiting scholar to the IMF Research Department under the AERC-IMF Visiting Scholar's Progamme. Her main research focus has been on the financial sector, covering issues of financial sector reforms, interest rate management and stock market development. She is also at present looking at issues of concern in creating an enabling environment for private sector development. In this regard she is involved in the World Bank Regional Private Enterprise Development project in Kenya, a research project on 'Understanding Reforms' with the Global Development Network and a project on 'Security Risk and Private Sector Growth' with KIPPRA. She has published in refereed journals including *Journal of African Business, Africa Finance Journal, African Development Review, Journal of International Development* and *African Journal of Economic Policy.*

Frederick Nixson is Professor of Development Economics in the School of Economic Studies (School of Social Science as of October 2004) at the University of Manchester. He lectured at Makerere University, Kampala, Uganda, before coming to Manchester in 1971. Since then he has worked in a number of countries including India, Mongolia, Vietnam, the Solomon Islands, Lesotho and North Korea and has lectured in China, Jamaica, Brazil and the Philippines. He has worked as a consultant for the EU, UNDP, UNCTAD, Asian Development Bank, World Bank and the Commonwealth Secretariat. He has authored, co-authored and co-edited 12 books and 80 papers in books and journals. His current research interests include the impact of privatization on poverty and the history of heterodox thinking in development economics.

Sanjiva Prasad is currently a business sector analyst at the Inland Revenue, UK. After completing his PhD at Cardiff Business School, the University of Wales, Cardiff, during which he was awarded the Royal Economic Society Scholarship, 1994–5, he has held numerous positions as an economist and analyst at a variety of institutions including HM Treasury (London) and at the UK Government's Export Credits Guarantee Department. He has also been a consultant to a number of private companies. Dr Prasad's research interests cover corporate finance issues in emerging financial markets.

Stuart Rutherford, a researcher, writer and practitioner of financial services for the poor, is based at the Institute for Development Policy and Management, University of Manchester.

Orlanda Ruthven is currently pursuing a PhD in Development Studies at Queen Elizabeth House, University of Oxford. Prior to this she worked for two years on the Finance and Development Research Programme of IDPM, undertaking 'financial diaries' and 'snapshot' surveys about saving, borrowing and expenditure behaviour among the poor of Delhi slums and villages in Eastern Uttar Pradesh, India. From 1996 to 2000 she worked as an Enterprise Development Adviser in DFID's London and Delhi offices.

Preface

The role of finance in development has become a major topic for research and debate in the last two decades. Although it is widely agreed that there are important relationships between finance and the development process, there is much less agreement on the exact nature of these relationships, particularly on the causality between finance and development: is financial development an essential prerequisite for general economic development, or is it more nearly a passive (if important) by-product of the development process? Development finance has become an important subject for teachers, researchers and policy makers. Despite this, there are relatively few convenient, up-to-date sources of collected information on finance and development. There are few textbooks on the subject, and no major journals devoted to finance and development, although there are numerous specialist finance or development journals. It could be argued that this has encouraged a certain amount of polarization in the field, with possible adverse implications for policy advice: development economists are rarely trained in finance, and financial economists are rarely trained in development. While one would expect that developing countries could learn from the financial experience of the industrial countries, and vice versa, it would be naïve to expect the solutions to policy problems in one country to be applicable a fortiori to apparently similar problems in other countries at different stages of development and with different institutional frameworks.

We believe therefore that this is an opportune time to take stock of the existing state of knowledge in the field of finance and development. To this end, we present in this volume a collection of surveys concerned with current issues in finance and development to be published as a book in a single volume. The contributions in the collection have been specially commissioned from leading researchers in the field. Each chapter aims to offer a comprehensive survey and synthesis of the subject with which it is concerned. The contributions should be accessible to postgraduate and advanced undergraduate students specializing in the area, and will form an essential work of reference for all professionals working in the field, whether in universities or elsewhere in the public or private sector.

We do not claim that the surveys will cover the entire field of finance and development. Many of the contributors are an outgrowth from a major research programme on finance and development funded by the UK Department for International Development (DFID) under the 'Finance and Development Research Programme'. The purpose of the research programme was to identify effective financial sector policies in relation to the objectives of promoting poverty-reducing economic growth in low-income countries. The intended outcome of the research was the provision of practical advice on the design and implementation of financial sector policies and reforms.

Some of the contributions have benefited from the seminars held at the universities of Birmingham, Loughborough, Manchester and Oxford under the ESRC Research Seminars on 'Finance for Economic Growth and Poverty Reduction'. Accordingly the emphasis within these chapters is on the relationships among finance, poverty and growth. We believe that this is an emphasis which most professionals would agree is particularly appropriate for this field.

Hence we would like to thank DFID and the ESRC for supporting the research, conferences and seminars that led to the final production of the chapters in the volume. Nevertheless the interpretations and conclusions expressed in this book are entirely our own and should not be attributed in any manner to DFID.

We are greatly indebted to the contributing authors for making available to us their original and previously unpublished papers rather than opting for the current tendency to send the contributions to top-rated journals. The editorial work was made particularly easy by the cooperation of the authors in revising their drafts as well as proofreading the galleys.

Finally, we are very grateful to Dymphna Evans who, as Commissioning Editor at Edward Elgar, generally encouraged the development of the volume. The production team at Edward Elgar, especially Karen McCarthy and Matthew Pitman, deserve a lot of credit for their patience and support during the gestation period for this final product.

Christopher J. Green
Loughborough

Colin H. Kirkpatrick
Manchester

Victor Murinde
Birmingham

May 2004

1. How does finance contribute to the development process and poverty reduction?

Christopher J. Green, Colin H. Kirkpatrick and Victor Murinde[1]

1. INTRODUCTION

At the outset, it is useful to ask the question: how, in theory, could finance contribute to the development process and poverty reduction? Although the first generation of neoclassical growth models attributed economic growth to exogenous technical change and population expansion (for example Solow, 1956, 1957), recent literature has shifted the spotlight to emphasize the key role played by finance in achieving economic growth in developing countries (Levine and Dermigüç-Kunt, 2001; Evans *et al.*, 2002). Meanwhile, since Myrdal's (1968) 'Asian Drama', important milestones have been achieved in understanding poverty. However, as pointed out by Green and Kirkpatrick (2002), the exact nature of the relationships among financial development, economic growth and poverty reduction remains unresolved.

One main hurdle in establishing these relationships is that the burgeoning literature on poverty is yet to be squarely interfaced with the recent developments in the literature on finance in developing countries, notwithstanding the clear promise shown by the seminal multidisciplinary study on 'Finance against Poverty' by Hulme and Mosley (1996). Recent studies bear testimony to the fact that some researchers are at least hammering away at this issue and there seems to be a small (albeit growing) body of evidence which supports the view that financial development can reduce income inequality and poverty levels, directly through widening access of the poor to financial services, and indirectly through the impact of finance-led growth on poverty reduction (Aghion, *et al.*, 1999). The recent International Conference on Financing for Development, which was held in Monterrey in March 2002, highlighted the initiatives as well as serious difficulties towards achieving the Millennium Development Goals. Hence, given the international community's commitment to the goal of halving world poverty by the year 2015, it is imperative to

understand better the ways in which finance contributes to economic growth
and poverty reduction, and to design effective policies that can make that
contribution a reality.

In this context, the purpose of this chapter is to draw on some of our case
studies and recent empirical work in order to provoke a debate on policy
dimensions as well as further research on finance for development and poverty reduction. In what follows, the chapter is structured into five sections.
Section 2 argues that finance does matter for economic growth; the discussion remains open on the question of whether higher growth does 'trickle
down' to facilitate poverty reduction. Section 3 looks at firm behaviour and
the role of financial markets and points to the potential for poverty reduction.
The stability of the financial system and implications for poverty reduction
are discussed in section 4. Section 5 considers the flow of funds and poverty
reduction, while section 6 highlights some recent work on directly testing for
the link between financial development and economic growth. The concluding section indicates some other policy conundrums and research issues.

2.   FINANCE DOES MATTER FOR ECONOMIC GROWTH

The subject of economic growth has enjoyed a renaissance in the last two
decades, as indicated by the vast theoretical and empirical literature on the
subject; see, for example, some recent surveys by Barro and Sala-i-Martin
(1995), Aghion and Howitt (1998), Evans (1997) and Temple (1999). The
seminal work is invariably Solow's (1956, 1957) model in which sustained
growth in output per head is only possible as a result of exogenous technical
change. However, the resurgence of interest in growth theory has been inspired largely by the Romer (1986)–Lucas (1988) paradigm of endogenous
growth, in which the key determinants of output growth may be endogenous
variables. In this paradigm, output per head can grow over time because of
endogenous forces within the economy, particularly human capital and the
knowledge base.

In general, attempts to delve into the causes of economic growth have
involved a number of empirical approaches. Probably the oldest and still
frequently-used approach is that based on growth accounting (see Senhadji,
2000). This essentially involves differentiating a Cobb–Douglas production
function with respect to time, and using the resulting equation to model the
rate of economic growth as a function of the change in factor inputs. Originally this type of model was estimated in cross-sectional regressions using
cross-country data, with a limited or negligible time dimension; see Fischer
(1993) and Senhadji (2000). Endogenous growth theory stimulated extensions to this approach, which typically involved cross-section regressions of

national growth rates on a wider range of variables, intended to capture cross-sectional variations in growth, including in particular indicators of human capital and the knowledge base. Such regressions were often not derived explicitly from a production function, but included instead a more-or-less ad hoc list of plausible explanatory variables, often called 'Barro regressions' following Barro (1991) and Barro and Lee (1994). This methodology was subjected to numerous criticisms, and more recent papers have attempted to improve on it in a variety of ways. The first approach, originated by Mankiw *et al.* (1992) is to make more explicit the equilibrium conditions and dynamics implied by the underlying growth model, mainly the Solow model, and to include human capital explicitly. The second approach employs panel data to make better use of the time domain, in order to test the convergence hypothesis implicit in Solow's original contribution. Knight *et al.* (1993), Knowles and Owen (1995), Islam (1995) and Murinde *et al.* (2004) are examples of this approach. Still a third approach is to develop completely different methodologies, such as that of Quah (1993, 1997), who has focused on describing income distribution dynamics.

However finance has also featured as an important argument in trying to disentangle the process of economic growth. A seminal contribution to the literature, stemming from Goldsmith's (1969) work, emphasizes the connection between a country's financial superstructure and its real economic infrastructure. It is argued that financial markets facilitate growth by enabling efficient intertemporal allocation of resources, although there remains some debate as to whether financial development causes economic growth or vice-versa. See, for example, Lyons and Murinde (1994) and Arestis *et al.* (2001). Indeed the issue of causality between financial development and economic growth may be described as the 'chicken and egg problem of finance and development'. It is useful to recall that almost a century ago, Schumpeter (1911) argued that financial intermediation through the banking system played a pivotal role in economic development by affecting the allocation of savings, thereby improving productivity, technical change and the rate of economic growth. Lewis (1955) suggested that the causality between finance and growth was not unidirectional; rather, there was a two-way relationship, where financial markets and institutions develop as a consequence of economic growth, and in turn act as a stimulus to growth. Over the years, research has built on these ideas by developing a greater understanding of the important ways in which financial development stimulates economic growth: by mobilizing savings, allocating capital funds, monitoring the use of funds and managing risk (see, for example, Murinde, 1996; Levine, 1997). Fry (1995) summarizes most of his work in which he specified and estimated simultaneous equation models in which financial development (as a measure of savings or investment) was determined simultaneously with economic growth. A consistent finding from most of the work by Fry was that improved financial inter-mediation, achieved by removing financial repression (through financial liberalization), has a positive impact on economic growth. It has also been argued that the financial system acts as the 'brain' of the economy, and hence serves to allocate scarce resources across time and space in the environment of uncertainty (Stiglitz, 1994). Under asymmetric information, the task of gathering information on the risk–return attributes of investment opportunities, and hence allocation of risk, is performed by financial institutions.

Arguably, the most important policy implication of the positive impact of financial development on economic growth relates to financial liberalization policy. Early work by McKinnon (1973) and Shaw (1973) identified financial repressions as a counterveiling force on economic growth.[2] Fry (1995) and Murinde (1996) present the theoretical McKinnon–Shaw model, its implications and limitations, and point to the key argument that the existence of negative real interest rates, fixed and overvalued exchange rates, and an overregulated financial sector curtail the ability of financial institutions and markets to function properly. The policy prescription consists of adoption of financial liberalization by allowing the market to determine allocation of resources through the price mechanism. For example, deregulation of nominal deposit rates was intended to achieve an increased volume of savings, while deregulation of loan rates was intended to improve the allocation of capital to productive uses; both would enhance the volume and productivity of physical capital and hence contribute to economic growth. Financial liberalization policy further provided an important component of the structural adjustment programmes which were initiated by the International Monetary Fund (IMF) and World Bank, and were designed to create stable long-run growth in developing countries (World Bank, 2001a). However, as Jalilian and Kirkpatrick (2002) have pointed out, there is no consensus on the effectiveness of financial liberalization in improving economic growth in developing countries. Rather it would seem to be that the results of financial liberalization, including the broader structural adjustment programmes, have been disappointing (see also the conclusions by Williamson and Maher, 1998).

The case study we present here is drawn from work which attempts to synthesize rival theories of economic growth, particularly those emphasizing finance. In the study, Evans *et al.* (2002) link and evaluate three different strands within the finance and development literature: the first strand is that derived from the neoclassical growth model, based on the seminal work of Solow (1956, 1957); the second strand is that inspired by the Romer (1986)–Lucas (1988) paradigm of endogenous growth; and the third strand stems from Goldsmith (1969), McKinnon (1973) and Shaw (1973). Specifically, the study investigates the contributions of human capital and financial development to economic growth in a panel of 82 countries covering 22 years

(1972–93). The main innovations in the chapter stem from the fact that a translog production function is used as a framework for estimating the relationships among economic growth and factor inputs, namely labour, physical capital, human capital (deriving from endogenous growth theory) and a monetary factor (money or credit, deriving from the theory of money in the production function).

A summary of the findings is presented in Table 1.1. First, it is found that finance makes a significant contribution to growth. Moreover this is true irrespective of whether money or credit is employed as a measure of the monetary factor. Second, the results associated with the money–capital interaction terms unambigously support the McKinnon–Shaw complementarity hypothesis and debt intermediation view, irrespective of the definition of the monetary variable used. The signs and significance levels of these coefficients are also consistent with developments in endogenous growth theory which emphasize the complementarities between financial markets and capital accumulation (Murinde, 1996). Third, it is found that the interaction between credit and human capital makes a significant contribution to growth, irrespective of the precise measure of human capital. Fourth, the results suggest that testing for the impact of human capital in isolation is likely to produce misleading results, mainly arising from the variations in the definitions of human capital used as well as the sharp differences in human capital development across a large sample of countries. Moreover, the study finds substantial evidence of (mostly intuitively reasonable) interaction effects among factor inputs, all of which give another reason why Barro regressions may be misleading. Overall, therefore, the results suggest that financial development is at least as important as human capital in the growth process.

However the estimates of the parameters associated with the initial income variable only provide ad hoc evidence that convergence in factor productivities may itself be factor-dependent. The precise impact of human capital and financial development on growth may perhaps depend in part on the quality of the input as much as on any single measure of its quantity.

Further research is clearly needed to allow for dynamics in an unbalanced panel and to tease out the endogeneity (and exogeneity) of the variables and interaction terms in the translog model. Moreover further research would be helpful to determine whether any one particular measure of money or human capital is superior to the others. This, in turn, suggests the need for further research at the micro and macro level to investigate the appropriate measures of these variables.

Table 1.1 The impact of human capital and domestic credit on GDP growth per work in 82 economies, 1972–92

Eq	Y72	K	CR	PS	K²	DC²	PS²	KY72	KCR	KPS	CRY72	CRPS
(1)	0.1E–06	0.159	0.587	–0.921	–0.007	–0.011	–0.072	–0.1E–04	0.027	–0.017	0.8E–05	0.054
(1)	0.1E–06	0.159	0.587	–0.921	–0.007	–0.011	–0.072	–0.1E–04	0.027	–0.017	0.8E–05	0.054
(1)	3.50**	1.18	6.14**	–2.74**	–0.63	–4.93**	–2.44*	–6.24**	9.17**	–2.35*	4.61**	6.44**
(2)	0.1E–05	0.089	0.599	–0.895	—	–0.011	–0.071	–0.1E–04	0.026	–0.019	0.9E–05	0.054
(2)	3.61**	1.18	6.44**	–2.68**	—	–4.89**	–2.41*	–9.29**	10.02**	–2.82**	4.69**	6.62**

Eq	Y72	K	CR	SS	K²	DC²	SS²	KY72	KCR	KSS	CRY72	CRSS
(3)	0.1E–05	0.256	0.348	–0.385	–0.006	–0.012	–0.021	–0.1E–04	0.027	–0.007	0.7E–05	0.027
(3)	3.36**	1.75†	4.37**	–2.16*	–0.52	–5.22**	–1.79†	–6.36**	8.98**	–1.03	3.64**	4.63**
(4)	–1E–05	0.193	0.358	–0.361	—	–0.012	–0.020	–0.1E–04	0.026	–0.008	0.7E–05	0.027
(4)	3.39**	2.52*	4.75**	–2.15*	—	–5.19**	–1.78†	–9.06**	9.80**	–1.45	3.64**	4.89**

Eq	Y72	K	CR	PE	K²	DC²	PE²	KY72	KCR	KPE	CRY72	CRPE
(5)	0.1E–05	0.137	0.441	–0.235	–0.004	–0.012	–0.009	–0.1E–04	0.027	–0.012	0.8E–05	0.030
(5)	3.40**	1.08	6.44**	1.72†	–0.36	–5.08**	–0.99	–6.79**	8.92**	–2.21*	4.53**	7.06**
(6)	0.1E–05	0.099	0.449	–0.105	—	–0.011	—	–0.1E–04	0.026	–0.013	0.8E–05	0.031
(6)	3.41**	1.22	6.73**	–2.27*	—	–5.09**	—	–9.32**	10.07**	–2.42*	4.55**	7.16**

Notes: A constant term is included in all regressions. Figures in parentheses are *t*-statistics, ** significant at the 1% level; * significant at the 5% level; † significant at the 10% level. Y72 = initial level of income; K = physical capital (perpetual inventory method with 5% depreciation rate; CR = money, measured as domestic credit; PS = human capital, measured as primary school enrolment; SS = human capital, measured as secondary school enrolment; PE = human capital, measured as public expenditure on education.
Test statistics and further diagnostics are available in Evans *et al.* (2002).

Source: Evans *et al.*, (2002).

6

3. FINANCE AND POVERTY REDUCTION THROUGH THE BEHAVIOUR OF FIRMS

One potential important link between finance and poverty reduction relates to the behaviour of firms and households. Prasad *et al.* (2001) survey the relevant literature and conclude that financing policy, capital structure and firm ownership are all strongly linked. The argument is that financing policy by firms requires managers to identify ways of funding new investment. The managers may exercise three main choices: use retained earnings, borrow through debt instruments or issue new shares. Hence the standard capital structure of a firm includes retained earnings, debt and equity; these three components of capital structure reflect firm ownership structure in the sense that the first and third components reflect ownership by shareholders while the second component represents ownership by debtholders. This is the pattern found in developing and developed countries alike (see La-Porta *et al.*, 1999). Capital structure also affects corporate behaviour (Hutton and Kenc, 1998). Thus financing policy, capital structure and firm ownership are all strongly linked in explaining how households form and modify their asset-acquisition behaviour through firms and capital markets, and thereby influence their incomes and returns to asset holdings, whether in the form of direct remuneration, capital gains or dividends.

There is a large volume of research on these issues in industrial countries, but virtually no work has been done on developing countries, apart from a limited amount of empirical research by, for example, Hamid and Singh (1992), Singh (1995), Brada and Singh (1999) and Prasad (2000). It is scarcely an exaggeration to state that, until recently, corporate finance did not exist as an area of research investigation in developing countries. Some of the reasons for this are clear. Many developing countries initially chose a state-sponsored route to development, with a relatively insignificant role assigned to the private corporate sector. In the poorer countries, irrespective of development strategy, there is only an embryonic corporate sector. Moreover most of the corporate financing needs were met by regional and international development banks, which either took an equity interest in the firms or provided the debt component of a firm's capital. However, in almost all these countries, development banks have experienced serious difficulties (Murinde, 1996; Murinde and Kariisa-Kasa, 1997). Thus there is a conspicuous gap in the empirical research on corporate finance in developing countries; this gap requires urgent attention, given that the research is likely to have profound policy implications for promoting poverty-reducing economic growth.

However we wish specifically to draw on two strands of empirical studies. The first is concerned with the issue of stock market development and the impact on companies, investors and policies aimed at revitalizing stock markets, particularly the modernization of trading systems, the liberalization of stock market regulations and changes in the regulatory regime. The second is concerned with company financing decisions and corporate capital structure, including dividend policy.

In the first strand, we draw on major case studies carried out in Kenya, India and a cross-section of African markets. For Kenya and India, the case studies use event study methodology to focus on the impact of stock market reforms, aimed at market revitalization on the efficiency of share pricing. The studies on Kenya analyse the main market microstructure characteristics of the Nairobi Stock Exchange, namely efficiency, volatility and liquidity. The analysis is conducted by comparing the state of market efficiency, the degree of volatility of stock returns and the level of liquidity in the period before and after the implementation of institutional changes, namely establishment of a market regulator, entry of foreign investors, changes in trading system and expansion of stockbrokerage market.

The main findings of our sample studies, summarized in Table 1.2, are threefold. First, the price discovery process shows efficiency gains, following the establishment of the market regulator and free entry of foreign investors, but not after the shift to an open out-cry trading system. Second, the revitalization period is characterized by a negative relationship between efficiency gains and volatility. Third, in general, the free entry of foreign investors has positive impact on market microstructure, including a temporary rise in liquidity, low volatility and efficiency gains.

These results are consistent with those obtained from a cross-section of ten African emerging stock markets, and provide a more general comparative

Table 1.2   The impact of revitalization reforms on Nairobi Stock Exchange microstructure

	Efficiency	Volatility	Liquidity
1. Changes in trading system			
1.1 Call to open outcry floor trading	±	–	+
1.2 Call auction to continuous auction	+	–	+
2. Establishment of market regulator	+	–	+
3. Entry of foreign investors	+	±	+

Note: The signs (+, – and ±) give the impact of the reforms in 1.1, 1.2, 2 and 3 on efficiency, volatility and liquidity; + is a positive impact, – is a negative (or inverse) impact, and ± is an indeterminate effect. For the full empirical results, including the magnitude of the impact, see Ngugi *et al.* (2002).

Source: Summarized from the evidence in Ngugi *et al.* (2002).

evaluation of the impact of stock market reforms in Africa. The evidence generally suggests that there are benefits of investments to improve market microstructure. For example, a comparative analysis across the sample demonstrates that markets with an advanced trading technology, a functional regulatory system and relaxed foreign investors' participation show high efficiency and low market volatility. Although direction of causality between efficiency and volatility varies across the markets, in general we infer that reforms which reduce volatility reap high efficiency. However, in some markets, the effects of the reforms are too recent to show any clear response pattern.

Moreover the results are consistent with those obtained by previous researchers, for example by Demirgüç-Kunt and Levine (1996), as well as the studies which are reviewed in Majnoni and Massa (2001). For example, for the Tel Aviv stock market, Amihud *et al.* (1997) show gains in efficiency of the price discovery process, increased liquidity and low volatility as a result of the adoption of a new trading system. Moreover, some studies suggest that the entry of foreign investors has been followed by increased liquidity and enhanced efficiency in the price discovery process, although market volatility has either remained unchanged or declined (see Kim and Singal, 2000). Nevertheless, for the Taiwan stock market, Chang *et al.* (1999) show no change in liquidity and efficiency of the price discovery process, while volatility increases with the continuous auction system.

The potential link of these sample studies to poverty reduction derives from the role that a stock market may play in facilitating asset ownership by firms and households. In this context, the drive to achieve market efficiency is desirable as efficiency allows households and firms to diversify their sources of investment capital and spread investment risk; this is because the stock markets play an important role in aggregating and conveying information through price signals, as noted by Amihud *et al.* (1997) and Caprio and Demirgüç-Kunt (1998). Particularly in small, emerging stock markets, efficient stock prices and yields provide benchmarks against which the cost of capital for and returns on investment projects can be judged, even if such projects are not financed through the stock market (Green, Maggioni and Murinde, 2000). Moreover, as they are forward-looking, stock prices provide a unique record of the shifts in investors' views about the future prospects of companies. Furthermore an efficient price discovery process is traditionally associated with low volatility, which promotes stock market effectiveness in allocating resources. High volatility distorts efficient resource allocation by making investors more averse to holding stocks. Risk-averse investors tend to demand a high risk premium, which increases the cost of capital and reduces market liquidity (Bekaert and Harvey, 1997; Kim and Singal, 2000). Liquidity is desirable because it reduces the required return by investors; illiquidity increases the cost of capital and acts as a constraint for stock markets to perform adequately their information processing and signalling functions (Amihud *et al.*, 1997).

But the behaviour of well regulated and efficient stock markets is only one part of the story, the other part is the use made of the markets by firms and households. Hence the second strand of the empirical research is concerned with corporate finance. The major case studies are based on India and Kenya, but additional evidence is based on research conducted on Zimbabwe and, for comparative purposes, on Thailand and Malaysia; see Mutenheri and Green (2003) and Ngugi *et al.* (2002a, 2002b). In Kenya a series of studies are undertaken, in order to examine company investment and financing decisions; the studies emphasize the impact of the various forms of uncertainty that are characteristic of Kenya as a developing economy. In addition, the studies examine the financing behaviour of firms listed on the Nairobi Stock Exchange, aiming to find out the implications of capital market development on capital structure, especially when firms are faced with market imperfections and an inflexible choice of external financing instruments. The results are reported in Table 1.3, and compared to evidence on many emerging and developed stock markets, based on the work by Rajan and Zingales (1995) and Booth *et al.* (2001).

In Table 1.3, it is shown that the traditional determinants of capital structure, namely tangibility, firm size and profitability, have clear and consistent effects on the gearing decisions of firms for emerging stock markets in 11 sample countries and seven OECD countries. First, the results are consistent with the trade-off theory, which seeks to balance the costs and benefits of debt, and predicts that equity financing is preferred when assets are intangible or highly specialized. Firms with high tangibility therefore tend to be highly geared. However, as the debt to equity ratio decreases, in line with agency theory, the cost of debt falls while the cost of equity rises. These agency cost effects become increasingly more important, until debt finance becomes the preferred form of financing. Firms with high tangibility therefore tend to be highly geared. Second, size matters: the bigger the firms, the more access the firms have to external finance. The inverse relationship between size and debt is driven by two agency costs of debt, namely underinvestment and asset substitution. Indeed evidence is found to show that the capital structure decision is influenced by growth opportunities and that, owing to agency costs, firms with lower levels of growth tend to be more highly geared. Third, highly profitable firms have the muscle to get access to extra debt financing. By incorporating information asymmetries, the pecking order hypothesis predicts that profitable firms will resort to debt financing less often than unprofitable firms. In contrast, the static trade-off theory predicts that profitability enhances the use of debt financing because profitable firms have access to cheaper debt.

Table 1.3 *Comparing empirical evidence on capital structure decisions for emerging and developed markets*

	Tax rate	Tangibility	Business risk	Firm size	Profitability	Growth opportunities
Part I Emerging stock markets						
Brazil	−ve(NS)	−ve	−ve(NS)	+ve(NS)	−ve	
India	−ve	−ve	+ve(NS)	−ve	−ve	+ve(NS)
Jordan	−ve	−ve	+ve	+ve	−ve	+ve
Kenya	−ve	−ve	+ve	+ve	−ve	+ve
Korea	−ve(NS)	−ve	−ve	+ve	−ve	−ve
Malaysia	−ve(NS)	−ve	+ve	+ve	−ve	+ve
Mexico	−ve	+ve	+ve	−ve(NS)	−ve	
Pakistan	−ve	−ve(NS)	−ve(NS)	+ve(NS)	−ve	−ve(NS)
Thailand	+ve	+ve(NS)	−ve	+ve	−ve	+ve
Turkey	−ve	−ve	−ve(NS)	+ve(NS)	−ve	−ve
Zimbabwe	+ve(NS)	−ve(NS)	−ve	−ve	+ve(NS)	−ve(NS)
Part II Developed stock markets						
Canada	+ve			+ve	−ve	−ve
France	+ve			+ve(NS)	−ve(NS)	−ve
Germany	+ve			−ve	−ve(NS)	−ve
Italy	+ve(NS)			+ve(NS)	−ve(NS)	−ve(NS)
Japan	+ve			+ve	−ve	−ve(NS)
UK	+ve			+ve	−ve(NS)	−ve
US	+ve			+ve	−ve	−ve

Notes:
1. The table provides summary results from comparative studies conducted for both developed and developing countries by Rajan and Zingales (1995) for G-7 countries; Booth *et al.* (2001) for 10 emerging markets, and Ngugi (2002) for Kenya.
2. We consider results for book value debt ratio and variables indicated to proxy for target debt ratio; +ve = positive relationship; −ve = negative relationship; and NS = insignificant relationship.

In general these results are consistent with the evidence discussed in recent work by Shyam-Sunder and Myers (1999), Chirinko and Singha (2000) and Myers (2001). However these determinants of financing decisions by firms are quite remote from the socioeconomic factors that relate to poverty reduction in developing countries. Hence the interesting question is: what socioeconomic variables tend to influence firm ownership and firm financing decisions at the micro and small-scale enterprises level, which may therefore relate to poverty reduction?

An attempt is made to incorporate a number of non-traditional determinants of firms' capital structure decisions in a study of some 2000 micro and small unquoted enterprises (MSEs) in Kenya, by Green, Kimuyu, Manos and

Murinde (2002). The study analyses the financing behaviour of these enterprises within the empirical framework of a heterodox model for the debt–equity
and gearing decisions of MSEs. The determinants of the success rate of loan
applications are also investigated by considering a comprehensive range of
non-traditional (heterodox) factors such as age of business and working owner,
gender of owner, education of owner, skills of owner, ownership type (family
or otherwise), ownership of land by entrepreneur, formality or non-informal-
ity of the business, and record keeping and other practices of the business –
factors which hitherto have not been used in the corporate finance literature
but are important in understanding the special case of MSEs in emerging
markets such as Kenya. The results emphasize three major findings. First,
MSEs in Kenya obtain debt from a wide variety of sources especially family
and friends, but including also cooperatives, banks, rotating savings and
credit associations (ROSCAs), non-governmental organizations (NGOs), and
other financial institutions. Second, the debt–equity and gearing decisions of
MSEs and their success rates in loan applications can all be understood by
using relatively simple models which include a mixture of conventional and
heterodox variables, including socioeconomic variables that are linked to
poverty reduction. Third, and in particular, measures of the tangibility of the
owner's assets and the owner's education and training have a significant
positive impact on the probability of borrowing and of the gearing level.
These findings have important policy implications for policy makers and
entrepreneurs of MSEs in Kenya. As Mullineux and Murinde (2002) point
out, good financial sector policies for enterpise development seem to promote
growth in the household and business sectors. Moreover, as King and Levine
(1993a, 1993b) show, the growth of enterprise (and enterpreneurship) does
strengthen the link between finance and growth, and directly encourages
innovation and productivity, which are some of the basic elements of current
poverty reduction strategies. Fourth, there is some tentative evidence that the
availability of credit for small business may have improved over time. Fifth,
and finally, the main key determinants of debt and loan-screening decisions
are a mixture of conventional and heterodox variables. Among the conventional variables, measures of the tangibility of the owner's assets, and objective
and subjective measures of income, are particularly important, both in the
debt and in the screening decisions. Among the more heterodox variables, the
level of education and training of the owners have a significant positive
impact on the probability of borrowing and of the resultant gearing level.

All these findings have important policy implications for policy makers
and entrepreneurs of MSEs in Kenya; the socioeconomic (and non-traditional) variables which importantly determine the financing choices made by
MSEs are linked to poverty reduction activities and could be further explored
in that light. Clearly further research on these issues is necessary.

4. THE STABILITY OF THE FINANCIAL SYSTEM AND IMPLICATIONS FOR POVERTY REDUCTION

As the recent East Asian crisis demonstrated, a financial crisis can seriously cripple the financial infrastructure of an economy, derail development programmes and dramatically worsen poverty (World Bank, 2001a, p. 165; 2001b, p. 76). A stable financial system is therefore vital for economic growth and poverty reduction strategies. Weak financial regulation, often as a consequence of over-hasty financial liberalization, has contributed directly to economic instability and decline (Brownbridge and Kirkpatrick, 2000).

Apart from the systemic effects of a financial crisis, localized bank failure can also threaten the viability of a financial system. Evidence from a large panel of 62 commercial banks in 11 African countries over the period 1991–8 suggests that the liquidity as well as quality of the assets of commercial banks can serve as reasonably reliable 'early warning' indicators of bank failure. Because the survival of commercial banks hinges upon public confidence, severe liquidity constraints are signals of doom and may induce bank runs, thus spreading banking failure across the entire banking sector (contagion effects). For this matter, central banks should exercise great caution in responding to bank failure: bailout policy should be considered only if bank failure is bound to lead to systematic disruption, otherwise individual weak banks should be allowed to fail (Tefula and Murinde, 2002).

In addition, an empirical study of efficiency in a cross-section of 82 commercial banks in Sub-Saharan Africa over the period 1991–8 suggests that commercial bank managers perform more efficiently through better management and control of the cost side compared to the revenue side of bank operations; hence managers are advised to keep a sharp eye on bank costs. This implies that central banks, which supervise and regulate the commercial banks, should take greater interest in the internal controls and budgetary performance of the commercial banks, in addition to the traditional focus on capital adequacy indicators (Tefula *et al.*, 2002).

Moreover, in the increasingly global network, the effects of bank performance are far-reaching. For example, Murinde and Ryan (2001, 2002) have argued that financial liberalization, implicit in the WTO and GATS protocols, will lead to a large shake-up of the African banking industry. However banks in most African countries have little to fear from liberalization, at least in terms of the continuing existence of a locally owned banking industry. Indeed the disciplinary benefits of the market are more likely to benefit the owners as well as the employees generally, and low-skilled local workers in particular. Increasing competition, especially from foreign entrants, is likely to put further pressure on older style lending policies, leading to more widespread use of auditing and accounting procedures and greater transparency (Murinde and Ryan, 2001, 2002).

However, in a case study of the limits to financial globalisation, Mullineux *et al.* (2001, 2003) emphasize that an important lesson from the financial crisis in Thailand is that a traditional central bank is not well suited to coping with a severe financial crisis. It is argued that, although financial reform is important, financial liberalization in an uncontrolled financial sector results in misallocation and mismatching of funds, especially arising from excessive lending by domestic banks (sometimes financed by international investors) and a lack of control over the actions of the borrowers.

Overall it may be argued that the financial sector should play an important role in promoting the growth of enterprises in poor countries. The strategies for stimulating enterprise finance should revolve around establishing effective bank regulation and supervision; setting an appropriate positive real interest rate; reducing unnecessary government intervention, guidance and direction (thus reducing opportunities for corruption and 'cronyism'); and addressing the credit rationing, financial exclusion and other problems, such as inadequate competition in banking, that arise from market failures (Mullineux and Murinde, 2002).

Hence it may be argued that the stability of the financial system in general, and the performance of banks in particular, have important implications for poverty reduction. One important dimension which could be explored here is the impact of bank failure and subsequent contagion effects of bank runs on households and firms in general, and on poverty reduction strategies in particular. The experience to date is that, in the aftermath of financial crises and bank failure, economic growth has fallen dramatically, severely affecting the most vulnerable and poorest people (see World Bank, 2001a). It may well be the case that some households immediately fall below the poverty line when banks fail, not only because they are clients of the bad bank but because of the contagion effects that lead to the collapse of other financial firms, non-financial firms and the effects on employment and consumption. Overall the World Bank (ibid.) shows that the countries which were badly hit by the Asian financial crisis of 1997 experienced an increase in poverty levels. Hence the implications of financial crises and bank failure for poverty reduction need to be very carefully investigated.

5.   FLOW OF FUNDS AND POVERTY REDUCTION

Flows of funds arise from the transactions which take place in an economy, involving purchases or sales of goods, services or assets and liabilities. National flow of funds accounts provide a record of these flows for the whole

economy; the corresponding accounts covering individual or corporate transactions are more usually called 'sources–uses' statements. The interpretation
and analysis of flow of funds data are important tasks for economic policy
advisors, for a main function of the flow of funds accounts is to show the
sources and uses of funds which a country needs for its growth, development
and poverty reduction. Flow of funds analysis can reveal information about
imbalances in the economy and changes in the distribution of funds.
Simulations of the effects of different economic policies on intersectoral
flows can give a clear picture of the channels through which policies may
affect different sectors of the economy and therefore the functional distribution of income in the economy.

We draw on some recent empirical studies which have proposed and implemented novel frameworks for the compilation and analysis of the flow of
funds in developing countries (see Green, Murinde, Suppakitjarak and Moore,
2000; Green and Murinde, 2003). We report here three case studies. The first
set of case studies are on India (Moore *et al.*, 2002a, 2002b, 2002c, 2002d).
India has a substantial base of flow of funds data comparable to many industrial countries, but one which has not so far been used for policy analysis. In
the case studies, flow of funds data are used to estimate a comprehensive
econometric financial model for the major sectors in the Indian economy:
households, businesses, banks and other financial institutions. Simulations of
the model are carried out, first, to evaluate the impact of interest rates and
credit controls on portfolio behaviour and, second, to study the effects of
monetary policy, financial controls and subsequent liberalization on different
sectors of the economy and the flow of funds.

In this set of case studies for India there are several more specific findings,
which may still bear some general lessons for other countries. First, there are
substantial interactions between bank reserve requirements (for cash and
liquid assets) on the one hand and interest rate ceilings imposed on the
banking system on the other. In the constrained regime, the combination of
reserve requirements and lending guidelines implies that Indian banks had
control over a relatively small proportion of their total portfolios. In general
secondary reserve requirements are imposed to create a captive market for
government debt and, in India, for the obligations of development banks.
Interest rate controls reduce the cost of financing this debt for the issuers and
again act as a tax on banks and their customers. It is widely believed that
releasing the controls will increase the flow of loans to the private sector and
may create a problem for the financing of government debt, since the captive
market is eliminated. However, it is found that, in India, a cut in secondary
reserve requirements combined with interest rate liberalization could lead to
increased bank holdings of government debt. This effect could arise because
liberalization may reduce interest rates: if firms can more easily raise funds

on the stock market, business demand for loans may decrease. If interest rates do fall, risk-free government debt becomes more attractive to banks than loans. This mitigates the problem of financing government activities in the short run, but does not produce the expected increase in the flow of bank lending to the private sector. Second, changes in bank rate are found to have a relatively minor effect on interest rates, again because of a strong substitution effect between cash and liquid assets in the banking system: a fall in bank rate primarily induces a switch from cash into liquid assets rather than from liquid assets into loans as might otherwise be predicted. Third, it is found that increases in real deposit rates do attract household savings into the banking system. This is consistent with the aim of financial liberalization and may well be one of the main channels through which liberalization increases the flow of funds into investment projects.

Although it is difficult to generalize results from one particular country, India's monetary controls share some features with those of other developing countries, especially in the use of interest rate and credit ceilings and reserve ratios for commercial bank holdings of government debt. This suggests that there may be some lessons to be learnt from the Indian experience, both in the operation of the controls and in the impact of liberalization.

The second case study involves Kenya, a country in which flow of funds data are much less well-established and which is therefore in line with most developing countries as far as information is concerned; see Green, Murinde and Ndungu (2002). For Kenya, more rudimentary flow of funds data are compiled, and a model is estimated to study the relationships between the financial and real sectors of the economy, emphasizing inter alia the role of the unofficial markets for credit in Kenya. This case study emphasizes the application of flow of funds as a policy device. Specifically, it is found that the flow of funds was a useful framework for studying the relationships between the financial and real sectors of the economy, including the linkages between the unofficial and official credit markets, during the period 1966–99. In addition, the flow of funds model is flexible enough to capture the main policy variables which underpin financial reform programmes in Kenya: these are the official interest rate, government spending, commercial bank loans, income tax and foreign reserves.

The third case study involves a broader evaluation of the flow of funds in some Sub-Saharan African countries (Chupabayeva *et al.*, 2002). The study starts with the entire set of Sub-Saharan Africa countries, but, after assessing the availability and quality of flow of funds data, it ends up with the sample of Kenya, Malawi, Namibia, Tanzania, Uganda, Zambia and Zimbabwe, for 1970–2000. In these countries data limitations are more severe still, and the study therefore concentrates on the banking system, where data are relatively good. Flow of funds models are estimated, aiming at understanding how

African banks behave in response to interest rate changes, often in the context of high inflation.

There are a number of lessons that can be learned from the case studies on flow of flunds; these are summarized in Box 1.1. One general lesson is that certain troublesome features of liberalized financial markets are also likely to be evident in developing countries. One example is that of 'distress borrowing'. In the industrial countries, a rise in interest rates intended to restrain credit expansion often produces the opposite effect, at least in the short run, with borrowing from banks increasing, particularly by businesses. This is a typical result of firms struggling to contain and to finance inventories as spending in the economy slows in response to the higher interest rates. The case studies discussed above contain evidence of this phenomenon in India and Kenya, particularly at times in the 1990s. If this proves to be a general characteristic of liberalized markets in developing countries, it underlines the need for gradualism in the implementation of policies intended either to raise interest rates or more generally to give a greater role to the market in interest rate determination. Market-determined interest rates are generally higher than interest rates which are constrained by central bank ceilings. However, it cannot be assumed that, if borrowing increases following liberalization, this is due to a more efficient allocation of credit and not to a greater incidence of financial distress. Thus the scope for orthodox policies in a particular country needs to be tempered by the institutional features of its regulations and by the pace of liberalization.

Overall, therefore, it may be argued that, in order to design effective financial sector policies for growth and poverty reduction, it is imperative to have an intimate understanding of the key relationships between the financial and real sectors of the economy and the role of the financial sector in the development process. Such fundamental insight into the mechanisms that link the financial and real sectors of developing countries can be derived primarily from the medium of the flow of funds, for 'a main function of the flow of funds accounts is to reveal the sources and uses of funds that are needed for growth and development' (Klein, 2000, pp. ix–xii). Although the growth and development dimensions are explicit in the flow of funds analyses in the case studies, poverty reductions issues are only implicit. Future research should go beyond growth and development dimensions in order to incorporate explicitly poverty reduction issues in flow of funds analysis for developing countries.

BOX 1.1   KEY FINDINGS FROM EMPIRICAL
          RESEARCH ON FLOW OF FUNDS IN
          DEVELOPING COUNTRIES

● Fundamental insight into the linkages between the financial
  and real sectors of developing countries can be derived primarily from the medium of the flow of funds, for a main
  function of the flow of funds accounts is to reveal the sources
  and uses of funds that are needed for growth, development
  and poverty reduction.
● Accurate and timely information is central to good policy
  making. Decisions taken in ignorance of the facts or as a
  result of guesswork are all too likely to be regretted at a later
  date. Thus small improvements in the collection of flow of
  funds data may easily lead to more substantial improvements
  in decision making.
● Financial liberalization policies provide effective mechanisms
  by which the informal financial sector can be successfully
  integrated into the formal financial institutions and markets.
● Differences between the liberalized and the previously controlled regimes in India stem from the way in which the
  controlled regime itself functioned, rather than from any features of the economy which are peculiar to India.
● Liberalizing the interest rate regime and giving markets a
  greater role in the economy will not necessarily complicate
  the task of monetary policy management. It is possible for
  developing countries to learn from the experience of industrial countries in this respect. Lessons learnt in the developing
  world may also be relevant in more industrialized economies.
● A key phenomenon of banks in industrial economies seems
  to hold true in African emerging markets: market-determined
  returns, which influence the asset formation behaviour of
  households and firms, are important in asset allocation through
  the banking sector. Further research should apply the flow of
  funds framework to explore the asset formation behaviour of
  the poor, which remains enigmatic.

Source: Moore *et al.* (2002a).

6. FINANCIAL DEVELOPMENT AND POVERTY REDUCTION

One important innovation in development research and policy has been the refocusing of the goals of development strategy from an exclusive concern with economic growth to 'growth with poverty reduction'. The prioritization of poverty reduction has also increased interest in the contribution that financial development can make to poverty reduction. For example, the profound argument made by Stiglitz (1994) is that market failure is a fundamental cause of poverty, and financial market failures, which mainly arise from market imperfections, asymmetric information and the high fixed costs of small-scale lending, limit the access of the poor to formal finance, thus pushing the poor to the informal financial sector or to the extreme case of financial exclusion. In addition, it is argued that improving the access of the poor to financial services enables these agents to build up productive assets and enhance their productivity and potential for sustainable livelihoods (see World Bank, 2001a). Hence the bottom line argument is that improving the supply of financial services to the poor can directly contribute to poverty reduction (Jalilian and Kirkpatrick, 2002). It is in this context that researchers and policy analysts have shown a renewed interest in the contribution of finance to development and poverty reduction, in order to obtain a better insight into the relationship among financial development, economic growth and poverty reduction and to obtain empirical grounds for formulating financial sector policies that can contribute to poverty reduction.

It has also been argued that financial development can have an indirect effect on poverty outcomes through its direct impact on economic growth. Dollar and Kraay (2000) argue that growth has been beneficial to the poor. In general, however, economic growth can generate different poverty outcomes (McKay, 2002; Jalilian and Kirkpatrick, 2002). Growth may reduce poverty through improving the position of some on the lower scale of the distribution; in some cases, growth may benefit the non-poor but may improve income distribution overall. Jalilian and Kirkpatrick (2002) take into account these considerations and specify a log-linear model to capture the interaction among financial development, economic growth and poverty reduction. In the model, the growth of per capita income in the poorest quintile of the population is determined by the growth of average per capita income in the entire population, and a vector of all other explanantory variables of mean income of the poor including proxies for macroeconomic policies, openness and globalization. The parameter estimates of the model give the magnitude and sign of the elasticity of poverty reduction with respect to growth and other determinants of poverty, including financial development variables. The basis for including proxies for financial development is that 'financial development potentially has two poverty impacts, first indirectly through its impact on the rate of mean income growth, and second, directly through improved supply of, and access to, financial services to the poor' (Jalilian and Kirkpatrick, 2002, p. 102). The model was tested on panel data covering 26 countries, including 18 developing countries, allowing for various measures of financial development, both income and headcount data for the poor as well as the Gini coefficient for inequality and the Theil inequality index. One important finding of the study is that a unit change in financial development improves the growth prospects of income of the poor in developing countries by almost 0.4 per cent. Overall the results are consistent with the argument that financial development does contribute to poverty reduction.

There are several important dimensions for extending existing studies on the impact of financial development on poverty reduction in developing countries. One possible innovation is to characterize financial development in terms of proxies for access to finance by the poor, reduction of information asymmetry in financial markets and better regulation to mitigate market imperfections and market failure, which are important arguments in the nexus between financial development and economic growth. Another promising research idea would be to broaden the definitions and measurement of poverty to allow for the most prevalent forms of poverty that plague developing countries, including disguised forms of rural poverty. The idea of these two innovations, taken together, provides a firm basis for undertaking empirical work to inform specific financial sector policies for poverty reduction. In addition, it would be interesting to extend existing studies on the impact of financial development on poverty reduction to identify clear threshold levels of financial development indicators that are necessary to induce a reduction in poverty measures. Recent econometric work by Hansen (1999, 2000), which propose and implement a reliable approach to sample splitting and measurement of threshold effects, could provide a sound empirical basis for investigating thresholds to guide financial policy measures that are required for poverty reduction.

7.   OTHER POLICY CONUNDRUMS AND RESEARCH ISSUES

The issues addressed in sections 2–6 above are arguably only the tip of the iceberg. A number of promising research ideas are proposed in these sections, especially section 6. There are further policy conundrums and research issues, but here we briefly point out only three, and hope that this chapter will provoke a debate on the other important issues.

The first issue relates to financial market imperfections, financial exclusion and poverty, especially in the context of rural financial markets and the microfinance revolution. It is noted, according to recent literature, that a fundamental cause of poverty is market failure in the sense that financial market imperfections often prevent the poor from borrowing (Stiglitz, 1994). To deal with possible financial exclusion, the 'microfinance revolution' has been recommended (Morduch, 1999). It is argued that providing the poor with effective financial services helps them deal with vulnerability and can thereby help reduce poverty. However the relationship is driven by complex livelihood imperatives.

The second issue relates to international financial flows and poverty reduction. It has been argued that economy-wide and international shocks may derail pro-poor strategies (World Bank, 2001a). The current poverty reduction frameworks, especially the millenium development goals (MDG) and the poverty reduction strategy papers (PRSPs), assume some high degree of capital inflows. Specifically, a major element of the trinity for poverty reduction in most developing countries is the Highly Indebted Poor Countries (HIPC) initiative; the other two elements are the PRSPs and the Medium Term Economic Framework (MTEF).

The third issue is that, while eradicating absolute poverty and reducing overall poverty remains the greatest global developmental challenge, there is relatively less consensus on the conceptualization, definition and measurement of poverty. In the literature, poverty is conceptualized and defined as a composite concept (Gordon and Spicker, 1999); as a lack of basic needs (Baratz and Grigsby, 1971, p. 120); as a deficiency in income/consumption (World Bank, 2001a, p. 26); as a limited command over resources (in Dreze and Sen, 1999); as lack of basic security and vulnerability (Duffy, 1995); as inequality and social exclusion (Spicker, 1993); and as defined by the poor themselves in the participatory poverty assessments (World Bank, 2001a). The main problems of measuring poverty relate to the different approaches commonly used, depending on the way poverty is perceived and defined. However the two major techniques include quantitative approaches, based on economics principles, and qualitative approaches, based on subjective principles. There is no consensus on the suitability of either approach (see Robb, 2002).

Thus, the important question remains: how does finance contribute to economic growth and poverty reduction? We do not know. But we are trying to find out.

NOTES

1. Useful comments on previous versions of this chapter were obtained from participants at the inaugural seminar of the 'ESRC Research Seminars on Finance for Development and

Poverty Reduction' held at the University of Birmingham on 29 November 2003. We take responsibility for remaining errors.
2. See, for example, Murinde (1996, ch. 5) on the McKinnon–Shaw model: the theory, evidence, usefulness and limitations.

REFERENCES

Aghion, P. and Howitt, P. (1998), *Endogenous Growth Theory*, Cambridge: MIT Press.

Aghion, P., Caroli, E. and Garcia-Penalosa, C. (1999), 'Inequality and economic growth: the perspectives from the new growth theories', *Journal of Economic Literature*, **37**(4), 1615–60.

Amihud, Y., Mendelson, H. and Lauterbach, B. (1997), 'Market microstructure and securities values: evidence from Tel Aviv Stock Exchange', *Journal of Financial Economics*, **45**, 365–90.

Arestis, P., Demetriades, P.O. and Luintel, K. (2001), 'Financial development and economic growth: the role of stock markets', *Journal of Money, Credit and Banking*, **33**(1), 16–41.

Baratz, M.S. and W.G. Grigsby (1971), 'Thoughts on poverty and its elimination', *Journal of Social Policy*, **1** (2), 119–34.

Barro, R.J. (1991), 'Economic growth in a cross-section of countries', *Quarterly Journal of Economics*, **106**(2), 407–43.

Barro, R.J. and Lee, J-W (1994), 'Sources of economic growth', *Carnegie-Rochester Conference Series on Public Policy*, **40**(June), 1–46.

Barro, R.J. and Sala-i-Martin, X. (1995), *Economic Growth*, New York: McGraw-Hill.

Bekaert, G. and Harvey, C.R. (1997), 'Emerging equity market volatility', *Journal of Financial Economics*, **43**, 29–77.

Booth, L., Aivazian, V., Demirgüç-Kunt, A. and Maksimovic, V. (2001), 'Capital structure in developing countries', *Journal of Finance*, **LVI**(1), 87–130.

Brada, J.C. and Singh, I. (1999), *Corporate Governance in Central Eastern Europe: Case Studies of Firms in Transition*. Armonk, NY and London: Sharpe.

Brownbridge, M. and Kirkpatrick, C. (2000), 'Financial regulation in developing countries', *Journal of Development Studies*, **37**(1), 1–24.

Caprio, G. Jr, and Demirgüç-Kunt, A. (1998), 'The role of long term finance: theory and evidence', *The World Bank Research Observer*, **13**(2), 171–89.

Chang, R.P., Hsu, S., Huang, N. and Rhee, S.G. (1999), 'The effects of trading methods on volatility and liquidity: evidence from Taiwan Stock Exchange', *Journal of Business Finance and Accounting*, **26**(1 and 2), 137–70.

Chirinko, R.S. and Singha, A.R. (2000), 'Testing static trade-off against pecking order models of capital structure: a critical comment', *Journal of Financial Economics*, **58**, 417–25.

Chupabayeva, G., Green, C.J. and Murinde, V. (2002), 'Flow of funds for the banking sector in African economies', paper presented at the 3rd Annual International Conference of the Finance and Development Research Programme, University of Manchester, April 2002.

Demirgüç-Kunt, A. and Levine, R. (1996), 'Stock market development and financial intermediaries: stylised facts', *The World Bank Economic Review*, **10**, 341–69.

Dollar, D. and Kraay, A. (2000), 'Growth is good for the poor', Development Research Group, World Bank.

Dreze, J. and Sen, A.K. (1999), *Hunger and Public Action*, Oxford: Clarendon Press.

Duffy, K. (1995), 'Social exclusion and human dignity in Europe', Council of Europe CDPS (95), 1 Rev.

Evans, A.D. (1997), 'The role of human capital, financial development and political stability in economic growth: evidence and interpretation from cross section and panel data', Unpublished PhD Thesis, University of Wales, July.

Evans, D., Green, C.J. and Murinde, V. (2002), 'The importance of human capital and financial development in economic growth: new evidence using the translog production function', *International Journal of Finance and Economics*, **7**, 123–40.

Fischer, S. (1993), 'The role of macroeconomic factors in growth', *Journal of Monetary Economics*, **32**, 485–512.

Fry, M.J. (1995), *Money, Interest, and Banking in Economic Development*, Baltimore and London: Johns Hopkins University Press.

Goldsmith, R.W. (1969), *Financial Structure and Development*, New Haven: Yale University Press.

Gordon, D. and Spicker, P. (1999), *The International Glossary on Poverty*, London: Zed Books Ltd.

Green, C.J. and Kirkpatrick, C.H. (2002), 'Finance and development: an overview of the issues', *Journal of International Development*, **14**(2), 207–10.

Green, C.J. and Murinde, V. (2003), 'The flow of funds: implications for research on financial sector development and the real economy', *Journal of International Development*, **15**, 1015–36.

Green, C.J., Maggioni, P. and Murinde, V. (2000), 'Regulatory lessons for emerging stock markets from a century of evidence on transactions costs and share price volatility in the London Stock Exchange', *Journal of Banking and Finance*, **24**, 577–601.

Green, C.J., Murinde, V. and Ndung'u, N. (2002), 'Flow of funds and policy modelling for Kenya', paper presented at the 3rd Annual International Conference of the Finance and Development Research Programme, University of Manchester, April 2002; forthcoming in *Finance and Development Research Programme Working Papers*.

Green, C.J., Kimuyu, P., Manos, R. and Murinde, V. (2002), 'How do small firms in developing countries raise capital? Evidence from a large-scale survey of Kenyan MSEs', Mimeo.

Green, C.J., Murinde, V., Suppakitjarak, N., and Moore, T. (2000), 'Compiling and understanding the flow of funds in developing countries', *Finance and Development Research Programme Working Paper, no. 21*, December.

Hamid, J. and Singh, A. (1992), 'Corporate financial structures in developing economies', *IFC Technical Paper* no.1, IFC, Washington, DC.

Hansen, B.E. (1999), 'Threshold effects in non-dynamic panels: estimation, testing and inference', *Journal of Econometrics*, **93**, 345–68.

Hansen, B.E. (2000), 'Sample splitting and threshold estimation', *Econometrica*, **68**, 575–603.

Hulme, D. and Mosley, P. (1996), *Finance Against Poverty*, vol. 1, London: Routldge.

Hutton, J. and Kenc, T. (1998), 'The influence of firms' financial policy on tax reforms', *Oxford Economic Papers*, **50**(4), 663–84.

Islam, N. (1995), 'Growth empirics: a panel data approach', *Quarterly Journal of Economics*, **110**(4), 1127–70.

Jalilian, H. and Kirkpatrick, C. (2002), 'Financial development and poverty reduction', *International Journal of Finance and Economics*, **7**(2), 97–108.

Kim, E.H. and Singal, V. (2000), 'Stock market openings: experience of emerging economies', *Journal of Business*, **73**(1), 25–66.

King, R.G. and Levine, R. (1993a), 'Finance, entrepreneurship and growth', *Journal of Monetary Economics*, **32**(3) (December), 513–42.

King, R.G. and Levine, R. (1993b), 'Finance and growth: Schumpeter might be right', *Quarterly Journal of Economics*, **108**(3) (August), 717–37.

Klein, L.R. (2000), 'Preface', in A.E. Fleming and M.M. Guigale (eds), *Financial Systems in Transition*, Singapore: World Scientific, pp. ix–xii.

Knight, M.E., Loayza. N. and Villanueva, D. (1993), 'Testing the neo-classical theory of economic growth', *IMF Staff Papers*, **40**(3) (September), 512–41.

Knowles, S. and Owen, P.D. (1995), 'Health capital and cross-country variation in income per capita in the Mankiw–Romer–Weil Model', *Economics Letters*, **48**(1) (April), 99–106.

La-Porta, R., Lopez de Silanes, F. and Shleifer, A. (1999), 'Corporate ownership around the world', *Journal of Finance*, **54**(2) (April), 471–517.

Levine, R. (1997), 'Financial development and economic growth: views and agenda', *Journal of Economic Literature*, **XXXV**, 688–726.

Levine, R. and Dermigüç-Kunt, A. (2001), *Financial Structure and Economic Growth: A Cross-Country Comparison of Banks, Markets and Development*, Cambridge, MA: MIT Press.

Lewis, W.A. (1955), *The Theory of Economic Growth*, London: Allen and Unwin.

Lucas, R.E. Jr (1988), 'On the mechanics of economic development', *Journal of Monetary Economics*, **22**(1) (July), 3–42.

Lyons, S. and V. Murinde (1994), 'Cointegration and Granger-causality testing of hypotheses on supply-leading and demand-following finance', *Economic Notes*, **23**(2), 308–16.

Majnoni, G. and Massa, M. (2001), 'Stock exchange reform and market efficiency: the Italy experience', *European Financial Management*, **7**(1), 93–115.

Mankiw, N.G., Romer, D. and Weil, D.N. (1992), 'A contribution to the empirics of economic growth', *Quarterly Journal of Economics*, **107**(2), 407–37.

McKay, A. (2002), 'Economic growth and distribution of poverty in developing countries', in C. Kirkpatrick, R. Clarke and C. Polidano (eds), *Handbook on Development Policy and Management*, Cheltenham, UK and Northampton, MA, USA: Edward Elgar.

McKinnon, R.I. (1973), *Money and Capital in Economic Development*, Washington, DC: Brookings Institute.

Moore, T., Green, C.J. and Murinde, V. (2002a), 'Flow of funds model of the capital structure of the business sector in India: evidence using the almost ideal demand system', paper presented at the 3rd Annual International Conference of the Finance and Development Research Programme, University of Manchester, April 2002.

Moore, T., Green, C.J. and Murinde, V. (2002b), 'Flow of funds simulation experiments in the financial sector in India', paper presented at the 3rd Annual International Conference of the Finance and Development Research Programme, University of Manchester, April 2002.

Moore, T., Green, C.J. and Murinde, V. (2002c), 'Modelling a flow of funds in the household sector and the policy implications for India', paper presented at the 3rd Annual International Conference of the Finance and Development Research Programme, University of Manchester, April 2002.

Moore, T., Green, C.J. and Murinde, V. (2002d), 'Modelling the flow of funds for the banking sector in India', paper presented at the 3rd Annual International Conference of the Finance and Development Research Programme, University of Manchester, April 2002.

Morduch, J. (1999), 'The microfinance promise', *Journal of Economic Literature*, **37** (4), 1569–1614.

Mullineux, A.W. and Murinde, V. (2002), 'Financial sector policies for enterprise development', in G. Wignaraja (ed.), *Enterprise Competition and Public Policies*, Basingstoke: Macmillan, ch. 4.

Mullineux, A.W., Murinde, V. and Pinijkulviwat, A. (2001), 'Accidents waiting to happen? The Thai banking crisis of 1997', *ID21 Communicating Development Research*, 2 October.

Mullineux, A.W., Murinde, V. and Pinijkulviwat, A. (2003), 'Reforming the traditional structure of a central bank to cope with the Asian financial crisis: lessons from the Bank of Thailand', in A.W. Mullineux and V. Murinde (eds), *Handbook of International Banking*, Cheltenham, UK and Northampton, MA, USA: Edward Elgar, ch. 17.

Murinde, V. (1996), 'Financial markets and endogenous growth: an econometric analysis for Pacific Basin Countries', in Niels Hermes and Robert Lensink (eds), *Financial Development and Economic Growth*, London and New York: Routledge, pp. 94–114.

Murinde, V. and Kariisa-Kasa, J. (1997), 'The financial performance of the East African Development Bank: a retrospective analysis', *Accounting, Business and Financial History*, **7**(1), 81–104.

Murinde, V. and Ryan, C. (2001), 'The implications of WTO and GATS for the banking sector in Africa', in V. Murinde (ed.), *The Free Trade Area of the Common Market for Eastern and Southern Africa*, Aldershot: Ashgate Publishing, ch. 7.

Murinde, V. and Ryan, C. (2002), 'The implications of the General Agreement on Trade in Services (GATS) for the banking sector in the Gulf Region', in C. Milner and R. Read (eds), *Trade Liberalisation, Competition & WTO*, Cheltenham, UK and Northampton, MA, USA: Edward Elgar, pp. 92–117.

Murinde, V., Agung, J. and Mullineux, A.W. (2004), 'Patterns of corporate financing and financial system convergence in Europe', *Review of International Economics*, **12**(4), 693–705.

Mutenheri, E. and Green, C.J. (2003), 'Financial reform and financing decisions of listed firms in Zimbabwe', *Journal of African Business*, **4**(2), 155–70.

Myers, S.C. (2001), 'Capital structure', *Journal of Economic Perspectives*, **15**(2), 81–102.

Myrdal, G. (1968), *Asian Drama: An Enquiry into the Poverty of Nations*, Harmondsworth: Allen Lane.

Ngugi, R. (2002), 'Four essays on corporate finance issues in emerging stock markets', unpublished PhD thesis, University of Birmingham.

Ngugi, R., Murinde, V. and Green, C.J. (2002), 'The response of the market microstructure to revitalisation: evidence from the Nairobi Stock Exchange', *Journal of African Finance*, **4**(1), 32–61.

Ngugi, R., Murinde, V. and Green, C.J. (2003), 'How have the emerging stock markets in Africa responded to market reforms?', *Journal of African Business*, **4**(2), 89–127.

Prasad, S.K. (2000), 'Corporate financial structures in developing economies', unpublished PhD Thesis, Cardiff Business School, University of Wales.

Prasad, S.K. Green, C.J. and Murinde, V. (2001), 'Company financing, capital structure and ownership: a survey and implications for developing countries', SUERF Studies, no. 12.

Quah, D. (1993), 'Empirical cross-section dynamics in economic growth', *European Economic Review*, **37**(2–3) (April), 426–34.

Quah, D. (1997), 'Empirics for growth and distribution: stratification, polarization and convergence clubs', *Journal of Economic Growth*, **2**(1), 27–59.

Rajan, R.G. and Zingales, L. (1995), 'What do we know about capital structure? Some evidence from international data', *Journal of Finance*, **L**(5) 1421–60.

Robb, C. (2002), *Can the Poor Influence Policy? Participatory Poverty Assessments in the Developing World*, Washington, DC: World Bank.

Romer, P. (1986), 'Increasing returns and long-run growth', *Journal of Political Economy*, **94**(5), 1002–37.

Schumpeter, J.A. (1911), *The Theory of Economic Development*, Cambridge, MA: Harvard University Press.

Senhadji, A. (2000), 'Sources of economic growth: an extensive growth accounting exercise', *IMF Staff Papers*, **47**(1), 129–57.

Shaw, E.S. (1973), *Financial Deepening in Economic Development*, New York: Oxford University Press.

Shyam-Sunder, L. and Myers, S.C. (1999), 'Testing static trade-off against pecking order models of capital structure', *Journal of Financial Economics*, **51**, 219–44.

Singh, A. (1995), 'Corporate financial patterns in industrialising economies: a comparative study', *IFC Technical Paper No. 2*, IFC, Washington, DC.

Solow, R. (1956), 'A contribution to the theory of economic growth', *Quarterly Journal of Economics*, **70**(1) (February), 65–94.

Solow, R. (1957), 'Technical change and the aggregate production function', *Review of Economics and Statistics*, **31**, 312–20.

Spicker, P. (1993), *Poverty and Social Security*, London: Routledge.

Stiglitz, J. (1994), 'The role of the state in financial markets', in *Proceedings of the World Bank Conference on Development Economics*, Washington, DC: World Bank, pp. 19–52.

Tefula, M. and Murinde, V. (2002), 'Identifying problem banks in Sub-Sahara Africa', *African Finance Journal*, **4**(2), 1–25.

Tefula, M., Murinde, V. and Kirkpatrick, C. (2002), 'Evidence on X-inefficiency in African commercial banks', Mimeo.

Temple, J. (1999), 'The new growth evidence', *Journal of Economic Literature*, **37**(1) (March), 112–56.

Williamson, J. and Maher, M. (1998), 'A survey of financial liberalisation', *Princeton Essays in International Finance*, no. 211.

World Bank (2001a), *World Development Report 2000/2001: Attacking Poverty*, New York: Oxford University Press.

World Bank (2001b), *Finance for Growth: Policy Choices in a Volatile World*, New York: Oxford University Press.

PART I

Financial markets and the macroeconomy

2. Savings and financial sector development: assessing the evidence

George Mavrotas*

1. INTRODUCTION

The relationship between financial sector development and economic development has been the subject of a booming literature in recent years.[1] However the relationship between savings mobilization and financial sector development has received less attention.[2] The lack of financial intermediation in developing countries is widely evidenced by the mismatch between institutional savings and investment. The need for investment is indisputable, and in the past it has been addressed through structural adjustment programmes, such as the introduction of development finance institutions and other such vehicles, which provide credit at below market rates for the purchase of capital. Many policies introduced into developing countries by donors, such as concessionary discount facilities in central banks, high reserve requirements and extensive use of specific credit programmes have discouraged deposit mobilization: the numerous small savers that exist, even in the poorest sectors of the least developed economies, have been overlooked as a potential source of internal funds. This is due to the fact that it is far easier for governments to accept donor funds than to mobilize the savings of its population, even though the latter method may, in total, provide more credit for fixed capital formation than the former (Mavrotas and Kelly, 2001a).The above clearly suggests the need for further research on this important issue.

What developing countries often lack is an appropriate financial sector, which could provide incentives for individuals to save, and acts as an efficient intermediary to convert these savings into credit for borrowers. In pursuit of such a financial system, many developing countries have implemented far-reaching financial reforms, including lifting restrictions on bank lending, the provision of market-based systems of credit allocation, lowering of reserve requirements and the easing of entry restrictions on the banking sector as well as privatization of state-owned banks. The experience related to the financial crisis in Asia in 1997 clearly suggests that, whilst this may be the ultimate aim of liberalization, the process must be correctly regulated (Stiglitz, 1999; Brownbridge and Kirkpatrick, 1999).

The main theoretical elements in support of financial liberalization as a policy goal are the fundamental theorem of welfare economics, and the efficient market hypothesis. The fundamental theorem states that competitive markets yield Pareto optimal equilibria, whilst the efficient markets hypothesis states that financial markets use information efficiently. A combination of the two ensure, by definition, efficiency of the real economy and also ensure that the financial markets reflect the fundamentals of the real economy. Market liberalization removes any market distortions that impede these free market conditions (Eatwell, 1996).

The present review will try to critically assess the literature associated with the relationship between savings mobilisation and financial sector development by looking mainly at aspects of the literature which have not been properly discussed before. Obviously, it is beyond the scope of the present review to cover in depth the voluminous literature on the determinants of savings. The interested reader can refer to the excellent reviews of Gersovitz (1988), Deaton (1989), and Schmidt-Hebbel *et al.* (1992) on the subject. Our main focus is on the interactions between private savings and financial sector development. Furthermore, the present review discusses a new booming literature on savings mobilization, namely social security reforms and the way they affect savings. Finally, we discuss the plethora of formal as well as informal institutions through which savings mobilization is influenced in developing countries. The rest of the chapter is organized as follows: section 2 will look at the nexus between financial sector development and savings mobilization; the importance of savings mobilization is also discussed, with reference to the appropriate literature, as well as the importance of financial sector development in the process of financial liberalization. Section 3 will look at other determinants of saving, including the causality between savings and growth, and the role of social security reforms. In the same section we also discuss recent empirical work carried out in the area of savings mobilization and financial sector development. Section 4 will discuss the formal and informal institutions that have been developed for development finance, and their effectiveness in acting as financial intermediaries. Finally, section 5 concludes the chapter and discusses the relevant policy lessons.

2. SAVINGS MOBILIZATION AND FINANCIAL SECTOR DEVELOPMENT: EXPLORING THE NEXUS

Financial sector development is one of the key elements of, and a necessary condition for, financial liberalization, and often the terms are used synonymously in the literature. Thus it is important to consider the process of financial sector liberalization in order to see the full picture of financial sector development and its effect on saving.

Financial Repression

Developing economies have historically been characterized by financial repression. This has tended to involve intervention by governments in allocating and pricing credit, controlling what banks and other intermediaries were able to do, using intermediaries as tax collection devices, and limiting competition, particularly from foreign institutions. Financial repression tends to be the unintended outcome of policies of financial restriction, in which ceilings are placed on interest rates by the government to provide firms with cheap capital, to facilitate expansion. In addition, the associated low deposit rates prevent funds from being attracted away from productive investment in physical assets. Such policies tend to reduce individuals' incentives to save in the form of monetary assets; the wide spreads offered, typically combined with high rates of inflation, meant that rates of return on deposits are frequently negative, so saving takes a non-monetary form. Such economies are described as having a low degree of financial depth, a typical measure of which is the ratio of money to GDP.

A financially repressed country has, at the best of times, a poorly developed financial sector. However matters are worsened during periods of high inflation, when real rates of interest are frequently negative, inducing disintermediation, in the form of further withdrawals of funds from the banking sector. This results in reduced productive investment, as households decrease investment, preferring instead to consume, and at the same time the funds that are available for productive investment are allocated inefficiently, because the market price rationing system is not at work (McKinnon, 1973; Shaw, 1973).[3]

The Centrality of Financial Sector Development

While the problems of financial repression originate from government control of interest rates, they are perpetuated by a lack of financial intermediation, which itself perpetuates and is perpetuated by a low level of monetization. A vicious circle seems to operate. Clearly, therefore, financial sector development, and in particular the development of financial intermediation, has a key role to play in the process of financial liberalization: the two processes are inextricably linked.

A widely documented problem in developing countries with poorly developed financial sectors is the mismatch between institutional savings and investment, resulting in a lack of investment in productive capital.[4] It is a commonly held fallacy that individuals in developing countries do not save; in fact it has been found that even in the poorest rural areas saving is rife, although frequently this does not occur in a monetized form in the main-stream financial system. This will be discussed further in section 3.

Early Financial Sector Reforms: Structural Adjustment and the Introduction of Development Finance Institutions

Based on the belief that the potential for saving in developing countries is negligible, a traditional first step in development policy has tended to be the introduction of development finance institutions (DFIs), institutions that provide credit for working capital at non-market rates, but offer no deposit facilities for individuals, and as such do not perform an intermediation role. They operate independently of the commercial banks, which act as deposit takers, and provide short-term loans and overdrafts. The development of a more sophisticated financial sector which provides a safe and attractive place for investors to place deposits would enable countries to move away from subsidized, state-provided credit, and move towards a market-based system that acts as an intermediary, channelling funds from savers to investors. In this way, the development of the financial system mobilizes domestic savings, rather than being reliant on external assistance. Kenrick Hunte (1997) provides a useful analysis of the role of savings mobilization in helping DFIs become independent of donor funds. He observed that traditional development finance institutions were dependent on donor funds; they purely supplied loans at subsidized rates. Some financial intermingling occurred (defined as the use by households of financial services from formal and informal institutions simultaneously), with individuals depositing at commercial banks. Development of the financial sector and the resulting mobilization of savings would provide a number of benefits for DFIs. They would be able to provide a basic set of financial services at a single institution, which Hunte saw as having three main effects: (a) it would minimize the saver–borrower transaction costs, (b) it would improve creditworthiness decision making, and (c) it would reduce the risk and cost of lending and improve recovery rates.

Traditionally it is in developing countries where financial sector intervention has been prevalent that financial sector reform is likely to have the largest impact. While regulation of interest rates and credit expansion is common in most repressed economies, in some developing countries banks were required to hold in excess of half of their liabilities in the form of reserve or liquid assets (often deposits at the central bank) and another large part of the portfolio was dominated by directed credit (Bandiera *et al.*, 2000). In practice, little power or responsibility was left to the banks. Thus the banks invested little in credit assessment or monitoring.

Analytical Framework for Modelling the Link between Saving and Financial Sector Development: the Life Cycle Model of Saving

Traditionally the models that look at the interface between saving and development are based on the life cycle or permanent income theory of consumption, and it will be useful here to review briefly these hypotheses, and then discuss the relevance of financial sector development to these models.[5] The model described below draws on Gersovitz (1988), but is typical of the style used by most authors.

Consider an individual who lives for T periods, receives income payments of y_i and consumes c_i. She neither receives nor leaves bequests. The only constraint on the individual's consumption is that the present value of lifetime consumption (C) cannot exceed the present value of lifetime income (Y):

$$C \equiv \sum_{i=0}^{T-1} \left[\frac{c_i}{(1+r)^i} \right] \leq \sum_{i=0}^{T-1} \left[\frac{y_i}{(1+r)^i} \right] \equiv Y. \qquad (2.1)$$

However, she is able to borrow or lend at interest rate r in period i if her objective, namely maximizing her discounted lifetime utility, V, does not require that $y_i = c_i$. V is defined as follows:

$$V \equiv \sum_{i=0}^{T-1} \delta^i U[c_i]. \qquad (2.2)$$

The decision maker's problem is solved for the two period model by the first order condition:

$$U'[c_0] = (1+r)\delta U'[c_1], \qquad (2.3)$$

which, along with condition (2.1) holding as an equality, yields optimal values of consumption, c_0^* and c_1^*. Current savings are then treated as a residual, which is why most models examining saving are formulated in terms of consumption rather than saving.

There are a number of key messages relating to the effects of interest rates, demography and other matters of interest that the standard life cycle model has been used to analyse. These will be considered later in the chapter. The permanent income hypothesis, proposed by Friedman (1957), is similar to the life cycle hypothesis, in that future, as well as current, resources affect saving. One of the main differences between the two hypotheses is that Friedman assumes consumers are infinitely lived.

The life cycle model assumes that saving varies over the course of an individual's life. Bayoumi (1993), using an overlapping-generations model, describes the effects of financial deregulation on household saving in the life cycle model. It is assumed that consumers live for a fixed number of periods and wish to smooth their consumption path. It is also assumed that the endowments available to individuals when they are young are small, so they would like to borrow when young in order to smooth consumption over their life cycle. Prior to financial liberalization, consumers have limited access to financial intermediation; they are unable to finance their desired level of consumption when young, as they have no financial assets and are unable to go into debt, so they are in a corner solution. After the initial period, consumers are able to use capital markets to smooth consumption over middle to old age. Because consumption was lower than desired when young, consumption is higher in middle and old age than it would have been, had they been able to follow the optimal consumption path over their entire lifetime.

Financial liberalization increases competition between providers of financial intermediation, thereby eliminating the constraint on going into debt. This means the young can now borrow in order to attain their optimal lifetime consumption path. This gives rise to two effects. There is an initial temporary effect. In the short term, there will be an increase in aggregate consumption, which will wane over time. The immediate increase reflects the fact that the consumption of the young increases as soon as financial deregulation occurs. There is no immediate effect on the borrowing of older consumers, as they are still affected by their inability to borrow while young. The effect dwindles as previously credit-constrained consumers drop out of the economy and overall consumption tends back to its original level. There is also a permanent effect. As young consumers are no longer credit constrained, they smooth their consumption. As a result, young consumers' saving becomes sensitive to wealth, real income, demographics and interest rates. This means that aggregate saving in the economy becomes more sensitive to these factors.

Thus, during youth and old age, an individual will dissave, and saving will occur while an individual is productive. Clearly such a model relies on a number of assumptions. There must be a system of financial intermediation that permits saving and dissaving to such a degree that it is hard to envisage the saving taking place in a non-monetary form. Therefore a major element of the process of financial liberalization is the reform of the financial sector, in order to generate institutions that provide more efficient financial intermediation. The intertemporal elasticity of substitution in consumption determines the extent to which individuals are prepared to defer consumption into the future, and therefore their propensity to save. This in turn will depend on the real rate of interest, which will both determine the preparedness of individuals to save in the financial sector and influence their consumption decision, depending on whether it is above or below the individual's subjective discount rate. The importance of all these factors will be considered in what follows, as will the importance of financial sector development.

The Role of the Rate of Interest

In the early works of McKinnon (1973) and Shaw (1973), it was argued that the liberalization of interest rates would end financial repression and cause financial deepening, thanks to the resulting increased efficiency of the intermediation process, and the effects of higher interest rates on savings. The difference between the hypotheses of the two authors was in the transmission mechanisms through which they believed this would occur.[6]

The neostructuralist critique
The neostructuralist critique provides a different view of the effect of liberalization to that proposed by McKinnon and Shaw. This critique, which includes authors such as Van Wijnbergen, Taylor and Liang among its proponents, considers the effect of incorporating informal loan markets into the original McKinnon–Shaw models and finds that the freeing of interest rates, far from resulting in output growth, may have the opposite effect.

Shahin (1996) performs a useful review of the neostructuralist views of the implications of financial sector liberalization on saving. They do not contend that an increased deposit rate motivates the movement of unorganized market funds into the banking system. However, since all assets held in informal loan markets are loaned out, whereas, owing to reserve requirements, only a portion of those in the banking system are, increasing deposit rates may convey contractionary moves to economic activity. The decrease in informal market funds increases the informal loan rate, or the cost of financing working capital, causing inflation. The combination of inflation and contraction could cause stagflation.

The interest elasticity of saving
The relationship between financial liberalization and savings, and in particular whether the increase in interest rates causes stagflation, as hypothesized by the neostructuralists, or is successful in promoting investment and growth, as proposed by McKinnon and Shaw, will depend on the interest elasticity of saving in the countries under consideration. This is a controversial question, which has attracted a large empirical literature, with rather inconclusive evidence.

It is notable that McKinnon (1991) acknowledges that aggregate savings, as measured in the GNP accounts, does not respond strongly to higher real interest rates (p. 22). Overall, then, it appears that a change in real interest rates has an ambiguous effect on saving, largely because of the competing income and substitution effects that changes in interest rates give rise to. However, even if higher real rates are unlikely to raise private saving and thus total private wealth, they can alter the portfolio composition of private wealth. Negative real interest rates on deposits cause a substitution of saving from monetary to real assets, such as the purchase of durables, and into foreign currency assets via capital flight. Both of these effects will result in reduced private saving as measured by official national accounts.

The Intertemporal Elasticity of Substitution in Consumption

Clearly one of the influences on the elasticity of the interest rate will be the willingness of the household to substitute consumption over time. Household decisions of how much to consume and how much to save, tend to be captured by models focusing on intertemporal optimization. In the absence of borrowing constraints, the first-order conditions of such models are well known: the ratio between marginal utilities in any two periods has to be equal to the expected discount rate. Individuals borrow and save as outlined above in order to smooth consumption over time. Any change in the discount rate will change the opportunity cost of consumption today, and thus in the absence of market imperfections would change the level of consumption (and therefore saving) today and in the future.

However the market is rarely free from imperfections, especially in developing economies, and as a result the elasticity of substitution is unlikely to be unity. It would seem likely that poorer households, being nearer the poverty line, would have less flexibility to substitute consumption between periods, thus their savings rate is likely to be inelastic relative to that of richer households. This intertemporal elasticity of substitution in consumption will vary across countries, and the degree of development will be a major determinant. Results cited in the IMF's *World Economic Outlook*[7] suggest that the interest elasticity of saving varies considerably with the level of wealth: in low-income countries the interest elasticity is close to zero, but it rises markedly in low middle-income countries, and increases further in upper middle and high-income countries. Thus the household saving rate in upper middle-income developing countries is likely to increase significantly as interest rates move up. This result is similar to that expected in industrial countries. So, while financial liberalization, and the resulting increases in interest rates, may have a number of positive effects, including increasing the efficiency of investment and strengthening economic growth, the direct impact of such policies on household saving behaviour is likely to be relatively small in low-income countries. This would suggest that the effects of financial deregulation outlined in the overlapping-generations model of Bayoumi (above) would be weaker in lower-income countries, on account of their lower intertemporal elasticity of consumption.

Clearly the rate of interest, and its effect on saving, is inextricably linked to the intertemporal rate of substitution of consumption. The indirect policy tool of using interest rates to manage current and future consumption is clearly less than effective. This has led to some countries to use tax reforms aimed at discouraging consumption directly, the rationale being that the opportunity cost of consuming today is higher in the face of a consumption tax. Thus direct action is taken to affect the intertemporal rate of substitution of consumption, rather than indirect, via the interest rate. Such reforms were used by Chile in the mid-1980s. However the effectiveness of such policies relies on the assumption that there is a high intertemporal substitution in consumption, as discussed previously, so poorer countries are less able to use such taxation tools.

Ricardian Equivalence and Savings Behaviour

The majority of studies looking at saving behaviour have relied on the use of aggregate, national saving data, rather than data at a disaggregated level. Aggregate data have the advantage of being, in general, more reliable, with more years of data being available for more countries. The use of private or household data can be limiting, owing to the lack of comparability across countries, and many authors justify using national saving as a reasonable proxy for private saving because private saving constitutes a large part of total saving. However assuming that one measure proxies for the other relies on the assumption that Ricardian equivalence holds. In essence, Ricardian equivalence states that public debt issues are macroeconomically indistinguishable from tax increases, and thus a change in public saving should be offset by an equal and opposite change in private saving.

A number of studies have tested the validity of the Ricardian equivalence hypothesis. Corbo and Schmidt-Hebbel (1991) use a 13–country data set to analyse the consequences of higher public saving. They found that, although government savings crowd out private savings, the magnitude of this effect is far below the one-to-one relationship suggested by the simple Ricardian equivalence doctrine. These results were echoed in the results of Edwards (1996), using a Latin American data set. More recently, Cardenas and Escobar (1998), by using Colombian data, found that increases in taxation over the permanent level of government expenditures reduced savings more than proportionally, thereby contradicting the hypothesis. This implies that higher levels of taxation during the 1990s had an adverse effect on private saving.

The general rejection of the Ricardian equivalence hypothesis implies that private and public saving are not perfect substitutes. Thus empirical rejection of Ricardian equivalence is seen by Schmidt-Hebbel *et al.* (1992) as a powerful argument in favour of using household saving data instead of aggregate data. Kelly and Mavrotas (2001), in their study of the determinants of private savings in India, obtain empirical results which seem to suggest some evidence of Ricardian equivalence, as the private savings variable is negatively related to the government savings variable. A similar finding was also found by the same authors in the case of Sri Lanka (Kelly and Mavrotas, 2002a).

Do Liquidity Constraints Matter?

The household's intertemporal optimization decision outlined above is likely to be complicated by liquidity constraints in developing countries, in the form of borrowing constraints. Such constraints tend to ease with development of the financial sector, as intermediation develops and facilitates more efficient saving and borrowing.

When a borrowing constraint is binding in the household's intertemporal consumption decision, the marginal utility of present consumption will exceed the expected utility of future consumption. Therefore, if liberalization reduces these borrowing constraints, saving ratios would be reduced, because a binding borrowing constraint induces an individual to consume less than they wish to, effectively forcing saving, or at least discouraging dissaving. In such a situation the consumption Euler equation no longer holds, as agents cannot borrow against future income. Studies such as that by Jappelli and Pagano (1994), using the loan-to-value ratio and consumption credit as proxies of borrowing constraints, have shown that liquidity constraints on households raise savings, strengthen the effect of growth on saving and, finally, increase the growth rate, if productivity growth is endogenous.[8]

Bandiera *et al.* (2000) use Euler equations to detect the extent of credit rationing and, in so doing, assess the impact of financial reform on the extent of liquidity constraints by estimating an augmented Euler equation for consumption, in which they assume that the fraction of the consumers that are liquidity- constrained varies with the degree of financial liberalization.

There is a large literature that has attempted to determine the importance of borrowing constraints by inferring that any dependence of the change in consumption on income might reflect the inability of households to smooth the intertemporal pattern of their consumption through borrowing. Corbo and Schmidt-Hebbel (1991) confirm the importance of this dependence, and have found some evidence that it has been higher for developing countries, for reasons outlined above. The inability to smooth is taken by them as evidence of the inapplicability of life cycle theories of borrowing for developing countries.

In the case of Colombia, Cardenas and Escobar (1998) tried to test the validity of the hypothesis that private savings rates have fallen following the relaxation of liquidity constraints as a result of the structural reform package implemented in the early 1990s. They find that liquidity constraints are indeed a significant factor in recent declines in private saving. However this is seen as a temporary effect.

The ratio of money to GDP is traditionally taken as a proxy for financial deepening, but it could also be used as a measure of the extent to which countries face a borrowing constraint. If the former is the case, its coefficient should be positive when included as an explanatory variable in a private savings regression; if the latter holds, it should be negative. Edwards (1996) finds that the coefficient is always significantly positive. Using alternative definitions of the index tested the robustness of this result, but the coefficient estimates were unchanged. Overall the results did not provide support for the view that borrowing constraints have resulted in lower savings.[9]

The Kelly and Mavrotas (2002a) findings for Sri Lanka seem to suggest that private saving is inversely related to the availability of credit (the credit constraint). This finding was also confirmed by the econometric analysis undertaken by the same authors using disaggregated savings time-series data on India (Kelly and Mavrotas, 2001). Their finding is also in line with the study by Loayza *et al.* (2000) which reports that the relaxation of credit constraints was responsible for a decrease in private savings in industrial and developing countries within the context of a dynamic panel data analysis.

The Role of the Financial Sector in Reducing Risk and Uncertainty

One of the key roles of saving is its precautionary motive to help mitigate future uncertainty. There are two factors that are important here: the liquidity of savings and the availability of insurance.

The liquidity of savings

Savings are an important precautionary device, to protect against uncertainty. However, in order to encourage individuals to save, it is vital that the savings can be liquidated when needed to cope with an income shock. This requires well developed financial markets. In order to mobilize individual savings, institutions must offer a positive rate of return to attract funds. By their size, stock markets, mutual funds and other financial institutions are able to diversify their portfolios to offer risky investments as elements of financial instruments which are of a size and risk profile that is suitable to the smaller investor (Gersovitz, 1988). The presence of stock markets means that such instruments are tradable, and so can be liquidated as and when necessary. If such returns and liquidity are not offered, savings rates will be lower, as in such circumstances savings will not offer their precautionary role.

The availability of insurance

The availability of insurance is an important factor in the question of savings mobilization: if the financial sector is sufficiently advanced to provide adequate insurance to individuals against future uncertainties, savings will be lower. For example, if a rural farmer in a developing country can insure against the loss of income resulting from a bad crop, she or he will not need to make precautionary savings to allow for this. Effectively, if the premium charged is actuarially correct, this will perform the consumption smoothing, for the individual savings will not be required for this purpose. However, if the premium is too high, insurance will not be taken, and if it is too low, insurance is not sustainable in the long term and there is a risk of default by the insurance company. Social security is another type of insurance that will be dealt with in section 3.

Information asymmetries

The key to having an effective insurance system is the presence of information. Moral hazard and adverse selection mean that determining actuarially correct premia is difficult (Stiglitz and Weiss, 1981). However financial sector development reduces information asymmetries, through the development of relationships between institutions and individuals. In particular, the deposit behaviour of individuals provides signals to lenders that help reduce informational opacity.

3. OTHER DETERMINANTS OF SAVINGS

Whilst the subject of interest for this review chapter is essentially the relationship between savings and financial sector development, it is important to consider briefly other determinants of saving, many of which indirectly affect the financial sector. A number of comprehensive general surveys of determinants of saving in developing countries have been undertaken, particularly notable examples being those of Deaton (1989), Gersovitz (1988), Schmidt-Hebbel (1992) and Obstfeld (1998). This section will pick up some of the key issues.

Savings and Growth: What Causes What?

The contemporaneous positive correlation between saving and growth has been widely discussed in the literature: it has been empirically verified by a number of authors, such as Houthakker (1961, 1965), Modigliani (1990), Maddison (1992) and Mankiw *et al.* (1992), among others. However, the direction of causality – in other words the lead–lag relationship between saving and growth – has remained a contentious issue. Both directions are supported by different economic theories. Traditional neoclassical models of economic growth, such as that of Solow (1956), and more recent models of endogenous growth (for example, Romer 1986, as well as Rebelo-style growth models), see savings leading growth. By contrast, the life cycle model of Modigliani and models of habit formation (see, for example, Deaton, 1992, and, more recently, Carroll *et al.* (2000) hypothesize that the relationship works in the other direction for reasons that are well known. However, as pointed out by Bosworth (1993), in life cycle models saving will also influence growth, as in a growing economy the young workers will anticipate future income increases and, as a result, will tend to increase present consumption and reduce savings. Without empirical investigation it is unclear whether the positive or negative effect will dominate.[10]

Traditional views related to the direction of causation between savings and growth have been challenged recently by a number of authors (Gavin *et al.*, 1997; Carroll and Weil, 1994; Jappelli and Pagano, 1994; Sinha and Sinha, 1998, and Sinha, 1997, among others). The new empirical literature on the subject seems to conclude that the direction of causation between the two variables runs from growth to savings and not vice versa. Gavin *et al.* (1997) examine the relationship between saving and growth, drawing on the experience of East Asia and Latin America in a cross-section data framework. They found that higher growth precedes saving; only after a sustained period of high growth do savings rates increase, and this may be with a delay that is quite significant. The most powerful determinant of saving over the long run is economic growth. Carroll and Weil (1994) used both cross-country panel data (from the Penn World Tables) and household level data to deal with the above issue and have concluded that there is evidence suggesting that growth indeed affects private savings positively. More recently, Rodrik (1999) reports similar findings using a qualitative analytical framework. Finally, Carroll *et al.* (2000) show, in the context of a habit formation model that, if utility depends partly on how consumption compares to a 'habit stock' determined by past consumption, an otherwise standard growth model can imply that increases in growth can cause increased savings.

However the vast empirical literature on the subject suffers from a number of shortcomings including preoccupation with the use of cross-section studies and inappropriate econometric techniques.[11] A detailed discussion of the above issue is provided in Attanasio *et al.* (2000), which is a striking exemption in the above empirical literature, adopting an appropriate dynamic specification of the panel data model, thus trying to have the best of both worlds: panel data and time series at the same time. In analysing the relationship between savings and growth, the authors consider in detail how the empirical results change when different econometric techniques are used, when the frequency of the data is changed and when different groups of countries are included in the sample.

Detailed econometric analysis has been carried out by Mavrotas and Kelly (2001b) on the savings–growth nexus. Using the most recent econometric techniques on this front (Toda–Yamamoto causality tests instead of the rather problematic Granger-causality type tests), as well as disaggregated savings data for India and Sri Lanka, the authors found that the conventional neoclassical view, that savings causes growth, does not hold when we look at gross domestic savings: in fact, evidence is found that growth causes savings, as hypothesized by life cycle models of savings behaviour. GDP growth is found to cause savings in India, while, in Sri Lanka, it appears that there is a bidirectional causality between private savings and growth. The above finding clearly demonstrates that the existing 'evidence' on the subject should be treated with caution, given the inappropriateness of the econometric analysis used (see, for instance, the problematic nature of standard Granger causality tests) in most of these empirical studies. At the same time, the above result clearly demonstrates the differing reaction of GDP growth to changes in private savings and gross domestic savings, a distinction not to be observed if only aggregate savings were examined. The same exercise was performed in the case of Pakistan by the same authors (for which relatively long time-series data were available) by distinguishing between gross domestic savings and private savings (Mavrotas and Kelly, 2000). The authors found evidence that private savings cause growth, but no evidence of causality in either direction between gross domestic savings (GDS) and growth was established. This is an interesting result, for a number of reasons, but particularly as it demonstrates the differing reaction of GDP growth to changes in private savings and GDS – a distinction that would not be observed if one examined only aggregate savings, and which has important policy implications. Furthermore the finding that private savings cause growth in Pakistan, thereby confirming the neoclassical growth theory, seems to run contrary to the results found for India and Sri Lanka (see above), highlighting the fact that causality is country-specific.

Income and Wealth Effects

It is commonly held that poor individuals save a smaller fraction of their income than the wealthy because they are closer to the line of subsistence; they have less flexibility in their consumption decisions, as discussed in section 2. However, according to the permanent income or life cycle theories, saving should be used simply to smooth consumption over time. As a result it is the time pattern of income that is important here; those with more volatile incomes should have higher savings rates according to these theories.

At the same time households, particularly those in developing countries, tend to be credit-constrained, and as a result are less able to smooth consumption, so it is likely that consumption (and therefore saving) would respond substantially to changes in income. Gupta (1987) finds that saving responds significantly and positively to temporary income shocks in developing countries. There is also likely to be a strong element of myopia present, as households are less than perfectly able to distinguish between temporary and permanent income shocks, meaning that they will consume more out of current shocks than predicted by consumption smoothing models (Campbell and Deaton, 1989).

Income growth is also important. If the young anticipate that their income will grow steadily, and are able to borrow against the increase, their dissaving in the early years of the life cycle may result in a negative relation between saving and growth (Deaton, 1989). Intertemporal optimization models see wealth as a key determinant of consumption or saving; in effect wealth provides a substitute for savings, hence greater wealth is predicted to reduce saving out of current income. Schmidt-Hebbel *et al.* (1992, p. 532) cite evidence from a study by Schmidt-Hebbel (1987), which uses five alternative measures of total wealth in an empirical intertemporal consumption model for Chile, and a study by Behrman and Sussangkarn (1989) using household level data on wealth and saving in Thailand. Both studies find that wealth has a strong negative effect on saving.

The Role of Demographic Factors

The effects of demography on saving can be analysed by extending the two-period life cycle model discussed in section 2 to a multi-period model. However, Gersovitz (1988) introduces a caveat here. Effectively, the increase in horizon corresponds to an increase in the life expectancy of adults, since the model is of a decision maker in full control of her initial consumption decisions (c_0). This should be borne in mind, especially in view of the fact that much of the increase in life expectancy in less developed countries (LDCs) has been through decreases in infant mortality rates, raising life expectancy at birth.

Demographic factors are supposed to be important elements of the entire saving process. Doshi (1994), Edwards (1995) and Faruqee and Husain (1995) report strong empirical evidence concerning the significance of demographic factors by estimating reduced-form savings equations in the context of a cross-section approach for a number of developing countries. Strong demographic effects have also been found in Horioka's study on Japanese savings (Horioka, 1991) as well as in Kang (1994) concerning Taiwan, Korea and Japan. Demographic changes in East Asia were also found responsible for the high savings rates in the region, according to Higgins and Williamson (1996). Cultural effects are also present in some cases (Carrol, Rhee and Rhee, 1994). Jappelli and Pagano (1994) found a significant negative relationship between dependency ratios and savings. Finally, Edwards (1996) finds that the coefficient on the age dependency ratio is significantly negative, indicating that demographics play an important role in explaining differences in private savings across time and countries.

The demographics coefficient (captured by the use of dependency ratios) was found to be negative and significant in the case of India in Kelly and Mavrotas (2001) but not significant in the case of Sri Lanka (Kelly and Mavrotas, 2002a). As only a single dependency ratio was used in the case of India, there is no clear evidence as to whether this result is driven by the young or old age dependency ratio; however theory suggests that the young dependency ratio is found to be negatively correlated with saving, while the old age dependency ratio is positively correlated with per capita income (and therefore, in theory, private saving). While the two ratios work in different directions, it is likely that the negative relationship will dominate in less developed countries, where the population is still growing at a relatively rapid pace: consequently this result is in line with expectations for India.

Uncertainty and Savings Behaviour

According to the Darberger–Laursen–Metzler effect,[12] a temporary improvement in the terms of trade is considered to increase the saving rate because it suggests a transitory boost in national income, which will increase national savings. An IMF study (1995) found that changes in the terms of trade have a strong positive effect on saving. However, other studies, for example that undertaken by Lopez-Murphy and Navajas (1998) on Argentina, found no correlation between private savings and terms of trade for the period 1970–95.

Political instability is also important as a determinant of savings behaviour since government savings is a fundamental component of national savings. There has been an extensive literature detailing the behaviour of governments. Edwards (1996) provides a useful summary of this literature. The incentive of the authorities to increase government savings will depend on two factors. First is the probability that the party in power will still be in power in the subsequent period; if this is low, then an incumbent party has little incentive to save, as the other party will gain the credit from the subsequent increased production of public goods. Thus the higher the degree of political instability, the lower government savings. A second determinant of governmental incentives to save is the degree of political polarization – in other words the degree of difference in the parties' preferences. A greater degree of polarization will, in theory, result in lower government savings. In

Edwards (1995), separate equations for government savings were estimated for 36 countries over the period 1983–92. The results obtained clearly confirm a priori expectations concerning the role of political instability and uncertainty in public savings.[13]

Foreign Capital and Savings

One of the most controversial parts of the savings literature is the relationship between foreign capital (in particular foreign aid) and domestic savings, in the recipient countries. The effect of foreign aid on domestic savings in developing countries has been mainly analysed in terms of the Harrod–Domar growth model and its two-gap versions associated with Hollis Chenery and his associates in the 1960s. More recent contributions in the area include Boone (1994) and Obstfeld (1998). Although vast, the empirical literature on the topic has failed to offer clear answers so far, owing to inappropriate econometric methodologies employed in most of the cases, simplistic modelling frameworks and lack of an aid disaggregation approach. Cassen (1994) and White (1992) assess the relevant literature and Mavrotas (2002) focuses on the aid disaggregation issue.

The Impact of Financial Sector Development on Savings: Recent Evidence

Recent evidence reported by Kelly and Mavrotas (2001, 2002a) seems to suggest that financial sector development (measured by three different indicators) has an overall positive and significant effect on private savings in the case of India and Sri Lanka. It is notable that it is not strictly correct to interpret the index of financial sector development, used in the above studies, as a measure of financial sector development, because each component may not be positively correlated with all the constituent variables. In view of the above, the authors tried to determine the influence of each variable on the dependent variable through the estimated regression coefficients of the retained principal components. Of the three measures employed, the measure of the activity of financial intermediaries seems to have the strongest effect in the case of Sri Lanka, followed by the measure of the absolute size, while the measure of the relative size of the financial sector seems to have only a relatively small impact. A similar methodology to reveal the true impact of each component was employed for India. Again the measure of the activity of financial intermediaries was found to have the strongest effect of the three measures used in the econometric analysis.

Do the results remain robust if we move from an individual country analysis to a panel data framework? To answer this important question and, at the same time, to shed some light on the experience of the Africa region with very low levels of savings, Kelly and Mavrotas (2002b) have recently carried out empirical work on the determinants of savings for a panel of 17 African countries for which relatively long time-series data were available. Different types of financial sector development indicators were employed (measuring the absolute and relative size of the financial sector as well as the activity of financial intermediaries) by the authors and an innovative econometric methodology was used related to a series of cointegration tests within a panel. The empirical results obtained vary considerably among different countries in the panel, thus highlighting the importance of using different measures of financial sector development rather than a single indicator. The evidence is rather inconclusive, although in most of the countries in the sample a positive relationship between financial sector development and private savings seems to hold.

Savings in the World: Recent Evidence from a World Bank Study

Loayza *et al.* (2000) use panel instrumental variables techniques (that allow correcting for endogeneity and heterogeneity through 'internal instruments') to assess the policy and non-policy determinants of savings for a panel developed and developing countries. Their main findings seem to suggest the following.

- Private savers respond very differently to temporary and permanent income changes, in line with the predictions of the permanent income hypothesis and life cycle hypothesis. Thus a policy change causing a permanent increase in private income will be almost fully reflected in increased consumption, while the same policy, if only temporary, has a significant effect on saving.
- Public sector saving is the most direct tool available to policy makers addressing the level of national saving. The reason is that private saving offsets only part of any increase in public saving. The authors find no positive reaction by private savers to higher government investment (on average consumers consider public capital to be 'real wealth').
- Inflation (a proxy of uncertainty) has a positive effect on private saving rates, consistent with the precautionary motive. But it is rather misleading to think that inflation stabilization could have an adverse effect on saving, because there is evidence that stabilization programmes that lower inflation raise growth that has a positive effect on private saving. The fiscal adjustment component of the stabilization has a positive effect on saving.
- There is a negative and significant effect of real interest rates on private saving. This suggests that the income effect outweigh the substitution

and wealth effects. The results are not robust, however, across country sub-samples. There is a robust negative effect of liberalization on both private and national saving. The rise in monetary and financial asset ratios to income caused by financial liberalization has an ambiguous effect on private saving. Financial liberalization, according to the authors, has an indirect channel to increase saving through its positive impact on growth.

- Regarding external borrowing, higher levels of foreign saving crowd out private saving (and hence national saving).
- Both the level and the growth rate of real per capita income have a positive impact on saving. The influence of per capita income is large and significant in developing countries, but smaller and insignificant in industrial countries. This seems to suggest, according to the authors, that the effect of the level of development on saving tapers off at medium or high levels of per capita income. Successful growth policies may be able to set in motion a virtuous cycle of saving, capital accumulation and growth.
- Finally, terms of trade windfalls are positively associated with private and national saving. Both urbanization and the old age dependency ratio are strongly positively correlated with per capita income, so that they dampen the positive effect of rising incomes on saving. The negative effect of young age dependency on saving suggest that developing countries with young populations that aim at accelerating their demographic transition and speed up the decline in young dependency ratios may witness a transitory increase in their saving ratios before reaching the next stage of demographic maturity, at which old age dependency rises swiftly and saving rates level off.

Social Security Reforms and Savings Mobilization

Reforming social security systems is an important route for mobilizing savings in developing countries. Private savings are affected by the extent and coverage of government-run social security systems in the sense that, if individuals perceive that when they retire they are going to receive high benefits from the government, they will tend to reduce the amount saved during their active days. Along the above lines, the development of new institutions in the social security sector could force savings in low income countries with depressed levels of saving.

In most countries, pension systems are state-run and are unfunded, defined benefit systems, that operate on a pay-as-you-go basis. There are a number of problems with such systems, such as the lack of a direct relationship between benefits and contributions, which can strain government budgets, and wage taxes that may distort labour markets and encourage tax evasion. It has been suggested by a number of authors, such as Edwards (1996) and Feldstein (1980),[14] that a switch to either fully funded, or at least partially funded, schemes would have a beneficial effect on the level of national savings in an economy, as part of a package of financial sector reform. However there has been an increasing empirical literature that has been less conclusive about the above hypothesized effect.[15] Public pension systems are intended to fulfil two primary objectives: to provide a compulsory saving mechanism and to alleviate poverty among the old. The compulsory saving mechanism forces the individuals who might be myopic with regard to their future needs or who might expect to rely on charity in their old age to save for themselves. In most countries a public pension system is the institution that delivers this service.

Unfortunately there is a contradiction in the objectives of these institutions. A good saving mechanism will have a tight link between the contribution and the benefits received, but the aim of poverty alleviation will divert contributions to benefit the poor. Most pension schemes around the world try to achieve both objectives through a single system, but they end up doing neither well. As a result of these difficulties, most pension reforms have attempted to use a hybrid of these mechanisms. Social security reforms comprise two elements: on the one side, a pillar of fully funded savings based on individual pension accounts, with investments made in a number of public and private long-term instruments, and a complementary state-run distributive pillar, to support the elderly poor.[16] Such a multi-pillar pension scheme, as described by Schwarz (1995), has one pillar devoted to providing a saving mechanism and the other to alleviating poverty.

Samwick (1998) models a voluntary scheme to privatize some or all of the current social security programmes. The scheme is structured to allow workers to buy themselves out of the current programme by saving in a dedicated retirement account. Samwick also set some recommendations to countries that want to follow a defined-contribution pension system. First of all there must be macroeconomic stability. The government must have credibility and must make an explicit recognition of the debt that was formerly implicit in the existing unfunded system (recognition bonds that are given to individuals that opt out and are taken as the first deposit on the private scheme). Furthermore taxation on retirement accounts must be low. Finally, the managers of the dedicated retirement account should be allowed to have access to the international capital markets and not be forced to hold excessive amounts of government debt.[17,18]

According to Samwick (1996), a combination of mandatory fully funded schemes with supplementary defined benefit arrangements relieves pressures on budgets while providing protection for retirees. The mandatory, fully funded pillar may lead to higher saving by making people aware of the need to save for the future, and through forced saving. It is also likely to deepen capital markets through private sector participation in the investment of pension funds. To the extent that the reforms lead to higher saving, they are likely to have a positive effect on growth. The increased capital market deepening that results from the reforms is also likely to contribute to higher output growth, which in turn would generate higher savings.

4. SAVINGS MOBILIZATION AND THE ROLE OF MICROFINANCE

Appropriately designed institutions are crucial to improving the mobilization of savings in developing countries. The poor tend to have limited access to formal financial services, and the lack of competition means that a high price is paid. This commonly takes the form of high interest payments on loans, but in fact the poor frequently pay for the chance to save: the nominal rates received on deposits are frequently low or even zero, meaning that the real interest rates are negative. In the absence of formal financial services, the poor rely on family and friends to provide loans on a reciprocal basis. A high value is placed on financial intermediation, as is evidenced by the informal financial institutions that have grown in developing countries. There exist a group of formal and informal financial institutions around the world that have developed to attend to the needs of the smaller saver and investor. Formal, state-introduced mechanisms traditionally worked on the assumption that the poor did not have the capacity to save, and needed direct credit to enable them to escape the poverty trap. Consequently, the institutions aimed to help the poor directly, through subsidy, rather than address their financial services needs. Empirical studies that will be reviewed in this section have shown that this has not occurred; given the appropriate incentives, even the poorest individuals have savings that could be mobilized.

There are two basic types of self-help groups that provide financial mutual aid; they have saving and lending as their primary functions. There are those with rotating funds known as 'rotating savings and credit associations' (ROSCAs) and those with non-rotating funds that Bouman (1995) calls 'accumulating savings and credit associations' (ASCAs). These groups have grown up in response to specific needs: there is no uniform type across countries, as will be seen below.

Both types of institution are voluntary and autonomous, and have their own objectives, rules and organization patterns. As financial institutions they are self-sufficient, self-regulating and have their own control mechanisms. They are thus independent of the legal, fiscal and financial authorities of their countries. Their great advantage is their flexibility, and this is where their comparative advantage over formal financial institutions lies.

ROSCAs

In a ROSCA, a group of individuals pool savings and these are returned to the members in rotation. The order of rotation varies between ROSCA. The ROSCA is governed by the principle of balanced reciprocity; this means that each member contributes the same amount, drawing from the fund as much as he puts into it. The ROSCA intermediates between savers and borrowers, allowing some to get funds before they could in the absence of the association, and allowing others to save more than they otherwise would. Once the rotation has finished, the association officially comes to an end, although in practice individuals tend to be perpetually involved in at least one ROSCA at any one time.[19]

The lifetime of the ROSCA depends on the number of participants, and the periodicity of the payments. Owing to the regularity of the payments, they must have a steady source of income, and so membership tends to stem from homogeneous groups (same occupation, residential area, social clubs). Aside from the financial intermediation role played by ROSCAs, Bouman sees that there is an illiquidity role. Contributions that are made to a ROSCA are recognized as being obligatory, and constitute a senior claim that must be respected by others. Thus individuals with money that they want to keep safe from greedy relatives will join a ROSCA in order to become illiquid (Bouman, 1995).

Adams and Canavesi (1989) performed a study of ROSCAs in Bolivia. They note that a significant proportion of the adult population participate in this sort of saving scheme, at least occasionally. Interestingly they found that such associations were common among employees of most formal financial intermediaries, suggesting that they offered benefits that could not be obtained from the financial intermediary in which they worked.

As ROSCAs have evolved in response to the specific needs of individuals, weaknesses in their structure tend to have been resolved over time. For example, under the standard, non-bid rotation of the funds, no interest is charged, meaning that late receivers save interest-free. The auction system of rotation gets around this problem, providing a more effective form of financial intermediation. The auction system also addresses another criticism of the traditional ROSCA, namely that a player cannot be sure when the fund will be received; by bidding appropriately, the element of chance is mitigated.

In some countries, the concept of interest payments on loans is still not culturally accepted. In these countries, a more acceptable way may be a 'last first' arrangement, such that those who receive their share later in one scheme receive it earlier in the next. Where interest payments are used, there is the risk identified by Adams and Canavesi (1989) that an individual could offer a deeply discounted bid in order to receive finance early on, and then renege on the repayments. To address this risk, many ROSCAs agree beforehand on a maximum bid that may not be exceeded. Adverse selection suggests that anyone offering an excessively high bid wants to benefit by being an early winner, and reneging.[20]

ASCAs

The term 'ASCA' was introduced by Bouman (1995) as a generic term to describe non-rotating savings and credit associations. They differ from ROSCAs[21] in that savings are not immediately redistributed between the members, but are allowed to accumulate to make loans. Usually the cycle lasts a year, after which partial or complete redistribution of the proceeds takes place and a new cycle starts. The main purpose of the ASCA is to save for specific purposes highly regarded by the members, such as community and social events. There is an order of priority for loans: emergencies and misfortunes, consumption loans and production loans. Contributions, interest payments and fines build up the fund. The contributions come from a more heterogeneous base of society. The amounts and regularity of payments are set in the membership agreement, but tend to be more flexible than ROSCA. The ASCA has a broader set of objectives than the ROSCA, and fulfils group rather than individual goals. To perform the lending activity, the ASCA has higher overheads than the ROSCA; they must hold records and have higher administration and supervision. There is also a magnitude difference: most ROSCAs are composed of no more than 50 members, while the ASCA membership could be greater than a thousand. This increases the chances of embezzlement and fraud, because of diminishing social control (Bouman, 1995).

Take-up of informal finance
Bouman (1995) cites evidence on take-up of ASCAs and ROSCAs from a number of sources. According to Siebel (1986), membership ranges from 50 to 95 per cent of the adult population in certain central African countries. However the spread of membership is far from uniform, and can be as low as 10–25 per cent in both rural and urban areas. Bouman (1995) notes that research in the Gambia and Uganda suggests that ROSCAs are more common in urban areas, and ASCAs in rural areas.

It is the role of such informal financial institutions as savings vehicles that comes as a surprise to many. In many countries, these associations are the sole deposit agents, either owing to the absence of formal financial institutions or because the formal institutions tend to tie savings in with borrowing, as discussed below. Schreider and Cuevas (1992) report that the informal financial groups in Cameroon handle about half of the total national savings of the country.

There is also evidence of the formal financial institutions' recognition of the importance of the role played by informal institutions. The work of Adams and Canavesi (1989) on Bolivia has shown banks using formally organized schemes to enable individuals to raise the finance required for deposits on houses and to obtain mortgages.

Microcredit Institutions (MCIs)

The Micro Credit Institutions (MCI) have been a success story in Bangladesh and are seen as the example to follow in the rest of the developing world. The Grameen Bank, the Bangladesh Rural Advancement Committee (BRAC) and the Association for Social Advancement (ASA) are based on the capacity of the poor to make savings out of their normal income. MCI lending provides loans, with small, frequent repayments. In effect, such lending is advances against savings. Use of such loans varies, tending to be either for consumer purchases or for business reasons. In the latter case, they may be repaid by the additional returns provided by the business expansion that the loan funds, but in general they are repaid through weekly saving. MCIs are first and foremost moneylenders; they act as financial intermediaries only to the extent that they supplement their loan funds, which come mainly from donor grants, with compulsory savings taken from customers. They are not in the business of acting as general deposit takers: all of their customers have outstanding loans. This means that such institutions are not attractive to the poorest groups; the poor are often unwilling to borrow, and under the group collateral approach of the MCIs, which means that grouped customers are jointly responsible for each other's loan repayments, there is an incentive to keep the poorest individuals out. Work by Rutherford (1998) on Bangladesh found a further reason why MCI tended to discriminate against the poor: branch staff are formally threatened with the loss of their job if repayment rates fall below 95 per cent. It appears that those excluded are those whose introduction to formal financial services would most conveniently have come via the opportunity to save.

Credit Unions

Savings and loans cooperatives, also known as credit unions,[22] are organizations owned and operated on a not-for-profit basis by its members according to democratic principles. Their purpose is to encourage savings, to use pooled funds to make loans, and to provide other related services to members and their families (Cuevas, 1988, p. 5). The democratic structure, the operating principles governing service to members and the social goals that characterize credit unions are likely to blend with and build upon the implicit principles of mutual trust and cooperation that exist in rural communities. They mainly flourish in rural areas and the established network usually exceeds the number of bank branches. Many observers regard them as the first step in the development of institutional finance. Worldwide, loans from credit unions grew at average annual rates substantially higher than credit received by the private sector from the banking system. The explanation for this fact is the different regulatory environment affecting the two types of institutions. Banks and other non-cooperative financial institutions are more likely to be influenced by policies aimed at increasing credit to the public sector than credit unions. Banks are also more prone to invest in government instruments if they perceive their loan demand is riskier than usual, thus reducing private sector credit. On the other hand, credit unions are in most cases unregulated or less regulated by the monetary authority, and the nature of the organization makes the level of risk implicit in their loan demand more stable than that faced by the banking institutions (Cuevas, 1988).

For Van Der Brink and Chavas (1997), two main limitations seem to be present in the development of credit unions: (a) an individual cannot withdraw savings that serve as a guarantee for another's individual loan, and (b) the limited capacity to reinvest savings locally. Finally, according to Bouman (1995) the disadvantage of the cooperative-type models is that, as they become permanent institutions, they tend to become formalized, static, bureaucratic and have greater operating costs, and are more susceptible to mismanagement and diminishing social control.

5. CONCLUSIONS AND POLICY LESSONS

There is a vast literature examining issues related to savings and development, the main aspects of which have been critically reviewed here. The link between financial sector development and saving is very important, though largely overlooked, with most authors examining the relationships between either financial sector development and growth or saving and growth. The present review has tried to shed more light on the important, though so far neglected, nexus between saving mobilization and financial sector development and the significant implications this implies for poverty-reducing growth in developing countries. We have tried to do this by critically evaluating the existing vast literature on both financial sector development and savings mobilization with a primary focus on the channels and the mechanisms through which the above nexus materializes. We have also considered aspects of the literature which have not been properly discussed before. Furthermore, the chapter has discussed a new booming literature on savings mobilization, namely social security reforms and the way they affect savings. Finally, we have discussed the plethora of formal as well as informal institutions by which savings mobilization is influenced in developing countries.

The following policy lessons seem to emerge from recent empirical work in the area of savings mobilization and in particular regarding the impact of financial sector development on savings. First, financial sector development does affect savings significantly, but knowing which type of financial sector development matters most is crucial for policy. Recent evidence seems to suggest that financial sector development has a rather significant and positive effect on private saving. The relevant policy implications are quite important. Financial reforms and policies strengthening the financial sector of the economy will have a strong boosting effect on private savings, which in turn may affect the entire growth process. However, knowing which type of financial sector development matters most is crucial for policy. As a recent study has put it:

> the importance of getting the big financial policy decisions right has thus emerged as one of the central development challenges of the new century. However, the controversy stirred up by the recent financial crises has pointed to the weaknesses of doctrinaire policy views on *how this is to be achieved*. (Emphasis added; World Bank, 2001, p. 1)

Recent empirical evidence reported in Kelly and Mavrotas (2001, 2002a, 2002b) clearly suggests that the measure of the activity of financial intermediaries seems to have the strongest effect on savings, followed by the measure of the absolute size, while the measure of the relative size of the financial sector seems to have only a relatively small impact. In view of the above findings, policies strengthening the efficiency of financial intermediaries will give rise to high returns on saving and should be prioritized. Having said this, policies which try to build better financial institutions (thereby increasing the confidence of savers), encourage competition and provide a wider variety of instruments for saving can further strengthen the overall saving mobilization process in developing countries with substantial gains in the area of poverty-reducing growth.

Second, liquidity constraints cannot be overlooked. The relevant policy dilemma is that, although policies strengthening the financial sector development can be associated with positive effects on savings, relaxing liquidity constraints may result in the opposite effect. Of course, the final impact on savings will depend on which of the two effects is greater. This is an important issue that should be borne in mind in the design of policies addressing savings mobilization in developing economies.

Third, introducing simple and straightforward banking procedures is essential to boost savings, along with improving access to saving institutions. The formalities, procedures and regulations in the formal financial sector for banking operation should be simplified to suit the needs of savers, in particular the small ones. Access to financial institutions is a crucial factor affecting savings mobilization. Rural savings mobilization, in particular, requires an institutional network which provides easy access to potential savers. The absence of institutions collecting deposits from the rural sector, especially in remote areas, may simply discourage saving or encourage consumption and perhaps wasteful expenditure, or it may lead to saving in a non-monetized form. In view of the above, it is rather important that the existing bank branches in developing countries be expanded to remote areas for the benefits of potential savers.

Fourth, improving the overall macroeconomic stability, the regulation and supervision of local banks and encouraging the provision of savings facilities to micro, small and medium-sized enterprises is crucial for savings mobilization. To strengthen savings mobilization, it is important that government initiatives in developing countries to improve the rate and levels of savings concentrate on micro, small and medium-sized enterprise deposits. Improving the overall macroeconomic stability and the regulation and supervision of local banks seem to be appropriate policy directions, along with encouraging the provision of savings facilities to micro, small and medium-sized enterprises (Brownbridge and Kirkpatrick, 1999; Maimbo and Mavrotas, 2001).

Fifth, the regulatory framework for microfinance institutions (MFIs) should be improved. Most individuals and small and medium enterprises continue to depend on informal and non-financial assets for their savings facilities and arrangements. Policy makers need to encourage the role played by MFIs, which, with a relatively smaller cost base, are a more viable option in the effective delivery of financial savings facilities to low-income individuals and small and medium-scale enterprises, especially in rural areas. At the same time, the challenge for MFIs is to create structures that make it easier for successful MFI clients to gain access to larger, more diverse and longer-term sources of finance.

Needless to say, as the present review makes clear, there is a strong need for further work in the above areas so that a much more conclusive picture can be obtained and further policy guidelines can be drawn. It is hoped that the present review has highlighted the key issues in the area of savings mobilization and financial sector development and, at the same time, will be of particular interest to those studying and/or trying to implement financial sector reforms for savings mobilization and sustainable growth in developing countries.

NOTES

* This work is part of the *Finance & Development Research Programme (FDRP)* funded by the Department for International Development (DFID) and managed by the Institute for Development Policy and Management, University of Manchester, UK. The interpretations and conclusions expressed in this chapter are entirely those of the author and should not be attributed in any manner to DFID or UNU-WIDER. An earlier version has been published in *Savings and Development*, **XXV**(1), 2001. I wish to thank in particular Colin Kirkpatrick (IDPM), William Kingsmill (DFID) and Victor Murinde (University of Birmingham) who have provided me with their insightful comments during the different stages of this research. I am also grateful to Roger Kelly for high-class research assistance well beyond the conventional standards during the first two years of this project. I am also indebted to seminar and conference participants in Manchester (July 1999, April and May 2001, April 2002), UNU-WIDER, Helsinki (October 2001), Nairobi (July 2001), the Money, Macro and Finance Conference in London (September 2000) and Berlin (July 2002). Finally, warm thanks to the members of the FDRP Advisory Panel for their comments during the several stages of this research. Needless to say, the usual disclaimer applies.

1. See Arestis and Demetriades (1997) for an excellent assessment of the literature.
2. Among the few exemptions are the study by Bandiera *et al.* (2000), which, by using data on a selected group of developing countries has concluded that financial sector development does not necessarily raise private saving, and Kelly and Mavrotas (2001), which shows a rather strong positive impact of different financial sector development indicators on private savings in India over the period 1972–97.
3. The cost of financial repression has been the subject of a voluminous empirical literature. Influential studies have been those by Fry (1978, 1980), Gupta (1984), Easterly (1997) and Giovannini (1983, 1985), among others. See Gibson and Tsakalotos (1994) for an excellent discussion.
4. See, for example, the works of Deaton (1989) and Gersovitz (1988).
5. Apart from models of saving behaviour rooted in the popular life cycle hypothesis, there exists a quite interesting strand of theoretical literature which focuses on the role of savings in the context of models of endogenous growth and financial sector development: see Mavrotas and Santillana (1999) for a discussion.
6. For a detailed discussion, see Gibson and Tsakalotos (1994).
7. IMF, 'Saving in a Growing World Economy', *World Economic Outlook*, May 1995.
8. Their sample, however, focuses on industrial countries, thus shedding little light on the relationship between financial sector development and savings as far as developing countries are concerned.
9. It is notable that the results of Edwards (1996) differ from those of Jappelli and Pagano (1994) and Schmidt-Hebbel *et al.* (1992); there are a number of possible reasons why, such as the share of private credit is a poor proxy for borrowing constraints.
10. It is possible that there is two-way causation; growth will affect savings through the mechanisms suggested by Modigliani, while savings are likely to have an impact on growth through their effect on capital accumulation. It is this very endogeneity of the rate of growth that makes testing for causality so complex. Deaton (1989) points out that the possibility that growth and saving cause each other simultaneously is an attractive option, since it suggests the possibility of multiple growth–saving equilibria.
11. These shortcomings have also been discussed in detail in connection with causality issues on financial development and growth in two comprehensive studies by Demetriades and Hussein (1996) and Arestis and Demetriades (1997) which conclude there are significant dangers from lumping together in cross-section equations countries with very different experiences which may reflect different institutional characteristics, different policies and differences in their implementation.
12. See Ostry and Reinhart (1992).
13. Concerning the nexus between political instability and government savings, see also Cukierman *et al.* (1992).

14. The model of Edwards (1996) found a significant negative coefficient on social security, consistent with the findings of Feldstein (1980), supporting the notion that the replacement of government-run, partially funded social security systems with privately-run funded systems will tend to result in higher savings rates. However the transition will reduce government savings in the short run, as the government will continue to have obligations to older retirees, but will receive no contributions from active workers.

15. See Arrau and Schmidt-Hebbel (1994), Diamond (1994), Schmidt-Hebbel (1995), Ribe (1994), Bailliu and Reisen (1997) and more recently Samwick (1998).

16. Such measures are seen by Arrau and Schmidt-Hebbel (1994) as a radical departure from the conventional pension paradigm in three ways: first, the substitution of a pay-as-you-go scheme by a fully funded arrangement for old age saving; second, more explicit separation of the distributive from the non-distributive aspects; finally, the private management of the collection of contributions, investment of pension fund savings and payment of pension benefits.

17. The problem in the developing countries is that not many non-government securities are present in the market. That is why it is important that the new security system develops alongside other financial market liberalization. Administrative expenses will tend to be higher in the developing countries with less experience in managing retirement accounts.

18. Examples of social security reforms in a number of countries (Chile, Colombia, Brazil, Argentina, Singapore and Malaysia) are discussed in Samwick (1996) and Diamond and Valdez-Prieto (1994).

19. Van Der Brink and Chavas (1997) develop a microfoundations model of a ROSCA based on the fieldwork at the Big Babanki of Cameroon for the period 1979–80; they determine efficiency conditions. They state that the default risk of private money lending through unconditional contracting within the context of a networking economy such as a village, characterized by insurance-motivated conditional contracting, is probably a major reason for the development of the ROSCA institution (p. 761).

20. Seibel and Shrestha (1988) report that the Nepalese Dhikuti has incremental payments in addition to the amounts bid. The recipient (winner) of the first fund pays more than the winner of the second, and so forth, diminishing stepwise to the last recipient who pays nothing.

21. For a detailed list of differences see Bouman (1995, p. 377).

22. Other names for this type of institution in Francophone Africa are *Co-opératives d'Epargne et de crédit, Caisses populaires* or *Banques Populaires*. In Latin America they are known as *Cooperativas de Ahorro y Credito*.

REFERENCES

Adams, D. and M.L. Canavesi (1989), 'Rotating savings and credit associations in Bolivia', *Savings and Development*, **13**(3), 219–35.

Arestis, P. and P. Demetriades (1997), 'Financial development and economic growth: assessing the evidence', *Economic Journal*, **107**, 783–99.

Arrau, P. and K. Schmidt-Hebbel (1994), 'Pension systems and reforms: country experiences and research issues', *Revista de Analisis Economico*, **9**, 3–20.

Attanasio, O., L. Picci and A. Scorcu (2000), 'Saving, growth and investment: a macroeconomic analysis using a panel of countries', *Review of Economics and Statistics*, **80**(2).

Bailliu, J. and H. Reisen (1997), 'Do funded pensions contribute to higher aggregate saving? A cross-country analysis', technical paper no.30, OECD Development Centre, Paris.

Bandiera, O., G. Caprio, P. Honohan and F. Schiantarelli (2000), 'Does financial reform raise or reduce savings?', *Review of Economics and Statistics*, **80**(2).

Bayoumi, T. (1993), 'Financial saving and household saving', *Economic Journal*, **103**, November.

Behrman, J. and C. Sussangkarn (1989), 'Do the wealthy save less?', cited in Schmidt-Hebbel *et al.* (1992).

Boone, P. (1994), 'The impact of foreign aid on savings and growth', working paper no. 1265, Centre for Economic Performance, London School of Economics.

Bouman, F.J.A. (1995), 'Rotating and accumulating savings and credit associations: a development perspective', *World Development*, **23**(3), 371–84.

Bosworth, B. (1993), 'Saving and investment in a global economy', The Brookings Institution, Washington, DC.

Brownbridge, M. and C. Kirkpatrick (1999), 'Financial sector regulation: lessons of the Asia Crisis', *Development Policy Review*, **17**(3).

Campbell, J. and A. Deaton (1989), 'Why is consumption so smooth?', *Review of Economic Studies*, **56**(3) (July), 357–73.

Cardenas, M and A. Escobar (1998), 'Saving determinants in Colombia: 1925–1994', *Journal of Development Economics*, **57**.

Carroll, C. and D. Weil (1994), 'Saving and growth: a re-interpretation', Carnegie-Rochester Conference Series on Public Policy, vol.40.

Carroll, C., J. Overland and D. Weil (2000), 'Saving and growth with habit formation', *American Economic Review*, **90**(3).

Carroll, C., B. Rhee and C. Rhee (1994), 'Are there cultural effects on saving? Some cross-sectional evidence', *Quarterly Journal of Economics*, **109**(3), 685–99.

Cassen, R. (1994), *Does Aid Work?*, 2nd edn, Oxford: Oxford University Press.

Corbo, V. and K. Schmidt-Hebbel (1991), 'Public policies and saving in developing countries', *Journal of Development Economics*, **36**(1) (July), 89–115.

Cuevas, C. (1988), 'Savings and loans co-operatives in rural areas of developing countries: recent performance and potential', *Savings and Development*, **13**(1), 5–18.

Cukierman, A., S. Edwards and G. Tabellini (1992), 'Seigniorage, political instability and inflation', *American Economic Review*, **76**.

Deaton, A. (1989), 'Saving in developing countries: theory and review', Proceedings of the World Bank Annual Conference on Development Economics, World Bank, Washington, DC.

Deaton, A. (1992), *Understanding Consumption*, Oxford: Oxford University Press.

Demetriades, P. and K. Hussein (1996), 'Does financial development cause economic growth? Time series evidence from 16 countries', *Journal of Development Economics*, **51**(2), 387–411.

Diamond, P. (1994), 'Privatisation of social security: lessons from Chile', *Revista de Analisis Economico*, **9**.

Diamond, P and S. Valdez-Prieto (1994), 'Social security reforms', in B. Bosworth, R. Dornbusch and R. Laban (eds), *The Chilean Economy: Policy Lessons and Challenges*, Washington, DC: The World Bank.

Doshi, K. (1994), 'Determinants of the saving rate: an international comparison', *Contemporary Economic Policy*, January.

Easterly, W. (1997), 'How much do distortions affect growth?', *Journal of Monetary Economics*, **32**(2) (November), 187–212.

Eatwell, J. (1996), 'International capital liberalisation: the record', CEPA Working Paper Series No.1, University of Cambridge.

Edwards, S. (1995), 'Why are saving rates so different across countries? An international comparative analysis', NBER Working Paper no. 5097, National Bureau of Economic Research, Cambridge, April.

Edwards, S. (1996), 'Why are Latin America's savings rates so low? An international comparative analysis', *Journal of Development Economics*, **51**, 5–44.

Faruqee, H. and A. Husain (1995), 'Saving trends in Southeast Asia: a cross-country analysis', IMF Working Paper WP/95/39, April.

Feldstein, M (1980), 'International differences in social security and saving', *Journal of Public Economics*, **14**(2) (October), 225–44.

Friedman, M. (1957), *A Theory of the Consumption Function*, New York: NBER.

Fry, M.J. (1978), 'Money and capital or financial deepening in economic development?', *Journal of Money, Credit and Banking*, **10**(4), 464–75.

Fry, M.J (1980), 'Saving, investment and growth and the cost of financial repression', *World Development*, **8**(4), 317–27.

Gavin, M., R. Hausmann and E. Talvi (1997), 'Saving behaviour in Latin America: overview and policy issues', in R. Hausmann and H. Reisen (eds), *Promoting Savings in Latin America*. Paris: OECD and Inter-America Development Bank.

Gersovitz, M (1988), 'Saving and development', in H. Chenery and T. Srinivasan (eds), *Handbook of Development Economics*, Amsterdam: North Holland.

Gibson, H. and E. Tsakalotos (1994), 'The scope and limits of financial liberalisation in developing countries: a critical survey', *Journal of Development Studies*, **30**(3).

Giovannini, A. (1983), 'The interest rate elasticity of savings in developing countries: existing evidence', *World Development*, **11**(7), 601–7.

Giovannini, A. (1985), 'Saving and real interest rates in LDCs', *Journal of Development Economics*, **8** (August).

Gupta, K.L. (1984), *Finance and Economic Growth in Developing Countries*, London: Croom Helm.

Gupta, K. (1987), 'Aggregate savings, financial intermediation and interest rate', *Review of Economics and Statistics*, **69**(2) (May), 303–11.

Higgins, M. and J. Williamson (1996), 'Asian demography and foreign capital dependence', National Bureau of Economic Research Working Paper 5560, May.

Horioka, C. (1991), 'The determinants of Japan's saving rate: the impact of the age structure of the population and other factors', *The Economic Studies Quarterly*, **42**.

Houthakker, H. (1961), 'An international comparison of personal saving', *Bulletin of the International Statistical Institute*, **38**.

Houthakker, H. (1965), 'On some determinants of saving in developed and underdeveloped countries', in E. Robinson (ed.), *Problems in Economic Development*, London: Macmillan.

Hunte, K. (1997), 'The impact of savings mobilisation on credit rationing: empirical evidence from Jamaica', *Savings and Development*, **22**(4).

IMF (1995), 'Saving in a growing world economy', *IMF World Economic Outlook*, May.

Jappelli, T. and M. Pagano (1994), 'Saving, growth and liquidity constraints', *Quarterly Journal of Economics*, **109**(1), 83–109.

Kang, K. (1994), 'Why did Koreans save so "Little" and why do they now save so "Much"?', *International Economic Journal*, **8**(4), 9–111.

Kelly, R. and G. Mavrotas (2001), 'On the determinants of savings in India: is there any role for the financial sector?', paper presented at the International Conference on Development and Business Finance: Policy and Experience in Developing Countries, IDPM, University of Manchester, 5–6 April 2001.

Kelly, R. and G. Mavrotas (2002a), 'Savings and financial sector development: futile or fruitful? Some new evidence from Sri Lanka', paper presented at the International Conference on Finance for Growth & Poverty Reduction: Experience & Policy, IDPM, University of Manchester, 10–12 April 2002.

Kelly, R. andG. Mavrotas (2002b), 'Private savings and financial sector development: panel cointegration evidence from Africa', paper presented at the 10th International Conference on Panel Data, Academy of Science, Berlin, 5–6 July 2002.

Loayza, N., K. Schmidt-Hebbel and L. Serven (2000), 'What drives saving across the world?', *Review of Economics and Statistics*, **80**(2).

Lopez-Murphy, R. and F. Navajas (1998), 'Domestic savings, public savings and expenditures on consumer durable goods in Argentina', *Journal of Development Economics*, **57**(1), 97–116.

Maddison, A. (1992), 'A long run perspective on saving', *Scandinavian Journal of Economics*, **94**(2).

Maimbo, S. and G. Mavrotas (2001), 'Savings mobilisation and financial sector development in Zambia', paper presented at the International Conference on Development and Business Finance: Policy and Experience in Developing Countries, IDPM, University of Manchester, 5–6 April 2001.

Mankiw, N., D. Romer and D. Weil (1992), 'A Contribution to the empirics of economic growth', *Quarterly Journal of Economics*, **107**(2), 407–37.

McKinnon, R. (1973), *Money and Capital in International Development*, Washington, DC: The Brookings Institution.

McKinnon, R. (1991), *The Order of Economic Liberalisation: Financial Control in the Transition to a Market Economy*, Baltimore: Johns Hopkins University Press.

Mavrotas, G. (2002), 'Foreign aid and fiscal response: does aid disaggregation matter?', *Weltwirtschaftliches Archiv*, September (3).

Mavrotas, G. and R. Kelly (2000), 'The relevance of private and gross domestic savings for growth in Pakistan', mimeo, School of Economic Studies, University of Manchester.

Mavrotas, G. and R. Kelly (2001a), 'Savings mobilisation and financial sector development: the nexus', *Savings and Development*, **XXV**(1).

Mavrotas, G. and R. Kelly (2001b), 'Old wine in new bottles: testing causality between savings and growth', *The Manchester School*, **69**.

Mavrotas, G. and M. Santillana (1999), 'Savings mobilisation: key issues', paper presented at the International Conference on Finance and Development Research Programme, University of Manchester, July 1999.

Modigliani, F. (1990), 'Recent development in saving rates: a life cycle perspective', Frisch Lecture, Sixth World Congress of the Econometric Society, Barcelona, Spain.

Obstfeld, M. (1998), 'Foreign resource inflows, saving and growth', in Klaus Schmidt-Hebbel and Luis Serven (eds), *The Economics of Saving*, Cambridge: Cambridge University Press.

Ostry, J. and C. Reinhart (1992), 'Private saving and terms of trade shocks: evidence from developing countries', *IMF Staff Papers*, **39**(September), 447–79.

Palley, T. (1996), 'The savings–investment nexus: why it matters and how it works', CEPA Working Paper no.1.

Ribe, F. (1994), 'Funded social security systems: a review of issues in four East Asian countries', *Revista de Analisis Economico*, **9**(1), 169–82.

Rodrik, D. (1999), 'Saving transitions', mimeo, Harvard University.

Romer, P. (1986), 'Increasing returns and long run Growth', *Journal of Political Economy*, **98**(5).

Rutherford, S. (1998), 'The savings of the poor: improving financial services in Bangladesh', *Journal of International Development*, **10**(1), 1–15.

Samwick, A. (1996), 'Discount rate heterogeneity and social security reform', *Journal of Development Economics*, **57**, 117–46.

Samwick, A. (1998), 'Is pension reform conducive to higher saving?', mimeo, World Bank, September.

Schmidt-Hebbel, K. (1987), 'Foreign shocks and macroeconomic adjustment in small open economies', cited in Schmidt-Hebbel *et al.* (1992).

Schmidt-Hebbel, K. (1995), 'Colombia's pension reform: fiscal and macroeconomic effects', Discussion Paper no. 314, World Bank, Washington, DC.

Schmidt-Hebbel, K., S. Webb and G. Corsetti (1992), 'Household saving in developing countries: first cross-country evidence', *World Bank Economic Review*, **6**(3).

Schreider G., and C. Cuevas (1992), 'Informal financial groups in Cameroon', in D. Adams and D. Fitchett (eds) *Informal Finance in Low-income Countries*, Boulder and Oxford: Westview Press, pp. 43–56.

Schwarz, A. (1995), 'Pension scheme: trade-offs between redistribution and saving', *Finance & Development*, **32**(2), 8–11.

Seibel, H.S. and B.P. Shrestha (1988), 'Dhikuti: the small businessman's informal self-help bank in Nepal', *Savings and Development*, **12**(2), 183–98.

Shahin, W. (1996), 'Could financial liberalisation ignore informal finance? A commentary', *Savings and Development*, **XX**, 105–15.

Shaw, E. (1973), *Financial Deepening in Economic Development*, Oxford: Oxford University Press.

Siebel, H.D. (1986), 'Duale finanzmarkte in Afrika', *Entiwicklung and landlicher Raum*, **1**, 14–16.

Sinha, D. (1997), 'Saving and economic growth in India', *Economia Internazionale*, **49**(4).

Sinha, D. and T. Sinha (1998), 'Cart before the horse? The saving–growth nexus in Mexico', *Economics Letters*, **61**(1).

Solow, R. (1956), 'A contribution to the theory of economic growth', *Quarterly Journal of Economics*, **70**.

Stiglitz, J. (1999), 'Responding to economic crises: policy alternatives for equitable recovery and development', *The Manchester School*, **67**(5).

Stiglitz, J. and A. Weiss (1981), 'Credit rationing in markets with imperfect information', *American Economic Review*, **71**(3), 393–410.

Van der Brink, R. and J-P Chavas (1997), 'The microeconomics of an indigenous African institution: the rotating savings and credit association', *Economic Development and Cultural Change*, 745–72.

White, H. (1992), 'The macroeconomic impact of development aid: a critical survey', *Journal of Development Studies*, **28**, 163–240.

World Bank (2001), *Finance for Growth: Policy Choices in a Volatile World*, Oxford: Oxford University Press.

3. Flow of funds: the relationship between finance and the macroeconomy

Christopher J. Green and Victor Murinde

1. INTRODUCTION

The flow of funds is an accounting framework and not a theory or a policy prescription. However, this framework and the data available within it provide the basis for a wide range of applied analyses of economic problems and policies. Most importantly, flow of funds analysis provides a general framework for studying the financial sector and its relationships with the real economy. Flow of funds has been widely used in the industrial economies as a basic information tool, in general empirical research, and for detailed financial policy analysis. See Green (1992) for a review of this work. Dawson (1996) provides several interesting examples of flow of funds applications.

A comprehensive search for relevant literature indicates that relatively little flow of funds work has been done for developing countries. In part, the paucity of work on flow of funds can be explained by an almost complete absence of sufficiently detailed data in most developing countries. Murinde (1996) gives examples of flow of funds data and applications in several developing countries; Fleming and Giugale (2000) provide examples for the transition economies of central and eastern Europe. The absence of flow of funds data in developing economies is unfortunate, for it can be argued that flow of funds analysis may be of more value in the developing world than in the industrial countries. Economic analysis and policy are based on both the prices and the quantities traded in an economy. The major industrial economies benefit from a vast range of organized and informal markets, which possess attributes of depth and liquidity, and whose *prices* provide much of the basic, timely information upon which economic policy is based. See Deacon and Derry (1994). In developing economies, where markets are more fragmented, and securities markets are invariably thin and illiquid, prices provide much less useful policy information. More information on *quantities*, particularly on the flow of funds, would be very valuable for policy makers. In addition, developing countries all have a continuing need to generate internal and external funds to finance public and private investment and a 'main function of the flow of funds accounts is to reveal the sources and uses of funds that are needed for growth and development' (Klein, 2000, p. ix). Thus the flow of funds could play an important role in developing countries to aid the study of financial sector development and resource mobilization issues so as to identify effective financial sector policies for promoting poverty-reducing economic growth.

In this chapter we aim to provide a selective survey of the leading theoretical and empirical issues surrounding flow of funds: its meaning and origin, problems of construction, its use in financial modelling and its role as a tool of analysis of intersectoral financial flows. The idea is to analyse the key relationships between the financial and real sectors of the economy and the role of the financial sector in the development process. We do not aim at a detailed survey of flow of funds modelling in industrial countries. Several such surveys are already available (Green, 1992; Dawson, 1996). Instead, we seek to summarize the main developments in flow of funds modelling and to evaluate those features of existing flow of funds models and data which are likely to need modifying for application in developing countries, in the light of the specific economic, financial and social structures of different developing countries. We argue that there is an intimate connection between the flow of funds, interest rates and asset prices, and hence incomes and expenditures, in an economy. We explore the reasons for lack of success at empirical flow of funds modelling and propose some 'promising research ideas' (PRIs) to develop and apply flow of funds analysis to study the relationship between financial sector development and the real economy, particularly to identify effective financial sector policies in developing countries.

In what follows, the rest of this chapter is divided into five sections. Section 2 outlines the basic principles of the flow of funds. Section 3 focuses on the construction and analysis of flow of funds models to underpin the evolution of financial institutions and markets and the determination of asset demands, interest rates and asset prices. Next, we turn more specifically to developing countries. Section 4 considers the conceptual issues involving flow of funds in developing countries, concentrating on possible applications, the analytical framework and data issues. Section 5 summarizes the main empirical studies of the flow of funds which have have been carried out in developing countries. Section 6 concludes by putting forward some PRIs for further research on flow of funds, in the context of financial sector development and the real economy.

2. THE PRINCIPLES OF FLOW OF FUNDS

Flows of funds arise from the transactions which take place in an economy, whether involving purchases or sales of goods and services or exchanges of assets and liabilities. These transactions generate flows of funds from one agent to another and from one sector to another. National flow of funds *accounts* provide a record of these flows for the whole economy; the accounts covering individual or corporate transactions are more usually called 'sources–uses statements'. Virtually all macroeconomic models call for the use of some part of the flow of funds. However the expression 'flow of funds *models*' has a more specific meaning, referring to a general approach to modelling and understanding the flow of funds as a whole, and its role in interest rate determination (Green, 1992).

Copeland (1952) is generally regarded as the pioneer of flow of funds analysis. He showed how comprehensive 'moneyflows' accounts could be compiled and used to analyse the US economy. He aimed to show all transactions in the economy, involving goods, services, assets and liabilities, and distinguishing between purchases and sales in each category. Indeed he originally conceived his work as an alternative to the national accounts. The implementation of flow of funds accounts in official statistics, first in the United States and later within the UN System of National Accounts (SNA; United Nations, 1968, 1993), was less ambitious than this, and flow of funds came to be seen as just one (albeit major) component of the whole national accounts system (see Dawson, 1991).[1] Even so, the level of detail proposed for the flow of funds in the SNA is such that it remains largely a blueprint for the relatively few industrial countries with well-funded statistical services. Among developing countries, only India has regularly compiled detailed flow of funds accounts, as we discuss in section 5 below.

For flow of funds analysis, two components of the SNA are particularly relevant. The first is the capital accumulation account which represents the transition between the national income accounts and the financial accounts. It shows sectoral savings including a provision for capital consumption (depreciation), capital transfers to or from the sector, and the non-official assets accumulated by the sector. The second component of the SNA is the capital finance account. It provides a breakdown of net lending (the balancing item of the capital accumulation account) and this is commonly called 'the flow of funds'.

Changes in the stocks of assets and liabilities are tracked through identities which state that the current stock is equal to the sum of the previous period's stock, net flows into or out of the stock through transactions (purchases or sales by any given sector), changes in valuation (capital gains or losses) and depreciation of the pre-existing stock. Net flows into or out of a stock correspond to entries in the capital accumulation or flow of funds account for any given sector. Entries for non-reproducible assets such as land reflect flows (purchases and sales) which do not enter into the current account. However one sector may sell land to another so as to augment its funds to purchase other assets. Intangible assets are also included in any complete representation of the flow of funds.

Flow of funds accounts show net transactions in financial instruments among broad sectors of the economy. They are typically presented in a matrix in which each row (i) represents an asset, and each column (j) a sector. Each cell (i,j) in the matrix shows net purchases(+) or sales(-) of asset i by sector j during the unit time period (usually a quarter or a year).[2] The row sums of the matrix are zero as net purchases of an asset must equal net sales, and each column (j) sums to the jth sector's surplus or deficit: its net acquistion of financial assets (NAFA). Sector NAFAs can be calculated either by summing each sector's transactions in assets and liabilities or from the income side through the capital accumulation account, and they therefore provide the immediate link between the flow of funds and national income accounts.

The accounting identities offer alternative means of estimating entries in the flow of funds matrix, but the estimates of the sectoral NAFAs arrived at from the income-expenditure side rarely correspond to those arrived at using flow of funds data (Dawson, 1991).[3] Indeed the resulting statistical discrepancy is often disturbingly large (US Commerce Department, 1977; Bank of England, 1985). Studies of savings behaviour invariably utilize data calculated from the income-expenditure side (World Bank, 1997) on the questionable assumption that these are more reliable than flow of funds data. In fact, much of the flow of funds is typically based on statistical reports from financial institutions and central government which, with some exceptions, are of census-like quality, whereas the national income accounts include a higher proportion of lower-quality sample survey data (Gorman, 1983). The relationships between flows of funds and asset stocks raise similar issues: the changes in stocks of assets and liabilities calculated from one source are rarely equal to the sum of the capital gains or losses and the flow of funds calculated from another source. In this reconciliation there may be three independent sources of data: for asset stocks, asset prices and flows of funds. Moreover the reconciliation is complicated by the fact that different transactions in any given interval may have taken place at different prices.

One approach to the problem of consistency is to pool the information provided by different data sources. Stone *et al.* (1942) proposed the use of least squares regression to reconcile the income, expenditure and output estimates of national income. For many years, official statisticians eschewed such 'purely statistical' methods of adjustment, preferring instead to provide users with data which included a discrepancy and to let them do their own adjustments if desired. Least squares adjustment may involve a large computational burden, as it can in theory involve adjusting every entry in the national accounts at every date and at each revision of the data. More recently a combination of improved computing power and the appearance of substantial residual errors in the national accounts of the United Kingdom led to a revival of interest in least squares adjustment (Barker *et al.*, 1984; Central Statistical Office, 1989) and, since 1992, the UK Office of National Statistics (ONS) has been charged with producing an annual set of fully reconciled national accounts and flow of funds data. See Baxter (1992). Integrated balance sheet and flow accounts pose more difficult problems, as they involve both arithmetic and geometric identities. These cannot be respected simultaneously by any linear adjustment procedure such as least squares (Lovell, 1963). Simple ad hoc procedures are often used in practice to reconcile such data (Green, 1984b), but it is an important methodological issue to develop more rigorous adjustment procedures for such integrated data.

3. THE FLOW OF FUNDS MODEL AND THE EVOLUTION OF FINANCIAL MARKETS

The flow of funds accounting matrix can be transformed into a flow of funds model by assuming that each cell in the matrix contains a variable to be explained by an asset demand function whose arguments may include interest rates and other variables. The column sums amount to sector budget constraints and state that each sector's net acquisitions of financial assets must sum to its total NAFA, which, as a first step, can be regarded as being determined independently of the flow of funds. Each row sum is interpreted as a market-clearing condition which states that, in equilibrium, desired net purchases of an asset must equal desired net sales. Desired net purchases or sales are determined by the asset demand functions. If the sectoral NAFAs are exogenous, an N market flow of funds model provides $N-1$ independent market-clearing conditions to determine $N-1$ endogenous variables. These are often thought of as $N-1$ interest rates with the (Nth) rate on currency fixed at zero. However interest rates do not have to be the equilibrating mechanism. In a fixed exchange rate system it is the monetary authorities' foreign exchange holdings which clear the exchange market: the authorities deal in foreign exchange so as to peg the exchange rate, given the movements in private demands and supplies. In effect, the monetary authority acts like a market maker, although the time horizon over which it expects to deal at the quoted rate is clearly longer than that over which a private sector market maker would deal. Knight and Wymer (1976) have argued that, conceptually, all financial markets can be viewed as having one sector which acts as market maker. This is a device which simplifies the computational task of solving a flow of funds model, but it is also rather arbitrary and has not proved popular with researchers. However, where interest rate movements are regulated, as remains common in developing countries, markets can only clear either by the intervention of some formal or informal market maker or by some scheme of rationing. Rationing schemes in empirical flow of funds models are discussed by, inter alia, Brainard and Smith (1982).

It is also useful to distinguish between complete flow of funds models and sector studies. Sector studies are the building blocks of a flow of funds model, but the central characteristic of a complete model is that it is a general equilibrium model, and therefore explains the flow of funds and the movement of interest rates jointly in a consistent framework. This requires modelling the market-clearing process as well as the demands and supplies of assets.

In discrete time, the evolution of financial markets in a complete flow of funds model can be thought of as follows. Each sector enters any given time period with a certain stock of assets and liabilities. The sectoral NAFAs, asset demands, and market-clearing conditions jointly determine the equilibrium flow of funds and the structure of interest rates and asset prices. The end-period values of the stocks of assets and liabilities are then equal to the sum of the beginning of period stocks, net capital gains on these stocks and the flow of funds. This is a temporary equilibrium, for the end-period stocks are carried over to the next period and, together with a new set of NAFAs and asset demands, will determine a new temporary equilibrium. A long-run equilibrium is one in which stocks are stationary from period to period in some well-defined sense.

Flow of funds analysis and forecasting using informal procedures is as old as the flow of funds itself. However the intellectual foundation for econometric modelling of the flow of funds was provided by Tobin and his associates (Tobin, 1963a, 1963b; Tobin and Brainard, 1963; Brainard, 1964). Initially this work focused on the relationships between stocks of financial assets and interest rates, but it soon became clear that static models of asset demands could not explain the characteristically autocorrelated time series properties of asset stocks. Tobin and Brainard's (1968) 'Pitfalls' paper advocated the use of general disequilibrium models. The characteristics of such models, explained by Smith (1975), are, first, that the short-run demand for any particular asset may differ from its long-run level, because of transactions and other adjustment costs; and, second, that the short-run demand for an asset has to be related not just to its own disequilibrium but also to the disequilibria in all other asset holdings which may spill over onto the demand for the asset in question.

The Pitfalls model is a generalized partial adjustment model whose solution determines the evolution of asset prices and stocks and hence the flow of funds. In a Pitfalls model, it is the demands and supplies of asset *stocks* which determine interest rates. Bain (1973) suggested that it could instead be the *flow* demands and supplies of funds which determine each period's interest rates more or less independently of the outstanding stocks of assets. The relation between a 'stock' and a 'flow' view of interest rate determination was clarified by Friedman (1977) who argued that the difference had to do mainly with the size of adjustment costs. The larger are the costs of adjusting asset stocks, the more important are financial flows in interest rate determination, and vice versa. In this sense, the Pitfalls model constitutes one class of flow of funds models. Adjustment costs in the financial markets of industrial countries are usually thought to be small, so it may be reasonable to suppose that it is the outstanding stocks of assets which are the major determinants of interest rates in these countries. In developing countries, however, adjustment costs may be larger and thus a flow view of interest rate determination may be more relevant.

Friedman (1977, 1979, 1980b) introduced the 'optimal marginal adjustment model' based on the argument that investors find it less costly to allocate new flows of funds than to rearrange existing portfolio holdings. Roley (1980) extended this model to allow adjustment speeds to differ as between inflows and outflows of funds; and Green (1984a) considered a scheme in which capital gains and net transactions incur different adjustment costs. These models are typically special cases of a general dynamic specification (Hendry *et al.*, 1984). An important problem with such models is that they are often difficult to derive from any underlying objective function. They therefore impose relatively few constraints on the coefficients, so that it can be difficult to evaluate the plausibility of the empirical results. In contrast, the Pitfalls model minimizes a quadratic cost function (Sharpe, 1973).

Early flow of funds models typically assumed that portfolio and consumption–saving decisions were separable, implying that portfolio demand functions and flow of funds models could be specified and estimated independently of the consumption function. Such separability is at the heart of the IS–LM model, and its logic was spelled out by Tobin (1969). However Buiter (1980) argued that it is never conceptually correct (except as an approximation) to separate portfolio and spending decisions if the model is to be properly specified. Tobin (1982) has shown how IS–LM can still be adapted to an integrated approach in which portfolio and consumption–saving decisions are taken simultaneously. In integrated flow of funds models, the sectoral NAFAs emerge endogenously as asset holdings and consumption are adjusted simultaneously in response to changes in variables, such as income and interest rates, which are taken as exogenous by individual agents, but may be endogenous from the point of view of the system as a whole (Purvis, 1978; Smith, 1978).

Tobin and Brainard analysed the Pitfalls model using calibrated coefficients and artificial data. Empirically estimated Pitfalls models have tended to have rather unsatisfactory properties. Estimated interest elasticities and adjustment speeds are often implausibly signed or are smaller than intuition would suggest is reasonable. This produces excessive volatility in interest rates when the model is simulated. Green and Kiernan (1989) showed that multicollinearity and measurement error among the interest rates can produce estimated coefficients which are substantially too small and sometimes of the wrong sign in relation to their true value. Multicollinearity is almost inevitable if assets are close substitutes, as their interest rates tend to move closely together; measurement error arises in the estimation of the unobserved expected real interest rates which are the explanatory variables. Moreover theory imposes few constraints on the signs and magnitudes of short-run interest rate coefficients. Hypotheses such as symmetry and homogeneity are invariably propositions about long-run (static) asset demands,[4] whereas it is the short-run demands which are largely responsible for the system-wide properties of the model. Even if the long-run demands are plausible, the short-run estimates can still give rise to implausible simulation paths for interest rates. The characteristics of the simulation paths are important if the model is be used for policy analysis.

The main practical difficulty in implementing flow of funds models is that they too easily become large and unwieldy. Johnson (1970) commented that the approach tends to produce models in which everything depends on everything else and nothing clear-cut can be said. Large size is not an intrinsic property of flow of funds models. Friedman (1980a) compared an eight-sector model of the US corporate bond market with a two-sector model, and concluded that disaggregation was only marginally useful in improving the performance of the model. In practice, though, it can be difficult to avoid undue size and, partly for this reason, flow of funds models have not proved popular in small-scale research. Hendershott's (1977) model of the USA contained considerable detail but explained only three market-clearing interest rates. Green's (1984a) model of the UK was more ambitious in attempting to explain seven market-clearing interest rates in a five-sector model, but he reported difficulty in simulating his model. Keating (1985) was more ambitious yet, but his model required strong and implausible theoretical restrictions to be estimated and solved (Courakis, 1988). These difficulties led some researchers to utilize a more Bayesian approach. This resolves the problems of multicollinearity and measurement error by imposing more plausible values on coefficients with large standard errors, but it can involve the prior specification of all the coefficients in the model, which is potentially a Herculean task. See Smith (1981). Backus *et al.* (1980) reported that the use of prior information was successful in removing most counterintuitive coefficients, and in producing reasonable model simulation properties in a large-scale model of US financial markets. Likewise Kearney and MacDonald (1986) found that prior information considerably improved the properties of a one-sector four-market model of the UK.

Sector studies are more numerous than complete flow of funds models but necessarily have less to say about interest rate determination. Included among these are some integrated portfolio and expenditure models, notably those of Backus and Purvis (1980) and Owen (1986). A more recent approach to sector studies has been to treat asset demands as analogous to consumer demand systems and utilize flexible functional forms to specify the demand functions (Aivazian *et al.*, 1990; Barr and Cuthbertson, 1991).

Flow of funds models are simulated by setting asset demands equal to supplies and solving for interest rates. The result is described as showing the effects on interest rates of shocks to asset supplies in a freely clearing market. However this implies that it is the exogenous asset supplies which determine the endogenous interest rates. If so, the traditional method of estimating asset demands by the regression of an asset quantity on interest rates is not meaningful since it amounts to regressing an exogenous variable on a collection of endogenous variables. This would suggest that the appropriate way of modelling interest rates is to regress each interest rate on asset supplies rather than the other way round. This insight was used by Frankel and Engel (1984), whose key contribution was to demonstrate the simple and intuitive link between portfolio demand functions and properly specified interest rate equations, and thus to exploit the connection between portfolio theory and asset pricing theory, particularly the Capital Asset Pricing Model (CAPM). This approach also delivers a parameterization which makes it easier to test certain theoretical hypotheses. Frankel and Dickens (1984) and Frankel (1985) estimated such 'inverted portfolio models' using postwar US data and obtained results which were broadly unsympathetic to the CAPM. Similar investigations by Green (1990) using UK data produced broadly similar results: the data rejected the CAPM but asset supplies made a significant contribution to the time variation in asset returns. These models have been extended to allow for autoregressive conditional heteroscedasticity in the error process, which is equivalent to allowing for time-variation in risks. See Bollerslev *et al.* (1988).

Inverted portfolio models are representative of a general shift in financial market research away from the flow of funds towards more direct modelling of asset prices and returns. Just as there is a close connection between flow of funds models and the CAPM, so there is also a connection between the integrated approach to modelling the flow of funds and the Intertemporal Capital Asset Pricing Model (ICAPM). The ICAPM starts from the hypothesis that agents trade assets (usually in perfect capital markets) to maximize an intertemporal utility function and to smooth consumption over time. Merton's (1973) ICAPM generates asset demands and a consumption function analogous to those considered in the Pitfalls literature. However Merton's specification is awkward to test, and Breeden's (1979) version has proven more popular. This emphasizes regression relationships among asset returns and the change in aggregate consumption and thus side-steps the flow of funds entirely. This approach has been applied to developing countries by Cashin and McDermott (1998). However, as we argued at the outset, a key stylized fact about developing economies is that organized markets are less perfect than in the industrial economies. Under these circumstances, aggregate consumption is not a sufficient statistic for asset returns, and portfolios and flows of funds are of independent significance. Thus, as a promising research idea (PRI), a next logical development in financial research is to reintegrate the flow of funds with consumption-based asset pricing theories. Such new theories of the flow of funds would be more rigorously founded than their predecessors and offer a better prospect of achieving a fully integrated account of the flow of funds and their relationships with interest rates, asset prices, incomes and expenditures.

4. CONCEPTUAL ISSUES IN FLOW OF FUNDS ANALYSIS FOR DEVELOPING COUNTRIES

Flow of Funds Applications

There are two main reasons for studying the flow of funds in developing countries. The first, shared with industrial countries, is that flow of funds analysis aids in broad macroeconomic policy making and analysis. Policy makers in developing countries need to understand the nature of any obstacles to efficient intersectoral financial flows and what policy alternatives are open to them for unblocking these obstacles. Thus an elaboration of the flow of funds is needed for a proper analysis of a wide range of issues such as the effects of fiscal and monetary policy, the crowding out of investment and the impact of foreign investment flows. By studying the pattern of intersectoral financial flows in a developing economy it is possible to isolate the activities of borrowers and lenders. For example, we can pinpoint the channels by which *domestic* and *external* sources of funds are reconciled with the claims on funds by competing sectors in the economy, particularly the claims for financing business investment. The flow of funds gives a decomposition of the sources and methods by which savings are accumulated in different economic environments: whether by the household sector, businesses, government or overseas, and whether in the form of liquid financial assets or as direct investment in illiquid tangibles, such as dwellings or inventories. This information permits an analysis of savings and investment requirements, and of the performance of financial intermediaries in channelling funds to their most effective uses.

The second reason for studying the flow of funds in developing economies is more specific to the nature of these economies. The mobilization and allocation of resources are the central issues for development, and properly specified flow of funds accounts tell exactly how financial resources are generated and distributed within an economy. Possible applications of the flow of funds would include many development issues, and are not confined to orthodox macroeconomic analyses. Here, therefore, we simply select and list some pertinent examples of (actual and possible) applications of the flow of funds.

The financial sector is at the heart of understanding the impact of financial repression and liberalization. The flow of funds can tell how the financial system in general, including both the parallel or curb markets and the organized banking system, allocates funds in the presence of rationing and other direct controls. Sen *et al.* (1996) have studied the impact of monetary policy in India where, until the liberalization of the 1990s, the Reserve Bank relied heavily on reserve ratios and credit controls as its main policy instruments. If markets are liberalized, flow of funds analysis permits an understanding of the impact of liberalization. See Moore *et al.* (2001) for a preliminary analysis of the impact of the Indian liberalization on bank portfolio behaviour.

There are many other developmental issues on which the flow of funds has an analytical bearing. A first instance is the question of market development: to what extent can shortfalls in flows from the foreign sector to the business sector be alleviated by the establishment and/or revitalization of stock markets? The flow of funds can help evaluate the effectiveness of different channels through which any particular sector of the economy seeks to raise funds. See Ngugi *et al.* (2000) for a survey of these issues. Second is the question of capital flight: how can capital flight be measured and what are its determinants and consequences? Within a flow of funds framework, capital flight can be seen as a particular type of portfolio flow with associated causes and consequences. Collier *et al.* (1999) have recently developed this interpretation. Murinde *et al.* (1996) and Lensink *et al.* (1998) applied a portfolio balance framework to estimate and analyse the magnitude and determinants of capital flight in selected African countries. Fitzgerald (1999) considered the inverse (but related) problem of sudden surges of capital *inflow*. Third, where parallel markets exist, as they do in most developing countries, the impact and effectiveness of liberalization measures depend crucially upon their effect on flows among the parallel markets and between the parallel and official markets. See, inter alia, Taylor (1983), Van Wijnbergen (1983) and Buffie (1991). Ideally, therefore, these flows should be estimated and monitored throughout any current reform programme. Fourth, many commentators have invested high hopes in microfinance as a potential tool for providing basic but effective financial services for the poorest groups in developing countries; see Morduch (1999) for a survey. Microfinance may offer consumption-smoothing opportunities which were previously unavailable to the poor, through small-scale saving and investment facilities. However an evaluation of the overall effectiveness of microfinance institutions calls for some monitoring of the flows of funds among households and small businesses that are generated by these institutions. See, inter alia, the studies reported by Hulme and Mosley (1996) and Mosley (2001). Clearly this is a micro-level application of the flow of funds. However one would expect there to be links between (effective!) macro-level economic policy and micro-level flows of funds. See Mosley (1999). As Shaw (1973) originally emphasized, one of the goals of financial liberalization is to improve financing sources and provisions at all levels in the economy. Overall, therefore, there is no shortage of potential applications for flow of funds in developing economies.

Modelling and Data

In principle there are as many ways to present the flow of funds as there are to utilize them: the presentation should depend on the objectives of the analysis, but also on the availability of data. Ideally the presentation of the flow of funds in developing countries should include considerable sectoral detail, distinguishing in particular between businesses and households and between central government and public enterprises. As Honohan and Atiyas (1993) observe, transactions involving households and businesses are among the most important in a modern economy. It is the household sector which typically provides the savings to finance business investment, even though most of these funds may be intermediated through the financial system. In addition most developing countries have a relatively large public enterprise sector whose investment and financing needs are linked to government policy. Structural measures such as privatization have an impact on the financing and investment decisions of formerly public enterprises, and thereby on financial intermediaries and government. Therefore public enterprises need to be understood as a separate sector distinct from general government.

However, developing countries rarely possess the resources to compile flow of funds statistics. Moreover the most difficult sectors for which to compile data are those which are particularly important, notably households and businesses. The important relationships between the formal and informal sector, emphasized by Shaw (1973), are even less susceptible to being documented within the official statistics. The practical difficulties involved in obtaining detailed up-to-date data might suggest the value of other approaches to analysing the flow of funds. One is to use a relatively aggregated framework, either concentrating on the sector surpluses and deficits following Honohan and Atiyas (1993) and Bahra et al. (1999; hereafter: BGM) or tailoring the framework to the availability of data, following Dawson (1991) or Murinde (1996). A further possibility is to retain a relatively detailed format, but to use calibration to simulate and understand the behaviour of the economy. Finally, there is considerable scope for sector and case studies to enlarge our understanding of particular areas of the economy, especially the informal sector, which will always remain largely outside the scope of the official statistics. Two recent examples of this approach are Schrieder (2000) and Copestake *et al.* (2001).

In this chapter we concentrate on applications involving relatively aggregated data, and utilizing the flow of funds as a whole rather than a sector approach. This is not because we believe that this is the only or indeed always the best approach, but we do believe it offers the clearest way to begin understanding the *overall* structure of developing economies. It should be emphasized that an aggregative approach is not proposed as an alternative to the SNA. Rather it offers a simplified setting within which flow of funds data can be gathered and analysed in countries where data are limited and resource constraints bite severely, especially on the national statistical services.

Even if resources were available, the methodology for preparing flow of funds accounts in the SNA is itself plagued by pitfalls. Two particular problems are worth mentioning. First, the estimation of flows by differencing successive balance sheet statements does not involve any adjustment for capital value changes. The proper procedure is to make valuation changes and to show these separately in a reconciliation account (of capital gains and losses), but these valuation changes are particularly difficult to estimate in emerging markets if trading is thin and prices are relatively volatile. Second, there is the problem of inflation. Kennedy (1988) argued that the analysis of sectoral savings and financing should be performed using data in real terms rather than nominal terms. He showed that inflation adjustments can dramatically change the pattern of intersectoral financial flows. However reliable inflation data are not always available in a timely fashion in developing countries and, where inflation is high and unevenly distributed across sectors, inflation adjustments can be difficult to perform consistently on the overall flow of funds. See also Honohan and Atiyas (1989).

Turning back to more aggregative approaches, the starting point for analysing financial flows in developing countries is the sector surpluses and deficits. On their own, these scarcely constitute flow of funds data, as they do no more than reflect the savings–investment balance and are an immediate by-product of any basic sectorized set of national accounts. Even so, a considerable amount can be learnt from these data about development needs and strategies. See Murinde (1996, ch. 2). At the economy-wide level, international flows of funds bridge the savings-investment gap.[5] At the sectoral level, financial flows help to meet the savings–investment gap of one sector *vis-à-vis* another, say households *vis-à-vis* the business sector, as in the work by Honohan and Atiyas (1989, 1993). More generally, the elasticity of financial flows between two economies or sectors, respectively, has important implications for the behaviour of savings, investment and financial markets, and thus for the nature of development strategy.

To answer more detailed questions, correspondingly more detailed flow of funds data are required. A simple and useful framework is given by Murinde (1996), reproduced here as Table 3.1. In part 1 of the table, rows represent income-expenditure flow variables; in part 2, rows represent stocks of assets and liabilities. Columns represent the main broad sectors of the economy. A single row distributes the stock or flow of a variable or asset over the supply-ing and demanding sectors, while a single column represents a sector's sources and uses of funds (flows) or a sector's balance sheet (stocks). The horizontal and vertical sums of the flows and of the stocks can be written out to explain how financial resources flow from one sector to another. The framework also

Table 3.1   Simplified accounting structure for a developing economy

	Private sector P	Banks sector B	Government sector G	Foreign sector F
1. Income-expenditure				
1.1 Income (Y)	Y^P			
1.2 Taxes (T)	T^P		T^G	
1.3 Consumption (C)	C^P		C^G	C^F
1.4 Investment (I)	I^P		I^G	I^F
Net acquisitions (S)	S^P		S^G	S^F
2. Assets and liabilities: balance-sheet accounts				
2.1 Capital (K)	K^P		K^G	K^F
2.2 Loans (L)	L^P	L^B	L^G	
2.3 Domestic money (M)	M^P	M^B	M^G	
2.4 Foreign money (R)			R^G	R^F
Net worth (W)	W^P	W^B	W^G	W^F

Note: The private sector (P) can be further disaggregated into the household sector and the business sector. The empirical disaggregation is conditional on data availability, for example from integrated household surveys.

Source: Murinde (1996).

offers a set of identities that demonstrate the sectoral balances that are consistent with financial flows.

Murinde's framework differs from the SNA in that the SNA distinguishes between its two components: the capital accumulation and capital finance accounts. These accounts are not made explicit in Table 3.1, although they are clearly implicit in the relationships which must hold over time between the income–expenditure account and the capital account, and within the capital account itself. The central advantage of Murinde's framework is that it offers a direct link between a simple flow of funds and standard macroeconomic models such as IS–LM. The intersectoral financial flows can be used to generate behavioural equations for consumption, saving and investment. Asset demands can be modelled through the capital account, and financial constraints, such as the government budget constraint and the foreign exchange constraint, can also be captured using this framework. Using this approach, Jha (1994) has explained the structure of simple macromodels for developing countries; Murinde (1996) has studied the pattern of intersectoral financial flows in selected African and Asian economies; and Green and Murinde (1998) have developed macroeconomic and financial models for transition economies.

The flow of funds matrix can be viewed using either a sector approach in which assets are distinguished by sector of origin, or an instrument approach in which assets are distinguished by their characteristics, such as risk, term to maturity or currency of denomination. Murinde's framework adopts an instrument approach. An alternative framework using a sector approach was proposed by the IMF (1981), and elaborated on by Dawson (1991). As shown in Table 3.2, this starts directly with the capital account but includes a rather more detailed breakdown of financial transactions.[6] However the primary emphasis is on the role of government and central bank: first, as distinct sectors in the economy and, second, as providers of assets and debt. Given its provenance and structure, this framework is best interpreted as a vehicle for understanding the impact of the authorities' monetary and debt policy on the main financial flows. Several of the studies reported in Fleming and Giugale (2000) are based on this general framework.

A third framework was proposed by Green *et al.* (2000; hereafter: GMSM). This adopts an instrument approach and retains Murinde's broad framework for the income–expenditure account but suggests a more detailed treatment of financial flows than does Murinde or Dawson (see Table 3.3). GMSM include certain important instruments which were omitted by Dawson and Murinde,[7] particularly private non-bank lending, corporate debt and equity. The inclusion of these instruments reflects the growth of non-bank institutions and markets (including stock markets) in most developing countries in recent years. Their omission from a comprehensive empirical financial model would

Table 3.2   Simplified flow of funds pro-forma

Classification of transactions ('rows')	Classification of sectors ('columns')
Capital account	Central bank
Gross capital formation	Central government
Gross saving	Commercial banks
Balance = sector surplus/deficit	Other domestic sectors
	Foreign
Financial transactions	Errors and omissions
Currency and deposits	Total
Bills, bonds, and loans	
Central government debt	
Central government loans	
Central bank advances	
Other loans and advances	
Other domestic debt	
Foreign assets	
Other claims and discrepancy, net	
Total financial transactions	

Source: Dawson (1991).

be quite misleading for many countries. Because it is more detailed, GMSM's framework imposes more data demands and is potentially more useful for empirical modelling than for theory. An important contribution of GMSM, following Murinde (1996), is to show how estimates of these relatively detailed data can be compiled for developing countries from international official sources, particularly the IMF publications, *International Financial Statistics* (*IFS*), the *Balance of Payments Yearbook* (*BOP*) and the *Government Finance Statistics Yearbook* (*GFS*).[8] These publications could be supplemented by sectoral national accounts data compiled by the United Nations and by country data, where these are available. Of course, it can be argued that compiling data from pre-existing secondary sources merely amounts to a rearrangement of what is already known. However, as Fleming and Giugale (2000) emphasize, a key advantage of the flow of funds is that it imposes internal consistency on analyses and forecasts, and provides an exposition of the complete financial implications of policy or other changes. By neglecting a sector or financing source which is not of immediate interest, partial equilibrium frameworks can easily generate misleading results. However it should also be emphasized that, insofar as data are drawn from different sources, the data presented may not always correspond to the concepts being measured. It would not be

Table 3.3 Flow of funds pro-forma

Classification of transactions ('rows')	Classification of sectors ('columns')
Current account	
1 Factor incomes	1. Central bank
2 Transfers	2. Public sector
3 Factor cost adjustment	3. Financial sector
4 Expenditures	4. Non-financial private sector
4.1 Consumption	5. Foreign
4.2 Exports	6. Total
4.3 Imports	
5 Balance = savings	
6 *Capital account*	
6.1 Gross fixed investment	
6.2 Other	
7 Balance = sector surplus/deficit	
8 Unidentified	
9 Total	
Financial transactions	
11 Total domestic currency	
12 Cash and bank reserves	
13 Public sector debt	
15 Bank deposits	
16 Deposits with OFIs	
17 Bank lending	
18 Lending by OFIs	
19 Corporate debt	
20 Equity	
21 Other domestic	
25 Total foreign currency	
26 Foreign reserves incl. net IMF	
27 Other foreign currency	
30 Total financial transactions	

Source: Green *et al.* (2000).

reasonable to sanctify the data used by current researchers; the main point is that this useful methodology will continue to be perfected as better data sets are generated.

5. EMPIRICAL STUDIES ON THE FLOW OF FUNDS IN DEVELOPING COUNTRIES

Notwithstanding the difficulties involved, several developing and transition countries have compiled one-time flow of funds accounts based on the SNA. Examples include Jamaica (Bank of Jamaica, 1976), Trinidad and Tobago (Central Statistical Office, 1977), Nigeria (Central Bank of Nigeria, 1983), and Estonia (Püss and Tammeraid, 1996).[9] Uniquely among developing countries, India has well-established flow of funds accounts prepared broadly along the lines of the SNA. Flow of funds were first prepared in India in 1964, and flow of funds data are available on an annual basis from 1951–2,[10] although there is a substantial lag in the production of the data, with the 1995–6 figures not being published until 2000. Nevertheless such a long run of data, and the high level of detail at which the accounts are prepared, would be regarded as a substantial achievement in most industrial countries. Indeed the original Indian data predate those in several of the major industrial countries. A detailed analysis of these data is beyond the scope of this chapter. The statistical basis of the accounts is summarized in Reserve Bank of India (2000a); the data themselves can be found in Reserve Bank of India (1999, 2000a, 2000b); some analyses are carried out in Sen *et al.* (1996), Sen and Vaidya (1999) and Moore *et al.* (2001).

The seminal analytical studies of the flow of funds in developing countries are those of Honohan and Atiyas (1989, 1993) who estimated sector surpluses and deficits for 17 developing countries regarded as having the best data availability for this purpose. Even so, Honohan and Atiyas were only able to compile data with an average span of about seven years per country.[11] They used their data to study the elasticity of financial flows between domestic sectors, following the work of Feldstein and Horioka (1980) on international flows. Their analysis captures the following relationships for each country:

$$GS_i - GK_i = FC_i, \tag{3.1}$$

where GS_i is sector i's gross savings including provisions for depreciation and GK_i is its gross capital formation (including stock accumulation). ($GS_i - GK_i$) gives the excess of each sector's GS over its GK, so that FC_i is the accumulation by sector i of financial claims on other sectors: its NAFA. Adjustments should also be made for capital transfers and for purchases and sales of land and intangible assets. One example of capital transfers, featured in the analysis of Korea, is government grants disbursed to the private sector.

The main conclusions of the Honohan–Atiyas studies are as follows. In general, the household sector is a net lender, lending to other sectors an average of 7 per cent of GNP. Indeed the household sector typically saves more than twice the amount of funds it needs to finance its own accumulation of real assets, lending the surplus to other sectors. This suggests that, even in developing countries, households may have the capacity to generate savings to finance capital accumulation by other sectors such as business and government. However the Honohan–Atiyas sample consists mainly of countries which are more open and which enjoy relatively high income levels; it is possible that less open or poorer countries may not reproduce this result.

In contrast, the business sector is a net borrower: typically, about half of real capital formation in the business sector is externally funded. This sector is thus an important beneficiary of an efficient intersectoral financial flows network.

Related work was carried out by Murinde (1996, ch. 2), who used the framework in Table 3.1 to construct empirical intersectoral financial flow tables from the published national accounts of four developing economies in Africa and Asia: Kenya,[12] Zimbabwe, Malaysia and Singapore. Murinde used these data to study the comparative performance of domestic and international finance as sources of domestic investment funds in these economies. In both Kenya and Zimbabwe it was found that the private sector generated virtually all the government tax revenue. As regards consumption expenditure, in Zimbabwe the private sector undertook consumption and investment expenditure far in excess of government expenditure. However Murinde noted that the scenario of high tax revenue and reasonable public expenditure control may not be reproduced in other Sub-Saharan African countries which have an underdeveloped corporate sector and an expanding government sector, and was unlikely to be sustainable in Zimbabwe. In terms of assets and liabilities, there was an active flow of capital resources between the private and the government sectors in Kenya. Much of domestic money was shown to be in the hands of the banking sector in Kenya and Zimbabwe; in addition, there was a higher proportion of domestic money in the private sector than in the government sector. However, in both Kenya and Zimbabwe, foreign money was predominantly in the hands of the government sector, reflecting the existence of exchange controls in these economies during the sample period. For Malaysia and Singapore,[13] Murinde reached the following conclusions. First, the private sector in Malaysia was a net lender to the government sector; second, capital formation was largely financed by domestic sources of funds; third, intersectoral flows were mostly achieved through the banking system; fourth, by end-1989, the Malaysian capital market had become a significant source of funds for business. Finally, even though the foreign sector did not provide a substantial amount of financing, there was no clear sign that the private sector reduced its investment in consequence; thus a shortfall in foreign finance did not cause the business sector to cut down on its investment, although this may have been partly because domestic savings were relatively high in these countries.

Summarizing, Murinde's results were broadly supportive of Honohan–Atiyas, although Murinde reached two additional conclusions. First, the government sector is sometimes a net lender, but in most developing economies this sector emerges as a net borrower. This mixed result depends on the tax effort and expenditure control in place in various developing economies. Second, the foreign sector is a residual provider of funds to the domestic economy. As such it cannot be relied upon as a main source of finance. This is an unfortunate scenario for developing economies which have serious foreign exchange bottlenecks (see Murinde, 1996).

Following the general approach of Green and Murinde (1998), BGM (1999) applied a more formal model to conduct simulation experiments to evaluate the impact of financial sector reform and liberalization in Poland and Estonia. BGM found that the results for these transition economies differed in certain key respects from the results for developing countries. In particular, there was evidence that foreign capital flows made an important contribution to financing domestic investment and that domestic and foreign funds were substitutes for one another in this respect. The results suggested that these economies were better integrated into the world capital market than many developing countries.

6. CONCLUSIONS AND PRIs

In this chapter, we have selectively surveyed the leading theoretical and empirical issues surrounding flow of funds analysis, as a financial modelling technique and as a tool of analysis of intersectoral financial flows. Below we highlight some of the main PRIs for further research on the key relationships between the financial and real sectors of low-income developing countries. In general, flow of funds analysis can be useful in shedding light on intersectoral financial flows and their volatility; the role of financial institutions in the economy, particularly in generating private savings and channelling them into productive investments; the requirements of the corporate sector for financing investment and their implications for interest rates and asset prices, and thereby for the economy as a whole; and the financial relationships between the formal and informal sectors.

1. Given the modern advances in constructing and estimating flow of funds, a major PRI involves incorporating these advances into the implementation of flow of funds analyses within a framework that is suitable for studying the relationship between financial sector development and the

real economy in developing countries. The techniques proposed by Dawson (1991), Murinde (1996) and GMSM (2000) offer a new and practical technology for assisting this process. It is straightforward to transform widely available IMF-source data into flow of funds data which can be used for policy analysis and design. These data are comparable across countries to the same extent as all IMF data. Although this may be thought to involve just a rearrangement of existing data, we have argued that the flow of funds framework adds value in itself. Furthermore these techniques provide a setting within which researchers and national statisticians can adapt existing data compiled for the IMF, and upon which they can build and extend their own flow of funds data at substantially lower cost than would be incurred in compiling these data from scratch.

2. A second PRI is to consider more precisely how the flow of funds framework may be applied by policy makers for the analysis of financial problems in developing countries. The studies by Murinde (1996), Green and Murinde (1998), Honohan and Atiyas (1989, 1993) and BGM (1999) suggest that flow of funds models may be used as a framework to set out and analyse the broad policy choices facing low-income developing countries with rudimentary financial markets.

3. In principle, empirical flow of funds models call for relatively detailed data, which are not generally available in developing countries. However considerable progress can still be made in understanding economic problems by using a simulation approach in which a detailed model is calibrated using benchmark values for parameters which are 'guesstimated' using a combination of existing home country data and consensus estimates of comparable parameters in foreign countries. A calibrated model may be used to carry out policy experiments accompanied by sensitivity analysis to assess how robust policies are in the face of the considerable uncertainty about the exact structure of the economy. This approach has been used by BGM (1999) with some success in the context of the transition economies of eastern Europe. In this PRI, therefore, it is argued that a simulation approach can be used as a tool for analysing financial policy choices for developing economies.[14] A flow of funds model can be used to simulate economic and financial policies in order to study the effects of financial sector reform on investment, output and financial flows, and to gauge the effects of monetary and fiscal policy on these variables.

4. Another PRI is to use flow of funds models to investigate the pattern of intersectoral financial flows in low-income countries, focusing on household choice (including consumption, saving and investment), the corporate sector (investment and financing), the banks (intermediation, debt and

equity financing), the government sector (taxation and spending) and the overseas sector (debt, aid and foreign direct investment). Evidence on intersectoral financial flows in developing economies will enable the identification of borrowing and lending sectors; for instance, to identify the extent to which the financing of business investment depends on the availability of foreign or domestic funds, and to determine the degree to which households accumulate financial assets, conditional on the state of economic development, domestic financial institutions or the availability of foreign sources of finance. Evidence on the pattern of intersectoral financial flows can help identify the types of assets and intermediaries which promote participation in the financial markets (broadly defined). In this way it is possible to identify the financial markets, institutions and instruments that are conducive to poverty-reducing economic growth.

5.   Finally, it is evident that much could be learnt from sector- and micro-level studies. Indeed individual studies are probably the only sensible method to document and understand the behaviour of informal and parallel markets and their relationship with the formal sector. The last PRI therefore is to engage in these studies with no less a priority than that given to the more macro-level, whole-economy research which is the main focus of this chapter.

NOTES

1.   Dawson (1991) carefully shows the conceptual relation of flow of funds accounts to the SNA. A brief review of the evolution of the SNA itself is presented, including the original 1953 version, the 1968 version and the current version, released in 1993.
2.   Copeland (1952) showed sources and uses separately, and this is the practice in the USA and some other countries. See also Dawson (1991). The reality is that it is practically difficult to identify consistently the gross sources and uses for many classes of transaction. Published data giving gross figures are often reporting the net sources or uses of certain components within the accounts, and are thus merely aggregating the data in a particular way.
3.   Dawson (1991) demonstrates methods of estimating a simple flow of funds system, especially for developing countries; see also an earlier application to Kenya by IMF (1981).
4.   Roley (1983) shows how symmetry restrictions can be tested in the context of a dynamic model.
5.   See the international study by Feldstein and Horioka (1980).
6.   In Tables 3.2 and 3.3, we save space by showing only the row and column heads of the accounts rather than complete matrices.
7.   These authors were well aware of these omissions, which were determined by the underlying objectives of their work.
8.   GMSM omit life insurance and pension funds from their proposed matrix, mainly because these data are not available in the international sources they use.
9.   This is not a comprehensive list, especially as it is confined to documents available in English. Other countries which have produced (national language) flow of funds data include Venezuela and Korea.

10. Indian flow of funds are on a fiscal year basis: 1 April–31March.
11. The length of the time series for a single country varied from just three years to 16 years.
12. For particular aspects of financial development, Table 3.1 is more helpful than the analysis in IMF (1981) for Kenya; however, IMF (1981) is more useful in incorporating fiscal aspects of the economy.
13. It is useful to recall that the economies of Malaysia and Singapore have common historical foundations (see Murinde and Eng, 1994).
14. The approach suggested here differs from some research where a flow of funds component is built into a large scale computable general equilibrium model (CGE). Not only is CGE modelling a different research problem from ours, but we also believe that this would be cumbersome without necessarily yielding positive value added. See Murinde (1996) on the comparison of flow of funds, social accounting matrices (SAMs) and CGEs.

REFERENCES

Aivazian, V.A., Callen, J.L., Krinsky, I. and Kwan, C.C.Y. (1990), 'Risk versus return in the substitutability of debt and equity securities', *Journal of Monetary Economics*, **26**(1), 161–78.
Backus, D. and Purvis, D. (1980), 'An integrated model of household flow of funds allocations', *Journal of Money, Credit and Banking*, **12**(2) (May), 400–421.
Backus, D., Brainard, W.C., Smith, G. and Tobin, J. (1980), 'A model of US financial and non-financial economic behaviour', *Journal of Money, Credit and Banking*, **12**(2) (May), 259–93.
Bahra, P., Green, C.J. and Murinde, V. (1999), 'Simulation experiments of the macroeconomic effects of financial sector reforms in Poland and Estonia', in C.J. Green and A.W. Mullineux (eds), *Financial Sector Reform in Central and Eastern Europe: Capital Flows, Bank and Enterprise Restructuring*, Cheltenham, UK and Northampton, MA, USA: Edward Elgar, pp. 277–304.
Bain, A.D. (1973), 'Surveys in applied economics: flow of funds analysis', *Economic Journal*, **83**(332) (December), 1055–93.
Bank of England (1985), 'Developments in UK banking and monetary statistics since the Radcliffe Report', *Bank of England Quarterly Bulletin*, **25**(3) (September), 392–7.
Bank of Jamaica (1976), 'Flow of funds accounts of Jamaica, 1976', Research Department, Kingston, Jamaica.
Barker, T.S., van der Ploeg, F. and Weale, M.R. (1984), 'A balanced system of national accounts for the United Kingdom', *Review of Income and Wealth*, **30**(4), 461–86.
Barr, D.G. and Cuthbertson, K. (1991), 'Neoclassical consumer demand theory and the demand for money', *Economic Journal*, **407** (July), 855–76.
Baxter, M.A. (1992), 'The production of fully reconciled UK national and sector accounts for 1988–1991', *Economic Trends*, **469** (November), 80–98.
Bollerslev, T., Engle, R.F. and Wooldridge, J.M. (1988), 'A capital asset pricing model with time varying covariances', *Journal of Political Economy*, **96**(1), 116–31.
Brainard, W.C. (1964), 'Financial intermediaries and a theory of monetary control', *Yale Economic Essays*, **4**(10) (Fall), 431–82.
Brainard, W.C. and Smith, G.N. (1982), 'A disequilibrium model of savings and loan associations', *Journal of Finance*, **37**(5) (December), 1277–93.

Breeden, D.T. (1979), 'An intertemporal asset pricing model with stochastic consumption and investment opportunities', *Journal of Financial Economics*, **7**, 265–96.

Buffie, E.F. (1991), 'Credit rationing and capital accumulation', *Economica*, **58**(231) (August), 299–316.

Buiter, W.H. (1980), 'Walras Law and all that: budget constraints and balance sheet constraints in period models and continuous time models', *International Economic Review*, **21**(1) (February), 1–16.

Cashin, P. and McDermott, C.J. (1998), 'Testing the consumption-CAPM in developing equity markets', *International Journal of Finance and Economics*, **3**(2), 127–42.

Central Bank of Nigeria (1983), 'Nigeria's flow of funds, 1970–1978', Lagos, Nigeria.

Central Statistical Office (1977), 'Flow of funds for Trinidad and Tobago, 1966–74', Ministry of Finance, Port of Spain, Trinidad and Tobago.

Central Statistical Office (1989), 'An investigation into balancing the UK national and financial accounts 1985–87', *Economic Trends*, **424** (February), 74–103.

Collier, P., Hoeffler, A. and Pattillo, C. (1999), 'Flight capital as a portfolio choice', Working Paper WP/99/171, December, International Monetary Fund, Washington, DC.

Copeland, M.A. (1952), *A Study of The Moneyflows in the United States*, New York: NBER.

Copestake, J., Bhalotra, S. and Johnson, S. (2001), 'Assessing the impact of microcredit: a Zambian case study', *Journal of Development Studies*, **37**(4) (April), 81–100.

Courakis, A.S. (1988), 'Modelling portfolio selection', *Economic Journal*, **392** (September), 619–42.

Dawson, J.C. (1991), 'The flow of funds accounts, the United Nations system of national accounts and the developing countries', in V. Galbis (ed.), *The IMF's Statistical Systems*, Washington, DC: International Monetary Fund.

Dawson, J.C. (1996), *Flow of Funds Analysis: A Handbook for Practitioners*, London: M.E. Sharpe.

Deacon, M. and Derry, A. (1994), 'Estimating market interest rates and inflation expectations from the prices of UK government bonds', *Bank of England Quarterly Bulletin*, **34**(3) (August), 232–40.

Feldstein, M.S. and Horioka, C. (1980), 'Domestic saving and international capital flows', *Economic Journal*, **90**, 314–29.

Fitzgerald, E.V.K. (1999), 'Capital surges, investment instability and income distribution after financial liberalization', Finance and Development Working Paper, no. 5, University of Manchester, May.

Fleming, A.E. and Giugale, M.M. (eds) (2000), *Financial Systems in Transition*, Singapore: World Scientific.

Frankel, J.A. (1985), 'Portfolio crowding out empirically estimated', *Quarterly Journal of Economics*, **100**(5), 1041–65.

Frankel, J.A. and Dickens, W.T. (1984), 'Are asset demand functions mean-variance efficient?', NBER working paper no.1113, June.

Frankel, J.A. and Engel, C.M. (1984), 'Do asset demand functions optimize over the mean and variance of real returns? A six-currency test', *Journal of International Economics*, **17**, 309–23.

Friedman, B.M. (1977), 'Financial flow variables and the short-run determination of long-term interest rates', *Journal of Political Economy*, **85**(4) (August), 661–89.

Friedman, B.M. (1979), 'Substitution and expectation effects on long-term borrowing behaviour and long-term interest rates', *Journal of Money, Credit and Banking*, **11**(2) (May), 131–50.

Friedman, B.M. (1980a), 'How important is disaggregation in structural models of interest rate determination', *Review of Economics and Statistics*, **62**(2) (May), 271–6.

Friedman, B.M. (1980b), 'The determination of long-term interest rates: implications for fiscal and monetary policies', *Journal of Money, Credit and Banking*, **12**(2) (May), 331–52.

Gorman, J.A. (1983), 'Data needs in flow of funds', *Review of Public Data Use*, **11**, 409–14.

Green, C.J. (1984a), 'Preliminary results from a five-sector flow of funds model of the United Kingdom 1972–77', *Economic Modelling*, **1**(3) (July), 304–26.

Green, C.J. (1984b), 'Integrated balance sheet and flow accounts: allocation of the residual adjustment', Bank of England Internal Memorandum, November; reproduced in R. Crossley, 'Integrated balance sheet and flow accounts for insurance companies and pension funds', Bank of England Technical Paper no. 17, September 1987, 36–45.

Green, C.J. (1990), 'Asset demands and asset prices in the UK: is there a risk premium?', *The Manchester School*, **58**(3) (September), 211–28.

Green, C.J. (1992), 'The flow of funds', in P. Newman, M. Milgate and J. Eatwell (eds), *The New Palgrave Dictionary of Money and Finance*, London, Macmillan, pp. 137–9.

Green, C.J. and Kiernan, E. (1989), 'Multicollinearity and measurement error in econometric financial modelling', *Manchester School*, **57**(4) (December), 357–69.

Green, C.J. and Murinde, V. (1998), 'Flow-of-funds and the macroeconomic policy framework for financial restructuring in transition economies', in J. Doukas, V. Murinde and C. Wihlborg (eds), *Financial Sector Reform and Privatisation in Transition Economies*, Amsterdam: Elsevier Science B.V., pp. 239–77.

Green, C.J., Murinde, V., Suppakitjarak, J. and Moore, T. (2000), 'Compiling and understanding the flow of funds in developing countries' , Finance and Development Working Paper, no. 21, University of Manchester, November.

Hendershott, P.H. (1977), *Understanding Capital Markets: Vol.I: A Flow of Funds Model*, Lexington: D.C. Heath and Co.

Hendry, D.F., Pagan, A.R. and Sargan, J.D. (1984), 'Dynamic specification', in Z.Griliches and M.D. Inviligator (eds), *Handbook of Econometrics*, vol. 2, Amsterdam, North Holland.

Honohan, P. and Atiyas, I. (1989), 'Intersectoral financial flows in developing countries', Working Papers, WPS 164, The World Bank, Washington, DC.

Honohan, P. and Atiyas, I. (1993), 'Intersectoral financial flows in developing countries', *Economic Journal*, **103**(418), 666–79.

Hulme, D. and Mosley, P. (1996), *Finance Against Poverty: Volumes 1 and 2*, London: Routledge.

IMF, *Balance of Payments Yearbook*, Washington, DC: International Monetary Fund.

IMF, *Government Finance Statistics Yearbook*, Washington, DC: International Monetary Fund.

IMF, *International Financial Statistics*, Washington, DC: International Monetary Fund.

IMF (1981), 'Workshop 4: flow of funds', *Financial Policy Workshops: the Case of Kenya*, Washington, DC: International Monetary Fund, pp. 128–53.

Jha, R. (1994), *Macroeconomics for Developing Countries*, London: Routledge.

Johnson, H.G. (1970), 'Recent developments in monetary theory: a commentary', in H.G. Johnson, *Further Essays in Monetary Economics*, London: Allen and Unwin, pp. 21–49.

Kearney, C. and MacDonald, R. (1986), 'A structural portfolio balance model of the sterling exchange rate', *Weltwirtschaftliches Archiv*, **122**(3), 478–96.

Keating, G. (1985), 'The financial sector of the London Business School model', in D. Currie (ed.), *Advances in Monetary Economics*, London: Croom Helm, pp. 86–126.

Kennedy, N.O. (1988) 'Inflation adjusted sectoral savings and financial balances', *Bank of England Quarterly Bulletin*, May.

Klein, L.R. (2000), 'Preface' in A.E. Fleming and M.M. Giugale (eds), *Financial Systems in Transition*, Singapore: World Scientific, pp. ix–xii.

Knight, M.D. and Wymer, C.R. (1976), 'A monetary model of an open economy with particular reference to the United Kingdom', in M.J. Artis and A.R. Nobay (eds), *Essays in Economic Analysis*, Cambridge: Cambridge University Press, pp. 153–66.

Lensink, R., Hermes, N. and Murinde, V. (1998), 'The effect of financial liberalisation on capital flight', *World Development*, **26**(7) (July), 1349–68.

Lovell, M.C. (1963), 'Seasonal adjustment of economic time series and multiple regression analysis', *Journal of the American Statistical Association*, **61**, 800–802.

Merton, R.C. (1973), 'An intertemporal capital asset pricing model', *Econometrica*, **41**(5), September, 867–87.

Moore, T., Green, C.J. and Murinde, V. (2001), 'Modelling the flow of funds in India', paper presented at the KIPPRA/DFID International Conference on Finance and Development, Nairobi, 10–11 July.

Morduch, J. (1999), 'The microfinance promise', *Journal of Economic Literature*, **37**(4) (December), 1569–614.

Mosley, P. (1999), 'Micro–macro linkages in financial markets: the impact of financial liberalization on access to rural credit in four African countries', Finance and Development Working Paper, no. 4, University of Manchester, March.

Mosley, P. (2001), 'Microfinance and poverty in Bolivia', *Journal of Development Studies*, **37**(4) (April), 101–32.

Murinde, V. (1996), *Development Banking and Finance*, Aldershot: Ashgate.

Murinde, V. and Eng, F.S.H. (1994), 'Financial development and economic growth in Singapore: demand-following or supply-leading?', *Applied Financial Economics*, **4**, 391–404.

Murinde, V., Hermes, N. and Lensink, R. (1996), 'Comparative aspects of the magnitude and determinants of capital flight in six Sub-Saharan African economies', *Savings and Development Quarterly Review*, **XX**(1), 61–78.

Ngugi, R., Murinde, V. and Green, C.J. (2000), 'Key microstructure and policy issues for emerging stock markets: what have we learned?', Finance and Development Working Paper, no. 16, University of Manchester, May.

Owen, P.D. (1986), *Money, Wealth and Expenditures*, Cambridge: Cambridge University Press.

Purvis, D.D. (1978), 'Dynamic models of portfolio behaviour: more on pitfalls in financial model building', *American Economic Review*, **68**(3) (June), 403–9.

Püss, S. and Tammeraid, T. (1996), 'Possibilities of flow of funds accounting arrangements in Estonia', in V. Vensel (ed.), *Economic Performance and Financial*

Sector Reform in Central and Eastern Europe, Tallinn: Tallinn Technical University Working Papers in Economics.

Reserve Bank of India (1999), *Report on Currency and Finance, Volume II, 1997–98*, Mumbai.

Reserve Bank of India (2000a), *Flow of Funds Accounts of the Indian Economy: 1951–52 to 1995–96*, Mumbai.

Reserve Bank of India (2000b), *Monthly Bulletin* (various issues), Mumbai.

Roley, V.V. (1980), 'The role of commercial banks' portfolio behaviour in the determination of treasury security yields', *Journal of Money, Credit and Banking*, **12**(2) (May), 353–69.

Roley, V.V. (1983), 'Symmetry restrictions in a system of financial asset demands: theoretical and empirical results', *Review of Economics and Statistics*, **65**(1) (February), 124–30.

Schrieder, G. (2000), 'Poverty, rural financial institution building and gender-sensitive demand analysis in the North-West and West province of Cameroon', *Savings and Development*, **XXIV**(1), 95–110.

Sen, K. and Vaidya, R. (1999), *The Process of Financial Liberalization in India*, Delhi: Oxford University Press.

Sen, K., Roy, T., Krishnan, R. and Mundlay, A. (1996) 'A flow of funds model for India and its implications', *Journal of Policy Modelling*, **18**(5), 469–94.

Sharpe, I.G. (1973), 'A quarterly econometric model of portfolio choice – part I: specification and estimation problems', *Economic Record*, December, 518–33.

Shaw, E.S. (1973), *Financial Deepening in Economic Development*, New York: Oxford University Press.

Smith, G. (1975), 'Pitfalls in financial model building: a clarification', *American Economic Review*, **65**(3) (June), 510–16.

Smith, G. (1978), 'Dynamic models of portfolio behaviour: comment on Purvis', *American Economic Review*, **68**(3) (June), 410–16.

Smith, G. (1981), 'The systematic specification of a full prior covariance matrix for asset demand equations', *Quarterly Journal of Economics*, May, 317–39.

Stone, J.R., Champernowne, D.G. and Meade, J.E. (1942), 'The precision of national income estimates', *Review of Economic Studies*, **9**(2), 111–25.

Taylor, L. (1983), *Structuralist Macroeconomics: Applicable Models for the Third World*, New York: Basic Books.

Tobin, J. (1963a) 'An essay on the Principles of debt management', in Commission on Money and Credit (ed.), *Fiscal and Debt Management Policies*, Englewood Cliffs, NJ: Prentice-Hall, pp. 143–218.

Tobin, J. (1963b), 'Commercial banks as creators of money', in D. Carson (ed.) *Banking and Monetary Studies*, Homewood, Illinois: R.D. Irwin, pp. 408–19.

Tobin, J. (1969), 'A general equilibrium approach to monetary theory', *Journal of Money,Credit and Banking*, **1**(1) (February), 15–29.

Tobin, J. (1982), 'Money and finance in the macroeconomic process', *Journal of Money, Credit and Banking*, **14**(2) (May), 171–204.

Tobin, J. and Brainard, W.C. (1963), 'Financial intermediaries and the effectiveness of monetary controls', *American Economic Review Papers and Proceedings*, **53**(2) (May), 383–400.

Tobin, J. and Brainard, W.C. (1968), 'Pitfalls in financial modelbuilding', *American Economic Review Papers and Proceedings*, **58**(2) (May), 99–122.

United States Department of Commerce, Office of Federal Statistical Policy and Standards (1977), *Gross National Product Data Improvement Report*, Report of the Advisory Committee on Gross National Product Data Improvement (The Creamer Report), Washington, DC: Government Printing Office.

United Nations, Department of Economics and Social Affairs (1968), 'A system of national accounts', *Studies in Methods*, series F, no. 2, United Nations, New York.

United Nations, Department of Economics and Social Affairs (1993), 'Revised system of national accounts', *Studies in Methods*, United Nations, New York.

Van Wijnbergen, S. (1983), 'Interest rate management in LDCs', *Journal of Monetary Economics*, **12**(3) (September), 433–52.

World Bank (1997), 'World Saving Database', 3rd revision, on-line at www.worldbank.org.

4. Stock market development: what have we learned?

Rose W. Ngugi, Victor Murinde and Christopher J. Green

1. INTRODUCTION

Since the early 1990s, many developing countries have launched new stock markets or revitalized existing ones in order to enhance the development of capital markets and facilitate access to long-term capital. Emerging stock markets (ESMs)[1] now exist in about 70 developing countries. Although the ESMs faced a declining trend after the Asian financial crisis, they almost outperformed their developed counterparts. In 1999, the ESMs took 30 per cent of the top 20 positions, ranked by market capitalization. The market liquidity of the ESMs increased phenomenally while most emerging market indices went up, partly reflecting growing demand in share trading (see Kim and Singal, 2000).

The revitalization of ESMs has involved institutional and policy reforms aimed at improving stock market performance by reducing costs of trading and volatility as well as increasing market liquidity and efficiency. The main institutional and policy reforms include adoption of new trading systems, relaxation of foreign investment restrictions, expansion of stock market membership, strengthening of the legal and regulatory frameworks and reform of taxation policy. See, for example, Röell (1992), Khambata (2000) and Kawakatsu and Morey (1999). It may be argued that there is a link between revitalization of ESMs, improved market microstructure and economic development. Precisely, the argument is that, if it has an efficient price discovery process, no excess volatility and provides liquidity at low costs, the stock market can make important contribution to the development process. The drive to achieve market efficiency is desirable as efficiency allows agents to diversify their sources of investment capital and spread investment risk by aggregating and conveying information through price signals (Caprio and Demirgüç-Kunt, 1998). In addition, efficient stock prices and yields provide benchmarks against which the cost of capital for and returns on investment projects can be judged, even if such projects are not in fact financed through the stock market (Green *et al.*, 2000). Moreover, as the stock prices are forward-looking, they provide a unique record of the shifts in investors' views about the future prospects of companies as well as the economy. Furthermore an efficient price discovery process is traditionally associated with low volatility, which promotes stock market effectiveness in allocating resources efficiently. High volatility distorts efficient resource allocation by making investors more averse to hold stocks. Risk-averse investors tend to demand a high risk premium, which increases the cost of capital and reduces the level of investment (see Bekaert and Harvey, 1997; Kim and Singal, 2000). Market liquidity is desirable because it reduces the required return by investors; illiquidity increases the cost of capital and acts as a constraint on stock markets adequately performing their information processing and signalling functions (Amihud *et al.*, 1997). Thus stock market development and improved performance in the main market microstructure attributes are integral components of the development process.

This chapter aims to survey a large body of theoretical and empirical literature on the key aspects of stock market development, including market microstructure and the relevant policy environment. The emphasis is on emerging stock markets, although the discussion also highlights some comparative major issues in developed stock markets. The remainder of this chapter is structured as follows. Section 2 discusses issues surrounding stock market efficiency. Section 3 surveys the main trading systems and related performance indicators, including costs of trading, volatility and liquidity. Section 4 examines the relationship between the stock market and macroeconomic policies. Section 5 presents the conclusions and promising research ideas.

2. STOCK MARKET EFFICIENCY

The Efficient Market Hypothesis: Evidence on Weak-form Efficiency

One issue that has attracted the attention of researchers as well as policy makers is whether the ESMs exhibit similar general characteristics, including the distribution behaviour of stock returns, to developed stock markets. The key element of the weak-form, semi-strong and strong form efficiency, identified by Fama (1970, 1991), is that stock prices incorporate all information such that changes in prices reflect news or unanticipated events; unanticipated information is incorporated instantaneously, so that it is impossible for investors to beat the market. In addition, it is argued that stock prices are rational, in the sense that they reflect only utilitarian characteristics such as risk. Also the efficient market hypothesis (EMH) is based on the assumption of a perfect market with no transaction costs (Papachristou, 1999).

Empirical tests for efficiency in ESMs tend to focus on the stochastic properties of stock returns to infer predictability of stock return. A number of methods are used to test for weak-form efficiency, including unit root tests, serial correlation tests and variance ratio tests. The unit root test and the serial correlation test distinguish between series with no random walk component (where the variance of the shocks to the random walk component is zero) and series with a random walk component (for which the variance of shocks to the random walk component is between zero and infinity). The EMH is rejected if stock returns are non-stationary or non-trend stationary (Richards, 1996). One drawback of the unit root test is that it does not distinguish between a stationary series and series with a very small random walk component. To overcome this weakness, some studies tend to use mean reversion tests; for example, Fama and French (1988) use a regression-based model that applies long-horizon returns. Mean reversion tests capture the slowly decaying temporary component of stock prices, which explains the long temporary swings that take prices away from fundamental values. These reversals are attributed to fads or irrational bubbles suggesting that financial markets display excess volatility and overreact to new information. Reversals are also consistent with the time-varying equilibrium expected returns generated by rational pricing in an efficient market. Shocks have no long-term effect on expected prices; the cumulative effect of a shock on expected returns must be exactly offset by an opposite adjustment in the current prices. Thus autocorrelated equilibrium expected returns lead to slowly decaying component of prices that is indistinguishable from the temporary price components of an inefficient market. See, for example, Gallagher (1999) and Majnoni and Massa (2001).

The variance ratio approach measures the size of random walk or permanent component in a series. The variance ratio at lag k is defined as the l/k times the variance of k-period return divided by the variance of the one period return (see Serletis and Sondergard, 1996; Kim and Singal, 2000). If stock prices have a random walk process, the variance of the k-period returns is equal to k-times the variance of one period return. If the variance ratio is less than one, then negative correlation is implied, while a variance ratio greater than one indicates positive serial correlation. A pure stationary process is reflected when the variance ratio approaches zero. However, the variance ratio test is constrained by the need for a long data set. It requires k to be large enough to capture mean reversion over the long horizon (Serletis and Sondergard, 1996). For example, it is proposed that the power of the ratio is preserved when k is less than one-half of the number of observations.

Table 4.1 summarizes empirical results from some key studies that have employed the above tests. In general, as shown in Table 4.1, the test results

Table 4.1 Summary of evidence on weak form efficiency tests

Market	Author	Unit root	Serial correlation	Regression-based model	Variance ratio test	Cointegration test	VAR test	IID test
				Part I Emerging stock markets (ESMs)				
Argentina	Richards (1996)	I(1)		Negative NS (3,6,12, 24); positive NS (36)		Accept the null		
Athens	Niarcholas and Alexakis (1998) Barkoulas and Travlos (1998)					Reject the null		Reject IID
Botswana		I(0)						
Brazil	Richards (1996)	I(1)		Negative NS (3, 12, 24, 36); positive NS (6)		Accept the null		
Chile	Richards (1996)	I(1)		Positive S (3,6,12); positive NS (24,36)		Accept the null		
Ghana	Osei((1998)		Reject the null					
Greece	Richards (1996)	I(1)		Positive S (6,36); positive NS (3,12,24)		Accept the null		
India	Gallagher (1999) Richards (1996)	I(1) I(0)		Negative NS (3); negative S (12,24,36); positive NS (6) Positive NS (3,6,12,24)		Reject the null Accept the null	0.11	
Jordan	Richards (1996)	I(1)	Reject the null	Monthly data = Ppositive		Accept the null		
Kenya	Muragu (1996)							
Korea	Titman and Wei (1999) Richards (1996)	I(1)		Positive S (12); positive NS (3,6,24); negative NS (36)		Accept the null		

Table 4.1 *continued*

Market	Author	Unit root	Serial correlation	Regression-based model	Variance ratio test	Cointegration test	VAR test	IID test
Malaysia	Richards (1996)			Negative S (12); positive NS (3); negative NS (6,24)		Accept the null		
Mexico	Richards (1996)	I(1)		Negative NS (3); positive NS (6,12, 24, 36)		Accept the null		
Nigeria	Inanga and Emenuga (1995)		Reject the null					
Pakistan	Richards (1996)			Negative S (12); positive NS (6); negative NS (3,24)		Accept the null		
Philippines	Richards (1996)			Positive NS (3,6,12,24)		Accept the null		
South Africa	Gallagher (1999)	I(1)				Reject the null	0.35	
Taiwan	Titman and Wei (1999)			Monthly data = positive				
	Richards (1996)			Positive NS (3,6); negative NS (12,24)		Accept the null		
Thailand	Richards (1996)	I(1)		Negative NS (3); positive NS (6,12, 24, 36)		Accept the null		
Venezuela	Richards (1996)			Positive NS (3,6,12); negative NS (24)		Accept the null		
Vienna	Huber (1997)				Reject/Accept RW Ho before/after			
Zimbabwe	Richards (1996)	I(1)		Positive S (3,6); positive (12); negative NS (24, 36)		Accept the null		
Zimbabwe	Jefferies and Okeahalam (1999)	I(1)						

94

Part II Developed stock markets

Country	Source					
Austria	Gallagher (1999)	I(1)			Reject the null	0.31
Belgium	Gallagher (1999)	I(1)			Reject the null	0.27
Canada	Serletis and Sondergard (1996)	I(1)	Daily data = positive; weekly and bi-weekly =			Reject IID
Canada	Gallagher (1999)	I(1)			Reject the null	0.62
Colombia	Richards (1996)		Negative S (12); positive NS (3,6); negative NS (24)	Short horizon > 1; Long horizon <1 negative	Accept the null	
Finland	Gallagher (1999)	I(1)			Reject the null	0.30
France	Gallagher (1999)	I(1)			Reject the null	0.09
Germany	Gallagher (1999)	I(1)			Reject the null	0.13
Italy	Gallagher (1999)	I(1)			Reject the null	0.07
Japan	Gallagher (1999)	I(1)			Reject the null	0.37
Netherlands	Gallagher (1999)	I(1)			Reject the null	0.34
Norway	Gallagher (1999)	I(1)			Reject the null	0.14
Sweden	Gallagher (1999)	I(1)			Reject the null	0.07
Switzerland	Gallagher (1999)	I(1)			Reject the null	0.27
UK	Al-Loughani and Chappell (1997)	I(1)				Reject IID
	Gallagher (1999)	I(1)			Reject the null	0.15
USA	Yadav et al. (1999)	I(1)				Reject IID
	Gallagher (1999)	I(1)			Reject the null	0.56

Note: The table is divided into two parts. In Part I we report the results for ESMs and in Part II we report the results for DSMs. Column 3 parentheses indicate the order of integration; column 5 positive/negative imply the sign of the β coefficient in the regression-based model; S is significant β; NS is insignificant β. Parentheses in column 5 are the horizons measured by the number of months. Column 9 IID is identically and independently distributed; column 8 values are of the coefficients for the temporary component.

Source: Based on the literature surveyed by the authors.

95

for weak-form efficiency are similar across the emerging and developed stock markets despite differences in stages of market development. What is particularly interesting, however, is that in almost all these studies predictability of stock returns is attributed to a number of key factors. The first factor is non-synchronous trading, which is characterized by portfolios of small stocks and thin markets in ESMs (Koutmos, 1999). The second factor is the presence of noise traders (Cochran and DeFina, 1995; Richards, 1996). The third factor is related to market fundamentals. However it is debatable whether some fundamentals are consistent with market inefficiency; for example, Fama (1991) argues that predictability of stock returns from dividend yields is not in itself evidence for or against market efficiency. While in an efficient market the forecast power of dividend yields implies that prices are high relative to dividends when discount rate and expected returns are low, it may be argued that low yields signal irrationally high prices that will move predictably back towards fundamentals values.

Event Studies and Semi-strong Efficiency

Event studies test for semi-strong efficiency (Fama, 1991). The main objective in event studies is to examine the stock market's response to a well-defined event through the observation of security prices around the event. The studies test for the existence of an information effect and its magnitude and identify factors that explain changes in the stock price on the event date. The hypothesis typically tested in event studies may be stated as follows:

$$E(AR_t \mid \Omega_{t-1}) = 0, \qquad (4.1)$$

$$AR_t = R_t - E(R_t), \qquad (4.2)$$

where E = expectations operator; Ω_{t-1} = information set in previous period; AR_t = abnormal returns; R_t is the ex-post security return conditional on experiencing the event being studied; $E(R_t)$ is the expected return in the absence of the event; and t = time subscript.

Kritzman (1994) and MacKinlay (1997) give a summary of the various steps involved in conducting event studies. The steps include defining the event of interest, determining the period over which the securities will be examined (event window), sample selection, determining the method of measuring the normal returns, and defining the estimation window and framework for abnormal returns. To make good inferences from the results, diagnostic tests are carried out, together with tests to reject the null hypothesis for a specified level of abnormal returns associated with an event.

The estimation of normal returns is conducted using either statistical models or economic models. As explained by MacKinlay (1997), statistical models follow statistical assumptions of asset returns, with no economic arguments, while the economic models rely on assumptions based on investor behaviour. However the market model, which is a statistical model, is widely used as it overcomes shortcomings of the main economic models such as the arbitrage pricing theory (APT).

Parametric and non-parametric methods are used to test the null hypothesis of no abnormal returns. Parametric tests assume normal distribution of the returns, and give an estimate of the size of the average effect of the event on stock returns. However, there is growing evidence that stock returns in developing markets are non-normally distributed, which implies that parametric tests are not always suitable for conducting event studies in ESMs. One widely used non-parametric test is the binomial test, which determines whether the percentage of post-event returns which are greater than the pre-event returns is significantly different from 50 per cent (Kim and Singal, 2000). The test is defined as $[|p - 0.5| - (0.5/N)]/(0.5/N^{0.5})$, where p = the proportion of total positive abnormal returns, N = the total number of observations in the event window. Kim and Singal (2000) and Amihud *et al.* (1997) use the binomial test and reject the null hypothesis that there are no abnormal returns.

Another popular non-parametric test used in event studies is the sign test for no difference between the pre-and post-event returns. The sign test requires that the abnormal returns are independent across securities. It involves calculating the sign of each abnormal return each day over the event window. See Corrado and Zivney (1992) for the construction of the test. One weakness of the test is that it may not be well specified if the distribution of abnormal returns is highly skewed.

In addition, a useful non-parametric test is the rank test. The test involves ranking the excess return in each security. To allow for missing returns, ranks are standardized by dividing each firm's excess return by a value equal to one plus the number of non-missing returns. Corrado and Zivney (1992) and MacKinlay (1997) compare the sign and rank tests and conclude that the latter is preferable to the former in obtaining non-parametric inferences concerning abnormal security price performance in event studies. However Giaccotto and Sfiridis (1996) recommend the sign test, in the special case where a researcher knows the exact day of the event, and the jackknife test in circumstances where a multiple-day window is used to capture the true event day.

An interesting issue, which has been raised with respect to the use of event studies in ESMs, is thin trading. Husnan and Theobald (1993) investigate the impact of thin trading on the results of event studies in the Indonesian stock market using different indexes. It is found that index sensitivity is indicated by the wide differences in the (cumulative) abnormal returns. These findings are consistent with those obtained by Maynes and Rumsey (1993), who conclude that the traditional procedures for conducting event studies are reasonably well specified for thickly and moderately traded stocks, but misspecified for thinly traded stocks. Specifically it is noted that the event study methodology may be severely misspecified when applied to infrequently traded stocks, if the return is forecast using the lumped or uniform treatment of missing trades or if the *t*-test is used. Similar observations are made by Cowan and Sergeant (1996).

In general, as noted by Fama (1991), evidence from event studies contains important inferences about semi-strong efficiency; efficient markets are expected to reflect quick stock price adjustment to information about investment decisions, dividend changes, changes in capital structure and corporate control transactions, among many examples of financial and economic events. However the evidence from existing studies seems to suggest that thin trading and market imperfections tend to distort the inferences that can be drawn from event studies in ESMs. In addition, it is common to find that dispersion of returns increases around the information event.

Second Moments of Stock Returns: from Efficiency to Volatility

In most existing studies, the analysis of the second moments of stock returns is undertaken in order to investigate the nature of the stochastic process that defines stock prices. In addition, the analysis is motivated by asset-pricing models, which predict that the expected return of a stock price is related to its covariance with one or more pricing factors.

Some existing studies suggest that the modelling of time-varying second moments is based on the autoregressive conditional heteroscedasticity (ARCH) model of Engel (1982). However the standard ARCH model has only one memory period and generates difficulties in selecting the optimal lag length and ensuring non-negativity of the coefficient of conditional variance. A generalized version of the ARCH model, the GARCH, introduces a lagged conditional variance to capture long memory. The model is composed of conditional mean return and conditional variance equations and generates empirical coefficients which can capture the persistence of volatility over time (see Koutmos, 1999; Choudhry, 1996; De Santis and Ìmrohoroglus, 1997). Knowledge on the persistency of volatility is important as markets do not adjust the future discount rate when shocks are not persistent (Choudhry, 1996). Overall, therefore, the GARCH model assumes martingale conditions, including unbiased expectations and clustering tendency of volatility. It is argued, however, that returns respond asymmetrically to shocks where negative shocks to returns generate more volatility than positive shocks of the same magnitude. Christie (1982) also shows a negative relationship between current returns and future volatility, where a reduction in the equity value of the firm raises its debt-to-equity ratio, in turn raising the riskiness of the firm as manifested by an increase in future volatility. If returns are less than expected they increase future volatility, and if they are higher than expected they reduce future return volatility. See also Glosten *et al.* (1993), who show that it is possible to have a positive as well as a negative relationship between current returns and current variance. To capture the asymmetric nature of returns, other versions of the GARCH model have been applied: for example, the exponential GARCH (EGARCH) by Nelson (1991) and the Glosten, Jaganathan and Runkle (GJR) model (see Glosten *et al.*, 1993). The advantage of EGARCH over the linear GARCH model is that by modelling the natural log of the conditional variance it guarantees positive values for all t and therefore there is no need to impose parameter restrictions. Volatility depends on both the size and sign of past standardized residuals. More recently, Bollerslev and Mikkelson (1999) find evidence that long-run dependence of stock market volatility is best described by a slowly mean reverting fractionally integrated GARCH process (FIGARCH).

In addition to testing for non-linear behaviour of second moments, some studies have gone further to investigate whether non-linearity portrays a chaotic dynamic process (see, for example, Serletis and Sondergard, 1996; Yadav *et al.*, 1999; Barkoulas and Travlos, 1998; Poshakwale and Murinde, 2001). The hypothesis is that if stock returns show non-linearity it is possible that a deterministic chaos process rather than a stochastic process defines the data-generation process. The presence of chaos indicates the possibility of improved short-term but not long-term predictability; implying a profitable non-linear trading rule would exist at least in the short run. Testing for the dynamics of deterministic chaos involves calculation of correlation integrals corresponding to different embedding dimensions as proposed by Grassberger and Procaccia (1983). This method measures how much space is filled up by a string of data.[2] However, the method has various weaknesses; for example, it is not possible to verify that a process has an infinite correlation dimension using a finite amount of data. An alternative method used is the Brock *et al.* (1987) (BDS statistic) to infer the deterministic chaotic dynamics. Rather than providing a direct test for non-linearity or chaos, BDS is used to infer the non-linearity dependence, which is a necessary but not sufficient condition for chaos. The procedure involves removing any stochastic and non-linear dependence in order to establish deterministic non-linear dependence.

Table 4.2 provides a summary of econometric results relating to the second moments of stock returns. It is shown that a number of studies use the student-*t* or the generalized error distribution (GED) test, reflecting the as-

Table 4.2   Summary of evidence from testing for efficiency and volatility

Market	Stock returns are predictable	Stock returns have a non-normal distribution	Stock return volatility is clustering	Time-varying risk premium is significant	Stock return volatility has an asymmetric response	Stock return volatility is persistent	Stock returns have a chaos process
			Part I Emerging stock markets (ESMs)				
Argentina	✓(DI, R)	✓(C, DI, BH)	✓(C, DI)	✗(C), ✓(DI)		✓(DI, C)	
Brazil	✓(DI, R)	✓(DI, BH)	✓(DI)	✗(DI)		✓(D)	
Chile	✓(DI, R)	✓(DI, BH)	✓(DI)	✗(DI)		✓(D)	
Colombia	✓(DI)	✓(DI, BH)	✓(DI)	✗(DI)		✓(D)	
Hungary		✓(PM)	✓(PM)	✗(PM)			
India	✗(G, DI), ✗(R)	✓(C, DI, BH)	✓(C, DI)	✗(C, DI)		✓(DI, C)	
Indonesia		✓(BH)					
Korea	✗(TW, DI), ✓(R)	✓(K, DI, BH)	✓+(K), ✗(D)	✗(DI)	✓(K)	✗(DI), ✓(K)	
Malaysia	✗(DI)	✓(K, DI, BH, FP)	✓(K, FP, DI)	✗(DI), ✓(FP)	✓(K, FP)	✓(DI, K); ✗(FP)	
Mexico	✓(DI, R)	✓(C, DI, BH)	✓(C, DI)	✗(C, DI)		✓(DI, C)	
Nigeria		✓(BH)					
Pakistan		✓(BH)					
Philippines	✓(DI)	✓(K, DI, BH)	✓(K, DI)	✓(DI)	✗(K)	✓(DI, K)	
Poland		✓(PM)	✓(PM)	✗(PM)			
S. Africa	✓(G)				✓(K)		
Taiwan	✗(TW, DI)	✓(K, DI)	✓(K, DI)	✗(DI)	✓(K)	✓(DI, K)	
Thailand	✓(DI, R)	✓(C, DI, BH)	✓(C, DI)	✗(C, DI)		✓(DI, C)	
Turkey	✓(DI)	✓(DI, BH)	✓(DI)	✗(DI)		✓(D)	
Venezuela	✓(DI)	✓(DI, BH)	✓(DI)	+(DI)		✓(D)	
Zimbabwe	✓(R)	✓(C, BH)	✓(C, DI)	✗(C)		✓(DI, C)	

Part II Developed stock markets

Australia	✓(G)	✗(FP)	✗(FP)	✗(FP)	✗(FP)
Belgium	✓(G), ✗(SS)				✗(SS)
Canada	✓(G)				
Finland	✓(G), ✗(DI)				
Germany	✓(G), ✗(DI)	✓(DI)	✓(DI)	✗(DI)	✓(DI)
Hong Kong	✓(G)	✓(FP, H)	✗(FP)	✗(FP)	✓(FP, H)
Italy	✓(G), ✗(DI)	✓(FP, DI)	✓(FP)	✗(DI, FP)	✓(DI, FP)
Japan	✓(G), ✗(DI)	✓(FP, DI)	✓(FP)	✗(FP, DI)	
Netherlands	✓(G)				
Norway	✓(G)				
Portugal	✓(BH)	✗(FP)			
Singapore	✓(K, DI, FP)	✓(K, FP)	✗(FP)	✓(K, FP)	✓(FP, K)
Sweden	✓(G)				
UK	✓(G), ✗(DI)	✓(FP, DI)	✓(FP)	✗(FP, DI)	✓(DI, FP)
US	✓(G, L), ✓(DI)	✓(FP, DI)	✗(FP)	✗(FP, DI)	✓(DP), ✗(FP), ✗(Y)

Note: The Table is divided into two parts. In Part I we report the results for ESMs and in Part II we report the results for DSMs. The tick (✓) affirms the indicated characteristic while the cross (✗) negates the indicated characteristic; parentheses represent the author(s) of the research finding. FP = Fraser and Power (1997); DI = De Santis and Imrohoroglu (1997); K = Koutmos (1999); TW = Titman and Wei(1999); SS = Serletis and Sondergard (1996); G = Gallagher (1999); Y = Yadav, Pandayal and Pope (1999); C = Choudhry (1996); BT = Barkoulas and Travlos (1998); BH = Bekaert and Harvey (1997); PM = Poshakwale and Murinde (2001); H = Henry (1998).

Source: Surveyed literature.

sumption that stock returns for emerging markets are non-normally distributed; for example, Choudhry (2000). In addition, it is shown that some studies use autoregressive variables to control for infrequent or thin trading in ESMs; for example, Poshakwale and Murinde (2001). In terms of specific results, the studies summarized in Table 4.2 suggest that stock returns are non-normally distributed in both ESMs and their developed counterparts. For example, De Santis and İmrohoroglus (1997) find that in both developed and emerging markets the skewness and excess kurtosis statistics are not equal to zero. Moreover Bekaert and Harvey (1997) find that the skewness and excess kurtosis statistics in 20 ESMs are significantly different from zero. Further test results indicate that the null hypothesis of unconditional normality can be rejected at the 5 per cent level in 15 of the countries. These results are consistent with those obtained by Koutmos (1999), who rejects normality using Kolmogorov–Smirnov statistics at the 5 per cent level for Korea, Malaysia, Philippines, Singapore, Taiwan and Thailand, for the period 2 January 1986–1 December 1995. Further supporting evidence is obtained by Choudhry (1996) who finds excess kurtosis in the ESMs in Argentina, Greece, India, Mexico, Thailand and Zimbabwe for the period January 1976–August 1994. Similarly, De Santis and İmrohoroglus (1997) find significant skewness in the markets in Greece, Mexico and Thailand. Other recent papers, which reject the null hypothesis for normal distribution, include Fraser and Power (1997). Comparing emerging and developed stock markets using data for Hong Kong, Japan, Singapore, Malaysia and Australia for the period 1 January 1988–14 October 1994, Fraser and Power (1997) find that the skewness statistic is significantly different from zero for all sample countries except Australia, while the excess kurtosis statistic is significantly different from zero for all the markets.

Another important finding from the existing studies summarized in Table 4.2 is that volatility clustering seems to display the same characteristics in both developed and developing markets. In a comparative study covering 14 emerging markets (Greece, Turkey, India, Korea, Malaysia, Philippines, Taiwan, Thailand, Argentina, Brazil, Chile, Colombia, Mexico and Venezuela) and four developed markets (Germany, Japan, UK and USA), De Santis and İmrohoroglus (1997) find a significant ARCH effect for all markets except Greece. The study uses the GARCH model and assumes GED for the conditional density function covering the period last week December 1988 to second week May 1996. Similarly, Fraser and Power (1997) find evidence of volatility clustering in the stock markets in Hong Kong, USA, Japan, Singapore and Malaysia for the period 1 January 1988–14 October 1994. These findings are consistent with those obtained by Choudhry (1996) for a group of emerging markets (Argentina, Greece, India, Mexico, Thailand and Zimbabwe). However, comparing the period before and after the October 1987 market crash, the results show no clustering for Zimbabwe for the period before the crash and no clustering for India, Mexico and Thailand for the period after the crash.

It is also shown in Table 4.2 that both the developed and emerging markets show asymmetry response to shocks, but with varying signs. Koutmos (1999) finds that on average the positive returns are more persistent than negative returns with an average of 1.4 degree of asymmetry for the conditional mean. Asymmetric tests for conditional volatility indicate a negative and significant coefficient for the sample of emerging markets except Philippines, implying that negative innovations increase volatility more than positive innovation. The degree of asymmetry was highest for Singapore and lowest for Philippines. On average a negative innovation increased volatility 1.5 times more than the positive innovation of equal sign. Like Koutmos (1999), Fraser and Power (1997) find a negative and significant asymmetric response for the Singapore market. However, all other markets (Japan, Malaysia, Hong Kong, Australia, UK and USA) show evidence of positive asymmetric response; for example, UK, Japan and Malaysia have positive and significant asymmetric response but USA, Hong Kong and Australia have positive and insignificant response.

Some other studies listed in Table 4.2 find evidence that the time varying premium is priced in ESMs. For example, Fraser and Power (1997) find a significantly negative coefficient for investors in the Malaysian market, which is interpreted to imply that investors in Malaysia are predominantly risk lovers. However, Choudhry (1996), using a GARCH-M model, finds no time varying risk premium in six emerging markets, while Poshakwale and Murinde (2001) also find an insignificant time varying premium for Hungary and Poland. The studies also show interesting findings relating to volatility spillover effects. Song *et al.* (1998) use GARCH models to analyse the relationship between returns and volatility and find that volatility transmission exists between the Shanghai and Shenzhen Stock Exchanges in China. Similarly Booth *et al.* (1997) use a GARCH model to investigate the impact of good news (market advances) and bad news (market retreats), and find evidence of price and volatility spillovers among the Danish, Norwegian, Swedish and Finnish stock markets.

Overall, therefore, the studies summarized in Table 4.2 suggest that stock returns in both emerging and developed stock markets can be characterized by a martingale process. The evidence further suggests that volatility clustering can be attributed to various factors including trade volumes, nominal interest rates, dividend yield, money supply and other external shocks, including oil prices. In addition, volatility persistency is found in all markets, implying that volatility exerts pressure on stock prices. However there are differences across the markets regarding the asymmetric response and price of a time varying premium. The chaos process is not confirmed in all markets, implying that stock returns are stochastic processes. It is noted also that differences in stages of market development do not affect the characteristics of stock return volatility. Thus, in conclusion, the studies suggest three main findings in ESMs: first, volatility transmission is asymmetric; second, spillovers are more pronounced for bad than good news; third, significant price and volatility spillovers exist but are few in number.

Behavioural Finance versus EMH

Almost all the literature on stock market efficiency is influenced by Fama's classification of EMH into weak-form efficiency, semi-strong efficiency and strong-form efficiency (Fama, 1970, 1991). However behavioural finance offers an alternative paradigm to the EMH. Specifically, behavioural finance has questioned the second argument of market efficiency, namely that stock prices are rational because they reflect only fundamental or utilitarian characteristics such as risk but not psychological or value-expressive characteristics such as sentiment (Statman, 1999). It is argued that investor choices and asset values are influenced by value-expressive characteristics such as overconfidence (Daniel and Titman, 1999). Evidence to support the behavioural finance critique is cited from the anomalies literature and the studies on stock market overreaction and underreaction; it is argued that cognitive bias could produce predictable mispricing of stocks because investors make systematic mistakes in the way they process information (see Thaler, 1999; Daniel and Titman, 1999). However researchers who support the EMH and related asset pricing models have responded by emphasizing the futility of behavioural finance because it offers neither a new methodology nor a new paradigm (Frankfurter and McGoun, 2001, 2002). A truce, suggested by Statman (1999), is that the discipline of finance would do well by taking a compromise position, to accept that investors cannot systematically beat the market (consistent with the EMH) and that value-expressive characteristics matter in both investor choices and asset prices (as argued by behavioural finance). The benefits would be that asset pricing models would reflect both value-expressive and utilitarian characteristics, suggested by behavioural finance and the EMH, respectively. One possible implication for future research on ESMs is to explore plausible ways of reworking standard asset pricing models to allow for behavioural finance assumptions of cognitive bias rather than rational prices, in the context of Statman (1999).

3. KEY MICROSTRUCTURE ISSUES

Introduction

Stock market microstructure refers to the institutional framework that defines the return-generating process. While the EMH analyses the characteristic behaviour of stock prices, the microstructure literature focuses on the institutional aspects that encompass the price discovery process and the trading mechanism (Madhavan, 1992).

Trading mechanisms differ in terms of their microstructure attributes (cost of trading, liquidity, volatility and efficiency) and partly show a trade-off in achieving a desired adequacy level. A trading mechanism that enhances efficiency in the price discovery process and provides liquidity at low costs and with no excess volatility is preferred by Bessembinder and Kaufman (1997) and Amihud *et al.* (1990). Below we examine the trading mechanism, including market making and trading systems, in relation to the price discovery process.

Market Making

For some ESMs, part-time agents facilitate initial trading. However, in more developed stock markets, professional securities dealers provide their services as agents of the investors. As part of the revitalization of ESMs, some markets have allowed stockbrokers to act as both agents and principals. In Table 4.3 we show that most ESMs use the services of the stockbrokers while developed markets are characterized by the presence of specialists or dealers who act as principals. It is argued that the presence of professional security traders reduces the length of time required to complete a transaction for non-synchronized buy and sell orders, increase trading frequency and reduce liquidity risk (see Huang and Stoll, 1996). However these services are provided at a cost to the investors. For example, in managing orders, stockbrokers earn income in the form of a commission charged to the customers. The value of the commission depends on the price of the share and is independent of whether or not the executed order is a market or limit order. Stockbrokers are strictly agents of investors and do not assume any risk. Dealers assume risk and derive their earnings from the difference between the sale (ask) and purchase (bid) price, the bid–ask spread (BAS).

The literature attributes the existence of explicit bid–ask spread to costs of adverse selection, costs of holding inventory and costs of dealer services. Costs of adverse selection are justified by the coexistence of informed and uninformed traders in the market. An uninformed trader trades for liquidity and pays the market maker a price in exchange for provision of immediacy services, while an informed trader aims to maximize expected profits at the expense of the market maker. As a result, the market maker charges both traders a spread to compensate for losses from trading with an informed trader. While Madhavan (1992) and Aitken *et al.* (1998) support this argument, Laffont and Maskin (1990) demonstrate that information-based trading need not result in a bid–ask spread. Depending on market conditions and price volatility, informed traders could choose to adopt a pooling or separating trading strategy. An informed trader strategically chooses the amount of information that will be conveyed by prices. In a perfect Bayesian equilibrium, large traders induce a pooling equilibrium, thereby concealing private information rather than revealing it through the selection of prices. In addition, Cornell and Sirri (1992) note that insider trading distorts share prices because insiders incorporate a large fraction of their information into share prices before the information is made public. Effectively, therefore, inside trading serves to reduce information asymmetry and the bid–ask spread.

In support of the adverse selection theory, Leach and Madhavan (1993) conclude that specialists widen the spread better to filter information from their traders as this is more likely to drive away noise traders than informed traders. In addition, Pagano and Röell (1996) find a negative relationship between the spread and transparency and conclude that BAS has an information asymmetry component. It is noted that transparency reduces information asymmetry and narrows the spread. Furthermore Huang and Stoll (1996) report empirical results which show the presence of a large order-processing component, reflecting adverse selection problems.

Inventory theory assumes a desired inventory level for the market makers, which is set at zero with a constant spread that is shifted up and down on a price scale to equalize the probability of receiving a purchase order and a sale order. Thus the level of inventory is portrayed as a simple random walk process with probability of one that it will reach either its upper or lower bound in a finite number of trades. Market makers optimize the bid and ask prices by shifting them downward (upward), decreasing (increasing) the width of the spread when a positive (negative) inventory has been accumulated. Flood (1991) uses a simple inventory control model to illustrate how market makers adjust the quotes. The model assumes no private information, a single monopolistic dealer who sets the quoted bid and ask prices, and a control variable, which is linear. Quotes are defined as:

$$q_t = v_t + \beta[I_t - I^*], \tag{4.3}$$

where I_t = level of inventory after the tth trade; I^* = desired inventory level, and q_t = half quote set at time t defined as $(q_t^a + q_t^b)/2$; where q_t^a is the ask quote and q_t^b the bid quote; v_t = market-clearing price where, if $q_t = v_t$, the incoming demand is zero. When the current inventory is above (below) the desired level quotes will be set low (high) to elicit a surplus (deficit) of buy orders oversell orders. Quote adjustments are defined by

$$r_t = q_t - q_{t-1} = v_t - v_{t-1} - \beta[I_t - I_{t-1}] = \mu_t + \beta z_t \qquad (4.4)$$

where μ_t = change in quote with the new information observed by the market maker on the order flows; z_t represents the net demands faced by the market makers, comprising the informed and liquidity traders. Quote revisions are influenced by a change in inventory level and a change in the fundamental value with additional information. Dealers adopt a price-inventory adjustment policy, which renders the inventory level a stationary stochastic process. Inventory control prevents large positive or negative inventory positions while stationarity allows control policy to be consistent and stable. Consequently trades have a non-persistent impact on quotes.

Although specialists' inventories are found to be stationary, Madhavan and Smidt (1993) observe that inventory imbalances are reversed over a number of trading days. Depending on the competitiveness of the dealers market, market makers require more than a single trading day to control inventory through prices. As a dealer, the specialist quotes prices that induce mean reversion towards a target inventory level while, as an investor, the specialist chooses a desired long-term inventory based on portfolio considerations and may periodically revise this target. However the obligation to maintain a fair and orderly market prevents a specialist from executing orders on only one side of the spread, constraining his ability to manage inventories using prices in the short run. In a competitive market, however, market makers can set bid and ask quotes to attract trades on only one side of the spread, limiting their exposure to trades that would aggravate unwanted inventory position and enhancing their ability to control inventory through prices.

BAS also includes a charge by market makers for being in the market and for handling the transaction. In general, the cost of dealer service includes order-processing costs, direct costs of servicing the uninformed traders and the oligopoly profit. De Jong *etal.* (1995) observe that order-processing costs are important determinants of the bid–ask spread, using London's SEAQ International and Paris Bourse data. Furthermore, it is shown that the risk preferences of the market maker play a major role in defining the width of the spread, while a risk-averse market maker has a smaller spread compared to a risk-neutral specialist, attributable to market order and inventory value uncertainty.

Trading Systems

As part of the current revitalization of ESMs, there is a growing shift in the trading systems from periodic coffeehouse trading forums, call auction floor trading, screen trading and continuous auction trading system (CATS). For example, the Tel Aviv Stock Exchange gradually shifted from a call auction trading system to a continuous trading system (Amihud *et al.*, 1997). The main objective of this reform was to create an efficient and well functioning market for trading securities. Similarly the Taiwan Stock Exchange switched from semi-automated CATS to a fully automated security trading system; perhaps as a consequence of this reform, transaction frequencies were increased as the momentum of a continuous trading system picked up (Chang *et al.*, 1999; Lang and Lee, 1999). The interesting question is whether the reforms in the trading systems have directly led to improvements in the market microstructure of ESMs: more efficiency, more liquidity and reduced volatility.

Table 4.3 provides a summary of the main reforms in trading systems which have been adopted by both ESMs and developed markets. Trading systems can be classified according to the method of matching orders into periodic *vis-à-vis* continuous market, to reflect the frequency of market clearing (Amihud *et al.*, 1990; Pagano and Röell, 1996). With technological advancement of the trading cycle, markets could also be classified as automated or manual driven (Amihud *et al.*, 1997). Differences in trading systems may also exist in terms of the way transactions are handled, type of transactions made, type of information available to market participants and the process of matching orders to sell and buy (Glen, 1994; Spulber, 1996).

In a periodic market, dealers accumulate orders and then execute all market orders simultaneously at a specified trading time and at a common price, while in a continuous market orders are booked or executed when they arrive. Limit orders are accumulated if they do not get crossed or executed against an offsetting order during trading and if they do not become stale at the end of trading. Comparing the periodic and continuous markets, Madhavan (1992) observes that the call auction is more efficient than the continuous markets, given the ability of the former to enhance liquidity and reduce market volatility. In addition, Madhavan demonstrates that, while there is a possibility that trading may be interrupted if information asymmetry is very high in a continuous market, periodic auction trading continues to operate even when market makers choose not to make the market, allowing assimilation of new information. Furthermore Comerton-Forde (1999) notes that prices in a call auction system are efficient because a call auction imposes an effective mechanism for dealing with asymmetric information problems, where the imposed delays in execution of trades force traders to reveal information

Table 4.3 Summary of empirical findings on stock markets and type of trading system

Stock market	Periodic trading system	Type of market maker			Trading cycle type of technology		Types of continuous trading system	
		Stockbroker	Specialist dealer	Dealer market	Manual	Electronic	Order-driven	Quote-driven
Emerging markets								
Egypt	✓✓				✓		✓	
Ghana		✓				✓	✓	
Israel		✓				✓	✓	
Jakarta		✓				✓	✓	
Korea		✓				✓	✓	
Malaysia		✓				✓	✓	
Mauritius		✓				✓	✓	
Nairobi	✓	✓		✓				
Nigeria	✓	✓			✓		✓	
South Africa		✓				✓	✓	
Taiwan		✓				✓	✓	
Thailand		✓			✓		✓	
Zimbabwe		✓				✓	✓	
Developed stock markets								
Australia	✓	✓				✓	✓	
Canada						✓	✓	
France	✓	✓				✓	✓	
Hong Kong		✓				✓	✓	
Italy		✓				✓	✓	
Japan	✓					✓	✓	
Singapore	✓	✓				✓	✓	
UK (LSE)	✓	✓				✓	✓	✓
US (NASDAQ)				✓✓		✓		✓✓
US (NYSE)	✓		✓			✓	✓	

Source: Based on literature surveyed by the authors.

through order placements. A call auction shows more market stability as the batching of orders over time eliminates price fluctuations caused by transactions bouncing between bid and ask quotes and reduces price volatility induced by a random order arrival sequence. Furthermore, as the orders accumulate over a fixed time interval the impact of a single large order becomes less secure. However low volatility is achieved at the expense of price discontinuity, which makes the market illiquid (Madhavan, 1992).

Continuous trading systems are classified into quote-driven and order-driven markets (Madhavan, 1992; Pagano and Röell, 1996). In a continuous auction market (order-driven market) investors' orders are executed through an auction process one by one upon placement such that prices are determined multilaterally. In an electronic continuous auction system, agents submit orders to a centralized system, which displays the best limit orders and automatically executes incoming market orders against them. As trades are executed, the transaction prices and quantities are automatically displayed on-screen so that all market participants can trace the recent history of the order flow. In some markets there is a specialist who posts the bid and ask quotes. In a continuous dealership market (quote-driven market) investors trade immediately with a market maker so that each order is satisfied separately by a single dealer who does not know the orders received by other dealers until they are reported to the central authority and displayed on the screen. Market makers display prices at which they are willing to buy and sell up to a specified size. In some markets there is limited exposure of public limit order.

The two continuous trading systems are differentiated by performance indicators including execution risk, execution costs, flexibility and transparency. Execution risk is measured by the amount of information available at the time of price formation and the probabilities of gathering information from the orders. Pagano and Röell (1996) observe that continuous auction markets have a positive execution risk as transaction prices generally depend on the random order flow coming from other traders. However a dealership market offers implicit insurance to agents who are averse to execution risk, reducing the riskiness of the transaction price; traders pay the bid–ask spread while the setting of price quotes in advance insulates traders from adverse price shocks arising from order flow imbalances.

Considering execution costs, Madhavan (1992) and Pagano and Röell (1996) observe that a dealership market has a higher execution cost than a continuous auction market as market makers face higher information asymmetry with limited information about recent trading history, which forces them to set wider spreads. Consequently, for any order flow placed by one potential informed trader and one potential uninformed liquidity trader, the continuous auction market is on average cheaper for liquidity traders than a dealership market.

Dealership markets are also preferred because they allow flexibility in handling different types of securities and different types of customers. Large trades are negotiated via personal contact so that there is scope to gather information and distinguish between informed and noise traders. This allows dealers to offer better prices to uninformed traders. However, for the continuous auction markets especially, it is impossible to weed out potential insider traders.

The markets can also be classified on the basis of their relative transparency (Pagano and Röell, 1996). Transparency is measured by the degree to which the size and direction of the current order flow are visible to the competing market makers involved in setting prices. While pre-trade transparency allows market professionals to infer their competitors' order flow from their pricing behaviour, post-trade transparency provides explicit information about recent trades. Continuous auction markets are indicated as more pre- and post-trade transparent, given that dealers display firm quotes, which give a vague indication of the real transaction prices. Furthermore, after negotiation, the dealer takes time to report to the Exchange and publish the information on the screen, reducing the public visibility of the recent trading history. In a transparent market, the price setters know about the order flow and are able to protect themselves against losses to insiders, narrowing the spread. As observed by Flood *et al.* (1999) using an experimental study, there is a trade-off between liquidity and price efficiency. In markets where all quotes are disclosed publicly, the opening spread is smaller and the volume of trading higher, but not efficient. However there is no evidence on the effect of pre-trade transparency on the spread.

Overall, while the majority of ESMs have periodic auction systems, most developed markets have adopted continuous trading systems as well as the call auction. Most of the reforms are aimed at encouraging investors to enter the market at a time of uncertainty by enhancing price discovery, increasing liquidity and reducing volatility. Given that the order book is open, investors are able to obtain indicative prices prior to actual trading, which helps to reduce the uncertainty caused by the overnight non-trading period. An order-driven trading system is more popular than a quote-driven market because of low information asymmetry associated with the former.

Empirical Evidence on Characteristics of Trading Systems

The performance of trading systems can be evaluated using several microstructure attributes, namely cost of trading, market depth, price efficiency, price volatility and market robustness (see Madhavan, 1992; Glen, 1994). Table 4.4 summarizes the main findings from selected comparative studies across the different trading systems in ESMs.

Table 4.4 Summary results of studies comparing markets with different trading systems

Microstructure variable	Definition of variable	Comparing shifts from call (CA) to continuous (CO) in the same market		Comparing order-driven and quote-driven markets	
		Taiwan stock exchange	Tel Aviv stock exchange	NASDAQ (NQ) vs NYSE (NY)	Paris Bourse (PB) and LSE (SEAQ)
Microstructural costs	Implicit costs of immediacy				
	Market model	CA < CO (Chang et al., 1999)			
		CA = CO (Lang and Lee, 1999)			
	Quoted spread			NQ > NY; (Bessimbinder and Kaufman, 1997)	PB < SEAQ; (Röell, 1992)
	Effective spread			NQ > NY; (Huang and Stoll, 1996); NQ < NY (Bessimbinder and Kaufman, 1997)	PB < SEAQ; (Röell, 1992)
	Realized spread			NQ > NY; (Bessimbinder and Kaufman, 1997)	Slow increase for large size (Röell, 1992)

Liquidity	Price impact of large order imbalances	CA > CO (Chang et al., 1999)
	Uses residuals derived from Schwert (1989) and proportionate change in volume traded	CA < CO (Lang and Lee, 1999)
		NQ > NY (Bessimbinder and Kaufman, 1997)
	Difference between period before and after for (a) the ratio of individual stock volume traded to total market volume; (b) the ratio of volume traded to absolute changes in prices (AMIVEST)	CA < CO (Amihud et al., 1997)
Volatility	Measured using 10 minutes returns	CA < CO (Chang et al., 1999)
	Measured using the Schwert (1989) metric	CA < CO (Lang and Lee, 1999)
	Standard deviation of closing prices	CA < CO (Amihud et al., 1997)
Efficiency	Event study method and relative return dispersion (RRD), which is mean value of the sum of squared error terms, estimated using a market model.	CA < CO (Amihud et al., 1997)

Source: Based on literature surveyed by the authors.

113

Cost of trading

Costs of trading for investors include the direct pecuniary costs composed of fixed costs (for example, taxes, stamp duties and commissions) and costs imposed by the market structure measured as the bid–ask spread. Indirect costs include the cost of acquiring and processing information about share values, companies, market movements and any other information, which may be relevant to the decision to buy and sell (see Green *et al.*, 2000).

As noted by Barclay *et al.* (1998) and Amihud *et al.* (1997), high costs of trading are undesirable because they lead to higher risk-adjusted returns where investors seeking to maximize their net returns demand compensation for investing in securities with high costs. Investors discount the value of these securities and increase the required rate of return. In addition, an increase in transaction costs causes a bias in investment decisions towards assets with a shorter pay-off-reducing average holding period (Green *et al.*, 2000; and Blukey and Harris, 1997). Thus high transaction costs reduce the incentive to trade and produce thinner markets, thus restraining the potential of the ESMs to mobilize the resources for investment.

The hypothesis that dealership markets have higher execution costs than the continuous auction markets owing to higher information asymmetry is tested by Huang and Stoll (1996). The study uses a sample of 175 NASDAQ (a competitive dealership market) firms and a paired sample of 175 NYSE (a specialist continuous auction market) firms for the period 1991. Execution cost is measured using a variety of bid–ask spread definitions.[3] The results show that execution costs are twice as large in NASDAQ as in NYSE. The lower frequency in price quote change is not attributed to higher inventory risk or to differences in realized spread. Overall results show that NASDAQ has a higher spread, but this is not attributed to adverse selection problems especially because the realized spread is lower in NYSE. In addition, higher quoted spreads are reported for the medium and smaller firms than for the large firms. Similarly the effective spread is higher in NASDAQ with substantial differences among the smaller and medium firms, but for the large firms the differences are not substantial; for both markets effective spread increases with declining firm size.

Further evidence on trading costs is obtained by De Jong *et al.* (1995) who compare a quote-driven market (London stock market, SEAQ) with an order-driven market (Paris Bourse) using data for the period 25 May to 25 July 1991. Average quoted spread in the Paris Bourse is estimated using the limit order book, while market maker quotes are used for the London Stock Exchange. It is found that the costs of immediate trading are lower in the continuous auction market especially for small transactions, while the effective and realized spread indicates that the few large transactions executed in the continuous auction market have a fairly low spread compared to those in the dealership market. Similarly, effective spread in the continuous auction market is flat in relation to trade size, while it declines with size in dealership market, failing to support the adverse selection and inventory control hypotheses that spread is an increasing function of size of transaction.

Analysis of microstructure costs in ESMs is very scanty. Bonser-Neal *et al.* (1999) analyse execution costs in the Jakarta Stock Exchange by estimating trading costs as earlier proposed by Chan and Lakonishok (1993). The Chan-Lakonishok method involves observing the open trade return as a measure of the initial impact of the trade, and then calculating the close trade return to check for any changes in the course of the day. The next step is to sum up the open trade and the close trade returns and compare the trade price with the volume-weighted average of all trade prices in that stock on the trade date. Bonser-Neal *et al.* (1999) find that, during the period of their study, when the trading system was operating on a manual order-based trading system, the estimated costs show that purchasers induced a 1.51 per cent average price for the open return, 0.31 per cent for the close trade and the cumulative open-to-close was 1.82 per cent. It is found that trading costs are lower for trades in large firms, the price impact of a trade was negatively related to firm size, and brokers with large execution costs tend to have large execution costs for sales. Trades initiated by foreigners have significantly greater execution costs. However execution costs are not significantly different from those estimated in developed stock markets even when the electronic trading cycle is used.

Liquidity

Liquidity in the ESMs can be defined as the ability to transact quickly without substantially moving prices (Glen, 1994). This definition captures a number of transactional properties of the market, namely tightness (the cost of turning around a position over a short period of time), depth (the size of an order flow innovation required to change prices by a given amount) and resiliency (the speed with which prices recover from a random uninformative shock). Market depth which measures the sensitivity of prices to order flow is influenced by the quality of information possessed by market makers such that the higher the information asymmetry the lower the market depth and, consequently, the lower the market liquidity (Madhavan, 1992). However it may be argued that, with a monopolistic market maker, liquidity is achievable even with extensive trading on private information. In addition, Cornell and Sirri (1992) explain that market liquidity increases with information asymmetry, as insiders are able to obtain superior execution for their trades relative to the contemporaneous liquidity traders, concluding that the presence of informed traders to the market does not necessarily reduce market liquidity.

In terms of the impact of structural reforms on market liquidity, Amihud *et al.* (1997) find liquidity gain and positive liquidity externalities when stocks are traded in a continuous auction session rather than the call auction, in the Tel Aviv Exchange market. Liquidity is proxied by the trading volume and the liquidity ratio. Trading volume is an increasing function of its liquidity, other things equal, while liquidity ratio measures the trading volume associated with a unit change in stock price. In a similar study, Chang *et al.* (1999) find no significant difference in liquidity between the call and continuous auction for the Taiwan Stock Exchange. Liquidity is measured as the ratio of trade volume to the sum of squared price changes, giving a measure of the volatility-adjusted trading volume (the quantity effect of liquidity). Thus a liquid market is characterized by a small impact on market prices by the execution of large orders. A high ratio implies that a large order can be executed with only a small price movement while a low ratio suggests the inability to absorb a large order without a large price movement. Liquidity is also measured as an implicit cost of market immediacy (the price effect of liquidity), by taking the ratio of long- to short-term return variances. This ratio is inversely related to the implicit costs of immediacy services. A smaller variance ratio reflects a noise market as it signifies greater friction in the market or market illiquidity. Results show consistently a greater variance ratio under call auction, implying more liquidity than the continuous market. But the results obtained by Lang and Lee (1999) from the Taiwan Stock Exchange show improved liquidity with a shift from the call auction to the continuous auction trading system. The study measures liquidity on the basis of the argument that unsystematic risk reflects on liquidity where price changes of high (low) liquid stock can(not) be easily predicted by the market model and the residuals of the market model are smaller (greater). The measure uses the squared residuals from the Schwert (1989) model and regresses the residuals on the percentage change of dollar volume to obtain a market-adjusted liquidity ratio. The results obtained indicate that liquidity improved more significantly for low turnover firms than for high turnover firms.

Volatility and trading systems

Volatility, which we discussed in section 2 in terms of the second moments of stock returns, is further explored here in the context of stock market reforms. Amihud *et al.* (1997) compare volatility for call auction and continuous auction trading systems in the Tel Aviv stock market. The results show reduced volatility as the market adopts a more continuous trading system. However Chang *et al.* (1999), using Taiwan stock market data, find lower volatility for the call auction system which is attributed to the fact that the call auction eliminates price fluctuation caused by transaction bouncing between bid and ask quotes and also price volatility induced by a random-order arrival sequence. These results are attributed to the dominance of individual investors who are not usually well informed and rational in their investment decision making and also to lack of transparency and adequate financial disclosure by the Taiwan Stock Exchange (TSE) listed companies. Similarly, Lang and Lee (1999) use the Schwert (1989) model to control for thin trading and find that high volatility is associated with continuous auction trading in the Taiwan stock market.

Trading systems and efficiency of the price discovery process
The efficiency of the price discovery process in ESMs can be described as the ability of the market to incorporate quickly and correctly new information into stock prices, thus allowing transaction prices to adjust to asset values. Lang and Lee (1999) attribute inefficiency in the price discovery process to various factors, including infrequent trading, market over- and underreaction, bid–ask bounce and the risk premium. These factors define the difference between the intrinsic value of security and the observed price including pricing error, which measures the deviations of the price actually observed in the market from efficient price. Amihud *et al.* (1990) observe that pricing errors are a product of imperfections in the structure of the market such as lack of perfect competitiveness and the existence of inventory control costs for the market makers. They use a simple price adjustment model to attribute the divergence of observed price of the security away from its intrinsic value to noise trading. It is noted that transitory liquidity needs of traders and investors and the errors in the analysis and interpretation of information induce noise trading. In addition, noise also reflects the price discovery process which defines the random arrival of buy and sell orders, the transitory state of dealers' inventory position and the price fluctuations between the bid and ask.

Madhavan (1992) observes that a large enough call auction provides more efficient prices than a continuous market because, as more traders participate in the auction, asymmetric information is reduced and prices tend to reflect the asset value. Analysing the impact of a newly introduced trading system in the Tel Aviv stock market, Amihud *et al.* (1997) find improved efficiency of the value discovery process with the new continuous auction trading system. Stock prices adjust faster to market information as noise in stock prices declines. In addition, Chang *et al.* (1999) find price discovery to be more efficient in a call auction than in a continuous auction for the Taiwan Stock Exchange, and suggest that continuous trading does not necessarily minimize pricing errors in the presence of uncertainty concerning the number of informed speculators.

Intra-day characteristics of microstructure factors
Some studies examine the intra-day characteristics of the microstructure attributes and find different patterns across the markets (see Table 4.5). Sev-

Table 4.5   Summary of results on intra-day characteristics of microstructure variables

Variable	Characteristic	Market
Spread	U-shaped	Hong Kong
	Decline in the course of the day	NYSE
Volatility	Open higher volatility than close	NASDAQ
	Hump-shaped	Italy
Depth	U-shaped	Hong Kong
Efficiency test using	Negative serial correlation at open	NYSE
autocorrelation	U-shaped	Hong Kong
	Positive serial correlation at open	Thailand

Source: Based on the literature surveyed by the authors.

eral factors explain the observed trends, including the presence of specialists, costs of adverse selection, the type of trading mechanism and the halt of trade effect. For example, Brock and Kleidon (1992) observe that specialists possess a monopoly power that they use to exploit the inelastic demand of investors to trade around the open and close by widening the bid–ask quotes. Furthermore Madhavan (1992) attributes the wide spread at open to high information asymmetry, which consequently reduces as the trading day advances. It is also observed that liquidity traders concentrate their trading on specific periods to minimize the adverse selection costs facing specialists resulting in simultaneous occurrence of heavy trading volume and narrowing of spreads at specific times during the day. The halt of trade effect is seen in the large amount of unprocessed information that accumulates overnight (Amihud *et al.*, 1990). In this section we review the intra-day characteristics of the microstructure attributes.

In terms of volatility, both emerging and developed stock markets report higher volatility for the open-to-open returns, which is attributed to the opening procedures and the halt of trade effect. For example, Shastri *et al.* (1995) analyse the intra-day volatility pattern of the Thailand Stock Exchange using the ratio of variance at open to close and find higher variance at the open, which is attributed to differences in the trading mechanism. In addition, Chang *et al.* (1995), analysing the intra-day volatility of the Jakarta Stock Exchange, find greater variance for open-to-open return, which they attribute to the halt of trade. However Comerton-Forde (1999), comparing the Australian stock market, which has a call auction pre-opening procedure, with the Jakarta Stock Exchange, which has no pre-opening procedures, finds that the Australian market has lower volatility and concludes that high volatility in the Jakarta stock market is attributable to the choice of opening procedure. Amihud *et al.* (1990) use Milan Stock Exchange data covering the period 2 January 1984 to 30 April 1987, and find that, when the call auction starts trading, volatility is higher than when it follows continuous auction. Volatility is lower with the last transaction, implying that continuous trading by the end of the trading day serves to correct errors or noise in prices set under call auction, so that the last price provides better information than the call price. In addition, Lam and Tong (1999) find hump-shaped volatility in both the morning and the afternoon sessions in the Hong Kong market and attribute the results to the differences in noise levels; the afternoon hump is lower than the morning session. It is noted that noise trading on asset prices is transient and, if traders cluster around a particular time, the noise level tends to be higher in that period and hence drives up the volatility. Informed traders use market depth as a camouflage while liquidity traders trade at the time when costs are low. Comparing the variance for the trading and non-trading sessions, the study finds a larger overnight variance compared to the midday break variance.

In terms of liquidity, heavy trading often characterizes the opening trade. For example, Comerton-Forde (1999) finds higher liquidity for the Australian stock market at the opening of the trading day. Similarly Ahn and Cheung (1999) find a U-shaped intra-day trade volume and an inverted U-shaped depth for the Hong Kong market and conclude that there is high liquidity in the mid-day and low liquidity at open and close of the trading day. This finding is consistent with the observation made by Lee *et al.* (1998) that the combination of wider (narrower) spread and smaller (greater) depth is sufficient to infer the decrease (increase) in liquidity. Spread is a measure of the price aspect of liquidity, while the depth measures the quantity aspect of liquidity. The study attributes the narrow depths and larger spread at the open and close to the limit order traders' strategy to avoid possible losses from trading with informed traders when the adverse selection problem is severe.

In terms of efficiency, the serial correlation approach shows mixed results across the markets. For example, Shastri *et al.* (1995) find positive serial correlation for both the open and the close, indicating that the adjustment coefficient is less than one, for the Thailand Stock Exchange. Serial correlation is larger for the close trading period, implying a low adjustment of transaction prices towards the security's value. This is consistent with the fact that the 10 per cent price limit is more binding on the closing prices than on the opening prices. Furthermore Lam and Tong (1999) find a U-shaped autocorrelation function for the Hong Kong market for both the morning and afternoon session. Highest autocorrelation is indicated for open-to-open return, which is attributed to trade clustering.

In terms of spread, the shape of the intra-day spread is found to be U-shaped or declining over the course of the day. However Madhavan (1992) proposes that market dealers should narrow spreads in early trading to attract an informed order flow so that information learned is exploited in subsequent trading. In an experimental study, Flood *et al.* (1999) illustrate that this is only possible in a competitive market where dealers widen their spreads after trading. For the NYSE market, Brock and Kleidon (1992) find a U-shaped intra-day spread which is attributed to the market power of the specialist. It is observed that, since a specialist can observe the order imbalances and has information on who is trading before deciding on the price of trade, he can set prices to earn monopoly profits, but such profits cannot be made during the rest of the day as the specialist must post bid and ask prices ex ante to incoming buy/sell orders. However Chan and Lakonishok (1993) find a narrowing inside spread near the close of the trading day using a data set of transactions made by 37 large money management firms covering the period July 1986 to end 1988. These results are consistent with the individual dealers' attempt to obtain optimal inventory position prior to the close by posting more competitive bid or ask quotes to divert order flow from other market makers. The results are also attributed to the fact that, initially, dealers avoid committing large trades, but, as the day progresses, they become more confident about the equilibrium values.

Calendar regularities

Research on stock markets in developed countries has accumulated evidence on the existence of calendar regularities in stock returns. The regularities are attributed to information arrival, information accumulation and settlement procedures. The hypothesis tested with respect to calendar regularities is that the process of return generation is continuous; the alternative hypothesis is that returns are generated only during the active trading periods; in this context, the EMH does not hold.

A common calendar regularity is the day-of–the week effect, where stock returns are lower over the periods Friday's close and Monday's close. The turn-of-the month effect shows returns are higher in January compared to other months, while holiday effects show returns are higher on trading days immediately prior to holidays. Arsad and Coutts (1997), however, note that these regularities are dying off in the US market. This is not the case in emerging markets, however. Wong *et al.* (1992) find a day-of-the-week effect for Singapore, Malaysia, Hong Kong, Thailand and Taiwan. Clare *et al.* (1998), using daily data from 3 January 1983–23 July 1993 for the Kuala Lumpur Stock Exchange composite index, find a marginally significant Monday effect and significant positive Wednesday and Thursday effects. They attribute the results to pre-1990 settlement procedures on the KLSE. However the results for the Singapore market, obtained by Tan and Tat (1998) using data for the period January 1975–December 1994, show weak calendar regularities for the periods 1975–84 and 1985–94.

Conclusion

Overall, therefore, the literature suggests that differences exist regarding the impact of changes in trading systems on stock market microstructure. We find that most changes in trading systems in emerging and developed markets have been evolutionary. For example, the shift to a continuous trading system in developed markets is generated by the growing size of trading volumes. However, in emerging markets, the shift to a continuous trading system is externally driven by the wave of revitalization. We also find that there is marked preference for trading systems that enhance efficiency and provide liquidity at low costs and with no excess volatility. Some markets aim to maximize the positive aspects of different trading systems.

4. STOCK MARKETS AND MACROECONOMIC POLICIES

Introduction

The relationship between the stock market and macroeconomic variables is perhaps the most actively researched topic within the theme of stock market development. It is interesting to note that most developing economies are revitalizing their stock markets at the same time as the countries implement financial liberalization policy programmes, including interest rate and exchange rate liberalization.

The Relationship between the Stock Market and Macroeconomic Policy Variables: the Theory

The existing literature suggests that several theoretical frameworks have been used to study the relationship between stock market behaviour and macroeconomic variables. First, some studies use equilibrium asset pricing models, such as the arbitrage pricing theory (APT), to study the relationship between stock returns and economic risk factors. Second, other studies use the discounted cash flow valuation model. Third, some researchers embed stock market behaviour within a broad macroeconomic framework; for example, in the context of a modified IS–LM framework or a simple *AK* model. In what follows, we discuss these models.

Equilibrium asset models

The most widely used equilibrium asset model is the APT model developed by Ross (1976). The model postulates that stock returns are defined by systematic risk, which encompasses economic policy variables; individual stock returns are assumed to respond differently to these variables. However the model does not spell out these variables. It assumes that stock returns can be decomposed into expected returns and unexpected returns, while the latter can be further decomposed into systematic and unsystematic news (see Roma and Schlitzer, 1996).

$$r_i = E(r_i) + \beta_{1i} f_1 + \ldots + \beta_{ki} f_k + \mu_i, \tag{4.5}$$

where $f_i = (F_i - E(F_i))$; f_i is the systematic risk; F_i is the economic factor; E is the expected value operator; μ_i is the unsystematic risk.

Given that the model does not explicitly identify the variables to include in estimation, empirical analysis involves identifying the risk factors using factor analysis or principal component technique (see, for example, Oyama, 1997). Factor analysis technique statistically extracts the components accounting for the variance–covariance structure from a set of variables. The analysis computes an index that explains the maximum amount of variation in the variance–covariance matrix of security returns and then searches for the index constrained to be orthogonal, that explains the unexplained portion of the variance–covariance matrix.[4]

To capture the contributions of macroeconomic risks to variations in expected return two methods are used: the two step procedure and the simultaneous estimation. The two-step procedure follows Fama and MacBeth (1973) where returns and betas are estimated from two different periods to correct for possible bias introduced by use of portfolio betas instead of single security betas. The process involves regressing the estimated returns on stocks in one period cross-section on the estimated betas in the preceding period in a portfolio setting. The simultaneous approach follows the work of McElroy and Burmeister (1988) and measures the factor coefficients for the common factors and then checks whether the common factors are priced. The model estimated takes the form

$$r_i = \lambda_0 + \sum_{j=1}^{k} b_{ij} \lambda_j + \sum_{j=1}^{k} b_{ij} f_j + \varepsilon. \tag{4.6}$$

Most of the existing studies tend to estimate this type of model using the iterated nonlinear seemingly unrelated regression estimation (Roma and Schlitzer, 1996). Extensions of the standard APT model include the specification of multifactor equilibrium asset models to derive a relationship among stock returns, exchange rate risk and interest rate risk (see Thorbecke, 1997). Similarly, Chen *et al.* (1986) use the valuation model to identify economic variables but borrow form the APT model to measure the risk factors.

Share valuation models

The share valuation model expresses stock prices as the present value of a stream of expected dividends. This model is used to identify possible macroeconomic factors that influence stock prices. For example, Chen *et al.* (1986), Roma and Schlitzer (1996) and Oyama (1997) use the valuation model to predict the main macroeconomic determinants of stock prices. It is hypothesized that stock prices are influenced by the spread between long-term and short-term interest rate (as a leading indicator of economic activities), expected and unexpected inflation (a test for the Fisher hypothesis and proxy for risk factor), industrial production (a proxy for corporate earnings) and the spread between the high- and low-grade bonds.

The discounted model shows that changes in stock prices can be explained by changes in expected dividend and change in the discount factor. In turn, unexpected movements in both real and nominal forces like expected level of real production, changes in expected inflation and changes in nominal interest rates influence changes in expected dividend. The discount factor is influenced by factors defining the long-term rate such as inflation, economic growth and the term premium. Dividend growth rate is defined by such factors as inflation and rate of economic growth. The model therefore indicates an indirect link between stock returns and economic variables through stock return fundamentals. However Oyama (1997) makes different assumptions to identify factors influencing stock returns in a share valuation model. The model assumes that the required rate of return, expected growth rate of dividends per share and dividend payout ratio depend on new investments initiated by retained earnings such that expected growth of dividend per share is defined as a product of retained earnings and the rate of growth on new investment. Furthermore the model assumes that firms rely fully on retained earnings to finance investment and that inflation pushes up corporate earning. Taking an expression for stock prices, the model defines stock prices as function of the investment financing strategy, real interest rates, risk premium for stock investment and the profitability of the firm.

Similarly, Feldstein (1980) uses the share valuation model and explicitly defines the net earnings received by the shareholders. Unlike Oyama (1997), where a proportion of the total earnings is distributed as dividend while the rest is used to finance investment, the model assumes all earnings are distributed as dividend. Total earnings are subjected to both corporate tax and personal income tax. The model assumes no corporate debt; it also assumes that inflation raises the effective tax rate on corporate source income. Furthermore it is assumed that equilibrium in the financial assets market is established when the demand price per share that individuals are willing to pay equates the net earnings per dollar of equity to net interest per dollar invested in government bonds.

Overall, therefore, the share valuation model justifies the use of a wide range of variables, which reflect economic activities, risk factors and corporate earnings. The model also justifies the use of predictable and unpredictable components of the economic variables.

Macroeconomic models

Macroeconomic models attempt to explain the direction of causality between the development of the stock market and the macroeconomic environment. Some of the models find no relationship (for example, Blanchard, 1981; Gavin, 1989), while other studies find ambiguous relationship (for example, Pagano, 1993) and yet studies find a significant relationship is indicated from stock market development to economic growth (for example, Atje and Jovanovic, 1993).

Blanchard (1981) and Gavin (1989) model the stock market value using an IS–LM framework. In the goods market it is assumed that total spending is influenced by the stock market value, current income, fiscal policy and the real exchange rate. It is assumed that the stock market value has a wealth effect and therefore influences consumption and determines the value of capital relative to its replacement costs. In the asset market, the model assumes no arbitrage between short-term bonds and shares such that share value is equated to return on bonds. The model is then analysed for anticipated and unanticipated changes in monetary and fiscal policy assuming fixed and flexible prices. The analysis indicates no direct relationship between the stock prices and output, but instead shows a simultaneous response of the two variables to policy change. It is also observed that, in this framework, the EMH hypothesis cannot be rejected as the models are driven by equilibrium in asset and goods markets. It is also demonstrated that a stable set of underlying fiscal policies play an important role in reducing volatility of real exchange rate and equity prices. Temporary changes in fiscal policies result in changes in the real exchange rate and equity prices in the same direction, while permanent changes cause changes in the opposite direction.

A simplified theoretical framework is offered by some related models, which analyse the relationship between the financial sector and economic development. For example, Pagano (1993) and Murinde (1996) use a simple (AK) endogenous growth model, defined as

$$Y_t = AK_t, \tag{4.7}$$

where Y is the aggregate output; A is the social marginal productivity of capital; K is the aggregate capital stock. The model assumes stationary population growth, and production of one good that is used either for consumption or for investment. Gross investment is defined in terms of incremental capital stock as $I_t = K_{t+1} - (1 - \sigma)K_t$, where K_t is physical and human capital; s is the depreciation rate. The model assumes a closed economy with no government, but with costs of intermediation such that capital market equilibrium is achieved when gross savings (excluding transaction costs) equal gross investment. By defining growth at $(t+1)$ as $g_{t+1} = ((y_{t+1})/(y_{t-1})) = ((k_{t+1})/(k_{t-1}))$, a steady state is defined as

$$g = A \frac{1}{y} - \sigma = A\phi S - \sigma. \qquad (4.8)$$

From this model, it is hypothesized that financial development will affect economic growth through savings rate (s), proportion of savings channelled for investment (ϕ), and the social marginal productivity of investment (A). Defining ($1-\phi$) as the commission and fees that are charged by securities, brokers and dealers, the model suggests the need to reduce transaction costs. However Pagano (1993) points out that the relationship between stock market development and economic growth could be ambiguous, depending on the channel of interaction.

An extension of the basic AK model is offered by Atje and Jovanovic (1993) by incorporating insights from Mankiw *et al.* (1992). The model assumes technology and population growth are exogenously determined. It predicts that the stock market will enhance economic growth because it increases the amount of savings used for investment.

In general, therefore, several theoretical frameworks have been used to study the relationship between stock market behaviour and macroeconomic variables. First, some studies use equilibrium asset pricing models, such as the APT, to study the relationship between stock returns and economic risk factors (see, for example, Ross, 1976; Kim and Wu, 1987; Jorion, 1990; Roma and Schlitzer, 1996; Flannery *et al.*, 1997; and Oyama, 1997). In these studies, the risk and return behaviour in stock markets is influenced by macroeconomic factors in such a way as to reflect the key aspects of market efficiency. As earlier noted, the EMH predicts that only when the stock market operates efficiently is it in a position to play its role effectively. Second, other studies use the discounted cash flow valuation model, which indicates an indirect relationship through the impact of these variables on expected future cash flows and discount factor. See, for example, Miller and Modigliani, 1961; Chen *et al.*, 1986; Roma and Schlitzer, 1996; and Oyama, 1997. Third, some researchers embed stock market behaviour within a broad macroeconomic framework. For example, Blanchard (1981) and Gavin (1989) use an IS–LM framework where the stock market is introduced as a factor influencing aggregate demand. In addition, Pagano (1993), Atje and Jovanovic (1993) and Murinde (1996) explore the relationship within the context of an endogenous growth model of the AK variety. These models also incorporate financial development theory by predicting a positive relationship between stock market development and economic growth, mainly because the stock market mobilizes long-term finance and facilitates efficient allocation of resources. See Caprio and Demirgüç-Kunt (1998), Boyd and Smith (1997) and Levine and Zervos (1996).

Evidence on the Relationship between the Stock Market and Macroeconomic Policy Variables

Although the theoretical work falls neatly into three main types of model, the empirical literature has tended to be piecemeal by focusing on the relationship between the stock market and some key macroeconomic policy variables, such as monetary policy. Hence, below, we review the empirical work in a piecemeal manner.

Monetary policy and stock prices

The relationship between monetary policy and stock prices can be explained by the monetary portfolio hypothesis, which predicts that change in the money supply results in change in the equilibrium position of money, in relation to other assets in the portfolio. Investors respond by adjusting the proportion of the asset portfolio held in money balances. However, because all money balances must be held, the system does not adjust until changes in the prices of various assets lead to a new equilibrium. See, for example, Dhakal *et al.* (1993). The relationship can also be explained through the credit channel. For example, Thorbecke (1997) observes that monetary policy affects stock returns by influencing the credit position and investment level of the firm. Tight monetary policy increases interest rates, worsening the cash flow net of interest and therefore the balance sheet position of the firm. As a result, creditworthiness of the firm is reduced, creating a credit constraint and reducing investment. Consequently the firm's value goes down and stocks are no longer attractive. The impact is felt more by firms with low creditworthiness.

However, as summarized in Tables 4.6 and 4.7, most empirical studies tend to investigate the impact of monetary policy on stock prices by specifying a simple equation consisting of the stock price index as well as expected and unexpected changes in monetary policy variables. It appears that the empirical results on the relationship between monetary aggregates and stock prices are ambiguous regarding the direction of causality and significance of anticipated and unanticipated changes in monetary policy. In addition, the channel

Table 4.6 Summary of literature on the relationship between stock prices and monetary and fiscal policy

	Monetary policy				Fiscal policy			
	CE	AR	UAR	GC MP⇒SP	AR	UAR	GC FP⇒SP	GC External MP⇒SP
Australia								✓(C)
Canada					✓(D)	✓(D)		
Hong Kong								✓(C)
Japan								✓(C)
Singapore		✓(EM)	✓(EM)		✓(EM)	✓(EM)		✓(C)
US	✓(ML)	✓(ML)	✓(ML)	✓(ML; P)	✓(ML)	✓(ML)	a(ML)	

Note: CE = contemporaneous response; UAR= unanticipated response; GC = granger causality; EML = the external monetary policy; MP = monetary policy; FP = fiscal policy; fi indicates the direction of causality tested; ML = McMillin and Laumas (1988); EM = Evans and Murinde (1995); P = Patelis (1997); D = Darrat (1988); C = Cheung (1997).

Source: Based on literature surveyed by the authors.

Table 4.7   Summary of empirical results on the relationship between the stock prices and monetary aggregates

Stock market	Cointegration between monetary aggregates (M1 and M2) and the stock prices (SP)		Granger causality between the monetary aggregates (M1 and M2) and stock prices (SP)	
	M1	M2	M1	M2
Part I Emerging stock markets				
India			✖(C)	✖(C)
Korea			M1⇔SP (C)	✖(C)
Malaysia	✖(HB)	✖(HB)	✖(C)	✖(C)
Mexico			✖(C)	✖(C)
Taiwan			✖(C)	✖(C)
Thailand			✖(C)	M2⇔SP(C)
Part II Developed stock markets				
Belgium			✖(M); M1⇒SP(HT)	✖(M)
Canada			✖(M); M1⇒SP(HT);	M2⇔SP(M) ✓(L)
France			✖(M); M1⇒SP(HT);	✖(M) ✓(L)
Germany			✖(M); M1⇒SP(HT);	✖(M) ✓(L)
Italy			M1⇔SP(M); M1⇒SP(HT) ✓(L)	M2⇔SP(M)
Japan			M1⇔SP(M); M1⇒P(HT) ✓(L)	M2⇔SP(M)
Netherlands			✖(M); M1⇒SP(HT) ✓(L)	M2⇔SP(M)
Singapore	✓(MY)	✓(MY)	SP⇔M1(MY)	M2⇔SP(MY)
Switzerland			M1⇔SP(M); M1⇒SP(HT)	
UK			M1⇒SP(M, HT); ✓(L)	M2⇔SP(M)
USA	✖(S, DKS)		✖(M); M1⇒SP(HT); ✓(L)	

Note: For Granger causality, ⇒ implies a unidirectional causality; ⇔ implies bidirectional-causality; parentheses represents the author(s) of the research findings; M = Mookerjee (1987); HB =Habibullah and Baharumshah (1996); MY = Moorkerjee and Yu (1997); ML = McMillin and Laumas (1988); C = Cornelius (1991); DKS = Dhakal *et al.* (1993); S=Serletis (1993); L = Lastrapes (1998); HT = Hashemzadeh and Taylor (1988).

Response of stock prices to anticipated changes in monetary aggregates (M1 and M2)		Contemporaneous response of stock prices to monetary aggregates (M1 and M2)		Lagged response of stock prices to monetary aggregates (M1 and M2)	
M1	M2	M1	M2	M1	M2
✓(HB)	✓(HB)				
			✓(M)		
✓(MY)	✗(MY)				✓(M)
✓(LM)					✓(DKS)

Source: Based on literature surveyed by the author

of relationship is not clearly identified. For example, some studies show evidence of both unidirectional and bidirectional causality in both developed and emerging markets; see Table 4.8. While narrow money shows unidirectional and bidirectional causality, broad money mainly reflects bi-directional causality. Further, the unidirectional causality is from narrow money to stock prices. For example, Moorkerjee and Yu (1997) find bidirectional causality for the Singapore market with both M1 and M2 for the period October 1984–April 1993. In an earlier study Moorkerjee (1988) shows similar results for Italy and Japan. Cornelius (1991) finds bidirectional causality with M1 for Korea and with M2 for Thailand.

Analyses of long-run relationships also show mixed results. For example, the hypothesis for a long-run relationship between stock prices and monetary aggregates is rejected for the Malaysian market by Habibullah and Baharumshah (1996) using data for the period January 1978–September 1992. The results imply that the market is efficient as stock prices incorporate all information in money supply and output. Similarly Serletis (1993) finds no long-run relationship between money and stock prices, implying long-run neutrality of money where permanent changes in money supply have no effect on real variables, as they are fully absorbed by the price level in the long run. However Moorkerjee and Yu (1997) obtain evidence for Singapore which shows that stock prices and monetary aggregates (M1, M2 and aggregate foreign exchange reserves) are cointegrated, for the period October 1984–April 1993. In addition, regression results using the anticipated and unanticipated variables show that the current and lagged anticipated M1 significantly influence stock prices while M2 is insignificant in both anticipated and unanticipated forms. This is interpreted to imply that broad money does not have any useful policy information.

Hence the empirical studies on ESMs are ambiguous regarding the direction of causality and the significance of anticipated and unanticipated changes in monetary policy. Most results show unidirectional causality from monetary policy variables to stock prices; others show bidirectional influence while some studies support and others reject long-run effects. Further research is necessary to specify more precise models and apply innovative testing procedures to shed further light on the impact of monetary policy on the stock market.

Fiscal policy and stock market

The impact of fiscal policy on stock markets tends to occur through various channels. Brean (1996) notes that taxation and other government fees raise the new issue barriers by increasing the transaction costs for new listings in the stock market in South Africa. In addition, discriminatory tax policies on different financial assets render inefficient the mobilization of domestic savings through the securities market. Furthermore Amihud and Murgia (1997) show that higher tax on dividends is a necessary condition for dividends to signal company value. However Hubbard and Michaely (1997) find that tax reforms have a temporary effect which is attributed to clientele effects and differences in liquidity.

Specifically with respect to ESMs, it has been argued that the impact of taxation on the capital market depends on the stage of market development (Brean, 1996). In a well-developed market, asset pricing reflects factors that affect profitability and risk, including taxation. However, when the market is not well developed, effects of taxation that would otherwise be reflected in returns or costs of capital fail to be properly priced and allocative effects of taxation fail to work through the mechanisms that link savings to interest rates or investment to expected return on investment.

Even in the context of developed stock markets, the empirical evidence on the relationship between fiscal policy and stock prices is very scanty (see Table 4.7). McMillin and Laumas (1988) investigate the effects of anticipated and unanticipated monetary and fiscal policy actions for the US stock market, using the employment rate for all workers, the rate of change in the import price deflator and the change in real cyclically-adjusted surplus scaled by real middle expansion trend GNP. Anticipated and unanticipated values are computed using the Kalman filter routine and then a stock return model is fitted with both anticipated and unanticipated variables, testing for the contemporary effects and speed of adjustment. Results show that anticipated fiscal actions have significant contemporaneous and lagged effects. Unanticipated fiscal actions, however, have little initial impact. Similarly, Darrat (1988) finds that the Canadian market is inefficient with respect to fiscal policy. Specifically the results indicate that most of the lagged coefficients for both unanticipated and anticipated fiscal policy are statistically significant, implying that the Canadian stock market is inefficient with respect to available information on fiscal policy. Evans and Murinde (1995) document similar results for the Singapore stock markets; they use the bivariate autoregressive (BVAR) method and find that both unanticipated and anticipated monetary and fiscal policy influence the stock market.

In general, therefore, although the evidence on the relationship between fiscal policy and stock prices is very scanty, the few existing studies seem to suggest that the stock market is inefficient with respect to available information on fiscal policy. However these findings can only be regarded as inconclusive; further research is necessary. In addition, the existing studies do not shed much light on the argument that the impact of taxation on the capital market depends on the stage of market development; clearly further research is also necessary on this issue.

Exchange rates and stock prices
Studies which investigate the relationship between stock prices and exchange rates include micro work that uses firm-level data and macro work that uses aggregate data. Micro-level studies investigate the economic exposure by firms with significant foreign trading activities. Most of the studies in the developed markets concentrate on multinational firms (for example Jorion, 1990; Bodnar and Gentry, 1993). These studies, however, do not show significant evidence on the contemporaneous relationship between stock returns and exchange rates, as noted in Table 4.8.

Bodnar and Gentry (1993) also find an insignificant contemporaneous effect. The study categorized the industries into non-traded and traded good industries covering the US, Canadian and Japanese industries and uses the following model for analysis:[5]

$$[R_{it} - rf_t] = \beta_{0i} + \beta_{1i}[R_{mt} - rf_t] + \beta_{2i}PCXR_t + \varepsilon_{it}, \qquad (4.9)$$

where R_{it} is the return on industry portfolio i in month t; rf_t is the risk-free rate of return in month t; R_{mt} is the return to national stock market in month t; $PCXR_t$ measures the percentage change in the trade weighted nominal exchange rate in month t; β_{1i} is the industry's exposure to changes in the overall stock market index, while, β_{2i} measures the industry's exposure to exchange rate fluctuations. The model is estimated using the SURE method for the USA and Canada, and OLS for Japan. The results indicate that, for the three countries, 20–35 per cent of industries had significant foreign exchange exposure, with more exposure in Canada and Japan. Except for the USA, non-traded goods industries indicated a gain with appreciation of local currency. Industry export and import ratios are associated with negative and positive exposures, respectively. For the USA and Japan, foreign-dominated assets show a significant negative exposure to exchange rate changes.

The same issue is revisited by Bartov and Bodnar (1994), who argue that the ambiguous results from earlier studies may be attributed to methodological problems. One of the problems anticipated is the sample selection problem. It is argued that firms with foreign activities do not necessarily have significant economic exposure because firms with widespread foreign operations are likely to hedge potential exchange rate exposure at low cost. Similarly firms with inherently large exposure are more likely to undertake hedging activities so that the endogeneity of hedging makes the detection of significant exchange rate exposure difficult on the basis of simple sample selection. To solve the sampling problem the study selects a sample of firms showing a negative correlation between reported foreign currency adjustments and corresponding fluctuations in the exchange rate. The following model is estimated:

Table 4.8 Summary results on the relationship between stock prices and exchange rates

	Lagged response of SP to E	Contemporaneous response of SP to E	Unidirectional causality from E to SP	No relationship between exchange rate to stock prices	Unanticipated response of SP to E (contemporaneous)	Cointegration between exchange rate to stock prices
			Part I Emerging stock markets			
India			✓(AM)			
Korea			✓(AM)			
Pakistan			✓(AM)			
Philippines		✓(AM)	✓(AM)			
			Part II Developed stock markets			
Denmark	✗(A)	✗(A)				
Finland	✗(A)	✗(A)				
France	✗(A)	✗(A)				
Germany	✗(A)	✗(A)				
Hong Kong			✓(Q)			✓(Q)
Italy	✗(A)	✗(A)	✓(Q)			✓(Q)
Japan					✓(MY)	
Netherlands	✓(A)	✓(A)				
Norway						
Singapore				✓(Q)		✓(Q)
Sweden	✗(A)	✗(A)				
Switzerland	✗(A)	✗(A)				
UK		✓(UK), ✗(A)				
USA	✓(BBo)					

Note: A= Aggarwal (1981); BBo = Bartov and Bodnar (1994); Q = Qiao (1996); MY= Moorkerjee and Yu (1997); AM= Abdalla and Murinde(1997).

Source: Based on the literature surveyed by the authors.

133

$$ASP_{it} = \alpha_0 + \sum_{j=0}^{n} C_j \Delta CUR_{i,t-j} + \varepsilon_{it}, \qquad (4.10)$$

where ASP_{it} = abnormal stock performance for security i in period t (per cent); $\Delta CUR_{i,t-j}$ = percentage change in a trade-weighted US dollar exchange rate index for the period t to j; α_0, C_j = parameter to be estimated; and ε_{it} = error term for firm i in period t.

Similar to the results from the previous studies, a contemporaneous effect is not found, notwithstanding the rigorous econometric procedures used. However, when lagged variables are incorporated to take care of any mispricing, the expected negative results are obtained. These results are interpreted to indicate that freely available public information on past changes in exchange rates is useful in explaining abnormal future stock price performance. Investors were thus seen to underestimate the impact of exchange rate change in every period, which was corrected with availability of additional information.

However some macro studies show a negative relationship between stock prices and exchange rate. For example, Solnik (1987) estimates a multivariate regression (SURE) model on several countries by regressing the change in the real exchange rate (Ds_t) on real stock returns (DRS_t), as indicators of changes in economic activity, and the change in the interest rate differential (Di_t) as follows:

$$DRS_t = a + bDs_t + cDi_t + e_t. \qquad (4.11)$$

The results show a negative relationship, which implies that a real appreciation of the US dollar is bad for domestic firms because it reduces their competitiveness, while real exchange rate depreciation stimulates the economy in the short run. The results are consistent with those obtained by Ma and Kao (1990), who show a negative relationship between exchange rate and stock prices for the US market using a two-step regression procedure. Specifically it is found that, while currency appreciation reduces the competitiveness of export markets, it has a negative effect on the domestic stock market; high exchange rate levels are associated with favourable stock price movements.

However some of the earlier studies have been criticized for ignoring the feedback effects between exchange rate changes and changes in stock prices. For example, Bahmani-Oskooee and Sohrabian (1992) make this criticism and then proceed to estimate and test a BVAR model for cointegration and causality, allowing for feedback effects. The results show a bidirectional causality between stock prices measured by the Standard & Poor's 500 index and the effective exchange rate of the dollar, at least in the short run. The cointegration analysis, however, reveals a long-run relationship between the two variables. Similarly, Abdalla and Murinde (1997) examine the relationship between exchange rates and stock prices for ESMs (India, Korea, Pakistan and the Philippines) and show unidirectional causality from exchange rates to stock prices in all the sample countries except the Philippines. Taking a wider market scope, Johnson and Soenen (1998) analyse the stock price reactions of 11 Pacific Basin stock markets to exchange rate changes with respect to the US dollar and Japanese yen for the period January 1985–June 1995. A significantly strong positive relationship is indicated with the yen while weak and mixed results are reported with regard to the US dollar.

All in all, most of the empirical studies show a negative relationship between the exchange rate and stock prices, which implies that a real appreciation of the exchange rate is bad for domestic firms because it reduces their competitiveness, while real exchange rate depreciation stimulates the economy in the short run. However some studies have uncovered a positive relationship, while most of the studies on ESMs tend to show bidirectional causality and are therefore inconclusive.

The stock market and capital flows
Most emerging markets have relaxed capital controls as part of the revitalization process, and have subsequently seen an upsurge of capital inflows. Despite the expectation that the inflow of capital would increase the liquidity of local stock markets (Litman, 1994; Aitken, 1998), the experience of emerging markets indicates that boom was shortly followed by bust. Richards (1996), citing *The Economist* (13 May 1995, p. 71), attributes the experience to investment fund managers' panic in fear of mass redemption, while Aitken (1998) attributes the response to herd-like behaviour in investment decisions portrayed by foreign investors.

Some studies, notably by Kim and Singal (2000), have questioned the argument which favours foreign investors in ESMs. It is argued that opening up to foreign investors exposes the domestic market to external shocks and this could increase stock price volatility and consequently raise the cost of capital, as shareholders demand a higher risk premium. Most empirical results fail to show that foreign investors' participation in emerging markets was characterized by market volatility (see Table 4.9). For example, Richards (1996) and Kim and Singal (2000) find no evidence that volatility has increased; rather results indicate that it has fallen. In addition, Chan *et al.* (1998) find no evidence of rational speculative bubbles following the 1997 crises in Asian markets (Hong Kong, Japan, Korea, Malaysia, Thailand and Taiwan). Moreover Kim and Singal (2000) and Aitken (1998) report efficiency gains in some markets (see Table 4.9).

Table 4.9   *A comparison of results for the period 'before' and 'after' the entry of foreign investors*

Stock market	Kim and Singal (2000)			Aitkens (1998)	
	'Before' (1976–91)	'After' (1991–96)	Change in frequency of trading	'Before' (1989–91)	'After' (1991–95)
Argentina	U	U	+	P	P
Brazil	P	U	–	P	P
Chile	P	P	–	U	U
Colombia	P	P	+	P	U
Greece	U	U	+	U	P
India	P	U	+		
Indonesia				P	U
Jordan				p	P
Korea	U	U	+*		
Malaysia				P	P
Mexico	P	U	–	U	U
Pakistan	U	P	–	P	U
Philippines	P	U	+	U	P
Portugal				P	U
Taiwan	U	U	+*	P	P
Thailand				P	P
Turkey	U	U	+*	U	P
Venezuela	P	P	+*	U	P
Zimbabwe	P	U	+*		

Note: Both studies use the variance ratio test for efficiency but differ in time period covered, especially the 'before' period; U is unpredictable stock returns; P is predictable stock returns; + is an increase in trading frequency in the 'after' period; – is the decline in trading frequency in the 'after'; * is statistically significant change.

Source: Based on the literature surveyed by the authors.

Stock prices and inflation

Two main arguments are advanced in the literature on the relationship between stock prices and inflation. The first is that equity securities provide a hedge against unanticipated inflation, because they represent claims on real assets; hence this argument predicts a negative relationship between stock returns and inflation. The second is the well-known Fisher effect, where expected real asset returns are assumed to be independent of inflationary expectations and a positive relationship between stock returns and expected inflation is predicted. Substantial empirical results reject the Fisher hypothesis, indicating a negative relationship between stock returns and inflation.

Some studies have tried to investigate rigorously the hypothesized negative relationship between stock prices and inflation. For example, Cochran and Defina (1995) test the proxy hypothesis using S&P500 within an error correction model. The results failed to support the proxy hypothesis, although Wei and Wong (1992) found that, in the postwar period, there was a spurious negative relationship between stock returns and expected inflation in all industries, with the exception of non-natural resource industry. Hence, as observed by Hess and Lee (1999), the relationship between stock prices and inflation could be positive, negative or insignificant, depending on the factors (supply and demand) influencing inflation.

Stock markets and economic growth

The interaction between the stock market and real economic activities involves two clear hypotheses. The first is that the stock market contains information that is helpful in forecasting real economic activities. The second is that the stock market has an impact on aggregate demand, particularly through aggregate consumption and investment. Fama (1991) argues that the stock market is a single leading indicator of the business cycle. This is contrary to Harvey (1989), who finds that the stock market is not a predictor of economic activities, given that changes in stock prices could reflect expected changes in economic activities and also changes in the perceived riskiness of stock cash flows. Consequently investors' perception about riskiness of cash flows could confound the information about expected economic activities, giving a different signal. The evidence tends to support the hypothesis by Fama (1991) that negative returns have significant effects on the unemployment rate for the US market. The results are consistent with the findings by Aylward and Glen (2000), who examine the relationship between stock prices and other economic variables in 23 emerging and developed markets (Argentina, Australia, Brazil, Canada, Chile, Colombia, France, Germany, Greece, India, Israel, Italy, Japan, Korea, Mexico, Pakistan, Peru, Philippines, South Africa, Taiwan, UK, Venezuela and the USA), supporting this hypothesis (see Table 4.10).

However the contribution of the stock market in the development process does not give conclusive results. For example, Levine and Zervos (1996) find a significant positive relationship between stock market development and long-run economic growth using the following model:

$$\text{Growth} = \beta X + \lambda(stock) + \mu, \tag{4.12}$$

Table 4.10 Summary results on the relationship between stock market and the real sector variables

	Cointegration between stock prices and GDP	Testing the hypothesis that stock prices predict GDP	Testing the hypothesis that IIP predicts stock prices		Testing the hypothesis that stock prices predict consumption	Testing the hypothesis that consumption predicts stock prices		Testing the hypothesis that stock prices predict investment
			CE	LR		CE	LR	
Argentina	✓(AG)	✓(AG)			✓(AG)			✓(AG)
Brazil	✓(AG)	✓(AG)			✓(AG)			✗(AG)
Chile	✓(AG)	✓(AG)			✓(AG)			✓(AG)
Colombia	✓(AG)	✓(AG)			✗(AG)			✗(AG)
Greece	✓(AG)	✓(AG)			✗(AG)			✓(AG)
India	✗(AG)	✗(AG)		✓(CS)	✗(AG)			✓(AG)
Israel	✓(AG)	✓(AG)			✓(AG)			✓(AG)
Korea	✗(AG)	✗(AG)			✗(AG)			✗(AG)
Malaysia	✗(BB)							
Mexico	✗(AG)	✗(AG)			✗(AG)			✓(AG)
Pakistan	✗(AG)	✗(AG)			✗(AG)			✓(AG)
Peru	✓(AG)	✓(AG)			✓(AG)			✓(AG)
Philippines	✓(AG)	✓(AG)			✓(AG)			✓(AG)
South Africa	✗(AG)	✗(AG)			✓(AG)			✓(AG)
Taiwan	✓(AG)	✓(AG)			✓(AG)			✓(AG)
Venezuela	✗(AG)	✗(AG)			✗(AG)			✓(AG)

Australia	✗ (AG)			✓ (AG)
Canada	✓ (AG)			✓ (AG)
Finland	✓ (AG)	✗ (A)	✗ (A)	✗ (AG)
France	✓ (AG)	✗ (A)	✗ (A)	✓ (AG)
Germany	✓ (AG)	✓ (A)	✓ (AG)	✓ (AG)
Italy	✓ (AG)		✓ (AG)	✓ (AG)
Japan			✓ (A)	✓ (AG)
Netherlands			✓ (AG)	
Norway		✗ (A)	✗ (A)	
Sweden			✓ (AG)	
Switzerland			✓ (AG)	
UK	✓ (AG)	✗ (A)	✓ (AG)	✓ (AG)
USA	✓ (AG)	✓ (A)	✗ (AG)	✓ (AG)

Note: CE = contemporaneous effect; LR = lagged effect; AG = Aylward and Glen (2000); A = Aggarwal (1981); IIP = industrial output

Source: Based on the literature surveyed by the authors.

where growth is measured as real per capita growth rate averaged over the relevant period; X is a set of control variables including initial income (log of initial real per capita GDP), initial education (log of initial secondary school enrolment rate), a measure of political instability (number of revolutions and coups), ratio of government consumption expenditure to GDP, inflation rate and the black market exchange rate premium; *stock* is the index for growth of the stock market; b is a vector of coefficient on variable X; l is the estimated coefficient of stock market growth; m is an error term.

Similarly Poterba and Samwick (1995) find significant results by analysing the relationship between stock market development and economic growth from the consumption side. This approach is based on the argument that stock market changes have an impact on economic growth through their predictive effect and wealth effect. The predictive effect implies that stock prices rise in anticipation of strong economic activity, including consumer spending. To capture the wealth effects, the study examines whether stock returns forecast changes in consumption across different bundles. However little evidence of wealth effects on consumption is portrayed.

In addition, the relationship between the stock market and economic growth may work through savings, as noted by Bonser-Neal and Dewenter (1999). It is noted that the impact of the stock market on savings depends on its effect on the savings return, riskiness of savings and response of individuals to these changes in return and risk. However the effect of a change in the rate of return on savings is ambiguous owing to the substitution effect and income effect. A sample of 16 ESMs is used, covering the period 1982–93. For the analysis, the following model is fitted:

$$S_{tj} = \alpha + \beta z_{tj} + cSMD_{tj} + e_{tj}, \tag{4.13}$$

where S_{tj} = private gross savings; Z_{tj} = economic factors determining savings, real interest rate, real GDP growth, dependency ratio, per capita income, current account surplus and budget surplus; SMD_{tj} = stock market development: defined as the overall market size (the ratio of market capitalization to GDP), liquidity measure of the market relative to the size of the economy (the ratio of value traded to GDP) and the turnover ratio (the ratio of value traded to market capitalization). The findings show a significant positive relationship between gross private savings and stock market size and liquidity.

Hence the evidence supports the key argument that there is a positive relationship between stock market development and economic growth. What is not so clear-cut is whether the mechanisms that link the two operate through the first or second hypothesis, or both.

Stock markets and other sources of investment financing
It has been argued that there is a unique role for both the banking and equity markets in developing countries (Demirgüç-Kunt and Vojislav, 1996). The evidence uncovered by Demirgüç-Kunt and Vojislav is that the existence of an active stock market increases the debt capacity of firms; in this context, equity markets and financial intermediaries complement one another so that an active stock market results in increased volumes of business for financial intermediaries. In addition, it has been argued that the development of stock markets facilitates reforms in the banking sector (Murinde, 1996). It is noted that most problems in the banking sector stem from unbalanced capital structures in the company sector, especially where equity markets are non-existent (Dailami and Atkin, 1990). In this respect, the development of capital markets in emerging markets has great implications for banking reform.

Similar conclusions are reached by Demirgüç-Kunt and Vojislav (1996), who investigate the view that stock market development tends to reduce the volume of bank business. It is found that stock markets serve an important role, as debt and equity are not substitutes. Furthermore it is shown that initial improvements in the functioning of a developing stock market produce a higher debt–equity ratio for firms making more business for banks.

In conclusion, the literature is persuasive enough about the existence of strong interaction between the stock market and macroeconomic variables in developing as well as developed economies. We present the summary and conclusions in section 5.

5. CONCLUSIONS AND PROMISING RESEARCH IDEAS

Conclusions

The body of theoretical and empirical work on ESMs is clearly growing, as a result of increasing research activity in this area. In this chapter, we have reviewed some key theoretical and empirical issues related to stock market development. In some parts we have drawn parallels from research work on developed stock markets. We summarize the main conclusions below.

Stock market efficiency
In general, what we have learned about stock market efficiency in ESMs can be summarized as follows. First, the test results for weak-form efficiency are similar across the ESMs and their developed counterparts, despite differences in the stages of market development. For example, unit root test results confirm that stock returns follow a random walk process in both emerging and developed stock markets, while mean reversion test results suggest that

we cannot accept weak-form efficiency across all the sample stock markets. However it is not possible to infer from the empirical results how close the ESMs are to the efficiency frontier, in order to rank the markets according to their efficiency levels. For this matter, it is very difficult to relate the stage of stock market development to the level of efficiency in each ESM.

Second, existing studies attribute the predictability of stock returns to various factors, including non-synchronous trading, presence of noise traders and the fundamentals. While there is consistency in the results for non-synchronous trading, the results on the presence of noise trading are rather mixed, while the role of fundamentals in relation to the EMH is still debatable. Whether these variables vary across the markets is yet to be documented. However one can assume that non-synchronous trading is more relevant for ESMs. Thus it would be interesting to analyse the specific factors that influence the predictability of stock returns across the ESMs.

Third, in the light of the evidence, it is debatable whether weak-form efficiency is a sufficient condition for market efficiency or just a general indicator of the stochastic process of stock prices. In addition, it is not altogether clear whether the methods used for studying weak-form efficiency provide adequate statistics that could be used to infer the state of market development.

Fourth, for both ESMs and their developed counterparts, it is found that stock returns are martingale. Also it is shown that the ARCH effect is significant in all markets. Volatility clustering is attributed to various factors, including trade volumes, nominal interest rates, dividend yield, money supply and external shocks such as oil prices. However the evidence does not shed light on whether factors determining volatility clustering vary across the ESMs.

Fifth, the evidence generally shows the presence of volatility persistency across the sample stock markets, implying that volatility exerts pressure on stock prices. Furthermore it is found that volatility can be detrimental to investment, especially because of the implied high cost of capital. These results suggest that ESMs, which are implementing structural reforms, should emphasize policies that can reduce market volatility.

Sixth, it is found that asymmetric response of stock returns to events differs across the markets, as does the pricing of time varying premia. Asymmetric response has implications for monitoring shocks in order to minimize their adverse effects. Also non-linearity and the chaos process cannot be confirmed in all markets, implying that stock returns are characterized as stochastic processes. Overall, however, the general results suggest that differences in stages of stock market development do not seem to affect the structure of stock return volatility.

Microstructure theory

Our review of microstructure theory focuses on the reforms which are being undertaken in ESMs. Overall what we have learned from the literature is that microstructure characteristics vary across the trading systems with more preference shown for trading systems that enhance efficiency and provide liquidity at low cost and with no excess volatility. However differences exist regarding the impact of changes in trading systems on stock market microstructure. We find that most changes in trading systems in both emerging and developed markets have been evolutionary.

Stock market and macroeconomic policies

Both the theoretical and the empirical literature are persuasive enough about the existence of a strong interaction between the stock market and macroeconomic variables in developing as well as developed economies. However two problems persist. First, the relationship is generally portrayed as ambiguous. Second, the transmission channels between the stock market and macroeconomic activity are not clearly identified. In general, the literature reviewed above leads to a number of observations.

First, the literature suggests that anticipated and unanticipated changes in monetary policy have a direct and significant effect on both the first and second moments of stock returns and market liquidity. In addition, the evidence suggests that monetary policy affects expected excess returns, mainly through the credit channel and portfolio allocation channel, rather than expected real returns.

Second, the relationship between stock prices and monetary aggregates is portrayed as ambiguous. Evidence from causality tests suggests a unidirectional as well as bidirectional relationship between stock prices and narrow money, while a bidirectional relationship is found between stock prices and broad money. Cointegration test results are rather mixed; some studies indicate a long-run relationship while others do not. In addition, contemporaneous and lagged effects suggest that the stock market is not efficient in incorporating new information from monetary policy.

Third, empirical work on the relationship between fiscal policy and stock prices is very scanty. However the few existing studies suggest that the stock market is inefficient with respect to available information on fiscal policy. Moreover, these findings can be regarded as but inconclusive. In addition, the existing studies do not shed much light on the argument that the impact of taxation on the capital market depends on the stage of market development; further research is necessary on this issue.

Fourth, both micro and macro studies show a negative relationship between the exchange rate and stock prices, which implies that a real appreciation of the exchange rate is bad for domestic firms because it reduces their competitiveness, while real exchange rate depreciation stimulates the economy in the short run. However some studies on ESMs have uncovered a positive relationship between exchange rates and stock prices, while others show bidirectional causality and are thus inconclusive.

Fifth, the evidence seems to support the key argument that there is a positive relationship between stock market development and economic growth. What is not so clear-cut is the mechanism that links the two.

Finally, the relationship between stock prices and inflation could be positive, negative or insignificant, depending on the factors (supply and demand) influencing inflation. There is continuing debate on the channel through which stock prices and inflation interact.

Promising Research Ideas

After taking stock of existing research on stock market development, we find that there are many gaps in our knowledge of ESMs. We shall only highlight some of the gaps implied by the summary of literature in Table 4.10, and thereby identify a number of what we believe are promising research ideas. Below, we summarize these ideas.

PRI 1   There is a need to identify the distributional characteristic of stock returns in ESMs, as the markets develop, and to identify how these characteristics differ from those of developed stock markets. Such analyses would include testing the EMH for predictability of stock returns, information effect of announcements at firm level and analysing the second moments of stock returns at various stages of the development of the stock markets.

PRI 2   There is a need to assess gains from investing in institutional changes in the revitalization process for the emerging markets, and any constraints in setting up an institutional structure that supports growth of a stock market. The idea is to examine the microstructure characteristics (including volatility, costs of trading, liquidity and efficiency of price discovery process) for the period before and after the reforms.

PRI 3   There is a need to assess the contribution of the stock market to economic growth, by modelling the mechanisms that link the stock market to the growth process: for example, analysing the implications of stock market performance on capital structure and investment behaviour, and analysing the impact of the stock market on savings. A related idea is to assess the complementarity and substitutability between the financial intermediaries and stock markets in their growth and contribution to development.

PRI 4 Table 4.10 indicates a very limited literature on the relationship between the stock market and the macroeconomic environment for ESMs. To be able to make generalities for ESMs, we propose exhaustive analysis of the response of ESMs to macroeconomic policy variables. The idea is to investigate the impact of liberalization processes (including floating of the exchange rate, relaxation of capital controls, trade liberalization, globalization and monetary and fiscal policy reforms) on stock market development. This also entails quantitative analysis of the information effect, speed of adjustment and differences in response across listed firms.

PRI 5 There is a need to assess the interaction between the domestic stock market and the global markets, especially given the popularization of regional integration and globalization. This would involve analysing the response of ESMs to the entry of foreign investors, finding the level of interactions across the markets and testing the robustness of ESMs to external shocks.

PRI 6 One idea is to take the challenge suggested by Statman (1999) that asset pricing models should reflect both value-expressive and utilitarian characteristics, thus reconciling behavioural finance and the EMH. Hence future research on ESMs may try to rework standard asset pricing models to allow for behavioural finance assumptions of cognitive bias rather than rational prices.

NOTES

1. According to IFC (2000, p. 3), the term 'ESM' refers to any stock market in a developing economy with potential to mature. Khambata (2000) categorizes the ESMs into four groups: group 1 – markets at early stages of development with few quoted companies, small capitalization, high concentration, low liquidity, high volatility and comparatively rudimentary institutional set-up; group 2 – higher liquidity, more quoted companies, foreign investor interest, small equity in relation to the economy; group 3 – market return less volatile, accelerated growth in trading activities and volume of shares issued, expanded capitalization and growing interest in developing mechanism to transfer risk; group 4 – more mature with high liquidity and trading activity, substantial financial depth, equity risk premium close to international competitive levels.
2. There are four steps to this measurement: (1) remove autocorrelation as this can affect some tests for chaos. This is accomplished by filtering the raw data using an autoregressive factor; (2) from *n*-histories of the filtered data define the dimensional space; (3)calculate the correlation integral; (4) calculate the slope of the relationship.
3. The various definitions of spread are as follows. Quoted spread captures the execution costs per trade; it is assumed that transactions will occur at the quotes. Effective spread is defined as the difference between quoted and actual transaction prices; it is assumed that trades do occur inside the quoted spread. Realized spread is used to decompose the effective spread on each trade into an adverse information component and the component realized by the dealer. The excess of the effective spread over the realized spread is used to measure the amount lost to informed traders. The realized spread is also referred to as the price reversal

as a dealer realizes earnings only if prices reverse. Roll-implied spread is based on the assumption that a bid–ask quote does not change in response to trades, something that would be implied if there is no informed trading and if quotes are not changed to equilibrate dealer inventories.

4. The procedure involves computing the variance–covariance matrix from the data on stock returns and performing a maximum likelihood factor analysis on the covariance matrix to estimate the number of factor loadings. The estimated factor loadings are then used to explain cross-sectional variation of the mean rates of return on equities (Oyama, 1997).

5. The theory in Bodnar and Gentry (1993) and Bartov and Bodnar (1994) predicts an indirect relationship between the exchange rate and the stock market. The economic theory argument is that profitability and the value of firms increase (decrease) with unexpected depreciation (appreciation) of the currency because of the impact on cash flows. It is also argued that exchange rate movements are felt by altering the domestic currency value of foreign currency-denominated fixed assets and liabilities. Another channel is through spillover effects for firms not involved in international trade or through the impact on foreign currency-denominated inputs. Bodnar and Gentry (1993) note that appreciation of home currency induces a shift of resources from traded to non-traded industries as long as capital is more sector-specific than other production inputs. Such reallocation causes the market value of capital in non-traded goods industries to rise relative to market value of traded good industries, such that there is a positive relation between the value of non-traded goods industries and appreciation of foreign exchange.

REFERENCES

Abdalla, I.S.A. and Murinde, V. (1997), 'Exchange rate and stock prices interactions in emerging financial markets: evidence on India, Korea, Pakistan and Philippines', *Applied Financial Economics,* **7**, 25–35.

Aggarwal, R. (1981), 'Exchange rates and stock processes: a study of US capital markets under floating exchange rate', *Akron Business and Economic Review,* **12**(2), 7–12.

Ahn, H.J. and Cheung, Y. (1999), 'The intra day patterns of spreads and depth in a market without market makers. The stock exchange of Hong Kong', *Pacific-Basin Finance Journal,* **7**(5), 539–56.

Aitken, B. (1998), 'Have institutional investors destabilised emerging markets?', *Contemporary Economic Policy,* **16**, 173–84.

Al-Loughani, N. and Chappell, D. (1997), 'Test for IID assumption implied by EMH', *Applied Financial Economics,* **7**(2), 173–6.

Amihud, Y. and Murgia, M. (1997), 'Dividends, taxes and signalling: evidence from Germany', *The Journal of Finance,* **52**(1), 397–409.

Amihud, Y., Mendelson, H. and Lauterbach, B. (1997), 'Market microstructure and securities values. Evidence from Tel Aviv stock exchange', *Journal of Financial Economics,* **45**, 365–90.

Amihud, Y., Mendelson, H. and Murgia, M. (1990), 'Stock market microstructure and return volatility: evidence from Italy', *Journal of Banking and Finance,* **14**, 423–40.

Arsad, Z. and Coutts, A.J. (1997), 'Security prices anomalies in London international stock exchange: a 60 year perspective', *Applied Financial Economics,* **7**, 455–64.

Atje, R. and Jovanovic, B. (1993), 'Stock markets and development', *European Economic Review,* **37**, 632–40.

Aylward, A. and Glen, J. (2000), 'Some international evidence on the stock prices as a leading indicator of economic activity', *Applied Financial Economics*, **10**, 1–14.

Bahmani-Oskooee, M. and Sohrabian, A. (1992), 'Stock prices and the effective exchange rate of the dollar', *Applied Economics*, **24**(4), 459–64.

Barclay, M.J., Kandel, E. and Marx, L.M. (1998), 'The effects of transaction costs on stock prices and trading volume', *Journal of Financial Intermediation*, **7**, 130–50.

Barkoulas, J. and Travlos, N.G. (1998), 'Chaos in an emerging capital market. The case of the Athens stock exchange', *Applied Financial Economics*, **8**(3), 231–43.

Bartov, E. and Bodnar, G.M. (1994), 'Firm valuation, earnings expectations, and the exchange rate exposure effects', *Journal of Finance*, **5**, 1755–85.

Bekaert, G. and Harvey, C.R. (1997), 'Emerging equity market volatility', *Journal of Financial Economics*, **43**, 29–77.

Bessembinder, H. and Kaufman, H.M. (1997), 'A cross exchange comparison of execution costs and information flow for NYSE listed stock', *Journal of Financial Economics*, **46**(3), 293–320.

Bianconi, M. (1995), 'Inflation and the real price of equities: theory with some empirical evidence', *Journal of Macroeconomics*, **17**, 495–514.

Blanchard, O. (1981), 'Output, the stock market and interest rate', *The American Economic Review*, **71**(1), 132–43.

Blukey, G. and Harris, R.D.F. (1997), 'Irrational analysts' expectations as a cause of excess volatility in stock prices', *Economic Journal*, **107**, 359–71.

Bodnar, G.M. and Gentry, W.M. (1993), 'Exchange rate exposure and industry characteristics: evidence from Canada, Japan and USA', *Journal of International Money and Finance*, **12**, 29–45.

Bollerslev, T. and Mikkelson, O.H. (1999), 'Long-term equity anticipation securities and stock market volatility dynamics', *Journal of Econometrics*, **92**, 75–99.

Bonser-Neal, C. and Dewenter, K.L. (1999), 'Does financial market development stimulate savings? Evidence from emerging stock markets', *Contemporary Economic Policy*, **17**(3), 370–80.

Bonser-Neal, C., Linnan, D. and Neal R. (1999), 'Emerging market transaction costs: evidence from Indonesia', *Pacific-Basin Finance Journal*, **7**, 103–27.

Booth, G.G., Martikainen, T. and Tse, Y. (1997), 'Price and volatility spillovers in Scandinavian stock markets', *Journal of Banking and Finance*, **21**(6), 811–23.

Boyd, J.H. and Smith, B.D. (1997), 'Capital market imperfections, international credit markets, non convergence', *Journal of Economic Theory*, **73**(2), 335–64.

Brean, D.J. (1996), 'Taxation and capital market development', in S. Mensah (ed.), *African Capital Markets: Contemporary Issues*, Nairobi: Rector Press Limited, pp. 76–85.

Brock, W.A. and Kleidon, A.W. (1992), 'Periodic market closure and trading volume', *Journal of Economic Dynamics and Control*, **16**, 451–89.

Brock, W., Dechert, W. and Scheinkman, J. (1987), 'A test for independence based on the correlation dimension', Working Paper, University of Wisconsin at Madison.

Caprio, G. Jr and Demirgüç-Kunt, A.(1998), 'The role of long term finance: theory and evidence', *The World Bank Research Observer*, **13**(2), 171–89.

Chan, K., Mcqueen, G. and Thorley, S. (1998), 'Are there rational speculative bubbles in Asian stock markets?', *Pacific-Basin Finance Journal*, **6**, 125–51.

Chan, L.K.C. and Lakonishok, J. (1993), 'Institutional trades and intraday stock price behaviour', *Journal of Financial Economics*, **33**, 173–99.

Chang, R.P., Rhee, S.G. and Soedigno, S. (1995), 'Price volatility of Indonesian stocks', *Pacific-Basin Finance Journal*, **3**, 337–55.

Chang, R.P., Hsu, S., Huang, N. and Rhee, S.G. (1999), 'The effects of trading methods on volatility and liquidity: evidence from Taiwan Stock Exchange', *Journal of Business Finance and Accounting*, **26**(1/2), 137–70.

Chen, N., Roll, R. and Ross, S. (1986), 'Economic forces and the stock market', *Journal of Business*, **59**(6), 383–403.

Cheung, D.W.W. (1997), 'Pacific Rim stock market integration under different federal funds rate regimes', *Journal of Business Finance & Accounting*, **24**(9/10), 1343–51.

Choudhry, T. (1996), 'Stock market volatility and the crash of 1987: evidence from six emerging markets', *Journal of International Money and Finance*, **15**(6), 969–81.

Choudhry, T. (2000), 'Meltdown of 1987 and meteor showers among Pacific-Basin stock markets', *Applied Financial Economics*, **10**, 71–80.

Christie, A. (1982), 'The stochastic behaviour of common stock variance: value leverage and interest rate effects', *Journal of Financial Economics*, **10**, 407–32.

Cochran, S.J. and Defina, R.H. (1995), 'New evidence on predictability in world equity markets', *Journal of Business Finance and Accounting*, **22**, 845–54.

Comerton-Forde, C. (1999), 'Do trading rules impact on market efficiency? Australian and Jakarta stock exchanges', *Pacific-Basin Finance Journal*, **7**, 495–521.

Cornelius, P.K. (1991), 'Monetary policy and the price behaviour in emerging stock markets', *IMF Working Paper*, WP/91/27.

Cornell, B. and Sirri, E.R. (1992), 'The reaction of investors and stock prices to insider trading', *Journal of Finance*, **47**, 1031–59.

Corrado, C.J. and Zivney, T.L. (1992), 'The specification and power of the sign test in event study hypothesis tests using daily stock returns', *Journal of Financial & Quantitative Analysis*, **27**, 465–78.

Cowan, A.R. and Sergeant, A.M.A. (1996), 'Trading frequency and event study test specification', *Journal of Banking & Finance*, **20**, 1731–57.

Dailami, M. and Atkin, M. (1990), 'Stock markets in developing countries: key issues and a research agenda', Working Paper WPS 515, The World Bank, Washington, DC.

Daniel, K. and Titman, S. (1999), 'Market efficiency in an irrational world', *Financial Analysts Journal*, **55**, 28–40.

Darrat, A.F. (1988), 'On fiscal policy and the stock market', *Journal of Money, Credit, and Banking*, **20**(3), 353–63.

De Jong, F., Nijman, T. and Röell, A. (1995), 'A comparison of the cost of trading French shares on the Paris Bourse and on SEAQ International', *European Economic Review*, **39**, 1277–301.

De Santis, G. and İmrohoroglus, S. (1997), 'Stock returns and volatility in emerging financial markets', *Journal of International Money and Finance*, **16**(4), 561–79.

Demirgüç-Kunt, A. and Vojislav, M. (1996), 'Stock market development and firm financial choices', *The World Bank Economic Review*, **10**(2), 341–69.

Dhakal, D., Kandil, M. and Sharma, S.C. (1993), 'Causality between the money supply and share prices. A VAR investigation', *Quarterly Journal of Business and Economics*, **32**, 52–74.

Engel, R. (1982), 'Autoregressive conditional heteroscedasticity with estimates of variables of UK inflation', *Econometrica*, **50**, 987–1008.

Evans, D. and Murinde, V. (1995), 'The impact of monetary and fiscal policy actions on the stock market in Singapore', *Savings and Development*, **XIX**(3), 297–313.

Fama, E.F. (1970), 'Efficient capital markets: a review of theory and empirical work', *Journal of Finance*, **25**(2), 383–423.

Fama, E.F. (1991), 'Efficient capital markets: II', *Journal of Finance*, **46**(5), 1575–615.

Fama, E.F. and French, K.R. (1988), 'Permanent and temporary components of stock prices', *Journal of Political Economy*, **96**, 246–73.

Fama, E.F. and MacBeth, J. (1973), 'Risk, return and equilibrium', *Journal of Political Economy*, **38**, 67–36.

Feldstein, M. (1980), 'Inflation and stock market', *The American Economic Review*, **70**(5), 839–47.

Flannery, M.J., Hameed, A.S. and Hameed, A.S. and Harjes, R.H. (1997), 'Asset pricing, time-varying risk premia and interest rate risk', *Journal of Banking and Finance*, **21**, 315–35.

Flood, M.D. (1991), 'Microstructure theory and foreign exchange market', *Federal Reserve Bank of St. Louis*, **73**(6), 52–70.

Flood, M.D., Huisman, R., Koedijk, K.G. and Mahieu, R.J. (1999), 'Quote disclosure and price discovery in multiple-dealer financial markets', *The Review of Financial Studies*, **12**(1), 37–59.

Frankfurter, G.M. and McGoun, E.G. (2001), 'Anomalies in finance: what are they and what are they good for?', *International Review of Financial Analysis*, **10**, 407–29.

Frankfurter, G.M. and McGoun, E.G. (2002), 'Resistance is futile: the assimilation of behavioural finance', *Journal of Economic Behaviour & Organisation*, **48**, 375–89.

Fraser, P. and Power, D. (1997), 'Stock return volatility and information: an empirical analysis of Pacific Rim, UK and US equity markets', *Applied Financial Economics*, **7**, 241–53.

Gallagher, L.A. (1999), 'A multi-country analysis of the temporary and permanent components of stock prices', *Applied Financial Economics*, **9**, 129–42.

Gavin, M. (1989), 'The stock market and exchange rate dynamics', *Journal of International Money and Finance*, **8**, 181–200.

Giaccotto, C. and Sfiridis, J.M. (1996), 'Hypothesis testing in event studies: the case of changes', *Journal of Economics & Business*, **48**, 349–70.

Glen, J. (1994), 'An introduction to the microstructure of emerging markets', *International Finance Corporation Discussion Paper*, no. 2, IFC, Washington, DC.

Glosten, L.R., Jaganathan, R. and Runkle, R.D. (1993), 'On the relation between the expected value and volatility of nominal excess return on stocks', *Journal of Finance*, **48**, 1779–801.

Grassberger, P. and Procaccia, I. (1983), 'Measuring the strangeness of strange attractors', *Physica*, 90, 189–208.

Green, C.J., Maggioni, P. and Murinde, V. (2000), 'Regulatory lessons for emerging stock markets from a century of evidence on transactions costs and share price volatility in the London Stock Exchange', *Journal of Banking and Finance*, **24**, 577–601.

Habibullah, M.S. and Baharumshah, A.Z. (1996), 'Money, output and stock prices in Malaysia: an application of cointegration tests', *International Economic Journal*, **10**(2), 121–30.

Harvey, C.R. (1989), 'Forecasts of economic growth from the bond and stock markets', *Financial Analyst Journal* (Sept/Oct), 38–45.

Hashemzadeh, N. and Taylor, P. (1988), 'Stock prices, money supply and interest rates: the question of causality', *Applied Economics*, **20**(12), 1603–11.

Henry, O. (1998), 'Modelling the asymmetry of stock market volatility', *Applied Financial Economics*, **8**, 145–53.

Hess, P.J. and Lee, B.S. (1999), 'Stock returns and inflation with supply and demand disturbances', *The Review of Financial Studies*, **12**(5), 1203–18.

Huang, R.D. and Stoll, H.R. (1996), 'Dealer versus auction markets: a paired comparison of execution costs on NASDAQ and the NYSE', *Journal of Financial Economics*, **41**, 313–57.

Hubbard, J. and Michaely, R. (1997), 'Do investors ignore dividend taxation? A reexamination of the citizens utilities case', *Journal of Financial and Quantitative Analysis*, **32**(1), 117–35.

Huber, P. (1997), 'Stock market returns in emerging markets: evidence from Vienna stock exchange', *Applied Financial Economics*, **7**, 493–8.

Husnan, S. and Theobald, M. (1993), 'Thin trading and index sensitivity in events studies: the case of the Indonesian stock market', *Research in Third World Accounting*, **2**, 353–67.

IFC (1997), *Emerging Stock Markets Factbook*, Washington, DC: IFC.

IFC (2000), *Emerging Stock Markets Factbook 2000*, Washington, DC: IFC.

Inanga, I.L. and Emenuga, C. (1995), 'Institutional, traditional and asset pricing characteristics of the Nigerian stock exchange', African Economic Research Consortium Research Paper, no. 60.

Jeffris, K.R. and Okeahalam, C. (1999), 'International stock market linkages in southern Africa', *South African Journal of Accounting and Research*, **13**(2), 27–51.

Johnson, R. and Soenen, L. (1998), 'Stock prices and exchange rates: empirical evidence from the Pacific Basin', *Journal of Asian Business*, **14**(2), 1–18.

Jorion, P. (1990), 'The exchange rate exposure of US multinationals', *Journal of Business*, **63**, 331–45.

Kawakatsu, H. and Morey, M.R. (1999), 'An empirical examination of financial liberalisation and the efficiency of emerging market stock prices', *The Journal of Financial Research*, **22**(4), 385–411.

Khambata, D. (2000), 'Impact of foreign investment on volatility and growth of an emerging stock market', *Multinational Business Review*, **8**, 50–59.

Kim, E.H. and Singal, V. (2000), 'Stock market openings: experience of emerging economies', *Journal of Business*, **73**(1), 25–66.

Kim, M.K. and Wu, C. (1987), 'Macroeconomic factors and stock returns', *The Journal of Financial Research*, **10**(2), 87–98.

Koutmos, G. (1999), 'Asymmetric price and volatility adjustment in emerging Asian stock markets', *Journal of Business Finance and Accounting*, **26**(1/2), 83–101.

Kritzman, M.P. (1994), 'About event studies', *Financial Analysts Journal*, **50**, 17–20.

Laffont, J. and Maskin, E.S. (1990), 'The efficient market hypothesis and insider trading on the stock market', *Journal of Political Economy*, **98**, 70–93.

Lam, P.H.L. and Tong, W.H.S (1999), 'Interdaily volatility in a continuous order-driven market', *Journal of Business Finance and Accounting*, **26**(7), 1013–36.

Lang, L.H.P. and Lee, Y.T. (1999), 'Performance of various transaction frequencies under call: the case of Taiwan', *Pacific-Basin Finance Journal*, **7**, 23–39.

Lastrapes, W.D (1998), 'International evidence on equity prices, interest rates and money', *Journal of International Money and Finance*, **17**, 377–406.

Leach, J.C. and Madhavan, A. (1993), 'Price experimentation and security market structure', *Review of Financial Studies*, **6**, 375–404.

Lee, J., Cheng, J., Lin, C.J. and Huang, C. (1998), 'Market efficiency hypothesis on stock prices: international evidence in the 1920s', *Applied Financial Economics*, **8**(1), 61–5.

Levine, R. and Zervos, S. (1996), 'Stock market development and long run growth', *World Bank Economic Review*, **10**, 323–39.

Littman, M.J. (1994), 'A world of opportunity-investing in overseas markets', *The CPA Journal*, **64**(3), 73–4.

Ma, C.K. and Kao, G.W. (1990), 'On exchange rate changes and stock price reactions', *Journal of Business Finance and Accounting*, **17**(3), 441–9.

MacKinlay, A.C. (1997), 'Event studies in economics and finance', *Journal of Economic Literature*, **35**(1), 13–39.

Madhavan, A. (1992), 'Trading mechanisms in securities markets', *Journal of Finance*, **XLVII**(2), 607–41.

Madhavan, A. and Smidt, S. (1993), 'An analysis of changes in specialist inventories and quotations', *Journal of Finance*, **XLVIII**(5), 1595–1628.

Majnoni, G. and Massa, M. (2001), 'Stock exchange reforms and market efficiency: the Italian experience', *European Financial Management*, **7**(1), 93–115.

Mankiw, G.N., Romer, D. and Weil, D.N. (1992), 'A contribution to the empirics of economic growth', *Quarterly Journal of Economics*, **107**(2), 407–38.

Maynes, E. and Rumsey, J. (1993), 'Conducting event studies with thinly traded stocks', *Journal of Banking & Finance*, **17**, 145–57.

McElroy, M.B. and Burmeister, E. (1988), 'Arbitrage pricing theory as a restricted non-linear multivariate regression model', *Journal of Business and Economic Statistics*, **6**(1), 29–42.

McMillin, W.D. and Laumas, G.S. (1988), 'The impact of anticipated and unanticipated policy actions on the stock market', *Applied Economics*, **20**(3), 377–84.

Miller, M. and Modigliani, F. (1961), 'Dividend policy, growth, and the valuation of shares', *Journal of Business*, **34**, 411–33.

Moorkerjee, R. (1987), 'Monetary policy and the informational efficiency of the stock market: the evidence from many countries', *Applied Economics*, **19**, 1521–32.

Moorkerjee, R. and Yu, Q. (1997), 'Macroeconomic variables and stock prices in a small open economy: the case of Singapore', *Pacific-Basin Finance Journal*, **5**, 377–88.

Muragu, K. (1996), 'Pricing efficiency of Nairobi stock exchange', in S. Mensah (ed.), *African Capital Markets Contemporary Issues*, Nairobi: Rector Press Ltd, pp. 140–42.

Murinde, V. (1996), 'Financial markets and endogenous growth: an econometric analysis for Pacific Basin countries, in N. Hermes and R. Lensink (eds), *Financial Development and Economic Growth Theory and Experiences from Developing Countries*. London: Routledge, pp. 94–114.

Nelson, D. (1991), 'Conditional heteroscedasticity in asset returns: a new approach', *Econometrica*, **59**, 347–70.

Niarchos, N.A. and Alexakis, C.A. (1998), 'Stock market prices, causality and efficiency evidence from the Athens Stock Exchange', *Applied Financial Economics*, **8**, 167–74.

Osei, K.A. (1998), 'Analysis of factors affecting the development of an emerging capital market, the case of Ghana stock market', African Economic Research Consortium Research Paper, no. 76.

Oyama, T. (1997), 'Determinants of stock prices: the case of Zimbabwe', IMF Working Paper, no. 117, IMF, Washington, DC.

Pagano, M. (1993), 'Financial markets and growth, an overview', *European Economic Review*, **37**, 613–22.

Pagano, M. and Röell, A. (1996), 'Transparency and liquidity: a comparison of auction and dealer markets with informed trading', *Journal of Finance*, **LI**(2), 579–611.

Papachristou, G. (1999), 'Stochastic behaviour of the Athens Stock Exchange: a case of institutional non-synchronous trading', *Applied Financial Economics*, **9**, 239–50.

Patelis, A.D. (1997), 'Stock return predictability and the role of monetary policy', *Journal of Finance*, **52**(5), 1951–72.

Poshakwale, S. and Murinde, V. (2001), 'Modelling volatility in East European emerging stock markets. Evidence on Hungary and Poland stock markets', *Applied Financial Economics*, **11**, 445–56.

Poterba, J.M. and Samwick, A.A. (1995), 'Stock ownership patterns stock market fluctuations and consumption', *Brookings Papers on Economic Activity*, **2**, 295–372.

Qiao, Y. (1996), 'Stock prices and exchange rates: experiences in leading East Asian Centers – Tokyo, Hong Kong and Singapore', *The Singapore Economic Review*, **41**(1), 47–56.

Richards, A.J. (1996), 'Volatility and predictability in national stock markets: how do emerging and mature markets differ?', *IMF Staff Papers*, **43**(3), 461–501.

Röell, A. (1992), 'Comparing the performance of stock exchange trading systems', in J. Fingleton and D. Schoenmaker (eds), *The Internationalisation of Capital Markets and the Regulatory Response*, London: Graham & Trotman.

Roma, A. and Schlitzer, G. (1996), 'The determinants of Italian stock market return: some empirical evidence', *Economic Notes*, **25**(3), 515–40.

Ross, S.A. (1976), 'The arbitrage theory of capital asset pricing', *Journal of Economic Theory*, **13**, 341–60.

Schwert, W. (1989), 'Why does stock market volatility change over time?', *Journal of Finance*, **44**, 1115–53.

Serletis, A. (1993), 'Money and stock prices in the United States', *Applied Financial Economics*, **3**, 51–4.

Serletis, A. and Sondergard, M.A. (1996), 'Permanent and temporary components of Canadian stock prices', *Applied Financial Economics*, **6**, 259–69.

Shastri, K.A., Shastri, K. and Sirodum, K. (1995), 'Trading mechanisms and return volatility: an empirical analysis of the stock exchange of Thailand', *Pacific-Basin Finance Journal*, **3**(2–3), 357–70.

Solnik, B. (1987), 'Using financial prices to test exchange rate models: a note', *Journal of Finance*, **42**(1), 141–9.

Song, H., Liu, X. and Romilly, P. (1998), 'Stock returns and volatility: an empirical study of Chinese stock markets', *International Review of Applied Economics*, **12**(1), 129–39.

Spulber, D.F. (1996), 'Market microstructure and intermediation', *Journal of Economic Perspectives*, **10**(3), 135–52.

Statman, M. (1999), 'Behavioural finance: past battles and future engagements', *Financial Analysts Journal*, **55**, 18–27.

Tan, K.S.R. and Tat, N.W. (1998), 'The diminishing calendar anomalies in the stock exchange of Singapore', *Applied Financial Economics*, **8**, 119–25.

Thaler, R.H. (1999), 'The end of behavioural finance', *Financial Analysts Journal*, **55**, 12–17.

Thorbecke, W. (1997), 'Stock market returns and monetary policy', *Journal of Finance*, **52**(2), 635–54.

Titman, S. and Wei, J.K.C. (1999), 'Understanding stock market volatility. The case of Korea and Taiwan', *Pacific-Basin Finance Journal*, **7**, 41–66.

Wei, K.C. and Wong, K.M. (1992), 'Tests of inflation and industry portfolio stock returns', *Journal of Economics and Business*, **44**, 77–94.

Wong, K.A., Hui, T.K. and Chan, C.Y. (1992), 'Day-of-the-week effects: evidence from developing stock markets', *Applied Financial Economics*, **2**(1), 49–56.

Yadav, P.K., Pandayal, K. and Pope, P.F. (1999), 'Non-linear dependence in stock returns: does trading frequency matter?', *Journal of Business Finance and Accounting*, **26**(5/6), 651–79.

5. Financial regulation in developing countries: policy and recent experience

Martin Brownbridge, Colin H. Kirkpatrick and Samuel Munzele Maimbo[1]

1. INTRODUCTION

The role of an effective regulatory regime in promoting economic growth and development has generated considerable interest among researchers and practitioners in recent years. Regulation by government is associated with mitigating market failures. From the 1960s to the 1980s, market failure was used to legitimize direct government involvement in productive activities in developing countries by, for example, extending public ownership of enterprises. However, following the apparent success of market liberalization programmes in developed countries, and growing evidence of the failure of state-led economic planning in developing countries, the role of the state was redefined and narrowed in the 1980s to one of ensuring an 'undistorted' policy environment in which markets could operate as an efficient mechanism for the mobilization and allocation of resources. Consequently markets were liberalized, often as part of structural adjustment programmes, with the aim of reducing the burden of regulation on the market economy. But, by the beginning of the 1990s, there was a recognition that the state had a key role to play in providing the regulatory framework for the operation of what are often imperfect or missing markets. Effective regulation is now recognized as essential for supporting market-led economic growth and development, and empirical analysis has confirmed that the quality of the regulatory regime has a significant impact on the functioning of markets and economic performance (World Bank, 2002; Jalilian *et al.*, 2003).

Since the 1980s, significant changes have taken place in the way that financial systems are regulated in developing countries (DCs). Economic regulations on the financial sector, such as controls over interest rates and directives to banks to lend to priority sectors of the economy to meet developmental or political objectives, have been reduced or removed as part of a policy of financial liberalization. The rationale for financial liberalization is that the market provides a more efficient mechanism than the state for mobilizing and allocating financial resources (Caprio *et al.*, 2001; Williamson and Mather, 1998). The period of financial liberalization also saw a significant increase in financial instability, with widespread financial distress afflicting banks and non-bank financial institutions in many developing countries, most notably in East Asia in the latter part of the 1990s. The damaging effects of financial instability on economic growth served to highlight the need for sound financial regulation and supervision to protect the stability of the financial system during the process of market liberalization.

Financial liberalization has been accompanied, therefore, by an increased emphasis on the prudential regulation and supervision of the financial system. Prudential regulation is the codification of public policy directed to ensure the soundness of banks and other financial institutions, while supervision is the means of ensuring compliance with regulation (Polizatto, 1991, p. 174). The objective of prudential regulation and supervision is to prevent systemic risk and to provide protection for small depositors.[2] This acknowledges that financial markets are subject to market failures, which in the absence of prudential regulation would threaten systemic risk and the deposits of small depositors. It also implies that prudential regulation and supervision can prevent, or at least mitigate, these market failures (Vittas, 1992, pp. 5–6).

This chapter examines the record of prudential reform in developing countries, analyses the weaknesses in their financial regulatory systems and discusses proposals for further reforms. We begin in section 2 by briefly examining the rationale for prudential regulation. Section 3 outlines the nature of the reforms to prudential systems which have been implemented in DCs. The empirical evidence on the success of prudential reforms in improving the safety and stability of the banking system is reviewed in section 4. Section 5 examines why prudential reforms have not been more effective in preventing banking crises in DCs, while section 6 examines the part played by prudential system weaknesses in the East Asian crisis of the late 1990s. Section 7 reviews proposals for further reform of the prudential systems of DCs, while section 8 concludes.

2.   THE RATIONALE FOR PRUDENTIAL REGULATION

Market failures characterize many different types of markets, but the financial sector, and banks in particular, are subject to heavier regulation than virtually any other industry. The reasons for this lie in the combination of several factors: banks are vulnerable to failure; bank failures entail serious negative externalities; there are significant principal–agent problems between bank owners and their depositors arising from imperfect information; and optimal regulation by the market is not feasible. While each of these factors alone is not unique to banks, the combination of these factors is shared by few other industries.

Banks, like firms in any industry, are vulnerable to insolvency through, for example, mismanagement or macroeconomic shocks. In addition, because of the nature of their liabilities, which are mostly short-term and fixed in value, and the illiquid and untransparent nature of their assets, banks are also vulnerable to illiquidity caused by bank runs if depositors believe, rightly or wrongly, that their bank may be unable to honour all of its liabilities because of financial distress (Diamond and Dybvig, 1983; Gorton, 1988). An illiquid bank may be rendered insolvent if it is forced to liquidate its assets at fire sale prices. Deposit insurance can reduce the risk of bank runs but at the cost of creating moral hazard which leads to excessive risk taking by banks and thus greater vulnerability of banks to insolvency.

Bank failures entail negative externalities, for several reasons. First, bank liabilities are used as a means of payment and banks themselves play a central role in the payments system; hence bank failures could disrupt the payments system which is crucial to the functioning of a modern economy. Second, banks have a comparative advantage in credit markets because they have private information (not available to other market participants) about their loan customers. This private information could be lost in a bank failure with the result that borrowers would face reduced access to credit. Systemic bank failures could lead to credit contraction with serious adverse macroeconomic affects. Third, bank failures may have serious social costs if they result in the loss of people's savings.

Agency problems between bank owners and depositors arise because of the combination of asymmetric information – a bank has superior information to its depositors about its own financial condition and prospects – and the fixed-value nature of deposit contracts, together with limited liability for bank shareholders.[3] This can provide adverse incentives for banks to take excessive risks with their depositors' funds: risks for which depositors are not properly compensated and which cannot be controlled or monitored optimally by depositors (Ncube and Senbet, 1997).

The justification for a bank regulator, representing the interests of depositors, is that the numerous, atomized bank depositors do not have the incentives to monitor banks optimally because of free-rider problems and also because they lack the expertise to do so. In almost all countries bank regulation is undertaken by a public regulator, since private regulation is subject to serious drawbacks, such as the difficulty of fully internalizing the benefits of optimal monitoring and regulation (Dewatripont and Tirole, 1994).[4]

Many of the factors discussed above, which provide a rationale for bank regulation, are more relevant in developing than in industrialized countries. Informational problems are more acute in DCs than in industrial countries: financial accounts are less reliable in the former and it is more difficult to enforce contracts. Also macroeconomic variables which affect the value of banks' assets are more volatile in DCs than in industrial countries (Goldstein and Turner, 1996). Consequently financial markets in DCs will be more prone to agency problems such as adverse selection and moral hazard, and banks will be vulnerable to financial distress (Long and Vittas, 1992, p. 54; Villanueva and Mirakhor, 1990, p. 521). In many DCs banks have a much more dominant role in financial markets than that in industrial countries, hence bank failures in DCs are likely to have a more serious impact on the availability of finance for industrial and commercial enterprises. These factors would strengthen the case for bank regulation but, to set against this, government failure, in this case regulatory failure, may be more likely in DCs than in industrial countries.

Economic theory has provided valuable insights into the design of bank regulation, focusing on issues such as the costs and benefits of deposit insurance and how to deter risk taking by banks subject to moral hazard through risk-sensitive capital requirements and deposit insurance premia, cash asset reserve requirements, market discipline and bank closure policy (Bhattacharya *et al.*, 1998; Berger *et al.*, 1995; Caprio and Honohan, 1999). A range of disciplines, other than economics, can also contribute to an understanding of the design of prudential regulation, including law, history, political science and sociology (Marquardt, 1987).

3. REFORMS TO PRUDENTIAL REGULATION OF BANKS AND NON-BANK FINANCIAL INSTITUTIONS

Developing countries began to implement major reforms to their prudential systems in the 1980s and early 1990s, often stimulated by banking crises which had occurred in the 1980s. In many cases, prudential reforms were part of broader programmes of financial sector reforms, including financial liberalization, funded by loans from the international financial institutions. Conditionalities related to bank regulation and supervision featured prominently in World Bank financial sector adjustment loans: 79 per cent of these loans included conditionalities related to bank supervision, 71 per cent to bank regulations and 64 per cent to non-bank regulations (Cull, 1997). The notion that prudential regulation was ignored by DCs which liberalized their financial systems is erroneous. Rather the key questions are whether the prudential reforms were properly implemented, whether they were properly sequenced with other financial sector reforms and, more fundamentally, whether the type of prudential reforms implemented in DCs were really appropriate given the institutional and political constraints in these countries.

Prudential reforms in DCs have followed a broadly similar pattern, with the adoption of an industrial country model of bank regulation and supervision. The model involves a set of detailed prudential regulations, set out in the banking law, which include minimum capital requirements on banks' activities and the composition of their asset portfolios, including restrictions on large loan exposures and insider lending, auditing and disclosure requirements of banks, and statutory powers for the regulator to supervise banks, to impose prudential directives on banks and to intervene in problem banks. Supervision is undertaken directly by a public agency and entails on-site inspections and off-site monitoring of banks based on the CAMEL principles, in which supervisors evaluate a bank according to its capital, asset quality, management, earnings and liquidity (Sheng, 1996, p. 51). Supervisors aim to inspect banks at regular intervals and banks are required to submit regular financial reports to the supervisors. The Basle Committee's Core Principles for Effective Banking Supervision, drawn up in 1997, set out the basic framework of this model (IMF, 1998a). Many developing countries have also set up deposit insurance schemes, to protect small depositors in the event of bank failures, enhance public confidence in the banking system and provide a mechanism for resolving failed banks (Kyei, 1995; Talley and Mas, 1992).

Reforms have also been introduced to extend the coverage of financial regulation to non-bank financial institutions (NBFIs). These include financial institutions involved in capital market activities such as trading securities, financial institutions which undertake banklike activities, such as taking deposits and extending loans (for example, finance companies, leasing companies and merchant banks) and microfinance institutions (MFIs). In many DCs, NBFIs have emerged as a rapidly growing sector, partly in response to financial liberalization and technological change which have facilitated the diversification of financial markets, but also, in some countries, because of the opportunities to take advantage of regulatory arbitrage: entry requirements and other prudential regulations are much lighter for NBFIs than for commercial banks.

The institutional structure of NBFI regulation is not uniform among DCs (which partly reflects differences in the structure of financial markets, such as whether or not there is universal banking), but in general capital market activities – the issuance and trading of securities – are regulated under specific capital markets legislation, and in many DCs by a separate capital markets regulator, whereas the NBFIs which take deposits and extend loans have been brought under the auspices of the bank regulator and are covered by banking legislation.

Interest in prudential regulation of microfinance institutions has been stimulated because increasing numbers of MFIs are mobilizing deposits from the public, both to enhance the self-sustainability of their operations and because of a recognition that poor people require access to a range of financial services besides microcredit, including savings and insurance facilities.

Research into the regulation of MFIs was pioneered by Berenbach and Churchill (1997) who surveyed existing methods of regulating MFIs in DCs. There are four basic regulatory options for MFIs: no regulation, self-regulation, regulation under the existing banking laws and regulation under specialized MFI regulations. Berenbach and Churchill recommend that regulations should be tailored to the risk profiles of MFIs, focusing on the areas where they are most vulnerable, but should be flexible in not imposing controls on MFIs which do not apply to their activities. They caution regulators not to move too quickly to establish regulations based on one institutional model as this may impede innovation by MFIs. Greuning *et al.* (1999) point out that what distinguishes different MFIs is the structure of their liabilities (for example, some MFIs only use donor funds, some use members' funds and some mobilize deposits from the public). External regulation of MFIs should be triggered by thresholds linked to the composition of their liabilities, and especially the mobilization of retail deposits from the public.

Kirkpatrick and Maimbo (2002) survey the literature on MFI regulation and also evaluate a number of proposed new models of regulation, which include certification or rating by a third party such as a credit union rating agency, and greater disclosure of information to the public to allow savers to make more informed choices as to where to deposit their money. Kirkpatrick and Maimbo point out that these new models all suffer from problems related to informational asymmetry: the MFIs know much more about their financial condition and the risks they face than does any outside party. The literature on regulating MFIs has yet to reach a consensus on the best way forward, and research will need to focus on identifying a consolidated set of core principles for microfinance regulations, rules and guidelines that national regulators can translate into specific supervisory benchmarks.

4. HOW SUCCESSFUL HAVE PRUDENTIAL REFORMS BEEN?

It is difficult to judge the success of the prudential reforms which have been implemented in DCs recently. The fact that there have been numerous banking crises in DCs in the 1990s, including DCs which had already been implementing prudential reforms for several years, might suggest that the prudential reforms have not been very effective. However it is not necessarily valid to assume that more bank failures imply less effective bank regulation. Prudential reforms have been accompanied by radical changes in structural conditions in financial markets as a result of financial liberalization and technological progress, which may have heightened the risk of financial fragility in banking systems. Moreover the prudential reforms themselves may have exposed the authorities and forced them to confront already existing distress in banks which had hitherto remained hidden because of poor accounting practices and regulatory forbearance. It would not be surprising if the introduction of stricter accounting rules, more rigorous on-site examinations by the supervisors, less willingness to extend liquidity support to insolvent banks and stronger bank intervention policies by the regulators led to an increase in bank failures, at least initially. Nevertheless it is evident that prudential systems in many developing countries still exhibit serious weaknesses.

A rapidly evolving field of research in recent years is the investigation of the relationship between prudential regulation and financial system stability using cross-country econometric techniques. Some of the initial work in this field established a link between financial liberalization and subsequent episodes of banking crises, which is mitigated to some extent when proxies for the quality of prudential regulation are taken into consideration: countries with weak prudential regulation were found to have a higher probability of suffering a banking crisis following financial liberalization than countries with stronger regulatory systems (Demirgüç-Kunt and Detragiache, 1998). Rossi (1999) uses a logit regression to investigate whether capital controls and measures of the tightness of bank regulation and supervision and the safety of deposits affect the probability of a banking crisis in a sample of 15 developing countries during the period 1990–97. Banking crises were found to be more likely where prudential regulations were laxer, where the safety of deposits was greater (through higher levels of deposit insurance or a history of bank bailouts) and where there were controls on capital outflows. These results support the conventional view that stronger official regulation and supervision improves banking system soundness and that depositors' safety nets create moral hazard which can increase vulnerability to a crisis.

The most comprehensive cross-country study of the links between a wide range of regulatory practices and the efficiency and stability of the financial sector was undertaken by Barth *et al.* (2001), who utilized a database covering 107 countries. The database included information from questionnaires on specific aspects of the regulatory system in each country, and enabled the researchers to investigate the efficacy of particular regulatory policies, including policies which are regarded as 'international best practice', such as minimum capital adequacy standards.

The regulatory policy explanatory variables used in their cross-country regressions included restrictions on banks undertaking fee-based and non-banking activities (such as underwriting securities); restrictions on foreign entry into the banking system and other barriers to entry; capital regulations; measures of official supervisory power, including the existence of prompt corrective action (PCA) rules and the authority of the supervisors to declare banks insolvent and restructure distressed banks; measures of regulatory forbearance; the stringency of loan classification and provisioning rules; restrictions on, or requirements for, asset diversification; the independence of the supervisory authority; and the average tenure of supervisors. Measures of the extent to which private sector monitoring of banks is possible (such as the percentage of the largest ten banks which were rated by international credit rating agencies) were also included as explanatory variables, along with the size and power of any deposit insurance scheme. These explanatory variables were used in two types of regressions: one in which the dependent variables were indicators of bank performance, such as the development of the banking system, and the other in which the dependent variable was the likelihood of experiencing a banking crisis. A weakness of the study, acknowledged by the authors, is that, while most of the explanatory variables are based on data pertaining to 1999, the data on banking crises related to the 1980s and 1990s. In many countries, regulatory systems were reformed and strengthened in the 1990s, partly as a response to the banking crises which these countries had suffered earlier. Consequently the regulatory systems which were in place prior to and during the banking crises were much weaker than those in place in 1999, and consequently the regressions will not fully capture the link between stronger regulatory systems and the likelihood of a banking crisis.

The results of the regressions indicated that restrictions on bank activities were negatively related to banking system development and efficiency, yet did not reduce the likelihood of a banking crisis. There was no robust relationship between capital requirements and banking crises, or between most measures of official supervisory power and banking crises. The researchers found a very strong link between the generosity of the deposit insurance scheme and the likelihood of suffering a banking crisis, which indicates that the moral hazard effects of deposit insurance are large. Moreover capital regulations were not able to offset the negative impact of deposit insurance on banking system fragility. Private sector monitoring of banks was associated with better bank performance but not with the likelihood of banking crisis.

The researchers also found that stronger regulatory powers and more stringent regulatory restrictions on banks' activities (such as restrictions on banks undertaking non-bank activities, including securities underwriting, denial of applications for bank licences and stronger official supervisory powers) were positively associated with higher levels of government corruption.

These cross-country empirical results are important because they cast doubt on the efficacy of the thrust of regulatory reform across the globe, which is to strengthen official prudential regulations' supervisory powers, and the results suggest that many of these policies may impede banking system development while doing little to enhance the financial stability of the banking system. Moreover, another major policy reform which is being implemented in many countries – the introduction of a deposit insurance scheme – was found to have a major destabilizing impact on financial sector soundness.

5. WEAKNESSES IN PRUDENTIAL SYSTEMS IN DEVELOPING COUNTRIES

Why have the regulatory reforms implemented by many DCs not been more effective in ensuring stable banking systems? This section draws on the recent experience of prudential regulation in a range of DCs and identifies a number of common areas of weakness in their prudential systems, while the following section looks in more detail at the role played by prudential system weaknesses in the East Asian financial crisis of the second half of the 1990s.

Weaknesses in Legislation

While banking laws were strengthened in most DCs, in some countries the revised legislation was not strict or comprehensive enough to deal with problems that emerged in the 1990s. The minimum capital requirements in the legislation enacted by several countries in Sub-Saharan Africa (SSA) were too low. This allowed too many undercapitalized banks, lacking adequate financial or managerial resources, to be set up in the 1990s, which subsequently failed as a result of mismanagement and fraud (Brownbridge, 1998).

Loan classification and provisioning rules were too lenient in many DCs, especially in SSA and East Africa. Consequently banks could conceal the impairment of their asset portfolios and failed to make adequate provision to cover likely losses. If loan classification and provisioning rules are weak, a bank's capital can be overstated, with the result that the minimum capital adequacy requirements, which are the cornerstone of prudential regulation, are rendered meaningless. Banks which were insolvent were able to publish financial accounts showing them to be not only solvent but in compliance with minimum capital requirements, because loans were not classified properly or the necessary provisions made.

Inadequate Supervisory Capacities

A key component of the prudential reforms has been the strengthening of supervisory capacities, through recruitment and training of supervisors, improvements in supervisory methodologies, much greater use of information technology and technical assistance. However the type of skills needed by supervisors are scarce in DCs and, because of financial constraints in the public sector, supervisory departments often struggle to retain skilled staff in the face of competition from the private sector, where salaries are much more attractive (Maimbo, 2001).

Strengthening supervisory capacities is also a lengthy process. Caprio (1996, p. 9) points out that it would take many DCs five to ten years to train their bank supervisors to the levels of expertise of the industrial countries. Mehran *et al.* (1998) show that, with the exception of Mauritius and Tanzania, the average experience of bank supervisors in SSA countries is only between two and five years, which suggests that inexperience must be a serious constraint on effective supervision. In some DCs, demands on supervisors have grown faster than supervisory capacity because deregulation has allowed a rapid pace of new entry of banks and deposit-taking NBFIs. Moreover it is the new entrants, which are often few and lack experienced management, that are most in need of close supervision.

Regulatory Forbearance

The failure by the regulators to enforce the prudential regulations properly – known as regulatory forbearance – is described by Honohan (1997, p. 21) as the 'Achilles' heel of any regulatory system'. One of the most common forms of regulatory forbearance is delay by the regulator in explicitly recognizing that a bank is insolvent and either intervening to close it down to prevent any further losses to its depositors, or forcing its owners to recapitalize the bank within a pre-specified time period, failing which the bank is closed. Honohan and Klingebiel (2000) distinguish between three degrees of regulatory forbearance. The most accommodating form of forbearance allows banks which are known by the regulator to be insolvent to remain open. An intermediate degree of forbearance involves the regulator allowing an undercapitalized bank to remain open under its existing management for an extended period of time, while a less accommodating form of forbearance involves the temporary relaxation or non-enforcement of prudential regulations such as loan provisioning rules. It is, however, difficult to assess empirically the extent of regulatory forbearance because much of the actual practice of bank supervision is not publicly observable, given that a degree of confidentiality is essential to maintaining public confidence in the banking system and the trust of the bankers. In many cases the extent of regulatory forbearance only becomes apparent after major bank failures occur and information on the events leading up to the failures are made public.

Regulatory forbearance has a number of causes. The regulators frequently face political pressure to exercise forbearance, because the owners or debtors of distressed banks are politically influential or because government fears that bank closures, with the attendant job losses and disruption to bank customers, will be politically unpopular. Political pressure for regulatory forbearance is likely to be strong in many DCs because of the concentration of political and economic power, including ownership of the banking system, in a few hands (Caprio and Honohan, 1999, pp. 10–11).

In addition to economic and political forbearance, Maimbo (2001) argues that in some cases a third form of forbearance was more prevalent, one which he referred to as bureaucratically institutionalized regulatory forbearance. In his study of the regulatory and supervisory process in Zambia, he found that this form of forbearance was not only embedded in the formal and informal administrative policies and procedures for effecting legislative and supervisory sanctions, but appears to have been part of the organizational culture of decision making within the regulatory agency: the Bank of Zambia. The process of implementing corrective action took an excessively long time, not only because of political and economic concerns but also because of the exhausting administrative policies and procedures, which had evolved in the department out of tradition and precedent rather than deliberate administrative design.

Bureaucratically institutionalised regulatory forbearance was most evident in the early stages of the regulatory process when the regulators had to deal with bank violations of the law, deteriorating financial conditions through regulatory meetings and remedial supervisory actions. Significant amounts of time and resources were expended in complying with bureaucratic policies and procedures that had evolved within the central bank out of precedent and tradition rather than well-thought-out organization design. These regulatory processes were further complicated by the decentralized responsibility structure in existence at the central bank operating within a highly-centralized decision-making environment.

In part, the continued exercise of regulatory forbearance may also be a result of 'regulatory capture'; the fear that disclosure of problems in the regulated banks may have adverse effects on the regulator's reputation and career prospects. Boot and Thakor (1993) present a formal model in which the regulator aims to maximize its reputation in the face of public or market uncertainty about its quality (quality is defined as the ability of the regulator to evaluate accurately the asset choice of the regulated bank). In a reputational Nash equilibrium, the regulator's optimal closure policy is more lax than the social optimum. This is because closure can signal failure of the regulator to monitor the bank adequately. Moreover, the worse is the public perception of the regulator's quality, the stronger are the incentives for the regulator to delay closure. This has important implications in DCs, where there is often much public cynicism about the ability and motives of public officials, and where any bank closures are likely to prompt the accusation that the regulators failed to do their job properly. Once the regulator extends forbearance to a distressed bank, a mutual dependence may develop between regulator and bank, with the former providing liquidity support to keep the bank afloat in order to avoid having to close the bank and realize the losses incurred by depositors and taxpayers.

Regulatory forbearance reflects a principal–agent problem in bank regulation which arises because of two factors. First, imperfect information prevents the principals – the public or their elected representatives – from being able to monitor adequately the actions of their agents, the regulators. Second, discretion is often granted to the regulators in the banking laws. For example, the banking laws often omit to delineate clear rules for when intervention should take place, leaving the decision to intervene to the discretion of the regulators (Glaessner and Mas, 1995).

Regulatory forbearance is very costly for taxpayers. Honohan and Klingebiel (2000) used econometric analysis to investigate whether the fiscal costs of banking crises in 34 countries were related to the bank intervention and resolution policies of these countries. The resolution of the banking crises in these 34 countries cost the government budget an average of 12 per cent of GDP. Honohan and Klingebiel found that the provision of liquidity support and of unlimited deposit guarantees, and two indicators of regulatory forbearance (allowing insolvent banks to remain open and the suspension of prudential regulations) all significantly raised the cost of a banking crisis.

Regulatory forbearance worsens moral hazard in the banking system. In particular, the owners of distressed banks have few incentives for prudent management when they have little, if any, of their own capital left to lose. Instead bank owners have incentives to 'gamble for resurrection' with what is left of their deposits and the liquidity support that they are able to obtain from the authorities, or even to loot what remains of the bank's assets (Akerlof and Romer, 1993). The result is usually an escalation of losses in what have been dubbed 'zombie banks' by Kane (1989): banks which are insolvent but remain open with liquidity support from the authorities. Furthermore, if regulators acquire a reputation for forbearance, bank owners and managers will have less reason to fear that imprudent bank management will be penalized, and therefore will be less constrained in taking imprudent risks.

Inappropriate Sequencing of Financial Sector Reforms

Poor sequencing of financial reforms contributed to banking crises in DCs which liberalized their financial systems. Strong prudential systems, the restructuring or liquidation of distressed banks and macroeconomic stability are prerequisites for successful financial liberalization, because the removal of controls over interest rates and the capital account of the balance of payments can increase opportunities for risk taking by banks (Alawode and Ikhide, 1997; Villanueva and Mirakhor, 1990). Most DCs did not follow the optimal sequence of financial sector reforms. In a sample of 34 countries, including 25 DCs, Williamson and Maher (1998) found that only three DCs strengthened prudential regulation prior to financial liberalization, with another three implementing prudential reform alongside liberalization. However implementing the optimal sequence of financial sector reforms in practice is complex, not least because strengthening prudential systems is a lengthy process. Sundararajan (1999) advocates a sequence of financial liberalization, bank restructuring and supervisory reforms involving three phases. In the first, preparatory, stage, prudential reforms focus on putting in place the legal and organizational basis for bank supervision, licensing and entry requirements, and a framework for orderly intervention and liquidation of banks, with financial liberalization confined to limited interest rate liberalization. In the second stage, direct credit economic controls are removed, accompanied by the phasing in of key prudential reforms and accounting standards such as off- and on-site bank supervision and the strengthening of capital adequacy ratios and asset portfolio restrictions. In the final stage, prudential issues become more complex and include the supervision of securities markets, the regulation of the market and liquidity risk of banks, the completion of reforms to accounting and disclosure rules and the management of liquidity risk in the payments system, while interest rates are made fully flexible.

6. REGULATORY LESSONS FROM THE FINANCIAL CRISES IN EAST ASIA

The financial crisis in East Asia was multifaceted, encompassing a balance of payments crisis, a banking crisis and a crisis in the corporate sector. Besides steep falls in exchange rates and asset prices, the financial sectors of the three worst affected countries (Thailand, Korea and Indonesia) were afflicted with numerous failures of banks and non-bank financial institutions (NBFIs). The financial fragility of banks and NBFIs in all three countries was caused by large non-performing loans, attributable to high rates of credit growth, excessive concentration on high-risk sectors such as real estate and insider lending.

Estimates of the share of non-performing loans (NPLs) in total banking system loans vary between 25 per cent and 35 per cent (see Table 5.1). Financial institutions also suffered from liquidity and foreign exchange mismatches on their balance sheets, in particular because they had invested short-term foreign exchange-denominated liabilities in longer-term domestic currency-denominated loans. In some cases financial institutions matched foreign currency-denominated liabilities with foreign currency-denominated loans, but the borrowers were businesses in the non-traded goods sectors which did not generate their income in foreign exchange, hence the financial institutions were simply transferring foreign exchange risks into credit risk.

Regulators intervened,[5] closed or recapitalized insolvent and undercapitalized banks (see Table 5.1). In Korea and Thailand, banks and NBFIs accounting for between 40 per cent and 50 per cent of the banking system's assets were intervened, closed or merged with public financial support, while in Indonesia, intervention, closure and/or merger affected banks comprising around 90 per cent of the banking system's assets (Lindgren *et al.*, 1999, p. 36). Hence in all three countries the financial crisis was systemic: it threatened the survival of a large share of the financial system rather than simply isolated financial institutions. The fiscal cost of the financial crisis, comprising the cost of repaying the liabilities of closed financial institutions or recapitalizing financial institutions with public funds, was huge, ranging from 13 per cent of GDP in Korea to 51 per cent of GDP in Indonesia.

Various explanations for the East Asian crisis have been advanced in the large literature on this subject. One set of explanations has focused on the volatility of international financial markets and utilizes currency crisis models, and especially second-generation or third-generation currency crisis models which are characterized by self-fulfilling expectations on the part of the investors and the possibility of multiple equilibria. Another set of explanations has analysed institutional problems in the East Asian economies: the misallocation of resources by poorly regulated financial sectors, the moral hazard arising from government guarantees of the liabilities of financial institutions and weak corporate governance characterized by a lack of transparency.

These explanations are not entirely mutually exclusive. There are currency crisis models in which weak prudential regulation and government guarantees of bank liabilities play a crucial role. Dooley (1998) models an emerging markets balance of payments crisis as an 'insurance crisis'. International capital is attracted into the banking system of an emerging market by the implicit government guarantee of banking system liabilities, backed by the government's foreign exchange reserves. Weak prudential regulation allows bank owners to appropriate bank assets. Once the value of insured bank liabilities exceeds the value of the government assets which back the implicit

Table 5.1 Bank failures in Thailand, Korea and Indonesia

Country	Interventions and closures	Non-performing loans as share of banking system's total loan (%)	Fiscal cost of recapitalizing financial institutions and repaying deposits (% of GDP)
Korea	17 merchant banks closed in 1998 and 1999 5 commercial banks closed in 1998 2 large commercial banks taken over by the government in December 1997 and recapitalized 5 commercial banks merged and recapitalized with public funds 2 other commercial banks recapitalized with public funds	25–30	13
Thailand	58 finance companies suspended in June and August 1997, of which 56 were closed permanently in December 1997 12 other finance companies intervened in 1998 6 commercial banks intervened in 1997–99. One of the intervened commercial banks was closed and 3 were merged with state-owned banks.	25–30	25
Indonesia	64 commercial banks closed between November 1997 and March 1999 54 banks brought under the supervision of the Indonesian Bank Restructuring Agency (IBRA) in February 1998 16 banks taken over by IBRA, of which 3 were closed subsequently 18 banks received public funds for recapitalization	30–35	51

Sources: Enoch (2000), Balino and Ubide (1999), Lindgren *et al.* (1999), World Bank (1999).

guarantee, the banks' creditors will withdraw their funds, precipitating a currency crisis. Similarly Dekle and Kletzer (2001) model a banking system characterized by agency costs, imperfect prudential regulation and government guarantees in which the banking system accumulates foreign debt and becomes progressively more fragile, followed by a banking and currency crisis. While there were clearly multiple factors contributing to the financial crisis in East Asia, it is difficult to fully explain the crisis without taking into account the institutional weaknesses in the financial sector, the deficiencies in prudential regulation and the moral hazard generated by implicit government guarantees (Miller and Luangaram, 1998; Corestti, Pesenti and Roubini, 1998a, 1998b).

Financial crises were not new to East Asia in the late 1990s. Several countries, including Thailand, Malaysia, the Philippines and Hong Kong, suffered bank failures in the 1980s, prompting reforms to strengthen regulation and supervision. Regulations were upgraded and minimum capital adequacy requirements were imposed in line with the Basle recommendations. Supervision was also strengthened with the adoption of CAMEL frameworks. It is notable that the countries in the East Asian region which went furthest in reforming their prudential systems, improving the regulatory framework, the quality of supervision and the enforcement of regulations, notably Hong Kong and Singapore, and to a lesser extent Malaysia and the Philippines, were able to avoid financial crises of the severity which afflicted Thailand, Korea and Indonesia, countries which had much weaker prudential systems (Brownbridge and Kirkpatrick, 1999; Dekle and Kletzer, 2001). The rest of this section analyses the key regulatory weaknesses in Indonesia, Thailand and Korea.

Institutionally Fragmented Regulation

In both Korea and Thailand, prudential regulation was undermined by institutional fragmentation, with regulatory authority split between the respective central banks and ministries of finance. In Korea, the commercial banks were supervised by the central bank, but the NBFIs, including the merchant banks, were supervised by the ministry of finance. The merchant banks, most of which were owned by Chaebols (large industrial conglomerates) were subject to much weaker regulations – related to provisioning rules and large loan exposures, for example – and only minimum supervision by the ministry of finance, which allowing them to engage in high-risk activities. Moreover the merchant banks themselves borrowed funds from the commercial banks. The fragmentation of regulation allowed regulatory arbitrage, whereby riskier activities were channelled towards the NBFIs which were less stringently regulated. Because of the need to address the problems caused by institutional fragmentation, financial system regulation in Korea was consolidated in a single supervisory body, the Financial Supervisory Commission, in April 1998 (Balino and Ubide, 1999, p. 10).

Weak Regulations and Accounting Standards

The asset classification and provisioning rules of the East Asian crisis countries were much laxer than international standards, and also relied too heavily on the value of loan collateral. As a consequence, financial institutions did not have to make adequate provisions for NPLs and for other assets such as securities, income was overstated by the inclusion of unpaid interest and the true extent of declines in the net worth of financial institutions was hidden (Rahman, 1998). Consequently the reported capital positions of financial institutions and their compliance with capital adequacy requirements were meaningless. The Korean authorities even relaxed the provisioning requirements for NPLs and losses incurred on securities holdings in 1995.

Had financial institutions been forced to classify NPLs accurately and make proper provisions, their capital would have been reduced accordingly. This would have forced them either to raise more capital or to curtail the growth of their lending to comply with the minimum capital requirements imposed by the banking regulations, which would have reduced their vulnerability to financial distress. The large loan exposure limits imposed on financial institutions in Korea were much laxer than the international norms. Merchant banks could lend up to 150 per cent of their capital to a single borrower, typically a Chaebol (Balino and Ubide, 1999, p. 19). Consequently default by just one borrower could render a merchant bank insolvent.

The regulations in Korea did not prevent maturity mismatches in foreign exchange exposures. Banks, and especially merchant banks, had much larger short-term foreign liabilities than short-term foreign assets. Short-term liabilities were almost double the short-term assets of Korean commercial banks at end-December 1997, while the merchant banks had short-term liabilities which were four times their short-term assets (ibid., p. 22). This was partly brought about because restrictions on short-term foreign borrowing were removed but restrictions on long-term borrowing remained in place. In addition, restrictions on foreign borrowing by non-financial corporations which did not have an international credit rating of BBB or above encouraged such corporations to borrow funds through domestic financial institutions which did have strong credit ratings, partly because of implicit government guarantees, and which could therefore raise funds from abroad. Consequently the regulations served to increase the vulnerability of domestic financial institutions to foreign exchange maturity mismatches and to credit risk.

Poor Enforcement of Regulations and Regulatory Forbearance

In all three countries prudential regulations were not strictly enforced. Breaches of prudential limits on insider lending and large loan exposures occurred in Korea and Indonesia. Insider lending regulations were difficult to enforce in some cases because of the lack of transparency in the financial accounts of financial institutions and because of political pressure (Folkerts-Landau *et al.*, 1995).

Regulatory forbearance meant that regulators only closed or intervened in the operations of a few banks prior to the financial crisis of 1997/98. Instead, distressed banks were often provided with financial support by governments to allow them to remain open. Consequently incentives for bank owners to pursue prudent management and incentives for depositors to avoid risky banks were weakened.

Regulatory forbearance was attributable to several factors. First, formal and transparent intervention and closure policies for failed banks and NBFIs were missing from the banking regulations in all three countries. Instead, regulation entailed large elements of discretion and dialogue between the regulators and financial institutions that they regulated (Stiglitz and Uy, 1996, p. 258), which provided scope for the regulators to exercise forbearance. Second, regulators faced strong political pressure not to enforce regulations against politically connected financial institutions or against financial institutions which had lent in an imprudent manner to politically connected borrowers. Political interference was pervasive in Indonesia, where the central bank had little effective independence to impose discipline on the banking industry (Anonymous, 1998, pp. 15–16). Third, there was an inherent conflict of interest between the role of central banks in enforcing economic regulations, such as the requirements for banks to lend a minimum share of their loan portfolios to priority sectors, which often involved lending to the more risky borrowers, and their role in enforcing prudential regulations.

Bongini *et al.* (2000) examined data on 186 banks and 87 NBFIs in Indonesia, Korea, Thailand, Malaysia and the Philippines. Of these financial institutions, 42 per cent experienced financial distress between July 1997 and July 1999 and 13 per cent were closed during this period. The researchers found that financial institutions categorized as 'connected' (defined as a financial institution in which the largest shareholder has a shareholding of more than 20 per cent in the financial institution and is either a family or an industrial conglomerate) had a higher probability of experiencing distress during 1997–9, which they interpreted as evidence of regulatory forbearance prior to the financial crisis. However connected financial institutions did not have a lower probability of being closed during 1997–9 than non-connected financial institutions, which indicates that the closure process during the financial crisis was transparent.

Implicit Government Guarantees

There were only very limited explicit government guarantees of the liabilities of banks and NBFIs in Korea, Thailand and Indonesia prior to the 1997/98 financial crisis. Korea had only limited deposit insurance from the mid-1990s, while Thailand had no official deposit insurance scheme and provided no explicit guarantee of banks' foreign borrowing. Nevertheless many analysts of the East Asian financial crisis have attributed an important role to the moral hazard created by implicit government guarantees, which arose because the incidents of bank closure in which creditors suffered losses had been relatively rare prior to the crisis of 1997/98. There had been incidences where creditors suffered losses (when 25 finance companies were closed in the mid-1980s in Thailand, their depositors had to bear 50 per cent of the losses) but this was the exception rather than the rule. There is also some evidence that international ratings agencies regarded the larger banks in Korea as enjoying government guarantees because they were 'too big to fail' and hence awarded them strong credit ratings (Balino and Ubide, 1999, p. 21).

The Bank of Thailand, in assessing regulatory and supervisory weaknesses in 1998, concluded that 'Moral hazard was also another important weakness of the system. The lack of a clearly stated policy stance on allowing financial institutions to fail gave a misleading sense of security to the market players. As in many countries in the region, the financial system in Thailand was characterized as one of "no entry, no exit", meaning that it is both difficult to get in as well as difficult to let a financial institution fail' (Bank of Thailand, 1998, p. 21).

If the holders, domestic and foreign, of the liabilities of financial institutions in Korea, Thailand and Indonesia did believe that their liabilities would be guaranteed by the governments of these countries, these beliefs were validated ex post. All of the liabilities of banks and NBFIs, including liabilities to non-residents, were eventually guaranteed by the governments of Korea, Indonesia and Thailand, because of the fear that bank runs would trigger systemic financial crises.

7. PROPOSALS FOR REFORMS TO PRUDENTIAL SYSTEMS

Recognition of the weaknesses in existing prudential frameworks in DCs has stimulated a number of proposals for further reform, some of which comprise incremental reforms to the standard prudential model and some of which entail more radical approaches. In this section proposals for a new generation of reform are divided into three categories. The first involves reforms which place more reliance on the market. The second involves stronger restrictions on banking activities, including some reversal of financial liberalization, such as deposit interest rate controls, while the third category involves strengthening the existing model through revisions to prudential regulations, such as strengthening capital adequacy requirements and bank intervention rules.

Market-based Approaches to Regulation

Greater reliance on the market to regulate risk taking by banks is advocated by Calomiris (1997) who doubts whether government supervisors have the skill or incentives to identify losses incurred by banks as diligently as would private sector agents with their own money at risk. Caprio (1996) argues that it is unrealistic to expect bank supervisors to act as the first line of defence against bank failures in DCs, given the constraints supervisors face in these countries, such as severe scarcities of the requisite skills, the length of time needed to train supervisors, political interference and weak accounting and legal frameworks. The findings of Barth *et al.* (2001) – reviewed in section 4 above – which cast doubt on the efficacy of government-imposed regulation and supervision, also provide support for more market-based approaches to bank regulation. The most obvious way to enhance incentives for market monitoring of banks is to restrict deposit insurance coverage to small amounts per depositor, to ensure that the bulk of bank deposits are not insured. However there are political costs to restricting deposit insurance to small deposits, which might reduce the credibility of such a restriction and thereby undermine incentives for private monitoring of banks. For politicians, restricting insurance only to small deposits may not be a time-consistent policy.

Calomiris (1997) advocates imposing a requirement that banks should finance a minimum percentage of their assets with subordinated and uninsured debt carrying a yield capped at a maximum premium above the riskless market interest rate. To mobilize subordinated debt with a capped yield, banks would have to convince potential private sector subordinated debt holders that the quality of the bank's asset portfolio and capital was sufficiently good to justify their providing such credit. Subordinated debt holders would have incentives to monitor the bank, and the threat of a run by informed debt holders would mitigate moral hazard on the part of the banks. Argentina introduced a requirement that banks should finance 2 per cent of total deposits in the form of subordinated debt, although without a maximum yield, in 1996.

While subordinated debt proposals may be applicable in some emerging markets, they require sophisticated market agents and so are unlikely to be feasible in low-income DCs where capital markets are very poorly developed and the veracity of audited accounts is unreliable. Consequently banks in low-income DCs would have great difficulty in mobilizing subordinated debt from genuine private sector investors irrespective of the quality of their asset portfolios. Furthermore, if a bank is insolvent or close to insolvency, uninsured subordinated debt takes on characteristics which are similar to those of equity capital, and consequently subordinated debt holders have sub-optimal incentives to impose conservative management on the bank to protect its deposits (Dewatripont and Tirole, 1994, p. 219).

Another approach which utilizes the market is to increase the requirements on banks to disclose details of their financial condition and to require banks to obtain credit ratings from private agencies on a regular basis. Both Chile and Argentina have strengthened disclosure requirements and provide less than full insurance for banks' liabilities. Argentina requires banks to make their balance sheet data publicly available on a monthly basis, requires quarterly external audits of banks and requires banks to obtain ratings from two established private credit rating agencies (Calomiris, 1997, IMF, 1998b, p. 161). However enhancing disclosure requirements in countries in which accounting standards are weak and audited accounts are unreliable is likely to have limited value. Even in countries with reliable accounting and auditing standards, the efficacy of disclosure requirements as an instrument to facilitate monitoring of banks by their depositors is limited. The acquisition and use of private information about borrowers, in a manner which is not feasible for depositors, provides one of the key motivations for the role of banks as financial intermediaries. The type of information which banks use to appraise their own borrowers is not publicly observable or verifiable (Marquardt, 1987, pp. 20–22). Borrowers seek loans from banks partly because they cannot credibly transmit information about their risk profiles directly to savers. If this were possible, the borrowers would raise funds more cheaply directly from capital markets.

Restrictions on Bank Deposit Rates

Restrictions on bank deposit rates have been advocated as a prudential instrument. One argument for such restrictions is that the combination of moral hazard arising from deposit insurance and weak prudential regulation gives banks incentives to take excessive risks and to bid up deposit rates in order to mobilize funds. Both depositors and the banks benefit if the banks' high-risk strategy pays off, but the deposit insurance fund bears the cost if the strategy fails. Deposit rate controls help to remove the incentives for depositors to fund risky banks. In this case, deposit rates are a second-best response to counter the weaknesses in deposit insurance and prudential regulation (McKinnon, 1988).

Hellmann *et al.* (1998) also advocate deposit rate controls. They contend that the increased competition induced by financial liberalization contributes to financial fragility because it reduces banks' franchise values and thus erodes incentives for prudent bank management. They model a banking market with freely determined deposit rates of interest in which, although raising capital requirements can induce more prudent bank management, this is not pareto efficient because banks are compelled to hold an inefficiently large amount of capital. In this model, an efficient pareto outcome can be induced through a combination of deposit rate controls and capital requirements. Hellman *et al.* (1998) view deposit rate controls as part of a wider strategy of regulations, which they term 'financial restraint', including restrictions on entry into banking markets, which create rents for banks. These rents enhance the franchise value of banks, thereby encouraging more prudent bank management, as well as encouraging greater deposit mobilization by banks.

There are, however, practical difficulties in using interest rate controls to promote more prudent bank management. First, it is not clear how the optimal interest rate ceiling can be determined. Second, prudential regulation is weak in DCs, not so much because the appropriate prudential regulations have not been put in place, but because of the difficulty in enforcing these regulations. These difficulties would apply equally to the enforcement of economic regulations, such as interest rate controls. If lending to high-risk borrowers is potentially profitable for banks and deposits can be mobilized by offering higher deposit rates, banks will have incentives to evade the interest rate controls.

Restrictions on Lending Growth and Foreign Exchange-denominated Lending

Overrapid expansion of lending by banks is often a cause of poor asset quality, because rapid growth of lending may outstrip the lender's capacity to appraise and monitor its borrowers and also because more marginal borrowers are likely to be brought into the credit market. However prudential regulations in most countries do not place restrictions on credit growth, other than indirectly through the capital adequacy requirement. Honohan (1997, p. 21) advocates 'speed limits' to restrict the rate of growth of banks' loan portfolios. He envisages that these would be used in markets with many new and inexperienced entrants, or to dampen a credit boom, but does not envisage their use as a tool of regulation on a permanent basis. Speed limits need not necessarily be applied to the entire loan portfolio, but could be restricted to the types of lending, such as real estate or foreign currency loans, which are regarded as posing the greatest risk to banks' financial soundness and which often grow rapidly after financial liberalization.

Mishkin (2000) argues for imposing restrictions on banks' borrowing and lending in foreign currencies, because domestic banks and firms which have foreign currency-denominated debt risk a deterioration in their net worth if the exchange rate depreciates. Even if domestic banks match their foreign currency assets and liabilities, an exchange rate depreciation would impair their asset portfolios if their borrowers have net liabilities in foreign exchange. Because of the adverse impact of exchange rate depreciation on the balance sheets of domestic banks and firms, the monetary authorities are restricted in using monetary expansion to promote recovery from economic crisis and in providing lender of last resort facilities to banks, as injecting liquidity into the economy could cause an exchange rate depreciation.

Strengthening Capital Requirements

Although most DCs have adopted bank capital requirements based on the Basle Capital Accord, Dziobeck *et al.* (1995) argue that stricter capital regulations are needed in DCs because the risks facing their banking systems are greater than in the industrialized countries as a result of a less stable economic environment and less developed financial infrastructures. DCs should, therefore, consider adopting higher minimum capital adequacy requirements than the 8 per cent of risk-adjusted assets specified in the Basle Accord. Both Singapore and Uganda have introduced capital adequacy requirements of 12 per cent, while Argentina has introduced an 11.5 per cent capital adequacy requirement. Moreover other elements of the capital adequacy requirement computation need to be reviewed. For example, the risk weights given to different types of loans are based on observed default probabilities in industrialized countries, which may be too low if applied to DCs.

Dziobeck, Frecaut and Nieto warn that higher capital requirements cannot compensate for deficiencies in other prudential regulations, such as inadequate provisioning. Furthermore bank capital in DCs is often elastic and of poor quality because bank owners are able to finance their equity holdings by borrowing from their own bank; hence in such cases raising capital requirements would neither reduce incentives for risk taking nor provide a buffer against losses (Goodhart *et al.*, 1998, pp. 107–8). Even if capital adequacy standards could be effectively enforced, some models of banking behaviour suggest that in some circumstances raising regulatory capital requirements may be ineffective in reducing risk taking on the part of banks or may even induce greater risk taking (Bhattacharya and Thakor, 1992; Gilbert, 1991).

Intervention Rules

The importance of regulatory forbearance as a source of weakness in prudential systems was highlighted in section 5 above. Two approaches which attempt to tackle this problem are the introduction of PCA rules and measures to increase the accountability of bank regulators. Publicly announced intervention rules aim to limit the discretion of the bank regulators to exercise regulator forbearance. An example of such rules are the PCA regulations, introduced in the United States in 1991, which specify graduated intervention by the regulators triggered by thresholds linked to capital adequacy.

The value of PCA regulations is threefold. First, PCA forces regulators to intervene in a distressed bank before it becomes insolvent. Hence the chances of successfully rectifying the bank's distress are higher than if intervention was to be delayed until the financial condition of the bank had worsened. Second, PCA regulations impose a legal requirement on the regulators to take specified actions and thus strengthen the incentives for regulators to intervene promptly. They also provide regulators with a defence against political pressure for regulatory forbearance. Third, by making PCA regulations part of the banking law, bank owners and managers will have less reason to believe that regulators will exercise forbearance in the event that their bank becomes distressed. Therefore the existence of publicly announced intervention rules will enhance the credibility of the regulators as enforcers of the regulations, and will thereby improve incentives for prudent bank management.

There are practical difficulties with implementing PCA rules in DCs (Brownbridge and Maimbo, 2003). Defining robust intervention rules may be difficult. The capital adequacy thresholds used in the USA may not convey useful information about the true financial condition of a bank in a DC, because an insolvent or capital-impaired bank can still produce a balance sheet showing that it is well capitalized if it fails to classify its non-performing loans accurately and make appropriate provisions. Regulators may not know that a bank has crossed an intervention threshold until long after the event, by which time it may already be insolvent. In addition, however strong the regulator's commitment may be, ex ante, to enforcing intervention rules, such rules are time-inconsistent in that, when faced with a major bank failure, governments often face very strong incentives to ignore the rules and bail out the bank rather close it down. For example, in the mid-1970s, the Chilean authorities repeatedly stated that they would not bail out insolvent banks, but they did so in 1977, when a large bank ran into trouble, because they feared the impact of its insolvency on the confidence of depositors and external creditors in the country's financial system (Diaz-Alejandro, 1985).

While acknowledging that allowing regulators discretion can lead to excessive forbearance, Enoch *et al.* (1997) argue that discretion and ambiguity by regulators in implementing intervention policies does have some value. It may not always be possible, or optimal, to enforce intervention rules, such as when a bank is 'too big to fail', in which case the rules lose their credibility. A rule-driven intervention policy could penalize bank management for problems, such as those arising from macroeconomic shocks, for which they are not responsible (Dewatripont and Tirole, 1994, pp. 220–21). Furthermore it may not be desirable to reveal publicly that a bank has received assistance from the authorities because it might undermine public confidence in that bank. Enoch, Stella and Khamis distinguish between ex ante and ex post transparency, and argue that some ex ante discretion in the operation of lender of last resort facilities, balanced by sanctions on those who are responsible for the bank's distress, should be combined with ex post transparency in which the regulators would have to make full disclosure of their intervention (for example, why, and how much, finance was provided, and what were the results) to the public.

Autonomy and Accountability of the Regulators

Enhancing the legal autonomy of the regulators from government may also help to insulate the regulators against pressure to exercise regulatory forbearance, but it is unlikely to be a panacea in countries where the legal framework is weak and, hence, nominally legally independent regulators may have little protection in practice from political interference.[6]

Regulatory forbearance reflects a principal–agent problem, as noted in section 5 above. Kane (1997) argues that it is the ability of government agents to conceal information from, and resist accountability to, the public which lies at the heart of many principal–agent problems. As such it is essential to make 'the costs generated by regulatory forbearance observable so that regulators can be disciplined in the press and in the labour market for post government employment' (ibid., p. 72). How this could best be achieved will depend upon the specific institutional characteristics of different DCs: for example, in countries which have independently minded parliamentarians, bank regulators could be required to submit a detailed annual report on their activities to a parliamentary committee, including the details of support given to banks and compliance with banking laws.

8.   CONCLUSIONS

In market-oriented economies, the financial system plays a crucial role in allocating resources but is vulnerable to instability and crisis. Financial crises can be very damaging for both economic output and the welfare of the poor in DCs, hence financial sector policy reforms have sought to strengthen the prudential regulation and supervision of the financial system, and especially the banking system (Jalilian and Kirkpatrick, 2002; Brownbridge and Kirkpatrick, 2002).

There is no doubt that many developing countries have made significant progress in reforming their prudential systems since the 1980s. Banking legislation has been upgraded, supervisory capacities have been strengthened, and policies and procedures for prompt corrective action have been put in place. Nevertheless serious institutional impediments to effective prudential regulation remain, including weak accounting standards, poor quality of information available to regulators and the market, acute shortages of the professional regulatory and supervisory skills needed for the politicalization of the regulatory process, and the difficulty of enforcing legal regulations. There is also emerging evidence from cross-country research that expanding regulatory controls over the banking system may do little to reduce the probability of a banking crisis occurring, while the introduction of deposit insurance schemes, which is another component of financial sector reforms in many DCs, may in fact make a banking crisis more likely.

What constitutes the best model for prudential regulation in DCs remains a matter for debate. Future reforms to the prudential system will need to address two key issues. The first issue is that public regulation alone is unlikely to provide effective bank regulation, because of the institutional and resource constraints facing public regulators and also because of the increasing complexity of the financial system. Therefore prudential policies must strive to strengthen market incentives for more stable banking systems, including the incentives facing the banks' owners and managers for more prudent bank management and the incentives facing depositors and other bank creditors for monitoring banks. Possibilities for strengthening market incentives include raising the franchise value of banks (by restricting entry into banking markets, for example) and requiring banks to disclose more information to the public and, more frequently, about their financial condition.

The second issue is how to reduce regulatory forbearance. This will require strengthening the incentives facing bank regulators to intervene more effectively and promptly in distressed banks. One reform which appears promising is to introduce PCA rules into banking legislation, which provide for mandatory regulatory intervention whenever banks pass predetermined thresholds of bank distress. It will also be necessary to protect the regulators from undue political interference, to make them more accountable for their actions.

For DCs, addressing the two issues noted above is critical. The rate of development of the financial system is accelerating in many countries, driven by liberalization and technological advances, and this is changing the nature of the risks which financial systems face. This has important implications for financial sector regulation, because it means that prudential regulatory systems will also have to be constantly reformed and improved if they are to keep pace with the challenges posed by the evolving financial system.

NOTES

1. The views expressed in this chapter are entirely the authors' and do not represent the views of the World Bank, its Board of Directors, its management or any of its member countries. Any errors or omissions remain the sole responsibility of the authors.
2. Systemic risk involves the potential for distress in one financial institution to become generalized within the financial system (Davis,1992, p. 122).
3. There are also similar agency problems between banks and their loan customers.
4. The rationale for bank regulation is not universally accepted. Benston and Kaufman (1996), for example, dispute that regulation of the banking system is warranted, except to reduce the negative externalities arising from government-imposed deposit insurance.
5. Here, intervene includes a number of regulatory management actions such as replacing and restricting the bank's operations, requiring additional reporting requirements, appointing a curator, and others aimed at improving a bank's strategic and operational management.
6. There are parallels here with literature on central bank independence and inflation (for example, Cukierman and Webb, 1995; Keefer and Stasavage, 1998).

REFERENCES

Akerlof, G. and Romer, D. (1993), 'The economic underworld of bankruptcy for profit', *Brookings Papers on Economic Activity*, 1–73.

Alawode, A. and Ikhide, S.I. (1997), 'Why should financial liberalisation induce financial crisis?', *Savings and Development*, **3**, 261–73.

Anonymous (1998), 'Cover story: going for gold', *Far Eastern Economic Review*, 2 April, 10–16.

Balino, T.J. and Ubide, A. (1999), 'The Korean financial crisis of 1997 – a strategy of financial sector reform', IMF Working Papers 99/28, International Monetary Fund, Washington, DC.

Bank of Thailand (1998), *Supervision Report* 1996/97, Bangkok, Bank of Thailand.

Barth, J., Caprio, G. and Levine, R. (2001), 'The regulation and supervision of banks around the world: a new database', World Bank Policy Research Working Paper 2588, Washington, DC.

Benston, G.J. and Kaufman, G.G. (1996), 'The appropriate role of bank regulation', *The Economic Journal*, **106**, 688–97.

Berenbach, S. and Churchill, C. (1997), 'Regulation and supervision of microfinance institutions: experiences from Latin America, Asia and Africa', occasional paper no. 1, the Microfinance Network, US AID, Washington, DC.

Berger, A.N., Herring, R.J. and Szego, G.P. (1995), 'The role of capital in financial institutions', *Journal of Banking and Finance*, **19** (3–4), 393–430.

Bhattacharya, S. and Thakor A.V. (1992), 'Contemporary banking theory', *Journal of Financial Intermediation*, **3**, 2–50.

Bhattacharya, S., Boot, A.W.A. and Thakor, A.V. (1998), 'The economics of bank regulation', *Journal of Money Credit and Banking*, **3** (4), 745–70.

Bongini, P., Claessens, S. and Ferri, G. (2000), 'The political economy of distress in East Asian financial institutions', World Bank Policy Research Working Paper 2265, Washington, DC.

Boot, A.W. and Thakor, A.V. (1993) 'Self-interest bank regulation', *American Economic Review, Papers and Proceedings*, **83**, 206–12.

Brook, P.J. and Irwin, T.C. (eds) (2003), 'Infrastructure for poor people: public policy for private provision', World Bank.

Brownbridge, M. (1998), 'Financial distress in local banks in Kenya, Nigeria, Uganda and Zambia: causes and implications for regulatory policy', *Development Policy Review*, **16** (2), 173–88.

Brownbridge, M. and Kirkpatrick, C. (1999), 'Financial sector regulation: the lessons of the Asian crisis', *Development Policy Review*, **17** (3), 243–66.

Brownbridge, M. and Kirkpatrick, C. (2002), 'Policy symposium: financial regulation and supervision in developing countries: an overview of the issues', *Development Policy Review*, **20** (3), 243–5.

Brownbridge, M. and Maimbo, S. (2003), 'Cleaner banking: is it possible?', ID21, DFID (Available at http://www.id21.org/society/S&bmb1g1.html).

Calomiris, G. (1997), *The Postmodern Bank Safety Net: Lessons from Developed and Developing Economies*, Washington, DC: AEO Press.

Caprio, G. (1996), 'Bank regulation: the case of the missing model', World Bank Policy Research Working Paper 1574, Washington, DC.

Caprio, G. and Honohan, P. (1999), 'Restoring banking stability: beyond supervised capital requirements', *Journal of Economic Perspectives*, **13** (4), 43–64.

Caprio, G., Honohan, P. and Stiglitz, J.E. (eds) (2001), *Financial Liberalisation: How Far, How Fast?*, Cambridge: Cambridge University Press.

Corestti, G., Pesenti, P. and Roubini, N. (1998a), 'What caused the Asian currency and financial crisis? Part I: a macroeconomic overview', Working Paper no. 6833, National Bureau of Economic Research, Cambridge, MA.

Corestti, G., Pesenti, P. and Roubini, N. (1998b), 'What caused the Asian currency and financial crisis? Part II: the policy debate', Working Paper no. 6834, National Bureau of Economic Research, Cambridge, MA.

Cukierman, A. and Webb, S.B. (1995), 'Political influence on the central bank: international evidence', *The World Bank Economic Review*, **9** (3), 397–423.

Cull, R.J. (1997), 'Financial sector adjustment lending: a mid-course analysis', World Bank Policy Research Working Paper 1804, Washington, DC.

Davis, E.P. (1992), *Debt, Financial Fragility and Systemic Risk*, Oxford: Oxford University Press.

Dekle, R. and Kletzer, K. (2001), 'Domestic bank regulation and financial crisis: theory and empirical evidence from East Asia', IMF Working Paper no, 63.

Demirgüç-Kunt, A. and Detragiache, E. (1998), 'The determinants of banking crises: evidence in developing and developed countries', *IMF Staff Papers*, **45**, 81–109, IMF, Washington, DC.

Dewatripont, M. and Tirole, J. (1994), *The Prudential Regulation of Banks*, Cambridge, MA: MIT Press.

Diamond, D. and Dybvig, P. (1983), 'Bank runs, deposit insurance and liquidity', *Journal of Political Economy*, **91** (3), 401–19.

Diaz-Alejandro, C. (1985), 'Good-bye financial repression, hello financial crash', *Journal of Development Economics*, **19** (102), 1–24.

Dooley, M. (1998), 'A model of crisis in emerging markets', National Bureau of Economic Research Working Paper no, 6300, Cambridge, MA.

Dziobeck, C., Frecaut, O. and Nieto, M. (1995), 'Non-G-10 countries and the Basle capital rules: how tough a challenge is it to join the Basle Club?', paper on policy analysis and assessment PPAA/95/5, IMF, Washington, DC.

Enoch, C. (2000), 'Interventions in banks during banking crisis: the experience of Indonesia', Policy Discussion Paper PDP/00/2, IMF, Washington, DC.

Enoch, C., Stella, P. and Khamis, M. (1997), 'Transparency and ambiguity in central bank safety net operations', IMF Working Paper WP/97/138, IMF, Washington, DC.

Folkerts-Landau, D., Schinasi, G.J., Cassad, M., Ng, V.K., Reinhart, C.M. and Spencer, M.G. (1995), 'Effect of capital flows on the domestic financial sectors in APEC developing countries', in Mohsin S. Khan and Carmen Reinhart (eds), 'Capital Flows in the APEC Region', *Occasional Paper 122*, Washington, DC: IMF, pp. 31–57.

Gilbert, R.A. (1991), 'Supervision of undercapitalised banks: is there a case for change?', *Federal Bank of St Louis Review*, **73** (3), 16–30.

Glaessner, T. and Mas, I. (1995), 'Incentives and the resolution of bank distress', *The World Bank Research Observer*, **10** (1) (Feb), 53–73.

Goldstein, M. and Turner, P. (1996), 'Banking crises in emerging economies: origins and policy options', BIS Economic Papers, no. 46, Bank for International Settlements, Basle.

Goodhart, C., Hartmann, P., Llewellyn D., Rojas-Suarez, L. and Weisbod, S. (1998), *Financial Regulation: Why How and Where Now?*, London: Routledge.

Gorton, G. (1988), 'Banking panics and business cycles', *Oxford Economic Papers*, **40**, pp. 751–81.

Greuning, H., Gallardo, J. and Randhawa, B. (1999), *A Framework for Regulating Microfinance Institutions*, Washington, DC: World Bank.

Hellmann, T., Murdock, K. and Stiglitz, J. (1995), 'Financial restraint: towards a new paradigm', in M. Aoki and H. Kim, M. Okuno-Fujiwara (eds), *The Role of Government in East Asian Economic Development: Comparative Institutional Analysis*, Oxford: Oxford University Press.

Honohan, P. (1997), 'Banking system failures in developing and transition countries: diagnosis and prediction', BIS Working Paper no, 39, Bank for International Settlements, Basle.

Honohan, P. and Klingebiel, D. (2000), 'Controlling fiscal costs of banking crises', World Bank Policy Research Working Paper 2441, Washington, DC.

International Monetary Fund (1998a), 'Towards a framework for financial stability', Washington, DC.

International Monetary Fund (1998b) 'International capital markets: developments, prospects and key policy issues', Washington, DC.

Jalilian, H. and Kirkpatrick, C. (2002), 'Financial development and poverty reduction in developing countries', *International Journal of Finance and Economics*, **7**, 1–12.

Jalilian, H., Kirkpatrick, C. and Parker, D. (2003), 'The impact of regulation on economic growth in developing countries: a cross country analysis', CRC Centre on Regulation and Competition, Working Paper 54, July, IDPM, University of Manchester.

Kane, E.J. (1989), 'The high costs of incompletely funding the FSLIC's shortage of explicit capital', *The Journal of Economic Perspectives*, **3** (4), 31–47.

Kane, E.J. (1997), 'Comment on "Understanding Financial Crises: A Developing

Country Perspective"', by Frederic S. Mishkin', *Annual World Bank Conference on Development Economics, 1996*, Washington, DC: World Bank, pp. 69–75.

Keefer, P. and Stasavage, D. (1998), 'When does delegation improve credibility? Central bank independence and the separation of powers', WPS/98-18, Centre for the Study of African Economies, Oxford.

Kirkpatrick, C. and Maimbo, S.M. (2002), 'The implications of the evolving microfinance agenda for regulatory and supervisory policy', *Development Policy Review*, **20** (3), 293–304.

Kyei, A. (1995), 'Deposit protection arrangements: a survey', IMF Working Paper WP/95/1 34.

Lindgren, C., Balino, J.T., Enoch, C., Gulde, A., Quintyn, M. and Teo, L. (1999), 'Financial sector crisis and restructuring: lessons from Asia', *IMF Occasional Paper 188*, Washington, DC: IMF.

Long, M. and Vittas, D. (1992), 'Changing the rules of the game', in D. Vittas (ed.), *Financial Regulation: Changing the Rules of the Game*, Washington, DC: World Bank, pp. 43–57.

Maimbo, S. (2001), 'The regulation and supervision of commercial banks: a study of the design, development and implementation of prudential regulations by the Bank of Zambia between 1980 and 2000', unpublished PhD Thesis, University of Manchester.

Marquardt, J.C. (1987), 'Financial market supervision: some conceptual issues', *Bank for International Settlements Economic Papers*, **19**, May.

McKinnon, R.I. (1988), 'Financial liberalisation in retrospect: interest rate policies in LDSs', in Gustav Ranis and T. Paul Schultz (eds), *The State of Development Economics: Progress and Perspectives*, New York: Basil Blackwell, pp. 386–410.

Mehran, H., Ugolini, P., Briffaux, J.P., Iden, G., Lybek, T., Swaray, S. and Hayward, P. (1998), 'Financial sector developments in Sub-Saharan African countries', *Occasional Paper 169*, Washington, DC: IMF.

Miller, M. and Luangaram, P. (1998), 'Financial crisis in East Asia: bank runs, asset bubbles and antidotes', *National Institute Economic Review*, **165**, 66–82.

Mishkin, F (2000), *The Economics of Money, Banking and Financial Markets*, 6th edn, Reading, MA: Addison Wesley Longman.

Ncube, M. and Senbet, L.W. (1997), 'Perspectives on financial regulation and liberalisation in Africa under asymmetric information and incentive problems', *Journal of African Economies*, supplement to 6 (1), Part II, pp. 29–88.

Polizatto, V. (1991), 'Prudential regulation and banking supervision: building an institutional framework for banks', in P. Collier (ed.), *Financial Systems and Development in Africa EDI Seminar Series*, Washington, DC: The World Bank.

Rahman, M.Z. (1998), 'The role of accounting and disclosure standards in the East Asian financial crisis: lessons learned', mimeo, UNCTAD, Geneva.

Rossi, M. (1999), 'Financial fragility and economic performance in developing economies: do capital controls, prudential regulation and supervision matter?', International Monetary Fund Working Paper WP/99/66, Washington, DC.

Sheng, A. (1996), 'Resolution and reform: supervisory remedies for problem banks', in A. Sheng (ed.) *Bank Restructuring: Lessons from the 1980s*, Washington, DC: World Bank, pp. 49–70.

Stiglitz, J. and Uy, M. (1996), 'Financial markets, public policy and the East Asian miracle', *World Bank Research Observer*, 11 (2) (August), 249–76.

Sundararajan, V. (1999), 'Prudential supervision, bank restructuring and financial sector reform', in R.B. Johnston and V. Sundarajan (eds), *Sequencing Financial*

Sector Reforms: Country Experiences and Issues, Washington, DC: International Monetary Fund, pp. 186–213.

Talley, S.H. and Mas, I. (1992), 'The role of deposit insurance', in D. Vittas (ed.), *Financial Regulation: Changing the Rules of the Game*, Washington, DC: The World Bank Economic Development Institute, pp. 321–51.

Villanueva, D. and Mirakhor, A. (1990), 'Strategies for financial reforms', *IMF Staff Papers*, 37 (3), 509–36.

Vittas, D. (1992), *Financial Regulation: Changing the Rules of the Game*, Washington, DC: World Bank.

Williamson, J. and Maher, M. (1998), 'A survey of financial liberalisation', *Princeton Essays in International Finance*, 211, Department of Economics, Princeton University.

World Bank (1999), *Global Economic Prospects*, Washington, DC: World Bank.

World Bank (2002), *World Development Report, Building Institutions for Markets*, Washington, DC: World Bank.

6. Banking regulation after recent financial crises: lessons for developing and developed countries

David T. Llewellyn*

1. INTRODUCTION

The objective of this chapter is to consider the experience of recent banking crises in both developed and developing countries, and to draw lessons most especially with respect to the regulation and supervision of banks, and the design of an optimal 'regulatory regime'. This will be done by setting out a series of general principles designed to lower the probability of banking distress. Just as the causes of banking crises are multidimensional, so the principles of an effective regulatory regime also need to incorporate a wider range of issues than externally imposed rules on bank behaviour. What will be termed a 'regulatory regime' also includes the arrangements for intervention in the event of bank distress and failures. This is because they have incentive and moral hazard effects which potentially influence future behaviour of banks and their customers and the probability of future crises.

The focus of the chapter is a consideration of alternative approaches to achieving the objectives of regulation: systemic stability and consumer protection. A central theme is that what are often regarded as 'alternatives' are in fact complements within an overall regulatory strategy. As the regulatory regime is wider than the rules and monitoring conducted by regulatory agencies, the skill in constructing a regulatory strategy lies in how the various components of the regime are combined.

When a particular regulatory problem emerges, the instinct of a regulator is often to create new rules. This implies an incremental approach to regulation by focusing upon the rules component of the regulatory regime. The chapter argues that there are serious problems with such an incremental rules approach in that it may blunt the power of the other mechanisms and may, in the process, reduce the overall effectiveness of the regime in achieving its core objectives.

Although there is considerable academic debate about whether or not banks should be regulated at all, this issue is not addressed. Some studies (notably those of Benston and Kaufman, 1995) argue that the economic rationale for bank regulation has not been robustly established and that, in some cases, banking problems have their origin in regulatory rather than market failure. In particular, emphasis is given to the moral hazard effects of safety-net arrangements. A similar approach is found in Schwartz (1995).[1]

A central theme is that the various components of the regulatory regime need to be combined in an overall regulatory strategy and that, while all are necessary, none is sufficient. While external regulation has a role in fostering a safe and sound banking system, this role is limited. Equally, and increasingly important, are the incentive structures faced by private banking agents, the efficiency of the necessary monitoring and supervision of banks by official agencies and the market, and corporate governance arrangements within banks. External regulation is only one component of regimes to create safe and sound banking systems which, if it is pressed too far, may blunt other mechanisms and in the process compromise the impact of the overall regime.

A sustained theme is that the regulatory regime is defined more widely than regulation externally imposed on financial institutions. In current conditions it would be a mistake to rely wholly, or even predominantly, on external regulation, monitoring and supervision by the 'official sector'. The world of banking and finance is too complex and volatile to be able to rely on a simple set of prescriptive rules for prudent and compliant behaviour. There is a danger of thinking only in terms of incremental change to regulation, rather than strategically with respect to the overall regime. This needs to be set in the context of trade-offs between the various components. In some circumstances the more emphasis that is given to one of the components (such as regulation) the less powerful becomes one or more of the others (such as market discipline on financial firms, or the effectiveness of corporate governance arrangements) and to an extent that may reduce the overall impact.

The skill in formulating regulatory strategy lies not so much in choosing between various options, but in combining the seven components of the regime. The objective is to move towards an optimal mix, combined with careful choice of regulatory instruments within each. It is not, therefore, a question of choosing between either regulation or market disciplines, or between regulation and supervision on the one hand or competition on the other. The concept of a regulatory strategy is that these are not alternatives but components of an overall approach to achieve the objective of systemic stability. A key issue for the regulator is how its actions can contribute not only to the objectives directly, but to the way they affect the other components of the regime: in particular, the issue is how regulation affects incentive structures within firms, and also the role that can be played by market discipline and monitoring.

The optimal mix of the components will change over time. It is argued that, over time and as the market environment in which banks operate becomes more complex, four structural shifts within the regulatory regime are desirable: (1) external regulation needs to become less prescriptive, more flexible and differentiated as between different institutions; (2) more emphasis needs to be given to incentive structures and the contribution that regulation can make to creating appropriate incentive structures; (3) market discipline and market monitoring of banks need to be strengthened; and (4) corporate governance mechanisms for banks need to be strengthened.

The outline of the chapter is as follows. Section 2 provides a brief overview of recent banking crises, while section 3 considers some common elements in banking crises. This is followed in section 4 by a discussion of the multidimensional nature of recent crises. Section 5 reviews the impact of liberalization where a distinction is made between the transitional effects associated with the shift from one regime to another, and the steady-state characteristics of a deregulated financial system. Section 6 discusses the nature of a regulatory regime and the trade-offs between its components, and proceeds to draw together the implications of the nature and origin of banking crises by setting out a set of principles designed to lower the probability of distress in the banking sector. Section 7 offers conclusions and an overall assessment.

2. RECENT BANKING CRISES

Given the incidence and variety of banking crises since the mid-1980s, banking crises (in both developing and industrial economies) are clearly not random or isolated events. Around the world, banks have had high levels of non-performing loans, there has been a major destruction of bank capital, banks have failed and massive support operations have been necessary. The failure rate amongst banks has been greater than at any time since the great depression of the 1920s. In the case of Indonesia, Malaysia, South Korea and Thailand, non-performing loans of banks recently amounted to around 30 per cent of total assets. Banking crises have involved substantial costs. In around 25 per cent of cases the cost has exceeded 10 per cent of GNP (for example in Spain, Venezuela, Bulgaria, Mexico, Argentina and Hungary). Evans (2000) suggests that the costs of crises amounted to 45 per cent of GDP in the case of Indonesia, 15 per cent in the case of Korea and 40 per cent in the case of Thailand. These figures include the costs of meeting obligations to depositors under the blanket guarantees that the authorities introduced to handle systemic crises, and public sector payments to finance the recapitalization of insolvent banks.

Almost always and everywhere banking crises are a complex interactive mix of economic, financial and structural weaknesses. Lindgren *et al.* (1996) give an excellent survey of the two-way link between banking systems and macro policy. The trigger for many crises has been macroeconomic in origin and has often been associated with a sudden withdrawal of liquid external capital from a country. As noted by Brownbridge and Kirkpatrick (1999), financial crises have often involved triple crises of currencies, financial sectors and corporate sectors. Similarly it has been argued that East Asian countries were vulnerable to a financial crisis because of 'reinforcing dynamics between capital flows, macro-policies, and weak financial and corporate sector institutions' (Alba *et al.*, 1998). The link between balance of payments and banking crises is certainly not a recent phenomenon and has been extensively studied (for example, Kaminsky and Reinhart, 1998; Godlayn and Valdes, 1997; Sachs *et al.*, 1996).

Almost invariably, systemic crises (as opposed to the failure of individual banks within a stable system) are preceded by major macroeconomic adjustment, which often leads to the economy moving into recession after a previous strong cyclical upswing. While financial crises have been preceded by sharp fluctuations in the macro economy, and often in asset prices, it would be a mistake to ascribe financial instability entirely to macroeconomic instability. While macro instability may be the proximate cause of a banking crisis, the crisis usually emerges because instability in the macro economy reveals existing weaknesses within the banking system. The seeds of a problem (overlending, weak risk analysis and control, and so on) are usually sown in the earlier upswing of the cycle: mistakes made in the upswing emerge in the downswing. The downswing phase reveals previous errors and overoptimism. In South East Asia, for instance, a decade of substantial economic growth up to 1997 concealed the effects of questionable bank lending policies.

A common experience in countries that have experienced banking crises is that expectations have been volatile, and asset prices (including property) have been subject to wild swings. A sharp (sometimes speculative) rise in asset prices is often followed by an equally dramatic collapse. An initial rise in asset prices has often induced overoptimism and euphoria, which in turn has lead to increased demand for borrowed funds and an increased willingness of banks to lend (Llewellyn and Holmes, 1991).

3.   SOME COMMON ELEMENTS IN BANKING DISTRESS

Analysis of recent financial crises in both developed and less developed countries indicates that they are not exclusively (or even mainly) a problem of the regulatory rules being wrong (see, for instance, Brealey, 1999; Corsetti *et al.*, 1998; Lindgren *et al.*, 1996). Five common characteristics have been weak internal risk analysis, management and control systems within banks; inadequate official supervision; weak (or even perverse) incentives within the financial system generally and financial institutions in particular; inadequate information disclosure, and inadequate corporate governance arrangements within banks and their large corporate customers. An unstable or unpredictable macroeconomic environment is not a sufficient condition for banking crises to emerge: it is an illusion to ascribe such crises to faults in the macro economy alone. The fault also lies internally within banks, and with failures of regulation, supervision and market discipline on banks.

While each banking crisis has unique and country-specific features, they also have a lot in common. Several conditions tend to precede most systemic banking crises. A period of rapid growth in bank lending within a short period, and unrealistic expectations and euphoria about economic prospects, often form the backdrop to subsequent crises. These are frequently aggravated by sharp and unsustainable rises in asset prices (part of euphoria speculation) which lead to unrealistic demands for credit and a willingness of banks to supply loans. In the process, inadequate risk premia are often incorporated in the rates of interest on loans. This is a version of the standard Fisher and Minsky thesis: debt accumulation in the upswing leading to problems for banks in the downswing.

During the period of substantial growth in bank lending, concentrated loan portfolios (often with a high property content) often emerge. This is partly because, in periods of rapid asset-price inflation, property appears to be either an attractive lending proposition or a secure form of collateral against bank loans. However it is in essence speculative lending and the bubble bursts when the overcapacity in the property sector becomes evident. This means that, while individual project risks may be accurately assessed, overall portfolio risks are often not. It is also the case that, in periods of rapid growth in bank lending, insufficient attention is given to the value of collateral, most especially in periods of asset-price inflation. Banks do not always operate as totally independent agents and in many crisis countries bank decisions have involved political influences and insider relationships. Such government involvement in lending decisions has the effect of weakening incentive structures and eroding discipline on lenders through the perception of an implicit guarantee.

The origins of crises have been both internal to banks and external. To focus myopically on one side misses the essential point that systemic crises have both macro and micro origins. In the final analysis, weak internal risk analysis, management and control systems are at the root of all banking crises. Instability elsewhere should not conceal, or be used to excuse, weaknesses in this area of bank management. It is also the case that banking crises often follow major changes in the regulatory regime which create unfamiliar market conditions. Periods of rapid balance sheet growth, most especially when they occur after a regime shift and in a period of intense competition, almost inevitably involve banks incurring more risk. There are several reasons for this: banks begin to compete for market share by lowering their risk thresholds; risks are underpriced in order to gain market share; internal control systems tend to weaken in periods of rapid balance sheet growth; growth itself generates unwarranted optimism and a growth momentum develops; and portfolios become unbalanced if new lending opportunities are concentrated in a narrow range of business sectors. When, as is often the case, fast-growth strategies are pursued by all banks simultaneously, borrowers become overindebted and take more risks, which in turn increases the vulnerability of the lending banks.

4. A MULTIDIMENSIONAL PROBLEM

The recent banking crises in South East Asia have, as always, been complex and the causes have been multidimensional. While evident macro policy failures and volatile and structurally weak economies have been contributory factors, fundamentally unsound banking practices, perverse incentive structures and moral hazards, and weak regulation and supervision have also been major contributory factors. A myopic concentration on any single cause fails to capture the complex interactions involved in almost all banking and financial crises. This suggests that the response to avoid future crises must also be multidimensional, involving macro policy, the conduct of regulation and supervision, the creation of appropriate incentive structures, the development of market discipline and the internal governance and management of financial institutions. As a prelude to a consideration of the principles to reduce the probability of future banking fragility, the remainder of this section briefly considers the main components of recent banking crises. While the experience of each country varies in detail, there is a remarkable degree of commonalty, including the experience of financial fragility, in some developed economies. A discussion of the factors behind the Scandinavian banking crises of the early 1990s is given in Andersson and Viotti (1999) and Benink and Llewellyn (1994).

Reflecting the multidimensional aspect of financial distress, the main causal factors are considered under eight headings: (1) volatility in the macro economy, (2) the inheritance of structural weaknesses in the economy, (3) bad banking practices, (4) hazardous incentive structures and moral hazard within the financial system, (5) ineffective regulation, (6) weak monitoring and supervision by official agencies, (7) the absence of effective market discipline against hazardous bank behaviour due partly to the lack of transparency and the disclosure of relevant information, and (8) unsound corporate governance mechanisms within banks and their borrowing customers.

The Macro Economy

Although growth in the countries of South East Asia had been strong for many years before the onset of recent crises, structural weaknesses in some of the region's economies were also evident. In many cases, exceptionally high investment rates concealed inefficiencies in the allocation of investment funds in the economy. Investment plans were often undertaken without reference to realistic assessment or measurement of expected rates of return. The financial and solvency position of many large investing companies was also seriously overstated by inaccurate accounting procedures.

Many financial crises have been preceded by sharp and speculative rises in real and financial asset prices (see, for instance, the experience of Indonesia, Malaysia, Philippines and Thailand, shown in Tables 6.1 and 6.2). Such sharp and unsustainable rises in asset prices have a bearing on subsequent financial distress through several channels. As already noted, the main route is through the effect on the demand and supply of bank credit. There is something of an accelerator effect in this: a rise in asset prices produces an increase in the value of collateral, which increases the borrowing capacity of agents and the willingness of banks to extend credit. This in turn reinforces the rise in asset prices.

A key factor in the macroeconomic background to recent banking crises has been the dependence on short-term capital inflows intermediated via the banking system. Table 6.3 shows the pattern of private capital flows to Asian countries over the 1990s and the dependence of the crisis countries (Indonesia, Korea, Malaysia, Philippines and Thailand) on volatile banking flows (the dominant component of the 'other' category in Table 6.3). The vulnerability to such volatile flows is shown in the $73 billion turnaround in 1997 with a net inflow of $41 billion in 1996, followed by a $32 billion net outflow in the following year. A substantial proportion of the short-term capital inflow was intermediated by domestic banks incurring short-term liabilities against foreign banks. The vulnerability of the crisis countries to an external illiquidity problem became substantial, and this was a pattern evident in crises faced by several other countries (see Cole and Kehoe, 1996; Sachs *et al.*, 1996). In this context one interpretation of the origin of the crises is that they were precipitated by a change of view by international investors about the economic prospects of the region, (for example, Corbett *et al.*, 1999). The issue is discussed in more detail in Corsetti *et al.* (1998).

Overall, strong economic growth was, at least at the margin, intermediated by domestic banks incurring foreign currency liabilities to foreign banks on

Table 6.1 Stock market price index

	1990	1991	1992	1993	1994	1995	1996	1997
Korea	696.00	610.00	678.00	866.00	1027.00	882.00	651.00	376.00
Indonesia	417.00	247.00	274.00	588.00	469.00	513.00	637.00	401.00
Malaysia	505.00	556.00	643.00	1275.00	971.00	995.00	1237.00	594.00
Philippines	651.00	1151.00	1256.00	3196.00	2785.00	2594.00	3170.00	1869.00
Singapore	1154.00	1490.00	1524.00	2425.00	2239.00	2266.00	2216.00	1529.00
Thailand	612.00	711.00	893.00	1682.00	1360.00	1280.00	831.00	372.00
Hong Kong	3024.00	4297.00	5512.00	11888.00	8191.00	10073.00	13451.00	10722.00
Taiwan	4350.00	4600.00	3377.00	6070.00	7111.00	5158.00	6933.00	8187.00

Table 6.2 Stock market price index (property sector)

	1990	1991	1992	1993	1994	1995	1996	1997
Indonesia	–	119.00	66.00	214.00	140.00	112.00	143.00	40.00
Malaysia	113.00	113.00	126.00	369.00	240.00	199.00	294.00	64.00
Philippines	32.00	34.00	39.00	81.00	80.00	87.00	119.00	59.00
Singapore	230.00	280.00	250.00	541.00	548.00	614.00	648.00	357.00
Thailand	74.00	82.00	168.00	367.00	232.00	192.00	99.00	7.00
Hong Kong	312.00	453.00	554.00	1392.00	862.00	1070.00	1682.00	941.00
Taiwan	61.00	71.00	57.00	137.00	109.00	59.00	55.00	55.00

Table 6.3 *Private capital flows to Asian countries*

	1990	1991	1992	1993	1994	1995	1996	1997
Asia								
Total net private capital inflows	19.1	35.8	21.7	57.6	66.2	95.8	110.4	13.9
Net foreign direct investment	8.9	14.5	16.5	35.9	46.8	49.5	57.0	57.8
Net portfolio investment	–1.4	1.8	9.3	21.6	9.5	10.5	13.4	–8.6
Other	11.6	19.5	–4.1	0.1	9.9	35.8	39.9	–35.4
Net external borrowing from official creditors	5.6	11.0	10.3	8.7	5.9	4.5	8.8	28.6
Affected countries' net private capital inflows[2]	24.9	29.0	30.3	32.6	35.1	62.9	72.9	–11.0
Net foreign direct investment[1]	6.2	7.2	8.6	8.6	7.4	9.5	12.0	9.6
Net portfolio investment	1.3	3.3	6.3	17.9	10.6	14.4	20.3	11.8
Other	17.4	18.5	15.4	6.1	17.1	39.0	40.6	–32.3
Affected countries' net external borrowing from official creditors	0.3	4.4	2.0	0.8	0.7	1.0	4.6	25.6

Notes:
[1] Net foreign direct investment plus net portfolio investment plus net other investment.
[2] Indonesia, Korea, Malaysia, the Philippines and Thailand.

Sources: International Monetary Fund, *International Financial Statistics* and *World Economic Outlook* database.

the basis of short-term inter-bank lines. Strategies based on funding high interest rate loans in domestic currency through low interest rate foreign currency deposits created a substantial interest rate and exchange rate exposure for banks.

The Inheritance

Many of the crisis countries had a long tradition of intrusive government involvement and ownership in the banking system and elsewhere in the economy. This frequently meant that funds were channelled to ailing industries under overt or covert political pressure. Bisignano (1998) argues that such selective credit allocation was a factor retarding the development of effective risk analysis and management systems in banks. In many South East Asian countries, directed lending in the pre-liberalization phase often carried explicit or implicit guarantees (see Corbett *et al.*, 1999; Stiglitz, 1999; Rodrik, 1999). In effect, banks have not always acted as market-oriented financial intermediaries but as a channel for the public policy support of industries that would not have received the scale of support through market mechanisms. In addition, the close connections between banks and industrial corporations, and the general influence of government in the economy and the support of certain industries, created a climate wherein neither borrowers nor banks would be allowed to fail. This in turn aggravated a tendency towards imprudent lending. These issues are discussed further in Martinez (1998).

This is not a problem restricted to the less developed countries of South East Asia. With respect to Japan, Suzuki (1986) has argued that heavy involvement of government in the financial intermediation process carries three potential hazards: capital may be allocated inefficiently and on non-market criteria, it may undermine the effectiveness of monetary policy, and it may undermine fiscal discipline.

The 'inheritance problem' also included weak corporate structures with powerful ownership links between companies in a way that enabled them to avoid normal market discipline on corporate behaviour. This in turn was often aggravated by weak corporate governance arrangements, and the non-feasibility for the market in corporate control to operate. Both of these weaknesses muted normal market disciplines.

Before financial liberalization was instigated, many of the crisis countries operated on the basis of fairly rigid public control and/or direction. Some of the subsequent problems emanated from losses (which were often concealed) incurred during the previously repressed financial regime. It is also evident that the true financial condition of many banks had been concealed in the pre-liberalization period through weak loan classification standards and an expectation that banks would be supported in the event of difficulty. In many

Latin American countries, accounting standards were lax, to the extent that banks were reporting positive net income even during a banking crisis (Rojas-Suarez and Weisbrod, 1995). Such questionable accounting practices are not exclusive to developing countries (Kim and Cross, 1995). In some cases, banks seem to have been able to determine loan-loss provisions on the basis of managing the level of declared capital rather than reflecting the true quality of loans (Beatty, *et al.*, 1993).

Bad Banking Practices

Several elements of 'bad banking' which were concealed during the optimism generated during the previous period of rapid economic growth also played a central role in the emergence of financial fragility and the subsequent failure of banks. Common examples of 'bad banking' include the following:

- banks operating on the basis of low capital ratios which were sometimes below minimum capital adequacy standards set by the regulatory authorities, and which were not addressed by the regulators;
- substantial foreign currency exposures incurred because foreign currency borrowing appeared to be cheap, because the alleged commitment to a fixed exchange rate was not questioned, and because of the general expectation of 'bailouts' in the event of difficulty;
- rapid growth in bank lending in a short period. As already noted, a common feature of bank crises (including those in advanced economies) is that they are preceded by a period of rapid growth in bank lending. This is indicated for the crisis countries of South East Asia in Tables 6.4 and 6.5, which show the high rates of growth in lending to the private sector. Rapid growth of bank lending is not in itself hazardous. However periods of rapid growth frequently conceal emerging problems: it is more difficult to distinguish good from bad loans (Hausmann and Gavin, 1998); it often involves banks lending in areas with which they are not familiar; herding behaviour develops; credit standards are weakened in a phase of euphoria; and some lending is based on speculative rises in asset prices. This has also been noted in the Scandinavia banking crises of the early 1990s (Benink and Llewellyn, 1994);
- weak risk analysis, management and control systems within banks;
- concentrated loan portfolios often with a substantial exposure to property and real estate either directly in the form of loans, or indirectly through the collateral offered by borrowers. The exposure to property of seven countries of South East Asia is given in Table 6.6;

Table 6.4   Bank lending to private sector (percentage growth)

	1991	1992	1993	1994	1995	1996	1997
Korea	20.78	12.55	12.94	20.08	15.45	20.01	21.95
Indonesia	17.82	12.29	25.48	22.97	22.57	21.45	46.42
Malaysia	20.58	10.79	10.80	16.04	30.65	25.77	26.96
Philippines	7.33	24.66	40.74	26.52	45.39	48.72	28.79
Singapore	12.41	9.77	15.15	15.25	20.26	15.82	12.68
Thailand	20.45	20.52	24.03	30.26	23.76	14.63	19.80
Hong Kong	–	10.17	20.15	19.94	10.99	15.75	20.10
China	19.76	20.84	43.52	24.58	24.23	24.68	20.96
Taiwan	21.25	28.70	19.46	16.18	10.00	6.00	8.92

Table 6.5   Bank lending to private sector (percentage of GDP)

	1990	1991	1992	1993	1994	1995	1996	1997
Korea	52.54	52.81	53.34	54.21	56.84	57.04	61.81	69.79
Indonesia	49.67	50.32	49.45	48.90	51.88	53.48	55.42	69.23
Malaysia	71.36	75.29	74.72	74.06	74.61	84.80	93.39	106.91
Philippines	19.17	17.76	20.44	26.37	29.06	37.52	48.98	56.53
Singapore	82.20	83.34	85.06	84.14	84.21	90.75	95.96	100.29
Thailand	64.30	67.70	72.24	80.01	91.00	97.62	101.94	116.33
Hong Kong	–	141.84	134.20	140.02	149.00	155.24	162.36	174.24
China	85.51	87.87	86.17	95.49	87.12	85.83	91.65	101.07
Taiwan	100.41	108.99	126.43	137.23	146.89	149.49	146.05	146.23

- bank lending on the basis of an unsustainable rise in asset prices;
- substantial connected lending by banks to companies within the same group and on the basis of poor (or non-existent) risk assessment and non-market criteria;
- the failure to incorporate risk premia in interest rates on loans. The BIS has noted that in many crisis countries the lending margin was low (and was declining during the period of rapid growth) which indicates that insufficient risk premia were being charged (BIS, 1998);
- inaccurate accounting standards and weak loan classification and provisioning, which had the effect of overstating the value of bank loans and hence the true capital position of banks.

Table 6.6   Banking system exposure to property

	Property exposure (%)	Collateral valuation (%)
Korea	15–25	80–100
Indonesia	25–30	80–100
Malaysia	30–40	80–100
Philippines	15–20	70–80
Singapore	30–40	70–80
Thailand	30–40	80–100
Hong Kong	40–55	50–70

Source: J.P. Morgan, *Asian Financial Markets*, January 1998.

An interesting perspective on the effect of excessive bank lending is given by an IMF team (Adams *et al.*, 1998). The growth of lending was substantially in excess of the growth of GDP in the distress countries of South East Asia. This produced high leverage ratios (ratio of credit to the private sector relative to GDP). The study notes that in many of the countries where bank distress was most marked (Korea, Malaysia and Thailand) loan leverage ratios rose to levels that were higher than those in industrial countries with more developed financial infrastructures. Several studies (for example, Demirgüç-Kunt and Detragiache, 1998; Kaminsky and Reinhart, 1998; Benink and Llewellyn, 1994) show that rapid credit growth and high and sharply rising leverage are significant factors in banking crises in both developing and developed countries.

The authors of the IMF study suggest that countries in the early stages of economic development normally have high loan growth with low leverage, but as they advance in their development they are expected to converge to the status of low-medium asset growth with high leverage. However, Korea, Thailand and Malaysia each had both high growth rates of bank lending and high leverage ratios. A somewhat different picture emerges for the Philippines (very high growth rate of bank lending but comparatively low leverage ratio) and Indonesia with a modest growth rate of bank lending and a modest leverage ratio.

Incentive Structures and Moral Hazard

A continuing theme of this chapter is that incentive structures and moral hazards faced by decision makers (bank owners and managers, lenders to banks, borrowers and central banks) are major components of the regulatory regime. This means that the regulator needs to consider the impact its own rules have on regulated firms' incentive structures: whether they might have perverse effects, and what regulation can do to improve incentives. Incentive structures are at the centre of all aspects of regulation, in that if they are perverse it is unlikely that other mechanisms in the regime will achieve the desired objectives. Regulatory strategy needs to consider not only how the various components of the regime directly affect the objectives, but also how they operate indirectly through their impact on the incentives of regulated firms and others. Some analysts ascribe recent banking crises in part to various moral hazards and perverse incentive structures such as fixed exchange rate regimes, anticipated lender-of-last-resort actions, what have been viewed as bailouts by the IMF, and safety-net arrangements.

Schinasi *et al.* (1999) argue that banks have complex incentives including internal incentive structures (incentives that motivate key decision makers involved with risk), corporate governance mechanisms (such as accountability to shareholders), the external market in corporate control, market disciplines which may affect the cost of capital and deposits, and accountability to bank supervisors. The presence of regulation and official supervision adds a particular dimension to the structure of incentives faced by decision makers. The key is to align incentives of the various stakeholders in the decision-making process: between the objectives set by regulators and supervisors (systemic stability and consumer protection) and those of the bank; between the overall business objectives of the bank and those of actual decision makers in the management structure, and between managers and owners of banks. Conflicts can arise at each level, which complicates incentives. A central role of regulation is to create incentives for managers to behave in a way consistent with the objectives that are set for regulation when these may not always be in the immediate interests of either managers or owners of banks.

Several potential adverse incentives can be identified in many of the countries that have experienced distressed banking systems:

- the expectation that the government's commitment to the exchange value of the domestic currency was absolute may have induced imprudent and unhedged foreign currency borrowing both by banks and by companies;
- expectations of bailouts or support for industrial companies (which had at various times been in receipt of government support) meant that the bankruptcy threat was weak;
- there was a belief in the role of the lender-of-last-resort and expectations that banks would not be allowed to fail. The IMF notes that the perception of implicit guarantees was probably strengthened by the bailouts in the resolution of earlier banking crises in Thailand (1983–7), Malaysia (1985–8) and Indonesia (1994);

- close relationships between banks, the government, other official agencies and industrial corporations often meant that relationships (such as lending) that would normally be conducted at arm's length became intertwined in a complex structure of economic and financial linkages within sometimes opaque corporate structures. This also meant that corporate governance arrangements, both within banks and with their borrowing customers, were often weak and ill-defined.

It has frequently been argued (for example, Drage and Mann, 1999) that, in the recent case of South East Asia, the expectation and actual injection of funds by the International Monetary Fund and World Bank (which in effect replaced private finance) effectively bailed out investors and, by shielding them from the full losses of their actions, may have had the effect of encouraging imprudent capital inflows and bank lending. It has also been claimed that the aftermath of the Mexico crisis sent a signal to investors that they are less likely to sustain losses by investing in short-term securities.

However this view has been challenged on the grounds that, in the case of South East Asia, investors did in fact lose value, and that governments are reluctant to resort to IMF facilities because of the resultant conditionality that is applied (Brealey, 1999). It is relevant in this regard that, in the years before the crisis, the countries of this region had grown at a faster rate, and for longer, than any countries in history. There were, therefore, powerful economic reasons for capital inflows irrespective of any expectation of bailouts in the event of sovereign problems. International fund managers were also motivated by a desire to develop globally diversified portfolios including assets in fast-growing regions. In addition, a substantial proportion of the inflows were in forms that could not expect any rescue. Overall the idea that capital inflows were motivated largely by the expectation of a bailout in the event of distress is less than convincing (Adams *et al.*, 1998). While potential moral hazard effects may be exaggerated, this is not to deny the central importance of identifying the incentive structures implicit in regulatory regimes, and the moral hazards that can arise.

If incentive structures are hazardous, regulation will always face formidable difficulties. There are several dimensions to incentive structures within banks: the extent to which reward structures are based on the volume of business undertaken; the extent to which the risk characteristics of decisions are incorporated into the reward structures; the nature of the internal control systems within banks; internal monitoring of the decision making of loan officers; the nature of profit-sharing schemes and the extent to which decision makers also share in losses, and so on. High staff turnover, and the speed with which officers are moved within the bank, may also create incentives for excessive risk taking. A similar effect can arise through herd behaviour.

It is clear that some incentive structures can lead to dysfunctional behavioural responses (Prendergast, 1993). This may often emerge when incentives within regulated firms relate to volume rather than risk-adjusted profitability, that is, there is a clear bias towards writing business. Thus bank managers may be rewarded by the volume of loans made. Many cases of bank distress have been associated with inappropriate incentive structures creating a bias in favour of balance sheet growth, and with moral hazard created by anticipated lender-of-last-resort actions. Dale (1996) suggests that profit-related bonuses were an important feature in the Barings collapse.

One potentially hazardous feature of bank management is the tendency towards herd behaviour. Fink and Haiss (2000) argue that there is often an unwillingness on the part of managers to risk rejection by the 'in-group' within the bank. They also argue that it is necessary to curb herd behaviour by altering the incentive structures faced by various stakeholders. Some analysts find that, under some circumstances, there can be a negative relationship between risk and return within banks. This may be because banks in distress seek risky projects. According to Prospect Theory, bankers have an asymmetric view of risk taking and risk avoidance. Performance expectations may raise the need or desire to take excessive risk (Kahneman and Tuersky, 1979).

There is a particular issue with respect to the incentive structure of state-owned, or state-controlled, banks as their incentives may be ill-defined, if not hazardous. Such banks are not subject to the normal disciplining pressures of the market, their 'owners' do not monitor their behaviour and there is no disciplining effect from the market in corporate control (i.e. retake-over market). Political interference in such banks (and the unwitting encouragement of 'bad banking' practices) can itself become a powerful ingredient in bank distress. Lindgren *et al.* (1996) found, for instance, that banks that are, or were recently, state-owned or controlled were a factor in most of the instances of unsound banking in their sample of crises.

Ineffective Regulation

In all crisis countries, banks have been regulated and supervised and, in principle, most countries nominally adopted standard international norms of regulation. However the adoption of such standards was often weak and uncertain. There were many elements of weak regulation in the origin of banking crises in recent years and which aggravated the effect of other dimensions of distress.

- Capital adequacy regulations were often either not fully in place or were not effectively enforced.
- Regulatory requirements for capital, while nominally conforming to the letter of international agreements, were nevertheless set too low in

relation to the nature of the risks in the economy and the risks being incurred by banks. Capital adequacy regulation often did not accurately reflect banks' risk characteristics (BIS, 1998).

- Rules with respect to classification of loan quality and provisions were often too lenient and ill-specified, with the result that provisions were insufficient to cover expected losses, and earnings and capital were overstated (Brownbridge and Kirkpatrick, 1999; Folkerts-Landau *et al.*, 1995).
- Rules with respect to exposure to single borrowers were often too lax (or not enforced).
- Regulation and supervision with respect to concentrated exposures (such as property) were often too lenient.
- Poor accounting standards enabled banks to evade prudential and other restrictions on insider lending (Rahman, 1998).
- Many governments and regulatory authorities were slow and hesitant to act in the face of impending solvency problems of banks. Such regulatory forbearance was often due to regulatory authorities having substantial discretion as to when and whether to intervene, and often being subject to political pressure of one kind or another.

Weak Monitoring and Supervision

As with all companies, banks need to be monitored. In addition to the standard principal–agent issues, banks are universally monitored and supervised by official agencies, such as central banks. In practice, 'some form of supervisory failure was a factor in almost all the sample countries' (Lindgren *et al.*, 1996). In many countries supervisory agencies did not enforce compliance with regulations (Reisen, 1998). In Korea and Indonesia especially, banks did not comply with regulatory capital adequacy requirements or other regulations (UNCTAD, 1998). In particular, connected lending restrictions were not adequately supervised, partly because of political pressure and the lack of transparency in the accounts of banks and their corporate customers.

There has often been a lack of political will on the part of supervisory agencies to exercise strong supervision. This may be associated with adverse incentive structures faced by politicians and others who may gain from imprudent banking (Fink and Haiss, 2000). While prudent banking is a public good, hazardous behaviour can be beneficial to some stakeholders. Others have noted the lack of political will to exercise strong supervision in the transitional economies of Eastern Europe (Baer and Gray, 1996).

A further dimension to supervisory failure has been that supervisory intensity has often not been adjusted in line with liberalization in financial systems and the new business operations and risk characteristics of banks that emerged in a more deregulated market environment. This is discussed in more detail in section 5. This was also the case with Scandinavian countries when, in the second half the 1980s, banks responded aggressively to deregulation. The nature and intensity of official supervision needs to reflect the nature of the regulatory environment. In practice, while the latter changed, this was often not accompanied by sufficiently intensified supervision.

Weak Market Discipline of Banks

Monitoring is conducted exclusively by official agencies whose specialist task it is. In well-developed financial regimes, the market also monitors the behaviour of financial firms. The disciplines imposed by the market can be as powerful as any sanctions imposed by official agencies. However, in practice, the disciplining role of markets (including the inter-bank market which is able to impose powerful discipline through the risk premia charged on inter-bank loans) was weak in the crisis countries of South East Asia. This was due predominantly to the lack of disclosure and transparency of banks and the fact that little reliance could be placed on the quality of accountancy data provided in bank accounts. In many cases standard accounting and auditing procedures were not rigorously applied, and in some cases there was wilful misrepresentation of the financial position of banks and non-financial companies. Market disciplines can work effectively only on the basis of full and accurate disclosure and transparency.

A further dimension relates to the potentially powerfully disciplining power of the market in corporate control which, through the threat of removing control from incumbent managements, is a discipline on managers to be efficient and not endanger the solvency of their banks. As put in a IMF study, 'An open and competitive banking market exerts its own form of discipline against weak banks while encouraging well-managed banks' (Lindgren *et al.*, 1996).

Unsound Corporate Governance Arrangements

In the final analysis, all aspects of the management of a bank are corporate governance issues. This means that if banks behave hazardously, this is, to some extent, a symptom of weak internal corporate governance. This may include, for instance, hazardous corporate structures of banks, lack of internal control systems, weak surveillance by (especially non-executive) directors, and ineffective internal audit arrangements. Corporate governance arrangements were evidently weak and underdeveloped in banks in many of the distress countries. Moral hazard can be created through lack of owner accountability and weak accountability of regulatory agencies (Krugman, 1998).

Some bank ownership structures tend to produce ineffective corporate governance. In some cases, particular corporate structures (such as banks being part of larger conglomerates) encourage connected lending and weak risk analysis of borrowers. This was found to be the case in a significant number of bank failures in the countries of South East Asia and Latin America. Some corporate structures also make it comparatively easy for banks to conceal losses and unsound financial positions effectively.

Assessment

The central theme of this section has been that recent banking crises have been multidimensional and a complex mix of several interacting pressures and weaknesses. A myopic focus on particular causal components is likely to produce a distorted picture and also to produce inadequate policy and reform proposals. The experience of many countries has demonstrated the lethal cocktail of fundamental and structural weaknesses in the economy, hazardous incentive structures, weak and ineffective regulation, inadequate official supervision and an inability or unwillingness of the market to impose discipline on banks. It follows that reform needs to proceed along several channels simultaneously, which in itself makes the reform process more demanding and challenging. We return to this issue in section 6.

5.   LIBERALIZATION: STOCK ADJUSTMENT VERSUS STEADY STATE

Many financial crises have been associated with changes in the regulatory regime and a process of liberalization. For decades, the economies of South East Asia were highly regulated, with interest rate ceilings, limitations on lending growth by financial institutions, restrictions on foreign entry into the banking system and so on. At various times during the 1990s, these restrictions were relaxed, and the pace of financial liberalization was accelerated.

Williamson and Mahar (1998) show that almost all of their sample of 34 economies (both industrialized and developing) that undertook financial liberalization over the 1980s and 1990s experienced varying degrees of financial crisis. Similarly Kaminsky and Reinhart (1998) found that, in the majority of cases in their sample of countries that had experienced banking crises, the financial sector had been liberalized during the previous five years. They conclude that financial liberalization helps predict banking crises across a range of countries. Goldstein and Folkerts-Landau (1993) observe a general pattern of deregulation inducing more competition being followed by increasing financial fragility.

Demirgüç-Kunt and Detragiache (1998) find that financial liberalization increases the probability of a banking crisis. However they also find that the probability is reduced the stronger are the institutional preconditions for liberalization and market discipline in terms of contract enforcement, lack of corruption, bureaucratic interference in lending decisions and so on. This reinforces the established wisdom that liberalization involves a significant change in the market environment and that, for the new regime to be stable and efficient, certain basic prerequisites of a well-functioning market system need to be in place. The key is that institutional structures and mechanisms need to be consistent with the prevailing market regime. Problems arise when a change to the market regime is made without there also being corresponding changes in institutional mechanisms.

While in both developed and less developed countries banking distress has often followed periods of deregulation and liberalization, a distinction needs to be made between the *transitional* effect of moving from one regulatory regime to another, and the characteristics of a *steady-state* liberalized financial system. The instabilities that may occur in the transition period do not necessarily carry over into the new steady state.

The Transitional Phase

The universal evidence is that financial liberalization enhances efficiency in the financial system and that financial repression distorts the incentives for saving and investment. However financial liberalization often creates instability in the transition period.

- One effect of increased competition that results from liberalization is an erosion of the economic rents enjoyed by financial firms associated with the previously uncompetitive environment. The subsequent lower profitability may induce financial institutions to take more risk.
- As discussed earlier, and noted by Corbett *et al.*, (1999), 'A key mistake, which led to the vulnerability of the financial system, appears to be that the old-style financial system continued into the new era of liberalisation.' This often included the continuation of old-style guarantees which are described in detail in Krugman (1999).
- In the stock adjustment phase (that is, during the period when the new regime is being introduced) uncertainty is created as financial firms are unfamiliar with the characteristics and management requirements of the new regime. Previously protected institutions need to adapt behaviour, though this may occur only with a considerable time lag. New behaviour patterns need to be learned. Some mistakes during the process of financial liberalization occur because banks do not adjust quickly

enough to the new regime. Behaviour which is appropriate under one regime may be totally inappropriate in another (see Benink and Llewellyn, 1994, for a more formal discussion).

- In the first instance, liberalization may increase inflationary pressure as banks' balance sheet restraints are lifted and financial firms increase their lending rapidly in a relatively short period. This is often associated with a sharp rise in asset prices. The implication is that financial liberalization needs to be accompanied by an appropriate stabilization policy to reduce the potential impact on inflation which can distort lending decisions.

- In many countries that liberalized their financial systems after decades of controls, banks responded in a remarkably similar way by substantially increasing the volume of lending in a short period. As a result of increased competitive pressures, banks lowered equilibrium and disequilibrium credit rationing and risk thresholds (Llewellyn and Holmes, 1991); bank lending margins were squeezed, and bank profitability at first rose as a result of this expansion, but later deteriorated sharply because of massive loan losses.

- The rapid growth in lending during the stock adjustment phase also increased risks because banks' internal control systems that were weak in the previous regime were carried forward into the new environment. This was compounded when banks adopted market-share strategies in a strongly expanding loans market.

- In general, periods of substantial growth of bank lending are likely to involve banks moving into more risky business and adopting a higher-risk profile (OECD, 1992). The removal of controls often unleashes a pent-up demand for credit, and suppliers of credit are freed to compete, which in some cases leads to a relaxation of standards (see also Schinasi and Hargreaves, 1993).

- The same competitive pressures may also make it difficult, in the short run, for banks to incorporate higher-risk premia in loan rates, with the result that bank loans are underpriced.

- The initial stock adjustment reaction often involves a phase of overreaction by lenders as balance sheet structures are taken beyond long-run sustainable positions. There are several reasons for this: reaction times in financial markets are short, adjustments can be made quickly and financial systems are often characterized by oligopolistic competition. As a result, competitive pressures induce firms to move together: the 'herd instinct'. Some analysts ascribe this to a property of the incentive structure within banks in that, in a world of uncertainty, the desire to avoid personal blame for mismanagement is liable to make risk-averse managers subject to peer-group pressure to follow the same strategy.

- Liberalization may also reveal inherent weaknesses in the banking system, with respect both to structure and to the traditional way of conducting business.
- In some cases, some basic infrastructure of markets had not been created ahead of liberalization: a strong legal framework to ensure that property rights are well-defined and easily exercisable; a legal framework for the pledging of collateral and the ability to take possession of collateral, and clearly defined bankruptcy laws and codes, along with weak enforcement mechanisms.
- If supervision is not intensified in line with liberalization, the financial system is more likely to become crisis-prone. When liberalizing their financial systems, the countries of South East Asia ignored the risks posed by rapid liberalization when it is not accompanied by significant strengthening of regulation and supervision of bank behaviour (Furman and Stiglitz, 1998). In this, they followed the earlier experience of the Scandinavian countries. Bisignano (1998) suggests that this experience represents a combination of 'excess momentum' by the private sector and 'excess inertia' by the regulatory authorities. Put another way, there is a trade-off between regulation and supervision in that, if regulation is eased to allow banks to conduct more business, there is an increased requirement for effective supervision of the way that business is conducted. The IMF has argued thus: 'bank supervision may need to be restructured before financial market liberalisation to cope with the new challenges and risks liberalisation entails.' (IMF, 1993).

These are essentially (though not necessarily exclusively) problems of transition. A distinction is made between what happens during a stock adjustment phase of liberalization, and the characteristics of a steady-state, deregulated financial system. Although the evidence indicates that a liberalized financial system is more efficient and contributes more substantially to economic development, when moving from one regime to another (especially from a highly controlled financial system to a more market-oriented system) instability may be created as new behaviour patterns need to be learned. The fact that instability may occur during the transitional, stock adjustment period does not necessarily mean that a deregulated financial system is inherently unstable, or even less stable than a regulated regime. Many of the financial crises experienced in recent years have been associated with the uncertainties and mistakes during the transitional phase during which liberalization measures were adopted. Crises have often been a property of uncertainty associated with regime changes (as the system moves from one regime to another) rather than the inherent characteristics of the new regime per se.

The policy implication is that care is needed in the process of liberalization and that supervision of financial institutions needs to move in step with liberalization. Deregulation without enhanced supervision is likely to be hazardous irrespective of the long-run benefits of liberalization and the erosion of financial repression. Liberalization has often not been accompanied by necessary changes in regulation and supervision, corporate governance reforms and enhanced market monitoring and control.

The Steady State

However, while some of the financial distress has been associated with the transition from one regime to another, it may also be the case that a more competitive market environment tends to be more risky. This is because the value of the banking franchise is reduced by competition. Keeley (1990), for example, analyses how deregulation and increased competition can induce banks to behave with less regard to risk because they lower the value of the banking franchise. The higher is the expected future value of the banking franchise, the more owners and managers have to lose through excessive risk taking which raises the probability of the bank failing. An IMF study (Goldstein and Folkerts-Landau, 1993) suggests that risks in banking increased over the 1980s owing to a combination of increased competition and the existence of safety nets. Similar conclusions are found in Caprio and Summers (1993) and Demsetz *et al.* (1997). Using data to proxy bank franchise values, Hellman *et al.* (1995) examine the relationship between bank franchise values and financial market liberalization as a test of the argument that moral hazard increases as banks' franchise values fall. Their results confirm that banking crises are more likely to occur in countries with a liberalized financial sector, and that franchise values tend to be lower when financial markets are liberalized. Shafer (1987) suggests that deregulation is likely to create financial markets with a permanently greater tendency to instability.

In many cases previous, highly regulated, regimes acted as a protection to financial institutions by effectively limiting competition. The extent of the economic rents that were created were probably underestimated by the regulatory authorities. In many cases the extent to which deregulation and liberalization would increase competition in the banking industry was underestimated, even though that was one of the public policy objectives. These errors inhibited appropriate responses in the areas of prudential regulation and monitoring and supervision.

The potential conflict and trade-off between stability and efficiency is highlighted by Sijben (1999), where efficiency considerations require deregulation and liberalization in financial systems, though by enhancing competition this may compromise the objective of stability. Hellweg (1995) suggests that the low rate of bank failures in Switzerland between the late 1930s and the 1970s was due, in part, to the absence of disintermediation threat and the generally weak climate of competition in the Swiss banking system. The resultant high margins in banking enhanced franchise values and also enabled capital to be quickly replenished following write-downs due to loan write-offs. In the Hellweg analysis, increased competition in the banking industry produces higher levels of risk in banks because it creates incentives for higher risk taking.

6.   THE *REGULATORY REGIME*

Having discussed some of the common origins of banking distress, we turn to consider a set of principles to reduce the future probability of crises. Emphasis has been given to inadequate regulation and supervision of banks. In the final analysis, regulation is about changing the behaviour of regulated institutions. A key issue is the extent to which behaviour is to be altered by externally imposed *rules*, or through creating *incentives* for firms to behave in a particular way.

A sustained theme is that a regulatory regime is to be viewed more widely than externally imposed regulation of financial institutions. Regulation is only one of seven key components. Regulation needs to be viewed and analysed not solely in the narrow terms of the rules and edicts of regulatory agencies, but in the wider context of a *regulatory regime*. This concept has seven components:

1.   the *rules* established by regulatory agencies (the regulation component);
2.   *monitoring and supervision* by regulatory agencies;
3.   the *incentive structures* faced by regulatory agencies, consumers and, most especially, regulated firms;
4.   the role of *market discipline* and monitoring;
5.   *intervention arrangements* in the event of compliance failures of one sort or another;
6.   the role of *corporate governance* arrangements in financial firms, and
7.   the *disciplining and accountability* arrangements applied to regulatory agencies.

In current conditions, it would be hazardous to rely wholly, or even predominantly, on external regulation, monitoring and supervision by official sector. The world of banking and finance is too complex and volatile for it to be possible to rely on a simple set of prescriptive rules for prudent behaviour.

The key to optimizing the effectiveness of a regulatory regime is the portfolio mix of the seven core components. All are necessary but none alone is sufficient. Particular emphasis is given to incentive structures because, in the final analysis, if these are perverse or inefficient, no amount of formal regulation will prevent problems emerging in the banking sector.

Trade-offs within the Regime

Regulatory stratregy is set in the context of trade-offs between the various components of the *regulatory regime*. In some circumstances the more emphasis that is given to one of the components (such as regulation) the less powerful becomes one or more of the others (such as market discipline on banks) and to an extent that may reduce the overall impact. Thus, while regulation may be viewed as a response to market failures, weak market discipline and inadequate corporate governance arrangements, causation may also operate in the other direction with regulation weakening these other mechanisms.

Within the regulatory regime, trade-offs emerge at two levels. In terms of regulatory strategy, choices have to be made about the balance of the various components and the relative weight to be assigned to each. For instance, a powerful role for official regulation with little weight assigned to market discipline, or alternatively a relatively light touch of regulation but with heavy reliance on the other components, might be chosen. The second form of trade-off relates to the way the components of the regime may be causally related. For instance, the more emphasis that is given to detailed, extensive and prescriptive rules, the weaker might be the role of incentive structures, market discipline and corporate governance arrangements with financial firms. This has been put by Simpson (2000) as follows: 'In a market which is heavily regulated for internal standards of integrity, the incentives to fair dealing diminish. Within the company culture, such norms of fair dealing as "the way we do things around here" would eventually be replaced by "It's OK if we can get away with it."' In other words, an excessive reliance on detailed and prescriptive rules may weaken incentive structures and market discipline.

Similarly an excessive focus on detailed and prescriptive rules may weaken corporate governance mechanisms within financial firms, and may blunt the incentive for others to monitor and control the behaviour of banks. Weakness in corporate governance mechanisms may also be a reflection of banks being monitored, regulated and supervised by official agencies. The way intervention is conducted in the event of bank distress (for example, whether forbearance is practised) may also have adverse incentive effects on the behaviour of banks and the willingness of markets to monitor and control their risk taking.

An empirical study of regulation in the United States by Billett *et al.* (1998) suggests that some types of regulation may undermine market discipline. They examine the costs of market discipline and regulation and show that, as a bank's risk increases, the cost of uninsured deposits rises and the bank switches to insured deposits. This is because changes in regulatory costs are less sensitive to changes in risk than are market costs. They also show that, when rating agencies downgrade a bank, the bank tends to increase its use of insured deposits. The authors conclude: 'The disparate costs of insured deposits and uninsured liabilities, combined with the ability and willingness of banks to alter their exposure to each, challenge the notion that market discipline can be an effective deterrent against excessive risk taking.' This type of evidence demonstrates that, under some circumstances, regulatory arrangements can have the effect of blunting market discipline.

The public policy objective is to optimize the outcome of a regulatory strategy in terms of mixing the components of the regime, bearing in mind the possibility of negative trade-offs. However the optimum mix in a regulatory regime will change over time as financial structures, market conditions and compliance cultures change. For instance, the combination of external regulation and market discipline that is most effective and efficient in one set of market circumstances, and one type of financial structure in a country, may become ill-suited if structures change. Also, if the norms and compliance culture of the industry change, it could become appropriate, at least for some firms, to rely less on detailed and prescriptive regulation.

Neither does the same approach and mix of components in the regulatory regime need to be the same for all regulated firms. On the contrary, given that banks are not homogeneous in their risk profiles, it would be sub-optimal to apply the same approach. A key strategic issue is the extent to which differentiations are to be made between different regulated firms.

Financial systems are changing substantially and to an extent that may undermine traditional approaches to regulation and, most especially, the balance between regulation and official supervision, and the role of market discipline. In particular, globalization, the pace of financial innovation and the creation of new financial instruments, the blurring of traditional distinctions between different types of financial firm, the speed with which portfolios can change through banks trading in derivatives and so on, and the increased complexity of banking business, create a fundamentally new (in particular, more competitive) environment in which regulation and supervision are undertaken. They also change the viability of different approaches to regulation which, if it is to be effective, must constantly respond to changes in the market environment in which regulated firms operate.

Having established the general framework of the regulatory regime, the following sections outline a set of general principles designed to reduce the probability of banking distress. They are focused on each of five of the core components: regulation, incentive structures, monitoring and supervision, the role of market discipline and corporate governance arrangements.

Regulation

Four particular issues need to be considered with respect to the regulation part of the regime: the weight to be given to formal and prescriptive rules of behaviour; the type of rules in the regime; the impact that rules may have on the other components of the regulatory regime; and the extent to which regulation and supervision differentiate between different banks.

Prescriptive rules

A former US regulator has noted that 'Financial services regulation has traditionally tended towards a style that is command-and-control, dictating precisely what a regulated entity can do and how it should do it ... generally, they focus on the specific steps needed to accomplish a certain regulatory task and specify with detail the actions to be taken by the regulated firm' (Wallman, 1999). His experience in the USA suggests that the interaction of the interests of the regulator and the regulated may tend towards a high degree of prescription in the regulatory process. Regulators tend to look for standards they can easily monitor and enforce, while the regulated seek standards they can comply with. The result is that regulators seek precision and detail in their requirements, while regulated firms look for certainty and firm guidance on what they are to do. Wallman suggests: 'The result is specific and detailed guidance, not the kind of pronouncements that reflect fundamental concepts and allow the market to develop on its own.'

The arguments against reliance on detailed and prescriptive rules are outlined in Goodhart *et al.* (1998). Although precise rules have their attractions for both regulators and regulated firms, there are several problems with a highly prescriptive approach to regulation.

- An excessive degree of prescription may bring regulation into disrepute if it is perceived by the industry as being excessive, with many redundant rules.
- Risks are usually too complex to be covered by simple rules.
- Balance-sheet rules reflect the position of an institution only at a particular point in time, although its position can change substantially within a short period.
- An inflexible approach based on a detailed rule book has the effect of impeding firms from choosing their own least-cost way of meeting regulatory objectives.
- Detailed and extensive rules may stifle innovation.

- A prescriptive regime tends to focus upon firms' processes rather than outcomes and the ultimate objectives of regulation. The precise rules may become the focus of compliance rather than the objectives they are designed to achieve. In this regard, this can give rise to a perverse culture of 'box ticking' by regulated firms. The letter of regulation may be obeyed but not the spirit or intention.
- A prescriptive approach is inclined towards 'rules escalation' whereby rules are added over time, but few are withdrawn.
- A highly prescriptive approach may create a confrontational relationship between the regulator and regulated firms, or alternatively cause firms to overreact, engaging in excessive efforts at internal compliance out of fear of being challenged by the regulator. In this sense, regulation may in practice become more prescriptive and detailed than originally intended by the regulator.
- Forcing a high degree of conformity on regulated firms causes an information loss. If firms are given leeway in satisfying the regulator's objectives, more may be learned about how different behaviour affects regulatory objectives, and also about the properties of different rules.
- In the interests of 'competitive neutrality', rules may be applied equally to all firms, although firms may be sufficiently heterogeneous to warrant different approaches. Treating as equal firms that in practice are not equal is not competitive neutrality, and a highly prescriptive approach to regulation reduces the scope for legitimate differentiations.
- A highly prescriptive rules approach may in practice prove to be inflexible and insufficiently responsive to market conditions.
- There is a potential moral hazard as firms may assume that, if something is not explicitly covered in regulation, there is no regulatory dimension to the issue.
- Detailed rules may also have perverse effects in that they are regarded as actual standards to be adopted rather than minimum standards, with the result that, in some cases, actual behaviour of regulated firms may be of a lower standard than they would have chosen without the rule. This is most especially the case if each firm assumes that its competitors will adopt the minimum regulatory standard (adverse incentive) or if firms who would adopt a higher standard were to exit the market (adverse selection).

The limitations of a prescriptive rules and rigid formula approach to regulation is highlighted in Estrella (1998) who argues that, while there is a clear role for regulation, what really matters is how the bank behaves and the quality of its risk analysis and management systems, rather than whether particular detailed rules are applied within the bank.

Types of rules

A second issue relates to the choice about the type of rules. This may have implications for enforcement as trade-offs are involved. Black (1994) distinguishes different types of rules along three dimensions: *precision* (how much is prescribed and covered in the rule), *simplicity* (the degree to which the rule may be easily applied to concrete situations) and *clarity*. The trade-off is between precision and ease of enforcement, in that the more precise is the rule the easier it is to enforce. On the other hand, the more precise is the rule the less flexibility is created within the overall regime.

Impact of rules

A third issue is whether the degree of precision in rules has a positive or negative impact on the other components of the regime. For reasons already suggested, precision and detail may have a negative effect on compliance and compliance culture. Conversely a regime based more on broad principles than on detailed and extensive rules has certain advantages: principles are easily understood and remembered, they apply to all behaviour, and they are more likely to have a positive impact on overall compliance culture. It might also be the case (as suggested in Black, 1994) that principles are more likely to become board issues, with the board of financial firms adopting compliance with principles as a high-level policy issue, rather than a culture of 'leaving it to the compliance department'. As put by Black, 'it helps chief executives to see the moral wood for the technical trees'.

Differentiation

A central issue in regulation for financial stability is the extent to which it differentiates between different banks according to their risk characteristics and their risk analysis, management and control systems. Most especially when supervisory resources are scarce, but also in the interests of efficiency in the banking system, supervision should be more detailed and extensive with banks which are considered to be more risky than others. In the UK, the Financial Services Authority (FSA) adopts a risk-based approach to supervision.

The objective of 'competitive neutrality' in regulation does not mean that all banks are to be treated in the same way if their risk characteristics are different. With respect to capital adequacy requirements, and reflecting the practice in the UK, Richardson and Stephenson (2000) argue that the FSA (and formerly the Bank of England) treats the requirements of the Basle Accord as minima and requires individual banks to hold more capital than the minima dependent upon the bank's risk exposure. Capital requirements are set individually for each bank. The authors list the major factors that are taken into account when setting individual banks' capital requirements. These include experience and quality of a bank's management; the bank's risk appetite; the quality of risk analysis, management and control systems; the nature of the markets in which the bank operates; the quality, reliability and volatility of the bank's earnings; the quality of the bank's capital and access to new capital; the degree of diversification; exposure concentrations; the complexity of a bank's legal and organizational structure; the support and control provided by shareholders; and the degree to which a bank is supervised by other jurisdictions. The authors note that 'these considerations imply that the appropriate margin above the minimum regulatory capital requirements will differ across banks'.

Goodhart *et al.* (1998) argue that, because regulation is not supplied through a market mechanism, the perception is that it is a free good, which means that it is likely to be overdemanded. If this is coupled with risk-averse regulators, there is an inherent danger of overregulation. In this context six main principles for the regulation component of the regime are outlined.

The objectives of regulation need to be clearly defined and circumscribed
Financial regulation should have only a limited number of objectives. In the final analysis the objectives are to sustain systemic stability and to protect the consumer. Regulation should not be overloaded by being required to achieve other and wider objectives, such as social outcomes. Constructing effective and efficient regulation is difficult enough with limited objectives and the more it is overburdened by wider considerations, the more likely it is to fail in all of them.

The rationale and motivation of regulation and supervision should be limited
The rationale for regulation lies in correcting for identified market imperfections and failures which, in the absence of regulation, produce sub-optimal results and reduce consumer welfare: such imperfections include externalities, economies of scale in monitoring, breaking a 'grid lock' and limiting moral hazard associated with safety nets (see Llewellyn, 1999). Regulation in general, and regulatory measures in particular, need to be assessed according to these criteria. In other words, regulation should be limited to correcting identified market imperfections and failures. If they do not satisfy any of these criteria, particular regulatory measures should be abandoned.

Regulation should be viewed in terms of a set of contracts
Laws, regulations and supervisory actions provide incentives for regulated firms to adjust their actions and behaviour, and to control their own risks internally. They can usefully be viewed as *incentive contracts* within a standard principal–agent relationship where the principal is the regulator and the agent is the regulated firm. Within this general framework, regula-

tion involves a process of creating incentive-compatible contracts so that regulated firms have an incentive to behave in ways consistent with systemic stability and investor protection. If incentive contracts are well designed they will induce appropriate behaviour by regulated firms. Conversely, if they are badly constructed and improperly designed, they may fail to reduce systemic risk (and other hazards regulation is designed to avoid) or have undesirable side-effects on the process of financial intermediation (for example, impose high cost). At centre stage is the issue of whether all parties have the right incentives to act in a way that satisfies the objectives of regulation.

The form and intensity of regulatory and supervisory requirements should differentiate between regulated institutions according to their relative portfolio risk and efficiency of internal control mechanisms
While the objective of 'competitive neutrality' in regulation is something of a mantra, this is not satisfied if what, in practice, are unequal institutions, are treated equally. In this respect, 'equality' relates to the risk characteristics of institutions. A hazard of a detailed and prescriptive rule book approach is that it may fail to make the necessary distinctions between non-homogeneous firms because the same rules are applied to all. In this regard, it reduces the scope for legitimate differentiations to be made.

In some areas the regulator could offer a menu of contracts to regulated firms requiring them to self-select into the correct category
There is an information, and possibly efficiency, loss if a high degree of conformity in the behaviour of regulated firms is enforced. If, alternatively, firms have a choice about how to satisfy the regulator's stated objectives, they would be able to choose their own, least-cost way of satisfying these objectives. One approach is for regulators to offer a menu of self-selecting contracts rather than the same contract to all institutions. Equally banks could offer their own contracts. A particular proposal in this regard is the pre-commitment approach which gives banks the possibility to pre-announce a maximum trading loss and incur regulatory penalties or other incentives in proportion to the extent to which pre-announced maximum losses are exceeded (this is discussed below).

Capital regulation should create incentives for the correct pricing of absolute and relative risk
If differential capital requirements are set against different types of assets (for example, through applying differential risk weights) the rules should be based on actuarial calculations of relative risk. If risk weights are incorrectly specified, perverse incentives are created for banks because the implied regu-

latory capital requirements are more or less than justified by true relative risk calculations. This in turn distorts the relative and absolute pricing of risks. A major critique of the current Basle capital requirements is that the risk weights bear little relation to relative risk characteristics of different assets, and the loan book carries a uniform risk weight even though the risk characteristics of different loans within a bank's portfolio vary considerably. This is recognized in the BIS discussion document on capital adequacy (Basle Committee, 1999a) which outlines a proposal for a wider range of risk weights attached to bank assets.

Incentive Structures

A maintained theme is that incentive structures and moral hazard faced by decision makers (bank owners and managers, lenders to banks, borrowers and regulators) are central components of the regulatory regime. The overall theme is twofold: (a) there need to be appropriate internal incentives for management to behave in appropriate ways, and (b) the regulator has a role in ensuring internal incentives are compatible with the objectives of regulation. Overall more understanding is needed about incentive structures within financial firms and whether, for instance, incentive structures align with the objectives of regulation. Research is needed into the way regulation affects positively and negatively incentives within regulated firms. The possibility that detailed rules may have a negative effect of blunting compliance incentives and other components of the regulatory regime have already been considered.

With respect to internal incentives for owners and management of financial firms, several procedures, processes and structures may reinforce internal risk control mechanisms. These include internal auditors, internal audit committees, procedures for reporting to senior management (and perhaps to supervisors) and making a named board member of financial firms responsible for compliance and risk analysis and management systems. In some countries (such as New Zealand) incentives faced by bank managers have been strengthened through increased personal liability for bank directors; bank directors are personally liable in cases involving disclosure of incomplete or erroneous information. The Financial Services Authority in the UK has recently proposed that, under some circumstances, individual directors and senior managers of financial firms should be made personally liable for compliance failures.

Supervisors can also strengthen incentives by, for instance, relating the frequency and intensity of their supervision and inspection visits (and possibly rules) to the perceived adequacy of the internal risk control procedures and internal compliance arrangements. In addition, appropriate incentives can be created by calibrating the external burden of regulation (number of inspection visits, allowable business and so on) to the quality of management and the efficiency of internal incentives.

Evans (2000) suggests several routes through which incentive structures in banks can be improved: greater transparency and information disclosure by financial institutions; subjecting local banks to foreign competition; ensuring a closer alignment of regulatory and economic capital; greater use of risk-based incentives by supervisors; and lower capital adequacy requirements for banks headquartered in jurisdictions which comply with the BIS core principles of supervision.

Deposit insurance has two opposing sets of incentive structures with respect to systemic risk. By reducing the rationality of bank runs (though this is dependent on the extent and coverage of the deposit insurance scheme and the extent of any coinsurance) deposit insurance has the effect of lowering the potential for financial instability. On the other hand, the moral hazard implicit in deposit insurance may increase risk in the system. Given that there is little firm empirical evidence for bank runs in systems without deposit insurance, the second factor probably outweighs the first. This reinforces the case for deposit insurance to be accompanied by regulation to contain risk-taking by banks. Reviewing the experience of bank crises in various countries, Demirgüç-Kunt and Datragiache (1998) argue: 'Our evidence suggests that, in the period under consideration, moral hazard played a significant role in bringing about systemic banking problems, perhaps because countries with deposit insurance schemes were not generally successful at implementing appropriate prudential regulation and supervision, or because the deposit insurance schemes were not properly designed.'

Bhattacharya *et al.* (1998) consider various schemes to attenuate the moral hazard associated with deposit insurance. These include cash reserve requirements, risk-sensitive capital requirements and deposit insurance premia, partial deposit insurance, bank closure policy and bank charter value. There is an additional issue with respect to the incentive structure faced by state-owned, or state-controlled, banks as incentives may be ill-defined, if not hazardous. Such banks are not subject to the normal disciplining pressures of the market, their 'owners' do not monitor their behaviour, and there is no disciplining effect from the market in corporate control. Political interference in such banks (and the unwitting encouragement of 'bad banking' practices) can itself become a powerful ingredient in bank distress. Lindgren *et al.* (1996) found that banks that are, or were recently, state-owned or controlled were a factor in most of the instances of unsound banking in their sample of banking crises.

In its consultation document on capital adequacy, the Basle Committee recognizes that supervisors have a strong interest in facilitating effective market discipline as a lever to strengthen the safety and soundness of the banking system. It argues: 'market discipline has the potential to reinforce capital regulation and other supervisory efforts to promote safety and soundness in banks and financial systems. Market discipline imposes strong incentives on banks to conduct their business in a safe, sound and efficient manner' (Basle Committee, 1999a).

The key challenge, therefore, is how to align the incentives of financial firms with those of the regulatory objectives and at the same time minimize moral hazard for both consumers and regulated firms. Two general principles are outlined.

There should be appropriate incentives for bank owners
Bank owners have an important role in the monitoring of bank management and their risk taking as, in the final analysis, bank owners absorb the risks of the bank. There are several ways in which bank owners can be appropriately incentivized.

- One route is to ensure that banks have appropriate levels of equity capital. Capital serves three main roles as far as incentive structures are concerned: a commitment of the owners to supply risk resources to the business and which they can lose in the event of the bank making bad loans, an internal insurance fund and the avoidance of the bank becoming the captive of its bad debtors. In general, the higher is the capital ratio the more the owners have to lose and hence the greater the incentive for them to monitor the behaviour of managers. Low capital creates a particular moral hazard in that, because of the small amount owners have to lose, the more likely they are to condone excessive risk taking in a gamble-for-resurrection strategy.
- Corporate governance arrangements should be such that equity holders actively supervise managers.
- Ownership structures should foster shareholder monitoring and oversight. This includes private ownership of banks to strengthen the monitoring of management performance and to minimize adverse incentives for managers.
- Supervisors and safety net agencies should ensure that owners lose out in any restructuring operations in the event of failure. Failure to penalize shareholders in the restructuring of unsuccessful banks was a major shortcoming in some rescue operations in Latin America.
- In some countries (such as New Zealand) the incentive on owners has been strengthened by experimenting with a policy of increased personal liability of bank directors.

There should be appropriate internal incentives for management
Creating the right incentive structures for managers of financial institutions is
as important as creating those for owners. Specific measures could include
the following.

- Strong and effective risk analysis, management and control systems to
  be in place in all financial institutions for assessing risks ex ante, and
  asset values ex post. This includes systems and incentives for timely
  and accurate provisions against bad or doubtful debts. In the final
  analysis, most bank failures are due to weaknesses in this area. Regulatory agencies have a powerful role in insisting upon effective systems
  of internal management and risk control in financial institutions by
  means of strict accountability of owners, directors and senior management.
- Managers should also lose if the bank fails. This requires penalties
  (including dismissal) for incompetence amongst bank managers. Remuneration packages may be related to regulatory compliance.
- Mechanisms need to be in place to ensure that loan valuation, asset
  classification, loan concentrations, interconnected lending and risk assessment practices reflect sound and accurate assessments of claims
  and counterparties. This also requires mechanisms for the independent
  verification of financial statements and compliance with the principles
  of sound practice through professional external auditing and on-site
  inspection by supervisory agencies.
- A requirement for large banks to establish internal audit committees.

The key is that there need to be effective internal incentives for management to behave in appropriate ways, and the regulator has a role in ensuring
internal incentives are compatible with the objectives of regulation. Combining appropriate incentives for owners and managers contributes to a
robust financial system and, in principle, the market would evolve such
incentives. However experience indicates that, in many areas, and most
especially when the competitive environment is changing and the regulatory regime is being adjusted, it is hazardous to rely on the market evolving
appropriate incentives.

Monitoring and Supervision

Because of the nature of financial contracts between financial firms and their
customers (for example, many are long-term in nature and involve a fiduciary
obligation) there is a need for continuous monitoring of the behaviour of all
financial firms. The key issue is who is to undertake the monitoring. Several

parties can potentially monitor the management of banks: bank owners, bank depositors, rating agencies, official agencies (for example, the central bank or other regulatory body) and other banks in the market. In practice, there can be only a limited monitoring role for depositors owing to major information asymmetries which cannot easily be rectified, and because depositors face the less costly option of withdrawal of deposits. Saunders and Wilson (1996) review the empirical evidence on the role of informed depositors. The funding structure of a bank may also militate against effective monitoring in that, unlike the case of non-financial companies, creditors tend to be large in number but with each having a small stake.

Because most (especially retail) customers, and many other creditors, are not in practice able to undertake such monitoring, and because there are substantial economies of scale in such activity, an important role of regulatory agencies is to monitor the behaviour of financial firms on behalf of customers. In effect, consumers delegate the task of monitoring to a dedicated agency.

However, in the process, adverse incentive effects may emerge in that, given that regulatory agencies conduct monitoring and supervision on a delegated basis, they may reduce the incentive for others to conduct efficient monitoring. The role of other potential monitors (and notably the market) needs to be strengthened in many, including well-developed, financial systems. This in turn requires adequate information disclosure and transparency in banking operations. There need to be greater incentives for other parties to monitor banks in parallel with official agencies. A major advantage of having agents other than official supervisory bodies involved in the monitoring of banks is that it removes the inherent danger of having monitoring and supervision being conducted by a monopolist with less than perfect and complete information. Two principles related to official monitoring and supervision are indicated.

Official agencies need to have sufficient powers and independence to conduct effective monitoring and supervision
This means they need to be independent of political authorities and able to license, refuse to license and to withdraw licences from banks. They need to have the authority and ability to monitor the full range of banks' activities and business and be able to monitor and assess banks' systems for risk analysis and control. Because of the moral hazard created in some bank structures, agencies need to have power to establish rules about ownership and corporate structure of banks, and be able to establish minimum requirements for the competency and integrity of bank management.

Less emphasis should be placed on detailed and prescriptive rules and more on internal risk analysis, management and control systems

Externally imposed regulation in the form of prescriptive and detailed rules is becoming increasingly inappropriate and ineffective. More reliance needs to be placed on institutions' own internal risk analysis, management and control systems. This relates not only to quantitative techniques such as value-at-risk (VaR) models but also to the management 'culture' of those who handle models and supervise traders. A shift in emphasis towards monitoring risk-control mechanisms is needed, together with a recasting of the nature and functions of external regulation away from generalized rule setting towards establishing incentives and sanctions to reinforce such internal control systems. The consultative document by the Basle Committee on Banking Supervision (Basle Committee, 1999a) explicitly recognizes that a major role in the supervisory process is the monitoring of banks' own internal capital management processes and 'the setting of targets for capital that are commensurate with the bank's particular risk profile and control environment. This process would be subject to supervisory review and intervention, where appropriate'.

Intervention Arrangements

A key component of a regulatory regime is intervention arrangements by regulatory agencies in the event of financial distress. The issue focuses on when and how intervention is to be made. The experience of banking crises (in both developed and developing countries) is that a well-defined strategy is needed for responding to the possible insolvency of financial institutions. The way such intervention is made has signalling and incentive effects for the future behaviour of financial institutions. The conditions under which intervention is made, the manner of intervention and its timing may, therefore, have powerful moral hazard effects. Important issues related to the credibility of intervention agencies also arise.

A key issue in this area relates to rules versus discretion in the event of bank distress: to what extent should intervention be circumscribed by clearly defined rules (so that intervention agencies have no discretion about whether, how and when to act), or should there always be discretion because all the relevant circumstances cannot be set out in advance? The obvious prima facie advantage of discretion is that it is impossible to foresee all future circumstances and conditions for when a bank might become distressed and close to (or actually) insolvent. It might be judged that it is not always the right policy to close a bank in such circumstances.

On the other hand, there are strong arguments against allowing discretion and in favour of a rules approach to intervention. Firstly, it enhances the credibility of the intervention agency in that market participants, including banks, have a high degree of certainty that action will be taken. Secondly, the danger of discretion is that it increases the probability of forbearance which experience suggests usually eventually leads to higher costs when intervention is finally made. Thirdly, and judging by the experience of some countries which have experienced banking distress, it removes the danger of undue political interference in the disciplining of banks. Experience in many countries indicates that supervisory authorities face substantial pressure to delay action and intervention. Fourthly, it is likely to have a beneficial impact on ex ante behaviour of financial firms. A rules-based approach, by removing any prospect that a hazardous bank might be treated leniently, enhances the incentives for bank managers to manage banks prudently so as to reduce the probability of insolvency (Glaessner and Mas, 1995). It also enhances the credibility of the regulator's threat to close institutions. Finally, a rules approach guards against the hazard associated with risk-averse regulators who themselves might be inclined not to take action for fear that intervention will be interpreted as a regulatory failure, and who might be tempted to allow a firm to trade out of its difficulty. This amounts to the regulator 'gambling for resurrection'. In this sense, a rules approach may be of assistance to the intervention agency as its hands are tied.

The BIS has argued as follows:

> Above all, reducing incentives to excessive risk-taking will depend on the credibility of the authorities' commitment to limiting intervention to the necessary minimum in the event of turmoil. In much the same way as the monetary authorities' anti-inflation commitment, it needs to be demonstrated in consistent action. (BIS, 1991)

The need to maintain the credibility of supervisory agencies creates a strong bias against forbearance. The overall conclusion is that there should be a clear bias (though not a bar) against forbearance when a bank is in difficulty. While there should be a strong presumption against forbearance, and that this is best secured through having clearly defined rules, there will always be exceptional circumstances when forbearance might be warranted in the interests of systemic stability. However, when it is exercised, the regulatory agency should be made accountable for its actions.

In some respects there is a trade-off between credibility and flexibility with respect to intervention arrangements. Bruni and Paterno (1994) analyse the trade-off between rules and discretion in bank supervision in a game-theoretic framework. They argue that time-consistency and credibility play a central role. They conclude that the optimum arrangement is for a 'no bailout commitment' fixed by law but with special exemptions. The transition to a 'no bailout' strategy is unlikely to be a smooth, trouble-free process because of the incentive structures of supervisors. This is partly a reflection of the interaction between the incentive structures of supervisors and those of politicians. Kane (1991) suggests that a conflict of interest can emerge (an 'incentive breakdown') and that this partly explains the bailout of the US savings and loans institutions in the 1980s. He argues that supervisors intervened under political pressure and that this resulted in a bailout of insolvent institutions.

Intervention arrangements also have important implications for the total cost of intervention (for example, initial forbearance often has the effect of raising the eventual cost of subsequent intervention) and the distribution of those costs between taxpayers and other agents. Different intervention arrangements may also have implications for the future efficiency of the financial system in that, for instance, forbearance may have the effect of sustaining inefficient banks and excess capacity in the banking sector.

All this amounts to the need for care when devising bank restructuring policies, and the need for appropriate incentives for intervention agencies. Several principles can be established to guide the timing and form of intervention.

The design and application of safety net arrangements[2]
It is well established that, depending upon how deposit insurance schemes are constructed (most especially with respect to which deposits are insured and the extent of any coinsurance), moral hazards can be created: depositors may be induced to act with less care, and under some circumstances they may be induced to seek risky banks on the grounds that a one-way-bet is involved. At the same time, insured institutions may be induced to take more risk because they are not required to pay the full risk premium on insured deposits, risk is therefore subsidized, banks may be induced to hold less capital and the cost of deposit protection is passed to others who have no say in the risk-taking activity of the insured bank.

The extent and coverage of deposit insurance schemes should be strictly limited
Maintaining the integrity of the banking system requires that some bank liability holders are to be protected from the consequences of bank failure, but this should be limited because such protection may create adverse incentives. In particular, and in order to avoid the potential moral hazards emerging, coverage should be explicit (rather than assumed) and restricted to comparatively small deposits. There should always be an element of coinsurance to the extent that less than 100 per cent of any deposit is insured.

There needs to be a well-defined strategy for responding to the possible insolvency of financial institutions

A regulatory regime that avoided any possibility of bank failure would certainly imply overregulation to an extent that would impose economic costs on society and the efficiency of the financial system. Occasional bank failures will always be a part of a well functioning financial system. This means it is necessary to have a strategy with respect to the way to respond to bank failures when they occur or when the predicament of individual banks is evidently deteriorating. A response strategy in the event of bank distress has several possible components: (a) being prepared to close insolvent financial institutions, (b) taking prompt corrective action to address financial problems before they reach critical proportions, (c) closing unviable institutions promptly, and vigorously monitoring weak and/or restructured institutions, and (d) undertaking a timely assessment of the full scope of financial insolvency and the fiscal cost of resolving the problem.

There should be a clear bias (though not a bar) against forbearance when a bank is in difficulty

A central issue for the credibility, and hence authority, of a regulator is whether rules and decisions are time-consistent. There may be circumstances where a rule, or normal policy action, needs to be suspended. The priors are in favour of a strong case for precommitment and rules of behaviour for the regulator. There is also a case for a graduated response approach since, for example, there is no magical capital ratio below which an institution is in danger and above which it is safe. Other things being equal, potential danger gradually increases as the capital ratio declines. This in itself suggests there should be a graduated series of responses from the regulator as capital diminishes.

Regulatory authorities need to build a reputation for tough supervision and, when necessary, decisive action in cases of financial distress. Supervisory authorities may, from time to time, face substantial political pressure to delay action in closing hazardous financial institutions. There is an additional danger of regulatory capture, and that a risk-averse regulator may simply delay intervention in order to avoid blame. The need to maintain credibility creates a strong bias against forbearance.

Time-inconsistency and credibility problems should be addressed through precommitments and graduated responses with the possibility of overrides

Some analysts have advocated various forms of predetermined intervention though a general policy of structured early intervention and resolution (SEIR). Goldstein and Turner (1996) argue that SEIR is designed to imitate the remedial action which private bond holders would impose on banks in the absence of government insurance or guarantees. In this sense it is a mimic of market solutions to troubled banks. An example of the rules-based approach is to be found in the prompt corrective action (PCA) rules in the USA. These specify graduated intervention by regulators with predetermined responses triggered by capital thresholds.

Under a related concept (the 'precommitment approach' to bank supervision) banks' own assessments of their capital needs (as determined by their own internal risk models) are used as the basis of supervision. At the beginning of each period the bank evaluates its need for capital and the bank is subsequently required to manage its risks so that its capital does not fall below the precommitment level. Penalties are imposed when capital falls below these levels. There are several advantages to a precommitment strategy: it avoids the necessity of detailed and prescriptive regulation, it creates powerful incentives for bank decision makers (the choice of an excessive amount of capital imposes costs on the bank, while choosing too low a level of capital risks the imposition of penalties) and it is flexible as it offers scope for each bank to choose a level of capital which is appropriate to its own particular circumstances. On the other hand, Estrella (1998) argues that the precise design of the penalty structure is likely to be complex.

However, even in a precommitment and graduated response regime there may be cases where predetermined rules are to be overridden. The problem, however, is that if this is publicly known the credibility of the regulator may be compromised, bearing in mind that it is to create and sustain such credibility that the precommitment rule is established in the first place. Can there be any guarantee that such an override would not turn regulation into a totally ad hoc procedure? One solution is to make the intervention agency publicly accountable for any actions and decisions not to intervene.

Intervention authorities need to ensure that parties that have benefited from risk taking bear a large proportion of the cost of any restructuring the banking system
This implies, for example, that shareholders should be the first to lose their investment, along with large holders of long-term liabilities such as subordinated debt. Also delinquent borrowers must not be given favourable treatment at public expense.

Prompt action should be taken to prevent problem institutions extending credit to high-risk borrowers, or capitalizing unpaid interest on delinquent loans into new credit
Execution of this principle is designed to reduce the moral hazard risk in bank restructurings that arises when institutions with low and declining net worth continue to operate under the protection of public policies designed to

maintain the integrity of the banking system. This implies that, when practicable, insolvent institutions should be removed from the hands of current owners, whether through sale, temporary nationalization or closure.

Society must create the political will to make restructuring a priority in allocating public funds while avoiding sharp increases in inflation. Use of public funds in rescue operations should be kept to a minimum and, whenever used, be subject to strict conditionally
This follows from previous principles in that their execution requires adequate funding to pay off some liability holders with negative net worth. Attempts should always be made to recover public funds over a period of time by, for instance, asset sales from resolution trusts and so on.

Barriers to market recapitalization should be minimized
A particular barrier that is often encountered relates to the market in corporate control. Governments or regulatory agencies frequently impose rules regarding the ownership of banks and the extent to which banks can be taken over through the market in corporate control. There are often particular limitations on the extent to which foreign banks are allowed to purchase domestic banks, even though this is frequently a solution for an insolvent bank which can be effectively recapitalized by being purchased by a stronger domestic or foreign institution.

Regulators should be publicly accountable through credible mechanisms
Regulatory agencies have considerable power through their influence over the terms on which business is conducted. For this reason agencies need to be accountable and their activities transparent. In addition, public accountability can be a protection against political interference in the decisions of regulatory agencies, and it can create incentives against forbearance. Difficulties can arise when it may be prudent for a central bank's success in averting a bank failure or systemic crisis to remain secret. One possible approach is to create an audit agency of the regulator, with the regulator being required to report on a regular basis to an independent person or body. The report would cover the objectives of the regulator and the measures of success and failure. The audit authority would have a degree of standing that would force the regulatory agency to respond to any concerns raised. In due course, the report of the regulator to the agency would be published.

Assessment
In the process of restructuring following a financial crisis financial market functioning needs to be restored as quickly as possible while minimizing market disruption. Balance sheet assets of weak institutions need to be re-

structured and placed on a sound footing. This should be designed to ameliorate the moral hazard that weak banks become the captive of their bad customers and, in the process, bad loans drive out good loans. In addition, the management and recovery of loans should be separated from the concurrent activity of banks so that a proper focus can be given to the efficient management of the continuing activity of banks.

Lessons can be learned about how to respond to crises when they emerge. The experience of Mexico, for example, demonstrates how a serious banking crisis can be managed and the banks restored to viability. The experience is instructive as an object lesson in how a banking crisis can be transformed if appropriate measures are taken. Several policy measures were adopted, both to restore the banking system and to lower the probability of similar crises recurring:

- foreign competition in banking was encouraged. There was subsequently a major influx of foreign banks and foreign capital into the banking sector associated with the privatization of banks and the relaxation of entry barriers. As a result, foreign ownership of banks in Mexico now exceeds 20 per cent;
- consolidation of the banking system was supported and encouraged;
- regulation and supervision was tightened and made more explicit;
- accountancy and disclosure standards and requirements were tightened;
- links between bankers and politics were broken.

When a banking crisis emerges, the policy strategy has to be to reconstitute the banking system (including recapitalizing banks) and to apply measures designed to lower significantly the probability of a crisis re-emerging.

Market Discipline

Monitoring is not only conducted by official agencies whose specialist task it is. In well developed regimes, the market also has incentives to monitor the behaviour of financial firms. The disciplines imposed by the market can be as powerful as any sanctions imposed by official agencies. The disciplining role of the markets (including the inter-bank market) was weak in the crisis countries of South East Asia in the 1990s. This was due predominantly to the lack of disclosure and transparency of banks, and the fact that little reliance could be placed on the quality of accountancy data provided in bank accounts. In many cases standard accountancy and auditing procedures were not rigorously applied, and in some cases there was wilful misrepresentation of the financial position of banks and non-financial companies.

Within the general framework of monitoring, a particular dimension is the extent to which the market undertakes monitoring and imposes discipline on the risk taking of banks. Given how the business of banking has evolved and the nature of the market environment in which banks now operate, less reliance can be placed on supervision by official agencies and a greater role needs to be played by the market. Market disciplines need to be strengthened. The issue is focused, not so much on market versus agency discipline, but on the mix of all aspects of monitoring, supervision and discipline. As has been noted,

> Broader approaches to bank supervision reach beyond the issues of defining capital and accounting standards, and envisage co-opting other market partici-pants by giving them a greater stake in bank survival. This approach increases the likelihood that problems will be detected earlier ... [it involves] broadening the number of those who are directly concerned about keeping the banks safe and sound. (Caprio and Honahan, 1998)

A potentially powerful disciplining power of markets derives from the market in corporate control which, through the threat of removing control from incumbent managements, is a discipline on managers to be efficient and not endanger the solvency of their banks. As put in a recent IMF study: 'An open and competitive banking market exerts its own form of discipline against weak banks while encouraging well-managed banks' (Lindgren *et al.*, 1996).

Some analysts (for example, Calomiris, 1997) are sceptical about the power of official supervisory agencies to identify the risk characteristics of banks compared with the power and incentives of markets. Along with others, Calomiris advocates banks being required to issue a minimum amount of subordinated and uninsured debt as part of the capital base. This would involve having private sector funds that could not be withdrawn from the bank and which would effectively be put at risk because the authorities would have no incentive to rescue the holders of such debt. Subordinated debt holders would therefore have an incentive to monitor the risk taking of banks. Discipline would be applied by the market as the markets' assessment of risk would be reflected in the risk premium in the price of traded debt. In particular, because of the nature of debt contracts, holders of a bank's subordinated debt do not share in the potential upside gain from the bank's risk taking, but stand to lose if the bank fails. They therefore have a particular incentive to monitor the risk profile of the bank compared with shareholders who, under some circumstances, have an incentive to support a high-risk profile. Movements in the price of a bank's subordinated debt also serve as a signal to official supervisors.

A scheme along these lines has been introduced in Argentina, whereby holders of subordinated debt must be entities of substance which are independent of the bank's shareholders, and it is required that the issue of debt must be in relatively lumpy amounts on a regular basis (ibid.). However, while there is a potentially powerful role for market discipline to operate through the pricing of subordinated debt, the interests of holders of such debt do not necessarily precisely coincide with those of depositors or the public interest more generally (Dewatripont and Tirole, 1994). It is not, therefore, a substitute for official monitoring. It is intended as a mechanism to extend the role of market monitoring. A further mechanism to enhance market discipline is to link deposit insurance premiums paid by banks to the implied risk of the bank as incorporated in subordinated debt yields or classifications of rating agencies.

The merit of increasing the role of market discipline is that large, well-informed creditors (including other banks) have the resources, expertise, market knowledge and incentives to conduct monitoring and to impose market discipline. For instance, it has been argued that the hazardous state of the Bank of Credit and Commerce International (BCCI) was reflected in market prices and inter-bank interest rates long before the Bank of England closed the bank.

Regulation should not impede competition but should enhance it and, by addressing information asymmetries, make it more effective in the marketplace

However well intentioned, regulation has the potential to compromise competition and to condone, if not in some cases endorse, unwarranted entry barriers, restrictive practices and other anti-competitive mechanisms. Historically regulation in finance has often been anti-competitive in nature, but this is not an inherent property of regulation. As there are clear consumer benefits and efficiency gains to be secured through competition, regulation should not be constructed in a way that impairs it. Regulation and competition need not be in conflict: on the contrary, properly constructed, they are complementary. Regulation can, therefore, enhance competition. It can also make it more effective in the marketplace by, for instance, requiring the disclosure of relevant information that can be used by consumers in making informed choices.

Discipline can also be exerted by competition. Opening domestic financial markets to external competition can contribute to the promotion of market discipline. There are many benefits to be derived from foreign institutions entering a country. They bring expertise and experience and, because they themselves are diversified throughout the world, what is a macro shock to a particular country becomes a regional shock, and hence they are more able to sustain purely national shocks compared with domestic institutions. It is generally the case that competition that develops from outside a system has a greater impact on competition and efficiency than internal competition. Foreign institutions tend to be less subject to domestic political pressures in the conduct of their business, and are also less susceptible to local euphoria which, at times, leads to excessive lending and overoptimistic expectations.

Regulation should reinforce, not replace, market discipline and the regulatory regime should be structured so as to provide greater incentives than exist at present for markets to monitor banks
In many countries, market discipline (for example, through disclosure) needs to be strengthened. This means creating incentives for private markets to reward good performance and penalize hazardous behaviour. Regulation and supervision should complement and support, and never undermine, the operation of market discipline.

Whenever possible, regulators should utilize market data in their supervisory procedures
The evidence indicates that markets can give signals about the credit standing of financial firms which, when combined with inside information gained by supervisory procedures, can increase the efficiency of the supervisory process. Flannery (1998) suggests that market information may improve two features of the overall process: it permits regulators to identify developing problems more promptly, and it provides regulators with the incentive and justification to take action more quickly once problems have been identified. He concludes that market information should be incorporated into the process of identifying and correcting problems.

If financial markets are able to assess a bank's market value as reflected in the market price, an asset-pricing model can in principle be used to infer the risk of insolvency that the market has assigned to each bank. Such a model has been applied to UK banks by Hall and Miles (1990). Similar analysis for countries which had recently liberalized their financial systems has been applied by Fischer and Gueyie (1995). On the other hand, as there are clear limitations to such an approach (see Simons and Cross, 1991), it would be hazardous to rely exclusively on it. For instance, it assumes that markets have sufficient data upon which to make an accurate assessment of the risk profile of banks, and it equally assumes that the market is able to assess efficiently the available information and incorporate this into an efficient pricing of bank securities.

There should be a significant role for rating agencies in the supervisory process
Rating agencies have considerable resources and expertise in monitoring banks and making assessments of risk. It could be made a requirement, as in Argentina, for all banks to have a rating, which would be made public.

Assessment

While market discipline is potentially powerful, it has its limitations. This means that, in practice, it is unlikely to be an effective alternative to the role of official regulatory and supervisory agencies.

- Markets are concerned with the private cost of a bank failure and reflect the risk of this in market prices. The social cost of bank failures, on the other hand, may exceed the private cost (Llewellyn, 1999) and hence the total cost of a bank failure may not be fully reflected in market prices.
- Market disciplines are not effective at monitoring and disciplining public sector banks.
- In many countries, there are limits imposed on the extent to which the market in corporate control (the takeover market) is allowed to operate. In particular, there are limits, if not bars, on the extent to which foreign institutions are able to take control of banks, even though they may offer a solution to undercapitalized banks.
- The market is able to price bank securities and inter-bank loans efficiently only to the extent that relevant information is available. Disclosure requirements are, therefore, an integral part of the market disciplining process.
- It is not self-evident that market participants always have the necessary expertise to make a risk assessment of complex, and sometimes opaque, banks.
- In some countries, the market in debt of all kinds (including securities and debt issued by banks) is limited, inefficient and cartelized.
- When debt issues are very small it is not always economic for a rating agency to conduct a full credit rating on the bank.

While there are clear limitations to the role of market discipline, the global trend is appropriately in the direction of placing more emphasis on market data in the supervisory process. The theme is not that market monitoring and discipline can effectively replace official supervision, but that it has a potentially powerful role which should be strengthened within the overall regulatory regime. In addition, Caprio (1997) argues that broadening the number of those who are directly concerned about the safety and soundness of banks reduces the extent to which insider political pressure can be brought to bear on bank regulation and supervision. A consultative document issued by the Basle Committee on Banking Supervision (1999a) incorporates the role of market discipline as one of the three pillars of a proposed new approach to banking supervision. The Committee emphasizes that its approach 'will encourage high disclosure standards and enhance the role of market participants in encouraging banks to hold adequate capital'.

Corporate Governance

There are several reasons why corporate governance arrangements operate differently with banks than with other types of firms. Firstly, banks are subject to regulation in the interests of systemic stability and consumer protection which adds an additional dimension to corporate governance arrangements. Regulation is partly a response to limitations in corporate governance mechanisms in banks. Secondly, banks are also subject to continuous supervision and monitoring by official agencies. This has two immediate implications for private corporate governance: shareholders and official agencies are to some extent duplicating monitoring activity, and the actions of official agencies may have an impact on the incentives faced by other monitors, such as shareholders and even depositors. However, for reasons already outlined, official and market monitoring are not perfectly substitutable. Thirdly, banks have a fiduciary relationship with their customers (for example, they are holding the wealth of depositors) which is generally not the case with other types of firm. This creates additional principal–agent relationships (and potentially agency costs) with banks that generally do not exist with non-financial firms.

A fourth reason why corporate governance mechanisms are different in banks is that there is a systemic dimension to banks and, because in some circumstances (such as presence of externalities) the social costs of bank failures may exceed private costs, there is a systemic concern with the behaviour of banks that does not exist with other companies. Finally, banks are subject to safety net arrangements that are not available to other companies. This has implications for incentive structures faced by owners, managers, depositors and the market with respect to monitoring and control.

All of these considerations have an impact on the two general mechanisms for exercising discipline on the management of firms: internal corporate governance and the market in corporate control. While there are significant differences between banks and other firms, corporate governance issues in banks have received remarkably little attention. A key issue, as noted by Flannery (1998), is that little is known about the way the two governance systems (regulation and private) interact with each other and, in particular, the extent to which they are complementary or offsetting.

A key issue in the management of financial firms is the extent to which corporate governance arrangements are suitable and efficient for the management and control of risks. The Financial Services Authority in the UK has argued as follows: 'Senior management set the business strategy, regulatory climate, and ethical standards of the firm ... Effective management of these activities will benefit firms and contribute to the delivery of the FSA's statutory objectives.' Corporate governance arrangements include issues of corporate structure, the power of shareholders to exercise accountability of managers, the transparency of corporate structures, the authority and power of directors, internal audit arrangements and the lines of accountability of managers. In the final analysis, shareholders are the ultimate risk takers and agency problems may induce managers to take more risks with the bank than the owners would wish. This in turn raises issues about what information shareholders have about the actions of the managers to which they delegate decision-making powers, the extent to which shareholders are represented on the board of directors of the bank, and the extent to which shareholders have power to discipline managers.

The Basle Committee has rightly argued that effective oversight by a bank's board of directors and senior management is critical. It suggests that the board should approve overall policies of the bank and its internal systems. It argues in particular that 'lack of adequate corporate governance in the banks seems to have been an important contributory factor in the Asian crisis. The boards of directors and management committees of the banks did not play the role they were expected to play' (Basle Committee, 1999b).

Useful insights have been provided by Sinha (1999) who concludes, for instance, that, while in the UK the regulatory authorities approve the appointment of non-executive directors of banks, such directors are generally considerably less effective in monitoring top management than is the case in manufacturing firms. Sinha compares corporate governance arrangements in banks and manufacturing firms in the UK and finds that top management turnover in banks is less than in other firms, and that turnover seems not to be related to share price performance. Prowse (1997) also shows that accountability to shareholders, and the effectiveness of board monitoring, is lower in banks than in non-financial firms.

An interesting possibility is the extent to which all this results from moral hazard associated with official regulation and supervision: this is a further example of possible negative trade-offs within a regulatory regime. It could be the case that, as regulatory authorities impose regulation and monitor banks, the incentive for non-executive directors and shareholders to do so is reduced. The presumption may be that regulators have more information than non-executive directors and shareholders, and that their own monitoring would only be wastefully duplicating that being conducted by official supervisors. Further research is needed into the role of non-executive directors and institutional investors in the effectiveness of corporate governance mechanisms in banks.

The Basle Committee has recognized that different structural approaches to corporate governance exist across countries. While it has not, therefore, taken a view with respect to any particular ideal model, the Committee encourages any practices which strengthen corporate governance in banks. The general principle should be as follows.

Corporate governance arrangements should provide for effective monitoring and supervision of the risk-taking profile of banks
These arrangements would provide for, inter alia, a management structure with clear lines of accountability; independent non-executive directors on the board; an independent audit committee; a four-eyes principle for important decisions involving the risk profile of the bank; transparent ownership structure; internal structures that enabled the risk profile of the bank to be clear, transparent and managed; and monitored risk analysis and management systems. According to the Basle Committee, good corporate governance includes the following:

- establishing strategic objectives and a set of corporate values that are communicated throughout the banking organization;
- setting and enforcing clear lines of responsibility and accountability throughout the organization;
- ensuring that board members are qualified for their positions, have a clear understanding of their role in corporate governance and are not subject to undue influence from management or outside concerns;
- ensuring that there is appropriate oversight by senior management;
- effectively utilizing the work conducted by internal and external auditors;
- ensuring that compensation packages are consistent with the bank's ethical values, objectives, strategy and control environment;
- conducting corporate governance in a transparent manner.

7. CONCLUSIONS AND ASSESSMENT

The concepts of a *regulatory regime* and *regulatory strategy* have been introduced. Seven components of the regime have been identified: each is important but none alone is sufficient for the objectives of regulation to be achieved. They are complementary and not alternatives. Regulatory strategy is ultimately about optimizing the outcome of the overall regime rather than any particular components. Regulation in particular needs to consider that, if it is badly constructed or taken too far, there may be negative impacts on the other components to the extent that the overall effect is diluted. However there may also be positive relationships between the components, and regulation can have a beneficial effect on incentive structures within financial firms.

Effective regulation and supervision of banks have the potential to contribute to the stability and robustness of financial systems, but there are also distinct limits to what they can achieve in practice. Although regulation is an important part of the regulatory regime, the other components are equally important. In the final analysis, there is no viable alternative to placing the main responsibility for risk management and general compliance on the shoulders of the management of financial institutions. Management must not be able to hide behind the cloak of regulation or pretend that, if regulation and supervisory arrangements are in place, this absolves them from their own responsibility. Nothing should ever be seen as taking away the responsibility for supervision of financial firms by shareholders, managers and the markets. On the contrary, regulation and supervision can be constructed in a way that enhances this responsibility.

The objective is to optimise the outcome of a regulatory strategy in terms of mixing the components of the regime, bearing in mind that negative trade-offs may be encountered. The emphasis is on the *combination* of mechanisms rather than alternative approaches to achieving the objectives. The skill of the regulator in devising a regulatory strategy lies in the way the various components in the regime are combined, and how the various instruments available to the regulator (rules, principles, guidelines, mandatory disclosure requirements, authorization, supervision, intervention, sanctions, redress and so on) are to be used.

Several shifts within the regulatory regime have been outlined in order to maximize its overall effectiveness and efficiency.

- Less emphasis to be given to formal and detailed prescriptive rules dictating the behaviour of regulated firms.
- A greater focus to be given to incentive structures within regulated firms, and how regulation might have a beneficial impact on incentives.
- Market discipline and market monitoring of financial firms need to be strengthened within the overall regime.
- There should be greater differentiation between regulated firms.
- Less emphasis to be placed on detailed and prescriptive rules and more on internal risk analysis, management and control systems. In some areas, externally imposed regulation in the form of prescriptive and detailed rules is becoming increasingly inappropriate and ineffective. For instance, with respect to prudential issues, more reliance should be placed on institutions' own internal risk analysis, management and control systems.
- Corporate governance mechanisms for financial firms need to be

strengthened so that owners play a greater role in the monitoring and control of regulated firms, and compliance issues are identified as being the ultimate responsibility of a nominated main board director.

Overall, the lesson of recent banking crises is that there needs to be more effective surveillance of financial institutions both by supervisory authorities and the markets. For markets to complement the work of supervisory agencies, there needs to be good and timely information about banks' activities and balance sheet positions. Regulation, supervision and information disclosure are not alternatives.

NOTES

* The author expresses his thanks to Jeffrey Shafer and Jacques Sijben for invaluable comments on an earlier draft of this chapter. The usual disclaimer applies.
1. The general economic rationale for financial regulation (in terms of externalities, market imperfections, economies of scale in monitoring, grid-lock problems, and moral hazard associated with safety nets) has been outlined elsewhere (Llewellyn, 1999). For purposes of the present chapter, the economic rationale for regulation is taken as given.
2. These include lender-of-last-resort and deposit insurance; they should create incentives for stakeholders to exercise oversight and to act prudently so as to reduce the probability of recourse being made to public funds.

REFERENCES

Adams, C., Mathieson, D., Schinasi, G. and Chadha, B. (1998), *International Capital Markets*, Washington: IMF.

Alba, P., Bhattacharya, G., Claessens, S., Ghash, S. and Hernandez, L. (1998), 'The role of macroeconomic and financial sector linkages in East Asia's financial crisis', mimeo, World Bank.

Andersson, M. and Viotti, S. (1999), 'Managing and preventing financial crises', *Sveriges Riksbank Quarterly Review*, 71–89.

Baer, H. and Gray, C. (1996), 'Debt as a control device in transitional economies: the experiences of Hungary and Poland', in R. Frydman, C. Gray and A. Rapaczynski (eds), *Corporate Governance in Central Europe and Russia*, Vol. 1, Budapest: Central European University Press.

Basle Committee (1999a), 'A new capital adequacy framework', consultative paper, BIS, Basle, June.

Basle Committee (1999b), 'Enhancing corporate governance for banking organisations', Basle Committee on Banking Supervision, BIS, Basle.

Beatty, A, Chamberlain, S. and Magliola, J. (1993), 'Managing financial reports on commercial banks', Wharton Financial Institutions Centre, paper no. 94-02, August.

Benink, H. and Llewellyn, D.T. (1994), 'De-regulation and financial fragility: a case study of the UK and Scandinavia', in D. Fair and R. Raymond (eds), *Competitive-*

ness of Financial Institutions and Centres in Europe, Dordrecht: Kluwer, pp. 186–201.

Benston, G. and Kaufman, G.(1995), 'Is the banking and payments system fragile?', *Journal of Financial Services Research*, September.

Bhattachary, S, Boot, A. and Thakor, A.V. (1998), 'The economics of bank regulation', *Journal of Money, Credit and Banking*, November, 745–70.

Billett, M., Garfinkel, J. and O'Neal, E. (1998), 'The cost of market versus regulatory discipline in banking', *Journal of Financial Economics*, 333–58.

BIS (1991), 'Annual Report', Basle, June.

BIS (1998), 'Annual Report', Basle, June.

Bisignano, J. (1998), 'Precarious credit equilibria: reflections on the Asian financial crisis', BIS, mimeo.

Black, J. (1994), 'Which Arrow? Rule type and regulatory policy', *Public Law*, June.

Brealey, R. (1999), 'The Asian crisis: lessons for crisis management and prevention', *Bank of England Quarterly Bulletin*, August, 285–96.

Brownbridge, M. and Kirkpatrick, C. (1999), 'Financial sector regulation: the lessons of the Asian crisis', *Development Policy Review*, **17** (3), 243–66.

Bruni, F. and Paterno, F. (1994), 'Market discipline of banks' riskiness: a study of selected issues', *Journal of Financial Services Research*, 313.

Calomiris, C. (1997), *The Postmodern Safety Net*, Washington, DC: American Enterprise Institute.

Caprio, G. (1997), 'Safe and sound banking in developing countries: we're not in Kansas anymore', Policy Research Paper, no. 1739, World Bank, Washington, DC.

Caprio, G. and Hanahan, P. (1998), 'Beyond capital ideals: restoring bank stability', unpublished paper, World Bank, Washington, DC.

Caprio, G. and Summers, L. (1993), 'Finance and its reform', Policy Research Paper no. 1734, World Bank, Washington, DC.

Cole, H. and Kehoe, T. (1996), 'A self-fulfilling model of Mexico's 1994–95 debt crisis', *Journal of International Economics*, **41**, 309–30.

Corbett, J., Irwin, G. and Vines, D. (1999), 'From Asian miracle to Asian crisis: why vulnerability, why collapse?', in D. Gruen and L. Gower (eds), *Capital Flows and the International Financial System*, Sydney: Reserve Bank of Australia, pp. 190–213.

Corsetti, G., Pesenti, P. and Rabini, N. (1998), 'What caused the Asia currency and financial crisis?', Banca D'Italia, discussion paper, December.

Dale, R. (1996), *Risk and Regulation in Global Securities Markets*, London: Wiley.

Demirgüç-Kunt, A. and Detragiache, E. (1998), 'Financial liberalisation and financial fragility', World Bank Annual Conference on Development Economics.

Demsetz, R., Saidenberg, M. and Strahan, P. (1997), 'Agency problems and risk-taking at banks', Federal Reserve Bank of New York Research Paper, no. 9709.

Dewatripont, M. and Tirole, J. (1994), *The Prudential Regulation of Banks*, Cambridge, MA: MIT Press.

Drage, J. and Mann, F. (1999), 'Improving the stability of the international financial system', *Financial Stability Review*, June, 40–77.

Estrella, A. (1998), 'Formulas or supervision? Remarks on the future of regulatory capital', Federal Reserve Bank of New York, *Economic Policy Review*, October.

Evans, H. (2000), 'Plumbers and architects: a supervisory perspective on international financial architecture, Occasional Paper no. 4, Financial Services Authority, London, January.

Fink, G. and Haiss, P. (2000), 'Lemming banking: conflict avoidance by herd instinct to eliminate excess capacity', paper presented at the SUERF Colloquium, Vienna, May.

Fischer, K. and Gueyie, J. (1995), 'Financial liberalisation and bank solvency', University of Laval, Quebec, August.

Flannery, M. (1998), 'Using market information in prudential bank supervision: a review of the US empirical evidence', *Journal of Money, Credit and Banking*, August, 273–305.

Folkerts-Landau, D., Schinasi, J., Cassard, M., Ng, V., Reinhart, C. and Spencer, M. (1995), 'Effects of capital flows on the domestic sectors in APEC countries', in M. Khan and C. Rheinhart (eds), *Capital Flows in the APEC Region*, IMF Occasional Paper, no. 122, IMF, Washington.

Furman, J. and Stiglitz, J. (1998), 'Economic crises: evidence and insights from East Asia', Brookings Papers, Washington.

Glaessner, T. and Mas, I. (1995), 'Incentives and the resolution of bank distress', *World Bank Research Observer*, **10** (1) (February), 53–73.

Godlayn, I. and Valdes, R. (1997), 'Capital flows and the twin crises: the role of liquidity', IMF Working Paper, 97/87, July.

Goldstein, M. and Folkerts-Landau, D. (1993), 'Systemic issues in international finance', World Economic and Financial Surveys, IMF, Washington.

Goldstein, M. and Turner, P. (1996), 'Banking crises in emerging economies', BIS Economic Papers, no. 46, BIS, Basle.

Goodhart, C., Hartmann, P., Llewellyn, D.T., Rojas-Suarez, L. and Weisbrod, S. (1998), *Financial Regulation: Why, How and Where Now?*, London, Routledge.

Hall, S. and Miles, D. (1990), 'Monitoring bank risk: a market based approach', discussion paper, Birkbeck College, London, April.

Hausmann, R. and Gavin, M. (1998), 'The roots of banking crises: the Macroeconomic context', IADB, Washington, mimeo.

Hellman, T, Murdock, K. and Stiglitz, J. (1995), 'Financial restraint: towards a new paradigm', in M. Aokí, H. Kim and M. Okuno-Fujiwara (eds), *The Role of Government in East Asian Economic Development: Comparative Institutional Analysis*, Oxford: Oxford University Press.

Hellweg, M (1995), 'Systemic aspects of risk management in banking and finance', *Swiss Journal of Economics and Statistics*, special volume, December.

IMF (1993), 'Deterioration of bank balance sheets', *World Economic Outlook*, 2.

Kahneman, D, and Tuersky, A (1979), 'Prospect theory: an analysis of decision under risk', *Econometrica*, 263–91.

Kaminsky, G. and Reinhart, C. (1998), 'The twin crises: the causes of banking and balance of payments problems', Board of Governors, Federal Reserve System, *International Finance Discussion Papers*, no. 554.

Kane, E. (1991), 'Financial regulation and market forces', *Swiss Journal of Economics and Statistics*, 326.

Keeley, M. (1990), 'Deposit insurance, risk and market power in banking', *American Economic Review*, December, 1183–201.

Kim, M. and Cross, W. (1995), 'The impact of the 1989 change in bank capital standards on loan loss provisions', mimeo, Rutgers University.

Krugman, P. (1998), 'Asia: what went wrong?', *Fortune*, 2 March.

Krugman, P. (1999), *The Return of Depression Economics*, London: Allen Lane.

Lindgren, C.J., Garcia, G. and Saal, M. (1996), *Bank Soundness and Macroeconomic Policy*, Washington: International Monetary Fund.

Llewellyn, D.T. (1999), 'The economic rationale of financial regulation', occasional paper no. 1, Financial Services Authority, London.
Llewellyn, D.T. and Holmes, M. (1991), 'Competition or credit controls?', Hobart Paper no. 117, Institute of Economic Affairs: London.
Martinez, P. (1998), 'Do depositors punish banks for bad behaviour?' Examining market discipline in Argentina, Chile & Mexico', World Bank Policy Research Working Paper, February.
OECD (1992), *Banking Under Stress*, Paris: OECD.
Prendergast, C. (1993), 'The provision of incentives in firms', *Journal of Economic Literature*, March, 7–63.
Prowse, S. (1997), Corporate control in commercial banks', *Journal of Financial Research*, **20**, 509–27.
Rahman, M. (1998), 'The role of accounting and disclosure standards in the East Asian financial crisis: lessons learned', mimeo, UNCTAD, Geneva.
Reisen, H. (1998), 'Domestic causes of currency crises: policy lessons for crisis avoidance', OECD Development Centre, technical paper 136, OECD, Paris.
Richardson, J. and Stephenson, M. (2000), 'Some aspects of regulatory capital', occasional paper no. 7, Financial Services Authority, London.
Rodrik, D. (1999), 'The new global economy and developing countries: making openness work', Overseas Development Council, Washington.
Rojas-Suarez, L. and Weisbrod, S. (1995), 'Financial fragilities in Latin America: 1980s and 1990s', occasional paper, no. 132, IMF, Washington.
Sachs, J., Torrell, A. and Velesco, A. (1996), 'Financial crises in emerging markets: the lessons from 1995', Brookings Papers 1, Brookings Institution, Washington.
Saunders, A. and Wilson, B. (1996), 'Contagious bank runs: evidence from the 1929–1933 period', *Journal of Financial Intermediation*, **5**, 409–23.
Schinasi, G. and Hargreaves, M. (1993), 'Boom and bust in asset markets in the 1980s: causes and consequences', *IMF World Economic Outlook*, December.
Schinasi, G., Drees, B. and Lee, W. (1999), 'Managing global finance and risk', *Finance and Development*, December.
Schwartz, A. (1995), 'Coping with financial fragility: a global perspective', *Journal of Financial Services Research*, September.
Shafer, J.R. (1987), 'Managing crisis in the emerging financial landscape', *OECD Economic Outlook*, no. 9, 55–77.
Sijben, J. (1999), 'Regulation versus market discipline in banking: an overview', University of Tilburg, Netherlands, mimeo.
Simons, K. and Cross, S. (1991), 'Do capital markets predict problems in large commercial banks', *New England Economic Review*, May, 51–6.
Simpson, D. (2000), 'Cost benefit analysis and competition', *Some Cost Benefit Issues in Financial Regulation*, London: Financial Services Authority.
Sinha, R. (1999), 'Corporate governance in financial services firms', Loughborough University Banking Centre Paper no 121/98.
Stiglitz, J. (1999), 'Must financial crises be this frequent and this painful?', in P.-R. Agenor *et al.* (eds), *The Asian Financial Crisis: Causes, Contagion and Consequences*, Cambridge: Cambridge University Press.
Suzuki, Y. (1986), *Money, Finance and Macroeconomic Performance in Japan*, New Haven: Yale University Press.
UNCTAD (1998), *Trade and Development Report*, Geneva: United Nations.
Wallman, S. (1999), 'Information technology revolution and its impact on regulation

and regulatory structure', in R. Littan and A. Santomero (eds), *Brookings-Wharton Papers on Financial Services*, Washington: Brookings Institution Press.
Williamson, J. and Mahar, M. (1998), 'A survey of financial liberalisation', *Princeton Essays in International Finance*, no. 211.

7. Policy issues in market-based and non-market-based measures to control the volatility of portfolio investment

Edmund Valpy Knox FitzGerald

1. INTRODUCTION

1.1 The Increasing Importance of Portfolio Investment

The increasing globalization of capital markets is widely regarded as a unique opportunity for poor economies to accelerate their rate of growth by gaining access to financial resources. Higher rates of private fixed capital formation are expected to result from financial liberalization, reducing poverty by generating new jobs at good wages and providing fiscal resources for human development (World Bank, 1997).

There are three main categories of private foreign investment flows: foreign direct investment (FDI) which involves investment *within* a firm where the foreign investor has a permanent interest in the subsidiary; foreign portfolio investment (FPI); and foreign bank lending (FBL) to banks, firms and governments in the recipient country.

Foreign portfolio investment is effected by purchases of bonds and equities issued by companies and governments, on both international and domestic capital markets. Large domestic corporations in developing countries are increasingly issuing international depository receipts or gaining listings on major stock markets, while foreign investors increasingly purchase bonds (particularly government paper) issued on domestic markets. As Table 7.1 indicates, FPI has accounted for about one-half of net private capital flows to 'emerging markets' (that is, developing and transition countries) during the 1990s.

The rapid growth of portfolio investment, in terms of capital flows across frontiers, is primarily due to the securitization of capital flows and the institutionalization of savings in industrial countries (UNCTAD, 1998c). Nonetheless, new equity issues (as opposed to secondary trading) are not very significant, as Table 7.2 indicates. Between 1996 and 1998, equity issues accounted for

Table 7.1 *Emerging market economies: net capital flows (US$ bn)*

	1991	1992	1993	1994	1995	1996	1997	1998
Net private capital flows	123.8	119.3	181.9	152.6	193.3	212.1	149.1	64.3
Net direct investment	31.3	35.5	56.8	82.7	97.0	115.9	142.7	131.0
Net portfolio investment	36.9	51.1	113.6	105.6	41.2	80.8	66.8	36.7
Net bank lending*	55.6	32.7	11.5	–35.8	55.0	15.4	–60.4	–103.4
Net official flows	36.5	22.3	20.1	1.8	26.1	–0.8	24.4	41.7
Change in reserves	–61.5	–51.9	–75.9	–66.7	–120.2	–109.1	–61.2	–34.7
Current account balance	–85.1	–75.6	–116.0	–72.0	–91.0	–91.8	–87.1	–59.2

Note: * 'other net investment' in the source table.

Source: IMF (1999).

Table 7.2   Gross private financing to emerging market economies

	1996	1997	1998
Total gross private financing	218.4	286.1	148.8
Bond issues	101.9	128.1	77.7
Other fixed income	9.4	10.0	0.5
Loan commitments	90.7	123.2	60.7
Equity issues	16.4	24.8	9.9

Source: IMF (1999).

only 8 per cent of gross private financing to emerging market economies. Rather it is bond issues – by corporations and governments – which account for most of the new market. In consequence, the effect of portfolio flows is felt mainly through their impact on the liquidity of local capital markets rather than directly on the management of local corporations (UNCTAD, 1998d).

1.2   Concerns about the Volatility of Portfolio Investment

In terms of the relative stability of the three categories of private flows, it is evident from Table 7.1 that FDI is the more stable flow in the aggregate during the 1990s. FBL is the most volatile of the three, becoming sharply negative when short-term bank credits are not renewed, and has been the main source of instability in recent emerging market crises. Aggregate FPI volatility lies between these two. Detailed statistical tests reveal that these patterns are repeated at the individual country level (UNCTAD, 1998d).

Opinions differ widely as to the origins of the evident volatility of exchange rates and capital flows, and the proper means of stabilizing them. Nonetheless, concern is growing that the impact of the volatility in short-term capital flows on developing countries is deleterious because of its effect on real exchange rates, domestic interest rates, asset values and domestic credit levels. National authorities are frequently forced to undertake sudden shifts in fiscal and monetary policy in order to offset such shocks, while international institutions become even further involved in policy conditionality and last-resort lending.[1]

This concern about the impact of short-term capital movements clearly goes beyond the traditional fear of systemic risk in the financial system arising from the differing maturity of assets and liabilities and the consequences of uncertain expectations being transmitted from one institution or market to others ('contagion'). The 'real economy', that is production, investment, wages, social services and so on, can be negatively affected by capital surges.

Failure to meet the standards required by foreign investors can be penalized by lower investment and growth as capital resources move elsewhere, leading to the danger of marginalization of those groups or nations not able to compete efficiently owing to lack of resources, skills or institutions (UNRISD, 1996). Moreover there are good reasons to believe that financial markets are inherently unstable, and have historically required strong institutions to control them (Kindelberger, 1996). Thus a considerable degree of intervention is probably required in order to ensure an orderly market in portfolio flows and to ensure that these flows support sustainable development. In consequence, it is not surprising that there is increasing interest in the regulation of portfolio flows in developing countries: controls that have only been lifted in recent decades by developed countries themselves (UNCTAD, 1998a).

2.　CAUSES AND CONSEQUENCES OF THE VOLATILITY OF FOREIGN PORTFOLIO INVESTMENT FLOWS

2.1　Systemic Characteristics of Flows towards Emerging Markets

The theoretical case for liberalizing international capital flows is based on four principles. First, free capital movements can facilitate a more efficient allocation of savings, channelling resources to countries where they can be used most productively, and thereby increasing growth and welfare. Second, access to foreign capital markets may enable investors to achieve a higher degree of portfolio diversification, allowing them to obtain higher returns at lower risk. Third, full convertibility for capital account transactions may complement the multilateral trading system, broadening the channels through which countries can obtain trade and investment finance. Fourth, liberalization may improve macroeconomic performance by subjecting governments to greater market discipline and penalizing unsound monetary and fiscal policies.

However global capital markets are characterized by asymmetric and incomplete information. The increasing international exposure of both equity funds in industrial countries and financial systems in emerging market economies has not been accompanied by a corresponding depth of information about the true value of the assets and liabilities. The speed and scale of shock transmission between markets has increased enormously thanks to technological advances in trading and settlement, which forces traders to act without knowledge of wider price movements, exacerbating fluctuations. There are also substantial agency problems for bank lenders and portfolio investors. Unlike multinational corporations involved in direct foreign investment, they can exercise little direct control over the asset acquired and thus cannot protect its market value. Banks can count on the international financial institutions to protect their interests to some extent, but as funds cannot count upon protection of asset value,[2] the logical response is to avoid assets which cannot be rapidly sold if things go wrong.

These information and agency problems lead logically to the two main characteristics of short-term investment in emerging markets.[3] First, international portfolio investors and bank lenders seek liquidity and use 'quick exit' as a means of containing downside risk. In consequence, indicators such as the 'quick ratio' of a country's short-term foreign liabilities to central bank reserves become critical to market stability, and can easily trigger self-fulfilling runs on a currency. Second, fund managers control risk, not by seeking more information or control, but by portfolio diversification based on an assumed lack of covariance between emerging market indices. The competition between funds for clients drives them towards seeking high-yield, high-risk markets, but by the same token leads them to make frequent marginal adjustments to their portfolios.[4]

High-risk emerging market assets with high returns have a positive attraction for global portfolio investors because the riskiness of their overall portfolio is considerably reduced by the low covariance between regional markets; but this does not prevent fund managers from switching frequently between markets in attempt to maximize short-term profitability. Although capital movements towards 'emerging markets' should depend upon 'fundamental valuation efficiency' on the part of international portfolio managers in assessing future income streams, because this is very difficult in practice and relies to a great extent on observing the behaviour of other investors, in practice misallocation is widespread and sudden corrections are frequent (Tobin, 1984).

The volatility of portfolio flows thus cannot be attributed to investor irrationality or even to 'speculation' except in the technical sense of international or intertemporal arbitrage (Hirschliefer and Riley, 1992). Rather it is the scale of these flows in relation to the size of the domestic capital market – in terms of both the proportion of the domestic capital stock that is effectively 'on the market' and the size of the local market in relation to the international market in which the non-resident investors operate – and the high covariance between asset prices within a given developing economy, or even region, which renders them problematic (UNCTAD, 1998d).

Shifts in international portfolio composition usually correspond to changes in perceptions of country solvency by international investors rather than to variations in underlying asset value. Because of the imbalance between borrowers and lenders (emerging market assets form a relatively small part of savers' portfolios in developed countries, but a large part of firms' and banks' liabilities in developing countries) marginal shifts in lenders' positions tend to destabilize borrowers' liquidity.[5] These surges are worsened by herding behaviour due to mean variance portfolio optimization as the market moves in a process of 'contagion' (IMF, 1999). As opportunities for diversification increase, the impact of news on the allocation of funds in a single country, relative to initial allocations, grows without bounds, resulting in massive outflows further threatening financial stability.[6] Therefore prudential regulation may be needed, of global lenders as much as of global borrowers.

2.2   Capital Market Stability in Open Developing Economies

Financial systems exist in order to facilitate the allocation of resources across space and time, in an environment of uncertainty and transaction costs (Levine, 1997). In general it is expected that the integration of stock markets internationally would reduce their volatility because of the portfolio diversification and increased liquidity and transparency of information this provides (Atje and Javanovic, 1993; Korajczyk, 1996). It is frequently argued (for example Levine, 1991) that the ability to trade corporate securities should help to fund long-term projects, reducing agents' productivity risks and increasing their liquidity; and a similar argument is extended to developing countries (Bencivanga et al., 1996). The selection and monitoring functions of financial markets are basically concerned with providing and processing information, but, as information is imperfect, financial markets are characterized by market failure and imperfections (Stiglitz, 1994); indeed stock markets can have a negative effect on growth if these markets are subject to excess volatility (De Long et al., 1989).

While resident financial investors evidently behave differently from non-residents, much of this difference arises from their respective portfolio compositions: resident investors have a much greater weighting of local assets ('home bias'). This home bias in turn results from asymmetric knowledge of local opportunities and control over local agents, plus the currency in which consumption is expressed (Brainard and Tobin, 1992). Access to information and control over investment outcomes also seem to differ between residents and non-residents, although here the distinction may well be between large and small investors rather than their location. Moreover, as the result of decades of overseas asset acquisition by domestic wealthholders in developing countries ('capital flight'), not only do their portfolios have a large foreign exchange-denominated component, but also much of what appears to be 'foreign' portfolio investment inflows is often in fact the reduction of external asset positions by domestic investors ('repatriation of flight capital').

The changes in the short-term asset holdings of non-residents are to a considerable extent *exogenous* to fluctuations in the real economy: output, investment, employment and wages. It is widely agreed that the larger part of the fluctuations in short-term capital flows to any one developing country is caused by changes in global capital markets (Calvo *et al.*, 1993;IMF, 1998). Moreover financial markets, particularly in developing countries, are supply-constrained (Stiglitz and Weiss, 1992) so that they are in stable disequilibrium with adjustments determined by creditors rather than debtors because demand is in effect infinitely elastic at the equilibrium interest rate. In consequence, changes in the asset demand pattern (reflecting international portfolio composition) of non-resident investors, rather than the supply of liabilities by residents, can be taken as the immediate cause of short-term capital flows.

Apart from the longer-term effects on saving and investment, portfolio capital inflows are generally regarded as being expansive in the sense of increasing domestic adsorption, unless they are fully sterilized by increasing reserves. However this expansive process is not the same as an autonomous rise in government expenditure (or even an export-led boom) because to create a flow the portfolio investment asset must have been acquired from (or sold to) a domestic agent and much depends upon that domestic agent's consequent response: to consume, invest or acquire external assets in the case of private agents, or to spend, invest or reduce debt in the case of government.

Short-term capital inflows often lead to an unsustainable appreciation of the exchange rate, which prevents export promotion and generates an import boom, while the expansion of domestic credit consequent upon asset sales to non-residents being deposited in the domestic banking system tends to result in unsafe loans at low rates of interest. The subsequent outflow usually forces cutbacks in domestic adsorption to restore external balance, which lead in turn to a fall in current output levels. Fragile financial institutions then often collapse under the pressure of bad debts and the fall of asset prices as interest rates rise and domestic activity declines (Rojas-Suarez and Weisbrod, 1994).

In sum, portfolio flows mainly affect domestic capital market liquidity and (through foreign demand for domestic currency in order to make asset purchases) the exchange rate. The direct impact on private fixed capital formation is not great, for two reasons: on the one hand, government bond sales and corporate commercial paper issues dominate the market, while on the other hand, most equity purchases are on the secondary market or initial offerings of privatized state enterprises.

2.3 Savings, Investment, Macroeconomic Volatility and Capital Surges

The impact of portfolio flows on economic development depends upon their net effect on savings and investment, and thus the key issue in evaluating the initial impact of these (and other) short term capital flows is the way in which the savings–investment balances of the public and private sectors react to an exogenous change in short term external liabilities.[7] A 'virtuous' debt cycle, requires, of course, that in the longer term the subsequent fixed capital formation is sustainable.[8]

It had been expected that financial liberalization would raise savings in developing countries (World Bank, 1997), but this has not been the case. There is in fact a strong substitution observed between external and domestic savings, with an elasticity of about 0.5 (Edwards, 1995; Masson *et al.*, 1995). Turner (1996) shows that, in the first half of the 1990s, private portfolio capital flows made the link between external savings and domestic investment more indirect, which has enhanced the likelihood of external savings being used to finance consumption rather than investment because consumers and financial markets react more rapidly than real investment to the relaxation of liquidity constraints. Short capital inflows appear to foster consumption through two channels. First, the positive wealth effect generated by the increase in asset prices and real exchange rate appreciation leads wealth holders to save less.[9] Second, domestic portfolio asset purchases by foreigners from domestic wealth holders increase the bank deposits of the previous owners and thus permit banks to expand consumer credit.

This outcome is reinforced by the orthodox policy response to short-term capital flows. In the IMF 'monetary programming model' (Khan and Huq, 1990), an autonomous inflow of capital will permit the government to relax monetary policy and increase growth; a subsequent outflow would lead to the opposite policy. In other words, policy becomes procyclical rather than stabilizing. Moreover bond yields (and thus interest rates) in small open economies exposed to the international capital market do not act so as to balance savings and investment. Broadly speaking, the domestic interest rate (i) is determined by the international interest rate ($i_\$$), the expected depreciation of the exchange rate ($E_e - E$) and the country risk proper (Y):

$$i = i_\$ + (E_e - E)/E + \rho.$$

Of these three terms, the first is clearly exogenous and fluctuates considerably in the short term; the second depends not only on the current macroeconomic policy of the government but also on expected policy in the future and fluctuations in *other* currencies; and, above all, the third term depends on foreign investors' perceptions of the country in the context of changing circumstances in the region and the world as a whole, and is the factor which determines the lack of substitutability between asset classes. The domestic interest rate is thus a consequence of much the same domestic and external factors that determine short-term capital flows, rather than acting as a domestic capital market-clearing mechanism.

There are four macroeconomic consequences of exogenous changes in short-term capital flows (FitzGerald, 1999c).[10] First the main direct transmission effects on the real economy are through variations in funds available to firms and in the demand for government bonds, while the main indirect effects are through variations in the real exchange rate and the level of economic activity. Second, the impact on the fiscal sector is mainly seen in sudden shifts in the perceived solvency of the public sector, and thus upon the level of debt believed by foreign investors to be sustainable; the effect of these fluctuations is felt in volatile levels of public investment, which reduce the efficiency of public provision of infrastructure and social services. Third, the impact on the firms sector is mainly through the supply of working capital, which generates asymmetric responses in terms of investment and output due to the impact on firms' balance sheets; the volatility of expected profits resulting from this has a strong depressive effect on private investment. Fourth, the impact on the household sector is the result of the employment and wage effects; these occur both directly through firms' response to short-term capital flows and as a result of the consequences of fiscal instability; and also indirectly through the effects of real exchange rate variations on real wages and aggregate employment levels.

The most damaging effect of volatile short-term capital flows is on private fixed investment, and thus on the growth of employment and productivity in the longer run. This is derived from the effect of this volatility on the expectations of firms about the profitability of investment through the impact of macroeconomic variables such as the real exchange rate and interest rates. Most investment expenditures are largely irreversible – sunk costs that cannot be recovered if market conditions turn out to be worse than expected. As firms can delay investments until more information arrives, there exists an opportunity cost of investing now rather than waiting.[11] In consequence, the value of a unit of investment must *exceed* the purchase and installation cost, by an amount equal to the value of keeping the investment option alive, which will increase exponentially with the level of uncertainty (Dixit and Pindyck, 1994). In consequence, if the goal of macroeconomic policy is to stimulate investment (and thus growth), macroeconomic stability and credibility may be much more important than particular levels of taxes or profit rates (Pindyck and Solimano, 1993). These findings apply a fortiori to the situation where short-term capital surges require abrupt compensatory movements in fiscal and monetary stances.

3. THE EXPERIENCE OF CAPITAL CONTROLS

3.1 The Motivation for Capital Controls

Recent financial market turmoil has prompted new interest in capital controls because emerging markets are adopting a more sceptical attitude towards short-term external finance in the wake of the crisis in East Asia. The IMF Articles of Agreement only require member countries to avoid imposing restrictions on current account transactions, such as those related to trade in goods and services and the remittance of profits and dividends. Specifically, Article VI.3 states:

> Members may exercise such controls as are necessary to regulate international capital movements, but no member may exercise these controls in a manner which will restrict payments for current transactions or which will unduly delay transfers of funds in settlement of commitments, except as provided in Article VII, Section 3(*b*) and in Article XIV, Section 2.

Several developed countries (including France, Spain and Italy) have in the comparatively recent past resorted to controls on the inflow or outflow of capital as a temporary expedient to stabilize domestic financial markets even though such controls have deliberately distortionary consequences and may increase the risk of a relaxation of macroeconomic discipline as well as discriminating against foreign investors. In developing countries, where domestic capital markets are imperfect and systems for financial supervision are not robust, there is a strong case for not liberalizing capital account transactions fully until these problems have been addressed (Eichengreen and Mussa, 1998). Nonetheless, the IMF Interim Committee agreed in 1997 that full convertibility for capital account transactions should be the ultimate objective for all Fund members.[12]

Johnston and Tamirisa (1998) examine the determinants of capital controls in 45 developing and transition countries. Their econometric evidence indicates that balance of payments and macroeconomic management, market and institutional evolution, and prudential factors are important in explaining recourse to capital controls. However macroeconomic variables appear primarily to motivate controls on capital inflows, while institutional and market structures appear to motivate financial regulations related to the operations of banks and institutional investors. Their findings indicate that capital controls in fact reflect the overall framework of economic regulation and the degree of financial market development, rather than just balance of payments management objectives.

3.2 The Design of Capital Controls

The focus of this chapter is on preventive controls, that is, on capital inflows, and specifically those with a temporary horizon. The controls may be in the form of a tax on capital inflows (Brazil, Chile, Colombia and Thailand) or quantitative restrictions on capital inflows (Czech Republic and Malaysia) including prudential measures directed at the domestic banking sector.

Leaving aside direct investment and real estate transactions on the one hand, and credit operations and provisions specific to commercial banks on the other,[13] the types of portfolio investment transactions possibly subject to controls are shares or other securities of a participating nature; bonds or other debt securities; money market instruments; collective investment securities; derivatives and other instruments. In all five categories there are possible inflows (purchase locally by non-residents or sale or issue abroad by residents) and outflows (sale or issue by non-residents, or purchase abroad by residents) to be considered. In addition there may be provisions specific to institutional investors, typically restricting their ability to invest abroad.[14]

Capital control measures on these transactions can be divided into three broad categories: price-based, quantity-based and regulatory. Price-based measures reduce the interest rate differential between domestic and foreign assets by lowering the rate of return on an asset for any level of risk. This would induce investors to reallocate their portfolios away from that asset on the familiar mean-variance criterion. On capital inflows this would include a tax rate on interest payments in the local currency, and entry tax (or stamp duty) on the investment in local currency or a tax on foreign debt issuance by domestic residents. All these taxes can be structured to depend on the maturity of the investment.[15] Keynes's original argument for a transactions tax was to lengthen investors' horizons for holding assets; and this proposal has been extended to emerging markets by Dornbusch (1996, 1997).[16]

Quantity-based capital control measures on portfolio capital inflows usually take the form of limits on the amount of foreign funds that can be invested in local currency.[17] In contrast to price-based (that is, tax) measures, the objective of quantitative capital controls is not to alter the return properties of local assets but rather to regulate the amount of foreign funds that can gain access to these assets. In other words, non-residents' portfolios are altered by asset rationing rather than by altering the mean-variance characteristics.

Quantitative restrictions have typically involved limitations on external asset and liability positions of domestic financial institutions (especially banks), on the domestic operations of foreign financial institutions; and on the external portfolios, real estate holdings or direct investment of non-bank residents. Measures implemented have included prudential limits or prohibitions on non trade-related swap activities, off-shore borrowing, banks' net foreign exchange positions (Czech Republic, Indonesia, Malaysia, Philippines, Thailand), caps on banks' foreign currency liabilities (Mexico) and even broad measures to prohibit residents from selling short-term money market instruments to foreigners (Malaysia). Often the type of instrument to be used is controlled rather than the volume, as when restricting the ability of domestic borrowers to issue bonds on international markets.

The advantage of price-based controls is that they can be built into the investors' risk–return calculations and are credible insofar as they are backed by a sound legislative and legal framework. Their disadvantage is that they represent a relatively weak brake on large capital surges in response to sudden changes in expected returns, where the tax payable on short stays may be very small compared to the gains (or losses) to non-resident investors from changing their portfolio composition rapidly.

The difficulty with quantitative restrictions is that they are subject to administrative discretion and thus investors cannot build their costs into their portfolio calculation. Their scope and application will be uncertain, introducing an unknown element of investor risk and amplifying the opportunities for corruption. In addition, the ability of even honest administrators to keep up with new forms of derivatives is limited.

Regulatory capital control measures attempt to combine the effects of price-based and quantity-based measures.[18] They involve the obligatory deposit of a proportion of portfolio purchases in local cash or government paper, and thus reduce the liquidity of the investor during the time period of the measure and cost her the yield difference. In consequence, they are more 'market-friendly' than quantitative restrictions. Although they do not generate explicit tax revenues, these measures can discriminate effectively between potential foreign investors according to their attitude to risk and thus encourage longer-term equity or bond holdings.

3.3 Circumvention of Capital Controls

In principle, the adoption of any measures aimed at preventing capital flows from enforcing the interest parity condition immediately introduces an incentive for circumvention (Dooley *et al.*, 1996). Whether this occurs depends upon the fixed, variable and penalty components of circumvention. The fixed cost refers to finding loopholes in the legislation and constructing appropriate financial instruments to take advantage of them, which becomes easier with financial market sophistication (if only off-shore) and in any case is a one-off cost which can become in effect a public good. The variable cost refers to the administrative expenses and yield losses involved in continued circumvention and varies with the volume of transactions; it is particularly high in the case of prudential measures. The penalty component reflects not only the respective fine but also the risk of punishment and the reputational consequences of conviction.

Insofar as all these costs can be reduced to an equivalent tax, and as tax can be administered transparently with considerable welfare benefits in terms of public revenues, this would seem to be an argument for price-based controls.[19] In practice, private operators will inevitably find ways to evade controls if there is sufficient incentive, if only by traditional methods such as the over- (or under-) invoicing of current account transactions, which are usually left uncontrolled owing to international trade commitments. In the 1990s, the existence of reasonably liquid secondary markets (increasingly off-shore) has made possible the construction of derivatives to avoid controls on maturities[20] and even 'synthetic sales' of long-term investments.[21]

In particular, the use of non-deliverable forward (NDF) and non-deliverable swap (NDS) contracts can be used to overcome quantitative restrictions,[22] including currency non-convertibility. NDF markets are found in Brazil, China, India, Korea, the Philippines, Poland, Russia, Taiwan and Vietnam, as well as in the Middle East. NDF and NDS contracts are off-shore transactions which require no delivery of the notional amounts of each currency at maturity: settlement takes place for the difference between the forward rate and the spot rate at maturity, funding constraints being avoided by payment of the difference in a major foreign currency.[23] They are commonly used to circumvent restrictions on forward markets but also to avoid entry taxes.

In consequence, controls may need to be wide-ranging and costly to evade in order to ensure their effectiveness. Policies to raise the cost of circumvention include measures such as broadening the coverage of controls (for example, to cover 'speculative FDI' in the case of Chile), stricter monitoring and enforcement and increased penalties for circumvention.

3.4 Evaluating Capital Control Regimes

The criteria for evaluating the effectiveness of a capital control regime are unclear. One approach is to measure the divergence of key variables (such as interest rates) between countries with and without controls. Another is to assess the government's ability to pursue an independent macroeconomic policy indefinitely. In either case it is unclear what size of yield differential is required to enhance the effectiveness of a policy regime. This would require a structural model encompassing the government's objectives and the economic constraints upon it. In consequence, observers can examine the same or similar data sets and reach very different qualitative conclusions regarding the effectiveness of capital controls. Those who see controls as a short-term device which grants the government time to react and adjust other policy instruments generally argue that controls can be effective. Those who analyse currency regime collapse suggest that such incidents are often preceded by controls, which cannot prevent and may even provoke such incidents.

Interpreting the effectiveness of capital controls on recorded flows is also a problem. Controlling for factors other than the controls is very difficult: total net capital flows are related to economic fundamentals such as yield differentials and changes in wealth, on the one hand, and expectations about the future macroeconomic position, on the other. The allocation between public and private securities depends on the current and expected fiscal stance and thus on government behaviour. Moreover, to the extent that controls themselves respond to fluctuations in capital flows, there is a strong element of endogeneity; and it would not be unexpected for new controls on inflows to be associated with increased inward flows, as in the case of Chile. Finally, the standard balance of payments classifications are not very informative as to the volatility, effective maturity and liquidity of the recorded flows.

Nonetheless, the extensive literature for the industrial and developing countries (Dooley, 1996; Gros, 1987; Obstfeld, 1995; Eichengreen and Mussa, 1998) suggests that the government can drive a significant wedge between domestic and international yields on similar short-term financial instruments for extended time periods. In the six cases (Brazil, Chile, Colombia, Czech Republic, Malaysia and Mexico) during the 1990s examined in Glick (1997) the composition of flows has been affected by the lengthening of maturities, particularly in the cases of Chile, Colombia and Malaysia, where the controls have been accompanied by an active monetary policy. In the case of Chile, Malaysia and to a lesser extent the Czech Republic, various combinations of taxes and quantitative restrictions were successful in reducing the volume of inflows of short maturities. In Brazil, controls seem to have been least effective, probably because they were accompanied by high interest rates originating in a combination of tight monetary policy and large fiscal deficits.

In addition, in four out of six cases, reserve accumulation slowed down after the imposition of capital controls, probably owing to a combination of reduced precautionary requirements and lesser sterilization by the authorities. Also, despite an easing of monetary policy in Chile and Malaysia and neutral monetary policies in Colombia and the Czech Republic, there was a general deceleration in monetary growth following the introduction of capital controls. This appears to reflect the slowdown in non-resident banking sector deposits (Malaysia), less off-shore borrowing by domestic banks (Chile and Colombia) as well as the slowing down of foreign exchange accumulation by central banks.

Quirk and Evans (1995) evaluated controls in Chile, Colombia and Malaysia by examining the impact on three variables: the magnitude of short capital flows and the composition of total flows, the disparity between onshore and off-shore deposit rates and the differentials between domestic and foreign interest rates. Controls do seem to have increased the gap between domestic and international interest rates, and to have lengthened the term structure of foreign investment. However circumvention appears quite quickly, and the interest rate 'wedge' is not large enough to prevent crises.

The specific case of Chile has attracted much attention, in particular the one-year 'unremunerated reserve requirement' (URR) on foreign inflows, introduced in 1991 at 20 per cent to dissuade portfolio inflows, and reduced to zero in 1998 in order to encourage them (Laurens and Cardoso, 1998). The review of a considerable number of detailed studies of the Chilean experience by De Simone and Sorsa (1998) reveals that there is strong evidence that controls were successful in driving the desired wedge between domestic and national interest rates, while the evidence for the effectiveness of controls in altering the composition of inflows towards the medium and longer-term maturities is positive but less strong. However they conclude that there is only mixed evidence that the URRs reduced total capital inflows and little evidence to support the conclusion that they had a significant effect on the real exchange rate.

In sum, the conclusion by Quirk and Evans (1995, p. 4) that 'recent experience suggests that although controls or taxes on inflows should not be viewed as a substitute for fundamental policy measures ... they might serve as temporary supplementary tools that could provide policy makers with time to react' seems to reflect the overall tone of the available literature. However the considerable implications of having more 'time to react' tend to be overlooked by orthodox economists. First, the emphasis on the 'interest rate wedge' supposes that changes in the relative price of capital are the main effect (intended and achieved) of controls, while it is clear in practice that the *liquidity* effect is also considerable, and is generally more significant in imperfect capital markets. Second, the fact that the effectiveness of controls depends upon the way they reinforce fiscal and monetary policies designed to stabilize the balance of payments means that the design and implementation of *active* macroeconomic management is crucial to the reduction of the volatility of portfolio flows. Capital controls might thus be regarded as having an enabling function in permitting effective market intervention rather than as being expected to reduce volatility on their own.

4. FISCAL AND MONETARY POLICY TO STABILIZE CAPITAL FLOWS

4.1 Stabilizing Capital Flows

As we have seen, the source of fluctuations in short capital flows varies widely: alterations in local conditions (both structural, such as banking liberalization and privatization, and policy shifts, such as in interest rates), changes in international capital markets (such as variations in prudential regulation or in domestic asset yields), or perhaps – and most importantly, as we have seen – shifts in the perceived risk associated with a particular market. Each source implies a distinct policy response: for instance, increased demand for money domestically can be countered by monetary accommodation, while a change in international perceptions of risk may be best handled by sterilization of capital flows, particularly if the policy objective is to maintain a stable real exchange rate in order to promote exports.

The overriding goal should be to maintain high rates of private investment in traded sectors through macroeconomic stability and low real interest rates. The hysteresis in exports and investment that fluctuations in exchange rates and interest rates generate is a strong argument for dampening exchange rate movements in the absence of full hedging facilities (Krugman, 1987).

The impact of the portfolio flows on liquidity depends upon the behaviour of domestic financial institutions, and thus upon the structure of financial regulation. There are two separate motives for financial regulation. The first is economic regulation (for example, over interest rates or credit allocation) which has been dismantled all over the world in order to improve market efficiency. However this may make financial systems more vulnerable to crises. The second category of regulation is prudential regulation to protect the stability of the financial system itself or to protect small investors as 'consumers'. In contrast to economic regulation, prudential regulation has not been dismantled and in many cases has been strengthened in response to financial crises.

The financial deregulation which has characterized emerging markets during the 1990s can be regarded as a permanent shock to the financial sector which alters the environment in which the intermediation is carried out (Bachetta, 1992). Specifically the lifting of regulations on asset portfolios and reserve ratios combined with privatization were designed to encourage better risk management and narrower margins, but may lead to excessive risk acquisition in the search for market share. Monetary policy has become more difficult to implement as the behaviour of monetary variables becomes more volatile with the reduction in market segmentation and consequently increased elasticities of substitution between assets (Melitz and Bordes, 1991).

The high real interest rates and lower reserve requirements associated with financial liberalization can thus actually increase banking fragility.

4.2 Open Market Operations

Sterilization of inflows leads to higher domestic interest rates, especially if the domestic currency assets investors want to hold are imperfect substitutes for short-term central bank paper or treasury bills supplied by the monetary authorities. This in turn can encourage even greater inflows and defeat the purpose of sterilization. If the domestic and foreign interest-bearing assets are not good substitutes, large changes in supply are required to affect the price. Even if they are poor substitutes, considerable relative price adjustment among domestic assets will ensue as the portfolio equilibrium is restored, with negative effects for productive investment.

The open market operations (OMOs) required for sterilization entail the sale of government or central bank securities by the central bank in order to remove the liquidity generated by central bank purchases of foreign currency. The liabilities of the central bank thus remain unchanged but the composition of assets changes with the reduction of claims on the government and increase in international reserves. There is a corresponding change in the composition of non-bank liabilities.

OMOs have been adopted by most countries, particularly in the early 1990s by Chile, Colombia, Indonesia and Malaysia. In come cases (Chile, Colombia and Indonesia, as well as Korea and the Philippines) the central bank issued new debt on its own behalf for this purpose; in others (such as Malaysia and also Sri Lanka) public debt was sold as the central bank depleted its own holdings. This form of sterilization has the advantage of not placing extra burdens on a weak domestic banking system, but it does lead to an increased fiscal burden as a high-yielding liability (domestic currency debt) is issued in exchange for lower-yielding assets (international reserves) and thus either a fiscal deficit is generated or expenditure must be reduced. Colombia increased the ratio of open market paper to the monetary base from less than 30 per cent in late 1990 to over 80 per cent by late 1991 in this way.

The impact of large changes in domestic bond yields interest rates can be serious, and may not be eased very much by the reduced country-risk premium; indeed the reduced rate of devaluation which often accompanies sterilization often raises ex post dollar yields even further. This would imply that OMOs slow down the convergence of domestic to foreign interest rates and do not lead, therefore, to any pronounced or sustained shifts in the composition of capital inflows as a result of such intervention. Despite heavy intervention, either the rate of devaluation slowed down or there was even revaluation. Argentina is an interesting contrast as it did not sterilize between

1989 and 1992; in the absence of OMOs, interest rates converged to world levels and short-term capital inflows levelled off by 1993, two years after the introduction of the currency board in 1991.

OMOs need not, however, lead to full sterilization, and thus exchange rate stability, because the active management of exchange rates within bands serves to discourage speculative flows, owing to the cost of risk of asset values to foreign investors. In a sense, the uncertainty has a similar effect to a transactions tax for risk-averse investors. It also reduces fluctuations in reserves and thus allows the monetary authorities some margin of independence in monetary policy.

4.3   Management of Reserve Requirements and Public Sector Deposits

The reserve requirements of banks may be increased in order to reduce the money multiplier: this offsets the increase in the monetary base due to central bank intervention in the foreign exchange market. In effect, the private sector rather than the central bank has to issue the domestic interest-bearing liabilities (or reduce other asset holdings) in order to finance the new reserves. When commercial banks have higher reserve requirements they are forced to absorb the monetary base (that is, the non-interest-yielding debt of the central bank) rather than interest-bearing loans to the private sector, who in turn issue interest-bearing securities or reduce their expenditure. Whether this decreased expenditure is on investment or consumption is an important consideration for longer-term growth.[24]

To prevent asset-switching (in order to avoid the cost of holding reserves) it may be necessary to increase the reserve requirement on *all* domestic currency deposits. Costa Rica, Malaysia, Sri Lanka and Peru have all used this option with some effect. This involves a lower fiscal cost than open-market operations. Reserve requirements are similar in effect to a tax on bank assets (the increase of reserve requirements in Malaysia from 3.5 to 11.5 per cent between 1989 and 1994 was equivalent to an additional 1 per cent tax on bank assets), a cost which is usually passed on to clients. Empirical evidence indicates that this leads to higher lending rates (where the banks are at a greater advantage than with depositors) which may stimulate further inflows and corporate borrowing abroad. In imperfect capital markets, reserve requirements have a much stronger effect on domestic credit markets by reducing liquidity.

Capital flows may be sterilized by shifting the deposits of the public sector (or quasi-public sector pension funds) from the banking system into the central bank: Malaysia, Taiwan and Thailand have sterilized capital inflows by this method. If government deposits are counted as part of the money stock then such a transfer is equivalent to an increase in reserve requirements;

but if they are not so counted, then the effect is the same as that of an OMO. If domestic assets are perfect substitutes, there is no interest rate effect; if they are not, the switch out of domestic assets will depress their prices and raise domestic interest rates.

This procedure has many advantages: it does not act as a tax on banks and it need not raise domestic interest rates overall; and there is no quasi-fiscal cost as is associated with standard sterilization. If there is an income lost to the public funds, the fiscal impact is less than that of sterilization. However it is difficult for banks to manage large deposit swings, and the cost of any market losses may be born by contributors, as it has been in the case of Employee Provident Funds in Malaysia. Moreover the available funds are limited by the scale of liquid assets already held by the public sector: government deposits held at the Bank of Thailand increased from 25 per cent of total government deposits at end-1987 to 82 per cent by mid-1992.

This procedure was used with considerable effect in 1998 by the Hong Kong government, which purchased 10 per cent of the Hang Seng index – about a quarter of the market's free float in view of the fact that many companies are still family controlled. In this way speculative attacks on the Hong Kong stock market (and, by extension, the exchange rate) were effectively warded off. As the market recovered by some 60 per cent between August 1998 and April 1999, the administration made a paper profit of some US$8 billion on US$10 billion invested: three times the budget deficit.

The resort to public sector deposit management requires, of course, fiscal solvency without debt overhang. It should also be preceded by an identification of the causes of the original fluctuation in short-term capital flows, particularly a judgment as to whether this represents a temporary or a permanent shock (Reisen, 1996). Flows which will soon be reversed would presumably be handled through compensatory reserve management, while permanent flows require some form of macroeconomic adjustment, in the absence of any clear basis for such a judgment, the proverbial admonition to 'treat all positive shocks as temporary and all negative shocks as permanent' may be a good guide.

4.4 Policy Design and Implementation

Following the Asian crisis, policy makers have shown increasing interest in the macroeconomic model pioneered by Chile, which couples trade openness and FDI encouragement with restrictions on short-term capital inflows.[25] The model has a number of components, each of which is used by other emerging markets to some extent. The first is *sterilized intervention*: the central bank has intervened in the foreign exchange market to prevent the real exchange rate from appreciating excessively, purchasing dollars in exchange for local currency to maintain the exchange rate within a 12.5 per cent band around a dollar–DM–yen reference rate. The impact on the money supply has been sterilized by massive placements of central bank promissory notes, albeit at the cost of additional fiscal burdens and high domestic interest rates. The second component is *investment regulations*: capital investment is subject to a number of laws and restrictions specifying minimum entry amounts and the time which must elapse before capital can be repatriated. Decree Law 600 requires FDI to enter Chile through a foreign investment contract with a specified minimum duration, which varies according to the industrial sector concerned. Capital cannot be repatriated until one year after entry, although there are no restrictions on the repatriation of profits. Law 18,657 creates Foreign Capital Investment Funds. Foreign portfolio investment (FPI) in public securities and equities is allowed, subject to a minimum amount of one million dollars, which must be invested within one year. Capital invested in these funds cannot be repatriated for a minimum of five years, but profit repatriation is not restricted. Finally, there are *reserve requirements*: the central bank has imposed reserve requirements on capital inflows, which attempt to discriminate between long-term capital investments and short-term 'non-productive' inflows. Short-term inflows are subject to a one-year reserve requirement of 30 per cent at zero interest. The aim is to reduce speculative capital inflows and increase the proportion of direct investment and long-term credit in the capital account. These 'market-friendly' controls have proved highly effective in practice.

Chile has also used several other policy instruments to restrict the speculative inflow of capital, including minimum conditions for external bond and equity issues, and reductions in the availability and increases in the cost of swap facilities at the central bank. The authorities have also taken measures to encourage capital outflows, including the liberalization of pension fund regulations, in order to avoid excessive money supply growth. These measures necessarily involve a degree of discrimination against foreign capital, particularly the portfolio entry regulations. Although in principle these could apply equally to asset repatriation by residents, effective discrimination against foreign nationals is held to be justified because they are believed to be less 'committed' to the host economy.[26]

Such 'fine-tuning' is not easy, particularly since much of its effect depends upon the reputation of the economic authorities. Indeed Obstfeld (1995) suggests that, because of the international integration of capital markets, the only way to reduce the shocks arising from external capital flows is either a completely clean float or an irrevocable currency union. However a pure float is probably unworkable in most developing countries owing to the fact that monetary aggregates do not provide a reliable policy anchor, particularly in a period of financial liberalization. In any case, the resulting fluctuations in real exchange rates would have the negative real-economy effects we have discussed above. Monetary union is not a feasible option for most developing countries and, for those (such as Mexico) for which it is a real prospect, the fiscal implications for the central economy of the region (for example, the USA) are probably unacceptable. In practice, therefore, the options appear to be the design of fiscal policy to reduce the pressure on domestic debt markets; sterilized intervention as the basis of monetary policy, combined with a strong reserve level and low real interest rates; high but flexible marginal reserve requirements on banks in order to mitigate the effects of capital flows on credit provision; and active management of the nominal exchange rate in order to maintain a stable, competitive real exchange rate.

4.5 Complementary Measures

Factors which are often cited as causes of financial crises in emerging markets (such as large current account deficits, overvalued real exchange rates and overinvestment in non-traded sectors) are in practice often the outcome of massive capital inflows in the first place (Reisen, 1996). All three of the balance of payments management policies discussed above (open-market operations, reserve requirements and public asset management) are made more effective by the existence of direct capital controls. This is for two reasons. First, the implicit asset differentiation between domestic and foreign assets and liabilities that controls create makes such interventions more effective precisely because it makes markets less efficient. In other words, stability can be attained at the cost of a loss of efficiency. As both enter into the objective function of investors in the real economy, there is a balance to be struck between the two. Second, controls over capital flows (if only in the form of registration) provide the means for the authorities to overcome the information and agency problems posed by monetary intervention. In other words, real-time knowledge of the scale and nature of flows, and who is generating them, allows the central bank to take prompt action and to exert 'moral suasion' on market agents. This, of course, is why industrial countries operated capital controls until a late stage in the development of their financial markets.

In Asia, these flows have mainly gone into short-term banking instruments, and in Latin America into securities, particularly government paper. Recent Latin American experience shows that two mutually reinforcing policies can help influence capital flows towards longer-term equity. First, it is necessary to keep nominal exchange risk substantial for short-term investors chasing high local returns by skilful parity management within credible bands. Second, excessive inflows should be discouraged by an implicit tax that varies with maturity. There is strong empirical evidence that this kind of policy management can have a strong impact on the composition and also overall size of flows (Ffrench-Davis and Reisen, 1998).

In addition, it is probably necessary to undertake specific national policy measures in order to support investment and employment during such episodes (FitzGerald, 1999c). Public investment programmes should be sustained by avoiding the use of short-term debt as a source of funds; undertaking a tax reform sufficiently extensive to generate a structural fiscal balance; and avoiding the refinancing of long-term external debt with short-term internal debt. High real rates of interest should be avoided by expansive monetary policy: they do little to stimulate aggregate savings, but clearly depress private investment and, in this context, attract volatile capital flows while increasing budgetary costs. It is helpful to ensure that long-term credit is available to firms in order to sustain private investment through the cycles caused by short-term capital flows, possibly by the provision of rediscount facilities at the central bank and tax incentives to long-term profit retention. Finally, small firms and home building should be protected from the effect of credit restrictions by dedicated loan schemes.

5. INTERNATIONAL REGULATORY ISSUES

5.1 The Effectiveness of International Financial Institutions

The existing international institutional 'architecture' to cope with the problems in emerging markets is based on the Bretton Woods bodies, and the IMF in particular. As an intergovernmental institution, the Fund is essentially a lender of last resort to developing country governments, against which facility it imposes policy conditionality in return for the restoration of liquidity:[27] specific monetary and fiscal policies in order to stabilize the economy, and structural reforms in order to restore long-term solvency. However recent emerging market crises are essentially related to private sector asset deflation and liquidity shortages, the root causes of which were not prevented (and possibly have been exacerbated) by IMF policies of fiscal retrenchment and high interest rates. In particular, as the emerging market crises unfolded, a number of apparently well-capitalized local banks were found to be insolvent, their fragility having been disguised by a failure to recognize the poor quality of their loan portfolios (BIS, 1998).

In response, the IMF has expanded its regular Article IV consultations with member countries to examine the quality of domestic banking supervision (IMF, 1998). Basle standards are being employed by an increasing number of industrial and industrializing countries, a trend likely to be reinforced by the publication in 1998 of the Basle Committee on Banking Supervision's *Core*

Principles for Effective Banking Supervision (reproduced in IMF, 1998). Although the Bank of International Settlements has no regulatory function as such, the Basle Committee members (central banks[28] and other supervisory agencies) do in practice establish best practice for bank regulators in all jurisdictions.

In addition, the Basle Committee has issued a report on *The Supervision of Cross-border Banking* (1996) agreed with the Offshore Group of banking supervisors, representing 19 off-shore financial centres.[29] The report provided a checklist of principles for effective consolidated supervision, intended to ensure that no internationally active banking group escapes the oversight of a regulator capable of effectively supervising its global operations. The report also contained principles which could be used to assess the quality of supervision in financial centres.[30] More importantly, the report represented a formal recognition by the Basle Committee that agreement among the leading industrialized countries alone was no longer sufficient to preserve the integrity of the international financial system in an increasingly integrated global economy.[31]

5.2 Beyond the Basle Approach

These measures in the 'Basle Approach' are restricted to bank supervision, as bank failures represent the greater threat to financial market stability. However Basle rules extend to the portfolio operations of banks and thus implicitly strengthen the supervision of securities markets. Most private short-term capital flows take the form of negotiable securities rather than bank credit, and the larger part of these securities is marketed by banks or by securities houses linked with these banks. The final purchaser may not be fully aware of the risk involved, relying on the reputation of the bank to ensure asset value.

Much of the responsibility for coping with reversible portfolio flows thus still falls on emerging market governments themselves, despite the fact that the large scale of the flows and their evident correlation means that some form of international action is also necessary. High-profile failures of a number of financial institutions among the leading industrialized countries have also highlighted the need for effective international supervisory standards. In addition, there is a growing recognition of the risk posed to the international financial system by the poor securities supervision in emerging markets.

The BIS itself bid successfully in 1996 to host the International Association of Insurance Supervisors (IAIS) and will soon bid to provide a secretariat for the International Organization of Securities Commissions (IOSCO). This could give the BIS the potential to supervise non-bank financial intermediaries as well as banks, although whether governments of the leading global capital markets will be willing to cede such authority is not yet clear.

The experience of financial turbulence in Latin America and Asia has led to a perceived need for greater monetary coordination at the regional level. In particular, as Latin American financial markets become more integrated, there is a growing interest in the harmonization of financial regulatory rules building on the European experience (FitzGerald and Grabbe, 1997). Within the North American Free Trade Agreement (NAFTA), the three central banks have become engaged in closer operational coordination in the wake of the 1995 peso crisis, but there is a marked reluctance to establish formal institutional mechanisms (FitzGerald, 1999b).

In addition, an UNCTAD Expert Meeting (UNCTAD, 1998b) suggested three further measures to stabilize international securities markets: first, the encouragement of closed-end funds as opposed to mutual funds, since investments in the former are relatively more stable because they are not bound by redemption obligations;[32] second, the issuance of American and global depository receipts and other similar instruments at the regional level (issued in the most stable and developed capital market within the region)[33] in order to deepen regional markets; third, special incentives for minimum holding periods (six months to one year) on a regional basis so as to ensure their effectiveness, and also to systematize both the differential taxation of portfolio assets and reserve requirements on non-resident holdings.[34]

Finally, in the wake of the Long Term Capital Management (LTCM) collapse, it has been suggested that bank lending to hedge funds investing in developed countries should be restricted in order to limit their ability to leverage their emerging market assets to such a large extent (Edwards, 1998).

5.3 International Investment Rules

Bilateral investment treaties, double taxation treaties, regional trade agreements and certain World Trade Organization (WTO) provisions play key roles in building investor confidence by locking in policy commitments over time (WTO, 1997a). Such new agreements, many of which refer to portfolio assets, are usually based on general standards of treatment, coupled with norms on specific matters such as expropriation, compensation, the transfer of funds and dispute settlement (UNCTAD, 1997). Such agreements are mainly designed to promote FDI, of course; however, by encouraging longer-term commitments by foreign investors, they also support more stable portfolio holdings.

Moreover clear international rules on the treatment of portfolio assets would help in private debt workouts in the wake of financial crises and possibly even help prevent them. Working out bad debts requires the disposal of securitized counterparty assets as the loan books of banks and other financial intermediaries are written down. In the absence of clear property rules, this can become very difficult, especially in a crisis. In consequence, private debtors are reluctant to participate in international bailout operations. Greater confidence in portfolio asset ownership might reduce the desire to withdraw from markets, speed up workouts and increase international private sector participation in rescue operations.

Unlike the original draft for the International Trade Agreement (ITO), the General Agreement on Tariffs and Trade (GATT) made no reference to investment issues.[35] However, by the late 1980s, many developing countries took a cautiously constructive approach to efforts to adopt investment disciplines in the Uruguay Round. In particular, the Fifth Protocol to the General Agreement on Trade in Services (GATS) on Financial Services (WTO, 1997b) expands market access in banking, securities and insurance as well as asset management and financial information, particularly by commercial presence, which has considerable implications for portfolio investment. The new commitments relax limitations on the forms of bank representation, expansion of existing operations and foreign ownership and control of local financial institutions. However, in view of the crucial importance of financial stability and depositor protection in all countries, many countries have chosen to schedule prudential measures under the GATS Annex on Financial Services.

Investment issues will be central to the next ('Millennium') round of WTO negotiations which began in 2000.[36] The WTO Working Group on the Relationship between Trade and Investment (WTO, 1998) argues that portfolio investment is inextricably bound up with direct investment, for two reasons: first, because foreign firms combine direct investment with portfolio investment in the process of establishing themselves within the host economy; second, because, while the conceptual definition of FDI is one of long-term involvement, in practice it is defined as an equity holding of over 10 per cent. In consequence, the asset definition of investment would probably include portfolio flows for the purposes of national treatment and investor protection.[37] A new set of multilateral investment rules would also have to include specific provisions for the financial services sector, including procedures for the recognition of another contracting party's financial regulation standards, transparency in authorisation procedures, and national treatment by self-regulating bodies such as stock markets. These would all stimulate longer-term portfolio investment.

At first sight, the inclusion of portfolio investment under multilateral disciplines based on national treatment and investor protection might seem to restrict the ability of governments to impose controls on volatile capital inflows. Contracting parties would thus have to be allowed to adopt temporary non-conforming measures in the event that cross-border capital transactions cause or threaten to cause external financial difficulties or serious difficulties for the conduct of monetary or exchange rate policies.[38]

5.4   International Taxation

International tax coordination would strengthen the effectiveness of tax-based measures in order to reduce the volatility of portfolio flows by reducing evasion and thus removing a source of volatility. Most developed countries have entered into double taxation agreements (DTTs) between themselves, and increasingly with developing countries.[39] There are two models used, which are similar in their general provisions but have very different implications for developing countries: the OECD Model Tax Convention (OECD, 1997), which is based on residence taxation, and the United Nations Model Double Taxation Convention between Developed and Developing Countries (1980), which is based on source (or 'territorial') taxation.[40] Under both models, fiscal income can be redistributed between two participating governments through the system of tax credits. The existing patchwork could be strengthened in order to stabilize international portfolio flows, through appropriate design of withholding taxes, without the need to establish a supranational tax authority.

A multilateral (or even regional) agreement on withholding taxes on portfolio assets would not only improve the fiscal revenue position of developing countries and reduce the attractiveness of tax incentives to foreign investors, but would also strengthen the effort to combat money laundering and financial fraud – again, stabilizing financial flows. In addition, there are current moves to establish withholding taxes on portfolio holdings in major financial centres in order to reduce the tax loss on the profits generated there (OECD, 1988b). The European Union, in particular, has found that the creation of a single market in financial services requires such a development (FitzGerald and Grabbe, 1997). In order to strengthen this process of fiscal capture by both developed and developing countries, it would be necessary to eliminate tax havens, or at the very least deny the benefits of international investor protection to firms registered there. Furthermore the reconsideration of tax credits on portfolio flows within existing DTTs in order to encourage longer-term holdings would be desirable, as would the application of the US 'pass-through' principle to tax havens (Plasschaert, 1994).

Finally, many foreign investors control their portfolio investments in LDCs through off-shore holding companies, often incorporated in tax havens. In some cases, this is done to avoid financial regulation,[41] as well as for tax evasion or money-laundering purposes; and, as we have seen in section 3.3, off-shore markets play a key part in the evasion of capital controls. The inclusion and protection of indirect ownership, in this context, is a potential problem for recipient LDCs, and should probably be excluded from multilateral investment protection as a positive disincentive to their use by foreign portfolio investors in emerging markets.

6. CONCLUSIONS

This chapter has explored the causes and consequences of the volatility in foreign portfolio flows (FPI) and the effectiveness of policy controls over these flows in the international context. There is a general agreement that public policy responses to the challenges posed by cross-border transactions are evolving towards 'market-based' procedures. These procedures should not, however, be interpreted as including only monetary and exchange rate policies but rather can and do include transparent and 'costable'[42] controls such as asset taxes and reserve requirements.

It is clear that policy must aim both to reduce the volatility of these flows and to shift their maturity towards that of foreign direct investment (FDI), in order to reduce the macroeconomic uncertainty caused by capital surges and thus support productive capital formation and broad employment creation. In practice such a policy could combine tax- and reserve-based direct control measures, an active policy of monetary intervention and a supportive international regulatory regime. In this context, controls have a significant role to play, but their effect is limited in time and most effective where the degree of integration into international capital markets is low. Larger and more open emerging markets must necessarily rely to a greater extent on monetary intervention and regulatory coordination.

The collective provision of prudential regulation of financial intermediaries is necessary in order to prevent not only fraud but also imprudent behaviour with wider consequences, and to protect vulnerable consumers of financial products. This presumes, however, the existence of a sound and transparent legal system that secures contracts and provides for efficient dispute settlement between contracting parties and between financial intermediaries and the regulators. This does not exist at the international level – indeed international investors have no status other than in municipal jurisdictions and only have recourse to essentially political mechanisms to solve investment disputes.

What is more, in practice the maintenance of an 'orderly market' at the domestic level involves de facto recognition of a small number of leading financial institutions ('market makers') who in principle stand ready to buy and sell assets at the current price (creating 'depth' and thus stability in the market) and can be called upon to take over the operations of insolvent financial intermediaries when necessary. These do not exist in the global market and, although as international banking and securities management becomes more concentrated they could emerge, there is no indication of how they might be coordinated or by whom.

Whatever domestic policy to control the volatility of portfolio investment is adopted, determined regulatory support from the international community is necessary. This must evidently include prudential supervision of large overseas investment funds by the securities regulators in developed countries, including restraints on bank lending to hedge funds. In addition, appropriate withholding tax agreements may be a necessary element in the construction of an orderly global capital market.

NOTES

1. In this context, the IMF (1999) forecast that net portfolio flows will be as low as US\$9 billion in 1999 appears realistic but worrying, while the somewhat optimistic projection of a recovery to US\$44 billion in 2000 implies yet another massive capital surge with all the attendant problems discussed in this chapter.
2. Bailouts can, of course, stabilize currencies (albeit at new lower levels) but, unlike banks with a contractual right to the nominal values of their loans, portfolio investors have no such guarantee.
3. Annual fluctuations in flows conventionally regarded as 'long term', such as foreign direct investment (FDI) and sovereign debt issues, may also reflect short-term liquidity considerations. However they are not considered here because, the *stock* of such capital cannot be readily sold by non-residents to residents through the domestic capital market in the short run and thus the same destabilizing consequences for the domestic economy do not occur.
4. Because depositors in (say) pension funds cannot know the eventual value of the asset acquired when they retire, they can only rely on the *current* return on the fund in question: this encourages short-termism by fund managers in order to gain market share. The bias is exacerbated by the system of bonuses as a form of remuneration which can only range between zero and (large) positive sums, thus placing a high option value on risk taking.
5. Financial liberalization in an economy such as Mexico meant not only that half of all Mexican equity and bond trade takes place on US stock markets, but also that the entire domestic money supply is, in effect, a contingent foreign exchange claim on the central bank because all peso securities can be converted into dollars on demand.
6. Even if information on the return (or risk) on a particular asset can be acquired at a cost, the benefit from this knowledge eventually declines as the opportunities for diversification increase; diversified investors have little incentive to search for information since they are shielded by low covariance and high liquidity (Hallwood and MacDonald, 1994).
7. These relationships are reflected in the 'accumulation balance', the national accounting identity which relates the savings of the public sector (S_g) and the private sector (S_p) and investment in the two sectors (I_g, I_p) on the one hand, and the changes in the short-term asset position of non-residents (A), long-term external debt and foreign investment stocks (D) and the level of reserves (R) on the other, which must hold ex post at all times.

$$(I_g - S_g) + (I_p - S_p) \equiv \Delta A + \Delta D + \Delta R$$

Public saving depends on fiscal revenue (T) and current expenditure (G), while private savings are disposable income ($Y - T$) less consumption (C), so we have

$$(I_g + G - T) + (I_p + C - Y + T) \equiv M - X \equiv \Delta A + \Delta D + \Delta R$$

Thus if short-term liabilities (A) rise ex ante and the other capital account items (D, R) are given, one of the left-hand-side variables must adjust ex post: the key issue in evaluating the effect of short-term capital flows is to determine which variable or variables do adjust, and what the consequences of this adjustment are.

8. Specifically, if the debt cycle is to end virtuously: (i) capital inflows should increase investment rather than consumption ($dI/dA > dC/dA$); (ii) the resulting investment should

be efficient in the sense of leading to factor productivity growth $(dY/dA > 1)$; (iii) investment should be in tradables to create the required trade surplus $(dX/dA > dM/dA)$; and (iv) marginal savings rates should exceed the average $(dS/dY > S/Y)$. This is, of course, true of both long- and short-term capital flows.

9. And also wage-earners, as an appreciating real exchange rate corresponds to a rising real wage rate (and vice versa): see FitzGerald (1999c).

10. By adapting the credit-constrained macroeconomic model in Blinder (1987) to the open developing economy with exogenous short-term capital inflows and outflows.

11. Moreover, firms are not in fact a homogeneous group in LDCs, and in practice react in quite different ways to similar macroeconomic shocks (FitzGerald, 1995). The affiliates of multinational corporations do not face the same liquidity constraints as local firms as they can always rely on their headquarters as 'lender of last resort', or raise credit from international banks with the international assets of the corporation as implicit collateral. Large domestic firms, often organized as 'groups', have preferential access to bank credit at any one time (frequently a bank within the group) and thus should suffer less from capital market fluctuations. Indeed it is often the case that banks are vulnerable to the non-financial firms in the group rather than the other way around. In contrast, independent domestic firms are the most vulnerable to shifts in bank credit. Small enterprises outside the formal credit system are also vulnerable to the business cycle because they rely on sub-contracts from larger firms or the expenditure of wages by their employees.

12. The IMF staff were instructed to draw up an amendment to the Articles of Agreement that would make the orderly liberalization of capital account transactions one of the Fund's central purposes.

13. And also excluding in practice personal capital movements (deposits, loans, gifts, endowments, inheritances and legacies) to residents from non-residents (inflows) and by residents to non-residents (outflows) as well as capital transactions by immigrants (such as settlement of debts).

14. For a detailed survey of regulations concerning foreign portfolio investment in emerging markets, see UNCTAD (1998d), Appendix II.

15. Examples include the 4 per cent interest tax and 1.2 per cent stamp duty in Chile (1991); the 1 per cent tax of stock market purchases by foreigners, 9 per cent tax on foreign purchases of bonds, and 7 per cent tax on the issuance of fixed-income securities abroad in Brazil (1994); and the 0.25 per cent fee for certain foreign exchange transactions in the Czech Republic (1995).

16. The case for such a tax is set out in ul Haq *et al.* (1996). The reasons why it would not in fact reduce volatility are set out in Arestis and Sawyer (1998).

17. Examples include the ban on foreign purchases of money-market instruments in Malaysia (1994), limits on short-term securities sales abroad in the Czech Republic (1995), restrictions on the types of securities that can be owned by non-residents in Korea and China and the restrictions on the use of proceeds from the issuance of global depositary receipts in India (1995).

18. Notable examples include the 30 per cent reserve requirement with a minimum maintenance period of one year for financial investment by non-residents in Chile (1992); the 100 per cent reserve requirement for commercial banks against non-resident deposits in Malaysia (1994); and the 30 per cent position limit against short open currency positions with non-residents in the Czech Republic (1995).

19. It should be noted that, although the foreign investor may appear to pay these taxes (or their equivalent) in the first instance, in a globally rationed capital market it is the domestic recipient who will end up carrying the cost of the controls in the form of higher bond yields.

20. For instance, since 1995, Brazil has imposed an entrance tax on foreign borrowing which declines with maturity, reaching zero for six years or more. By simultaneously issuing long (that is, over six year) bonds and writing put options with a one-year maturity, holders could sell the bond to the issuer at any time and thus hold what was in effect a tax-free short bond.

21. For example, the Malaysian decision in 1998 that the principal value of FPI could not be

repatriated for at least a year, while FDI could be freely repatriated, led to two-part arrangements being made. First, portfolio and direct investors exchange holdings to allow the former to repatriate their funds; and second, an off-shore swap of the respective earnings cash flows is arranged so that both parties still receive the original return on their investment.

22. For a practical explanation of forwards and swaps operations, and of derivatives trading generally, see Valdez (1997).

23. If a spot market does not exist at the time of maturity, the spot rate can be an official rate or index, which may create arbitrage opportunities between the domestic and off-shore rate. If the off-shore investor (usually a bank) wishes to hedge, it may do so with a loan in the domestic currency, and thus reduce the insulation of domestic markets that the controls are designed to create.

24. See section 2.3 above.

25. That is, until its recent partial dismantling.

26. This is because foreign investors are believed to have less information about any one emerging market than nationals, and are also in a better position to switch between emerging markets rapidly. They thus are more likely to leave in response to bad news (FitzGerald, 1999a).

27. This contrasts markedly with last resort lending by central banks, which offer unlimited funds on request, but at penal interest rates.

28. Brazil, China, Hong Kong, Korea, Mexico, Russia, Saudi Arabia and Singapore were invited to join the BIS in 1996.

29. Including Hong Kong, Singapore, the Cayman Islands and the Isle of Man.

30. Including the standards and procedures for authorization, the supervisory authority's ability to gather information about the banks and banking groups it authorizes, and the powers available to the supervisory authority to take action against authorized institutions which breach their authorization requirements.

31. The report was endorsed by banking supervisors from 140 countries at the 1998 biannual International Conference of Banking Supervisors in Stockholm.

32. However, closed-end funds trade at a discount and there is thus less investor interest.

33. Such as a 'South-East Asian depository receipt'. However, it is not at all obvious that extensive trading in Mexican stocks in New York ameliorated the 1994–5 crisis.

34. However this is a strong disincentive for US mutual funds, for example which are legally required to redeem shares within a period of three to seven days, so that the imposition of a minimum holding period would represent a very strong disincentive to investments by those funds.

35. Although as early as 1954 the original GATT text was modified to allow for quantitative restrictions in cases of perceived balance of payments crises; Article XVIIIb was rather vague.

36. See FitzGerald (1999d) for a fuller discussion.

37. The definition of investment in terms of 'expecting a return' would automatically exclude, however, government procurement and construction contracts, and so on.

38. As was done in Section VI of the MAI draft (OECD, 1998a). However it was proposed that such measures should only be allowed with permission from the IMF, which was inappropriate in view of the need for rapid and flexible action in balance of payments crises.

39. There are now over 1700 such treaties in existence (IBFD, 1998): 34 per cent of all DDTs are between developed and developing countries, and a further 17 per cent between developing countries.

40. In theory, developing countries would benefit most from a multilateral withholding tax treaty based on the source principle, for two reasons. First, the gains from taxing income of foreign investors would be greater than the loss from not taxing income from their own residents' assets held abroad, because a developing country has a net external liability position. Second, the full taxation of these assets held abroad by the authorities in that country on the source principle would make capital flight much less attractive. Although when applied unilaterally the source principle may encourage nationals or residents to

invest abroad ('capital flight'), it is often adopted because tax administrators have great difficulty in finding out how much foreign income accrues to their residents. The residence principle, although based on overall capacity to pay, has proved to be of limited significance in countries whose residents do not have substantial (recorded) investments in other countries, and whose fiscal administration is not well equipped to ensure its application. Moreover, to the extent that developed countries do not tax non-residents, they too stimulate capital flight from developing countries.

41. LTCM was registered in Bermuda.
42. That is, taxes and reserve requirements can be computed as costs by the investor involved, permitting rational economic calculations.

REFERENCES

Arestis, P. and M. Sawyer (1998), 'What role for the Tobin tax in global governance?', (mimeo) University of East London.

Atje, R. and B. Javanovic (1993), 'Stock markets and development', *European Economic Review*, **37**, 632–40.

Bachetta, P. (1992), 'Liberalization of capital movements and the domestic financial system', *Economica*, 465–7.

Bencivanga, V.R., B. Smith and R.M. Starr (1996), 'Equity markets, transaction costs and capital accumulation', *World Bank Economic Review*, **10**(2), 241–65.

BIS (1998), *Sixty-Eighth Annual Report*, Basle: Bank for International Settlements.

Blinder, A.S. (1987) 'Credit Rationing and Effective Supply Failures' *Economic Journal* 97: 327–352.

Brainard, W.C. and J. Tobin (1992), 'On the internationalization of portfolios', *Oxford Economic Papers*, **44**.

Calvo, G., L. Leiderman and C. Reinhart (1993), 'Capital inflows and real exchange rate appreciation in Latin America: the role of external factors', *IMF Staff Papers*, **40**.

DeLong, J.B., A. Scleifer, L. Summers and R.J. Waldemann (1989), 'The size and incidence of losses from noise trading', *Journal of Finance*, **44** (3), 681–96.

De Simone, F. and P. Sorsa (1998), 'A review of of capital account restrictions in Chile in the 1990s', *IMF Working Paper 99*, Washington, DC: International Monetary Fund.

Dixit, A.K. and R.S. Pindyck (1994), *Investment under Uncertainty*, Princeton, NJ: Princeton University Press.

Dooley, M. (1996) 'A survey of literature on controls over international capital transactions', *IMF Staff Papers*, **43** (4).

Dooley, M., D. Mathieson and L. Rojas-Suarez (1996), 'Capital mobility and exchange market intervention in developing countries', *IMF Working Paper*, WP/96/131, Washington, DC: International Monetary Fund.

Dornbusch, R. (1996), 'It's time for a financial transactions tax', *The International Economy*, Aug/Sept.

Dornbusch, R. (1997), 'Cross-border payments taxes and alternative capital account regimes', *International Monetary and Financial Issues for the 1990s*, Geneva: UNCTAD.

Edwards, F.R. (1998), 'Hedge funds: implications of LTCM's collapse' (mimeo), Colombia University Graduate School of Business, New York.

Edwards, S. (1995), 'Why are savings rates so different across countries? An international comparative analysis', NBER Working Paper 5097.

Eichengreen, B. and M. Mussa (1998), 'Theoretical and practical aspects of capital account liberalization', *IMF Occasional Paper 172*, Washington, DC: International Monetary Fund.

Ffrench-Davis, R. and H. Reisen (1998), *Capital Flows and Investment Performance: Lessons from Latin American Experience*, Paris: OECD Development Centre.

FitzGerald, E. (1995), 'Hamlet without the prince: structural adjustment, firm behaviour and private investment in semi-industrialized economies' in P. Arestis and V. Chick (eds), *Finance, Development and Structural Change*, Aldershot, UK and Brookfield, US: Edward Elgar, pp. 27–45.

FitzGerald, E.V.K. (1999a), 'Global capital market volatility and the developing countries: lessons from the East Asian crisis', *IDS Bulletin*, **30** (1), 19–32.

FitzGerald, E.V.K. (1999b), 'Trade, investment and the NAFTA: the economics of neighbourhood', in V. Bulmer-Thomas and J. Dunkerley (eds), *The United States and Latin America: Analysis of the New Agenda*, London: Macmillan; Cambridge, MA, Harvard University Press, pp. 99–122.

FitzGerald, E.V.K. (1999c), 'Capital surges, investment instability and income distribution after financial liberalization', in W. Mahmud (ed.), *Adjustment and Beyond: the Reform Experience in South Asia*, Basingstoke: Macmillan in association with the International Economic Association, pp. 129–51.

FitzGerald, E.V.K. (1999d), *The International Development Dimension of Multilateral Investment Rules*, London: Department for International Development (DfID/IEPD).

FitzGerald, E.V.K. and H. Grabbe (1997), 'Financial services integration: the European experience and lessons for Latin America', *Integration and Trade*, **1** (2), 85–124.

Glick, R. (ed.) (1997), *Managing Capital Flows and Exchange Rates: Perspectives from the Pacific Basin*, Cambridge: Cambridge University Press.

Gros, D. (1987), 'The effectiveness of capital controls: implication for monetary autonomy in the presence of incomplete market separation', *IMF Staff Papers*, **34**.

Hallwood, C.P. and R. MacDonald (1994), *International Money and Finance*, 2nd edn, Oxford: Blackwell.

Haq, M.U., I. Kaul and I. Grunberg (eds) (1996), *The Tobin Tax: Coping with Financial Volatility*, New York: Oxford University Press.

Hirschliefer, J. and J.G. Riley (1992), *The Analytics of Uncertainty and Information*, Cambridge: Cambridge University Press.

IBFD (1998), *Annual Report 1997–1998*, Amsterdam: International Bureau of Fiscal Documentation.

IMF (1998), *International Capital Markets*, Washington, DC: International Monetary Fund.

IMF (1999), *World Economic Outlook (May)*, Washington, DC: International Monetary Fund.

Johnston, R.B. and N.T. Tamirisa (1998), 'Why do countries use capital controls?', *IMF Working Paper* WP/98/181, Washington, DC: International Monetary Fund.

Khan, M.S. and N.U. Huq (1990), 'Adjustment with growth: relating the analytical approaches of the IMF and the World Bank', *Journal of Development Economics*, **32**, 155–79.

Kindelberger, C.P. (1996), *Manias, Panics and Crashes: A History of Financial Crisis* 3rd edn, Basingstoke: Macmillan.

Korajczyk, R. (1996), 'A measure of stock market integration for developed and developing countries', *World Bank Economic Review*, **10** (2), 267–89.

Krugman, P. (1987) 'A model of balance of payments crises', *Journal of Money, Credit and Banking*, 16 (2).

Levine, R. (1991), 'Stock markets, growth and tax policy', *Journal of Finance*, **46**.

Levine, R. (1997), 'Financial development and economic growth: views and agenda', *Journal of Economic Literature*, **35** (2).

Masson, P., T. Bayoumi and H. Samiei (1995), 'International evidence on the determinants of private savings', *IMF Working Paper 95/91*, Washington, DC: International Monetary Fund.

Obstfeld, M. (1995), 'International currency experience: new lessons and lessons relearned', *Brookings Papers on Economic Activity*, 1, 119–220.

OECD (1997), *Model Double Taxation Convention on Income and Capital*, Paris: Organization for Economic Cooperation and Development.

OECD (1998a), *Multilateral Agreement on Investment: Consolidated Text*, Paris: Organization for Economic Cooperation and Development.

OECD (1998b), *Harmful Tax Competition: An Emerging Global Issue*, Paris: Organization for Economic Cooperation and Development.

Pindyck, R.S. and A. Solimano (1993), 'Economic instability and aggregate investment', *Working Paper 4380*, Cambridge, MA: NBER.

Plasschaert, S. (ed.) (1994), *Transnational Corporations: Transfer Pricing and Taxation*, London and New York: Routledge for the United Nations.

Quirk, P.J. and O. Evans (1995), 'Capital account convertibility: review of experience and implications for IMF policies', *IMF Occasional Paper 131*, Washington, DC: International Monetary Fund.

Reisen, H. (1996), 'Managing volatile capital inflows: the experience of the 1990s', *Asian Development Review*, **14** (1), 72–96.

Rojas-Suarez, L. and S.R. Weisbrod (1994), 'Financial market fragilities in Latin America', *IMF Working Paper 117*, Washington, DC: International Monetary Fund.

Stiglitz, J.E. (1994), 'The role of the state in financial markets', *Proceedings of the World Bank Conference on Development Economics 1993*, Washington, DC: World Bank.

Stiglitz, J.E. and A. Weiss (1992), 'Asymmetric information in credit markets and its implications for macroeconomics', *Oxford Economic Papers*, **44**, 694–724.

Tobin, T. (1984), 'On the efficiency of the financial system', *Lloyds Bank Review*, **153**.

Turner, P. (1996), 'Comments on Reisen', in R. Hausmann and H. Reisen (eds), *Promoting Savings in Latin America*, Paris: IDB and OECD Development Centre.

UN (1980), *United Nations Model Double Taxation Convention between Developed and Developing Countries*, New York: United Nations (E.80.XVI.3).

UNCTAD (1997), *World Investment Report 1997: Transnational Corporations, Market Structure and Competition Policy*, Geneva: United Nations Conference on Trade and Development.

UNCTAD (1998a), *Trade and Development Report, 1998*, Geneva: United Nations Conference on Trade and Development.

UNCTAD (1998b), *Report on the Expert Meeting on the Growth of Domestic Capital Markets* (TB/B/COM.2/12), Geneva: United Nations Conference on Trade and Development.

UNCTAD (1998c), 'The growth of domestic capital markets, particularly in developing countries, and its relation with foreign portfolio investment' (TD/B/COM.2/EM.4/1), United Nations Conference on Trade and Development, Geneva.

UNCTAD (1998d), 'Foreign portfolio investment: implications for the growth of emerging capital markets' (GDS/GFSB/4), United Nations Conference on Trade and Development, Geneva.

UNRISD (1996), *States of Disarray: The Social Effects of Globalization*, Geneva: UN Research Institute for Social Development.

Valdez, S. (1997), *An Introduction to Global Financial Markets*, Basingstoke: Macmillan.

World Bank (1997), *Private Capital Flows to Developing Countries: The Road to Financial Integration,* New York: Oxford University Press.

WTO (1997a), *Annual Report 1997*, Geneva: World Trade Organization.

WTO (1997b), *Fifth Protocol to the General Agreement on Trade in Services*, Geneva: World Trade Organization (S/L/45).

WTO (1998), *Report (1988) of the Working Group on the Relationship between Trade and Investment to the General Council*, WT/WGTI/2, Geneva: World Trade Organization.

PART II

Households, firms and financial institutions

8.   Finance and poor people's livelihoods

Susan Johnson, David Hulme and Orlanda Ruthven

1.   INTRODUCTION

Views about the way in which financial services should be provided for poor people are changing. The dominant approach has, until recently, been pro-duction-based and suggested that poor people lack the financial capital that will enable them to invest and engage in productive activity, in particular making use of their labour. This view reflects, at the household level, the macroeconomic analysis that identified capital constraints to growth as a key cause of slow development.

In line with this analysis, efforts to provide credit for poor people from the 1950s to the 1990s focused on the direct provision of credit, usually subsi-dized, through government agricultural credit schemes and NGO initiatives. Such credit was in the main aimed at the agricultural sector, often in the context of the introduction of new agricultural technologies. This approach started to take root in the informal enterprise sector in the mid-1970s. At this time, research started to demonstrate the importance of the informal sector as a source of employment and potential economic growth (ILO, 1972) and development interventions started to focus on directing credit to it. The performance of these credit programmes was generally found to be poor, both in agriculture and enterprise, state or NGO-based (Adams *et al.*, 1983; Adams and von Pischke, 1992). In the 1980s, an approach which used group-based lending and regular repayment brought new hope. However regular repay-ment was invariably a problem for more rural and agriculturally based households, leading to the gradual withdrawal of credit programmes from this sector. For a decade, from the late 1980s to late 1990s, the provision of credit to informal sector enterprise was the core intervention of NGOs work-ing in the sector.

Since the late 1990s, there has been the beginning of a further shift in analysis and understanding of poor people's financial needs. Livelihood ap-proaches suggest that poor people use the resources they have to construct livelihood strategies in response to the risks and opportunities that they face.

This perspective converges with growing insights into the operation of informal financial systems to offer a more holistic perspective on the financial service requirements of poor people. The approach suggests the need to shift emphasis from the provision of credit for specific productive purposes to the provision of financial services which allow poor people to manage more effectively the financing of their livelihood strategies.

This chapter first reviews the evidence from the growing literature on informal financial mechanisms. This evidence of the diversity, complexity and detail of financial arrangements demonstrates the multidimensional nature of poor people's needs for financial intermediation. This analysis has given rise to a more in-depth understanding of how poor people manage their money. But, even then, it is critically important to recognize that informal financial intermediation (see section 2) in many instances offers far more than simply loans and savings. Rather, that poor people may enter into informal financial arrangements because they enable them to develop social relationships with others that also help them to better cope with crisis and hardship. The livelihoods approach is then briefly reviewed in section 3. This allows the complex and multidimensional reality of poor people's livelihoods to be better understood. When finance is seen in the context of livelihoods, the wider context of social relations must be addressed, as it is social axes of difference such as class, gender, age and ethnicity that fundamentally affect the options that poor people have open to them. Hence exclusion from these services can also be socially based.

Section 4 presents material from recent research in India and Kenya. This evidence demonstrates the way in which poor people use financial services to achieve a range of livelihood needs and the way that different types of financial service enable them to do this. However the question of exclusion remains. While the evidence suggests that poor people make extensive use of informal financial services, the poorest may be excluded because of their material and social poverty.

2.   LEARNING FROM INFORMAL FINANCE

Informal Financial Systems: Diverse and Ubiquitous

Debates over the role of moneylenders in development have a long history that is largely based on South Asian experience. For example, accounts dating back to the late eighteenth century reveal the concern of the British colonial administration in India about the role and extent of indebtedness among peasant farmers, in particular its role in creating landlessness (McGregor, 1998). This concern was not without moral and religious significance for the British, whose attention then turned to attempting to alleviate the problem through various forms of credit provision.

The analysis of the relationships involved in moneylending has become the core of a political economy analysis of agriculture and the rural economy, a view that has interpreted the high interest rates charged by moneylenders as exploitative. For example, Bhaduri's (1977) seminal contribution argues that usurious interest rates are a deliberate strategy used by moneylenders to accumulate land, since borrowers will be unable to repay and therefore forfeit the land. Other studies (Harriss, 1983; Aleem, 1990) demonstrate the ways in which moneylenders may interlink credit contracts with other aspects of agriculture, such as the supply of inputs, sale of outputs or supply of labour. Olsen (1994), for example, observed in southern India the ways in which merchant moneylenders locked borrowers into relationships with lenders that would ensure the provision of groundnuts at prices beneficial to them.

An alternative view of interest rates in moneylending relationships is that they reflect the shortage of liquidity in the rural economy and the risk and convenience of the service that moneylenders offer (Wai, 1957). New institutional economists argue that, by analysing the risk of default to lenders and the low transactions costs to borrowers due to the convenience of the service, both the charging of these high rates by lenders and the choice of paying them by borrowers can be understood (see also Chapter 9 of the present volume). However this view also accepts that the degree of competition in the market also determines the extent of monopolistic profit that can be charged. Moreover it has been pointed out that such arrangements often contain high degrees of flexibility, in that repayment dates can be renegotiated, payment may be made in kind and so on (Adams, 1994).

In the early 1960s, anthropologists drew attention to rotating savings and credit associations (ROSCAs) that could be found across Asia, Africa and Latin America and in immigrant communities in developed countries (Adams and Fitchett, 1992; Geertz, 1962; Ardener, 1964; Bouman and Hospes, 1994; Ardener and Burman, 1995). ROSCAs are systems in which a number of people form a group and contribute an agreed amount on a regular basis. At each meeting the fund is usually given to one person who takes all of the money, until everyone in the group has received the money in turn. The order of rotation may be determined by ballot, by age or seniority or other social systems of preferment. Alternatively the payout may be auctioned, with the person willing to take the largest discount receiving the payout. The remainder of the funds are then divided amongst those who have not yet won the payout. Hence ROSCAs are a very basic and simple form of financial intermediation that has a very high degree of flexibility: the amount to be saved, the number of people in the system, the regularity of contributions, the number of people to receive a payout on each occasion, the use to which funds can be put, can all be determined by those participating.

Thus, for example, 'merry-go-rounds' (the term for ROSCAs in Kenya) are found in both urban and rural locations. In rural areas women may meet weekly or monthly and contribute very small amounts. Such groups are often based on lineage relationships with women who are from, or married into, a particular lineage. The funds may be given in cash or used by the group to buy particular items such as kitchen utensils, jumpers, clothes and so on. In these cases, the group agrees at the beginning of the cycle what they would like to buy and each time they meet the next person in the cycle receives the item. While many women in central Kenya have access to income flows on their own account, many may only receive the funds that their husbands give them for buying food. They then save small amounts to contribute to the merry-go-round. The ROSCA provides a means of saving small amounts and equipping the house or buying clothes for sums that she is unlikely otherwise to be able to command at one time. At the same time, the meeting of the group gives the women an opportunity to meet and pursue related social activities. Alternatively groups may simply provide cash payouts, and this is usually the norm in ROSCAs that operate in markets or urban areas. Women may set up or join groups in order to finance virtually any aspect of expenditure, from buying cooking fat to raising funds to renew stock for business or to pay school fees (Johnson, 2001).

One of the key debates surrounding ROSCAs has been their potential as a developmental mechanism: to what extent can they operate as a modernizing mechanism to facilitate a transition into a modern economy? While Geertz proposes that ROSCAs are a product of the shift from agrarian society to a more commercialized one, Ardener thinks they may instead be a cause of the shift (Geertz, 1962; Ardener, 1964). Nelson did indeed find that a ROSCA amongst a group of commercial beer brewers in the Mathare valley of Nairobi had enabled them to move from self-financing their own activities with the ROSCA, to the ROSCA becoming the basis of a land-buying cooperative and hence was the platform for the shift to a more formal and complex institutional form (Nelson, 1995). Aredo (1993) similarly sees *iddir* (social insurance funds) in Ethiopia as developmental, having examined their large-scale development in certain urban environments. Hospes (1995), on the other hand, criticizes this discourse for its concentration on the ROSCA model's capacity to mobilize rural savings rather than recognition of the capacity that it demonstrates of poor people to save, organize and regulate themselves.

While ROSCAs are now well known, there are related savings mechanisms that operate on similar lines. First are Accumulating Savings and Credit Associations (ASCAs) (Bouman, 1995). In these, members of the group save into a central fund from which they then take loans. Interest on the loans is also paid into the fund and hence it accumulates. The members may then receive dividends from the fund in relation to the amount of their savings in it. Second are savings clubs, which usually involve saving in the fund, but these savings are not withdrawn or taken as loans. The fund is usually then divided on an agreed occasion; for example, in the UK, such systems were often run as a means of accumulating savings for Christmas expenditure ('Christmas clubs') and the fund would be divided just before Christmas.

Money lending, ROSCAs, ASCAs and savings clubs have now been shown to operate in a huge number of countries and have dominated much of the informal financial literature. The variations in their mode of operation are huge: whether used by men or women, to finance virtually any form of investment from rickshaws to taxis, or consumption expenditure from cooking fat to clothes, and it is this diversity that demonstrates their flexibility in responding to the basic financial needs of poor people. However there is a range of less well-known informal financial mechanisms which poor people also use to save and take loans.

First, there are various types of money guards and deposit takers who offer private informal arrangements for making savings. These include the *alajos* in Nigeria who move door-to-door collecting savings. A customer can withdraw whenever she likes and is charged a day's savings per month that is deducted from the withdrawal (Rutherford, 1997). These arrangements are very similar to other west African systems such as *susu* in which deposit takers move around the markets collecting savings. Loans may also be taken from the *susu* collector. Other money guards may be local trusted shopkeepers who may not charge for the service but for whom the savings represent extra working capital. In some cases, according to Rutherford, this has also become formalized, with the shopkeeper offering a card and imposing a small service charge when the set period of making daily deposits is over and the lump sum is withdrawn.

On the lending side, one of the most common forms of borrowing is from friends and relatives. These arrangements can usually be distinguished from those of moneylenders in that an interest rate is not charged, although this is not necessarily the case. But the importance of these arrangements is that they are easy and convenient and again highly flexible as negotiation is integral to the arrangement made.

Another very common form of lending is pawnbroking, which allows the use of pledged items to raise funds and is one of the easiest ways to raise money quickly. These arrangements tend to occur informally when regulations get in the way of licensed provision (ibid.). In India, Rutherford notes that pawnbrokers generally like to lend against gold but other items can be used – even cooking pots. As he further points out, because the collateral for the loan is unambiguous, the pawnbroker does not need to know customers well and can lend to more or less anyone at any time though a constant concern is to avoid stolen goods.

Finally, there is a range of informal mechanisms that offers basic forms of insurance. Insurance is required to provide for core life cycle events and contingencies such as death and burial, fire, flood and other natural calamities. In rural central Kenya, such burial funds are often organized amongst lineage groups who make contributions on an ad hoc basis on the death of a member or his family. Over time, some of these groups have evolved into making regular contributions to a fund held in a bank or cooperative in order to ensure the availability of funds when they are required. The payout may also be made in the event of a house burning down. Rutherford (ibid.) describes the way in which small-scale traders and shopkeepers in a slum of Dhaka in Bangladesh organized daily contributions banked by a committee in order to have funds to draw on when their shops and workshops have been damaged by fire or damaged by the bulldozers of the City Corporation.

Rutherford (ibid.) draws attention to this variety of informal finance mechanisms and the abundant evidence of their presence worldwide to argue that they clearly demonstrate poor people's needs for a variety of financial services.

The Financial Service Needs of Poor Households: the Demand Side

Until recently, ideas about the financial service needs of poor households were gross simplifications of the realities of their day-to-day experiences and actions. Most of those engaged in trying to work out how to help poor people gain access to more and better financial services implicitly adopted analytical frameworks grounded in modernization theory. Poor people were seen as pursuing 'traditional' ways of making a living and needed assistance to take on modern ways. Peasants needed to become capitalist small farmers, while those not directly involved in agricultural production would set up small businesses (if they could not acquire a full-time job in the formal sector). Foreign aid and technical assistance were required to develop financial service provision. Such gross simplifications made it easier to design blueprint projects (50 000 farmers each needing a US$200 loan to grow High Yielding Variety (HYV) rice made a neat US$10 million aid facility).

These gross simplifications also matched the poverty conceptualizations of that era. Poverty was an economic phenomenon, so it could be rapidly resolved by directly increasing the income of poor people. Poor people had low incomes that had to be used immediately, because of their poverty, so they could not make savings. Value judgments also filtered through. Poor people were childlike (in terms of behaviour and lack of experience with money) and thus needed constant supervision to ensure that, if they acquired a loan, they did not become indebted because of wasting it on non-productive expenditure, such as celebrations, weddings, food for consumption or burying their dead.

While some commentators, particularly anthropologists (see earlier), challenged these ideas, it took decades for a fuller appreciation of the financial service needs of poor people to inform development policy and action. One area in which early progress was made was risk and vulnerability. Throughout the 1980s, economists and rural sociologists pointed out that mitigating risk and trying to manage vulnerability was an important activity for poor people that often involved informal financial services and surrogates. This was a 'breakthrough', in analytical terms, as it forced onto the agenda a recognition of the unpredictability of life for the poor and of their need for services to manage emergencies and shocks.

A second 'breakthrough' came with the recognition that poor people actively pursued economic diversification both to survive and to improve their position (see section 3). As a strategic choice, poor households weave together several different streams of income. Finally, changing conceptualizations of poverty have helped to drive forward thinking about the financial service needs of the poor. As the concept of poverty as capability deprivation (Dreze and Sen, 1989; Sen, 1999) has gained ground, the need of poor people to finance health, education, social networks and other activities has been seen as valuable, rather than wasteful.

So we now appreciate that poor people have complex and changing livelihoods, and small and uncertain incomes, a major part of which has to go on the purchase of food and relatively unpredictable expenditure patterns. For many non-food items, and at times for food, poor households have no cash-in-hand to make purchases: this occurs even for very small-scale items (for example, a bus fare, cooking fuel, a kitchen utensil). Thus poor people need financial services more frequently and urgently than other groups, and the poorest need them most of all (Sinha and Lipton, 1999). If they cannot obtain them 'the only alternative is that they must go without, an all-too-common outcome' (Rutherford *et al.*, 2002, p. 114).

In his influential work Rutherford (2000) has argued that poor people can meet their need for 'lump sums' of money in three main ways. The first is to sell assets that they hold, or expect to hold (for example, next season's crop); second is the mortgaging or pawning of assets. Both of these entail that the user has assets. This is problematic for poor people given that poverty is characterized by low levels of assets and that asset disposal for them is not a sustainable means of survival. The third approach does not share this limitation . It 'enables poor people to convert their small savings [from day-to-day economic activities] into lump sums' (ibid., p. 6).[1] It comprises three mechanisms: saving up, saving down and saving through, which 'are at the heart of all financial services for the poor, whether they are informal or formal, large

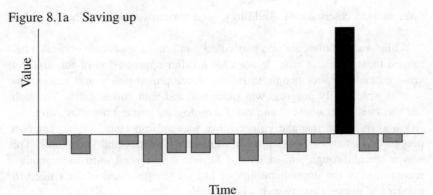

Figure 8.1a Saving up
Value
Time
Figure 8.1b Saving down
Next cycle may begin
Value
Time
Figure 8.1c Saving through
Value
Time
Usefully large lump sum withdrawn
Savings

Source: Adapted from Rutherford (2000, pp. 7–8).

Figure 8.1 Saving

or small' (ibid.). 'Saving up' (Figure 8.1a) involves a series of small savings (daily, weekly or monthly and regularly or irregularly) being built up and eventually withdrawn as a lump sum. It has the advantage of being 'unencumbered' as it does not involve debt or the right of a lender to place conditions on the use of the lump sum. Its problem is that poor people have few places (hiding places, friends and contacts, institutions) where they can safely keep their savings.

'Saving down' (Figure 8.1b) involves acquiring a lump sum or loan first and then using micro-savings to repay the loan over time. In effect this is 'advances against future savings' (ibid., p. 7). As with saving up, the problem for most poor people is that there are few people or institutions that will provide them with 'saving down' services. In addition, because of the lack of competition, access to such services may at times come at a very high cost.

Finally, there is 'saving through' (Figure 8.1c), when a user makes a continuous flow of savings that are converted into a lump sum at an intermediate time. Sometimes the user is a net saver, at other times he or she is a net borrower. This is a very user-friendly mechanism, allowing the user to meet the need for planned lump sums (such as school fees or agricultural inputs) and unplanned lump sums (such as medical expenses or a funeral). Unfortunately such services are rarely available to poor people.[2]

So the complex, dynamic and unpredictable needs of poor people lead them to search for ways of saving up, saving down or saving through so that they can gain access to lump sums on a rapid and flexible basis with a good degree of security (that is, the service provider will not run off with their savings) and at a reasonable price (that is, one at which they judge the terms and conditions to be commensurate with the utility of the service). Relatively few such financial service providers exist, however, and so in many cases poor people patch together a portfolio of informal services (see next section) and, sometimes, formal services (see section 4) in an attempt to meet their needs.

Informal Finance: Insurance and Social Safety Nets

The usefulness of many informal financial mechanisms to poor people is not limited to the ways in which they enable people to turn flows of income into lump sums. There are a number of ways in which these mechanisms for financial intermediation (especially group-based mechanisms) offer social benefits through the social relationships that such groups embody and can generate (Ardener, 1995). As a result Bouman (1995), amongst others, argues the limitations of an instrumental view of ROSCAs as development vehicles since he recognizes that ROSCAs serve more purposes than simply financial ones.

Platteau and Abraham (1987) argue that credit contracts that are reciprocal, such as loans from friends and relatives, because they are embedded in social relations, can reduce risk. They call them 'quasi-credit', because such contracts do not usually involve interest rates, fixed repayment dates or collateral. These contracts enable the smoothing out of income streams with high degrees of intertemporal and interpersonal variability. Hence they argue that attempts to unlink credit from other social relations when replacing traditional mechanisms with formal services, can lead to efficiency losses as the means through which these mechanisms reduce information and transactions costs can increase efficiency in the context of uncertainty.

Platteau has also attempted to delineate boundaries between financial intermediation and insurance. He argues that insurance mechanisms in developing countries are based on a norm of 'balanced reciprocity' rather than 'conditional reciprocity', where the ex ante utility of eliminating or reducing the effects of a negative event are valued, and which is the usual basis of insurance in developing countries. To explain this he uses the example of mutual aid in Senegalese fishing communities, where he suggests that the variability of income flows on a daily basis offers opportunities for members of such mutual aid groups to benefit from support from each other on a frequent basis. In this case mutual aid and balanced reciprocity are strongly convergent. A fisherman who has been able to make a catch one day will be able to assist another who has not, with their situations being reversed on another day. In contrast to the fishing communities, he argues that agrarian societies are more likely to use state-contingent lending where the terms of repayment may be adjusted to take account of shocks affecting either borrower or lender. State-contingent loans can also assist in mitigating unexpected shocks and hence act as a risk-pooling mechanism but he argues that these are also more akin to balanced reciprocity because the repayment periods under situations of favourable or unfavourable shocks are little different: hence the insurance element of these arrangements is not particularly significant and does not operate in the same way on the basis of need. From this he argues that agrarian societies prefer insurance based on credit transactions because they better embody the 'balanced reciprocity' norm.

There are a number of aspects of the argument for 'balanced reciprocity' rather than mutual aid that deserve further examination. First, the literature on microcredit group-based lending involves a discussion of screening mechanisms whose purpose is to ensure that only those with the ability to pay join groups. As Ghatak argues, where borrowers have local information about each other, positive assortative matching occurs and safe borrowers will end up with safe partners while risky borrowers will end up with risky partners (Ghatak, 2000). Presumably if this is the case for microcredit groups it is sensible to suggest that it is also true of indigenous savings mechanisms and indigenous group-based insurance systems. This means that there is a priori selection into ROSCAs (and ASCAs) on the basis of an individual's risk profile. The individual's risk profile in the view of others is a consequence of his or her socioeconomic status. This status is affected by factors such as gender, class, caste, age and ethnicity. The function of groups intent on financial intermediation is therefore to exclude those who are seen as bad risks and to ensure balanced reciprocity rather than redistribution. So it is not surprising that Platteau finds that only limited redistributive transfers operate *within* the framework of a ROSCA. Those with greater diversity could be expected to involve greater elements of redistribution but this would in turn undermine ROSCAs as a system of financial intermediation.

It is clear, however, that many group-based intermediation mechanisms may involve a range of activities, both financial and social. Members of a ROSCA may have a facility for collecting a regular contribution towards an insurance fund with payouts agreed under certain circumstances. Thus it may not be within the transactions of the ROSCA itself that redistribution is most likely to occur. Nevertheless the argument Platteau makes for 'balanced reciprocity' is still valid, since it is most likely that those in the group will have tended to select themselves because they have similar risk profiles and hence even social assistance is likely to occur in a more 'balanced' way than if groups involved a wider range of socioeconomic profiles. Norms of 'balanced reciprocity' may still prevail in these relationships, and members who transgress them may eventually be dropped from the group.

However, as Ardener (1995) suggests, the interaction between the social and economic functions of ROSCAs are inseparable. Velez-Ibanez (1983, p. 113) argues (after Lomnitz) that ROSCAs are an important means 'by which individuals can successfully counter the basic uncertainty of a marginal existence by generating methods of economic solidarity that mobilise available resources efficiently'. While offering the material means to purchase gifts and to enable crucial ritual obligations to be met, he argues that 'Accumulating money to meet such obligations selects for an increased number of social links, and with that increase, access to more favors' (ibid., p. 114) and he enumerates such favours as reduced prices in the marketplace, an introduction to a job, assistance in child care or medicine for a child and so on. While a feature of these favours may indeed be balanced reciprocity, these favours may operate well beyond the bounds of the ROSCA itself. As a 'cultural invention' that allows people to meet both biological and sociocultural needs (Velez-Ibanez, 1983), he describes ROSCAs as adaptive to varied circumstances and argues that it is this adaptability that has contributed to their continued use.

3. FINANCIAL SERVICES IN THE CONTEXT OF LIVELIHOODS

Introducing Livelihood Approaches

At the same time as analysts of microfinance were building up their understanding of the complex financial needs and behaviours of poor people in the 1990s, research by rural development specialists sought to deepen understanding of the complex and dynamic ways in which poor people survive, especially in rural areas and with an emphasis on providing better guidance for pro-poor policy. This resulted in the development of 'sustainable rural livelihoods' analytical frameworks (Carney, 1998; Scoones, 1998) that have been adapted to 'rural livelihoods' (Ellis, 2000), 'multiple livelihoods (Murray, 2001) and 'urban livelihoods' (Rakodi, 2002). While there are differences between each of these frameworks, for the main part they are similar.[3] Here we briefly demonstrate why these frameworks permit a more comprehensive understanding of the way poor people use financial services to enhance their lives.

At the heart of livelihoods analysis is the idea that households (groups of people who live under the same roof and eat together) pursue livelihood strategies (dynamic sets of economic activities) to maintain their security and well-being and, often, to improve their economic and social position. Households construct their strategy around the deployment of a portfolio of assets or capitals (human, social, physical, financial and natural) to meet present needs and, at the same time, develop this asset base to achieve aspirations for the future and for transfer to the next generation. The strategies pursued by a household depend on the structure of its asset portfolio, household composition and the broader physical and socioeconomic context within which it operates. For poor households the vulnerability context is of central importance as their strategies have to focus more on short-term survival than on longer-term economic and social goals. The main elements of the livelihoods framework are summarized in Figure 8.2.

For specific households the composition of the five assets upon which they can draw is a key determinant of strategy (Box 8.1). The application of the framework entails the recording of a household's assets and an understanding of how these are utilized: they can be stored, exchanged, accumulated, depleted or employed to generate a flow of benefits. Underpinning the asset pentagon is the idea that households with more assets will have more livelihood options to achieve their aspirations and a greater capacity to manage risk and vulnerability, as shown in Figure 8.3. Households can invest to secure more of an asset (for example, using income to buy a tool or pay school fees), substitute one asset for another (for example, using savings to

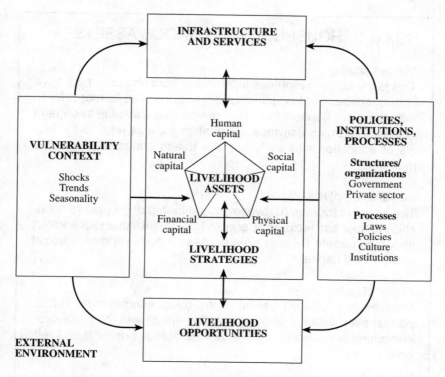

Source: Rakodi (2002, p. 9).

Figure 8.2   The livelihoods framework

buy land) or dispose of an asset to overcome a shock (for example, selling their radio to pay for medical expenses, so maintaining human capital). The more assets a household controls the greater the choice of options.

The concept of vulnerability is central to the livelihoods framework as poor people are exposed to high levels of risk from crises, stress and shocks. Carney (1998) provides guidelines on how the analysis of vulnerability can be structured and Rakodi (2002, p. 14) usefully distinguishes three main forms:

- long-term trends (demographic, changes to the natural resource base, climatic, technology, complex political emergencies) that can raise or lower the overall likelihood of risk;
- recurring seasonal shocks, such as prices or employment opportunities, that can be partly planned for; and
- short-term shocks, such as illness, accident, natural disaster or communal violence.

BOX 8.1   HOUSEHOLD LIVELIHOOD ASSETS

Human capital
This is the labour resources available to households, which have both quantitative and qualitative dimensions. The former refer to the number of household members and time available to engage in income-earning activities. Qualitative aspects refer to the levels of education and skills and the health status of household members.

Social and political capital
The social resources (networks, membership of groups, relationships of trust and reciprocity, access to wider institutions of society) on which people draw in pursuit of livelihoods represent social and political capital.

Physical capital
Physical or produced capital is the basic infrastructure (transport, shelter, water, energy, communications) and the production equipment and means which enable people to pursue their livelihoods.

Financial capital
This is the financial resources available to people (including savings, credit, remittances and pensions) which provide them with different livelihood options.

Natural capital
Natural capital is the natural resource stocks from which resource flows useful to livelihoods are derived, including land, water and other environmental resources, especially common pool resources.

Source: Carney (1998, p. 7)

The policies, institutions and processes box of the framework captures a vast array of phenomena. Institutions are public (government departments, state banks, parliaments, local governments, police, aid agencies), commercial (informal enterprises, formal businesses at local, national and international levels) and civic (local associations, religious groups, social movements and

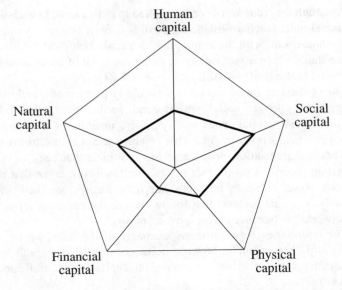

Note: The example displays a household that is high in social and natural capital, but low in human and financial capital, and moderately endowed with physical capital. For making comparisons between households, assets always need to follow the same order round the perimeter of the pentagon. Then the area of the pentagon gives an approximate 'view' of the relative asset endowment of the social units that are being compared.

Source: Ellis (2000, p. 49).

Figure 8.3   Plotting asset status on a pentagon

NGOs). Processes can be formal and informal and include laws, policies, social norms, 'rules of the game' and incentives. They maintain and transform how institutions and individuals behave and embody a complex set of power relations between classes, genders, age groups, ethnic, religious and regional social formations and countries. They have a great influence on the ways in which households can use their assets.

Livelihood frameworks offer many potential benefits: they permit an analysis of how people survive, prosper or decline that incorporates the complexities of their lives and does not simply see them as 'small farmers' or 'self-employed businessmen'; it recognizes the agency of poor people in setting goals and choosing strategies for their achievement; it appreciates that life is not stable and steady but involves risks and shocks; it recognizes the value of assets that have often been neglected, particularly human and social capital. It is not unproblematic, however, and although there is not space to explore criticisms here the reader should be aware of some of the major criticisms.

- Although the framework can be applied to individuals, households and spatial units (such as village or ward) it is most commonly applied to the household, with the assumption that households can be identified, are stable, share assets and agree on strategy. All of these assumptions can be challenged (see Ellis, 2000, pp. 18–21).

- The concept of social capital is particularly problematic as this can be applied to 'private' social networks and 'public' norms. Where household 'social capital' ends and 'policies, institutions and processes' begin remains unclear. And what of anti-social capital, forms of networking, association or adverse incorporation that seek to damage certain groups of people? Critics of the framework argue that it mentions power relations but does not fully incorporate them into the analysis. In the sections that follow we use the narrower term 'social networks' as our focus is on 'private' networks.

- The boundaries between many elements of the framework are ambiguous. For example, at what point does physical capital become infrastructure; is urban land physical capital or natural capital or both?

- The framework is very instrumentalist. As well as providing a means of making a living, assets can give meaning to a person's world and be a central component of personal identity.[4]

The Livelihood Framework and Financial Services for Poor People

Using the livelihood framework to understand how poor people use financial services, and identifying ways in which interventions in financial markets might assist poor people, offers a number of benefits. Figure 8.4 shows the change in a household's asset pentagon over time. For those with a specialist interest in financial services the framework draws together nine lessons that have emerged from empirical research on microfinance over the last 20 years.

1. *The agency of poor people.* It has long been recognized that credit is fungible when it enters the household in the form of money; that is, it may be used for purposes for which it was not intended. When poor people's livelihoods are understood as being multidimensional and they are seeking to achieve a range of objectives, it is easier to understand why attempts to control what poor people do with credit are generally futile. Poor people need to be given opportunities to change their strategies rarther than coerced to do so.[5]

2. *Household diversity and optimal investments.* Livelihood approaches confirm the heterogeneity of households due to their different endowments of assets and their differing dynamics and strategies. Hence it is easy to

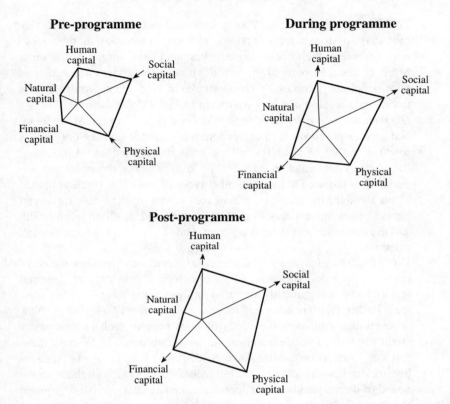

Note: For explanatory text see Box 8.1.

Source: Adapted from DFID Sustainable Livelihoods Guidance Sheets, 2.3 (www.livelihoods. org).

Figure 8.4   Change in a household's asset pentagon over time

recognize why approaches which have sought to identify 'optimal' in-vestments, usually in the form of particular physical assets such as livestock, ploughs, machinery and so on, and provide them on credit have tended to flounder and not produce the expected results.

3.   *Household financial capital portfolios.* Like other types of capital, finan-cial capital is best understood as a portfolio: poor people seek to build a range of places within which they can both save and acquire credit. They are therefore likely to make use of a number of savings mechanisms and borrow from a range of sources, depending on how these fit the strategies they are employing.

4. *The relative risk to assets.* Poor people will only use financial service providers to store wealth (savings, pensions, insurance) if their risk–return profile or their convenience makes them more attractive than other forms of asset. In parts of the world where such services are available, poor people still choose to create stocks in kind (goats, grain, bricks, trees, land) because of a lack of trust in financial organizations.

5. *Overemphasis on investment in physical and natural assets.* Much financial service provision for poor people has assumed that the only assets worth investing in are physical and natural, such as land, machinery, irrigation systems and so on. Livelihood approaches recognize the importance of the need to invest in other types of asset also (such as human assets through, for example, school fees loans) or to be able to protect human assets against shocks due to sickness and death, through health and life insurance and funeral schemes, and to cope with old age through pensions.

6. *Vulnerability and finance.* While financial services can be a key means of coping with risks, stresses and shocks, formal providers of financial services have not generally ventured into providing these kinds of services. Rather this has been left to informal providers (see above). New products that can meet the needs of poor people, such as emergency credit products, health insurance and so on are needed.[6] Without these services, poor people often have to dispose of other assets, such as livestock or household assets, on unfavourable terms to fulfil these needs. Speed of delivery and ease of access are the key characteristics required to address the supply side of this market.

7. *The substitutability of financial capital.* Financial capital can be made available to poor people relatively easily and (in dynamic economies at least) may enable them to make rapid and beneficial adjustments to their livelihood strategies. As a result financial service specialists can point to the need for an analysis of how to develop appropriate financial services as a component of any development programme.

8. *Collateral.* Conventional banking has denied poor people access to financial services because of its insistence on land or property as collateral. Group-based lending systems have enabled poor people to use their social networks as a form of collateral through joint liability contracts. Livelihood frameworks enable the range of ways by which loans can be secured to be recognized: physical capital (jewellery, radios, furniture, land), human capital (payments from labour at source) and social networks.

9. *Social and political relationships and finance.* Social and political relationships are important to the ways in which people gain access to finance. Social relationships enable access to reciprocal borrowing from

friends and relations or social networks that makes it possible for them to join ROSCAs or ASCAs. The formal political dimension of these relationships has been one of the reasons why past subsidized credit has tended to go to the better off because of the patronage relationships which they have used to gain access to this resource. An analysis of the social and political context is therefore very important in considering how financial service development can take place and whether new services can be based on pre-existing social networks, or whether it is necessary to create new local level institutions. Such analyses can also help scheme designers identify in advance those poor people who are likely to be excluded from new financial services.

Apart from enabling the role of financial services to be better understood in the context of the wider livelihood strategies that poor people engage in and the vulnerabilities they face, this approach also enables financial services to be seen as an integral part of all economic and social development activities rather than a discrete or 'add on' component.

4.   CASE STUDIES FROM INDIA AND KENYA

This section provides case studies from recent research in India and Kenya that demonstrate empirically the way in which poor people use financial services to support their livelihood strategies. The Indian evidence indicates the diverse range of services that poor households used and the complexity of the strategies that they employed to meet their livelihood needs. The evidence from Kenya highlights that the type of financial intermediary also matters. User-owned financial systems were popular because of the assistance these offered in meeting a wider range of livelihood needs and helping to protect against shocks.

The Financial Life of the Poor in North India[7]

Researchers in north India studied the financial behaviours and preferences of 49 carefully selected urban and rural households over a 12-month period (Patole and Ruthven, 2002; Ruthven, 2002; Ruthven and Kumar, 2002). Half of the sample lived in Delhi slums and half in two villages in Koraon, Allahabad District, Uttar Pradesh. Interviews occurred every fortnight so that 'financial diaries' could be constructed of all of the formal and informal financial services that were used.[8] This methodology permitted deep insights into the financial lives of these people and uncovered complex behaviours that surveys do not hear about. In addition, 82 households living adjacent to the sample were interviewed, together with a wide number of key informants (moneylenders, bank staff, district officials, microfinance institutions – MFIs).

First, all of the households, however poor, had money which they needed to manage and actively sought out financial services to do this. The quest for services was not simply to meet present needs but also had a strategic orientation towards the future: people joined new MFIs and entered into social relationships with the idea that useful financial services could be reached through this contact to meet future needs. Households had different goals, ranging from bare survival to becoming wealthy, but they all had strategies and planned for the future in some way.

Second, vulnerability was a key contextual factor in shaping the behaviours and the services to which they gained access. Commonly, people needed access to loans to overcome both anticipated problems (such as a lack of food during the lean season) and unanticipated problems (such as medical expenses, loss of employment or funeral costs). Knowing that at times access to capitals would be needed on a creditor basis – in cash or in kind – had a profound influence on the portfolios of financial services that our respondents developed.

Thirdly, respondents used a wide array of devices to get credit and to store wealth. In all, 48 different types of financial service were used by interviewees: the 'average' household used eight different devices and engaged in 22 'deals' during the year. In effect, they ran a portfolio of financial services to pursue a variety of planned activities and to react to unplanned events.

To develop this range of services, all of the different capitals had to be related to each other but also highlighted the particular importance of social relationships in securing livelihoods. Financial services for poor people in India remain closely embedded in social networks. All of our urban and 86 per cent of our rural households borrowed from friends, neighbours and relatives during the year (on average Rs.6100[9] per household in urban areas and Rs.7600 in rural areas over the year). More than 50 per cent of households made informal loans during the year. The costs which people bear (for which they require finance) are also closely tied to social relations. For most poor people, life cycle events (marriages and funerals) are the greatest expense they ever bear. In Koraon, a third of expenditure among the 'poorest' was on ceremonies, a much higher proportion than other groups. Owing to the high sums involved, such families cannot afford to borrow on interest or repay over tight schedules. The most popular way to finance such events is through reciprocal gifts. Households accumulate 'savings' in the form of gifts to family members over several years. When their turn comes (to bury a parent or marry a daughter) they 'draw down' these gifts, receiving back what they gave plus an increment. Half of our rural respondents gave and received an average of Rs.4450 in this way during the research year.

Smoothing consumption and cashflow also depended considerably on trust and reputation with local shopkeepers and service providers. Credit was taken from shopkeepers in the form of goods (60 per cent of urban and 50 per cent of rural households) and 57 per cent of our rural group took services on credit (for example, for a doctor's consultation, tractor hire). Particularly noticeable in the more remote part of Allahabad District where some of our rural households were based was the exchange of goods and services 'in kind', and the lower use of financial services, because of the lower levels of monetization of the economy.

In urban areas the links between the human capital, deployed in the labour market, and financial services were important. This was particularly the case for women in domestic service who often took advances on wages and, much less often, sometimes left wages with employers: in effect the employer became a moneyguard. Although poor, some women who worked as domestics had bank accounts that their employers had opened for them. The insistence of the formal banks that borrowers must have collateral (that is, a land title) was a major obstacle to their outreach and only five of our 48 households, all among the wealthiest in the sample, received bank loans.

Making savings through physical capital, especially jewellery, natural capital (goats, cattle and pigs) or social networks (getting friends to mind it) were the commonest savings devices for poorer households. In addition, poor households 'hid' an average of Rs.1800 in their home over the year: cash-on-hand to deal with unexpected needs. The research revealed big differences between the portfolios of the poorest people and those of the 'better off' (these were non-poor but not wealthy – they lived in slums and villages in undeveloped regions). The poorest have little or no access to formal banks, insurance or other services; they commonly have an urgent need for finance which they are unable to meet, so have to 'do without' (for example, do without health services, miss meals or not take part in a social event); they are most likely to have to go to moneylenders and pay 'high' rates of interest.[10]

Financing Livelihoods through User-owned Financial Mechanisms in Central Kenya

Research has been carried out on the financial landscape in the highland tea and coffee growing areas near to the market town of Karatina in Central Kenya (Johnson, 2004). The results of a supply side survey of formal financial service providers in Karatina indicated that formal sector banks, non-bank financial institutions (NBFIs) and parastatals accounted for 80 per cent of deposits by value, 55 per cent of loans by value and 49 per cent of savings accounts. Microfinance organizations accounted for 1 per cent of savings, 4 per cent of loans and 2 per cent of accounts. Savings and Credit Cooperatives (SACCOs) along with NGO-promoted ASCAs accounted for 20 per cent of deposits, 28 per cent of loans and 49 per cent of accounts. The demand-side survey indicated that users were likely to make use of a wider range of savings services than sources of loans. Furthermore ROSCAs were the most frequently used savings service, followed by bank accounts and then SACCOs. On the loan side, SACCOs were the most frequently used, followed by loans from friends and relatives. These data demonstrate the importance of both SACCOs and informal group-based mechanisms in financial intermediation.

User-owned mechanisms – both formally registered SACCOs and informal group-based systems –therefore appear to merit further investigation. While the importance of SACCOs in part reflects the historical position of coffee as a cash crop in the area, there were new areas of SACCO development in the transport and business sectors during the 1990s. Moreover there were wide-spread reports that both ROSCAs and ASCAs had also increased in number in the period since 1997; and in particular that their use had increased among men, while in the past they had mainly been associated with women.

This trend can be explained by the following factors. First, it is important to note the general deterioration in the Kenyan economy since 1997, precipitated by drought, poor economic management and the absence of aid flows. Against this background lump sum payments that men used to receive from coffee or other business ventures have declined. This has driven them into ROSCAs and ASCAs that enable flows of income to be converted into lump sum payments required for school fees, investments and other expenditure for which they tend to have responsibility.

Second, users see borrowing from the banks as increasingly difficult. Government fiscal policy has used treasury bills to finance spending and this has been an important factor in producing high and volatile bank lending rates during the 1990s. These have acted as a disincentive to borrowers when business opportunities are higher risk. In this context borrowers have become increasingly wary of mortgaging land for fear they might lose it.

Third, user-owned financial mechanisms offer products with characteristics that are more appropriate to the circumstances people face. In these mechanisms, the member's entitlement to a loan is usually very clear and based on a multiple of savings. In the words of an informant: 'nobody is there to deny you a loan … it is not like a bank, because in a SACCO you have a right but in a bank it is not a right but a privilege'. Second, members set the interest rate on loans, which can be as high as 10 per cent per month in an ASCA. Members know that, not only will the interest rate not change without their knowing or voting for it, but also the interest they are paying will accrue to them as dividends at the end of the year. This contrasts strongly with the volatility of the interest rates in the banks in the 1990s and people also recognize that they are paying themselves for the service rather than a third party. Third, when circumstances arise which result in repayment difficulties, members know that they will have a range of options in dealing with the situation. In SACCOs, loan products include school fees and emergency loans which can be used to cater for a crisis. In informal groups, members have the opportunity to explain themselves ('voice') which can result in negotiating an alternative payment schedule; or, in some cases, the member may be given an additional loan to overcome the circumstances. Members can also appeal to others in the group to assist them with a payment, or swap places with them in the order to receive the money from a ROSCA. Fourth, the member is usually risking only his or her existing savings, future income (from salaries or cash crops) or possibly household items – land is not at risk.

In this research it became clear that the social support that members could gain access to via the group was also very important. As one woman astutely remarked: 'If I take my money to the bank then when I have a problem, who will help me?' The example of a women's group in Karatina demonstrates why she felt this:

> Three women were interviewed who were members of a group of 90 business-women in Karatina. The group runs a merry-go-round and a welfare fund. The welfare fund is Kshs250[11] per month that is banked and the merry-go-round is Kshs1000 that is balloted and given to nine people at each meeting. To join it is necessary to have three guarantors in the group and new members must now make a non-refundable contribution equivalent to the average value of the group's funds. They described the assistance a member would get in case of a problem. For example, in the case of being admitted to hospital the group will give you Kshs4000. If a member dies then they will bury the member and contribute Kshs8000 if it is a member, their husband or child. They described with great pride how, when a single mother in the group had recently died, they bought the coffin, hired the vehicles themselves to go to the funeral, and paid off the hospital bill. Indeed, members can be fined if they are selected as representatives to attend a funeral and do not turn up. One of the members commented that the group supports you during happiness and sadness, morally and financially.

Women were significantly more likely to use ROSCAs than men, while young educated men were significantly more likely to borrow from friends or relatives. Women argued that men were not vulnerable to shame as a social sanction enforcing repayment in the same way as women. This is part of the explanation why ROSCAs are a lower cost financial intermediation mecha-nism for men than women. It also became clear that young men are particularly excluded from the financial market because they not only lack collateral with which to gain access to banks but they have not been socialized in ways that enable them to comply with social sanctions. If unmarried, they cannot gain access to such mechanisms via a wife either.

This case study therefore indicates the importance of user-owned informal group systems in terms of the way that they enable a wider range of livelihood needs to be met, particularly through the access to support they offer in times of crisis.

5. CONCLUSIONS

This chapter has reviewed the evidence on informal financial systems to demonstrate their diversity and complexity. This evidence also suggests that the people who use them have a wide range of financial service needs. Since poor people by definition have little money, their ability to manage it effectively using these systems is even more important. Rutherford's analysis of how these systems enable poor people to 'save up', 'save down' and 'save through' presents a holistic device for analysing the patterns of cash flow that these informal services deliver and suggests means through which new services might mimic these devices.

The development of livelihood analysis frameworks in the wider rural development literature contributes a further analytical context in which to analyse the financial service behaviour of poor people. This, allied to the adoption of qualitative research methods that yield detailed data on 'what' poor people do, provides insights that aid understanding and have policy relevance. Empirical work confirms that poor people seek out financial services for a range of different reasons – to accumulate financial capital or borrow for investment, consumption or risk management – and, that they do this to meet present and future needs. Commonly, this entails managing a portfolio of informal and, sometimes, formal financial relationships. Poor people need financial services that help them to manage the opportunities and problems of their lives, and not only agricultural or microenterprise loans.

The livelihood approach also enables the way in which poor people use the combination of assets and relationships that they have to be recognized. In particular, social networks are central to the access to informal financial services, such as loans from neighbours or membership of ROSCAs. These, in turn, enable social networks to be extended and new possibilities for financial relationships to be developed. Where financial services are not available or reliable, storing wealth in physical or natural forms becomes more likely.

Both of our case studies, which present data from very different contexts, show that informal financial services remain most important for poorer people despite state and non-governmental activities. The flexibility and convenience of the informal sector is something that both government and commercial providers find hard to match. However informal financial services are not equally accessible to all poor people and some, especially the very poor, those who are unable to be economically active (such as the elderly) and those who experience social exclusion (such as women and scheduled castes), find it as hard to gain access to informal financial services as to formal services.

In conclusion, livelihoods frameworks are useful for gaining an understanding of the ways in which poor people construct complex portfolios of financial services to meet present and potential future needs. They recognize the agency of poor people in ways that the supply-led analyses of the past could not envisage.

NOTES

1. It must be observed that these mechanisms are not available to that minority of the poor who are not economically active and whose 'flow' of income is dependent on others, for example, for transfers, gifts and alms, which means that even micro-savings are not feasible.
2. The reader will observe that in effect this is a current account with an overdraft facility, a service that many better off people take for granted.
3. To try and summarize these differences in a nutshell: Ellis is concerned about the normative and ecological notion of 'sustainable' and prefers the idea of 'secure' livelihoods; Murray prefers to drop the normative element and emphasize the diversity of livelihoods and that they do not fit neatly into a rural–urban divide. He, along with many others, is concerned that the framework does not deal adequately with power and social relationships.
4. See Bebbington (1999) for a discussion of a broader view of assets and their roles in people's lives than is usual in livelihood analysis.
5. A classic example of failed coercion is the provision of fertilizer to 'small farmers' to increase their productivity. As one of the authors observed in the 1990s in Malawi, this often led to the recipients of 'rural finance' selling some of their fertilizer to local estates at a discount. The cash received was then used to buy food, to maintain human capital essential for crop production, and invested in small-scale trading. The recipient incurred additional costs in discounting the price of fertilizer and managing the substitution. The local estate received a subsidy from poor people!
6. A notable exception is SANASA in Sri Lanka. Primary cooperatives provide members with small, emergency loans at short notice. This is a profitable product that is greatly appreciated by poor people.
7. For more details of this work see O. Ruthven (2002), 'Money matters: uncovering the financial life of the poor in north India' on the IDPM website (www.man.ac.uk/idpm). Also see Patole and Ruthven (2002), Ruthven and Kumar (2002) and Ruthven (2002).
8. For the full text of the 'diaries', visit www.man.ac.uk/idpm/research/financeanddevelopment.
9. The exchange rate was approximately US$1 = Rs.43.
10. The rates that moneylenders charge are higher than friends and neighbours (usually interest-free) and banks charge. However, given the moneylenders' costs and risks, the three moneylenders we studied did not charge excessive rates (see Ruthven, 2002).
11. Kshs73 = US$1.

REFERENCES

Adams, D. and J.D. von Pischke (1992), 'Microenterprise credit programs: déjà vu', *World Development*, **20**(10).

Adams, D.W. (1994), 'Using contracts to analyze informal finance', in F.J.A. Bouman and O. Hospes (eds), *Financial Landscapes Reconstructed*, Boulder, Colorado: Westview Press.

Adams, D.W. and D.A. Fitchett (eds) (1992), *Informal Finance in Low-Income Countries*, Boulder, Colorado: Westview Press.

Aleem, I. (1990), 'Imperfect information, screening and the costs of informal lending: a study of the rural credit market in Pakistan', *World Bank Economic Review*, **4**(3), 329–49.

Ardener, S. (1964), 'The comparative study of rotating credit associations', *Journal of the Royal Anthropological Institute*, **94**(1), 201–29.

Ardener, S. (1995), 'Women making money go round: Roscas revisited', in S. Ardener and S. Burman (eds), *Money-Go-Rounds: The Importance of Rotating Savings and Credit Associations for Women*, Oxford/Washington, DC: Berg, p. 326.

Ardener, S. and S. Burman (eds) (1995), *Money-Go-Rounds: The Importance of Rotating Savings and Credit Associations for Women*, Oxford/Washington DC, Berg.

Aredo, D. (1993), 'The Iddir: a study of an indigenous informal financial institution in Ethiopia', *Savings and Development*, **1**, 77–89.

Bebbington, T. (1999), 'Capitals and capabilities: a framework for analysing peasant viability, rural livelihoods and poverty', *World Development*, **27**(12), 2021–44.

Bhaduri, A. (1977), 'On the formation of usurious interest rates in backward agriculture', *Cambridge Journal of Economics*.

Bouman, F.J.A. (1995), 'Rotating and accumulating savings and credit associations: a development perspective', *World Development*, **23**(3).

Bouman, F.J.A. and O. Hospes (eds) (1994), *Financial Landscapes Reconstructed*, Boulder, Colorado: Westview Press.

Carney, D. (1998) 'Implementing the sustainable rural livelihoods approach', in D. Carney (ed.), *Sustainable Rural Livelihoods: What Contribution Can We Make?*, London: DFID, pp. 3–23.

Dreze, J. and A. Sen, (1989), *Hunger and Public Action*, Oxford: Clarendon Press.

Ellis, F. (2000), *Rural Livelihoods and Diversity in Developing Countries*, Oxford: Clarendon Press.

Geertz, C. (1962), 'Rotating savings and credit associations: the middle rung in economic development', *Economic Development and Cultural Change*, **10**(3).

Ghatak, M. (2000), 'Screening by the company you keep : joint liability lending and the peer selection effect', *Economic Journal*, **110**(July), 601–31.

Harriss, B. (1983), 'Money and commodities: their interaction in a rural Indian setting', in J.D. Von Pischke, D.W. Adams and G. Donald (eds), *Rural Financial Markets in Developing Countries*, Baltimore: Johns Hopkins University Press.

Hospes, O. (1995), 'Women's differential ise of ROSCAs in Indonesia', in S. Ardener and S. Burman (eds), *Money-Go-Rounds: The Importance of Rotating Savings and Credit Associations for Women*, Oxford/Washington, DC: Berg.

ILO (1972), *Employment, Incomes and Equality: A Strategy for Increasing Productive Employment in Kenya*, Geneva: International Labour Organisation.

Johnson, S. (2001), 'From fragmentation to embeddedness: towards an institutional analysis of financial markets', FDRP working paper no. 29, IDPM, University of Manchester.

Johnson, S. (2004), 'Milking the elephant: financial markets as real markets in Kenya', *Development and Change*, **35**(2), 249–75.

McGregor, A. (1998), 'Credit, debt and morals: local and universial models in development practice in South Asia', mimeo.

Murray, C. (2001), 'Livelihoods research: conceptual and methodological issues', CPRC Background Paper 5, IDPM, University of Manchester.

Nelson, N. (1995), 'The Kiambu group: a successful women's ROSCA in Mathare Valley, Nairobi (1971 to 1990)', in S. Ardener and S. Burman (eds), *Money-Go-Rounds: The Importance of Rotating Savings and Credit Associations for Women*. Oxford/Washington, DC: Berg.

Olsen, W. (1994), 'Distress sales and rural credit: evidence from an Indian village case study', in T. Lloyd and O. Morrissey (eds), *Poverty, Inequality and Rural Development*, Basingstoke: Macmillan.

Patole, M. and O. Ruthven (2002), 'Metro moneylenders – microcredit providers for Delhi's poor', *Small Enterprise Development*, **13**(2), 36–45.

Platteau, J.-P. and A. Abraham (1987), 'An inquiry into quasi-credit contracts: the role of reciprocal credit and interlinked deals in small-scale fishing communities', *Journal of Development Studies*, **23**, 461–90.

Rakodi, C. (2002), 'A livelihoods approach – conceptual issues and definitions', in C. Rakodi and T. Lloyd-Jones (eds), *Urban Livelihoods: A People-Centred Approach to Reducing Poverty*, London: Earthscan, pp. 3–22.

Rutherford, S. (1997), *A Critical Typology of Financial Services for the Poor*, London: ACTIONAID.

Rutherford, S. (2000), *The Poor and Their Money*, New Delhi: OUP.

Rutherford, S., M. Harper and J. Grierson (2002), 'Support for livelihood strategies', in C. Rakodi and T. Lloyd-Jones (eds), *Urban Livelihoods: A People-Centred Approach to Reducing Poverty*, London: Earthscan, pp. 112–32.

Ruthven, O. (2002), 'Money mosaics: financial choice and strategy in a West Delhi squatter settlement', *Journal of International Development*, **14**, 249–71.

Ruthven, O. and S. Rumar (2002), 'Fine-grain finance: financial choice and strategy among the poor in rural North India', Finance and Development Working Paper 57, IDPM, Manchester.

Ruthven, O. and S. Rumar (2003), 'Making and breaking poverty in Koraon, Uttar Pradesh', paper presented at the conference 'Staying Poor: Chronic Poverty and Development Policy', University of Manchester, 7–9 April (www.chronicpoverty.org).

Scoones, I. (1998), 'Sustainable rural livelihoods: a framework for analysis. Sussex', IDS Working Paper no. 72.

Sen, A. (1999), *Development as Freedom*, Oxford: Clarendon Press.

Sinha, S. and M. Lipton (1999), 'Damaging fluctuations, risk and poverty: a review', background paper for World Development Report 2000, World Bank: Washington DC.

Velez-Ibanez, C.G. (1983), *Bonds of Mutual Trust: The Cultural Systems of Rotating Credit Associations among Urban Mexicans and Chicanos*, New Brunswick, NJ: Rutgers University Press.

Von Pischke, J.D., D. Adams and G. Donald (eds) (1983), *Rural Financial Markets in Developing Countries: Their Use and Abuse*, Baltimore: Johns Hopkins University Press.

Wai, U.T. (1957), 'Interest rates outside the organised money markets of underdeveloped countries', *IMF Staff Papers*, **6**, 80–142.

9. Finance for the poor: the way forward?

Thankom Arun, David Hulme, Imran Matin and Stuart Rutherford[1]

1. INTRODUCTION

Since the 1980s, microfinancial services have generated considerable interest among academics, donors and development practitioners as an alternative to the documented failures of government rural credit assistance to reach low-income households (Hulme and Mosley, 1996; Johnson and Rogaly, 1997). The failures are attributed to causes such as urban biased credit allocation, higher transaction costs, interest rate restrictions, high default rates and corrupt practices. The reasons for poor loan recovery are related to inappropriate design features, leading to incentive problems, and politicization that made borrowers view credit as political largesse (Lipton *et al.*, 1997). These failures stimulated a set of innovative financial institutions in several corners of the world which began to prosper and attract attention, especially in Bolivia, Bangladesh and Indonesia. These microfinance institutions (MFIs) share a commitment to serving clients that have been excluded from the formal banking sector.

The development of the microfinance sector is based on the assumption that the poor possess the capacity to implement income-generating economic activities but are limited by lack of access to and inadequate provision of savings, credit and insurance facilities. This approach also breaks from the directed credit strategies by reducing the government involvement and by paying close attention to the incentives that drive efficient performance (Morduch, 1999). The developments in microfinancial services have been based on a prototype delivery model that is considered the best answer to capture financial needs of the poor in various socioeconomic and institutional systems. However, after two decades of experience, a better understanding of the financial service preferences and behaviours of the poor and poorest is still needed to expand the scope of microfinance initiatives in addressing the concerns about welfare implications of MFIs (Morduch, 2000; Matin and Sinha, 1998; Gulli, 1998; Rutherford, 1999).

Following this introduction, Section 2 of the chapter explores the fallacy of the misconceptions regarding the poor and savings. Section 3 reviews the role of informal providers and mutual finance in relation to saving by the poor. Section 4 explores the recent microfinance initiatives in the formal sector, with the distinctiveness of MFIs and the possible welfare impacts of MFIs being discussed in section 5. Section 6 draws out the main conclusions of the chapter and highlights the importance of matching demand and supply initiatives in microfinance.

2. THE POOR AND SAVINGS

The popular conception about the inability of the poor to save is not true. The nature of the 'Lilliputian economy' in which the poor operate involves high levels of insecurity and risk that lead to the use by the poor of savings and credit mechanisms as substitutes for insurance (Platteau and Abraham, 1984; Alderman and Paxson, 1994; Fafchamps, 1995). The poor may save money as it goes out (keeping a few coins back from the housekeeping money) as well as when it comes in (deducting savings at source from wages or other income). Also *reciprocal lending*, which is very common among the poor, making up the bulk of financial transactions for poor people (Matin and Sinha, 1998; Dreze *et al.*, 1997), demonstrates the poor's capacity and willingness to save. However the idea behind savings is to get a large lump sum, which is not possible through their daily patterns of living. The interconnectedness of the roles of savings, credit and insurance leads one to think about the motivation behind savings which can be expected to be in broadly three categories of life cycle needs, emergencies and opportunities.

Life cycle needs such as childbirth, education, marriage, home-building, old age, funeral expenses, festivals and the desire to bequeath a lump sum to heirs vary from region to region. These can be anticipated as they require relatively large sums of money to be amassed. The amount of cash needed to meet such expenses is much larger than can normally be found in the household. Emergencies also create a sudden and unanticipated need for a large sum of money. Idiosyncratic emergencies such as sickness or injury, the death of a breadwinner, the loss of employment and theft, or the covariant emergencies such as war, floods, fires and cyclones, create a sudden need for more cash than can normally be found at home. There may be opportunities to invest in an existing or new business, to buy land or other productive assets, or to pay a bribe to get a permanent job.

Other than savings, the poor can obtain lump sums through selling assets, and through mortgage and pawn. In a large number of cases, poor people sell in advance assets that they do not currently have but expect to hold in the future, such as the sale of crops. The second method, mortgage and pawn, enables poor people to convert assets into cash and back again, which may not always be realized. However both these methods require the user to have a stock of wealth in the form of an asset of some sort, of which poor people often have very few. The saving method enables the poor to convert the small savings into lump sums through a variety of mechanisms such as savings deposit, loans and insurance. The savings strategy helps the poor to develop an asset base to protect against risks and shocks in the future. However the success of this strategy depends on the understanding of the informal arrangements that the poor themselves innovate and use varies from region to region.

The financial diaries[2] prepared by poor households in urban and rural areas in Bangladesh and in India reveal that the respondents patch together a wide array of informal financial arrangements with semi-formal and formal services. All households in the samples engage in money-managing practices and on average the Bangladeshi households push or pull through financial services and devices each year a sum of money ($839) equivalent to two-thirds of their annual cash income. In the Indian case, households enter a fresh financial arrangement (with a moneylender, money guard, savings club or formal provider, among others) on average every two weeks. In Bangladesh, among 42 households, 33 types of service or device have been used. These households see financial services as a day-to-day activity, neither as a right or privilege nor as a reward or enticement for engaging in some form of approved behaviour. These diaries reveal that poor people want reliable, convenient and flexible ways to store and retrieve cash and to turn their capacity to save into spending power, in the short, medium and long term on a continuing basis (Morduch and Rutherford, 2003).

This experience shows the fallacy of the prevalent conception that the poor in general cannot save. This leads to an overemphasis on the promotional role of financial services as credit for investment. The better conceptualizations of the poor as a heterogeneous group, of vulnerable households with complex livelihoods (Carney, 1998; Scoones, 1998; Ellis, 2000), explores the need for microfinancial services to be redesigned as client-centred organizations to help the poor to be more likely to achieve the goals that they seek to achieve.

3. MUTUAL FINANCE, INFORMAL PROVIDERS AND SAVINGS

Credit can be provided in different forms and varied institutional arrangements such as standard loan or through different informal channels. Informal providers are a mixed group, such as moneylenders, pawnbrokers and traders, who have in common the fact that they provide unregistered sources of credit. The main sources of informal financial credit services are (i) lending by individuals on a non-profit (and often reciprocal) basis; (ii) direct but inter-mittent lending by individuals with a temporary surplus; (iii) lending by individuals specializing in lending, whether on the basis of their own funds or of intermediated funds; (iv) individuals who collect deposits or 'guard' money; and (v) group finance (for a detailed discussion on these various categories, see Matin *et al.*, 2002). Informal providers are ready to accept collateral in different forms that are unacceptable to formal providers. They are part of a localized scale of financial intermediation and have much better information regarding the activities and characteristics of borrowers.

The type of informal finance that makes the greatest contribution to addi-tive savings[3] is mutual finance: group-based or reciprocal financial services. Other than the mutual finance schemes, the level of intermediation is either absent or very localized for informal finance. Moneylenders normally rely on their own funds and do not accept receipts (Binswanger and Rosenzweig, 1984). The major attractions of mutual finance arrangements as effective financial intermediaries are (i) reciprocity, or the inbuilt provision of borrow-ing at short notice which serves as a kind of access to a liquidity-guaranteeing function which is especially important to business; (ii) being able to save in small instalments; (iii) provision of a disciplined environment for saving; (iv) convenience and absence of formalities; and (v) meeting liquidity prefer-ences by permitting savings to be hidden away from the demands of friends and relatives.

Getting access to a useful lump sum through building mutual savings is central to informal group finance schemes. In such arrangements, groups of individuals pool their savings and lend primarily to each other. The credit extended by group finance arrangements is the financial product which incor-porates the functions of savings and insurance, which the poor households tend to use to a greater extent than the non-poor. The two main methods of group financing are savings services provided by rotating savings and credit associations (ROSCAs,[4] where the case rotates evenly between all the group members), and accumulating savings and credit associations (ASCRAs, where some members borrow and others do not).

In ROSCAs, the equal periodic savings of every member are pooled to-gether and given to each member in turn. The number of poolings depends on the number of members and the cycle comes automatically to an end when each member has taken their turn. In an ASCRA, the pooled savings of the members may accumulate until such time as one or more members are willing to take them on loan. ROSCAs are often classified under informal credit and considered predominantly a means of acquiring indivisible con-sumer durables (Besley *et al.*, 1990). ASCRAs lack the clarity of ROSCAs, which demands more management skills to succeed. However ASCRAs can be put to uses like insurance more easily than ROSCAs, and manage intermediate savings over longer periods of time. The continuing prevalence and growth of these arrangements have negated the apprehension about the viability of these arrangements in the long run and Brink and Chavas (1991) show that these institutions are built on sound microeconomic foundations.

As mentioned elsewhere, credit often serves as an insurance substitute in informal finance.[5] However a substantial number of households, particularly the most poor, appear ill-equipped to handle risks even to a smaller extent (Alderman and Paxson, 1994; Morduch, 1997). Many of the risks faced by low-income households are insurable and it has been proved that well designed insurance products can have a significant development impact (Brown, 2001). Many of these mechanisms are costly: for instance, in rural India, households may sacrifice as much as 25 per cent of average income to reduce exposure to shocks. However insurance products which could reduce the vulnerability of poor people to negative income shocks, a salient dimension of the vicious circle in which the poorest are trapped, are a priority area for experiment and innovation (Mosley, 2001).

4. MICROFINANCE AND THE FORMAL PROVIDERS

The increasing levels of transaction costs in small-size loans have an impact on formal sector institutions in financing the poor, while the charging of a standardized price makes the transactions unattractive to the poor as well. However in many countries (for example, Kenya, Malawi and Sri Lanka) the post offices run savings schemes that are widely used by low-income households, and in some countries (such as Sri Lanka and the Philippines) formal banks engage in pawnbroking. Recently certain examples emerging from different countries indicate that the formal sector is trying to develop new methods to link with microfinance initiatives. Here we review three such schemes form Indonesia, Bangladesh and India.

The Bank Rakyat Indonesia's Unit Desa (UD) Scheme

The Bank Rakyat Indonesia (BRI) is notable for its success in delivering conventional banking services to low-income clients. In 1984, BRI established the Unit Desa (UD) or village bank system to reach the rural clientele. The scheme operates as a separate profit centre and has received a high degree of autonomy of operation from BRI. The scheme has developed products that have enabled it to work profitably with low-income households and it is more convenient for bank clients. The flexibility in saving services is an important aspect of the UD scheme, which offers convenient banking hours, a friendly atmosphere, unconstrained withdrawals and a range of incentives including bonuses and raffles. Deposit mobilization has been very successful under this scheme which relies on agents who have extensive knowledge about borrowers and local systems. A client may also take out loans with a range of convenient terms and repayment frequencies. The Unit Desa scheme also proved highly resilient to the shock of Asia's financial crises in the late 1990s.

The Gono Bima (Popular Insurance) Scheme of Bangladesh

In Bangladesh, Delta Insurance, a large private insurance company, launched a *Gono Bima* (popular insurance) in 1994. It markets a life insurance product that has been designed to reach the poor in large numbers and has clearly benefited from the experience of MFIs like Grameen Bank. The product is a ten-year contractual savings account with fixed monthly premium payments leading to a one-time lump sum payout at maturity, along with accumulated interest.

The insurance element is provided by the guarantee that the death of the insured at any time during the term will trigger a full payout as if the term had been completed. The bureaucratic procedures such as medical examinations are minimal in the delivery mechanism of this scheme. Gono Bima rents simple office accommodation in rural and urban centres staffed by field workers who collect the premium from customers arranged in groups in the villages and slums. The smallest monthly premium accepted is about two dollars. The office then relends the premium income to its customers in loans whose terms are similar to those of the Grameen Bank. However the scheme is now facing major problems because of administrative problems that threaten its financial viability.

Self-help Groups (SHGs) in India

The SHG programme in India, a distinctive microfinance programme which is based on the existing banking network in delivering financial services to the poor, is a recent phenomenon (Arun and Mosley, 2003). The Reserve Bank of India (RBI) has instructed all commercial banks to participate and extend finance to SHGs, extending this to regional rural ranks (RRBs) and cooperative banks in 1993. As in most group lending, peer pressure operates among the members and no group member may receive a loan while any member is in default on their loan instalments. Also the members are aware that, to obtain loans from banks, they have to produce evidence of credit history which could develop through the repeated rotations of savings to mutual credit among the members. The groups themselves, however, clearly build on the traditional institution of the ROSCA, and provide access to both savings and credit for the asset-less poor. Such groups are eligible for loans from banks, usually accompanied by training, after six months of savings and credit operations.

The formal financial institutions extend loans to highly performing SHGs[6] in certain multiples (mostly in the range of one to four times) of the accumulated savings of each SHG. The RBI has allowed banks to decide on the interest rates to be charged to the SHGs. These loans are sanctioned to the SHG as a whole and do not contain any instructions on disbursement among the members. The groups will prioritize the purposes for which loans are to be given to its members, which vary from emergency and consumption needs to acquisition of income-generating assets. The group is collectively responsible for the repayments as well. The individual members maintain their own accounts with SHG; banks or NGOs do not have direct contact with individual members.

5. WELFARE IMPACTS OF MFIs

MFIs are different from small-scale commercial and informal financial institutions and from large government-sponsored schemes. MFIs are independent of government and/or have a high degree of autonomy from bureaucrats and politicians. The primary clientele of these institutions are those who face severe barriers in gaining access to financial services. There is also an acceptance that what households need is access to credit, not cheap credit. Some of these MFIs are financially successful, boast repayment rates above 95 per cent and constantly check the levels of subsidy and inefficiency. The real innovations in these schemes are the concepts such as a group lending contract and incentives for loan repayments. Repayment incentives may include several devices, such as larger repeat loans, access to loans for other group members and cashback facilities for clients who repay on time. Many MFIs permit people to acquire useful lump sums through loans and allow borrowers to repay the loan in small, frequent and manageable instalments, further supported by quick access to larger repeat loans. The flexibility in repayment options is an important feature of MFI operations which allows borrowers to repay out of existing income, freeing the borrower to invest the loan according to their needs.

The studies have shown the positive impacts of microfinance initiatives on socioeconomic variables such as children's schooling, household nutrition status and women's empowerment (Johnson and Rogaly, 1997). The ways in which financial services affect household welfare and food security can be grouped into income generation, cost efficient management of assets and liabilities, and diversion of use for immediate consumption needs (Zeller,

1996). Income generation decreases the cost of income smoothing by allowing households to engage in more risky but also more profitable activities. However some studies have argued that there is a significant difference between income generation and reducing poverty (Wright, 1999). The use to which income is put is an important variable in determining the poverty which is neither linear nor static. The second and third methods are related to decreasing the cost of consumption smoothing through allowing households to hold and retain better combinations of assets and liabilities or through increasing liquidity for direct consumption smoothing.

However there are apprehensions about the capacity of microfinance institutions to provide services and products for the poorest of the poor category (Hulme and Mosley, 1996). The real challenge in serving them is to identify the beneficiaries from various categories, such as financial services alone, non-financial services along with finance, and non-financial services before participating in market-oriented finance (Meyer, 2002). Hulme (2000) has further argued that, outside Bangladesh, the MFIs have not even scratched the surface of poverty. The exclusion of the poorest is probably driven by the emphasis on credit delivery by MFIs, which pay little attention to the needs of the poorest regarding savings.

6.   THE WAY FORWARD: BALANCING SUPPLY AND DEMAND

Although the microcredit developments of the 1970s and 1980s contributed to the understanding of poverty reduction, the emphasis is shifting from the microcredit–poverty alleviation equation to one that recognizes the intrinsic importance of building sustainable financial systems that offer a wide-ranging menu of financial services, including savings and insurance, to poor people. For instance, in Bangladesh, studies have identified the limitations of the horizontal expansion of a single service which leaves a large range of other needs of existing clients and new markets unmet (Chaudhury and Matin, 2002). Along with the loan provision, opportunities for opening savings accounts and deposit services are especially important for the poor. As we explained earlier, the mobilization of the savings of the poor requires an understanding of the nature of such savings, which may be tiny and temporary surpluses that accrue to the household with high frequency and seasonality.

The failure of MFI to attract the poorest of the poor may be due to their limited understanding of the limitations of their current products and the possible innovations which could be made to make products relevant to the needs of the poorest. The majority of studies have focused on the demand-side forces and found that not all categories of the poor can make good use of the services. However the demand-side constraints are to be seen along with the supply-side limitations, such as the limited nature of the service provision (Arun and Hulme, 2003). It could be argued that better product design and delivery methods would alter demand in ways that deepen outreach. CGAP (1998) has assessed the relative emphasis that existing MFIs place on (a) identifying and reaching the poor, (b) attracting the poor and (c) discouraging or excluding the non-poor. The study shows that most emphasis is placed on identifying and reaching the poor and the least on attracting the poor, which lies at the centre of the financial service outreach arguments.

Diverse and flexible financial services can provide positive incentives to attract the poorest and reduce the likelihood of their exclusion.[7] It is argued that the provision of a wide range of financial services will fulfil the needs of clients, improve outreach depth, and enhance the access to sources of funding. The first microfinance revolution took a supply-side perspective and showed that the poor are bankable. The second revolution highlighted demand-side concerns to meet the complex livelihood needs of the poor. It is also important to recognize the enhanced interest among the formal sector to engage in microfinance provisions, at least in certain countries. There is a need to improve the design and outreach of MFIs on a continuous basis and to put these institutions in a perspective which matches demand and supply concerns.

NOTES

1. The main ideas presented in this paper are based on two earlier works: I. Matin, D. Hulme and S. Rutherford (1999), 'Finance for the poor and poorest: deepening understanding to improve provision', Finance and Development Working Paper No. 9, IDPM, University of Manchester; I. Matin, D. Hulme and S. Rutherford (2002), 'Finance for the poor: from microcredit to microfinancial services', *Journal of International Development*, **14**, 273–94.
2. These financial diaries were collected by researchers from the Institute for Development Policy and Management (IDPM), University of Manchester in 1999–2001. Financial diaries, each covering a full year, were prepared by poor, very poor and near-poor households through the help of two-weekly visits by researchers.
3. Additive savings are savings which would not have been mobilized by the formal sector in the absence of the informal.
4. The four main ways in which ROSCA users can decide the order in which a lump sum is taken are by prior agreement, by agreement at each round, by lottery and by bidding for the lump sum.
5. Morduch (1997).
6. The performance of SHGs who have been in existence for at least six months has been evaluated on the basis of a set of factors identified in the checklist of the National Bank for Agriculture and Rural Development (NABARD), such as loan recoveries, nature and participation of group meetings, accumulated savings and maintenance of accounts.
7. In Sri Lanka, for example, the Federation of Thrift and Credit Cooperatives (SANASA) poorest clients use savings services more than credit services (Hulme and Mosley, 1996) and small, high-cost emergency loans more than larger, lower-cost investment loans.

REFERENCES

Alderman, H. and C. Paxson (1994), 'Do the poor insure? a synthesis of the literature on risk sharing institutions in developing countries', *International Economic Association Moscow Conference*, **4**.

Arun, T. and D. Hulme (2003), 'Balancing supply and demand – the emerging agenda for microfinance institutions', *Journal of Microfinance*, **5**(2).

Arun, T. and P. Mosley (2003), 'SHGs in India – a magic bullet for poor rural women', paper presented to the ESRC seminar series on Finance and Development, 30 October, University of Manchester.

Besley, T., S. Coate and G. Lowry (1990), 'The economics of RoSCAs', Centre for International Studies, discussion Paper No. 149, Princeton University.

Binswanger, H.P. and M.R. Rosenzweig (1984), 'Contractual arrangements: employment and wages in rural labour markets in South Asia', New Haven: Yale University Press.

Brink, R. and J-P. Chavas (1991), 'The microeconomics of an indigenous African institution', Cornell Food and Nutrition Policy Programme, Working Paper 15, Ithaca, New York.

Brown, W. (2001), 'Microinsurance – the risks, perils and opportunities', *Small Enterprise Development*, **12**(1), 11–24.

Carney, D. (1998), *Sustainable Rural Livelihoods: What Contribution Can We Make?*, London: DFID.

CGAP (1998) 'How microfinance providers target the poor?', Washington, DC: PACT Publications.

Chaudhury, I. and I. Matin (2002), 'Dimensions and dynamics of microfinance membership overlap – a micro study from Bangladesh', *Small Enterprise Development*, **13**(2), 46–55.

Dreze, J., P. Lanjouw and N. Sharma (1997), 'Credit transactions in a North Indian village', mimeo, Delhi School of Economics.

Ellis, F. (2000), *Rural Livelihoods*, Oxford: Oxford University Press

Fafchamps, M. (1995), 'Risk sharing, quasi-credit and the enforcement of informal contracts', Stanford University.

Gulli, H. (1998) *Microfinance and Poverty*, Washington, DC: Inter-American Development Bank.

Hulme, D. (2000), 'Is microdebt good for poor people? A note on the dark side of microfinance', *Small Enterprise Development*, **11**(1),26–8.

Hulme, D. and P. Mosley (eds) (1996), *Finance Against Poverty*, vols 1 and 2, London: Routledge.

Johnson, S. and B. Rogaly (1997), 'Microfinance and poverty reduction', Oxfam Poverty Guidelines, Oxford.

Lipton, M., A. de Haan and S. Yaqub (1997) 'Credit and employment for the Poor', *Politica Internazionale*, **5** (Sept.–Oct.), 153–66.

Matin, I and S. Sinha (1998), 'Informal credit transaction of microcredit borrowers', IDS Bulletin, **29**(4).

Matin, I., D. Hulme and S. Rutherford (2002), 'Finance for the poor: from microcredit to microfinancial services', *Journal of International Development*,**14**, 273–94.

Meyer, R.L. (2002) 'Track record of financial institutions in assisting the poor in Asia', Asian Development Bank Institute Research Paper, 49, ADB Institute, December.

Morduch, J. (1997), 'Between market and state: can informal insurance patch the safety net?', mimeo, Princeton University.

Morduch, J. (1999), 'The microfinance promise', *Journal of Economic Literature*, **XXXVII** (December), 1569–614.

Morduch, J. (2000), 'The microfinance schism', *World Development*, **28** (4), 617–29.

Morduch, J. and S. Rutherford (2003), 'Microfinance: analytical issues for India', paper submitted for the World Bank, South Asia Region.

Mosley, P. (2001), 'Insurance against poverty? The "new generation" agricultural micro insurance schemes', *Small Enterprise Development*, **12**(1), 51–8.

Platteau, J.P. and A. Abraham (1984), 'An inquiry into quasi-credit contracts: the role of reciprocal credit and interlinked deals in small scale fishing communities', *Journal of Development Studies*, **23**(4).

Rutherford, S. (1999), *The Poor and Their Money*, Delhi: Oxford University Press.

Scoones, I. (1998), 'Sustainable rural livelihoods: a framework for analysis', *IDS Working Paper*, **72**, IDS, Brighton.

Wright, G. (1999), 'Examining the impact of microinsurance services – increasing income or reducing poverty?', *Small Enterprise Development*, **10**(1),38–47.

Zeller, M. (1996), 'Rural finance for food security for the poor : implications for research and policy', Food Policy Review no. 4, IFPRI, Washington, DC.

10. Rural financial markets

Susan Johnson

1. INTRODUCTION

The term 'rural financial market' was adopted in the early 1980s to reflect the changing analysis of the context of rural credit (Von Pischke *et al.*, 1983). The term refers to 'relationships between buyers and sellers of financial assets who are active in rural economies' (p. 4) and to the financial intermediation process involved in the transferring of financial claims using both formal and informal organizations. It was the outcome of the convergence of financial repression thinking with an improved understanding of informal financial markets and the financial intermediation needs of rural households.

Financial sector reform policies have been in operation since the 1980s and a considerable body of work has developed in theorizing and investigating their consequences. The thinking on rural financial markets supported the analysis of reform for rural credit policy. Nevertheless, the analysis of the operation and consequences of reform has still mainly focused on the formal financial sector. While the majority of economic actors in low-income countries do not directly or significantly participate in the formal financial sector, the financial arrangements in which they do participate are generally regarded as irrelevant to the operation of formal financial sector reform since the scale of individual transactions is small.

Despite this, reform policy has considerably influenced the way in which interventions to provide financial services for poor people are designed and implemented. Donor interest in the provision of financial services through the development of self-sustaining microfinance institutions (MFIs) has expanded significantly in the 1990s, but, despite the proliferation of interventions, analysis rarely goes beyond examining the impact on individual users to an analysis at the level of the financial market.

Chapter 8 explained the way in which poor people use a range of financial services to support their need to finance accumulation, life cycle events and coping with emergencies. Chapter 9 then reviewed the development of the emerging microfinance industry. The present chapter first considers a number of definitions of informal finance, before moving on to review theories relating to its role in financial markets. Since informal finance plays an important role in supporting poor people's livelihoods, the relationship between informal finance and financial sector reform is a key issue for poverty reduction. The final section therefore considers how these theories have affected approaches to intervention in rural financial markets, before concluding.

2. INFORMAL FINANCE: AN OVERVIEW

One of the underlying 'stylized facts' of the analysis of financial repression is that financial systems in developing countries are dominated by commercial banks (Fry, 1995, p. 4). While it is clearly true that commercial banks are the dominant institutional form within the formal financial sector, research has increasingly demonstrated the extensive and pervasive presence of informal financial arrangements in low-income economies as a whole (Wai, 1992). Indeed the vast majority of transactions fall outside the regulated formal sector (Aryeetey and Udry, 1997). Since informal arrangements are more likely to be used by poor people, the size of individual transactions is relatively small, another reason why formal sector policy has tended to ignore them. Estimates of the size of informal financial arrangements are of course difficult, but figures that are available suggest that informal arrangements have supplied anywhere between 30 and 95 per cent of the credit needs of rural or urban populations (Germidis *et al.*, 1991). These figures also tend to exclude informal arrangements based on reciprocity between relatives and friends; if these were included, the extent and importance of informal arrangements would be even greater. But even without these, some evidence suggests that the size of flows circulated through informal finance within the household and non-corporate sector is substantially larger than flows channelled through formal institutions (Nissanke and Aryeetey, 1998, p. 279).

The term 'informal' usually refers to those parts of the economy that fall outside governmental regulation. In the context of finance, this has led to a definition of the informal sector which 'describes participation in all commercial saving and lending activity taking place outside of formal or established financial institutions'(Aryeetey, 1995, p. 3). This definition draws a distinction between 'commercial' and 'non-commercial' forms of finance in which 'non-commercial' arrangements are excluded. However group arrangements are usually treated as part of the definition of the informal sector. This draws on Adams's threefold distinction (see Callier, 1990) between non-commercial arrangements based on reciprocity between relatives, friends and neighbours, commercial arrangements such as those engaged in by moneylenders and deposittakers, and group arrangements such as ROSCAs.

This approach therefore excludes financial arrangements that are based on reciprocal social relations, although group arrangements can clearly involve both commercial and non-commercial aspects. Evidence in a range of anthropological studies suggests that financial arrangements between friends and neighbours form part and parcel of the web of financial arrangements in a community through which people seek to diversify risks, develop social insurance or accumulate capital (Platteau and Abraham, 1987). It has been proposed that the presence of an interest rate might adequately take account of the difference between commercial and non-commercial arrangements. However Adams (1994) points out that the terms of informal financial contracts, especially the costs of borrowing, encompass a range of characteristics of which the interest rate is only one; for example, the presence of tied transactions. He also points out that informal contracts may not specify a repayment date or repayment schedule. This suggests that distinguishing reciprocity from commercial arrangements may in fact be rather difficult in practice. Moreover the above definition suggests that group arrangements are part of the informal sector, but these also operate in ways that use norms of reciprocity or redistribution, for example, many groups operate welfare funds (Nagarajan *et al.*, 1995, p. 309).

Bell discusses the policy relevance of these definitional concerns in the context of the All India Credit survey (Bell, 1990), where he takes issue with findings that the banks and cooperatives have successfully brought about the downfall of moneylenders. He suggests that 'the lender's guise is very much in the eye of his clients' (p. 190) and might to some be a relative, and to others a farmer or trader. Therefore, if the influence of public policies on informal lending is to be understood, he suggests that it is necessary to understand what a category such as 'moneylender' means in practice.

There are two views of the origins of informal finance, although they are not necessarily mutually exclusive. One view proposes that informal arrangements pre-date formal arrangements and that in this way the financial sector is intrinsically dualistic. The other view emphasizes that it exists because of financial repression: that it has developed as a response to controls and deficiencies of the formal sector and is in this sense a reaction to financial regulation and repression. These differing views have implications for analysis of the sector's contribution to allocative efficiency and hence to policy conclusions.

The first view suggests that informal finance may make a net additive contribution to efficiency due to (assumed) inherently greater operational efficiency (Ghate, 1988). The second view, on the other hand, suggests it may make an 'ameliorating contribution' to allocative efficiency in the context of regulation, in that it provides credit to sectors not reached by the formal sector – assuming that returns in these sectors are high. The government, through regulation, may be attempting to address what it understands to be a divergence between private and social returns, for example, by reducing the availability of credit for activities such as land speculation. Liberalization may therefore only produce improvements in allocative efficiency if the government has incorrectly identified deviations of private from social returns or has implemented a sub-optimal regulatory response.

As has been pointed out in the literature, these different views of the origins of the informal sector drive different policy responses (Germidis *et al.*, 1991). Where the informal sector is seen as a response to financial repression, the need is for institutional and operational reforms via financial deregulation. However liberalization may itself be a sub-optimal response in terms of overall allocative efficiency if government policy was in the first place erroneous, and the informal sector may instead provide a second-best solution, whereas, if its origins lie in inherent dualism, policy focus needs to be on the transformation of the informal sector through (for example) making links between informal and formal sector financial institutions.

As financial liberalization policies were being designed and implemented in the late 1980s and early 1990s, there was some recognition of the importance of the informal sector (World Bank, 1989; Asian Development Bank, 1990; Callier, 1990; Germidis *et al.*, 1991). In particular this was partly born of a view that there was a risk that financial sector reform programmes might in fact be frustrated (Acharya and Madhur, 1983) given the size and inherent strengths of the informal sector, resulting from its flexibility and responsiveness (Adams and Fitchett, 1992). More broadly there arose a view that financial systems development and deepening was unlikely to be achieved by focusing on formal sector institutions alone (Germidis *et al.*, 1991, p. 15). This gave rise to policy recommendations:

- the development of linkages between formal and informal financial agents;
- the potential for formal financial institutions to learn from the practices of informal agents, and themselves 'informalize' or 'mimic' them, so creating additional competition;
- transforming informal into formal financial institutions;
- regulating parts of the informal sector in order to improve market structure.

However, while it has been pointed out that an adequate understanding of informal finance is a prerequisite for satisfactory financial policy analysis, it does not appear that an adequate understanding has yet been established, since there is a need for detailed institutional knowledge and investigation of the transmission mechanisms involved (Aryeetey *et al.*, 1997; Aryeetey and Udry, 1997).

3. THEORIES OF THE ROLE OF INFORMAL FINANCE IN FINANCIAL MARKETS

Different theoretical frameworks have been used to analyse the role of informal finance in the financial market with different consequences for policy: first is neoclassical economics; second is the new institutional economics, which has developed the neoclassical tool-kit to deal with imperfect information and transactions costs; third is the approach of political economy, which has particularly analysed credit and its links to input and output markets.

Neoclassical Approaches

The concern, indicated above, was that linkages between the informal and formal credit markets might act to frustrate the intended effects of monetary and credit policy because of highly elastic supplies of 'black' liquidity originating in the informal sector. To examine this, Acharya and Madhur set up a model in which demand from the formal sector spills over into the informal sector. With this assumption, and borne out by evidence based on the Indian financial market, credit rationing in the commercial bank sector results in spillover into the informal market and hence an increase in interest rates in the informal sector also. They argue that the removal of formal interest rate controls will only fail to have an impact on informal interest rates under special circumstances. These are the cases where, first, the supply of informal credit is infinitely elastic and hence shifts in the demand function will have no effect on price; second, where supply in the informal credit market is related to the formal market in a one-for-one inverse relationship so that a contraction in commercial bank credit results in an equal expansion of supply in the informal market with no net effect on price; third, where there is absolutely no spillover effect and hence the supply and demand schedules in the informal market are unaffected (Acharya and Madhur, 1983). The implications of their analysis for liberalization are that removing restrictions on credit supply will result in a reduction in informal sector interest rates as demand returns to the formal market.

Roemer presents a partial equilibrium analysis that, by contrast to Acharya and Madhur, allows for a spillover of supply as well as demand into the informal market. This model assumes a segmented market prior to regulation with the informal market demanding a risk premium over the formal market. The impact of credit controls which pushes interest rates below the pre-existing equilibrium in the formal market then changes both the supply and demand for funds in the informal market as a result of both a spillover of unmet demand from the formal market and a supply of funds for investment seeking returns higher than those the formal market can offer.

These neoclassical models therefore suggest that the impact of regulation may, under certain conditions of the supply and demand curves, be to *lower* rates in the informal market. The impact of reversing this process through removing controls on interest rates would therefore be to raise informal market rates. This would benefit, first, borrowers who have been squeezed out of the formal market and therefore can return to the formal market without facing the risk premia of the informal market, and second, money-lenders who deal only with the informal market, who would be able to raise rates and capture a larger market share since there would at the same time be a return of funds from the informal to the formal sector. Liberalization would therefore reduce the welfare of borrowers who had access to funds at controlled interest rates and those with no access to the formal sector, since they would now face higher rates in the informal segment (Roemer, 1986).

The transmission mechanism proposed here assumes that the impact of regulation is to drive deposits and other sources of funds available for lending into the informal market. Roemer concludes by suggesting that arguments for deregulation that are made on the basis of increasing savings channelled through the formal sector will result in reduced savings channelled through the informal system. But Aryeetey considers Roemer's view that supply will spill over into the informal market in the same way as demand as unrealistic. First, he argues that it is often not permitted by law; second, it ignores problems of information deficiencies in the assessment of risk; third, the transactions costs of lending to insecure borrowers would rise, which would reduce the risk premium (Aryeetey, 1995). However there remains the possibility that there can be some spillover of savings by those with funds to invest and who may be able to become informal sector lenders.

These theoretical arguments, therefore, present scenarios of prices and quantities in the informal market rising, falling or staying the same as a result of liberalization, depending on the assumptions made. The key issue then is the empirical question of the extent and nature of the interaction between the formal and informal parts of the market on both the supply and demand side. It is therefore necessary to understand the extent to which demand is indeed 'specific' to each sector or 'non-specific' and capable of moving between sectors (Nissanke and Aryeetey, 1998). Ghate, for example, suggests that there is a spectrum of credit needs which at the extremes are specific to each of the formal and informal markets. Hence lending for long-term fixed capital in the large-scale sector can only be supplied by the formal sector, while short-term consumption credit needs can only be fulfilled by the informal sector. Needs in the spectrum in between these two extremes might be supplied by either sector (Ghate, 1988).

On the supply side, the question of interlinkages also arises: the extent to which excess funds can flow from the formal into informal markets, for example, via moneylenders who borrow from banks, and the extent to which informal sector providers deposit funds into the formal system for on lending. These types of relationship are termed 'financial layering' (Floro and Yotopoulos, 1991) and, although they may raise the costs of intermediation in a fully integrated market (Fry, 1995), they present an improvement on complete separation.

These views of the financial market therefore suggest that the degree of fragmentation of the financial market is the major concern and that policies to integrate the market better are the key component of improving the efficiency outcomes of financial sector reform policy and overall financial sector development. In order to establish the impact of financial sector reform in the informal market, it is necessary to establish empirically the extent and nature of interlinkages between the formal and the informal financial systems on both the supply and demand side.

New Institutional Economic Approaches

The analysis of informal credit transactions has been at the core of much new institutional economic analysis that has sought to incorporate the effects of imperfect information and transactions costs. The work of Stiglitz and Hoff has demonstrated how credit markets are subject to particular information, monitoring and enforcement problems due to the intertemporal basis of their transactions (Stiglitz and Weiss, 1981; Hoff *et al.*, 1993). These features give rise to moral hazard and adverse selection in credit transactions. Moral hazard is the situation in which lending (or insurance) affects the behaviour of the borrower who may take less care or take more risks if the funds at stake are not their own. This helps explain the use of collateral as a feature of credit markets. Adverse selection refers to the fact that, if price alone is used to allocate credit, projects able to produce the highest returns are also likely to be riskier, hence lowering the portfolio quality of the lender.

The imperfect information paradigm has been used to explore a number of features of informal financial arrangements. First there is the view, much favoured by the 'Ohio School', including Dale Adams, Douglas Graham and J.D. von Pischke, that information problems and transactions costs can explain the interest rate differences between formal and informal providers. Interest rates comprise four components: the cost of funds, risk of default, transactions costs of providing the service and a monopolistic component dependent on the alternatives available to the borrower. The 'Ohio School' therefore argue that informal financial arrangements, especially moneylenders, charge relatively high interest rates because they face high risks of default and lack the legal means to enforce contracts. They argue that the political economy school has overemphasized the monopoly element involved in pricing on the basis that moneylenders usually lend as a part of their business and not as their sole business and hence that there often is competition in the lending market. They further argue that the cost of funds in low-income countries is necessarily high owing to the general scarcity of liquidity and the opportunity cost of funds (see also Wai, 1957, p. 139). Furthermore they argue that a direct comparison of interest rates with formal sector interest rates is an inadequate comparison of the actual costs of borrowing since the transactions costs involved in formal sector borrowing are considerably higher than the interest rate. These transactions costs include the physical costs of travel to local banks as well as the opportunity cost of time necessary to undertake the trip; the payment of administration fees for loan applications; the likelihood that bribes are necessary to bank officials and the social inaccessibility of banks to poor people are imputed as further, though unmeasurable, costs of the transaction.

Further examples of the use of new institutional economics (NIE) to help explain informal financial arrangements have included the view that interlinked transactions between credit and other goods or service markets (inputs, outputs or labour) can also be understood by the need to overcome information problems about the future behaviour of clients in time based transactions (Hoff *et al.*, 1993). Third, informal financial arrangements are able to make use of local sources of knowledge and specific social mechanisms to overcome screening, monitoring and enforcement costs: for example, that rotating savings and credit associations (ROSCAs) are able to operate thanks to the degree of 'insider' knowledge they have about each member and their ability to enforce compliance through the use of local social sanctions, such as non-cooperation in other aspects of daily life.

The NIE thesis therefore suggests that, once differences in information, transactions costs and default risks are taken into account, returns across these lending activities will be comparable and that there is a unified underlying market for funds. Nissanke and Aryeetey (1998) therefore distinguish between a *segmented* market and a *fragmented* market on the basis that fragmentation is evident when returns adjusted for risks and transactions costs are not comparable between markets. The term 'segmentation', on the other hand, describes a process of normal specialization between products on which returns are evened out once risk-adjusted returns are examined. Many researchers have recognized the segmentation of informal financial markets and suggested that this is due to variables such as locality, type of lender and the trade, service or sector being financed (Ghate, 1988, p. 67). Remaining variations in returns are therefore explained in terms of imperfections in the market due to, for example, barriers to entry.

Despite the extensive development of this theoretical approach, the application of the theory faces considerable empirical problems. The most pervasive of these is the problem of measuring information and transactions costs. Aleem advances an analysis of moneylenders in Pakistan in which he incorporates screening, transaction and default costs into the cost of lending in order to examine whether higher interest rates over the formal market are indeed justified (Aleem, 1990). He tentatively concludes that lenders' average costs exceed their marginal costs and suggests that a Chamberlinian model of imperfect competition in which there are few barriers to entry can explain it. In this case the model involves many lenders but strong product differentiation between them. This product differentiation, he argues, is caused by imperfections in the flow of information on the supply side (in terms of lenders' screening processes) and on the demand side because borrowers do not have sufficient information about the terms and conditions offered by other lenders. He further explains that borrowers find it difficult to move between lenders because of the long screening process they would be submitted to (the process tended to be carried out over at least a year with the lender observing borrower characteristics with small initial loans), because they could not be sure of the outcome of this process and the terms they would eventually be offered. Further, since borrowing was related to marketing all of the harvest through a particular lender, the borrower would not wish to jeopardize his relationship with his existing lender by approaching another and using multiple lenders was not an option. Finally, they would have problems obtaining credit from another lender if their current lender were to refuse to give them a loan.

Floro and Yotopoulos, in testing the NIE in the context of agricultural credit in the Philippines, test the hypothesis that interest rates reflect transactions costs of lending 'as determined by the character of personalistic relations between the parties' (Floro and Yotopoulos, 1991, p. 17). The analysis examines interlinked transactions with other markets. The approach therefore attempts to adjust returns on transactions in relation to the related costs involved in other markets. The authors conclude that these 'personalistic relations' enable information barriers and moral hazard problems to be overcome between particular groups of borrowers and lenders. However these 'personalistic relations' are constructed on the basis of social and political institutions such as kinship which, they point out, underlie the character-based lending that takes place. Information problems are therefore being overcome through the use of underlying social institutions.

Examining credit transactions in a village in Northern Nigeria, Udry (1993) finds that the majority of credit transactions occur within the village and between kin, which enables the moral hazard problem to be minimized as information on wilful default is readily available. He also finds that the use of collateral and interlinking of contracts with other markets is hardly used. He concludes that credit transactions in this context are therefore state-contingent contracts; that is, the lender can readily verify whether the circumstances leading to default are merited owing to the failure of the investment as a result of adverse shocks. However the borrower does not tend to be regarded as being in default and will pay lower interest rates than if the investment is a success, so resulting in a degree of risk pooling across households which can cope with idiosyncratic risks to individual households. The village presents a boundary to state-contingent lending of this kind and covariant risks faced by the village cannot be dealt with; rather these are diversified through long distance trading relationships with traders acquiring credit that they on-lend locally. Given this situation, formal sector lenders cannot compete with lenders within the community in making state-contingent loans without the development of forms of collateral.

In a study of informal financial arrangements in four African countries, the view that interest rates are higher in the informal sector for reasons of default risk and higher transactions costs is tested on data collected from informal financial providers about their methods of screening, monitoring and enforcement, and their records of actual default. Nissanke and Aryeetey (1998) conclude that, contrary to the theory, costs incurred by lenders are lower in the informal sector than in the formal sector. They found that transactions costs were influenced by proximity to the lender and the extent of personal relations, and that the strength of such factors as social cohesion and community organization influenced perceptions of risk (p. 245). Furthermore the experience of default in these arrangements also resulted in lower costs for these lenders, suggesting that risk-adjusted returns are not comparable across market segments. The authors therefore conclude that the market for funds is strongly fragmented and they find little evidence of financial layering on the supply side to overcome this fragmentation and enable greater integration in the market. The study concludes that, rather than liberalization resulting in a reduction in the size of the informal sector, as the parallel theory of its origins suggests, the informal sector has shown growth and dynamism in responding to increasing demand from the real sector in the context of a more liberal economic and political climate. The regulatory environment, amongst other factors, has not developed in ways that enable such fragmentation to be overcome (p. 281).

These studies demonstrate that the analysis of imperfect information and transactions costs adds a considerable dimension of understanding to informal financial arrangements. Aleem's study suggests that lenders can develop an information base on borrowers that means that they become locked in and face high exit costs from a particular arrangement. This allows the lender to raise prices and extract rent from this information base despite oversupply in the market as a whole. Moreover he suggests that methods of information sharing exist between moneylenders that present borrowers with problems of movement between lenders. Other researchers have also offered evidence of the difficulties clients face in leaving tied credit arrangements if they attempt to sell their crop elsewhere (Bell, 1993, p. 151; Olsen, 1994, p. 161). These tactics, along with the heavy interlinking of arrangements with output markets, suggest that additional factors may be at work in fragmenting the market, not least the path-dependence involved in information accumulation by lenders about their clients over time which enables information itself to become an instrument of economic power (Harriss-White, 1999, p. 272).

The studies by Floro and Yotopoulos and by Nissanke and Aryeetey are more explicit about the presence of factors at work in the market that are not explained by their analysis. Both studies suggest that remaining variation in their results that is not accounted for by transactions, information and default costs might be explained by the presence of personal and social relations. Thus, while the NIE can explain the transmission of information and reduced transactions costs in informal financial arrangements through the presence of social institutions, these costs are clearly not open to measurement. Having revealed the role of deeper social structures, it is not able to offer a systematic analysis of the influence of these institutions on market operation and hence presents an incomplete explanation of empirical results. Moreover, in studying the multiplicity and detail of informal financial arrangements in The Gambia, Shipton concludes that transactions costs are too simple a concept to capture the 'reasoning behind rural Gambian's individual or collective decisions about entrustments and obligations' (Shipton, 1994, p. 284) and the multidimensional nature of these social ties and cultural traditions, and that 'if these financial systems are to be understood as markets, they are certainly not unified or discrete ones' (p. 311).

Political Economy and 'Real Market' Approaches

By contrast to the NIE's attempt to explain high interest rates through information, transactions and default costs, Bhaduri's classic contribution argues that usurious interest rates charged by moneylenders are based on the need for lenders to further accumulate land since those who are unable to pay will forfeit their land (Bhaduri, 1977; 1981). The political economy approach has given rise to extensive evidence that markets interlink and interlock, with powerful agents able to incorporate credit relations into the wider exchange and production relations of labour markets, trade or asset accumulation. These relationships have been extensively documented and while research has tended to suggest that such arrangements are more common in Asia than in Africa, Nissanke and Aryeetey's study (1998) reports that interlinked transactions exist in Tanzania as a means of gaining usufruct rights in land in the absence of a land market (p. 231). The operation of such arrangements has been termed 'financial repression from below' (McGregor, 1994).

Political economists have been at pains to point out that markets are 'the hollow core at the heart of economics … which has no adequate tradition for analysing actually existing markets' (Crow, 1998). They have particularly sought to demonstrate that participation in markets is differentiated along axes of class but also recognize the role of variables such as gender, space and time. Research into informal financial arrangements both in the political economy tradition and elsewhere has clearly demonstrated the diversity, complexity and detail involved in their functioning. Financial 'landscapes' are understood as rooted in agroecological conditions, socioeconomic relations and political–administrative structures (Bouman and Hospes, 1994). In highlighting the deviation of these 'real' markets from those of 'abstract' neoclassical theory, Mackintosh directs attention to four questions in addressing the 'black box' of markets (Mackintosh, 1990): first, the terms on which people come to market, access to resources being a means through which they establish dominant positions; second, who has power and control over the terms on which markets operate; third, the social stratification of trade relationships; and, finally, the way in which markets are suppressed rather than developed.

There are many studies of informal financial arrangements that demonstrate the intricate relationship between these arrangements and aspects of wider social institutions (Adams and Fitchett, 1992; Bouman and Hospes, 1994). For example, Hospes' study of the financial landscape in Ambon, Indonesia is one in which an actor-structure approach is used. As a result he finds that 'social systems sustained by actors who are not only participants of these systems but also of other social systems, such as ethnic community, an extension program, an office, a neighbourhood, a religious society, a group of entrepreneurs … affect or somehow embed "financial systems"' (Hospes, 1996, p. 13). The result of such a view is to see that the dualistic formal and informal divide needs to be overcome in order to see formal and informal institutional arrangements, be they club law, local government directives, commercial, ethical or religious concerns, as 'regulative complexes' (p. 10) in which financial arrangements take place.

4. INTERVENTION IN RURAL FINANCIAL MARKETS

Political economy analyses of moneylender exploitation were a strong rationale for past state-subsidized credit provision. The objectives of credit projects, especially those in South Asia, have often involved reducing the dependence of borrowers on moneylenders and the power relationships they represent.

The approach to building self-sustaining MFIs that charge interest rates to cover costs has challenged this rationale and many credit providers have accepted the view that access rather than price is the critical factor for poor people.

Notwithstanding this development, an indicator that is often used to assess impact is moneylender dependence. But such an indicator, if it is to be useful, needs to reflect the wider context of the financial market and the underlying power relations which money lending represents, as well as the circumstances of poor people's livelihoods. Questions must be asked about whether the market niche of moneylenders is really being eroded, or simply being converted or channelled into other types of production and exchange relationship. Is it as easy as shifting dependence from the moneylender to the MFI, who act as new patrons? Evidence has been presented from Bangladesh demonstrating that households participating in MFI programmes borrow as much from informal sources (moneylenders) as other households and cross-finance their debt repayments to either source (Sinha and Matin, 1998).

As was explained above, the idea of building sustainable microfinance institutions converged with financial repression thinking. The Ohio School had earlier criticized subsidized lending both through the state in the form of agricultural credit schemes, for example, and through NGOs taking the view that this was 'undermining' the market with cheap credit (Adams *et al.*, 1984). Along with the proponents of financial repression, they considered that subsidized credit led to allocative inefficiency and also argued that cheap credit could erode the inbuilt mechanisms of indigenous lending practices (Nagarajan *et al.*, 1995). By contrast, building financial organizations that could cover their costs and be financially self-sustaining was viewed as widening the market for financial services in a sustainable way.

However, while cheap credit to users may no longer be seen as good practice, grants and subsidized capital for the establishment of MFIs is still the norm. Drawing on infant industry arguments, Hulme and Mosley argue that subsidies are valid because the benefits of developing the technology of lending to poor people involves externalities of knowledge which cannot be internalized by the organization itself (Hulme and Mosley, 1996). However the case made is a general theoretical one and has not been applied to specific financial markets to demonstrate the legitimacy of subsidies in a particular context. This would require the development of criteria to be used in assessing what a 'correct' level of subsidy might be which would avoid undermining already existing financial service providers.

With the consequent proliferation of donor support for MFIs, concern has turned to assessment of the impact of these interventions. The approach favoured by the 'New World' proponents (Otero and Rhyne, 1994) is to analyse measures of outreach and sustainability of the financial organization that involves examining the numbers and coverage of people reached, and measures of financial performance of the organisation itself. This approach, described by Hulme as the 'intermediary school' of impact assessment, judges the intervention to be 'beneficial because it has widened the financial market in a sustainable fashion' (Hulme, 2000, p. 82). However these assessments seem somewhat premature since, beyond the financial service organization, impact on informal services and the financial market has not actually been examined (Johnson, 1998).

Before a market analysis is further explored, it is worthwhile asking why proponents of the intermediary school might have neglected an analysis of the impact of MFIs in the market. There are two possible reasons. The first is that it is too methodologically difficult and therefore not worthwhile. Key concerns are the issues of fungibility and attribution. Fungibility refers to the situation where it is hard to trace the exact use of funds, whether by a household or by an MFI. Second, the problems of attribution in impact assessment are related to those of fungibility in that it is almost impossible to set up a methodologically rigorous means of finding out what changes are the result of the intervention. These arguments have been used to argue that assessing the impact of credit provision on users is not worthwhile. Given such problems at the user level, the idea of attempting to assess the impact on markets is clearly even more methodologically problematic.

The second reason is more fundamental. It is the view that it is not necessary to look beyond the creation of a profitable MFI that is fit and can survive in the market. This approach adopts a Schumpeterian model of innovation, which allows for the creative destruction of competitors in search of ever greater allocative efficiency (Bhatt, 1987). But others argue that aid is about more than improving efficiency alone and, for those concerned with poverty elimination, requires an analysis of the distributional consequences deriving from market power (DFID, 1997). This approach therefore still needs to find the means to move beyond assessing the development of the MFI itself and on to assessing the impact of the organization on the wider financial market.

In considering this concern, the Ohio School has suggested that 'the route to better RFM performance is not well marked' (Von Pischke *et al.*, 1983, p. 12). They argue that a well functioning rural financial market should have certain characteristics. It should

- mobilize rural savings as well as disburse credit,
- grow to meet expanding opportunities without the need for subsidies,
- expand the array of vehicles for attracting savings,
- offer varied and flexible lending terms and conditions,
- have institutions which are healthy and expanding,

- have active competition among formal and informal borrowers and lenders.

Also,

- the costs of financial services should fall as a result of innovation,
- the economically active population should have expanding access,
- the capability of the rural financial market (RFM) to take part in larger financial markets should grow.

When considering the shifting of the 'frontier' of financial development, von Pischke gives further indications as to how the broader impact of a particular project or financial organization on financial development might be established. He asks (Von Pischke, 1991, pp. 364–76): 'are project instruments innovative, have they proved catalytic, novel or trivial, do project instruments promote competition and reduce transaction costs?' These are questions which have been considered by the intermediary school (Rhyne, 1994), but while it is relatively straightforward to establish whether the instruments offered have been innovative (in the sense, for example, that they fall outside the mainstream of banking sector products) it is rather harder to measure and assess transactions costs, and methods of doing this have not been significantly developed.

At the level of the financial market, von Pischke concentrates on the question of whether projects have successfully lengthened term structure; that is, whether they have overcome the risks of borrowing short to lend long. Since the role of a financial intermediary is to overcome the risk of using funds taken in on relatively short-term deposits and turn them into loans for much longer periods of time, the ability to manage liquidity and price risks successfully is crucial. He proposes means of analysing the MFI's assets and liabilities to establish whether this is being achieved. Additionally, he poses two further questions: whether injecting liquidity into tight financial markets has a greater impact on these markets than where liquidity is not a problem, and whether the intervention has successfully developed banking habits.

Von Pischke does not indicate the means of answering these last questions. Indeed it is notable that, in discussing the assessment of projects on financial market development and the macroeconomic and macrofinancial level, he has more questions than answers about the specific approaches and indicators to be used. This framework for impact assessment on financial markets concentrates on improving their efficiency in allocating resources for investment consistent with the financial repression case. In line with the operationalizing of new institutional economics approaches, reducing transaction costs and managing risk are the main indicators of whether or not this has been achieved, despite the inherent difficulties in their measurement.

5. CONCLUSIONS

This chapter has reviewed the theoretical and policy debates surrounding rural credit and rural financial markets over the last 20 years. It has shown that theoretically based analyses of reforms indicate the need for a detailed understanding of the transmission mechanisms and linkages between formal and informal sectors if the impact is to be traced. While the new institutional economics analysis of transaction and information costs has been instrumental in expanding the analysis of informal financial arrangements, it at the same time reveals the importance of social relations that it cannot adequately accommodate in its analysis. At the same time, political economy and real market thinkers suggests that there is still some way to go before economics has an adequate analysis of rural financial markets that can deal with the wider complex of social and political relations that influence the way in which poor people gain, or do not gain, access to and make choices about the financial relationships in which they do engage.

From a policy perspective, while improved understanding of the informal financial sector has been at the core of many policy prescriptions for rural financial markets, it is apparent that the impact of these changes has not been extensively researched. Although theory suggests that the nature of the interlinkages between the informal and formal sector may be critical for the outcomes of reform, few studies exist to indicate what the impact has been in practice of financial sector reform on the options that poor people have for financing their livelihoods. Further research is required, especially to investigate the micro-level applications of these theories to the agricultural sector. In addition, it is important to assess the impact of existing interventions in rural financial markets.

REFERENCES

Acharya, S. and S. Madhur (1983), 'Informal credit markets and black money: do they frustrate monetary policy?', *Economic and Political Weekly*, **18**, 8 October, 1751–6.

Adams, D.W. (1994), 'Using contracts to analyze informal finance', in F.J.A. Bouman and O. Hospes (eds), *Financial Landscapes Reconstructed*, Boulder, Colorado: Westview Press.

Adams, D.W. and D.A. Fitchett (eds) (1992), *Informal Finance in Low-Income Countries*, Boulder, Colorado: Westview Press.

Adams, D.W., D.H. Graham and J.D. Von Pischke (eds) (1984), *Undermining Rural Development with Cheap Credit*, Boulder, Colorado: Westview Press.

Aleem, I. (1990), 'Imperfect information, screening and the costs of informal lending: a study of the rural credit market in Pakistan', *World Bank Economic Review*, **4**(3), 329–49.

Aryeetey, E. (1995), *Filling the Niche: Informal Finance in Africa*, Nairobi, Kenya: East African Educational Publishers.

Aryeetey, E. and C. Udry (1997), 'The characteristics of informal financial markets in Sub-Saharan Africa', *Journal of African Economies*, **6**(1), 161–203.

Aryeetey, E., L. Senbet and C. Udry (1997), 'Financial liberalisation and financial markets in Sub-Saharan Africa: a synthesis', *Journal of African Economies*, **6**(1) (Supplement), 1–28.

Asian Development Bank (1990), *Asian Development Outlook*, Manila, Philippines: Asian Development Bank.

Bell, C. (1990). 'Interactions between institutional and informal credit agencies in rural India', *World Bank Economic Review*, **4**(3), 297–328.

Bell, C. (1993), 'Interactions between institutional and informal credit agencies in rural India', in K. Hoff, A. Bravermand and J. Stiglitz (eds), *The Economics of Rural Organization: Theory, Practice and Policy*, Washington, DC: World Bank.

Bhaduri, A. (1977), 'On the formation of usurious interest rates in backward agriculture', *Cambridge Journal of Economics*, **4**(2), 103–15.

Bhaduri, A. (1981), 'Class relations and the pattern of accumulation in an agrarian economy', *Cambridge Journal of Economics*, **5**(1), 33–46.

Bhatt, V.V. (1987), 'Financial innovations and credit market evolution', *Economic and Political Weekly*, **22**(22), M45–54.

Bouman, F.J.A. and O. Hospes (eds) (1994), *Financial Landscapes Reconstructed*, Boulder, Colorado: Westview Press.

Callier, P. (1990), *Financial Systems and Development in Africa*, Washington, DC: World Bank.

Crow, B. (1998), 'Market and class in rural Bangladesh', paper presented at ISS, The Hague, 15 October.

DFID (1997), *Eliminating World Poverty: A Challenge for the 21st Century*, London: Department for International Development.

Floro, S.L. and P.A. Yotopoulos (1991), *Informal Credit Markets and the New Institutional Economics: The Case of Philippine Agriculture*, Boulder, Colorado: Westview Press.

Fry, M.J. (1995), *Money, Interest and Banking in Economic Development*, Baltimore and London: Johns Hopkins University Press.

Germidis, D., D. Kessler and R. Meghir (1991), *Financial Systems and Development: What Role for the Formal and Informal Financial Sectors?*, Paris: OECD Development Centre.

Ghate, P.B. (1988), 'Informal credit markets in Asian developing countries', *Asian Development Review*, **6**(1), 64–85.

Harriss-White, B. (ed.) (1999), *Agricultural Markets from Theory to Practice: Field Experience in Developing Countries*, London and New York: Macmillan/St Martin's Press.

Hoff, K., A. Braverman and J.E. Stiglitz (eds) (1993), *The Economics of Rural Organization: Theory, Practice and Policy*, Washington, DC: World Bank.

Hospes, O. (1996), *People That Count: Changing Savings and Credit Practices in Ambon, Indonesia*, Amsterdam: Thesis Publishers.

Hulme, D. (2000), 'Impact assessment methodologies for microfinance: theory, experience and better practice', *World Development*, **28**(1): 79–98.

Hulme, D. and P. Mosley (1996), *Finance Against Poverty: Effective Institutions for Lending to Small Farmers and Micro-enterprises in Developing Countries*, London: Routledge.

Johnson, S. (1998). 'Programme impact assessment in microfinance: the need for analysis of real markets', *IDS Bulletin*, **29**(4), 21–30.

Mackintosh, M. (1990), 'Abstract markets and real needs', in H. Bernstein and B. Crow (ed.), *The Food Question*, London: Earthscan.

McGregor, J.A.M. (1994), 'Village credit and the reproduction of poverty in contemporary rural Bangladesh', in J.M. Acheson (ed.), *Anthropology and Institutional Economics*, Lanham, Maryland: University Press of America, pp. 261–81.

Nagarajan, G., R. Meyer and D. Graham (1995), 'Effects of NGO financial intermediation on indigenous self-help village groups in The Gambia', *Development Policy Review*, **13**(3), 307–16.

Nissanke, M. and E. Aryeetey (1998), *Financial Integration and Development: Liberalization and Reform in Sub-Saharan Africa*, London and New York: Routledge.

Olsen, W. (1994), 'Distress sales and rural credit: evidence from an Indian village case study', in T. Lloyd and O. Morrissey (eds), *Poverty, Inequality and Rural Development*, Basingstoke: Macmillan.

Otero, M. and E. Rhyne (eds) (1994), *The New World of Micro-enterprise Finance*, London: IT Publications.

Platteau, J.-P. and A. Abraham (1987), 'An inquiry into quasi-credit contracts: the role of reciprocal credit and interlinked deals in small scale fishing communities', *Journal of Development Studies*, **23**, 461–90.

Rhyne, E. (1994), 'A new view of finance program evaluation', in M. Otero and E. Rhyne (eds), *The New World of Microenterprise Finance*, London: IT Publications.

Roemer, M. (1986), 'Simple analytics of segmented markets: what case for liberalization?', *World Development*, **14**(3), 429–40.

Shipton, P. (1994), 'Time and money in the Western Sahel: a clash of cultures in Gambian rural finance', in J.M. Acheson (ed.), *Anthropology and Institutional Economics*, Lanham: University Press of America, pp. 283–327.

Sinha, S. and I. Matin (1998), 'Informal credit transactions of micro-credit borrowers in rural Bangladesh', *IDS Bulletin*, **29**(4), 66–80.

Stiglitz, J. and A. Weiss (1981), 'Credit rationing in markets with imperfect information', *American Economic Review*, 71, 393–410.

Udry, C. (1993), 'Credit markets in Northern Nigeria: credit as insurance in a rural economy', in K. Hoff, A. Braverman and J. Stiglitz (eds), *The Economics of Rural Organization: Theory, Practice and Policy*, Washington, DC: World Bank.

Von Pischke, J.D. (1991), *Finance at the Frontier: Debt Capacity and the Role of Credit in the Private Economy*, Washington, DC: World Bank.

Von Pischke, J.D., D. Adams and G. Donald (eds) (1983), *Rural Financial Markets in Developing Countries: Their Use and Abuse*, Baltimore: Johns Hopkins University Press.

Wai, U.T. (1957), 'Interest rates outside the organised money markets of underdeveloped countries', *IMF Staff Papers*, **6**, 80–142.

Wai, U.T. (1992), 'What have we learned about informal finance in three decades?', in D.W. Adams and D.A. Fitchett (eds), *Informal Finance in Low-Income Countries*, Boulder, Colorado: Westview Press.

World Bank (1989), *World Development Report: Financial Systems and Development*, Washington, DC: World Bank.

11. Small and medium sized enterprises in developing economies

Frederick Nixson and Paul Cook

1. INTRODUCTION

There is general agreement that small and medium sized enterprises (hereafter SMEs) have played a crucial role in the process of economic development. They contribute to employment, the production of appropriate goods and services and exports (Berry and Levy, 1994). Widespread research has identified the importance of finance for the development of SMEs and the constraints faced by them in this area, particularly with respect to their access to credit (Levy, 1993). Some studies (for example, Parker *et al.*, 1995) have found that around 90 per cent of small enterprises surveyed indicated that the limited access to credit was a major constraint to new investment.

The access problems faced by SMEs in low-income countries have largely been with respect to formal sector banking institutions. Collier and Mayer (1989) have argued that commercial banks are more likely to be sources of finance for smaller enterprises in poorer countries since the role of financial institutions is related to the life cycle of enterprises and economies. As the corporate sector develops, capital and money markets become more important vehicles for the financing of larger enterprises. Improvements in the efficiency of financial intermediation and financial liberalization, that reduce oligopolistic behaviour in the banking sector, are likely to lead to new sources of finance for smaller enterprises, and we are likely to witness a movement away from debt to equity-based forms of finance, as illustrated by the experience with venture capital in Malaysia (Boocock, 1995).

Improved access to finance, according to transactions cost theory, will reduce the cost disadvantages of SMEs relative to larger enterprises. However, whether financial liberalization as such will lead to better access to credit for SMEs remains an open question, with experience so far not providing an encouraging picture for low-income countries (Steel, 1994). A survey of SMEs in Kenya (Kariuki, 1995) showed that access to credit declined after liberalization, as a result of higher nominal interest rates and increases in other transactions costs. Meier and Pilgrim's (1994) study of enterprises in Bangladesh, Nepal and the Philippines found that only enterprises towards the upper end of the size distribution had viable access to formal sector finance. Formal sector credit was also found to be out of reach for smaller enterprises in Ghana and Tanzania (Dawson, 1993). It was clear from the experience of Sri Lanka that the access problem for smaller enterprises was not likely to be solved simply by encouraging competition among private banks but would require additional forms of support (Levy, 1993).

In general, therefore, the advantages claimed for SMEs are various, including the encouragement of entrepreneurship; the greater likelihood that SMEs will utilize labour-intensive technologies and thus have an immediate impact on employment generation; the fact that they can usually be established rapidly and put into operation to produce quick returns; that SME development can encourage the process of both inter- and intraregional decentralization; and that they may well become a countervailing force against the economic power of larger enterprises. More generally the development of SMEs is seen as accelerating the achievement of wider economic and socioeconomic objectives, including poverty alleviation.

This chapter draws upon previous papers discussing both specific and general issues relating to SMEs and finance. Cook and Nixson (2000) identified gaps in research, examined the impact of economic policy reforms on SME development and identified various approaches to issues of SME finance. Kayanula and Quartey (2000) discussed trends in SME financing in the context of financial sector reforms and provided a description of financial institutions of particular interest to SMEs in Ghana and Malawi.

The remainder of this chapter is structured as follows. Section 2 considers questions of definition. Section 3 briefly discusses issues relating to the relationship between SMEs and economic development. Section 4 looks at financial structure and the demand for and the supply of finance to SMEs. Section 5 presents the survey data, analysis and empirical results, while section 6 concludes with a discussion of policy issues.

2. DEFINITION OF SMEs AND GROWTH IN RESEARCH ACTIVITY

It should already be clear from this brief overview that the scope for confusion with respect to terminology and definition is immense. Some studies and authors (for example, UNIDO, 1997; Mead, 1999; Daniels, 1999) refer to micro and small enterprises (MSEs); other authors use the term 'small-scale industry' (for example, Weiss, 2002) while yet other studies use the term SMEs (World Bank, various publications).

Terminology matters for a number of reasons. Apart from the more general development issues touched on above (that is, in Mead's (1999) terminology, whether small scale-scale enterprises are to be viewed as survivalist activities or are they part of a dynamic growth process), we face the question whether the SME sector is viewed as a continuum or as a series of segments (McGrath and King, 1999, p. 6). Do we see MSEs / SMEs as being located within the informal sector, however defined, or do we see them as capitalist small enterprises (Mkandawire, 1999, p. 34)? In practice, of course, SMEs will straddle both the informal and formal sectors of the low-income economy, with presumably over time a shift of enterprises from the former into the latter sector. Recognizing the heterogeneity of the SME sector has important implications for policy, as we shall argue in section 6 below.

With respect to issues of definition and measurement, numerous measures are used to identify and define SMEs. Such measures can include, for example, the value of the fixed assets of the enterprise and enterprise turnover, but the great majority of empirical studies define SMEs with respect to the number of workers employed in the enterprise. There is no consistency in definitions across countries, however, and any measure used must in some sense be arbitrary.

The definitions of SMEs have been shaped by increased research activity in the area. Earlier work on the internal workings of small and medium-sized enterprises was mainly concerned with the size of small firms and providing explanations for their growth. Staley and Morse (1965) examined the stages small firms pass through as an economy grows. They postulated several reasons why small firms in low-income countries initially grow rapidly before their share in total industrial activity begins to decline. Rapid growth of small firms could be explained where demand was rising as rural incomes were growing and where infrastructure costs still favoured small firms locating near fragmented markets, where subcontracting and local assembly was common, as for example in varieties of machine-shop activities, and where smaller firms produced a range of differentiated and innovative products serving small total markets. But as Anderson (1982) pointed out, these propositions had not been quantitatively tested by the early 1980s.

Earlier researchers were also preoccupied with investigating the extent to which small firms form the foundation for larger firm growth. As Anderson (1982) reported, the body of that research claimed that

> firms practically always begin as very small entities, with low amounts of capital drawn from the savings of the owner or borrowings from friends and relatives; initial levels of employment are low, typically less than a dozen, though the figure varies with the nature of the business; the social and occupational backgrounds of the owners vary greatly; and the firms that expand into medium or large scale activities do so continually or in steps. Expansion can be very fast for some firms,

though the growth rates appear as broadly distributed as their final sizes. (ibid., p. 923).

However work directed towards the internal workings of enterprises has been hampered by the lack of basic data on the management and characteristics of smaller firms. Considerable effort has been expended on attempting to gather consistent and measurable information about small firms. Industrial censuses in a large range of low-income countries have not been undertaken annually; they have concentrated on larger enterprises; they have only infrequently surveyed small enterprises and have often been published with long delays. As a consequence, useful time series data for smaller enterprises from official sources are largely absent.

This has had implications for research efforts into small enterprises in developing countries in three important ways. First, a considerable amount of time has been spent on gathering baseline information on small firms. This has involved identifying the population and constructing samples, devising methods to deal with delinquent returns and editing the results in a consistent manner. Second, information collected tends to be more qualitative than quantitative because of the poor record keeping and lack of cross-referencing sources through formal channels that can be used to confirm the reliability of surveyed data. This tends to limit their use in statistical analysis. Third, surveys are more often conducted on an ad hoc basis at a point in time. Few compare different points in time and fewer still have attempted to use the same database for follow-up work. As a result time series work on the small-scale sector is relatively scarce. The preoccupation with gathering baseline data and the restricted nature of the data that have eventually been collected have resulted in a preponderance of studies that have attempted to describe and report on the characteristics and features of the small-scale sector rather than test theoretical propositions about relationships and the expected behaviour of the small firm sector. This is not to suggest that theorizing and testing of theories is completely absent in relation to work on small enterprises in low-income countries, but, in comparison with work in industrialized countries or in relation to research on the behaviour of larger foreign-owned enterprises in low-income countries, it is quantitatively much less evident.

In contrast to the earlier work, a distinctive feature of the current spate of empirical work undertaken in low-income countries rests with its concentration on attempting to identify the constraints facing the development of the small-scale sector (Levy, 1993). Most surveys have sought to capture the range of factors that inhibit the growth and development of small firms. A large proportion of this information has been collected from smaller firms through questionnaires asking owners and managers to give their views either on the kind of constraint they face, whether it be related to such factors as access to finance, poor managerial skills and lack of training opportunities and the high cost of inputs, or on the severity of the constraints, often ranking them on an ordinal scale. Few studies have concentrated on a particular constraint, so that finance has most often been identified as an inhibiting factor as part of a larger investigation into a wider range of variables. The results in terms of the significance of financing acting as a constraint to development are mixed and it is difficult to draw firm conclusions about the subject. Interpretation is complicated because of the qualitative nature of the surveys and the fact that enquiries have almost exclusively been directed at firms that exist rather than following the histories of those that have eventually failed.

In summary, it cannot be denied that a considerable amount is known about the behaviour of smaller firms in a range of areas relating to growth, efficiency, management, investment and employment. A smaller proportion of this work is theoretical in nature. The vast majority of studies, particularly those relating to low-income countries, are empirical, and in general surveys have been used to generate basic information on smaller enterprises where official enumeration is lacking. The dilemma facing researchers is how to maximize the use of existing surveys and forgo the need for newer enquiries which may waste resources and time by duplicating or replicating existing sources of information. What seems clear is that, in the past, there has been a too distinct separation between theoretical work that advances hypotheses about the small-scale sector and empirical work that has not clearly sought to test hypotheses but instead has been involved with describing the characteristics of small enterprises. In part, this can best be explained by the preoccupation with gathering original data that in some way has crowded out initiatives to apply the data to test theories. Alternatively it may simply reflect data inadequacies once they had been collected. Whatever the reasons, it is apparent that work in relation to low-income countries, where these data problems most evidently exist, has lacked the formalized hypothesis, data collection and testing approaches widely adopted in other branches of industrial studies.

3. SMEs AND ECONOMIC DEVELOPMENT

A dynamic and growing small and medium-sized enterprise sector can, in principle, contribute to the achievement of a wide range of development objectives. Such objectives include the following:

- the more efficient utilization of resources;
- the generation of employment opportunities through the development and utilization of labour-intensive ('appropriate' or intermediate) technologies;

- the development of innovative entrepreneurial capabilities (the 'seed-bed' role);
- greater intra- and interregional balance;
- the more effective mobilization and utilization of domestic savings;
- the greater use of locally available resources and the production of more 'appropriate' products meeting the 'basic needs' of poor people;
- enhancing the acquisition of managerial, marketing and technical skills through training and 'learning by doing';
- the achievement of distributional and poverty alleviation objectives;
- greater national control of the economy.

The rationale for the promotion of SMEs has shifted over the postwar period. Lewis (1955, ch. 3) discussed the development of 'cottage industries' and emphasized their advantages with respect to economizing in the use of scarce capital and supervisory skills. He noted, however, that their prospects depended on their ability to improve their techniques of production and the quality of raw material inputs and on governments improving the organization of marketing and finance facilities directed to the development of such enterprises. He argued (ibid., p. 140) that 'cottage industry' should survive insofar as it 'can be made to compete on an economic basis with factory industry'; that is, 'cottage industries' had to improve their efficiency, and a case for their protection could only be made in countries where there was surplus labour.

Staley and Morse (1965) identified a 'developmental approach' to SME promotion, focusing on the determinants of their size and growth and the extent to which SMEs formed the foundations for the emergence of larger enterprises. They emphasized the need for improved efficiency and the encouragement of SMEs to adopt new methods, move into new lines of production and in the longer run, wherever feasible, to become medium- or even large-scale producers. Sutcliffe (1971, pp. 239–41) also emphasized the need to improve the efficiency (productivity) of SMEs: 'If small-scale industry is in the long run to play a dynamic role in the industrialization process, then it will have to be because it is efficient enough to compete with other production methods and not because it is an inefficient sponge for urban underemployment.'

Mkandawire (1999) notes that, in the 1970s, the promotion of SMEs was related to strategies of 'growth with equity'. With the consolidation of the neoclassical counterrevolution, SMEs were defended on the grounds of static allocative efficiency (Steel, 1993). In the 1990s, the focus on 'pro-poor' growth strategies and poverty alleviation once more led to attention being given to 'broad-based' strategies based on the creation of income and employment opportunities, in those regions and sectors where poverty is most acute, based on small-scale, labour-intensive activities and enterprises.

There are clearly inconsistencies between the objectives listed above. Mkandawire (1999) notes the likely conflict between the development of a dynamic and entrepreneurial SME sector and the sustainability of other 'livelihood' activities, leading perhaps to greater social differentiation and new sources of poverty. SMEs will come under increasing pressure to become competitive as economies become more 'open' under policies of trade liberalization. SMEs may find their position in the domestic market threatened by cheaper, mass-produced imports, and will have to respond by raising productivity and increasing the quality and reliability of their products. Such pressures will be even greater if SMEs are to enter overseas markets. Raising the productivity of the SME sector will typically require not only improving the training of managers and workers but also investing in new plant and machinery. Competitiveness depends on productivity and the latter, in part at least, depends on the amount of capital per unit of labour. There will almost certainly be a conflict, therefore, between the short-term goals of poverty alleviation through the use of labour-intensive technologies and the need to increase productivity and competitiveness through investment in both human and physical capital.

More recent research in fact seems to provide support for the more critical perspective on SMEs. There is no evidence that supports the view that SMEs exert a causal impact on economic growth or that they reduce poverty. Daniels (1999) highlights the importance of employment by micro and small enterprises in Kenya, but finds that returns to individual micro and small enterprises vary widely, with below-average earnings in general and, where they represent the sole source of income, income levels are typically below the absolute poverty line.

SMEs suffer from a number of weaknesses that may well constrain their ability to survive or grow. Specialized management is rare, with only one or very few persons performing a wide variety of tasks: production, administration, marketing and many other functions. Imperfect capital markets and policy-induced distortions may make institutional credit difficult if not impossible to obtain, especially for very small enterprises. SMEs may face highly imperfect markets for the purchase of inputs and the sale of their outputs (markets dominated by few merchants or middlemen may be monopsonistic in structure). Infrastructural facilities may be absent or deficient, and public programmes of technical and marketing assistance may often not reach the smaller firms most in need of such help.

Such problems are of course widely recognized and the great majority of less developed economies have specific programmes aimed at alleviating these constraints. But such programmes – industrial estates, extension services, training programmes, subsidized credit – use scarce resources with a high opportunity cost. Thus to argue that the SME sector deserves support at the expense of other activities is to argue that the benefits accruing as a result of committing resources to SME development are at least as great, if not greater than, the benefits that would accrue from alternative uses (Page, 1984).

From this perspective, the promotion of SMEs is not an alternative to an industrial development policy but an integral part of such a policy. SMEs are not alternatives to larger-scale enterprises, but rather complement them through the development of linkages and subcontracting relationships. Some SMEs might well become larger-scale enterprises themselves, either through internal growth or through takeovers and amalgamations, often part of deliberative government policy. Anderson (1982) concluded that a significant part of the growth of large-scale enterprises might well be found in the expansion of once small enterprises through the size distribution. The promotion of SMEs does not presuppose the absence of state intervention but rather 'presupposes a proactive and interventionist policy and state capacity to pursue such policies' (Mkandawire,1999, p. 33).

This perspective is in part reflected in the more recent work that has examined the successful growth and export competitiveness that has been achieved by clusters of small enterprises in countries as diverse as Italy, Brazil and Pakistan. Explanations for this success focus on flexible specialization and the notion of collective efficiency capturing external economies (Schmitz, 1995). The attempt to explain the success of clusters looks to their historical roots and the building up of social capital (Bazan and Schmitz, 1999). This process was found to be instrumental in mobilizing the effective use of resources although, in general, the research on finance in relation to clustering is limited.

4.   FINANCIAL ISSUES AND SME DEVELOPMENT

Most research on SMEs has been undertaken in developed market economies, especially the United States of America and the United Kingdom, and has tended to concentrate on enterprises at the upper end of the SME size distribution. Although a great deal is known about the characteristics and behaviour of SMEs in low-income countries, a number of fundamental questions remain unanswered, in part because of the lack of empirical data, but also because of the weakness of the theoretical foundations of much of the research and the absence of empirically testable hypotheses relating to the determinants of SME performance and growth (Cook and Nixson, 2000). Such unanswered questions include the following: are there systematic relationships between enterprises of different sizes and ownership patterns and access to finance? Are there systematic relationships between different forms of finance and enterprise performance? What factors determine the supply of different forms of finance, with respect both to formal and informal sector institutions?

If it is indeed the case that much of the growth of large-scale industry, which eventually predominates as industrialization proceeds, is rooted in the expansion of once small firms through the size distribution, then the focus of attention inevitably turns to an examination of the factors that constrain the growth of small and medium size enterprises.

As Schmitz (1982, p. 430) noted, the growth constraints identified in the literature can be grouped into two categories: those of an internal nature (entrepreneurship, management) and those of an external nature (access to resources, exploitation by larger enterprises). Of the external constraints identified, the limited access of SMEs to the resources of the organized financial sector has been most commonly highlighted. As Schmitz (p. 441) further notes, however, this constraint can be subdivided: the limited access to formal sector credit and the high interest rates paid by SMEs may simply be a reflection of underlying market conditions (the unstable and risky conditions of production) or else the constraint is the result of 'distortions in the views and practices of those in charge of the credit institutions'.

These two constraints are not, of course, mutually exclusive. There are a number of reasons why SMEs have limited access to formal institutional finance, including the high transactions costs and risks associated with lending to SMEs, given the vulnerabilities of SMEs to changing economic circumstances, the high mortality rate of such enterprises and the possibility of loan defaults; the inability or unwillingness of SMEs seeking loans to provide proper accounts and other documentary information required by lending institutions; and, in part as a result of the above factors, a bias on the part of financial institutions in favour of larger borrowers.

If there is a bias in favour of large-scale enterprises, it may well be policy-induced, as argued by the neoclassical school, via government intervention in financial markets through the use of interest rate ceilings and directed credit ('financial repression'). With fixed lending rates, financial institutions may not be able to add an appropriate margin for risk to cover the possibility of default. Banks and other financial institutions will thus require high levels of collateral as security that SMEs are unlikely to possess (Weiss, 2002). As already noted above, however, the neoclassical policy of financial liberalization may not be sufficient on its own to overcome the marginalization of SMEs with respect to access to formal sector credit.

But financial markets may fail in a more fundamental sense. Financial markets are inherently imperfect because of information asymmetries. Full information on the likelihood of the project's success will not be available to lenders and, even in a fully liberalized market, it may be rational for lenders not to raise interest rates to market-clearing levels but rather to ration credit on the basis of the perceived creditworthiness of applicants (Weiss, 2002; see also Weiss, 1995, ch. 9). In this situation, even profitable SMEs, if perceived to be of high risk, will remain marginalized.

This is, not of course, a new problem and most countries have attempted to address the issue by establishing public sector institutions designed to provide credit to SMEs, sometimes accompanied by other, complementary, services. Private sector institutions will find it difficult to provide a large flow of credit in small loans to SMEs with poor accounting records and no collateral (Levitsky, 1986). Public sector institutions attempt to fill this gap but perhaps at a high cost, in part as a result of high levels of default on loans. Berry and Mazumdar (1991, p. 56) argue that the general consensus is that very low interest rates are not of importance to SMEs when the latter do not borrow from the formal financial sector and that 'it is also rather generally accepted that many [SMEs] blame lack of credit when the root cause lies elsewhere, e.g. managerial or marketing problems'.

If interest rates are too low, they undermine the market and increase the risk of moral hazard, which arises from the possibility of institutions passing on losses to governments, under the guarantees agreed upon, rather than attempting to improve procedures and reduce losses over time (Anderson, 1982, p. 935). On the other hand, if interest rates remain too close to commercial rates, they reduce the benefits to SMEs. In some instances, the informal sector may well provide for the credit needs of SMEs but, in general, as enterprises grow, their capital needs are less likely to be satisfied by the informal sector and eventual access to formal sector credit becomes important. In general, SMEs will have weak bargaining positions vis-à-vis formal sector institutions, hence the need for new forms of financing, for example credit guarantee and credit insurance arrangements, adapted to local economic, social and institutional conditions.

When enterprises plan to borrow to meet working capital or fixed investment needs, their decisions will be based on the transactions costs of dealing with the various segments of the financial market (Aryeetey *et al.*, 1994). For both borrowers and lenders, effective demand for, and the supply of, finance, is determined by incentives, costs, risks and information (see Table 11.1).

All enterprises, whatever their size, will use varying combinations of internal finance (retained earnings) and external finance (the issue of equity, bank loans and the issue of debt instruments) to finance their working capital and investment needs. Their capital structures will reflect the relative importance of these various sources and may well reflect a 'pecking order' (enterprises exhibiting a strong preference for internal sources of finance before resorting to external sources). Different types of enterprises have significantly differing needs with respect to the types of financial services they require and the

Table 11.1   A framework for demand and supply of finance

Factor	Lender	Borrower
Incentives	Interest rate on loan; Building client base.	Opportunity to expand sales and capacity which is determined by market demand and competition.
Costs	Time spent screening, monitoring and ensuring repayment of loans.	Interest rate; Time spent in applying for credit.
Risks	Arrears or default if borrower is unable or unwilling to repay.	Inability to repay loan may lead to bankruptcy.
Information	Inadequate knowledge of customer's reputation and business prospects; difficulty of appraising small loans accurately.	Inadequate knowledge about dealing with banks or availability of credit; lack of adequate financial accounts on the firm; uncertainty about ability to increase sales enough to repay loan.

Source: Adapted from Aryeetey *et al.* (1994).

difficulties that they face in gaining access to finance. As enterprises grow, the size and composition of their financial requirements change. The balance between fixed and working capital will change and there is likely to be a shift from predominantly informal to formal sector institutions as sources of credit.

In the great majority of surveys of SME finance in low-income economies, the amounts of initial start-up capital are small (although relatively significant with respect to per capita incomes) and are acquired from personal savings or family sources, and gifts or loans from relatives and friends. Credit is rarely used to establish an SME (UNIDO, 1997, p. 86). Once operations have begun and production has been expanded, there are likely to be higher demands for working capital, which may initially be met from internal cash flows and retained profits. As internal sources of finance become insufficient, however, external financing options have to be explored, including advances from customers and suppliers, trade credit and a variety of other short-term, informal sources. Subcontracting has been of particular importance in a number of East and South East Asian economies, and where there is a complementary relationship between the larger firm and SMEs, the provision of credit and technical assistance may well be part of the overall relationship (Berry and Mazumdar, 1991).

As SMEs grow, the demand for fixed capital is likely to increase, and informal sources will be less able to meet these needs. As the UNIDO (1997, p. 87) study notes, at this stage of development, access to a variety of sources of external finance, in particular formal financial markets, becomes critical, and lack of access may well be detrimental to the growth of both micro-enterprises and SMEs with otherwise good potential and prospects. There is a tendency for enterprise owners and managers to overstate the problems they have in obtaining credit and, as noted above, poor management may well be the primary cause of liquidity problems and lack of creditworthiness (UNIDO, 1997, p. 89; Berry and Mazumdar, 1991, p. 56). Nevertheless 'there are many enterprises experiencing a growth in demand that warrants expansion beyond the limits imposed by the self-financing approach. Lack of access to credit does curtail the ability of some MSEs [and SMEs] to explore highly profitable opportunities, and the growth of the MSE [SME] sector could be accelerated if external financing were more readily available' (UNIDO, 1997, p. 89).

These conclusions are drawn from numerous case studies. Levy (1993) found that lack of access to finance was the leading (non-price) constraint on SMEs in both Sri Lanka and Tanzania, although he emphasized that SMEs operated in a complex environment and faced a diverse array of constraints. Aryeetey *et al.* (1994) found that in Ghana there were two SME applications for bank loans for every one awarded and that, even when loan applications were successful, the applicants received much less than originally requested. The gap between supply and demand was in part the result of problems of imperfect and costly information, high perceived risk and transaction cost and enforcement problems associated with lending to SMEs. In Sub-Saharan Africa, Aryeetey and Nissanke (1998) highlight the problems of market segmentation and fragmentation, with weak links between the segments constraining the transmission of price and policy signals across the system. Banks have yet to develop the capacity for risk management and prefer to concentrate their lending on their traditional clientele (large, established customers). In the Philippines, Saito and Villanueva (1981) found evidence supporting the argument that the higher costs associated with smaller loans, and the default risk expenses, helped explain why credit went predominantly to the larger enterprises.

To summarize some of the main points of the above discussion: virtually all studies on the constraints to the growth of SMEs (their 'graduation' to larger enterprises) point to the problems of finance (Mkandawire, 1999; UNIDO, 1997). Financial liberalization may be a necessary, but it is not a sufficient, condition for the reduction in the fragmentation of the financial sector that characterizes so many economies, especially those of Sub-Saharan Africa (Aryeetey *et al.*, 1997). Imperfections and rationing in credit markets are not simply 'policy-induced distortions' but are inherent in the structure of financial markets. Government policy has thus an important role to play in encouraging the growth of investment in the SME sector, but the provision of credit should be linked to the creation of an institutional structure that supports and monitors the performance of SMEs and provides the necessary managerial and technological support (UNIDO, 1997, p. 100).

5. EMPIRICAL EVIDENCE FROM GHANA AND MALAWI

Characteristics of the Survey Enterprises

Sample surveys of SMEs and financial institutions were conducted in Ghana and Malawi in 1999 (for full details, see Quartey, 2003; Kayanula, 2004). SMEs were defined as any non-agricultural activity undertaken for commercial purposes employing between six and 100 people. Enterprises employing between six and 29 people were classified as small-scale; enterprises employing between 30 and 100 people were classified as medium-scale. The enterprise surveys were restricted to a radius of 50 kilometres around the main urban centres in the two countries; 208 usable questionnaires from SMEs were obtained for Ghana and 189 for Malawi. In addition, information was obtained from 22 financial institutions in Ghana and nine financial institutions in Malawi.

For Ghana, 69 per cent of the sampled enterprises were engaged in manufacturing activities, 26.5 per cent were in services, with the remainder in construction and mining and quarrying. For Malawi, 37 per cent of sampled enterprises were engaged in manufacturing activities, 31 per cent were engaged in distribution and 32 per cent were engaged in other service sector activities. The sectoral distribution of enterprises in the Ghana survey is broadly similar to other Ghanaian studies that show that manufacturing and services dominate the SME sector. In Malawi, it is likely that manufacturing SMEs are underrepresented in the sample.

For Ghana, 85 per cent of the sampled enterprises were established by their owners, 9 per cent were inherited and 5 per cent were acquired by purchase; 87 per cent of the sampled enterprises were owned privately by Ghanaian citizens, and 74 per cent were managed by their owners, with 20 per cent employing salaried managers. For Malawi, 77 per cent of sampled enterprises were established by their owners, 15 per cent were inherited and 6 per cent acquired by purchase; 83 per cent of sampled enterprises were owned privately by Malawian citizens, and 85 per cent were managed by their owners, with 7 per cent employing salaried managers.

For Ghana, 84 per cent of entrepreneurs interviewed were male, which probably underrepresents female entrepreneurs who have traditionally dominated the services sector, especially trading. For Malawi, 86 per cent of entrepreneurs interviewed were men. As in Ghana, it would appear that female entrepreneurs are underrepresented in the sample, although it is not clear why this is the case.

With respect to the educational background of enterprise owners, virtually all interviewees had some degree of formal education in both countries. In Ghana, 9 per cent of interviewees were university graduates and 17 per cent had professional qualifications. Enterprise owners either had been salaried employees who had left their employment to set up their own business (60 per cent of interviewees), had operated other businesses (18 per cent) or had been employed in another SME (16 per cent). In the case of Malawi, 6 per cent of interviewees were university graduates and 12 per cent had professional qualifications; 46 per cent of enterprise owners had been salaried employees prior to establishing their own business and a further 31 per cent had previous experience of owning an SME.

Sources of Finance

The principal sources of finance for start-up capital include owner's savings and/or retained profits, gifts from friends and relations, moneylenders, suppliers' credits, bank loans, non-governmental organizations (NGOs) and SME-support institutions. It is clear from the data presented in Table 11.2 that owners' savings were the most important source of start-up capital in both countries, accounting for 63.6 per cent of the total in Ghana and 75.8 per cent in Malawi. These figures are consistent with those found in other studies (for example, Aryeetey et al., 1994; Daniels and Ngwira, 1993). Small enterprises were, not surprisingly, more dependent on this source of finance than medium-sized enterprises. Loans from friends and relations were the second most important source of finance.

With respect to bank loans, 7.4 per cent of respondents in Ghana and 4.3 per cent of respondents in Malawi had access to the formal sector for start-up capital. Medium-sized firms, mainly in the manufacturing sector, in both countries, were more likely to use bank loans for this purpose.

The picture was similar with respect to sources of finance to meet working capital, raw material and plant and equipment needs. Friends and relations are relatively more important as sources of finance in Ghana than in Malawi, and suppliers' credits are also marginally more important (but never account for more that 5–10 per cent of the total supply of finance). Once again,

Table 11.2   Sources of finance for start-up

	Ghana		Malawi	
	No. of respondents	% of total responses	No. of respondents	% of total responses
Own savings	180	63.6	157	75.8
Friends and relations	53	18.7	11	5.3
Moneylender	3	1.1	1	0.5
Bank	21	7.4	9	4.3
Donor	0	0.0	3	1.4
NGO	1	0.4	3	1.4
Supplier credit	7	2.5	4	1.9
Loan from SME support institution	0	0.0	5	2.4
Equity	11	3.9	4	1.9
Other	7	2.5	10	4.8

Source: Survey data.

medium-sized firms are more likely to have access to bank finance and suppliers' credits, confirming the generally held view that, for whatever reasons, the majority of small enterprises and many medium-sized enterprises are effectively excluded from formal sector sources of credit. For these particular enterprise samples, neither moneylenders nor SME support institutions were more than marginal sources of finance.

The Supply of Finance

As noted above, a number of financial institutions were surveyed in both countries. Even though SMEs were overwhelmingly dependent on own sources of finance and that of friends and family members, SMEs did make efforts to acquire formal sector credit. According to the survey data, 43 per cent of surveyed enterprises in Ghana and 46 per cent of surveyed enterprises in Malawi had obtained support from formal sector financial institutions at one time or another. In Ghana, it was estimated that SMEs had a 42 per cent chance of success in their loan application, with the major reasons for failure relating to the inadequacy of their bookkeeping and financial records, high default rates and the high transactions costs associated with relatively small loans. In Malawi, the success rate was estimated at 37 per cent. Although the informal financial sector was an important source of finance, it was relatively unattractive to SMEs in both Ghana and Malawi, given the high interest rates, short repayment periods and the limited lending capacity characteristic of this sector (see also Aryeetey *et al.*, 1994).

Both countries have a variety of institutions, formal, semi-formal and informal, which directly or indirectly attempt to cater for the needs of SMEs (fuller details are given in Quartey, 2003; Kayanula, 2004), and both countries have undergone various processes of financial liberalization. Nevertheless weaknesses remain. It would appear that small enterprises, and those located in rural areas in particular, are in effective marginalized by the formal financial sector, and it is clear from the data presented above that the majority of SMEs find it difficult or impossible to acquire formal sector credit and depend on own financing or less-preferred informal sector institutions. The problems referred to in section 4 above are writ large in the two country case studies. We briefly discuss the policy implications of this analysis in section 6 below.

Finance and Enterprise Performance

Based on the sample survey enterprise data, an attempt was made, using the analysis of variance (ANOVA) and multiple regression analysis, to examine the way in which the availability of finance, and the types of finance that SMEs had access to, influenced various dimensions of enterprise performance (defined with respect to the growth of sales revenue over the period 1995–7), taking into account various enterprise characteristics. The results are suggestive and illustrative, and although they pass the appropriate statistical tests for significance, they nevertheless should be interpreted with caution and regarded as orders of magnitude only.

From the literature review, a number of hypotheses were identified and the attempt was made to test them empirically. The hypotheses can be grouped around two main issues, namely, the determinants of access to external finance and the determinants of external performance. The hypotheses are as follows:

- the performance of enterprises is influenced by access to external finance;
- the performance of enterprises is influenced by type of ownership;
- location influences the access of the SME to external finance;
- the gender of the entrepreneur influences access to external finance;
- the gender of the entrepreneur is an influence on enterprise performance;
- the level of education of the entrepreneur influences access to external finance;

- the level of education of the entrepreneur influences enterprise performance;
- the size of the enterprise influences access to external finance.

The results drawn from the analysis must be regarded as tentative, but they are nevertheless suggestive and generally consistent with what has been found in other studies. With respect to access to external finance, the results suggest that the size of the enterprise influences access, with medium-sized enterprises enjoying an advantage in this respect; the location of the SME influences access: a rural location is a disadvantage while an urban location enjoys better access to both finance and inputs; the gender of the entrepreneur is important in Ghana, with females having an advantage (female-owned enterprises, however, do not perform better that male-owned enterprises, a reflection perhaps of the small number of female-headed enterprises in the Ghana sample); in Malawi, male and female entrepreneurs appear to have equal access to finance; the level of education influences access: the higher the level of education, the better the access to external finance. In Malawi, the type of enterprise ownership and management (owner-managed or salaried manager-managed) does not appear to influence enterprise performance. In Ghana, on the other hand, salaried manager-managed enterprises appear to perform better.

The attempt was made to use two-stage least squares regression analysis to ascertain the determinants of enterprise growth, access to finance and size. The inadequacy of the sample data means that there are limits to what econometric analysis can achieve. Data on the profitability of enterprises are not available, for example, as the majority of SMEs do not keep adequate records. Enterprise growth was measured as growth in sales for the three years covered by the surveys, but again there are reasons to doubt the accuracy of such data. Where enterprises are very small, a small absolute increase in sales or employment will give high rates of growth that may be misleading. In addition, problems of multicollinearity arise when we attempt to disentangle access to finance, the size and age of the enterprise and its rate of growth.

For the Ghanaian sample, an urban location, the use of salaried managers, access to finance and the level of education of the entrepreneur all exert a significant and positive effect on growth. It is also found that small firms grow faster than medium-sized firms when growth is defined as growth in sales, although when growth is defined with respect to value added, medium-sized firms grow faster than small firms. With respect to access to finance, it is found that firm size exerts a positive and statistically significant effect, that is, the SMEs' access to finance improves as they increase in size. Logically, if medium-sized firms have better access to finance and access to finance is an important determinant of growth, then medium-sized firms should grow more rapidly than small firms, with respect to any measure of enterprise growth. Obviously, for a variety of reasons, some small firms will grow more rapidly than their larger counterparts. We must therefore interpret this result with some caution.

For the Malawian sample, similar results are obtained. An urban location, access to finance, access to raw materials and the education level of the entrepreneur are significant for growth. But female-headed enterprises do not grow as rapidly as those with male proprietors and, unlike the case of Ghana, where there is some evidence of positive export activity in the SME sector, in Malawi, the impact of exports on enterprise growth is statistically insignificant.

What stylized picture emerges from these country surveys? In general, the most marginalized enterprises are small or very small, located in rural areas, owned or managed by proprietors/entrepreneurs with limited formal education and few business skills and with little access to formal sector finance or managerial/technical inputs. Such an enterprise will have few or no networking opportunities, will find it very difficult to grow and will be very vulnerable to changes in market conditions, for example the easier availability of imported consumer goods following trade liberalization. Many female proprietors may well find themselves in this position.

The more successful SME may well be larger or growing more rapidly, owing to its access to formal sector credit. It will be located in an urban area with a more educated or skilled owner/proprietor, it may well have better networking opportunities and may even be able to engage in exporting. But in the majority of sub-Saharan countries, including Ghana and Malawi, it is highly unlikely that SMEs will be able in the very near future to emulate the example of economies such as Taiwan or Hong Kong where, at least for much of their early period of industrialization, SMEs played an exceptionally important role in the development process.

6.   CONCLUSION: POLICY ISSUES AND IDEAS FOR FURTHER RESEARCH

Policy Issues

The conclusions drawn from the sample surveys of SMEs in Ghana and Malawi are consistent with other similar studies and reinforce what most policy makers are already well aware of. The availability of credit to SMEs is important in terms both of their performance and of growth prospects. The great majority of studies, as we have noted already, argue that the limited availability of credit is an important constraint. Rural SMEs appear to be at a particular disadvantage in this respect and there is evidence that female entrepreneurs do not have equal access to credit when compared with male entrepreneurs. Programmes that attempt to assist SMEs must thus become both rural and gender aware. Education appears as an important determinant of performance and access to finance and, consistent with what is found in other studies, policy must focus on the provision of relevant training in the areas of management, bookkeeping, accountancy, marketing and so on. If SMEs are to export, they will need additional financial and technical assistance and market information before they can be expected to improve their performance.

At the macroeconomic level, financial liberalization may be necessary but not sufficient to promote SME development. SMEs should benefit from the more rapid development of the financial sector, but financial liberalization may well lead to higher real rates of interest which have a disproportionate impact on SMEs. At the same time, trade liberalization may undermine the position of SMEs in the domestic market because of increasing imports of cheap, mass-produced commodities.

There is general agreement in the literature that governments have an important role to play in stimulating the development of the SME sector, through the provision of credit, the creation of an institutional structure to support and monitor the performance of SMEs and the provision of managerial and technical support. Credit subsidization has proved to be effective in a number of countries, including the Republic of Korea, Taiwan, China and Japan. Special credit programmes directed at SMEs have been successful in Indonesia and Korea (UNIDO, 1997, p. 100). Such programmes have failed in many other countries, however, not least because of the inability or unwillingness of borrowers to pay back subsidized loans that are often regarded as gifts.

Before support policies can be expected to succeed, it must be recognized that there needs to be greater consistency with respect to what is being referred to: micro, small, medium-sized enterprises, informal versus formal sectors, rural versus urban sectors, and so on. SMEs are not 'a unified and distinct analytical category in any meaningful sense' (Lyberaki and Smyth, 1990, p. 141). From this it also follows that policies towards SMEs need to be tailored to the specific economic, social, institutional and cultural circumstances of individual countries. Policies cannot be taken 'off the shelf'. Furthermore individual sectors will differ with respect to their needs for finance and technical and managerial assistance. The links between policy and improved enterprise performance are not always clear and, as noted by McGrath and King (1999), the links between education and enterprise in particular are poorly understood.

The focus of this research has been on finance and SMEs and it is in this area that there is general agreement that new forms of financing should be explored. These may range from the provision of micro credit to the very smallest enterprises, improving the bargaining position of SMEs vis-à-vis the commercial banks, perhaps through cooperation between SMEs, to strengthening the capacities of existing financial institutions to deal more effectively with the SME sector, through the reduction of transactions costs, for example, and the development of appropriate institutions in the semi-formal or informal sectors. Official development assistance and NGOs have an enhanced role to play in this respect. Another option is what is called 'mezzanine' financing (Durie, 1998) which carries a low rate of interest but the financing is construed in such a way that it allows the lenders to participate in the success of the company in a manner similar to equity participation.

In many countries, there is the lack of an 'organic policy' for SMEs, in spite of the rhetoric to the contrary. Confusion over definitions and the often undifferentiated policy packages exacerbate the relative ineffectiveness of the overall policy approach. It needs to be emphasized that SME promotion is not an end in its own right, but rather a means to an end. As Lyberaki and Smyth (1990, p. 142) argue, policies towards SMEs must form a continuum with national industrialization policies and general economic policy measures to promote development defined with respect to each country's specific aims and objectives. It would appear to be the case that, in both of our case study countries, this important insight is yet to be translated into a holistic and effective menu of approaches to the promotion of SMEs.

Ideas for Further Research

In general at least four strands of research can be indicated that combine theoretical and empirical perspectives on SMEs, within which promising research ideas can be pursued. First, research is needed on the forms of finance used by small and medium-sized enterprises and made available by lending institutions and investors. In particular, a clear picture is required of the financing differences between firms of different sizes and the differences in financing in relation to types of ownership structures. Cross-country and regional differences may also exist in these respects.

Second, research is required into the relation between different financial forms and firm-level performance. Existing research on small size and performance has not isolated the importance of different forms of finance. Methods should be devised to examine the relationship between different financial structures of firms and a range of performance measures (including output, productivity, employment and survival rates).

Third, research is required relating to the behaviour of small and medium-sized firms with different forms of finance. We need to predict how different forms of finance will affect the allocation of profits between income (dividend flows), investment and consumption and their effect on other forms of expenditure relating to innovation, marketing and human resource development through training. In particular, the links need to be made between different forms of finance and the impact of small firm development on poverty alleviation.

Finally, research is required on the supply side of finance, involving formal and informal sector lending institutions and savers, and the macroeconomic environment, including economic policies, promotional policies and the role played by private, international and non-governmental organizations.

A final point needs to be made. Smallness of factory or plant size is not in and of itself a virtue. The development of SMEs must be a coherent part of a development programme aimed at the achievement of explicit socioeconomic objectives which vary both over time and between countries. Appropriate and effective policy packages for SME development will similarly vary and it cannot be assumed that there will exist a standard policy package. The conditions under which SMEs can realize their employment and growth potential have to be identified and the links with poverty alleviation and other development objectives clearly established.

REFERENCES

Anderson, Dennis (1982), 'Small industry in developing countries: a discussion of issues', *World Development*, **10**(11), November, 913–48.

Aryeetey, E. and Nissanke, M. (1998), *Financial Integration and Development: Financial Gaps Under Liberalisation in Four African Countries*, London: Routledge.

Aryeetey, E., Hettige, H., Nissanke, M. and Steel, W.F. (1997), 'Financial market fragmentation and reforms in Ghana, Malawi, Nigeria and Tanzania', *World Bank Economic Review*, **11**(2).

Aryeetey, E., Baah-Nvako, A., Duggleby, T., Hettige, H. and Steel, W.F. (1994), 'Supply and demand for finance for small scale enterprises in Ghana?', World Bank Discussion Paper, no. 251.

Bazan, L. and Schmitz, H. (1999), 'Social capital and export growth: an industrial community in Southern Brazil', IDS Discussion Paper no. 361, Institute of Development Studies, University of Sussex, Brighton.

Berry, A. and Mazumdar, D. (1991), 'Small-scale industry in the Asian–Pacific Region', *Asian–Pacific Economic Literature*, **5**(2), September, 35–67.

Berry, A. and Levy, B. (1994), 'Indonesia's small and medium-size exporters and their support systems', Policy Research Working Paper no. 1402, World Bank, Washington, DC.

Boocock, J.G. (1995), 'Risk capital of SMEs in Malaysia', in M.M. Woods (ed.), *Malaysia in International Business*, Chapman and Hall, pp. 233–7.

Collier, P. and Mayer, C. (1989), 'The assessment: financial liberalisation, financial systems and economic growth', *Oxford Review of Economic Policy*, **5**(4), 1–12.

Cook, Paul and Nixson, Frederick (2000), 'Finance and small and medium-sized enterprise development', Finance and Development Research Programme, Paper no. 14, mimeo, IDPM, University of Manchester.

Daniels, L. (1999), 'The role of small enterprises in the household and national economy in Kenya: a significant contribution or a last resort?', *World Development*, **27**(1), 55–65.

Daniels, L. and Ngwira, A. (1993), *Results of the Nation-wide Survey on Micro, Small and Medium Enterprises in Malawi*, New York: PACT Publications.

Dawson, J. (1993), 'Impact of structural adjustment on the small enterprise sector: a comparison of the Ghanaian and Tanzanian experiences', in A. Helmsing and T. Kolstee (eds), *Small Enterprise and Changing Policies: Structural Adjustment Financial Policy and Assistance Programmes in Africa*, London: IT Publications, pp. 71–90.

Durie, D. (1998), 'Financial instruments for the enterprise development', Final Report, AESMEC'98, Asia–Europe SME Conference, Naples, Italy, May, Consorzio Ferrara Richerche.

Kariuki, N. (1995), 'The effects of liberalisation on access to bank credit in Kenya', *Small Enterprise Development*, **6**(1), 15–23.

Kayanula, D. (2004), 'Finance and small and medium-sized enterprise (SME) development: a study of the SME sector in Malawi', University of Manchester, PhD thesis, mimeo.

Kayanula, D. and Quartey, P. (2000), 'The policy environment for promoting small and medium-sized enterprises in Ghana and Malawi', Finance and Development Working Paper no. 14, Institute of Development Policy and Management, University of Manchester.

Levitsky, J. (1986), 'Assessment of bank small scale enterprise lending', World Bank Industry Department, mimeo.

Levy, Brian (1993), 'Obstacles to developing indigenous small and medium enterprises: an empirical assessment', *The World Bank Economic Review*, **7**(1), 65–83.

Lewis, W.A. (1955), *The Theory of Economic Growth*, London: George Allen and Unwin.

Lyberaki, A. and Smyth, I. (1990), 'Small is small: the role and functions of small-scale industries', in Meine Pieter van Dijk and Henrik Secher Marcussen (eds), *Industrialisation in the Third World: The Need for Alternative Strategies*, London: Frank Cass.

McGrath, S. and King, K. (1999), 'Enterprise in Africa: new contexts, renewed challenges', in K. King and S. McGrath (eds), *Enterprise in Africa*, London: Intermediate Technology Publications.

Mead, D. (1999), 'MSEs tackle both poverty and growth (but in differing proportions)', in K. King and S. McGrath (eds), *Enterprise in Africa*, London: Intermediate Technology Publications.

Meier, R. and Pilgrim, M. (1994), 'Policy-induced constraints on small enterprise development in Asian countries', *Small Enterprise Development*, **5**(2), 32–8.

Mkandawire, T. (1999), 'Developmental states and small enterprises', in K. King and S. McGrath (eds), *Enterprise in Africa*, London: Intermediate Technology Publications.

Page, J. (1984), 'Firm size and technical efficiency: application of production frontiers to Indian survey data', *Journal of Development Economics*, **16**(1–2), 129–52.

Parker, R.L., Riopelle, R. and Steel, W.F. (1995), 'Small enterprises adjusting to liberalisation in five African countries', World Bank Discussion Paper no. 271, African Technical Department Series.

Quartey, P. (2003), 'Finance and small and medium-sized enterprise development in Ghana', University of Manchester, PhD thesis, mimeo.

Saito, K. and Villanueva, D. (1981), 'Transactions costs of credit to the small-scale sector in the Philippines', *Economic Development and Cultural Change*, **29**(3).

Schmitz, H. (1995), 'Collective efficiency: growth path for small-scale industry', *Journal of Development Studies*, **31**(4), 529–66.

Schmitz, Hubert (1982), 'Growth constraints on small-scale manufacturing in developing countries: a critical review', *World Development*, **10**(6), June, 429–50.

Staley, E. and Morse, R. (1965), *Modern Small-Scale Industry for Developing Countries*, New York: McGraw-Hill.

Steel, W. (1993), 'Analysing policy framework for small enterprise development', in A. Helmsing and T. Kolstee (eds), *Small Enterprise and Changing Policies: Structural Adjustment, Financial Policy and Assistance Programmes in Africa*, London: IT Publications, pp. 39–49.

Steel, W. (1994), 'Changing the institutional and policy environment for small enterprise development in Africa', *Small Enterprise Development*, **5**(2), 4–9.

Sutcliffe, R.B. (1971), *Industry and Underdevelopment*, London: Addison-Wesley.

UNIDO (1997), *Industrial Development: Global Report 1997*, Oxford: Oxford University Press for UNIDO.

Weiss, John (1995), *Economic Policy in Developing Countries: The Reform Agenda*, Englewood Cliffs, NJ: Prentice Hall/Harvester Wheatsheaf.

Weiss, John (2002), *Industrialisation and Globalisation: Theory and Evidence from Developing Countries*, London: Routledge.

12. Company financial structure: a survey and implications for developing economies

Sanjiva Prasad, Christopher J. Green and Victor Murinde

---

1. INTRODUCTION

The financial structure of a company arises from the ways in which it finances new investment. There are three main funding choices which are then reflected in a firm's capital structure: employ retained earnings, borrow using debt instruments or issue new shares. These components of capital structure also reflect firm ownership in the sense that retentions and equity correspond to shareholder interests while borrowing gives rise to claims by debt holders. This is the broad pattern found in developing and developed countries alike (see La-Porta et al., 1999).[1] Capital structure also affects corporate behaviour (Hutton and Kenc, 1998). Thus financial structure is concerned with the closely-linked relationships among financing policy, capital structure and firm ownership. The development of these relationships is a key factor in explaining how economic agents acquire and utilize assets through firms and capital markets, and create returns, whether in the form of direct remuneration, capital gains, debt interest or dividends.

There is a large volume of research on company financial structure in industrial countries, but virtually no work has been done on developing countries (LDCs), apart from a limited amount of empirical research pioneered particularly by Singh: for example, Hamid and Singh (1992), Singh (1995) and Brada and Singh (1999). It is scarcely an exaggeration to state that, until recently, corporate finance did not exist as an area of research for LDCs. Some of the reasons for this are clear. Many LDCs initially chose a state-sponsored route to development, with an insignificant role assigned to the private corporate sector. In the poorer countries, irrespective of development strategy, there is only an embryonic corporate sector and most corporate financing needs have been met by regional and international development banks. However, in almost all these countries, development banks have experienced serious difficulties (Murinde, 1996; Murinde and Kariisa-Kasa, 1997). Thus there is a conspicuous gap in the empirical research on corporate finance in LDCs; this gap requires urgent attention, given that the research is likely to have profound policy implications for promoting poverty-reducing economic growth.

In this chapter, we conduct a critical survey of the key literature in order to isolate the leading theoretical and empirical issues surrounding company financing, capital structure and ownership that are particularly relevant for developing economies. We aim to take stock of existing knowledge in the area and identify the main strands of the theoretical and empirical literature, considering the policy implications of existing knowledge, and spelling out the current policy problems which should be addressed by future research. As the subject area is vast, the survey is highly selective. Well-known theories are not discussed at length; only the main arguments within the literature are summarized. Also we concentrate, as far as possible, on the *direct* relationships among financing, capital structure and ownership. We do not cover the numerous topics, such as dividend policy, which indirectly relate to capital structure but which are the subject of a substantial literature in their own right. In the empirical part of the survey, we again concentrate on research involving the direct description and analysis of capital structure and ownership, especially orthodox regression studies whose main goal is usually to understand the temporal and, more particularly, the cross-sectional differences among companies' capital structures. We do not cover research based on event studies or on interview and survey research methods. These each constitute a vast and varied literature in their own right and they have been the subject of several recent surveys. MacKinlay (1997) has surveyed event study methods; Ang and Jung (1993) and De Haan *et al.* (1994) have surveyed interview and survey methods. In reviewing the empirical work, we do not dwell in detail on each individual set of results from the industrial countries. Rather we summarize the main results, and seek to evaluate their implications for LDCs. Of course, we also draw on the small body of research that *is* directly concerned with LDCs.

The literature as a whole is fragmented, and there are numerous ways in which a review could be organized. We chose to follow the approach of Harris and Raviv (1991) in organizing the survey around the 'driving forces' behind financing and capital structure. The theoretical component of the survey draws heavily on Masulis (1988) and Harris and Raviv (1991), but also extends their work by examining the impact of managerial shareholdings, corporate strategy and taxation on the firm's capital structure. Sections 2 to 5 of the chapter cover the leading issues in the theoretical literature: section 2 summarizes the seminal contribution of Modigliani and Miller (1958); section 3 focuses on agency theory and capital structure; asymmetric information models are discussed in section 4; and section 5 addresses the issue of taxation. The empirical component of the survey distinguishes first between univariate and multivariate studies, the former aimed at documenting basic facts and testing general descriptive hypotheses, the latter using a regression approach to test more specific, theoretical hypotheses.

Univariate studies of developed and LDCs are discussed in section 6. Section 7 contains a brief overview of the main empirical methods used in multivariate research before we turn to the research results themselves. Most multivariate studies can be interpreted either as a precise test of a certain theory or as a test of the role of particular variables in determining capital structure, with such variables usually serving as measures of some specific theoretical predictions. Accordingly, section 8 discusses studies that investigate the following: the impact of ownership and control on capital structure; the role of business groups, a particularly important issue in many developing economies; the influence of bankruptcy costs; corporate strategy and capital structure; and tests of the pecking order hypothesis against trade-off theories. In section 9, we organize the results by explanatory variable, and review particularly the influence on capital structure of tangibility, size, profitability, growth, risk, non-debt tax shields and the industrial classification of firms. The major empirical research findings are organized in a way that allows comparisons to be made between theoretical predictions and empirical results. We identify promising research ideas (PRIs) for future research relating to corporate finance and development, and these are set out in the final section, 10.

2. THE BACKGROUND: MODIGLIANI–MILLER AND THE TRADITIONAL THEORIES

The traditional view (TV) of corporate finance was based on a firm's weighted average cost of capital (r_a) that is, the weighted sum of debt and equity costs or the minimum overall return that is required on existing operations to satisfy the demands of all stakeholders. TV begins with the observation that debt is generally cheaper than equity as a source of investment finance. Hence a firm can lower its average cost of capital by increasing its debt relative to its equity (that is, its leverage), provided the firm's cost of debt and equity remain constant. However this process cannot be extended indefinitely because higher levels of debt increase the likelihood of default, resulting in debt holders and shareholders each demanding greater returns on their capital. Therefore the r_a schedule is U-shaped when plotted against leverage, with the cost of debt and equity both rising at an increasing rate as bankruptcy risk increases. The corresponding company market value schedule is an inverted

U-shape. Optimal leverage occurs where r_a is minimized and the value of the firm is maximized.

The TV was overturned by the celebrated paper of Modigliani and Miller (MM, 1958). MM assumed a perfect capital market and used a simple arbitrage mechanism to derive three, now well-known, propositions relating to the value of the firm, the equity cost of capital and the cut-off rate for new investment. MM's Proposition I states that the market value of any firm is independent of its capital structure. Hence the firm's average cost of capital is also independent of its capital structure. It does not have an optimal, market value-maximizing, debt–equity ratio: any degree of leverage is as good as any other. This is a consequence of the perfect capital markets assumption, which implies that the r_a and the market value schedules are both horizontal, when plotted against leverage. Proposition II states that the rate of return required by shareholders rises linearly as the firm's debt–equity ratio increases. That is, the cost of equity rises so as to offset exactly any benefits accrued by the use of cheap debt. However some criticisms of this proposition show that a disparity normally exists between the capitalization rate and the cut-off rate (Peyser, 1999). Proposition III states that a firm will only undertake investments whose returns are at least equal to r_a.

There are two essential differences between the conclusions of MM and TV. First, under TV, the firm's value and cost of capital are related to its capital structure, whereas MM's Proposition I states that they are independent of capital structure. Second, under MM's Proposition II, if management aimed to maximize shareholder returns, they would maximize outstanding debt up to 100 per cent of capital. Clearly this cannot be precisely true, since a firm which is 100 per cent debt-financed is technically bankrupt.[2] However, Proposition II does imply a linear relationship between shareholders' rate of return and firm leverage. Therefore, at low levels of debt, the cost of equity rises faster under MM than under TV. At higher levels of debt, as the risk of default increases, the cost of equity rises faster under TV than under MM's Proposition II.

A direct argument for the TV is that firms may have a comparative advantage over households in the debt market, because of lower transactions and information costs. If so, investors can borrow more cheaply if they borrow indirectly by purchasing the shares of a levered firm. Investors who are high-cost borrowers will be willing to pay a higher premium for the shares of levered firms than will low-cost borrowers. Also, as a firm's leverage increases, the number of investors willing to hold its shares will decrease. The counterargument in the spirit of MM is to question the assumption that firms do, in fact, have a comparative advantage in the debt market. If they do not, investors will be indifferent between the shares of a leveraged firm and home-made leverage: a combination of shares in an unleveraged firm and their own debt.

MM's propositions do have to be modified to accommodate taxation, a topic we take up in detail in section 5, and financial distress. Proposition II implies that maximizing the return on shareholders' equity is equivalent to 100 per cent debt financing. This is based on two assumptions: first, that the firm does not face any costs of financial distress which increase as leverage increases; and second, that the marginal rate of return which debt holders require remains constant as leverage increases. In reality, it is more likely that the higher the leverage of a company, the greater will be the costs of restructuring and possible liquidation. Moreover, as leverage rises, the risk of default also rises, resulting in debt holders demanding a higher rate of return for them to hold an additional unit of debt. Accordingly the value of a firm will be inversely related to its probability of financial distress and to the discount at which its assets may be disposed of in a forced sale.

In general, therefore, market imperfections such as taxes and financial distress affect the firm's capital structure. These are discussed in the next three sections.

3. AGENCY THEORY AND CAPITAL STRUCTURE

3.1 Agency Costs

The seminal work on agency theory and capital structure is Jensen and Meckling (1976); key subsequent contributions include Ross (1973), Shavell (1979), Fama (1980, 1990), Arrow (1985) and Jensen and Meckling (1992). The basic model is that of an owner-managed firm that wishes to finance projects in excess of its own resources. The firm has two options: to issue equity or to use debt. If the firm issues equity, the owner–manager's fractional interest within the firm decreases. This increases the incentives for an owner–manager to undertake excessive perk consumption since the costs to the owner of such activities have been lowered as a result of a reduction in his fractional interest. Such costs include: (i) the monitoring expenses of the principal (the equity holders); (ii) the bonding expenses of the agent (the manager); and (iii) the money value of the reduction in welfare experienced by the principal as a result of the divergence between the agent's decisions and those which maximize the welfare of the principal. If markets are efficient, potential external investors anticipate such actions by the owner–manager (James, 1999) and the price of new equity will be discounted to allow for the monitoring costs of external shareholders. This 'underpricing' of new equity (Rock, 1986) suggests that the owner–manager would prefer to finance projects using debt rather than equity.

However debt also incurs agency costs because of the conflict of interest between external lenders and the owner–manager. Debt increases the owner–

manager's incentive to invest in high risk projects which, if successful, offer high returns which accrue exclusively to the owner–manager, but also increase the likelihood of failure when the owner–manager's exposure is limited to the value of his equity holdings. Debt holders, on the other hand, do not share the profits of success, but will share in the costs of a bankruptcy: they are incurring extra risk without additional expected returns. Debt holders can be thought of as having written a European put on the firm's assets, with bankruptcy corresponding to exercise of the put by shareholders. As the amount of debt increases, debt holders will demand a higher premium to compensate them for the increased probability of failure. Thus the agency costs of debt include the opportunity costs caused by the impact of debt on the investment decisions of the firm; the monitoring and bonding expenditures by debt holders and the owner–manager; and the costs associated with bankruptcy and reorganization (Hunsaker, 1999).

Since equity and debt both incur agency costs, the optimal debt–equity ratio involves a trade-off between the two types of cost. Agency costs associated with equity are at a maximum when the owner–manager's share of equity is zero, and the firm is wholly owned by outside shareholders. These costs fall to zero as the owner–manager's equity share rises to 100 per cent. Similarly the agency costs of debt are at a maximum when all external funds are obtained from debt. As the level of debt falls, agency costs are reduced: first, because the amount of wealth that can be reallocated away from debt holders falls, and second, since the fraction of equity held by the owner–manager is reduced, her share of any reallocation also falls. The total agency cost schedule is therefore a U-shaped function of the ratio of debt to outside equity, and the optimal ratio of debt to outside equity is that which minimizes total agency costs.

When a firm is close to bankruptcy, shareholders have no incentive to inject new capital into value-increasing projects since the returns of such a venture will accrue mainly to debt holders. Thus the higher is a firm's leverage, the less is its incentive to invest in value-increasing projects; this will have implications for the nature of debt contracts, and for the characteristics of highly levered firms (Myers, 1977). First, we would expect bond contracts to include features which prevent asset substitution, such as the sale of profitable parts of the business to finance new high-risk projects. Second, industries which have limited scope for such asset substitution should have higher levels of debt (for example, regulated public utilities and banks). Third, firms with low growth prospects and strong cash flows should also have high amounts of debt that would use up resources that would otherwise be used for perquisites. Such firms are typically thought to be those in 'mature' industries, such as steel, chemicals, brewing and tobacco.

3.2   Conflicts between Shareholders and Managers

Conflicts between shareholders and managers take several distinct forms. First, managers prefer to have greater perquisites and lower effort, provided that they do not have to pay for these through lower wages or by a lower market value of their personal equity holdings (Jensen and Meckling, 1976). Second, managers may prefer short-term projects, which produce early re-sults and enhance their reputation quickly, rather than more profitable long-term projects (Masulis, 1988). Third, managers may prefer less risky investments and lower leverage to lessen the probability of bankruptcy, with its associated job losses (Hunsaker, 1999). Fourth, managers will generally wish to mini-mize the likelihood of employment termination. As this increases with changes in corporate control, management may resist takeovers, irrespective of their effect on shareholder value (Garvey and Hanka, 1999). Managers and share-holders may also disagree over a firm's operating decisions. Managers will typically wish to continue operating the firm even if liquidation is preferred by shareholders (Harris and Raviv, 1990).[3] They may also prefer to invest all available funds even if shareholders want to receive dividends (Stultz, 1990).

A varied menu of solutions has been proposed to limit or resolve these problems. Jensen (1986) argued that managers will attempt to evade share-holder control by financing less profitable projects using internal funds, which are subject to a minimum of external monitoring. Shareholders can prevent management from undertaking unprofitable expansion by reducing free cash flow, either by increasing a firm's dividend or by increasing its leverage. As Hunsaker (1999) points out, increased leverage also increases the risk of bankruptcy, and therefore limits management's consumption of perquisites. The optimal capital structure is then determined by trading off the benefit of debt in preventing investment in value-decreasing projects against the cost of debt in impeding investment in value-increasing projects. Firms which have more value-increasing investment opportunities than value-decreasing oppor-tunities will have less debt, *ceteris paribus*.

Other vehicles for removing shareholder–manager conflicts include the provision of incentive-compatible managerial contracts and the role of the managerial labour market in exerting discipline on managerial behaviour. Shleifer and Vishny (1989) develop a model in which a manager has an incentive to invest the firm's resources in those assets that are more highly valued under that manager than under the next best alternative manager. By this means, the manager counters any potential disciplining devices and can demand higher compensation, together with greater autonomy. Shleifer and Vishny show that, when investment projects are irreversible, the firm overinvests in projects whose value is greater under one particular manager than under the next best manager. Such projects incur two distinct types of cost: the first is a social cost because investments are not value-maximizing; the second is a transfer of economic rent from shareholders to managers. This helps explain why managers like growth: growth promotes those areas specific to the manager's skills and provides management benefits through entrenchment. However Jensen and Meckling (1976), Green (1984) and Smith and Warner (1979) argue that management can be disciplined by the use of convertible debt. Convertibles reduce the agency costs of monitoring because they give lenders an opportunity to share in a firm's profits. It may be expected that, the greater the growth opportunities available to a firm, the greater the probability that management will overinvest. If discipline is effective, this implies a positive relationship between firm growth opportunities and the level of convertible debt, and a negative relationship between growth and ordinary (long-term) debt.

Williamson's (1988) transactions cost approach provides an alternative framework for analysing shareholder–manager conflicts. In this approach, debt and equity are regarded as vehicles for corporate governance rather than as financial instruments per se; see, for example, Core *et al.* (1999), Brada and Singh (1999) and Vilasuso and Minkler (2001). Williamson argued that financial structure is affected by the specificity of the assets that a firm owns, that is, the extent to which its assets can be redeployed in different projects. The more specific the asset, the lower will be its liquidation value. In this context, debt acts as a straitjacket for investment opportunities: credit will not be provided for very specific projects since, in the event of liquidation, the amount realized will be low. Thus leverage should decrease as asset specificity rises. Equity holders are less affected by specificity, since they surrender the firm's assets to lenders at liquidation. Overall, as asset specificity rises, the costs of debt and equity rise, with the costs of debt rising faster than equity. Thus redeployable assets should be financed by debt, whilst equity should be used for non-redeployable assets. Williamson argued that this conclusion was at odds with the prevailing literature, as it suggests that debt is a neutral financial instrument with equity being the instrument of last resort. However this conclusion was foreshadowed by the pecking order theory of Myers (1984) and Myers and Majluf (1984) that we discuss in section 4.

Corporate strategy may also influence capital structure, although this relationship has not been widely debated in the mainstream corporate finance literature. Strategy consists of those actions and plans that influence the portfolio of activities in which the firm is involved and how they are financed. Several authors have argued that firms which adopt single and related strategies are more conservative and therefore most risk-averse, while those which pursue unrelated strategies are likely to be less risk-averse. See Barton and Gordon (1987, 1988), Lowe *et al.* (1994) and Krishnaswami *et al.* (1999). This runs counter to standard diversification arguments, and suggests that strategic focus implies less risk-taking behaviour. Riah-Belkaoui and Bannister (1994) suggest that a firm's capital structure can be directly affected by its organizational structure; specifically, that the adoption of a multidivisional ('M-form') strategy is associated with an increase in free cash flow. If so, and as noted above, the capital market may force such firms to finance new capital by debt rather than by equity in order to reduce management's misuse of cash (Jensen, 1986).

3.3 Conflict between Shareholders and Debt Holders

Smith and Warner (1979) identify four major sources of conflict between shareholders and debt holders. The first is *dividends*: in theory, a firm could sell its assets and pay a liquidating dividend to its shareholders with the bondholders being left with valueless claims. In practice, this is usually precluded by corporate law. The second is *claim dilution*: as a firm issues additional debt, existing debt will fall in value if the newly issued debt has higher priority. Even if it does not, existing debt will fall in value if the risk of bankruptcy is perceived to have increased. The third source of conflict is *asset substitution*: bonds are priced in relation to the risk of the project which is being financed. Lenders' claims will be diluted if the firm substitutes projects that increase the firm's variance, thus transferring wealth from debt holders to shareholders. Finally there is *underinvestment or misinvestment*: a firm in financial difficulties has an incentive to reject low-risk, low positive net present value projects whose benefits accrue mainly to bondholders, in favour of high-risk, high net present value projects whose benefits will accrue to shareholders if they materialize.

Myers (1977) argues that, the greater is the proportion of growth assets in a firm, the greater is the potential conflict of interest between shareholders and debt holders, because the easier it is to alter a firm's market value and risk in such a way as to benefit shareholders at the expense of debt holders. To minimize these conflicts, firms with high growth opportunities should have higher leverage and use more long-term debt than firms in mature industries. Alternatively, if capital market participants have rational expectations and perfect information, they will anticipate these conflicts of interest and counteract them by adjusting the price and conditions on a firm's bonds. In fact information in capital markets is far from perfect and the two main competing hypotheses concerning the impact on firm value of debt holder–shareholder conflicts are built on the assumption of imperfect information: the Irrelevance hypothesis and the Costly Contracting hypothesis.

The Irrelevance hypothesis predicts that the conflict of interest between debt holders and shareholders does not change the value of the firm. According to Smith and Warner (1979), if a firm's investment is given, debt covenants will only alter the distribution of payoffs between debt holders and shareholders, and will not alter the overall value of the firm. If, however, a firm's investment is not given, dividend payouts, asset substitution and underinvestment may cause changes in the investment policies of the firm. In principle, therefore, the value of the firm may change if shareholders engage in activities that maximize their wealth at the expense of debt holders. Galai and Masulis (1976) argue that a redistribution of wealth from debt holders to shareholders will result from an increase in the risk of the firm, an increase in debt or a distribution of assets to shareholders. However, as Jensen and Meckling (1976) observe, if investors are aware of the conflict between shareholders and debt holders and discount any bonds which are issued, shareholders will be unable to gain from any such actions, since the proceeds from the sale of debt will be correspondingly less.

The Costly Contracting hypothesis predicts that the use of contracts to control shareholder–debt holder conflicts will increase the value of the firm. By the imposing of restrictive covenants on debt, the value of the firm will increase, for two reasons. First, the covenants reduce the costs which debt holders incur if shareholders do not maximize the value of the firm; second, they reduce the monitoring costs of debt holders. This leads to increased monitoring, improved management decisions and hence an increase in the value of the firm. However restrictive covenants involve costs, particularly the transactions costs of writing the contracts. In principle, therefore, the benefits of covenants can be traded against their costs to arrive at a unique set of optimal contracts that will maximize the value of the firm. In this setting, information asymmetry and monitoring problems play an important role. See Krishnaswami *et al.* (1999).

Agency costs have several important implications for the features of debt contracts. Green (1984) and Masulis (1988) argue that convertible debt will have lower agency costs than plain debt. Since conversion rights enable debt holders to share in any positive wealth transfers to shareholders and to gain from any increase in risk, shareholders have fewer opportunities to engage in wealth-transferring activities. Thus convertible debt tends to moderate shareholder–manager conflicts *and* shareholder–debt holder conflicts. Such debt issues should therefore be less discounted than plain debt issues. More specifically, Thatcher (1985) argues that the gain accruing to convertible bondholders from investments in profitable low-risk projects, which would otherwise be rejected by shareholders, is reduced to the conversion premium, since debt holders have less incentive to convert. This allows shareholders to capture most of the profits in such profitable low-risk projects, thereby reducing the agency problem.

A problem with covenants is that the partitioning of debt into separate classes with different rights creates a new potential for conflict of interest among the various classes of debt holders. According to Masulis (1988), such conflicts are greatest during periods of financial distress. Bulow and Shoven (1978) focus on conflicts arising from differences in the seniority and time priority of debt. When a firm has negative net worth, shareholders will not subscribe to more shares, but short-term debt holders may extend additional credit in exchange for a partial payment of their existing claims so that the firm can avoid default (Hunsaker, 1999). This is beneficial to the firm since it prevents immediate bankruptcy and allows short-term debt to be paid off, thereby maintaining the time priority of short-term debt. On the other hand, if bankruptcy is declared, the claims of long-term debt will be accelerated, which in turn may result in non-payment to short-term debt holders if the long-term claims are of senior or equal standing to the short-term debt claims. Given the multitude of different bond covenants used in practice, it is not altogether surprising that the theoretical literature has produced a host of special cases, but fewer general conclusions about the implications of covenants. See Smith and Warner (1979).

If debt covenants can help resolve shareholder–debt holder conflicts, other constraints may also perform this function. Since dividends are the main route by which shareholders divert cash from debt holders, it is natural to consider constraints on dividend payments. Wald (1999) develops a model in which conflict arises, not because of information asymmetries, but because of incomplete contracts: debt contracts cannot cover all possible future contingencies. Wald shows that a dividend constraint can solve the moral hazard problem that arises in the presence of incomplete contracts. In this setting, more profitable firms that can afford higher dividends will have lower debt–equity ratios so as to avoid hitting the dividend constraint.

A further important issue in situations of conflict and imperfect information is that of managerial reputation. Diamond (1989) analyses reputation in a model in which a firm can invest in a safe asset, a risky asset or a combination of the two. Firms investing in a safe project will not default; those investing in the risky project may default. Investors, ex ante, cannot distinguish between firms, consequently the lending rate will reflect their beliefs about the riskiness of a firm's investment. Diamond assumes that investors can only observe defaults. Hence, the longer the period of non-default, the better is a firm's reputation as a safe firm and the lower will be its borrowing costs. This suggests that older firms will choose the safe project to maintain reputation. Younger firms with a lesser reputation may choose risky projects with higher prospective returns; but, if they survive, they will eventually choose the safe project. Accordingly older firms will have lower business risk and lower levels of debt, *ceteris paribus*.

If there is a high level of managerial share ownership, reputation is less important, as there are fewer outsiders. However this does not lead to unambiguous conclusions about leverage levels. Kim and Sorensen (1986) argue that firms with high inside ownership will issue *more* debt (and possibly excessive debt) than those in which ownership is more dispersed. This is because firms with high inside ownership face higher equity agency costs and lower debt agency costs, arising from the lesser divergence of managerial and shareholder interests. In addition, such firms may issue more debt than is optimal simply for the insiders to maintain control. Grossman and Hart (1982) point out that higher leverage also commits managers to generating the cash flows required to meet debt repayments and consequently reduces the possibility of management engaging in excessive perquisites. This in turn increases the value of the firm's equity and correspondingly reduces the agency costs of issuing equity as external investors perceive that management have reduced their 'shirking'. However other theories suggest that firms with high inside ownership will issue *less* debt. Jensen (1986) argues that owner-managers will prefer lower debt levels so as to increase their discretion over the use of free cash flow. Friend and Lang (1988) and Hunsaker (1999) point out that lower debt levels reduce the risk of bankruptcy, and so help preserve the management's stake in the firm. Thus owner-managers will have a level of debt which is lower than optimal, and the greater the concentration of management ownership the lower will be the firm's level of debt. A further consideration is that well-diversified external shareholders would be willing to incur higher debt levels than those which would rationally be sought by less diversified risk-averse owner managers (Short and Keasey, 1999).

The key issue here is the extent to which shareholder–debt holder conflicts will persist in the presence of a high degree of insider ownership. It is natural to suppose that, the higher the proportion of shares owned by the management, the more difficult it becomes for outsiders to discipline owner-managers, without the aid of high levels of debt. However Grossman and Hart (1982) show that, if we start from a situation in which managers have no equity, then, as management ownership increases, owner-managers' and external shareholders' interests are increasingly tied together. The dispersion of external shareholders is also important. For example, Zeckhauser and Pound (1990) and Chen and Steiner (2000) argue that the presence of a few large external shareholders in a firm may prevent owner-managers from adjusting debt ratios to suit their own interests. Large external shareholders can act directly as monitors and help to lower some of the agency problems of debt financing. Thus such firms should have a higher level of debt than those firms with no large external shareholders. Large external shareholders may also act as a signal to the market that managers are less able to engage in profit-reducing activities, thereby mitigating the need for debt to be used as a signal of firm quality. These arguments suggest that investment funds have an important role to play in the monitoring process.

4. THEORIES OF ASYMMETRIC INFORMATION BETWEEN FIRMS AND THE CAPITAL MARKET

4.1 Interactions between Investment and Capital Structure: the Pecking Order Hypothesis

It is generally agreed that there are important informational asymmetries between borrowers and investors. In this section, we follow Harris and Raviv (1991) in outlining three main theoretical strands of literature on asymmetric information: the interaction of investment and capital structure, signalling with debt, and models based on marginal risk aversion.

Myers and Majluf (MyM, 1984) is the seminal contribution to this literature,[4] which draws attention to the use of debt to avoid the inefficiencies in a firm's investment decisions which would otherwise result from information asymmetries. The nature of the asymmetric information in this case is that managers know more about their companies' prospects, risks and values than outside investors. This creates the possibility of adverse selection and moral hazard. Potential investors purchase company securities whose quality they cannot ascertain *ex ante*, and which may turn out to be 'lemons' (Akerlof, 1970). Asymmetric information between investors and firm insiders may lead to underpricing of a firm's existing equity by the market. This has the effect of also underpricing new equity which is used to finance new investment projects. If management's objective is to maximize the return to all shareholders, the net effect is that new investors obtain a higher capitalized cash flow from this investment than pre-existing shareholders, which may cause the project to be rejected even when it has a positive net present-value (NPV) (Rock, 1986). In principle, the problem of underpricing of new equity could be solved by using financial securities that may not be undervalued by the market, particularly internally generated funds. In contrast to MM, this suggests that there will exist a specific hierarchy or 'pecking order' of securities to be used in the financing of projects. Moreover, if a firm has financial 'slack', but asymmetric information means that the market does not know this, managers will not issue new equity, even if it involves passing up a good investment opportunity, so that the interests of present shareholders are protected. If investors understand this point, the market will assume that a decision not to issue shares is good news. If management does propose a new share issue, it will be interpreted as bad news, and the share issue will precipitate a fall in the firm's share price. MyM also show that, if a firm can issue debt, it will do so rather than issue equity, and this will result in the *ex ante* value of the firm being higher, since the loss in market value is reduced thanks to the reduction in underinvestment losses.[5]

These arguments lead to the Pecking Order hypothesis, which Myers (1984) summarized as follows. First, firms prefer internal over external funds to finance new investment. They may choose not to issue new securities and miss a positive NPV investment rather than issuing equity at a low price which disadvantages existing shareholders. Second, managers adapt target dividend payout rates to their investment opportunities, given the downward inflexibility of dividends. In setting the target payout rates, they aim to ensure that 'normal' investment plans can be met by internal finance. Third, if retained earnings are less than planned investment, the firm first depletes its financial slack (cash and marketable securities). If, instead, retained earnings exceed investment, it first invests in cash or marketable securities, and then pays off debt. If the firm is persistently in surplus, it may increase its target payout rate. Fourth, if financial slack is depleted and a sufficiently favourable investment opportunity is presented, the firm will resort to external finance. In this event, it starts with the safest security (plain debt) and then hybrid securities such as convertible bonds. As it climbs up the pecking order, a firm faces increasing costs of financial distress inherent in the risk class of debt and equity securities. Only when it runs out of debt capacity, and the potential costs of financial distress become important, will it finally resort to a new equity issue. Thus internal finance is at the top, and equity is at the bottom, of the pecking order. A single optimal debt–equity ratio does not exist: a result which takes us back to the original no-tax MM Proposition I, but by a very different route. The original MM propositions would suggest that firm financial policy is irrelevant and this is obviously not an implication of the Pecking Order hypothesis.

Like the MM propositions, MyM's Pecking Order hypothesis has generated substantial debate. MyM's model is not easily applied to new firms, an omission which was rectified by Narayanan (1988) whose conclusions are broadly consistent with those of MyM. However, if the model is extended to allow the firm to choose its capital structure before its investment decision, it transpires that the use of debt or hybrid securities, such as preferred stock, tends to cause underinvestment (Heinkel and Zechner, 1990). This implies that the firm does once more have an optimal capital structure, consisting of a mixture of debt and equity, a result that remains robust when the analysis is extended to include corporate taxes.

Brennan and Kraus (1987) argue that MyM's model only incorporates equity and riskless debt. Since the pecking order theory relies in part on the costs of distress and bankruptcy, this is potentially an inconsistency. They present a counterexample in which the essential ingredients are asymmetric information and the existence of a signalling equilibrium in which the market will still underprice shares as lemons.[6] In their model, if a firm chooses a financing mix that minimizes the cost of raising investment funds, then, depending on the structure of the investment payoff function, it is possible that investors can infer the main parameters of this function (and hence firm quality) from the financing mix chosen. This amounts to costless signalling of information to the market, or a form of revealed preference. If the market can infer a firm's financial position from its observable financial policy, the firm cannot improve on the pricing of its securities by changing that policy. In this model, the cost-minimizing financial policy includes a share issue, and will often involve using part of the proceeds of the issue to retire debt. Constantinides and Grundy (1989) show that similar arguments are applicable to firms in which managers have an equity stake. Such firms can invest in positive NPV projects by issuing sufficient amounts of a hybrid security, such as convertible debt, so as to undertake the projects and repurchase some of the firm's existing equity. Evidently both these results contradict the pecking order prediction that equity is the financing of last resort.

4.2 Signalling with the Proportion of Debt

This literature is concerned with the ability of firms to signal their true financial position to outsiders, by the capital structure that they choose. Typically it is assumed that the investment opportunity is fixed. The seminal contribution in this strand of literature is due to Ross (1977); more recent contributions, such as Hunsaker (1999), link the role of debt to bankruptcy. The basic model assumes two types of firm facing different, positive present value, investment projects, one of which (A) is superior to the other (B). A signalling equilibrium for these firms can be established using a particular cut-off value of debt as a signal of the firm's type. If the actual value of debt issued exceeds the cut-off value, the market perceives the firm to be of type A (a high-quality, high-leverage firm); alternatively, if debt is less than the cut-off value, the market perceives the firm to be of type B (low quality and leverage). If a firm signals itself to be of type A, it must not issue more debt than the net present value of the investment project for firm A, otherwise it will go bankrupt. Similarly, if the firm is of type B, it must not issue more debt than the NPV of the investment project for firm B. This constitutes an equilibrium provided that each firm has no incentive to signal incorrectly. If type A managers signal that they are of type B, they will issue less debt, and therefore will not raise sufficient funds to finance the type A investment project. Their compensation is therefore less than if they signal correctly. If type B managers signal that they are of type A, then the amount of debt issued is greater than the present value of the type B project, and bankruptcy occurs. Type B managers will signal truthfully if the marginal gain of a false signal is less than the cost of bankruptcy. Since both types of firm signal truthfully, outsiders can infer the quality of the firm from its debt level. Ross's model has three main implications. First, in a recapitulation of MM, the cost of capital is independent of the financing decision of the firm, despite each firm having its own unique level of debt. Second, the level of bankruptcy risk rises as the amount of debt issued by the firm increases. Third, the value of the firm is positively related to its debt–equity ratio: higher-quality firms issue more debt.

A limitation of Ross's (1977) model is that management does not hold shares in the firm; management compensation is determined by a contingent contract, related to the value of the firm. Heinkel (1982) considers the case of the owner-managed firm. As before, a costless signalling equilibrium is one where the value-maximizing decisions of insiders determine the optimal level of debt to be issued. Heinkel proves that, the greater the quality of the firm, the less the amount of debt issued. For a low-quality firm to misrepresent itself as high-quality, it must issue more underpriced debt and reduce the amount of its overpriced equity. Similarly, for a high-value firm to misrepresent itself as a low-value firm, it must issue less overpriced debt and more underpriced equity. These actions by themselves are beneficial to outsiders but detrimental to insiders in the firm. Thus value-maximizing insiders have no incentive to signal incorrectly and their financing decisions will support a costless, fully revealing equilibrium. However this model implies that high-quality firms will have *low* levels of debt, which is exactly the reverse of Ross (1977) which holds that high-quality firms have *high* levels of debt! This again underlines the point that, in recent models of capital structure, small changes in assumptions can produce large changes in results.

Debt may also be used as a signal in the context of entry into a new market. Poitevin (1989) develops a model in which there is an incumbent firm and a new entrant, and the financial structure of each firm is endogenous. There are two types of entrants: a low-cost firm and a high-cost firm. In a separating equilibrium,[7] the entrant's type can be inferred by observing its financial policy. If financial policy is consistent with a low-cost entrant, investors agree to provide finance. If any other financial policy is observed, investors assume that the firm is high-cost, and will not finance its investment. The incumbent will finance using only equity that is actuarially fairly priced (since his marginal cost and thus firm value is known). The low-cost entrant will partially finance with debt. The level of debt chosen is such that it would bankrupt the high-cost firm with certainty; and it is this property of the financing decision which enables the low-cost firm to signal truthfully that it is low-cost. High-cost entrants cannot masquerade as low-cost because the resulting high level of debt and probability of bankruptcy will be too high. The advantage of debt is that the capital market places a higher value on the debt-financed firm because it is perceived to be low-cost; the disadvantage of debt is that it makes the entrant prone to be attacked by the all-equity incumbent via a price war, threatening the entrant with bankruptcy. The model suggests why younger firms may be more financially vulnerable than established firms. Investors can assess the value of the incumbent and its securities more easily than they can the entrant and its securities.

4.3   Models based on Marginal Risk Aversion

Models based on marginal risk aversion invariably assume that the firm has an owner–manager who is risk-averse.[8] Therefore the level of debt incurred depends in part on the degree of risk aversion of the entrepreneur. The more risky a project, the smaller will be the entrepreneur's desired stake. Leland and Pyle (1977) consider an entrepreneur who wants to undertake an investment project and plans to hold a certain fraction of the firm's equity. The remaining equity is raised from outside lenders. As before, a signalling equilibrium exists in which the entrepreneur's ownership increases with the quality of the firm, because the amount of equity retained by the entrepreneur is interpreted by the market as a signal of quality. Since entrepreneurs are known to be risk-averse, one who takes a high stake in a risky project must be confident of its success. Entrepreneurs with inferior projects will not choose a higher equity stake (to signal a higher-quality firm), because it would increase their exposure to the project's idiosyncratic risk, and thus reduce their utility. The equilibrium has several properties. First, a project will be undertaken only if its true market value exceeds its cost. Second, the market treats higher entrepreneurial ownership as a signal for a more favourable project. Third, entrepreneurs make larger investments in their own projects than would be the case if they could costlessly communicate their true expected return. Thus the entrepreneur suffers a welfare loss of investing more than is optimal in a project, so as to communicate its worth. This may cause some profitable projects to be rejected. Leland and Pyle suggest that intermediaries which specialize in information gathering and monitoring of entrepreneurial projects could reduce this welfare loss by offering entrepreneurs better terms of finance. Fourth, an increase in the specific risk of the project, or the risk aversion of the entrepreneur, will reduce their equilibrium stake in the project. Fifth, an increase in the specific risk of a project will result in a greater expected utility for the entrepreneur.

5.   THEORIES OF THE IMPACT OF TAXATION ON CAPITAL STRUCTURE

The theoretical literature has examined two main aspects of the impact of tax on the firm's capital structure. The first concentrates on the corporate tax deductibility of debt; the second looks at the way in which taxes influence the decisions of the firm's security holders, and hence their willingness to hold the firm's securities. Modigliani and Miller (1963) recognized at an early stage that their perfect capital markets assumptions need modifying to allow for corporate tax. Debt typically offers a tax shelter, because interest is deducted before taxable profits are struck. In the presence of corporate taxes, MM showed that the value of the firm as a whole rises as the level of leverage increases, suggesting that firms have no constraint on the incentive to issue debt, other than the direct threat of bankruptcy.

However owners of debt and shares are also subject to tax on their security income, and this affects their after-tax returns. King (1974, 1977) was among the first to consider these issues more generally, and he pointed out that the marginal tax rate applicable to securities depends both on the official tax rates and on the system under which tax is collected. Under the *classical system* operated in most countries, debt interest is a deductible expense for firms, but is taxed as income in the hands of debt holders. Dividends, on the other hand, are effectively taxed twice: once in the hands of the firm at the corporate profits tax rate, and then a second time in the hands of shareholders at the rate appropriate to dividend income, which may be different from the rate applicable to interest or other income, and may differ among individual recipients. Under the *imputation system*, the double-taxation of dividends is partially relieved by an 'imputation': a tax credit which enables shareholders to credit the profits tax already paid by a firm to their own tax liability on account of their dividend income from that same firm.[9]

King (1977) examined the financing decisions of a firm whose objective is to minimize the overall tax liability of its shareholders. This is a reasonable objective in the world of MM, in which taxation is the only factor that can be used to distinguish among securities. To summarize his results, we define as follows: z = the capital gains tax rate; c = the corporate profits tax rate; t = the marginal rate of tax on dividend income; and u = the marginal rate of tax on interest income. King distinguished three cases which, for simplicity, we set out under the classical system:

1. if equity is given, and $(1 - u)/((1 - c)(1 - z)) > 1$, the firm chooses debt over retentions;
2. if retentions are given, and $(1 - u)/((1 - c)(1 - t)) > 1$, the firm chooses debt over equity, a result which recapitulates that of Modigliani and Miller (1963);
3. if debt is given, and $(1 - t)/(1 - z) > 1$, the firm chooses equity over retentions.

The intuition underlying these results is that one minus the marginal tax rate can be interpreted as the after-tax retention rate of each £1 of profit associated with any form of financing. To minimize its tax bill, the firm chooses the financing which gives the highest retention rates.

King's analysis still suggests that, abstracting from other issues, exogenous tax rates imply all-or-nothing financing decisions. In contrast, Miller (1977) argues that marginal income tax rates are, in fact, heterogeneous, as shareholders typically include a combination of taxable and tax-exempt entities. In Miller's view, the firm will issue debt until, at the margin, the corporate tax savings are equal to the personal tax loss, that is, until the (marginal) corporate tax rate is equal to the investor's personal tax rate. Since these two rates cannot be controlled by the firm, at equilibrium, the tax structure determines the aggregate level of debt, but not the amount issued by a single firm. Miller's analysis suggests that aggregate leverage is determinate, but irrelevant for the individual firm. However it can also be argued that the marginal (personal) lender faces an upward schedule of the return that is required to lend an additional unit of funds, because of heterogeneous personal tax rates. Likewise any individual firm typically has pre-existing non-debt tax shields, and will face an increasing probability of distress as debt increases. Thus the marginal (corporate) borrower will also face rising costs of debt, because the value of the potential tax shield will tend to fall as leverage increases.

As Auerbach and King (1983) point out, the existence of a Miller tax equilibrium depends on there being institutional constraints on corporate and individual behaviour, to rule out tax arbitrage, for example. Moreover the nature of the equilibrium depends crucially on the exact nature of the constraints. Small 'realistic' changes in the constraints, allowing for different kinds of tax-exempt institutions, for example, can generate equilibria with a distinct optimal debt–equity ratio for each firm. This argument was developed by DeAngelo and Masulis (1980), who incorporate into the analysis non-debt tax shields such as depreciation and investment tax credits. Their results overturn Miller's irrelevancy theorem without the need for bankruptcy, agency or any other leverage-related costs. They argue that firms with large non-debt tax shields relative to their cash flow will have less debt in their capital structure, because the non-debt tax-sheltered expenditures effectively exhaust the firm's tax-saving capacity. There is a negative relationship between the value of the marginal corporate tax saving and the amount of debt issued: the higher is leverage, the higher is the probability that the potential tax shield from additional debt will be partially or totally lost. The optimum level of debt occurs when the marginal corporate tax benefit of debt is equal to its marginal personal tax disadvantage.

Subsequent contributions to this literature have further emphasized the role of constraints in supporting an interior optimum capital structure, but have extended the analysis to allow for bankruptcy. This is sometimes called the Tax Shelter Bankruptcy Cost model. Kim (1978) applies mean variance analysis to show that, when firms are subject to taxes and to costly bankruptcies, corporate debt capacity occurs at less than 100 per cent debt financing.

Brennan and Schwartz (1978) also study the impact of corporate taxes and bankruptcy on the relationship between capital structure and valuation. The issue of debt has two effects on the value of the firm: first, it increases the tax savings as long as the firm survives; but second, it reduces the probability of survival. Depending on which is the stronger of the two, the value of the firm might rise or fall as a result of a debt issue. The optimum value of debt is that at which the marginal tax benefit associated with one extra unit of debt is equal to the expected marginal cost of default (which rises as the firm's gearing increases). Among the predictions of this model are first, that firm value increases the most following a debt issue by firms with the lowest business risk; second, that, as the maturity of debt increases, the optimal leverage ratio falls; and third, that an increase in earnings risk also reduces the optimal leverage ratio. Masulis (1988) notes that, within these models, debt is usually subject to a higher personal tax rate than is equity, although the differential is assumed to vary among investors. This implies that investors who currently prefer equity must be persuaded to switch to debt by a price reduction. This is an additional factor that diminishes the overall tax advantage of debt.

One immediate problem with theories of an optimal debt ratio based on bankruptcy costs is that there is debate about the quantitative importance of such costs. The seminal study by Warner (1977) of US railroad bankruptcies found that the direct costs of bankruptcy were practically trivial. Altman (1984) argued that, once the indirect costs are taken into account, bankruptcy costs are much larger, and certainly sufficient to influence firm behaviour. In this respect, an important contribution of the Tax Shelter Bankruptcy Cost model is to establish that there is an interaction between the tax system and financial distress. As Mayer (1986) points out, corporate tax payments are non-negative: national tax authorities typically allow companies to carry forward losses, but not to claim immediate tax refunds on account of current losses. Financially distressed firms encounter tax exhaustion well before they are close to bankruptcy, and this imposes an immediate and significant cost on the use of debt for such firms, independently of the immediate costs of bankruptcy per se.

6. UNIVARIATE EMPIRICAL RESEARCH

A vast volume of work has investigated empirically the capital structures of firms in the industrial economies. There have also been some empirical studies of firms in developing economies, most of which aim at documenting basic facts, and are based on the analysis of financial ratios. They may therefore be classified as univariate empirical studies. On its own, a set of financial ratios does not necessarily provide much information; accordingly, in this section, we emphasize *inter*-country comparisons among industrial countries and between industrial and LDCs. Moreover, since few specific hypotheses are tested in the papers under review, we follow Mayer (1990), and classify the results in a set of observations, each one representing a broadly accepted stylized fact. In making these observations, we begin by noting that a distinction is usually drawn between firms in 'market-based' or 'Anglo-Saxon' financial systems (especially the USA and UK) and those in 'bank-based' or 'European' systems (especially Germany and Japan). See, for example, Mayer and Alexander (1990).

Observation 1

Regardless of whether a market-based or bank-based capital structure is observed, retentions are the dominant source of finance for firms in the main industrial countries. Observation 1 is drawn from our synthesis of findings by Corbett and Jenkinson (CJ, 1996[10]), Mayer (1988, 1990), Borio (1990) and Wright (1994). CJ examine corporate capital structures at the aggregate level in Japan, Germany, the UK and USA, for the period 1970–89. Internal funds were the main source of finance in all countries, with the UK financing the highest proportion (97.3 per cent) of its investment by retentions, and Japan financing the lowest (69.3 per cent). Similar results are reported by Mayer (1988) for France, Japan, Germany, the UK and USA for 1970–85. The UK was again the highest user of retentions (107 per cent of investment[11]) while Germany was the lowest with 67 per cent. This finding is supported by Mayer (1990), Murinde *et al.* (1999) and Borio (1990). Moreover Wright (1994) finds that the level of retained earnings employed by non-North Sea industrial and commercial companies in the UK has remained essentially the same over the period 1982–94.

Observation 2

Firms found in bank-based financial systems have higher leverage than firms in market-based ones. This is almost part of economic 'folklore', and it can be found in Borio (1990), Bisignano (1990) and many others. Borio's study of developed economy corporate capital structures finds that countries are either 'high leverage', such as Japan, Germany, France and Italy, or 'low leverage', such as Canada, the UK and USA. A similar conclusion is drawn by Bisignano (1990), who surveys the aggregate capital structures of Japanese, German and US firms.[12]

However there are many qualifications to observation 2. First, it depends on the precise definition of leverage used in the calculations. Rajan and

Zingales (1995) observe that, if leverage is calculated as a ratio of debt to total assets, at *book value*, then Canadian firms (at 36 per cent) are the most highly geared of the G-7 economies, with German firms being the lowest at 20 per cent; the gearing levels of US and Japanese firms are comparable at 35 per cent and 31 per cent, respectively. If, however, leverage is calculated as the ratio of debt to debt-plus-equity, at *market value*, then UK and German firms have the lowest gearing, at 16 per cent, with Italian companies having the highest, at 28 per cent. CJ (1996) find that British and American firms are more highly geared than German firms if book values are used to calculate the ratio of debt to debt-plus-equity.

Second, CJ (1996) note that, although US and UK firms are located in market-based financial systems, the proportion of internal funds employed by US firms increased from 74.5 per cent in 1970 to 103.7 per cent in 1989; and US and UK firms both reduced their reliance on market-based sources of finance over this period. They suggest that this was due to financial innovation over the period. Bisignano (1990) also notes that US firms' dependence on new equity issues has fallen, especially during the 1980s. He suggests that merger activity may have been responsible for this development.

Third, Atkin and Glen (1992) report that, since World War II, bonds have constituted a significantly higher fraction of external finance for US firms than new equity. Moreover loans (mortgages and commercial paper) and trade credit each provided more new finance than did equity. These data highlight some important changes in the capital structure of US firms post-World War II: a decline in equity and bank finance and an increased use of directly intermediated debt.

Fourth, the dependence of Japanese firms on debt is neither long-standing nor persistent. Elston (1981) notes that, during the 1930s, 60 per cent of all funds employed by Japanese firms were equity. This fell to 17 per cent in the mid-1970s, compared to 40 per cent for West Germany, 50 per cent for the UK and 60 per cent for the USA. More recently, however, Japanese firms have relied less heavily on bank debt and more on retained earnings and non-bank external sources. The previously strong *keiretsu* relationships between affiliates have also become weaker as a result of changes in banking law which forced bank portfolios to become more diversified. This is generally reckoned to have increased the cost of debt, but has allowed firms to be freer to raise funds from equity. During the 1970s, equity issued increased from 6 per cent to 10 per cent of total external finance, while bond financing increased from 4 per cent to 8 per cent in the same period. Moreover the internationalization of Japanese business, together with the increasing flow of overseas investment, has given rise to a natural desire to raise funds from abroad. Atkin and Glen (1992) also find that there has been a marked reduction in Japanese leverage since the 1970s, falling from

400 per cent (of equity) in 1977 to 100 per cent in 1988. The authors assert that this decrease can be explained in part by the liberalization of the Japanese financial markets.

Bisignano (1990) notes several differences in the financial behaviour of firms in 'bank-based' financial systems. In 1965–89, for example, the issues of securities and bonds by German firms were small in comparison to their Japanese and US counterparts, a difference that cannot be explained by regulatory or other market restrictions. Since the mid-1970s, holdings of the German corporate sector by banks have fallen, as they have in Japan, but, unlike the case of Japan, bank lending is still the dominant source of finance. Overall it appears that Japanese firms, which have, historically, been closer to German firms, are now approaching those of the USA. See Rajan and Zingales (1995) and Borio (1990). Indeed there are similar patterns of corporate finance for firms within both market-based and bank-based systems. UK and US firms have relied less on market sources of finance, whilst those in Germany have increased theirs. Of the four countries studied by CJ (1996), Japan was the only one to rely more heavily on external than on internal sources. Bertero (1997) notes that the French financial system could be classified as a bank-based system, but there are features which are either unique to France or more like other systems. Typically the French system was more of an overdraft system, like that of the UK, rather than a German- or Japanese-type bank system. More recently French firms have increased their use of retained earnings at the expense of short-term debt and have also increased their use of equity and bonds. Bertero asserts that the latter has been as a result of increased capital market efficiency caused by financial reform. See also Cobham and Serre (2000). Cobham et al. (1999) draw parallel conclusions for Italy.

The 'battle of the systems', regarding the relative merits of bank-based and market-based financial systems, is integral to the developing policy debate on the evolution of financial systems in developing and transition economies. See Murinde and Mullineux (1998). It is therefore important to observe that, in the industrial countries, it can safely be concluded that many of the stereotypes of firms within market-based and bank-based financial systems have broken down, or perhaps never did exist in the precise form that the 'folklore' would have it. Firms in all countries are increasingly influenced by the global capital market in which securities are traded and international banks are active. But each country's system of corporate finance retains some of its own distinctive features, partly because of its historical development and partly because of current economic circumstances, particularly the existing regulatory regime.

Observation 3

Firms located in developing economies rely less heavily on internal finance than those found in developed economies. Observation 3 was proposed by Hamid and Singh (1992) who analyse the corporate finance characteristics of the top 50 manufacturing firms in India, Thailand, Jordan, Malaysia, Taiwan, Mexico, Pakistan, Zimbabwe and South Korea over the period 1980–87. They find that firms in these countries used less internal finance than their developed economy counterparts. They attribute this to different growth rates, and to lower retention ratios, rather than, for example, to the distorting influences of inflation which has had a major influence in at least some developing economies. Atkin and Glen (1992) and Singh (1995) reach similar conclusions. The use of internal finance does vary across LDCs, just as it does across the industrial economies. Atkin and Glen (1992) survey macroeconomic data on the corporate sector in several developing economies (Zimbabwe, Pakistan, Malaysia, India and South Korea) and find that Zimbabwean and Pakistani firms rely most heavily on internal finance: 58.5 per cent and 58.3 per cent, respectively, of all sources, whilst South Korean firms were least dependent, with 12.8 per cent. See also Guariglia (1999). They argued that, as South Korea has a more advanced financial system, it provides a greater number of external financing options for investment projects; indeed South Korean firms do use a greater amount of external finance, both equity and long-term debt, than do Pakistani firms. Cobham and Subramaniam (CS, 1998) find that Indian firms use more equity and fewer retained earnings than their UK counterparts.

Observation 4

Equity and debt are equally important as the major source of firm finance in LDCs, although one is more important in some countries and the other is more important elsewhere. Hamid and Singh (1992) and Singh (1995) find that firms in developing economies rely more heavily on equity than on debt to finance growth relative to their counterparts in the developed economies. However gearing levels do vary quite widely among LDCs and in comparison with the industrial countries. They find that companies in Jordan, Malaysia, Taiwan, Mexico, Pakistan and Zimbabwe have gearing levels that are similar to those of firms in developed economies, whereas firms in Thailand and South Korea have higher levels. Broadly similar results are reported by Booth *et al.* (2001); they also emphasize that there are important inter-country differences in debt ratios in LDCs.

Singh (1995) argues that the dependence of firms in emerging markets is due to three factors: first, active government sponsorship, such as privatization, and specific policies that promote capital market development; second, financial liberalization, which has resulted in higher real interest rates and lower demand for bank finance; and third, rising price–earnings ratios that have reduced the cost of equity capital. Cobham and Subramaniam (CS) (1998) note that these conclusions are puzzling, given LDCs' lax accounting and auditing protocols, which increase information imperfections, their less well-defined property rights, and still small and inefficient capital markets. Taken together, these factors suggest that firms would use bank finance rather than the capital markets. The puzzle may be resolved partly by a more detailed investigation of the debt component. Thus Booth *et al.* (2001) note that long-term debt levels are typically much lower in LDCs than in the industrial countries, which is consistent with a greater use of bank finance and lesser use of capital markets in LDCs.

India has been more extensively investigated than many other LDCs, particularly because the corporate sector is well established and data are generally excellent. Hamid and Singh (1992) and Singh (1995) find that Indian firms have gearing levels that are similar to those of companies in developed countries. However CS (1998) argue that these studies suffer from small-sample bias. To correct for this, they conduct a micro-study using two large data sets for India and one for the UK.[13] They find that Indian firms employed more bank-based and bond finance than their UK counterparts, but that the gearing levels of the largest Indian firms were broadly similar to those of their larger UK peers. CS note that debt ratios tended to be lower for smaller firms, and they suggest that this is due to smaller firms having lower agency costs since they will most likely issue new equity to existing shareholders who are already familiar with the firm, rather than to the public directly.[14] Largely consistent with CS, Green *et al.* (2003) find that quoted Indian companies have broadly similar debt ratios to their peers in the industrial countries, but that unquoted (and therefore generally smaller) companies have lower debt ratios. They attribute this difference to the impact of a public quotation in improving information and reducing the agency costs of debt. In other words, when companies go public, it improves their access to debt markets. Interestingly Green *et al.* (2003) find that the impact of market liberalization in India in the 1990s tended to reduce debt ratios, as more companies came to the stock market in this era.

Observation 5

As yet there is no evidence that the broad determinants of firm debt ratios in developing economies are substantively different from those in the industrial countries. In their early study, Glen and Pinto (1994) found that factors such as risk, the cost of capital, tax, and governance and control issues all played a role in helping to understand company financing decisions in LDCs, just as they do in the industrial countries. However theirs was a very broad-based study and they acknowledged that government controls and capital market constraints loom much larger in the developing world and clearly have a major impact on company financing decisions. Regression evidence is available in the study of Booth *et al.* (2001) and they arrive at broadly similar conclusions. However these conclusions are based more on the signs of coefficients in their estimated models and less on their significance, which is often too low to assert the conclusion with a high degree of confidence. Clearly there is more work to be done in this area, in cross-country studies as well as in country-specific studies.

Summing up the Stylised Facts

Although we have set out five more or less consensual observations, it will be clear that, overall, it is difficult to generalize about corporate capital structures, within the industrial countries, within LDCs or in comparisons between the two. Depending on the country, the time period and the data definitions, different studies come to different conclusions. Perhaps the root of the differences in corporate capital structures may lie in the different underlying circumstances faced by individual firms. If firms in the same country all faced exactly the same circumstances and constraints, we would expect to see greater uniformity of results within individual countries. It would appear particularly important, therefore, to survey the various tests of theories of corporate capital structure, as these theories seek the source of cross-sectional differences among firms in more fundamental differences of circumstance among individual firms: their industry, shareholders, bond-holders, managements and workforce. We therefore turn next to the multivariate research results.

7.   MULTIVARIATE EMPIRICAL RESEARCH: A BRIEF REVIEW OF METHODOLOGIES

Various methods have been employed in multivariate empirical research on capital structure. Although the most popular involve the use of ordinary least squares (OLS) regressions to analyse cross-sections or panels of company data, linear structural modelling has also been employed. Company data are usually taken from the published accounts of individual companies, many of which are widely available from the websites of individual firms, or from specialist information companies. Cross-sections are still the most widely used but, in the last 15 years, greater emphasis has been placed on panel data.

Here a cross-section of companies is tracked through time, typically for between five and ten years. An important advantage of panel data is that they offer substantially more observations, and the time dimension allows for easier testing of a wider range of hypotheses than is possible with a single year's cross-section. However the use of panel data does pose new econometric problems (Hsiao, 2003).

7.1   Single-equation Models

The basic empirical model is a regression of some measure of firm leverage (d_i) on a vector (X_i) of explanatory variables:[15]

$$d_i = f(X_i). \tag{12.1}$$

The explanatory variables typically consist of empirical proxies that are intended to capture certain latent (unobservable) attributes of the firm. Most empirical research assumes a linear relationship between the underlying latent variable and its proxy. Titman and Wessels (1988) note that linearity is an unreliable assumption for a number of reasons: first, the relationship between the true unobserved determinant and the observed proxy may be imperfect, resulting in errors-in-variable problems when used in regressions; second, measurement errors in the proxies may be correlated with those of the dependent variable, creating a spurious relationship even though the unobserved variable may be unrelated to the dependent variable; third, proxy variables may be chosen mainly by goodness-of-fit criteria; and fourth, it is difficult to use measures of one attribute that are unrelated to other variables of interest.

In principle, a linear structural model, such as LISREL, can be used to overcome some of these problems, as it explicitly specifies the relation between the unobservable attributes and the observable variables. See Titman and Wessels (1988) and Chiarella *et al.* (1992) for examples of its application. LISREL consists of a measurement model and a structural model which are estimated simultaneously. In the measurement model, unobservable firm-specific attributes are related to observable variables such as accounting data:

$$x = \Lambda e + \delta. \tag{12.2}$$

Here x is a vector of q observable indicators; e is a vector of m unobservable attributes; hence Λ is a $q \times m$ matrix of regression coefficients and δ is a $q \times 1$ vector of measurement errors. In the structural model, measured debt ratios are specified as functions of the attributes defined in the measurement model:

$$y = \Gamma e + \varepsilon. \tag{12.3}$$

Here y is a vector of p individual firm debt ratios; hence, Γ is a $p \times m$ matrix of factor loadings and ε is a $p \times 1$ vector of disturbance terms. See Jöreskog and Sörbom (1981) for a detailed exposition of this method.

The form of non-linearity that can arise in corporate financial decisions is often of the all-or-nothing variety as when, for example, the Pecking Order hypothesis predicts that a firm will not issue new equity in the current time period. Discrete variable techniques (LOGIT and PROBIT) can be used to model such decisions. See, for example, Greene (2000) for an exposition. The LOGIT method can be used to model the relationship between the probability of a firm switching from one branch of a decision to another, subject to a vector of explanatory variables. For example, Gardner and Trzcinka (1992) test Myers's (1977) theory of the relationship between a firm's growth opportunities and its debt levels. They do this by estimating a LOGIT model giving the relationship between a firm's growth rate (and other variables) and the probability of its choosing all-equity financing versus debt and equity. The LOGIT model is naturally applicable to problems of binary choice. Where there are several possible outcomes, or a multi-step decision tree is to be analysed, the probit model or sequential LOGIT or PROBIT is more applicable.

7.2 Multi-equation Models

Single-equation methods implicitly assume that capital structure decisions can be thought of in a series of binary, or at least simple, steps: choice of debt–equity ratio, whether or not to issue debt or equity and, later, how much to issue, and so on. Arguably, though, the capital structure decision is better thought of as a single decision, involving the question as to what type of financing to use and, simultaneously, that of how much of each type to use. A convenient example is Jensen *et al.* (1992) who estimate a cross-section model of the simultaneous determination by firms of debt, dividends and insider finance. Three (linear) equations are estimated as follows:

$$\text{Debt} = f(\text{Dividends, Insider, } X_1, X_2, X_3, X_4), \qquad (12.4a)$$

$$\text{Dividends} = f(\text{Debt, Insider, } X_1, X_2, X_6, X_7), \qquad (12.4b)$$

$$\text{Insider} = f(\text{Debt, Dividends, } X_1, X_2, X_5, X_8) \qquad (12.4c)$$

with X_1 = business risk, X_2 = profitability, X_3 = R&D spending (a proxy for agency costs), X_4 = fixed assets, X_5 = size, X_6 = growth rate, X_7 = investment and X_8 = the firm's industry classification. This model is a simultaneous equations model in the sense that the endogenous variables all appear as explanatory variables in each other's equation; that is, dividends, debt and insider financing are assumed to have an impact on each other independently of the other explanatory variables.

The problem with a system such as (12.4) is that it can only be identified if sufficient exogenous variables are excluded from all three equations. This can be arbitrary and each exclusion restriction has the effect of restricting the impact of the exogenous variables to effects that have to come via the other endogenous variables. In contrast, Chowdhury *et al.* (CGM, 1994) argue that financing decisions are better treated by analogy with portfolio decisions. This suggests re-specifying (12.4) as a system of demand equations, or perhaps more properly as supply equations of liabilities. CGM (1994) analyse the determinants of UK companies' short-term financial decisions using a panel of 694 firms covering 1969 to 1983. The following equation was estimated:

$$f_{it} = \alpha_i + \sum_k \tau_{ik} m_{kt} + \sum_j \mu_{ij} F_{jt-1} + \sum_l \delta_{il} M_{lt-1} + \sum_h \phi_{ih} Z_{ht} + u_{it} \quad (12.5)$$

The endogenous variables (f_i, $i = 1 \ldots 4$) are the short-term or 'quick' financial flows;[16] F_j are the corresponding stocks of quick finance assets and liabilities; m_k are the cash flows generated by all other (mainstream) activities; M_l are the stocks of assets and liabilities associated with mainstream activities and Z_h are other explanatory variables (both firm-specific and economy-wide); α_i, τ_{ik}, μ_{ij}, δ_{il}, ϕ_{ih} are parameters and u_{it} are the error terms. This specification is somewhat analogous to Brainard and Tobin's (1968) methods for modelling financial asset demands, and is foreshadowed by the early contribution of Heston (1962). Chowdhury and Miles (1989) use the same approach to analyse UK companies' debt, dividend and equity decisions. Given the appropriate degree of aggregation, total external long-term funding is just the sum of equity and debt raised, less dividends paid. If these variables are treated as a simultaneous system of supply functions of liabilities, with common explanatory variables, any one of the three equations is redundant, because the parameters of any one equation can be inferred from the parameters of the other two. See Greene (2000). Since equity issues are typically intermittent, whereas debt and dividends are more usually regular flows, the efficient estimation of an equation for equity flows poses more difficult econometric problems than does the estimation of debt and dividend equations. Chowdhury and Miles exploit this point to estimate equations for debt and dividends, which have the same general linear structure as (12.5) with a common set of explanatory variables which test for the effects of taxation, macroeconomic variables, the cost of funds, external regulatory controls, bankruptcy and other risk proxies, learning and expectations proxies, and firm size.

It would appear that the system approach is a methodological improvement on the single-equation approach, especially, as noted earlier by Brainard and Tobin (1968), because it forces the investigator to confront the broader implications of any estimated model. For example, a model may appear to offer a sensible explanation for debt and dividends, but its implications for equity issues may be nonsensical. However the models of Jensen *et al.* and Chowdhury and Miles are essentially static cross-section explanations of capital structure, and do not consider adjustment mechanisms. Fischer *et al.* (1989) observe that, if adjustment costs are large, firms will rarely be at or close to their long-run equilibrium, and theoretical and empirical studies should therefore focus less on long-run trade-offs and more on understanding how managers respond to adjustment costs. Myers (1984) and Shyam-Sunder and Myers (1999) also emphasize this point, which suggests the need for a dynamic multivariate approach to modelling capital structure.

The response to this argument is limited to a relatively few papers, in part because many balanced panels of company accounts data do not have a time dimension which is sufficiently long to estimate the necessary dynamics. Chowdhury *et al.* (1990) develop and estimate the dynamic and the long-run implications of their model, but argue that, if short-term finance is a buffer, the long-run equilibrium is either notional or largely irrelevant. Homaifa *et al.* (1994) use an autoregressive distributed lag (ADL) model to study the capital structure decisions of a panel of 370 US firms for the period 1979–88. Possibly the most complete attempt to reconcile static and dynamic theories of capital structure is due to Vogt (1994), who constructs a partial stock adjustment model to test the Pecking Order hypothesis. His model assumes that there is a value-maximizing capital structure for each firm, but that transactions costs, information asymmetries and corporate control issues prevent the firm from instantaneously reaching this point and give rise to an adjustment mechanism. If the existence of a target capital structure is rejected then there is support for the Pecking Order hypothesis.

8.   MULTIVARIATE EMPIRICAL RESEARCH: MAIN EMPIRICAL FINDINGS

8.1   Ownership and Control Structures and the Financial Structure of the Firm

The empirical literature on ownership and control can be divided into two themes. The first examines the influence of ownership structure on dividend policies. The second investigates the impact of management shareholdings on the firm's debt ratio. Although clearly relevant to capital structure, dividend policy is a major subject in its own right and the literature on this topic is well surveyed by Short (1994). Accordingly, in this section we concentrate on the impact of management shareholdings on debt ratios.

Zeckhauser and Pound (1990) test whether large shareholders improve corporate performance by encouraging performance tilting, the practice which arises under asymmetric information between shareholders and managers and results in improvements of corporate performance without the diminution of managerial effort or excess pay. This is because large shareholders can exploit economies of scale in information costs, which reduces the agency (monitoring) costs of debt. If true, this implies that the leverage of firms with at least one large shareholder should be higher than that of a firm that does not have a large shareholder. In fact Zeckhauser and Pound (1990) find that there is no significant difference in leverage ratios between such groups of firms. They conclude that large shareholders appear to perform a monitoring function only for equity owners and do not have a positive impact on debt holders.

This theme is pursued by Friend and Hasbrouck (1988) who investigate whether there is a systematic relationship between insider (manager) holdings and debt. Two proxies are used: a fractional variable (the largest fraction of shares that is held by an insider) and an absolute variable (the market value of equity held by the largest insider). *A priori*, there could be either a negative or a positive relationship between debt and insider holdings: negative, if the rise in bankruptcy costs for insiders outweighs the reduction in their agency costs; positive, if the reverse is true. Friend and Hasbrouck find that, when both the fractional and absolute insider holdings are included, the former becomes positive and significant whilst the latter becomes more negative. In addition, the explanatory power of the fractional variable dominates that of the absolute variable. These results provide weak support for the hypothesis that insider ownership does reduce the agency cost of debt. However, in these regressions, causality runs from insider holdings to the debt ratio. Friend and Hasbrouck suggest that reverse causality may also occur: a high level of debt increases the risk of the firm's shares, and may drive out outside shareholders.

Friend and Lang (1988) extend Friend and Hasbrouck's work in several ways. First, the sample of firms is divided into two equal-sized groups: closely held companies (CHCs) where the dominant insider shareholders hold more than 13.825 per cent of overall equity, and publicly held corporations (PHCs) where managers hold less than 13.825 per cent. Second, Friend and Lang argue that those firms who have dominant insider shareholders will have less debt than those companies who do not. Consequently CHCs should have lower debt levels than PHCs. Moreover, if there are economies of scale in information gathering, firms with large external shareholders may monitor the behaviour of managers more effectively than those without. Therefore, each group was subdivided into two further groups: CHC_0 and CHC_1 (closely-held companies with and without non-managerial principal investors, respectively); and PHC_0 and PHC_1 (publicly held companies with and without non-managerial principal investors, respectively). Friend and Lang include as an additional explanatory variable the fraction of equity (FRO) held by dominant non-managerial stockholders who are not either an officer or a director but hold more than 10 per cent of outstanding shares. Finally, they used the log of a firm's market value (LMV) as an explanatory variable. When LMV was used with the other explanatory variables, the coefficient for FRO was positive and statistically significant in each of the CHC_0, CHC_1, PHC_0 and PHC_1 sub-samples. The last result was contrary to *a priori* expectations. When LMV was excluded, the coefficients were statistically significant but changed sign from positive to negative in all sub-samples. Since LMV dominates FRO, these results confirm Friend and Hasbrouck's finding that the links between insider ownership and leverage are relatively weak.

Kim and Sorensen (1986) also test the influence of insider equity holders on firm leverage. They examine whether cross-sectional variations in corporate leverage ratios can be related to agency costs. Firms were classified into three groups: high, average and low inside ownership. Insider ownership is defined as owning more than 25 per cent of the outstanding equity of the firm. The sample of low or diffuse insider ownership firms consisted of those in which less than 5 per cent of the outstanding equity is held by insiders. The third sample of average insider ownership firms consisted of those with 50 per cent insider ownership and 50 per cent diffuse ownership. Debt was defined as the book ratio of long-term debt to total capitalization. It transpired that insider firms had between 6 per cent to 7 per cent higher debt-to-capitalization ratios than diffuse ownership firms in the same industry. This suggests that large firms who are heavily owned by insiders do tend to finance projects with greater amounts of long-term debt. Other studies examining the impact of shareholder concentration on a firm's capital structure obtain conflicting results. Zeckhauser and Pound (1990) find a negative relationship between large shareholders and firm leverage, whereas Amihud *et al.* (1990) and Hussain (1995) find the relationship to be positive.

Firth (1995) considers the impact of institutional shareholders and management interest on the firm's capital structure. In contrast to Friend and Lang (1988) and Friend and Hasbrouck (1988), Firth uses the whole of the sample data with managerial shareholder ownership expressed as a continuous variable instead of pre-classifying firms into groups, which may be misspecified. Firth tested whether there is a negative relationship between executive shareholdings and a firm's debt–equity ratio, and if there is a positive dependence between the level of institutional shareholdings and a firm's debt–equity ratio. The former hypothesis represents the human capital motivation while the latter is an implication of the usual value maximizing argument. Firth concludes that there is sufficient empirical evidence to support either hypothesis. The capital structure of the firm depends on the relative influence and power of substantial institutional shareholders.

A final point concerns the measurement of insider shareholdings. Using *par* values to measure firms' capital, Chen and Steiner (2000) find a clear positive relationship between managerial ownership and leverage. This provides evidence against the hypothesis that managers prefer to reduce the risk associated with their individual portfolios in the firm: instead of reducing leverage, they actually gear up. However, as noted by Firth (1995) and by Friend and Hasbrouck (1988), there tends to be a negative relationship between the proportion of the *market* value of the shares held by management and the firm's gearing level. This is more consistent with theory, which would suggest that managements are influenced by the current values of their undiversified portfolios to spread risk: one method of reducing risk is to maintain low capital gearing. Thus a possible interpretation of these results is that managers are more concerned with the market values of their holdings than with their par values.

8.2 Business Groups

An important factor in many emerging markets is the existence of numerous business groups. A business group may be defined as a collection of independent companies, usually from various industries, that are linked together either formally or informally. A formal link is achieved through cross-shareholding, where firms in the group hold the shares of other members. An informal link may include family or other social ties such as religion or ethnicity, or situations where firms in the group share directors. In many groups, though by no means all, effective control of firms in the group is exercised by the same insider group of shareholders.[17] In most cases, the link between firms in a business group is stable, in the sense that each individual firm in the group is an independent legal entity with separate management and board of directors, rather than a subsidiary company (Granovetter, 1995). The best-known business groups internationally are probably the Japanese *keiretsu* and the Korean *chaebol*. However business groups are present in many emerging markets, particularly in Asia and Latin America (Khanna and Palepu, 2000a, 2000b).

A common explanation for the business group phenomenon is that it has evolved to mitigate problems of informational asymmetry and capital market imperfections. *A priori*, this does not seem consistent with the wide range of countries in which groups are found, and the equally wide range of (different) countries in which they are not found. Whatever the historical reasons for the emergence of groups, interlocking ownership or other relationships might be expected to affect company financing decisions in general and capital structure in particular.

Research on business groups has concentrated on their effectiveness and profitability (Khanna and Palepu, 2000a, 2000b); here we are concerned with their implications for capital structure. Guillen (2000) argues that the group structure mitigates capital market failures: the group as a whole gains superior access to external resources because of its size and reputation, and it then provides an efficient internal capital market to allocate these resources. Groups may have access to private savings, as they are typically connected to wealthy families. Group reputation can be based on the group's track record for efficient internal allocation of capital. Reputation may also relate to the ability of the controlling entity to monitor and influence the behaviour of the management teams of member firms effectively (Shleifer and Vishny, 1986). On the other hand, since the group is a conglomerate, it may suffer from the inefficiencies and rent seeking associated with conglomeration (Jensen, 1986). There is potential for conflicts of interests between controlling and minority shareholders in group-affiliated firms, especially if the controlling entity pursues objectives other than shareholder wealth maximization, such as investment in unprofitable projects owing to family or group-wide considerations (Khanna and Palepu, 2000a).

Hirota (1999) explores the determinants of capital structure of between 407 and 546 Japanese firms in four cross-sections: from 1977, 1982, 1987 and 1992. He seeks to explain the leverage of these firms by a combination of conventional capital structure variables (non-debt tax shields, asset tangibility, growth opportunities, business risk, profitability and size) and Japanese institutional variables, including bank relationships (measured by the proportion of debt due to the largest bank lender), *keiretsu* membership, regulation of new equity issues (measured by a dummy representing firms who satisfy the voluntary code enforced by major Japanese security companies between 1973 and 1996) and a variable representing a firm's incentive to exploit free cash flows (a firm-specific debt–equity yield differential). Almost all the variables in both groups entered the regressions with the expected sign in each of the four cross-sections, and most were significant. *Keiretsu* membership contributes significantly to explaining leverage independently of the standard variables, suggesting that there is more to firm financial behaviour in Japan than is captured by a standard model. The results are consistent with the market failure hypothesis as *keiretsu* membership is associated with higher leverage in each of the cross-sections. Gul (1999) reports broadly similar findings to Hirota (1999), but for a shorter list of explanatory variables. He investigates a panel of more than 1000 Japanese firms covering 1988–92 and finds that *keiretsu* affiliation is associated with significantly increased leverage. Gul and Kealey (1999) obtain comparable results for Korea: *chaebol* membership is associated with increased leverage. However Wiwattanakantang (1999), who studied a cross-section of 270 Thai firms, found that group membership did not significantly affect leverage in these firms.

Group membership is often related to family ownership in LDCs, as many groups are effectively owned by an extended family. We know of no capital structure studies which look at the importance of families within business groups. However several authors have examined family ownership per se in developing economies. Hussain (1995) studies family-owned firms in Indonesia, and tests whether the influx of foreign capital has altered the firm's capital structure via the proportion of shares held by these families. The main finding is that the inflow of foreign capital, which has reduced the concentration of family ownership, has resulted in reduced leverage. Wiwattanakantang (1999) investigated the impact of family ownership within the context of a more general model of leverage, which also controlled for group membership as noted above. Here too the results show that family firms are more highly levered than more widely-held companies. These results are all consistent with the findings for firms in the industrial countries. They are suggestive of the importance of aligning owners' and managers' interests in order to mitigate the agency problems of debt, and indicate that family ownership may be one method of achieving this.

Finally, Prasad (2000) studied the financing decisions of a sample of 165 Malay and 174 Thai companies in a panel covering the period 1987 to 1995. Although he finds numerous detailed differences in the behaviour of firms as between the two countries, overall a conventional capital structure model performs equally well in both countries. However Prasad found little evidence that family ownership was an important factor in either Malaysia or Thailand over and above conventional capital structure determinants. Overall, given the relative paucity of studies on this subject and the sometimes inconclusive results, it seems more than usually clear that further research on this issue is needed.

8.3   The Influence of Bankruptcy Costs on the Firm's Capital Structure

In the majority of existing empirical studies, the impact of bankruptcy costs on the firm's financial structure is investigated directly. For example Ang *et al.* (1982) examine whether there is a relationship between bankruptcy costs and the capital structure of the firm. Three types of costs are associated with bankruptcy: first, administrative expenses paid to various third parties involved in the bankruptcy proceedings; second, the indirect costs of reorganization and the shortfall in realized value when assets are liquidated; and third, the loss of tax credits when the firm goes bankrupt. Haugen and Senbet (1978), Miller (1977) and Warner (1977) argue that the last two costs are the most relevant ones when a decision about the liquidation of the firm is about to be made. Such costs would be borne by the security holders of the firm regardless of how much equity and debt the firm carries and are irrelevant to the firm's capital structure. Ang *et al.*'s paper studies the direct administrative costs of corporate bankruptcy, concentrating in particular on the possible scale effects of such costs. Warner (1977) argues that such costs are a concave function of the market value of the firm at the time of bankruptcy. Accordingly, Ang *et al.* estimated two equations, one with a quadratic functional form and the other with a logarithmic form. In each case, they regressed the cash amount of administrative expenses on the liquidating value of the firm, including funds used to pay for the administrator's expenses. The non-linear terms proved to be significant and consistent with Warner's hypothesis. The results also imply that bankruptcy costs are about 2 per cent of the firm's liquidating value if the firm's value is in excess of US$1m. However these results are based on a restricted sample of small companies located within a specific geographical region, and may not be representative of US firms in general.

The direct costs of bankruptcy are estimated by Bradbury and Lloyd (1994) for New Zealand via an analysis of 27 corporate receiverships for the period 1980 to 1987. They estimate two non-linear functions similar to Ang *et al.* relating bankruptcy administration costs to firm size, but they also innovate by estimating how sensitive bankruptcy costs are to different measures of firm size. They too conclude that there are fixed costs associated with bankruptcy and that administration costs are a concave function of the firm's liquidation value. However one deficiency of this study is that it excludes indirect bankruptcy costs, owing to lack of data. Similarly Altman (1984) investigates the impact of direct and indirect bankruptcy costs as well as the likelihood of bankruptcy for a sample of 12 US retailers (1970–78) and seven industrial bankruptcies (1975–78). Indirect costs are measured in terms of forgone sales and profits. That is, the difference between actual and estimated profits was applied. For both industrial and retailing firms, it was found that, in general, there was a marked decrease in the value of the firm in the period prior to bankruptcy, a decrease that was especially acute for industrial corporations. Marked increases in the costs of individual firms were observed, with the greatest increases occurring in the period immediately prior to bankruptcy. Thus, for both types of firms, bankruptcy costs cannot be treated as trivial. Interestingly it was noted that the likelihood of a firm entering bankruptcy was correctly interpreted by security analysts who discounted the market value of the firm up to three periods prior to bankruptcy. Chen and Merville (1999) also find that the indirect costs of financial distress may be considerable. In a sample of 1041 US firms covering 1982–92, they find that the annual average loss per firm due to financial distress was 10.3 per cent of market value, per annum. This estimate is substantially larger than most previous estimates mainly because Chen and Merville include the cost of lost investment opportunities. Firms in distress are constrained in their ability to finance new investments for the reasons discussed in previous sections, particularly the concerns of debt-holders that the firm may not survive to realize the rewards of a potentially profitable investment opportunity; and this effect turns out to be particularly important in Chen and Merville's results.

8.4 The Impact of Corporate Strategy on the Firm's Capital Structure

Whitley (1992) observes that developing economy firms follow corporate structures that are similar to those of conglomerates. This suggests that the issue of the relationship between a firm's strategy and its capital structure has special relevance to the financial behaviour of firms in a developing economy. The empirical literature on these issues can be divided into two groups. The first examines the direct impact of diversification strategies on capital structure while the second explores the influence of firm-specific assets on capital structure. In this section we concentrate on the first group of studies.

Econometric testing of the impact of corporate strategy on a firm's capital structure was started by Barton and Gordon, (BG, 1988). Strategy is a proxy for management values, goals and motivations for firm diversification. It must therefore also include managers' preference for debt and equity. A central issue here is the impact of diversification on risk, which in turn influences the firm's gearing. Firm strategies which involve diversification into unrelated activities have the lowest risk associated with them since there is no order to the process of diversification; the reverse is true for firm strategies which involve diversification into related activities. A sample of 279 *Fortune-500* US industrial firms covering the period 1970–74 was divided into four groups: single strategy, dominant strategy, related strategy and unrelated strategy. The main results were as follows. First, there was sufficient evidence for not rejecting the hypothesis that corporate strategy does influence the capital structure decisions of the firm. Second, the average debt level was significantly lower in single strategy firms than in all other categories, but there was no significant difference between the average debt level of firms following dominant strategies and the average debt level of the whole sample. Third, the average debt level of firms that adopted a related corporate strategy was lower than that for firms in the unrelated category. Finally, firms with an unrelated strategy had the highest debt ratios of all, and these debt levels were significantly higher than those for single and related category firms.

Lowe *et al.* (1994) extend BG's work by investigating whether the corporate strategy of the firm influences its capital structure in a sample of Australian public companies for the period 1984 to 1988. In contrast to BG, they report that the gearing of firms which adopt either a single firm, a dominant firm or a related firm strategy is *not* affected by that strategy, but the gearing of firms which adopt an unrelated strategy *is* affected by the strategy. Riahi-Belkaoui and Bannister (1994) also consider the impact of corporate strategy on the financial structure of the firm. They conduct a longitudinal study to capture the effects of the implementation of a decentralized M-form (multidivisional) organization structure on the firm's capital structure. Data for a period of five years before and five years after the point of restructuring was collected from COMPUSTAT and Moody's Industrials Manual for 62 firms. Covariates of firm size, growth in total assets and growth in GNP are used as control factors for the early or late adaptation of M-form structures. This is motivated by the belief that late adapters learn from the experience of early movers and so can restructure faster and more efficiently. The results indicate that those firms that adopt a change in structure to form a multidivisional organization are associated with a shift in capital structure and a significant increase in long-term debt in comparison with those with a hierarchical structure.

All the work reviewed so far has concentrated on large firms. Jordan *et al.* (1998) extended the analysis by examining the role of strategy in smaller UK firms. The influence of strategy should be different from that in large firms, since the ownership and risk characteristics of small firms are distinct from those of large firms. The role of competition may be more important than that of corporate strategy in determining the demand for funds by smaller firms. Jordan *et al.* test for the impact of both competitive and corporate strategies, using a sample of 275 small UK firms for the period 1983–93, which (like BG and Lowe *et al.*) was split according to whether the firm adopted a corporate or a competitive strategy. It was found that corporate strategy per se did not influence smaller firms' capital structure. However, when the same analysis was applied to firms that used competitive strategies, it was found that competitive strategy did influence capital structure.

Overall, therefore, it seems clear that strategy does influence the firm's capital structure, but further research is required to identify the precise channels through which this influence is felt, as the results of the main studies do not offer a clear consensus on this point.

8.5 Testing the Pecking Order Hypothesis

According to the Pecking Order hypothesis, information asymmetries between the firm and the market imply that firms prefer to finance using retained earnings, followed by debt and finally by equity. There are two main ways in which the Pecking Order hypothesis is tested within the literature. The first is by examining the impact of profitability on the firm's leverage. A negative dependence suggests that the firm will, for a given dividend, prefer retained earnings over debt and so adhere to the Pecking Order hypothesis. However this approach does not specifically test for the hypothesis in isolation since the influence of a number of other capital structure determinants is simultaneously investigated. The second approach does involve specifically testing for the Pecking Order hypothesis.

Klein and Belt (1994) use a LOGIT model to test the likelihood that a firm will choose internal over external sources of finance, and to model the probability of choosing between debt and equity. This study was carried out for all non-financial and non-regulated firms in the USA for the period 1983–88. It was found that faster growing and more operationally efficient firms tended to employ external over internal finance, and that the most efficient firms preferred to use debt over equity. Both of these results provide support for the Pecking Order hypothesis. However Marsh (1982) used the same general LOGIT model approach, but found that the deviation of the current debt ratio from the firm's target debt ratio helped explain the probability of debt and equity issues. This would suggest that firms are adjusting towards a target capital structure, a hypothesis that is not consistent with the pecking order model.

Baskin (1989) examines whether US firms adhere to the Pecking Order hypothesis by constructing a structural model for 378 firms for 1972. Unlike previous models, that of Baskin (1989) argues that the existence of a pecking order is, in part, due to the stickiness of dividend payments that restrict the free use of retained earnings. Dividend stickiness is a central hypothesis of the celebrated Lintner model in which the past level of dividends influences current dividends, so that high past dividends increase the expectation of larger future ones. This in turn increases the demand for free cash flow and hence the firm's demand for debt (Lintner, 1956). Baskin (1989) finds support for Lintner's argument and for a pecking order: the payment of high levels of past dividends statistically increases the demand for leverage; dividend payments are sticky; and the demand for debt is significantly negatively related to past profitability. Overall this provides interesting support for the traditional Pecking Order hypothesis in the context of the Lintner dividend model.

Unlike the previous approaches, Allen (1993) investigates the Pecking Order hypothesis via the impact of past returns and growth on firm leverage. Using a sample of 89 Australian industrial and commercial firms for the period 1954 to 1982, he found a significant negative relationship between past profitability and debt ratios which rejects the static optimal capital structure model and provides support for the Pecking Order hypothesis. Chua and Woodward (1993) assert that, if the hypothesis is correct, there should in addition be negative relation-ships between liquidity and leverage, and between internally generated cash flows and leverage. Therefore leverage is regressed against internally generated cash flows, external funds required and liquidity for a sample of 43 private Canadian firms for the period 1983 to 1988. Liquidity and internally generated funds did indeed have a negative impact on leverage, providing further support to the Pecking Order hypothesis.

Claggett (1991) employs a sample of 253 US firms from 13 industries for 1979–88 to examine the hypothesis versus an optimal capital structure, which is, however, time-varying in response to variations in the business risk of the industry. He examines these two hypotheses by considering a firm with an initial low level of debt. If the Pecking Order hypothesis is adhered to, the firm will prefer to use internally generated funds over external funds. Accord-ingly the firm's capital structure should move away from rather than towards the industry's mean over time. Likewise, for firms that have higher levels of debt, for any given income stream, retained earnings will be lower, resulting in the firm employing more debt, in turn causing their gearing levels to move away from the industry's norm over time. If, on the other hand, there is an optimal capital structure, firms' capital structures will tend to converge over time, once allowance is made for time variations in the optimal capital struc-ture itself. Claggett (1991) finds weak evidence that firms' capital structures do indeed tend to converge over time, as found also by Lev (1969), Marsh (1982) and Murinde *et al.* (1999),[18] using a wide range of different method-ologies. Taken together, these studies suggest the existence of optimal industry target leverage levels for individual firms. However there is some evidence of asymmetries in convergence as between firms having an above-average in-dustry leverage ratio and those having a below-average leverage ratio. This may provide a partial reconciliation between the optimal capital structure theory and the pecking order models of the firm.

Shyam-Sunder and Myers (1999) argue that it is possible to discriminate between pecking order and static trade-off theories by a simple comparison between two OLS regressions:

$$\Delta D = b_0 + b_1(D_t^* - D_{t-1}) + u_t \text{ and } \Delta D_t = a_0 + a_1 DEF_t + v_t \qquad (12.6)$$

Here ΔD_t is the change in a firm's debt ratio, D_t^* is the optimal debt ratio and D_{t-1} the actual ratio in the previous period. DEF_t is the firm's (flow) financing requirement, defined as the difference between committed pay-ments (capital spending, dividends, working capital and debt repayment) and free cash flow. Shyam-Sunder and Myers argue that, for non-distressed firms, we would expect to find $0 < b_1 < 1$ if the static trade-off theory is true, and $a_0 = 0$ and $a_1 = 1$ if the Pecking Order hypothesis is true. They employ a sample of 157 US firms for which sources and uses data are available from 1971. They find that $0 < b_1 < 1$, that a_1 is positive but less than unity, and that the pecking order model has higher explanatory power than the trade-off model. Shyam-Sunder and Myers also perform simulations of firm debt policy under the two different hypotheses, and conclude that the power of their test is such that the Pecking Order hypothesis should be preferred to the trade-off model. This is questioned by Chirinko and Singha (2000) who argue that the analysis is not robust to changes in the underlying model, particularly in the specification of alternative hypotheses. For example, the regression of ΔD_t on DEF_t cannot easily distinguish between the pecking order as proposed by Myers and Majluf (1984) and different financing priorities such as internal financing followed by a preference for equity over debt.

Fama and French (2002) carry out a comprehensive set of comparisons between pecking order and trade-off theories using models for dividends and for leverage, and covering US firms over the period 1965–99. As they observe, many of the variables held to determine dividends and leverage are common to both theories. This makes it difficult for a standard 'horse race' between regressions to distinguish adequately between the two theories, notwithstanding that they have very different implications for corporate behaviour. Indeed key differences between the theories emerge for only two variables. First, they find that leverage is negatively related to profitability in line with the pecking order and contrary to trade-off theory; second, they find that, for non-dividend paying firms, highly levered firms make fewer new issues than less levered firms. This is contrary to pecking order theory and consistent with trade-off theory. Overall, therefore, the authors conclude that it is difficult to decide which of the two theories is more consistent with the data, and further that this difficulty will persist given the many common determining variables which the two theories share.

Thus the evidence on the Pecking Order hypothesis is still inconclusive. One difficulty in comparing the pecking order with theories of optimal capital structure is that the former is an essentially dynamic model containing predictions of how a firm will behave over time and is more naturally tested in that context. This requires time series data on individual firms and, where such data are readily available, they mostly have a relatively short time dimension. Many of the records of company accounts in the major industrial countries date back to the previous century, but compiling these data for the purposes of investigating capital structure questions is a Herculean task. See Shannon (1932). The problems in this respect are likely to be more acute in studies of developing counties. On the other hand, static trade-off theories are naturally tested using panel or cross-section data, of which there is a general abundance, even in LDCs. This suggests that there may be value in giving further consideration to the ways in which the two classes of theory can be compared within a cross-sectional context.

9. EMPIRICAL RESULTS ON GENERAL CAPITAL STRUCTURE THEMES

9.1 Empirical determinants of capital structure

The discussion so far has concentrated on the testing of specific theories. Many of these studies have generated further interesting empirical results as a by-product of the main theoretical tests. In addition, there are many other studies that are more empirically oriented, and aim to examine the influence on leverage of certain specific variables. The hypotheses tested are motivated by theoretical or empirical concerns, and involve the use of a variety of more or less ad hoc variables that aim to measure the underlying concepts to be tested. In this section, therefore, we examine these results, organizing the discussion according to the main variables that have been found by a large number of studies to influence the firm's capital structure. Table 12A.1 sets out in summary form the results of these studies, most of which examine the role of specific firm characteristics in determining leverage. This table indicates a number of common characteristics that are thought to determine capital structure: tangibility, size, profitability, growth, risk, non-debt tax shields and industry group. Each of these will now be discussed briefly in turn and will allow a comparison between a priori expectations and empirical findings. Text tables provide a compact summary of the results for these main variables.

A few caveats apply when making this type of cross-study comparison. First, proxies are invariably applied for explanatory variables and are difficult to interpret. We make comparisons taking the results at face value, and ignoring any differences in measurement, definition and techniques, except insofar as these differences are crucial to an understanding of the results. Second, leverage can be expressed as a ratio to either the market or the book value of equity. The former is consistent with the theory of capital structure. However, like the vast majority of the empirical literature, the following results, together with those of Table 12A.1, are mostly derived using the book value of equity. There are several reasons for this. First, the market value of equity and leverage is dependent upon factors orthogonal to the firm; consequently any changes in the leverage ratio when using market values may not reflect any underlying alteration within the firm. Second, the market value of leverage is not always readily obtainable although, where data are available, they suggest that there is a high correlation between market and book values of leverage (Bowman, 1980). Thus empirical differences between book and market values should not be that great. Third, Baskin (1989) suggests that the book debt ratio more accurately indicates the financing mix that managers actually obtain from outside sources. Fourth, and finally, book ratios better reflect management's target debt ratios (Thies and Klock, 1992).

9.2   Tangibility

The tangibility of assets represents the effect of the collateral value of assets on the firm's gearing level (Rajan and Zingales, 1995). Its *a priori* direction of influence is debatable. Theories that support a positive relationship were developed by Galai and Masulis (1976), Jensen and Meckling (1976) and Myers (1977), who argue that stockholders of leveraged firms have an incentive to invest sub-optimally, and thus transfer wealth away from the firm's bondholders. If debt can be secured against assets, the borrower is restricted to using loaned funds for a specific project, and creditors have an improved guarantee of repayment, depending on the value of the assets used as collateral. Clearly no such guarantee exists if unsecured debt is used. MyM argue that the process of selling debt secured against assets with known values will reduce the information costs of issuing debt, while Scott (1977) asserts that a transfer of wealth from unsecured to secured creditors will occur when secured debt is used.

The possibility of a negative relationship between leverage and tangible assets is argued by Grossman and Hart (1982), who claim that the agency costs of managers consuming more than the optimal level of perquisites will increase for firms that have low levels of assets used as collateral. This is because shareholder monitoring costs of capital outlays for firms with fewer assets that can be used as collateral will be higher than for those that have more collaterizable assets. Shareholders will therefore prefer firms with low levels of collateral assets to have higher gearing levels, *ceteris paribus*. Thus, contrary to Rajan and Zingales (1995) who argue for a positive relationship, overall the theory suggests that the influence of the collateral value of the firm's assets on its leverage is *indeterminate*.

The empirical results on tangibility are in fact mixed (Table 12.1), although a majority of studies provide support for a positive impact of tangibility on leverage. This suggests that the evidence supports the hypothesis that leverage reduces the ability of the firm to invest sub-optimally, and that tangibility diminishes the information asymmetries associated with the issue of debt. Thus we may tentatively conclude that the evidence supports the hypothesis that stockholder–debt holder conflicts of interest are reduced by firms securing debt against assets.

Table 12.1   The influence of tangibility on firm leverage (section 9.2)

+	−	Insignificant
Friend and Hasbrouck (1988)	Barton and Gordon (1988)	Titman and Wessels (1988) [−]
Friend and Lang (1988)	Van der Wijst and Thurik (1993)[2]	Lowe *et al.* (1994) [+]
Jensen, Solberg and Zorn (1992)	Cornelli *et al.* (1996)	
Thies and Klock (1992)	Wiwattanakantang (1999)	
Downs (1993)		
Van der Wijst and Thurik (1993)		
Rajan and Zingales (1995)		
Shenoy and Koch (1996)		
Jordan *et al.* (1998)		
Hirota (1999)		
Colombo (2001)[1]		
Mutenheri and Green (2003)[3]		

Notes:
Signs within square brackets represent the direction of influence of insignificant coefficients.
1.   Found for short-term debt only.
2.   Found for long-term debt only.
3.   Post-reform period.

9.3   Size

As discussed in section 8.3, several authors have shown that there are economies of scale in bankruptcy, reflected in a quadratic relationship between a
firm's bankruptcy costs and its liquidation value. Titman and Wessels (1988)
argue that larger firms tend to be more diversified than their smaller counterparts and are therefore less prone to collapse. Likewise the liquidation values
of smaller firms are lower than their larger counterparts, suggesting that
bondholders are more likely get a partial payment at bankruptcy, and therefore that the agency costs of debt will be lower for larger companies.
Accordingly a positive dependence is expected to be observed between leverage and firm size. The converse argument is that firm size can be viewed as a

proxy for information asymmetries between the firm and the market: the larger the firm, the more complex its organization and the higher the costs caused by information asymmetries (Rajan and Zingales, 1995). Overall, therefore, theory suggests that the influence of firm size on leverage is *indeterminate*.

Table 12.2 shows that a majority of studies considered have found a positive relation between firm size and leverage, although again some studies show a negative relation. Titman and Wessels (1988) suggest that the negative relationship could arise from small firms using more short-term finance than their larger counterparts. That is, smaller firms have higher transactions costs

Table 12.2   The influence of size on firm leverage (section 9.3)

+	−	Insignificant
Barton and Gordon (1988)[1]	Barton and Gordon (1988)[1]	Kim and Sorensen (1986) [−]
Friend and Lang (1988)	Titman and Wessels (1988)	Lowe *et al.* (1994) [+]
Crutchley and Hansen (1989)	Kale *et al.* (1991)	Van der Wijst and Thurik (1994) [+]
Chiarella *et al.* (1992)	Munro (1996)	Mutenheri and Green (2003)[2]
Downs (1993)		
Chowdhury *et al.* (1994)		
Homaifa *et al.* (1994)		
Klein and Belt (1994)		
Hussain (1995)		
Rajan and Zingales (1995)		
Cornelli *et al.* (1996)		
Shenoy and Koch (1996)		
Jordan *et al.* (1998)		
Hirota (1999)		
Wiwattanakantang (1999)		
Colombo (2001)		

Note:
Signs within square brackets represent the direction of influence of insignificant coefficients.
1.   Dependent upon firm strategy.
2.   Post-reform period.

when they issue long-term debt or equity. Such behaviour may cause a small-firm risk effect: by borrowing more short term, these types of firms will be more sensitive to temporary economic downturns than larger, more longer-geared firms.

9.4 Profitability

Traditional theories of financial development point to a positive dependence between leverage levels and profitability. The argument here is that the market will be reluctant to offer funds to those firms who are currently unprofitable. Profitable firms are also more likely to seek exploitable tax shelters, again suggesting that leverage should increase with profitability (Fama and French, 2002). On the other hand, the Pecking Order hypothesis of Myers (1984) and MyM implies a negative relation between leverage and profitability: more profitable firms can use retentions as they do not require external financing; less profitable firms will finance initially with debt. Once again therefore, theory suggests that the influence of profitability on leverage is *indeterminate*.

Unlike the previous two attributes, the empirical evidence on profitability is almost evenly split between a positive relationship and a negative relationship (Table 12.3). Thus, as Fama and French (2002) argue, the debate as to whether firms adhere to the static theory or the Pecking Order hypothesis remains unresolved.

9.5 Growth

Jensen and Meckling (1976) and Myers (1977), among others, argue that, when the firm issues debt, the managers can engage in asset substitution, and transfer wealth from debt holders to shareholders. This calls for increased monitoring by debt holders, which in turn suggests that rapidly growing firms will avoid debt so as to reduce the risk of missing profitable investment opportunities. This is consistent with the increased operating efficiency hypothesis of Higgins (1977), who argues that firms that are better managed rely less on outside financing. This implies a negative relation between leverage and growth. However Smith and Warner (1979), among others, suggest that the moral hazard could be reduced by the firm issuing convertible debt; and Myers (1977) argues that if, the firm issues short-term rather than long-term debt, this problem will also be resolved. Therefore there could equally well be a positive relation between growth and leverage. Once again, theory suggests that the influence of growth on leverage is *indeterminate*.

As with profitability, the main empirical research that has examined the influence of growth on firm leverage suggests that the overall direction of impact remains unresolved (Table 12.4). These conflicting results may be due

Table 12.3   The influence of profitability on firm leverage (section 9.4)

+	−	Insignificant
Barton and Gordon (1988)	Kester (1986)	Titman and Wessels (1988) [−]
Friend and Hasbrouck (1988)	Friend and Lang (1988)	Mutenheri and Green (2003)[3]
Chowdhury and Miles (1989)	Allen and Mizuno (1989)	
Chiarella *et al.* (1992)	Chowdhury and Miles (1989)[1]	
Jensen, Solberg and Zorn (1992)	Thies and Klock (1992)	
Downs (1993)	Lowe *et al.* (1994)	
Chowdhury *et al.* (1994)[2]	Van der Wijst and Thurik (1993)	
Hussain (1995)	Chowdhury *et al.* (1994)	
Cornelli *et al.* (1996)	Rajan and Zingales (1995)	
Boyle and Eckhold (1997)	Jordan *et al.* (1998)	
	Hirota (1999)	
	Wiwattanakantang (1999)	

Notes:
Signs within square brackets represent the direction of influence of insignificant coefficients.
1. Found for past profitability only.
2. Found under the net profit ratio which is defined as net profit divided by sales.
3. Post-reform period.

to the fact that the growth measure tends to pick up the positive dependence between leverage and tangibility. For example, there is an indirect link between leverage and growth, with firms borrowing against plant, machinery or other assets when they are required to expand to meet the increase in sales that accompanies growth. An equally important factor stems from the arguments of Smith and Warner (1979) and Myers (1977) which suggest that care needs to be taken to distinguish among different types of debt. A positive relationship between growth and short-term debt ratios is reported by Hall *et al.* (2000) in a study of 3000 unquoted small and medium-sized UK companies. However many studies do not distinguish carefully between long-term and short-term debt; and unless this is done, a negative relationship between leverage and growth is probably to be expected.

Table 12.4   The influence of growth on firm leverage (section 9.5)

+	−	Insignificant
Kester (1986)	Kim and Sorensen	Downs (1993) [+]
Titman and Wessels	(1986)	Klein and Belt
(1988)	Barton and Gordon	(1994) [−]
Chowdhury and Miles	(1988)	Munro (1996) [−]
(1989)	Kale *et al.* (1991)	
Thies and Klock	Chiarella *et al.* (1992)	
(1992)	Gardner and Trzcinka	
Homaifa *et al.* (1994)	(1992)	
Boyle and Eckhold	Lowe *et al.* (1994)	
(1997)	Rajan and Zingales	
Jordan *et al.* (1998)	(1995)	
Mutenheri and Green	Burton *et al.* (1996)	
(2003)[1]	Hirota (1999)	
	Gul (1999)	
	Wiwattanakantang	
	(1999)	
	Hall *et al.* (2000)	

Note:
Signs within square brackets represent the direction of influence of insignificant coefficients.
1.   Post-reform period.

9.6   Firm Risk

The theoretical literature argues that, the greater the risk faced by a firm, the lower its debt level because each additional unit of debt increases the likelihood of bankruptcy for the firm (DeAngelo and Masulis, 1980). For firms who have variability in their earnings, investors will have little ability to forecast accurately future earnings based on publicly available information. The market will see the firm as a 'lemon' and demand a premium in order to lend funds to it. Furthermore an increase in earnings risk will typically lead to an increase in the risk of default. This results in leverage becoming less attractive at the margin, implying that the optimal level of firm gearing falls. In addition, any increase in the variability of the firm's income implies that banks and other lenders of finance will have a greater probability of forfeiting their funds. In turn, they will be less willing to lend or will charge a higher risk premium in comparison with firms who have lower levels of risk. Therefore we would expect a *negative* relationship between leverage levels and business risk. However Scott (1977) and Jaffe and Westerfield (1987) suggest that the relationship may not be monotonic; indeed under certain conditions it may be positive. Risky firms have a higher option value than safer firms: their probability of financial distress is higher, but so also is their probability of escape from distress (Green and Murinde, 2004).

Indeed we see from Table 12.5 that a negative relationship is not supported by the empirical evidence, with almost as many studies finding a positive as a negative relationship. Kale *et al.* (1991) find that the relationship is not monotonic, as suggested above. Thies and Klock (1992) argue that the positive relationship that they find is due to credit rationing: firms are restricted in the extent to which they can borrow long-term, and therefore make up any deficiencies using short-term debt. Shenoy and Koch (1996) suggest there is a bidirectional relationship between risk and leverage: high risk reduces

Table 12.5   The influence of risk on firm leverage (section 9.6)

+	−	Insignificant
Kim and Sorensen (1986)	Friend and Hasbrouck (1988)	Kester (1986) [+]
Barton and Gordon (1988)[3]	Friend and Lang (1988)	Titman and Wessels (1988) [−]
Crutchley and Hansen (1989)	Barton and Gordon (1988) [3]	Allen and Mizuno (1989) [−]
Kale *et al.* (1991)[1]	Chowdhury and Miles (1989)	Hussain (1995) [−]
Gardner and Trcinka (1992)	Mackie-Mason (1990)	Wiwattanakantang (1999)
Thies and Klock (1992)[2]	Jensen, Solberg and Zorn (1992)	
Lowe *et al.* (1994)	Thies and Klock (1992)[4]	
Shenoy and Koch (1996)	Downs (1993)	
Mutenheri and Green[5] (2003)	Boyle and Eckhold (1997)	
	Hirota (1999)	

Notes:
Signs within square brackets represent the direction of influence of insignificant coefficients.
1. Under a quadratic risk measure.
2. Found for short-term debt only.
3. Dependent upon firm strategy.
4. Found for long-term debt only.
5. Post-reform period.

leverage, but high leverage increases risk of bankruptcy. This suggests a reconsideration of the estimation and testing procedures for these variables.

9.7 Non-debt Tax Shields

The basic point about corporate tax is that the firm will exploit the tax deductibility of debt interest payments to reduce its tax bill. Therefore firms that have other tax shields, such as depreciation deductions, have less need to exploit the debt tax shield. Indeed, if a firm in this position issues excessive debt, it may become 'tax-exhausted' in the sense of having potential tax shields which it is unable to use. Ross (1985) explains that firms face a decline in the expected value of their interest tax savings as outstanding non-debt tax shields increase. Thus the incentive to finance with debt diminishes as non-debt tax shields increase: debt is 'crowded out'. There is a further effect that arises from the risk of bankruptcy (DeAngelo and Masulis, 1980). At low leverage levels, the marginal tax shield is positive since it can be fully employed to reduce the company's overall tax liability. At higher leverage levels, the marginal advantage of debt is negative as a result of the increased probability that the potential tax shield from an extra unit of leverage will be partially or totally lost through bankruptcy. These arguments would all suggest that there should be a *negative* relationship between leverage and non-debt tax shields. However arguments also exist for a *positive* relationship. Scott (1977) and Moore (1986) suggest that firms with substantial non-debt tax shields invariably have considerable collateral assets which can be used to secure debt; and secured debt is less risky than that which is unsecured.

It is also worth emphasizing that, even if the effect of non-debt tax shields on the supply of debt is known, the effect on leverage may nevertheless be uncertain. For a given firm size, if the supply of debt falls, equity or retained earnings must rise, *ceteris paribus*. However, if a change in the non-debt tax shields of the firm is associated with a change in the size of the firm, the supply of equity and retained earnings may change endogenously, thus also changing the firm's leverage. This is most likely to be an issue for firms in conditions of financial distress. In these conditions, a firm may sell collateral assets, reducing its non-debt tax shields, and shrink in size, in an effort to stave off bankruptcy. Even if, for example, debt is reduced, the leverage ratio may either decrease or increase as a result of the change in the size of the firm associated with the reduction in debt.[19]

The preponderance of the evidence would suggest that there is, in fact, a negative relationship between non-debt tax shields and leverage (Table 12.6). However a number of studies do find a positive relationship. Moreover there may be indirect relationships between tax shields and leverage which cannot easily be uncovered by a simple cross-sectional study. For example, Zarowin

Table 12.6   The influence of non-debt tax shields on firm leverage (section 9.7)

+	−	Insignificant
Gardner and Trzcinka (1992)	Bowen, Daly and Huber (1982)	Titman and Wessels (1988) [−]
Downs (1993)	Kim and Sorensen (1986)	Allen and Mizuno (1989) [−]
Homaifa *et al.* (1994)	Crutchley and Hansen (1989)	Van der Wijst and Thurik (1993) [±][2]
Boyle and Eckhold (1997)	Mackie-Mason (1990)	
	Kale *et al.* (1991)	
	Jensen, Solberg and Zorn (1992)	
	Homaifa *et al.* (1994)[1]	
	Shenoy and Koch (1996)	
	Hirota (1999)	
	Wiwattanakantang (1999)	

Notes:
Signs within square brackets represent the direction of influence of insignificant coefficients.
1.   Found for past NDTS.
2.   Negative influence found on long-term debt whilst a positive impact was noted for short-term debt.

(1988) detects a negative dependence between non-debt tax shields and common stock returns, suggesting that stockholders do not attribute positive value to tax shields in the way one might expect. A possible explanation for this and related results is that the estimated relationship between tax shields and leverage depends on the way in which the tax shields are measured. This issue is taken up by Downs (1993) who examines whether non-debt tax shields crowd out debt financing. The sample is drawn from the USA for the period 1968–85 across ten two-digit industries. Normally depreciation and related items are scaled by the firm's total assets so as to remove firm-specific heterogeneity and to reduce heteroscedasticity. Downs argues that this procedure ignores the maturity structure of non-debt tax shields and, in particular, that of depreciation, since the firm's long-term debt ratio will take into account the value of its present *and* its future tax shields. Downs proposes instead that the present value of the future stream of depreciation charges should be applied. As depreciation increases in relation to pre-tax cash flows, the value of the tax shield provided by debt interest payments, and its present value, decreases. Therefore a better scaling of depreciation charges would be provided by using pre-tax cash flows as divisor, rather than the firm's total assets. However pre-tax cash flows alone will underestimate debt crowding out per se, as they ignore the present value of the firm's future cash flows. To rectify this, the present value of these cash flows should be employed. Once this is done, Downs does indeed find a positive relationship between non-debt tax shields and leverage.

9.8 Industrial Classification

The identification and usage of firms' industrial classification are important aspects of financial market research. Kahle and Walking (1996) note five applications of industrial classification: first, to identify control firms within the same industry; second, to describe the industrial composition of the sample; third, to filter firms for specific investigations; fourth, to determine whether mergers and acquisitions are horizontal, vertical or conglomerate; and fifth, to explain the capital structure characteristics which are the focus of this chapter. Kahle and Walking argue that researchers have been 'cavalier' in their application of these classifications, and several important issues have not been addressed: (i) consistent classification of firms across different databases, (ii) consistency of corporate classification when different procedures are applied, (iii) successful identification of utilities and financials, and (iv) consistent grouping over time. In relation to (iii), utilities are typically regulated whereas financials are regulated *and* have special capital characteristics, invariably being highly leveraged. Thus these two groups are generally isolated and will have a higher level of conformity between various classification procedures. In general, the more specialized the industry, the greater the accuracy of its classification across different categorizing procedures. In terms of (iv), as the firm progresses over time, its very structure, nature and industry may change. The transformation of American Can from a manufacturing firm into a financial services conglomerate is just one of the more dramatic examples of this process.

Kahle and Walking (1996) argue that, in general, errors in the use of industrial classification schemes are expected to be proportional to the level of classification employed: a detailed four-digit US SIC code will be more sensitive than a coarser two-digit code to changes in corporate nature and product mix over time. For example, using the first digit of the US SIC code will only classify firms into very broad categories, and this creates a number of very unlikely industries: 'It is doubtful that Olympia Brewing perceives Helena Rubinstein or Standard Oil as competitors. All three are in the industry 2XXX' (Bowen *et al.*, 1982, p. 11). Bowen *et al.* (1982) argue for a four-digit classification. However, while a coarse partition can create anomalies in comparisons *among* firms, a finer partition creates instead the potential for classification errors and anomalies *within* firms. Firms with a range of business activities, especially but not exclusively conglomerates, become increasingly difficult to allocate accurately to one particular group at detailed levels of any industrial classification scheme. This suggests the desirability of a coarser classification, such as the two-digit SIC codes, and this is the conclusion reached, for example, by Clarke (1989).

The errors created under (i) to (iv) above are found within developed capital markets where corporate data are widely published under tight institutional and regulatory rules. In developing markets, company information is not widely distributed and published under such a rigid framework. See, *inter alia*, Kitchen (1986) and Whitley (1992). This suggests that the problems involved in using industrial classifications will be more acute in LDCs. In particular, the problem of comparability *within* firms is likely to be more acute as there is a greater preponderance of industrial conglomerates than there is in the industrial countries. See Prasad (2000). This also points to the desirability of a coarser classification scheme.

There are several reasons for thinking that the industry in which a firm operates will have a significant effect on its capital structure. Titman (1984) begins with the argument that the firm will choose a level of leverage that will maximize its liquidation costs. As the likelihood of liquidation increases, the firm's current income stream will tend to fall because, post liquidation, the after-sales service of the firm will effectively disappear. Prior to liquidation, therefore, consumers are less likely to purchase durable goods from the firm at risk, because of the expected increase in maintenance costs of the product, following the firm's disappearance. The more specialized the product, the lower is the liquidation value of the firm, because the harder it is to replace the after-sales service. *A priori*, this suggests that there will be *inter*-industry differences in leverage across industries, as firms producing more specialized products seek a level of leverage to help offset their lower liquidation costs.

Available evidence does suggests that firms located within different industries do have different gearing levels (Table 12.7). Harris and Raviv (1991) note that Drugs, Instruments, Electronics and Food have low leverage while Paper, Textiles, Mill Products, Steel, Airlines and Cement have high leverage. The authors also note that utilities are more heavily geared than non-utilities. However it should be pointed out that identifying capital structure differences between industries does not necessarily explain them, since there is not a one-for-one relationship between a firm's industrial group and the degree of specialization of its product.

Table 12.7   The influence of industrial classification on firm leverage (section 9.8)

Significant	Insignificant
Bowen *et al.* (1982)	Friend and Hasbrouck (1988)
Titman and Wessels (1988)	Hussain (1995)
Allen and Mizuno (1989)	
Munro (1996)	
Jordan *et al.* (1998)	

9.9   Other Variables[20]

A key reason for using debt is its tax advantages: the higher the tax rate, the larger the advantages of using debt. There are fewer studies which directly investigate the impact of tax rates on corporate leverage and the evidence they produce is mixed, partly because of the difficulty in measuring the true tax rates faced by individual firms. Chowdhury and Miles (1989) as well as CGM support the expected positive relationship, while Homaifa *et al.* (1994), Hussain (1995), Kim and Sorensen (1986), Lowe *et al.* (1994) and Mackie-Mason (1990) find an indeterminate influence. Booth *et al.* (2001) find a negative relation between the calculated average tax rate and leverage in a sample of 727 firms from ten developing economies covering varying time periods from 1980–90. Graham (1996) estimated firm-specific marginal tax rates for 10 000 US firms for 1980–92 allowing for the carry-forward and carry-back of losses, investment tax credits and the Alternative Minimum Tax. This is a more accurate measure of true tax rates, and he finds a small but significantly positive cross-sectional relationship between tax rates and leverage, as we would expect.[21] The tax system is particularly important in LDCs where companies and the urban sector tend to bear much of the tax burden. Clearly, therefore, tax and corporate capital structure in developing economies is an important PRI.

The studies surveyed also find that past leverage levels are negatively related to present ones. This suggests that firms do have a target capital structure and that they employ an adjustment mechanism. The negative dependence suggests that any adjustments that take place decline with time, thereby indicating a converging capital structure path. However the evidence of Chowdhury and Miles (1989) is that costs of adjustment do not influence the firm's capital structure.

Other variables provide further evidence that it is difficult to distinguish between the pecking order and trade-off theories. Support for a pecking order is provided by the negative relation between liquidity and gearing found by Jordan *et al.* (1998), Shenoy and Koch (1996), and Lowe *et al.* (1994). However several studies find that liquidity does not have a significant impact: see Chiarella *et al.* (1992) and Mackie-Mason (1990). CGM find a negative dependence between equity and debt, suggesting that these two liabilities are substitutes for each other, which is more consistent with trade-off theories.

There is also some support for Williamson's (1988) hypothesis that the more specialized assets of a firm will be financed by equity rather than debt. Downs (1993) and Titman and Wessels (1988) find a negative relation between debt and the uniqueness of a firm's assets. Munro (1996) finds that the higher are the fixed assets of a firm, the greater is its leverage, which suggests that the firm uses its assets as collateral to secure debt.

Perhaps more surprising is the number of studies that effectively estimate a demand equation for debt without including its price or cost as a determinant. However Thies and Klock (1992) find a positive relationship between debt and interest rates, as do CGM. The application of interest rates on debt is a clear PRI that needs to be explored further. Likewise few studies investigate the impact of inflation on the demand for debt. Inflation reduces the real cost of employing debt via the erosion of the real value of the principal. Accordingly we would expect a positive dependence between leverage and inflation, and this is the finding of Homaifa *et al.* (1994).

10.   CONCLUSION AND PRIs

The review carried out in this chapter has concentrated on the main issues in the literature on corporate financing and capital structure. We have sought to codify the major hypotheses about corporate financial behaviour, the extent to which they may be expected to be relevant to low-income LDCs, and the state of the evidence concerning these hypotheses. In this section, we summarize the main points and suggest PRIs for a research programme on capital markets and development.

In the last 50 years, *theoretical research* has come full circle from the traditional view of corporate capital structures. In the traditional view, the firm's cost of capital and its value are interdependent. MM's seminal paper turned this theory on its head and argued that the cost of capital is actually independent of capital structure. However, when the perfect capital market assumptions underlying MM are relaxed, it transpires that we move back towards the traditional view. Imperfections in the capital market can be divided into three groups: agency costs, information asymmetries and taxation.

Agency costs arise in several situations involving shareholders, managers, and debt holders. To alleviate shareholder–manager agency costs, the firm issues debt over equity. However this can lead to further costs involving shareholders and debt-holders, where there are two schools of thought: the Irrelevance Hypothesis and the Costly Contracting Hypothesis. The former states that agency costs do not affect a firm's value, while the latter asserts that they do, but this effect can be mitigated by the use of covenants. In this context, we also reviewed the impact of ownership structure on a firm's capital structure; the results of this research are still in their relative infancy. This issue is particularly important for developing economies where the role of institutional factors is particularly pronounced, including the prevalence of business groups in many countries; and it is a clear PRI for future work. See Whitley (1992).

The literature on information asymmetries emphasizes the difference between the information possessed by the firm and that possessed by the market, and it can be summarized in three main results. The first is MyM's Pecking Order hypothesis which argues that firms do not have a unique long-run optimal capital structure, but instead use a financing instrument of first choice, which is conditional on the state of each firm and of the market. The theory explains how a firm chooses its incremental financing but not how (or if) it chooses a particular long-run level of leverage. The second result, suggested by managerial risk aversion, argues that there will be a positive relationship between the level of equity held by management and the quality of the firm. However this result is also consistent with the shareholder–manager agency cost literature, and illustrates a general problem in this field: two very different theories generating similar empirical predictions. The third result involves management's use of debt as a device with which to signal the quality of the firm. One of the implications of the model that is employed here is that the level of the firm's bankruptcy risk rises as its gearing increases. This is identical to that noted under the traditional view and further illustrates the theoretical literature coming full circle. However the link between gearing and the quality of firm management is still one which has to be resolved. This is a clear PRI for theoretical work.

The third group of market imperfections is that associated with tax. The relative levels of personal, corporate and capital taxes, together with the type of tax system (classical or imputation), will influence the capital structure of the firm. In general, a firm will choose its leverage to set the marginal tax benefits of debt equal to its costs. This gives rise to an optimal, static capital structure, but one which may be augmented by considerations of bankruptcy risk and non-debt tax shields.

A main conclusion that emerges from our survey of *empirical work* is that only a limited number of studies have examined the financial behaviour of firms within developing economies and capital markets. Thus we do not yet know how far theories that have been formulated for firms in developed capital markets can be applied to those in LDCs. This deficiency constitutes a critical PRI that must be addressed. It is also a primary question that would need to be addressed by any research programme on capital markets and development, given that policies towards asset formation contribute to growth and poverty reduction.

Existing empirical research can be divided into those that employ univariate methods and those that apply a multivariate model. With regard to the former, we find that, following financial liberalization in many countries, the capital structures of firms in traditional market-based and bank-based financial systems are beginning to converge. Moreover, regardless of the level of development, firms in most countries rely heavily on retained earnings as a source of finance. For LDCs, however, some studies suggest that firms follow a reversed pecking order in their financing, a result which is at variance with the evidence from the industrial countries, and is therefore an important further PRI.

The results from multivariate models tend to confirm that management is concerned with the value of the firm, as basic theory would suggest. By gearing up their firms, managers enhance earnings per share and market value. Large shareholders play a positive role in capital markets by lowering monitoring costs and thus reducing the agency costs of debt. Bankruptcy costs are a concave function of the liquidation value of the firm. However research so far has concentrated only on a small number of firms, and on the direct costs of bankruptcy. Widening this research to include more firms and to study indirect costs are both interesting PRIs.

Direct testing of the Pecking Order hypothesis employed several distinct methodologies, but there is considerable evidence to support this hypothesis. However there is also support for trade-off theories, and we have drawn attention to the difficulty of comparing pecking order and trade-off theories: the former being essentially a time series hypothesis and the latter a cross-sectional hypothesis. For this reason we cannot conclude in favour either of pecking order theory or of optimal capital structure theory. Clearly this is an important subject for further research: hence a PRI.

Specific firm characteristics that have been found to influence capital structure include tangibility, size, profitability, growth, risk, non-debt tax shields and industrial classification. Larger companies in industrial countries appear to use tangible assets as collateral for debt, whilst smaller firms may face fewer information asymmetries. However the combination of inadequately defined property rights and inefficient capital markets may undermine these observations in the context of developing economies. The impact of firm growth on capital structure is ambiguous, as is the impact of risk. These are all clearly important factors in LDCs and constitute PRIs for future work.

Equally important, this review has highlighted three major *omissions* from the empirical literature surveyed. First, there is considerable evidence to suggest that many firms do have a target capital structure. Insofar as this target may not be reached instantly, an adjustment mechanism is applied which must be included within any capital structure model. This issue has scarcely been tackled by the empirical literature. Second, the empirical literature has mainly concentrated on the determinants of leverage. Although a firm's capital structure can be inferred from the identity: total assets ≡ debt + equity, there are advantages in considering both variables explicitly. Moreover there are substantial differences between the management and use of shareholders' funds which are retained profits and those which derive from the issued share capital of a company. A study of leverage sheds no explicit light on the retentions–equity decision, and a considerable amount of information that could be used to explain the financial behaviour of firms is lost. An interesting PRI would be to consider the simultaneous impact of the determinants of capital structure on both equity and debt, following Chowdhury and Miles (1989), so as to produce a more informed picture of the financial behaviour of the firm. Third, few studies have considered the direct impact of the cost of debt, or any other liability, on the firm's capital structure decision. Research has so far effectively constructed a demand function for debt without including its price: the interest rate that is charged. This is important from the firm's point of view since it is the actual cost of using debt. An exciting PRI would investigate the impact of liability prices on the financial behaviour of the firm. It would determine whether these liability prices can better explain corporate capital structure than those firm-specific characteristics that have mainly been employed in the literature so far.

In conclusion, the empirical literature on corporate capital structure is fragmented, and has so far paid relatively little attention to LDCs. In this chapter, we have substantially extended and updated the review of empirical work contained in Harris and Raviv (1991).[22] We have also aimed to classify the empirical results more systematically than has previously been attempted. Our summary of the relationships among firms' characteristics and their capital structures enables comparisons to be made between theoretical predictions and empirical results and, more importantly, it provides a benchmark that can be used by future researchers in the construction of capital structure models. This should help reduce the, at times, ethereal and ad-hoc methodologies that have been employed in many empirical studies.

NOTES

1. La-Porta *et al.* (1999) survey firm ownership around the world. See also the literature on ownership and firm value: for example, Griffith (1999).
2. If the firm is bankrupt, its shares are worthless, and lenders become the new owners of the firm. They will now demand the same rate of return on their capital since they bear all the

firm's business risk. This implies that firms perpetually oscillate between 100 per cent equity finance and 100 per cent debt finance; and we do not in fact observe such oscilla-tions.

3. Since higher levels of debt make default more likely, firms with higher liquidation values will have more debt than those with lower liquidation values, *ceteris paribus*.
4. Cleary (1999) is representative of some recent contributions.
5. More recent work by Guariglia (1999) suggests also that there exists a strong linkage between internal finance and inventory investment, especially work-in-progress and mate-rial inventories.
6. The concept of a signalling equilibrium is discussed in section 4.2.
7. A separating equilibrium is one in which the two different firms can be correctly identified by outsiders on the basis of the contracts offered by the respective firms. This concept is due to Rothschild and Stiglitz (1976).
8. In most developing economies, owner-managed firms predominate; almost all local firms start as owner-managed and expand their businesses for later flotation on the stock market. The firms are usually risk-averse, although Green *et al.* (2001) found evidence to suggest that, in Poland, firms are risk-lovers.
9. Imputation systems typically involve some complexity in the exact manner in which the imputation is calculated, and set against the firm's profits tax on the one hand and the individual's dividend tax on the other. A detailed discussion of such systems is beyond the scope of this survey.
10. See also Corbett and Jenkinson (1997).
11. This shows that retained earnings have been used to retire other sources of finance.
12. Wensley and Walker (1995) note that Japanese firms carry more leverage than New Zealand firms.
13. For India, the samples are composed of 1013 firms for 1980–92, and a further 1650 firms for 1975–90. The UK sample consists of 2000 firms for 1982–1990.
14. This suggests that there are important *intra*-country differences in capital structure.
15. The '*i*' subscript is used to index a cross-section of, say, *n* firms: $i = 1,\ldots, n$.
16. They consist of trade credit given and received, bank borrowing and liquid assets.
17. The nature of the group relationship varies across countries but one particular model tends to predominate in any particular country.
18. Murinde *et al.* (1999) empirically test for convergence in the EU in terms of the structure of the financial systems as well as the patterns of corporate financing activities by banks, bond markets, stock markets and non-financial companies (NFCs) themselves through retained earnings; the results show convergence in terms of capital market activities only.
19. Of course, this is a general point in connection with any study of leverage. One cannot always assume that firm size is, in some sense, exogenous to the analysis.
20. The following observations are based particularly on the further information in Table 12A.1.
21. For the USA, Graham's procedure required seven years' pre-sample data to calculate each year's marginal tax rate. Therefore it cannot easily be applied in many circumstances, depending on local tax rules, the availability of data and the survival rate of individual firms.
22. It should be emphasized that the objective of Harris and Raviv's paper was to provide a detailed survey of the theoretical literature, with an intentionally shorter overview of the empirical evidence.

REFERENCES

Akerlof, G.A. (1970), 'The market for "lemons": quality and the market mechanism', *Quarterly Journal of Economics*, **84**, 488–500.
Allen, D.E. (1993), 'The Pecking Order hypothesis: Australian evidence', *Applied Financial Economics*, **3**, 101–12.

Allen, D.E. and Mizuno, H. (1989), 'The determinants of corporate capital structure: Japanese evidence', *Applied Economics*, **21**, 569–85.

Altman, E. (1984), 'A further empirical investigation of the bankruptcy cost question', *Journal of Finance*, **39**, 1067–89.

Amihud, Y., Baruch, L. and Travlos, N.G. (1990), 'Corporate control and the choice of investment financing: the case of corporate acquisitions', *Journal of Finance*, **45**, 603–16.

Ang, J.S. and Jung, M. (1993), 'An alternate test of Myers' pecking order theory of capital structure: the case of South Korean firms', *Pacific-Basin Finance Journal*, **1**, 31–46.

Ang, J.S., Chua, J.H. and McConnell, J.J. (1982), 'The administrative costs of corporate bankruptcy: a note', *Journal of Finance*, **37**, 219–26.

Arrow, K. (1985), 'The economics of agency', in J. Pratt and R. Zeckhauser (eds), *Principals and Agents: The Structure of Business*, Boston: Harvard Business School Press.

Atkin, M. and Glen, J. (1992), 'Comparing corporate capital structures around the globe', *The International Executive*, **34**, 369–87.

Auerbach, A.J. and King, M.A. (1983), 'Taxation, portfolio choice and debt–equity ratios: a general equilibrium model', *Quarterly Journal of Economics*, **98** (4), November, 587–609.

Barton, S.L. and Gordon, P.J. (1987), 'Corporate strategy: useful perspective for the study of capital structure', *Academy of Management Review*, **12**, 67–75.

Barton, S.L. and Gordon, P.J. (1988), 'Corporate strategy and capital structure', *Strategic Management Journal*, **9**, 623–32.

Baskin, J. (1989), 'An empirical investigation of the pecking order hypothesis', *Financial Management*, **18**, 26–35.

Bertero, E. (1997), 'The banking system, financial markets and capital structure: some evidence from France', *Oxford Review of Economic Policy*, **10**, 68–78.

Bisignano, J. (1990), 'Structures of financial intermediation, corporate finance and central banking', mimeo, Bank of International Settlements, Basle, Switzerland.

Booth, L., Aivazian, V., Demirgüç-Kunt, A. and Maksimovic, V. (2001), 'Capital structures in developing countries', *Journal of Finance*, **56**(1), 87–130.

Borio, C.E.V. (1990), 'Leverage and financing of non-financial companies: an international perspective', BIS Economic Papers no. 27, May, Bank of International Settlements, Basle, Switzerland.

Bowen, R.M., Daly, L.A. and Huber, C.C. (1982), 'Evidence on the existence and determinants of inter-industry differences in leverage', *Financial Management*, **11**, 10–20.

Bowman, R.G. (1980), 'The importance of a market value measurement of debt in assessing leverage', *Journal of Accounting Research*, **18**, 242–54.

Boyle, G.W. and Eckhold, K.R. (1997), 'Capital structure choice and financial market liberalisation: evidence from New Zealand', *Applied Financial Economics*, **7**, 427–37.

Brada, J.C. and Singh, I. (1999), *Corporate Governance in Central Eastern Europe: Case Studies of Firms in Transition*, Armonk, NY and London: Sharpe.

Bradbury, M. and Lloyd, S. (1994), 'An estimate of the direct costs of bankruptcy in New Zealand', *Asia–Pacific Journal of Management*, **11**, 103–11.

Bradley, M., Jarrell, G. and Kim, E.H. (1984), 'On the existence of an optimal capital structure: theory and evidence', *Journal of Finance*, **39**, 857–78.

Brainard, W. and Tobin, J. (1968), 'Pitfalls in financial model building', *American Economic Review*, **58**, 99–122.

Brennan, M. and Kraus, A. (1987), 'Efficient financing under asymmetric information', *Journal of Finance*, **42**, 1225–43.

Brennan, M. and Schwartz, E.S. (1978), 'Corporate income taxes, valuation and the problem of optimal capital structure', *Journal of Business*, **51**, 593–607.

Bulow, J. and Shoven, J.B. (1978), 'The bankruptcy decision', *Bell Journal of Economics*, **14**, 437–55.

Burton, B.M., Lonie, A.A. and Power, D.M. (1996), 'Corporate growth opportunities and the market response to new financing announcements', Discussion Papers in Accountancy and Business Finance, Department of Accountancy and Business Finance, University of Dundee, UK.

Chen C.R. and Steiner T.L. (2000), 'Tobin's q, managerial ownership and analyst coverage – a nonlinear simultaneous equations model', *Journal of Economics and Business*, **52**(4), 365–82.

Chen, G.M. and Merville, L.J. (1999), 'An analysis of the underreported magnitude of the total indirect costs of financial distress', *Review of Quantitative Finance and Accounting*, **13**(3), 277–93.

Chiarella, C., Pham, T.M., Sim, A.B. and Tan, M.M.L. (1992), 'Determinants of corporate capital structure: Australian evidence', in S.G. Rhee and R.P. Chang (eds), *Pacific Basin Capital Markets Research*, vol. 3, Amsterdam: Elsevier.

Chirinko, R.S. and Singha, A.R. (2000), 'Testing static tradeoff against pecking order models of capital structure; a critical comment', *Journal of Financial Economics*, **58**, 417–25.

Chowdhury, G. and Miles, D. (1989), 'Modelling companies' debt and dividend decisions with company accounts data', *Applied Economics*, **21**, 1483–507.

Chowdhury, G., Green, C.J. and Miles, D. (1990), 'What determines the bank borrowing and liquid lending of UK companies? Explanations based on aggregated and disaggregated data', in T. Barker and M.H. Pesaran (eds), *Disaggregation in Econometric Modelling*, New York: Routledge, pp. 300–24.

Chowdhury, G., Green, C.J. and Miles, D. (1994), 'UK companies' short-term financial decisions: evidence from company accounts data', *The Manchester School of Economics and Social Studies*, **62**, 395–411.

Chua, J.H. and Woodward, R.S. (1993), 'The pecking order hypothesis and capital structure of private companies', *Financial Management*, **22**, 18–19.

Claggett, E.T. (1991), 'Capital structure: convergent and pecking order evidence', *Review of Financial Economics*, **1**, 35–48.

Clarke, R.N. (1989), 'SICs as delineators of economic markets', *Journal of Business*, **62**, 17–31.

Cleary, S. (1999), 'The relationship between firm investment and financial status', *Journal of Finance*, **54**(2), April, 673–92.

Cobham, D. and Serre, J-M. (2000), 'A characterization of the French financial system', *Manchester School*, **68**(1), January, 44–67.

Cobham, D. and Subramaniam, R. (1998), 'Corporate finance in developing countries: new evidence for India', *World Development*, **26**(6), 1033–47.

Cobham, D., Cosci, S. and Mattesini, F. (1999), 'The Italian financial system: neither bank based nor market based', *Manchester School*, **67**(3), June, 325–45.

Colombo, E. (2001), 'Determinants of corporate capital structure: evidence from Hungarian firms', Applied Economics, **33**, 1689–701.

Constantinides, G.M. and Grundy, B.D. (1989), 'Optimal investment with stock repurchase as Signals', *The Review of Financial Studies*, **2**, 445–66.

Copeland, T.E. and Weston, J.F. (1988), Financial Theory and Corporate Policy, 3rd edn, Reading, MA: Addison-Wesley.

Corbett, J. and Jenkinson, T. (1996), 'The financing of industry, 1970–89: an international comparison', *Journal of the Japanese and International Economies*, **10**, 71–96.

Corbett, J. and Jenkinson, T. (1997), 'How is investment financed? A study of Germany, the United Kingdom and the United States', *The Manchester School Supplement*, **65**, 69–93.

Core, J.E., Holthausen, R.W. and Larcker, D.F. (1999), 'Corporate governance, chief executive officer compensation and firm performance', *Journal of Financial Economics*, **51**(3), March, 371–406.

Cornelli, F., Portes, R. and Schaffer, M.E. (1996), 'The capital structure of firms in central and eastern Europe', CEPR Discussion Paper no. 1392, Centre for Economic Policy Research, London.

Crutchley, C.E. and Hansen, R.S. (1989), 'A test of the agency theory of managerial ownership, corporate leverage and corporate dividends', *Financial Management*, **18**, 33–46.

De Haan, L., Koedik, K.G. and De Vrijer, J.E. (1994), 'Buffer stock money and pecking order financing: results from an interview study among Dutch firms', *De Economist*, **14**, 287–305.

DeAngelo, H. and Masulis, R.W. (1980), 'Optimal capital structure under corporate and personal taxation', *Journal of Financial Economics*, **8**, 3–29.

Diamond, D.W. (1989), 'Reputation acquisition in debt markets', *Journal of Political Economy*, **97**, 828–62.

Downs, T.W. (1993), 'Corporate leverage and non-debt tax shields: evidence on crowding out', *Financial Review*, **28**, 549–83.

Elston, C.D. (1981), 'The financing of Japanese industry', *Bank of England Quarterly Bulletin*, **21**, 510–18.

Fama, E. (1980), 'Agency problems and theory of the firm', *Journal of Political Economy*, **88**(2), 288–307.

Fama, E. (1990), 'Contract costs and financing decisions', *Journal of Business*, **63**(1), 71–91.

Fama, E.F. and French, K.R. (2002), 'Testing trade-off and pecking order predictions about dividends and debt', *The Review of Financial Studies*, **15**(1), 1–33.

Firth, M. (1995), 'The impact of institutional stockholders and managerial interests on the capital structure of firms', *Managerial and Decision Economics*, **16**, 167–75.

Fischer, E.O., Heinkel, R. and Zechner, J. (1989), 'Dynamic capital structure choice: theory and Tests', *Journal of Finance*, **44**, 19–40.

Friend, I. and Hasbrouck, I. (1988), 'Determinants of capital structure', in J. Chen (ed.), *Research in Finance*, London: JAI Press.

Friend, I. and Lang, L.H. (1988), 'An empirical test of the impact of managerial self-interest on corporate capital structure', *Journal of Finance*, **43**, 271–81.

Galai, D. and Masulis, R. (1976), 'The option pricing model and the risk factor of stock', *Journal of Financial Economics*, **3**, 631–44.

Gardner, J.C. and Trzcinka, C.A. (1992), 'All-equity firms and the balancing theory of capital structure', *Journal of Financial Research*, **15**, 77–90.

Garvey, G.T. and Hanka, G. (1999), 'Capital structure and corporate control: the effect of anti-takeover statutes on firm leverage', *Journal of Finance*, **54**(2), pp. 519–46.

Glen, J. and Pinto, B. (1994), 'Debt or equity? How firms in developing countries choose', IFC Discussion Paper no. 22, IFC, Washington, DC.

Graham, J.R. (1996), 'Debt and the marginal tax rate', *Journal of Financial Economics*, **41**, 41–73.

Granovetter, M. (1995), 'Coase revisited: business groups in the modern economy', *Industrial and Corporate Change*, **4**, 93–130.

Green, C.J. and Murinde, V. (2004), 'The impact of tax policy on corporate debt in a developing economy: a study of unquoted Indian companies', Loughborough University Department of Economics Research Paper, ERP04-04, January.

Green, C.J., Lensink, R. and Murinde, V. (2001), 'Demand uncertainty and the capital–labour ratio in Poland', *Emerging Markets Review*, **2**(2), June, 184–97.

Green, C.J., Murinde, V. and Suppakitjarak, J. (2003), 'Corporate financial structures in India', *South Asian Economic Journal*, **4**(2), 245–73.

Green, R.C. (1984), 'Investment incentives, debts and warrants', *Journal of Financial Economics*, **13**, 115–36.

Greene, W.H. (2000), *Econometric Analysis*, 4th edn, New York: Macmillan.

Griffith, J.M. (1999), 'CEO ownership and firm value', *Managerial and Decision Economics*, **20**(1), February, 1–8.

Grossman, S.J. and Hart, O.D. (1982), 'Corporate financial structure and managerial incentives', in J. McCall (ed.), *The Economics of Information and Uncertainty*, Chicago: University of Chicago Press.

Guariglia, A. (1999), 'The effects of financial constraints on inventory investment: evidence from a panel of UK firms', *Economica*, **66**(261), 43–62.

Guillen, M.F. (2000), 'Business groups in emerging economies: a resource-based view', *Academy of Management Journal*, **43**(3), 362–80.

Gul, F.A. (1999), 'Growth opportunities, capital structure and dividend policies in Japan', *Journal of Corporate Finance*, **5**(2), 141–68.

Gul, F.A. and Kealey, B.T. (1999), 'Chaebol, investment opportunity set, and corporate debt and dividend policies of Korean companies', *Review of Quantitative Finance and Accounting*, **13**(4), 401–16.

Hall, G., Hutchinson, P. and Michaelas, N. (2000), 'Industry effects on the determinants of unquoted SMEs' capital structure', *International Journal of the Economics of Business*, **7**(3), 297–312.

Hamid, J. and Singh, A. (1992), 'Corporate financial structures in developing economies', IFC Technical Paper no.1, IFC, Washington, DC.

Harris, M. and Raviv, A. (1990), 'Capital structure and the informational role of debt', *Journal of Finance*, **45**, 321–49.

Harris, M. and Raviv, A. (1991), 'The theory of capital structure', *Journal of Finance*, **46**, 297–355.

Haugen, R.A. and Senbet, L.W. (1978), 'The insignificance of bankruptcy costs to the theory of optimal capital structure', *Journal of Finance*, **23**, 383–93.

Heinkel, R. (1982), 'A theory of capital structure relevance under imperfect information', *Journal of Finance*, **37**, 1141–50.

Heinkel, R. and Zechner, J. (1990), 'The role of debt and preferred stock as a solution to adverse investment incentives', *Journal of Financial and Quantitative Analysis*, **25**, 1–24.

Heston, A.W. (1962), 'An empirical study of cash, securities and other current accounts of large corporations', in D.D. Hester and J. Tobin (eds), *Studies of Portfolio Behaviour*, New York: John Wiley & Sons, pp. 66–117.

Higgins, R.C. (1977), 'How much growth can a firm afford?', *Financial Management*, **6**, 7–16.

Hirota, S. (1999), 'Are corporate financing decisions different in Japan? An empirical study on capital structure', *Journal of the Japanese and International Economies*, **13**, 201–29.

Homaifa, G., Zietz, J. and Benkato, O. (1994), 'An empirical model of capital structure: some new evidence', *Journal of Business Finance and Accounting*, **21**, 1–14.

Hsiao, C. (2003), Analysis of Panel Data, 2nd edn, Cambridge: Cambridge University Press.

Hunsaker, J. (1999), 'The role of debt and bankruptcy statutes in facilitating tacit collusion', *Managerial and Decision Economics*, **20** (1), 9–24.

Hussain, Q. (1995), 'Implications of foreign capital inflows and shareholder concentration on financial sector: a case study of Indonesia', mimeo, School of Economics and Law, University of Gothenburg, Sweden.

Hutton, J. and Kenc, T. (1998), 'The influence of firms' financial policy on tax reforms', *Oxford Economic Papers*, 50(4), 663–84.

Jaffe, J.F. and Westerfield, R. (1987), 'Risk and the optimal debt level', in T.E. Copeland (ed.), *Modern Finance and Industrial Economics: Papers in Honour of I. Weston*, Oxford: Blackwell.

James, H.S. (1999), 'Owner as manager, extended horizons and the family firm', *International Journal of the Economics of Business*, **6**(1), 41–55.

Jensen, M.C. (1986), 'Agency costs of free cash flow, corporate finance and takeovers', *American Economic Review*, **76**, 323–39.

Jensen, M.C. and Meckling, W.H. (1976), 'Theory of the firm: managerial behaviour, agency costs and ownership structure', *Journal of Financial Economics*, **3**, 305–60.

Jensen, M.C. and Meckling, W.H. (1992), 'Specific and general knowledge, and organizational structure', in L. Werin and H. Wijkander (eds), *Contract Economics*, Cambridge, MA: Blackwell.

Jensen, G.H., Solberg, D.P. and Zorn, T.S. (1992), 'Simultaneous determination of insider ownership, debt and dividend policies', *Journal of Financial Quantitative Analysis*, **27**, 247–61.

Jordan, J., Lowe, J. and Taylor, P. (1998), 'Strategy and financial policy in UK small firms', *Journal of Business Finance and Accounting*, **25**, 1–27.

Jöreskog, K.G. and Sörbom, D. (1981), *LISREL V, Analysis of linear structural relationships by the method of maximum likelihood*, Chicago: National Education Resources.

Kahle, K.M. and Walking, R.A. (1996), 'The impact of industry classifications on financial research', *Journal of Financial and Quantitative Analysis*, **31**, 309–55.

Kale, J.R., Noe, T.H. and Ramirez, G.G. (1991), 'The effect of business risk on corporate capital structure: theory and evidence', *Journal of Finance*, **46**, 1693–715.

Kester, C.W. (1986), 'Capital and ownership structure: a comparison of United States and Japanese manufacturing corporations', *Financial Management*, 5–16.

Khanna, T. and K. Palepu (2000a), 'Is group affiliation profitable in emerging markets? an analysis of diversified Indian business groups', *Journal of Finance*, **55**(2), 867–90.

Khanna, T. and K. Palepu (2000b), 'The future of business groups in emerging markets: long-run evidence from Chile', *Academy of Management Journal*, **43**(3), 268–85.

Kim, E.H. (1978), 'A mean-variance analysis of optimal capital structures', *Journal of Finance*, **23**.

Kim, W.S. and Sorensen, E.H. (1986), 'Evidence on the impact of the agency costs of debt in corporate debt policy', *Journal of Financial and Quantitative Analysis*, **21**, 131–44.

King, M.A. (1974), 'Taxation and the cost of capital', *Review of Economic Studies*, **41**(1), 21–35.

King, M.A. (1977), *Public Policy and the Corporation*, London: Chapman and Hall.

Kitchen, R.L. (1986), *Finance for the Developing Countries*, Chichester: Wiley.

Klein, D.P. and Belt, B. (1994), 'Sustainable growth and choice of financing: a test of the pecking order hypothesis', *Review of Financial Economics*, **3**, 143–54.

Krishnaswami, S., Spindt, P.A. and Subramaniam, V. (1999), 'Information asymmetry, monitoring, and the placement structure of corporate debt', *Journal of Financial Economics*, **51**(3), 407–34.

La-Porta, R., Lopez de Silanes, F. and Shleifer, A. (1999), 'Corporate ownership around the world', *Journal of Finance*, **54**(2), April, 471–517.

Leland, H. and Pyle, D. (1977), 'Informational asymmetries, financial structure and financing intermediation', *Journal of Finance*, **32**, 371–88.

Lev, B. (1969), 'Industry averages as targets for financial ratios', *Journal of Accounting Research*, Autumn, 290–99.

Lintner, J. (1956), 'Distribution of incomes of corporations among dividends, retained earnings, and taxes', *American Economic Review*, **46**, 97–113.

Lowe, J., Naughton, T. and Taylor, P. (1994), 'The impact of corporate strategy on the capital structure of Australian companies', *Managerial and Decision Economics*, **15**, 245–57.

Mackie-Mason, J. (1990), 'Do firms care who provides their financing?', in R.G. Hubbard (ed.), *Asymmetric Information, Corporate Finance and Investment*, Chicago and London: University of Chicago Press.

MacKinlay, A.C. (1997), 'Event studies in economics and finance', *Journal of Economic Literature*, **35**(1), 13–39.

Marsh, P. (1982), 'The choice between equity and debt: An empirical study', *Journal of Finance*, **37**, 121–44.

Masulis, R.W. (1988), *The Debt/Equity Choice*, Cambridge, MA: Ballinger.

Mayer, C. (1986), 'Corporation tax, finance and the cost of capital', *Review of Economic Studies*, **53**, 93–112.

Mayer, C. (1988), 'New issues in corporate finance', *European Economic Review*, **32**, 1167–89.

Mayer, C. (1990), 'Financial systems, corporate finance and economic development', in R.G. Hubbard (ed.), *Asymmetric Information, Corporate Finance and Investment*, Chicago: University of Chicago Press.

Mayer, C. and Alexander, I. (1990), 'Banks and securities markets: corporate financing in Germany and the United Kingdom', *Journal of the Japanese and International Economies*, **4**, 450–75.

Miller, M.H. (1977), 'Debt and taxes', *Journal of Finance*, **32**, 261–75.

Modigliani, F. and Miller, M.H. (1958), 'The cost of capital, corporation finance and the theory of investment', *American Economic Review*, **48**, 261–97.

Modigliani, F. and Miller, M.H. (1963), 'Corporate income taxes and the cost of capital: a correction', *American Economic Review*, **53**, 433–43.

Moore, W. (1986), 'Asset composition, bankruptcy costs and the firm's choice of capital structure', *Quarterly Review of Economics and Business*, **26**, 51–61.

Munro, J.W. (1996), 'Convertible debt financing: an empirical analysis', *Journal of Business Finance and Accounting*, **23**, 319–34.

Murinde, V. (1996), *Development Banking and Finance*, Aldershot: Ashgate.

Murinde, V. and Kariisa-Kasa, J. (1997) 'The financial performance of the East African Development Bank: a retrospective analysis', *Accounting, Business and Financial History*, **7**(1), 81–104.

Murinde, V. and Mullineux, A.W. (1998), 'Introductory overview: issues surrounding bank and enterprise restructuring in Central and Eastern Europe', in A.W. Mullineux and C.J. Green (eds), *Economic Performance and Financial Sector Reform in Central and Eastern Europe*, Cheltenham, UK and Northampton, MA, USA: Edward Elgar, 1–20.

Murinde, V., Agung, J. and Mullineux, A.W. (1999) 'Convergence of European financial systems: banks or equity markets?', in M. Fischer and P. Nijkamp (eds), *Spatial Dynamics of European Integration: Political and Regional Issues at the Turn of the Millennium*, Munich: Springer-Verlag.

Mutenheri, E. and Green, C.J. (2003), 'Financial reform and financing decisions of listed firms in Zimbabwe', *Journal of African Business*, **4**(2), 155–70.

Myers, S.C. (1977), 'Determinants of corporate borrowing', *Journal of Financial Economics*, 5, 147–75.

Myers, S.C. (1984), 'The capital structure puzzle', *Journal of Finance*, **34**, 575–92.

Myers, S.C. and Majluf, N.S. (1984), 'Corporate financing and investment decisions when firms have information that investors do not have', *Journal of Financial Economics*, **13**, 187–221.

Narayanan, M.P. (1988), 'Debt versus equity under asymmetric information', *Journal of Financial and Quantitative Analysis*, **23**, 39–51.

Peyser, P.S. (1999), 'Firm theoretic limitations on proposition III', *Review of Quantitative Finance and Accounting*, **12**(1), 65–88.

Poitevin, M. (1989), 'Financial signalling and the "Deep-Pocket" argument', *Rand Journal of Economics*, **20**, 26–40.

Prasad, S.K. (2000), 'Corporate financial structures in developing economies', unpublished PhD thesis, Cardiff Business School, University of Wales.

Rajan, R. and Zingales, L. (1995), 'What do we know about capital structure? Some evidence from international data', *Journal of Finance*, **50**, 1421–60.

Riah-Belkaoui, A. and Bannister, J.W. (1994), 'Multidivisional structure and capital structure: the contingency of diversification strategy', *Managerial and Decision Economics*, **15**, 267–76.

Rock, K. (1986), 'Why new issues are underpriced', *Journal of Financial Economics*, **15**, 187–212.

Ross, S. (1973), 'The economic theory of agency: the principal's problem', *American Economic Review*, **63**(2), 134–9.

Ross. S. (1977), 'The determination of financial structures: an incentive signalling approach', *The Bell Journal of Economics*, **8**(1), 23–40.

Ross, S. (1985), 'Debt and taxes and uncertainty', *Journal of Finance*, **40**, 637–57.

Rothschild, M. and Stiglitz, J.E. (1976), 'Equilibrium in competitive insurance markets: an essay in the economics of imperfect information', *Quarterly Journal of Economics*, November, 629–49.

Scott, J.H. (1977), 'Bankruptcy, secured debt and optimal capital structure', *Journal of Finance*, **32**, 1–19.

Shannon, H.A. (1932), 'The first five thousand limited companies and their duration', *Economic History*, **2**, 396–424.

Shavell, S. (1979), 'Risk sharing and incentives in the principal and agent relationship', *The Bell Journal of Economics*, **10**(1), 55–73.

Shenoy, C. and Koch, P.D. (1996), 'The firm's leverage–cash flow relationship', *Journal of Empirical Finance*, **2**, 307–31.

Shleifer, A. and Vishny, R.W. (1986), 'Large shareholders and corporate control', *Journal of Political Economy*, **94**(3), pp. 461–88.

Shleifer, A. and Vishny, R.W. (1989), 'Management entrenchment: the case of managerial specific investments', *Journal of Financial Economics*, **25**, 123–39.

Short, H. (1994), 'Ownership, control, financial structure and the performance of firms', *Journal of Economic Surveys*, **8**, 203–49.

Short, H. and K. Keasey (1999), 'Managerial ownership and the performance of firms: evidence from the UK', *Journal of Corporate Finance*, **5**(1), 79–101.

Shyam-Sunder, L. and Myers, S.C. (1999), 'Testing static trade-off against pecking order models of capital structure', *Journal of Financial Economics*, **51**, 219–44.

Singh, A. (1995), 'Corporate financial patterns in industrialising economies: a comparative study', IFC Technical Paper no. 2: IFC, Washington, DC.

Smith, C. and Warner, J. (1979), 'On financing contracting: an analysis of bond covenants', *Journal of Financial Economics*, **7**, 117–61.

Stultz, R. (1990), 'Managerial discretion and optimal financing policies', *Journal of Financial Economics*, **26**, 3–27.

Thatcher, J.S. (1985), 'The choice of call provision terms: evidence of the existence of agency costs of debt', *Journal of Finance*, **40**, 549–61.

Thies, C.F. and Klock, M.S. (1992), 'Determinants of capital structure', *Review of Financial Economics*, **1**, 40–52.

Titman, S. (1984), 'The effect of capital structure on the firm's liquidation decision', *Journal of Financial Economics*, **13**, 137–51.

Titman, S. and Wessels, R. (1988), 'The determinants of capital structure choice', *Journal of Finance*, **43**, 1–19.

Van der Wijst, R. and Thurik, R. (1993), 'Determinants of small firm debt ratios: analysis of retail panel data', *Small Business Economics*, **5**, 55–65.

Vilasuso, J. and Minkler, A. (2001), 'Agency costs, asset specificity, and the capital structure of the firm', *Journal of Economic Behaviour and Organisation*, **44**(1), 55–69.

Vogt, S.C. (1994), 'The role of internal financial sources in firm financing and investment decisions', *Review of Financial Economics*, **4**, 1–24.

Wald, J. (1999), 'Capital structure with dividend restrictions', *Journal of Corporate Finance*, **5**(2), 193–208.

Warner, J.B. (1977), 'Bankruptcy costs: some evidence', *Journal of Finance*, **32**, 337–47.

Wensley, P. and Walker, G. (1995), 'Capital structure differences between Japan and New Zealand', *International Company and Commercial Law Review*, **6**, 47–55.

Whitley, R. (1992), *Business Systems in East Asia: Firms, Markets and Societies*, London: Sage.

Williamson, O.E. (1988), 'Corporate finance and corporate governance', *Journal of Finance*, **43**, 567–91.

Wiwattanakantang, Y. (1999), 'An empirical study on the determinants of the capital structure of Thai firms', *Pacific-Basin Finance Journal*, **7**, 371–403.

Wright, K. (1994), 'Company profitability and finance', *Bank of England Quarterly Bulletin*, **34**, 241–9.

Zarowin, P. (1988), 'Non-linearities and nominal contracting effects: the case of the depreciation tax shield', *Journal of Accounting and Economics*, **10**, 89–110.

Zeckhauser, R.L. and Pound, J. (1990), 'Are Large Shareholders Effective Monitors? An Investigation of Share Ownership and Corporate Performance', in R.G. Hubbard (ed.), *Asymmetric Information, Corporate Finance and Investment*, Chicago: University of Chicago Press, pp. 149–80.

APPENDIX   SUMMARY OF RECENT EMPIRICAL RESEARCH ON CORPORATE CAPITAL STRUCTURE

General Notes for Tables 12A.1 to 12A.6

Unless stated otherwise, the dependent variable is the book value of a leverage measure.

+/–   positive/negative coefficients, respectively; and statistically significant.

?   coefficients have indeterminate sign; and statistically significant.

ns   coefficients not significant.

si   coefficients significant (sign is immaterial).

Blanks within the tables represent variables that were not tested for.

Table 12A.1   Summary of recent empirical research on corporate capital structure

	Authors					
Determinant	Barton and Gordon (1988)	Boyle and Eckhold (1997)	Burton, Lonie and Power (1996)	Bowen, Daly and Huber (1982)	Kester (1986)	Allen and Mizuno (1989)
Dividend		+				ns
Risk	?[1]	–			ns	?[2]
Profitability	+	+			–	–
NDTS		+		–		ns
Tangibility	–					
Growth	–	+	–		+	
Past growth					ns	
Size	?[1]					
Industrial group				si		si
Country classifications					si	
Earning power		+				

Notes:

1. Dependent upon the strategy followed by the firm; of the four types, two were positively related and two negatively related; overall, impact of this attribute was indeterminate.
2. When the market value of leverage was employed, risk had a significant negative impact on firm leverage; when the book value of leverage was used, risk had an insignificant impact on leverage.

Table 12A.2 Summary of recent empirical research on corporate capital structure

Determinant	Jensen, Solberg and Zorn (1992)	Kale et al. (1991)	Klein and Belt (1994)[1]	Kim and Sorensen (1986)[2]	Lowe et al. (1994)	Friend and Hasbrouck (1988)[3]
Dividend	−					
Risk	−	+[4]		+	+	−
Profitability	−				+	−
NDTS	−	−		−		
Tangibility	+				ns	+
Operational efficiency			+			
Growth		−	ns	−	−	
Size	−		+	ns	ns	ns
Information asymmetry			+			
Tax				ns	ns	
Tax subsidy	−					
Liquidity (cash holdings)					−	

Notes:
1. Results taken from Table 5, regression 1, p. 150.
2. Results taken from Table 2 using the book value of leverage.
3. Results taken from Table 6, p. 14.
4. Quadratic risk measure employed here.

Table 12A.3 Summary of recent empirical research on corporate capital structure

	Authors					
Determinant	Crutchley and Hanson (1989)	Bradley *et al.* (1984)	Chowdhury and Miles (1989)	Chiarella *et al.* (1992)	Cornelli *et al.* (1996)	Chowdhury, Green, Miles (1994)
Dividend						+
Risk	+		−			
Profitability			−	−	−	+
Past profitability			+			
NDTS	−			−		
Tangibility				ns	−	
Growth			+	+		
Size	+			+	+	+
Tax			+			+
Past tax			+			
State ownership					si	
Liquidity (cash holdings)				ns		
Cost of funds			ns			
Costs of adjustments			ns			
Investment			+			+
Leasing			+			
Stock building						+
Miscellaneous sources						−
Miscellaneous expenses						+
Capital issues						−
Sale of fixed assets						ns
Equity						−
Past leverage						−
Interest rates						?[1]
Tax discrimination						ns
Rate of return on capital						−
Net profits (% of sales)						−

Notes:
1. Dependent upon the rate applied: negative influence is found with the inter-bank rate and a positive one with the Certificate of Deposit (CD) rate.

Table 12A.4 *Summary of recent empirical research on corporate capital structure*

Determinant	Downs (1993)[1]	Gardner and Trzcinka (1992)	Homaifa et al. (1994)	Hussain (1995)	Jordan et al. (1998)	Friend and Lang (1988)
Risk	–	+		ns	+	–
Profitability	–			–	+	–
NDTS	+	+	+			
Past NDTS			–			
Tangibility	+				+	+
Growth	ns	–	+		+	
Past growth			–			
Size	+		+	+	+	+
Past size			–		–	
Tax			ns	ns[2]		
Past tax			–			
Industrial group				ns	si	
Liquidity (cash holdings)					–	
Uniqueness	–					
Past leverage			–			
Market conditions			–			
Past market conditions			–			
Inflation			+			
Past inflation			–			

Notes:
1. Results of estimates when the sample was unrestricted and was allowed to vary across industries.
2. A negative dependence was noted for this variable post-1988.

Table 12A.5   *Summary of recent empirical research on corporate capital structure*

Determinant	MacKie-Mason (1990)	Munro (1996)[1]	Rajan and Zingales (1995)[2]	Shenoy and Koch (1996)	Titman and Wessels (1988)	Thies and Klock (1992)
Dividend				+		
Risk	−			+	ns	?[1]
Profitability			−		ns[4]	−
NDTS	−			−	ns	
Tangibility			+	?[3]	ns	+[2]
Operational leverage						ns
Growth		ns	−		?[5]	+
Size		−	+	+	−	
Investment				+		
Tax	ns					+
Industrial group		si			si	
Liquidity (cash holdings)	ns					
Past liquidity				−		
Intangibles		−				
Uniqueness				?[3]	−	
Leverage		−				
Past leverage				−		
Interest rates						+

Notes:
1. A negative/positive coefficient was found on this variable in the equation for long/short-term debt.
2. Coefficient for long-term debt was insignificant.
3. This attribute has a positive coefficient in two of the four equations, and negative in the other two.
4. Significant only when the market value of equity was used.
5. Coefficient was negative when using the market value of equity, and positive when using the book value.

Table 12A.6 **Summary of recent empirical research on corporate capital structure**

Determinant	Vogt (1994)	Van der Wijst and Thurik (1993)	Hirota (1999)	Wiwattana-kantang (1999)	Colombo[3] (2001)	Mutenheri and Green[4] (2003)
Dividend						−
Risk			−	−		+
Profitability		−	−	−	−	+
NDTS	ns		$-^2$	−		
Tangibility		?[1]	+	+	+	+
Market/book				−		
Growth			−			+
Size	ns		+	+	+	+
Tax						−
Inventories					+	
Investment					+	
Liquidity (cash holdings)	−					+
Cash flow					−	−
Inflation						−
Stock market						−

Notes:
1. A negative/positive coefficient was found for this variable in the equation for short/long-term debt.
2. Significant in one out of four cross-section equations; significant at the 10% level in the whole (pooled) data set.
3. The dependent variable is short-term debt/total assets.
4. Post-reform period.

Index